GW00716664

BIBLIOGRAPHY
OF THE WRITINGS OF
SIR WINSTON
CHURCHILL

BIBLIOGRAPHY
OF THE WRITINGS OF
SIR WINSTON
CHURCHILL

VOLUME II

RONALD I. COHEN

thoemmes

Thoemmes Continuum, an imprint of
The Continuum International Publishing Group
The Tower Building, 11 York Road, London, SE1 7NX
80 Maiden Lane, Suite 704, New York, NY 10038

www.continuumbooks.com

ISBN 08264-7235-4

British Library Cataloguing-in-Publication Data

A catalogue record for this book is available from the British Library.

Library of Congress Cataloging-in-Publication Data

Cohen, Ronald I.
  Bibliography of the writings of Sir Winston Churchill / Ronald I. Cohen
    p. cm
  Includes bibliographical references and index.
  ISBN 0-8264-7235-4 (set)
  I. Churchill, Winston, Sir, 1874–1965—Bibliography. I. Title

Z8169.45.C64 2004
[DA566.9.C5]
016.941084'092—dc22

2003062603

Typeset by Fakenham Photosetting Ltd
Printed on acid-free paper in Great Britain by Antony Rowe Ltd., Chippenham

CONTENTS

LIST OF ABBREVIATIONS

AC	American Catalogue of Books
AuCChMT	Churchill Memorial Trust Library, Canberra
AuM	Melbourne Public Library
AuNL	National Library, Canberra
AuNSWSL	Mitchell Library, State Library of New South Wales, Sydney
AuVM	Melbourne Public Library
AuVSL	State Library of Victoria, Melbourne
BA	Bermuda Archives, Hamilton
BeNL	Koninklijke Bibliotheek / Bibliothèque royale, Brussels
Blanchard	Robert G. Blanchard, *The First Editions of John Buchan: A Collector's Bibliography*, first edition (Hamden, CT: Shoestring Press, 1981)
Bliss	Carey S. Bliss, *Bibliography of Cheney Miniatures* (Los Angeles: Dawson's Book Shop, 1974)
BLOI	British Library of Information, New York
CaAC	Calgary Public Library, Calgary, Alberta
CaACU	University of Calgary Library, Calgary, Alberta
CaAE	Edmonton Public Library, Edmonton, Alberta
CaAEGA	Alberta Government Library, Neil Crawford Site, Edmonton, Alberta
CaAEKC	Simona Maaskant Library, King's University College, Edmonton, Alberta
CaAEP	Alberta Legislative Library, Edmonton, Alberta
CaAEU	University of Alberta, Edmonton, Alberta
CaBPR	Prince Rupert Public Library, Prince Rupert, British Columbia
CaBVA	Vancouver Public Library, Vancouver, British Columbia
CaBVAS	Simon Fraser University, Vancouver, British Columbia
CaBVAU	Walter C. Koerner Library, University of British Columbia, Vancouver, British Columbia
CaBVIP	Legislative Library, Victoria, British Columbia
CaBVIV	McPherson Library, University of Victoria, Victoria, British Columbia

CaMW	Winnipeg Public Library, Winnipeg, Manitoba
CaMWU	Elizabeth Dafoe Library, University of Manitoba, Winnipeg, Manitoba
CaNBFL	Legislative Library, Fredericton, New Brunswick
CaNBFU	Harriet Irving Library, University of New Brunswick, Fredericton
CaNBSAM	Ralph Pickard Bell Library, Mt. Allison University, Sackville, New Brunswick
CaNBSU	Ward Chipman Library, University of New Brunswick, Saint John
CaNFCBM	Sir Wilfred Grenfell College, Ferriss Hodgett Library, Memorial University of Newfoundland, St. John's
CaNFSM	Memorial University of Newfoundland, St. John's
CaNSH	Halifax City Regional Library, Halifax, Nova Scotia
CaNSHD	Killam Library, Dalhousie University, Halifax, Nova Scotia
CaNSHL	Legislative Library of Nova Scotia, Halifax, Nova Scotia
CaNSHV	Mount Saint Vincent University, Halifax, Nova Scotia
CaNSLF	Library, Fortress Louisbourg National Historical Site, Louisbourg, Nova Scotia
CaNSSX	University College of Cape Breton Library, Sydney, Nova Scotia
CaNSWA	Acadia University, Wolfville, Nova Scotia
CaOBRAC	Bracebridge Public Library, Bracebridge, Ontario
CaOGU	McLaughlin Library, University of Guelph, Guelph, Ontario
CaOGWE	Silvercreek Education Centre, Terry James Resource Library, Guelph, Ontario
CaOH	Hamilton Public Library, Hamilton, Ontario
CaOHM	Mills Memorial Library, McMaster University, Hamilton, Ontario
CaOKQ	Douglas Library, Queen's University, Kingston, Ontario
CaOKR	Royal Military College of Canada Library, Kingston, Ontario
CaOL	London Public Library, London, Ontario
CaOLU	D. B. Weldon Library, University of Western Ontario, London, Ontario
CaOME	Erindale College, University of Toronto, Toronto, Ontario
CaOOC	Ottawa Public Library, Ottawa
CaOOCC	Carleton University Library, Ottawa

CaOOE	Library of the Department of Foreign Affairs and International Trade, Ottawa
CaOOM	Canmet Library (formerly Canada Centre for Mineral and Energy Technology, Department of Energy, Mines and Resources), Ottawa
CaOOMC	Canadian Housing Information Centre, Canada Mortgage and Housing Corporation, Ottawa
CaOOND	Library of the Department of National Defence, Ottawa
CaOONL	National Library, Ottawa
CaOONMA	National Aviation Museum Library, Ottawa
CaOONMC	Canadian War Museum Library, Ottawa
CaOOP	Parliamentary Library, Ottawa
CaOOU	University of Ottawa
CaOPAL	The Chancellor Paterson Library, Lakehead University, Port Arthur, Ontario
CaOPALE	Education Library, Lakehead University, Port Arthur, Ontario
CaOTMCL	Metro Toronto Reference Library, Toronto, Ontario
CaOTP	Toronto Public Library, Toronto, Ontario
CaOTTC	John W. Graham Library, Trinity College, University of Toronto, Toronto, Ontario
CaOTU	Robarts Humanities & Social Sciences Library, University of Toronto, Toronto, Ontario
CaOTUTF	Fisher Rare Book Library, University of Toronto, Toronto, Ontario
CaOTY	Scott Library, York University, Toronto, Ontario
CaOTYL	Law Library, Osgoode Hall Law School, York University, Toronto, Ontario
CaOWA	University of Windsor, Windsor, Ontario
CaOWTL	Wilfrid Laurier University, Waterloo, Ontario
CaOWTU	University of Waterloo, Waterloo, Ontario
CaPCU	University of Prince Edward Island, Charlottetown
CaQLB	Bishop's University, Lennoxville, Quebec
CaQMBM	Bibliothèque de la Ville de Montréal, Montreal, Quebec
CaQMFA	Bibliothèque, Musée des beaux-arts, Montreal, Quebec
CaQMG	Webster Library, Concordia University, Montreal, Quebec

CaQMHE	Myriam and J.-Robert Ouimet Library, École des hautes études commerciales, Montreal, Quebec
CaQMJ	Jewish Public Library, Montreal, Quebec
CaQML	Concordia University Library, Loyola Campus, Montreal, Quebec
CaQMM	McLennan Library, McGill University, Montreal, Quebec
CaQMU	Université de Montréal, Montreal, Quebec
CaQWSMM	Westmount Public Library, Westmount, Quebec
CaSRU	University of Regina Library, Regina, Saskatchewan
CaSSU	University of Saskatchewan Library, Saskatoon, Saskatchewan
Cahoon	Herbert Cahoon, *The Overbrook Press Bibliography 1934–1959* (Stamford, CT: The Overbrook Press, 1963)
CB	Private collection, Halifax, Nova Scotia
CJZ	Private collection, Mission Viejo, California
Cockalorum	Christopher Sandford, *Cockalorum, A Sequel to Chanticleer and Pertelote, Being A Bibliography of the Golden Cockerell Press, June 1943–December 1948* ([London]: Golden Cockerel Press, [1948])
C.V.	*Companion Volumes* to the official biography (*WSC*), begun by Randolph S. Churchill (Volumes I and II) and completed by Martin Gilbert (Volumes III-VIII) (London: Heinemann, 1967–82)
C.W.P.	*Churchill War Papers*, Volumes I-III (London: Heinemann, 1993–2000)
DAT	Private collection, Hertfordshire, England
DkNL	Det Kongelige Bibliotek, Copenhagen
DLJ	Private collection, Vancouver, British Columbia
DN	Private collection, Sacramento, California
DT	Private collection, Ashburn, Virginia
ECB	English Catalogue of Books
ER	Private collection
EsNL	Biblioteca Nacional de España, Madrid
FBW	Collection of the late F. Bartlett Watt, Toronto, Ontario
FD	Private collection, Ontario
FrAv	Bibliothèque municipale, Avignon
FrNL	Bibliothèque nationale, Paris
FrPaBp	Bibliothèque du Centre culturel portugais, Paris

GPO	Government Printing Office, Washington, DC
HAC	Collection of the late Harry A. Cahn, London
Hanneman	Audre Hanneman, *Ernest Hemingway: A Comprehensive Bibliography*, 2nd printing with corrections (Princeton: Princeton University Press, 1969)
Henderson	George Henderson, *W. L. Mackenzie King: A Bibliography and Research Guide* (Toronto: University of Toronto Press, 1998)
HMSO	Her (or His) Majesty's Stationery Office, London
HrNL	Nacionalni i Sveučilišna Biblioteka, Zagreb
IeDTc	Trinity College, Dublin
IsTaL	Sha'ar Zion Municipal Library, Beit Ariella, Tel Aviv
ItBoU	Biblioteca di discipline umanistiche dell'Università degli studi di Bologna
ItNL	Biblioteca nazionale centrale Vittorio Emmanuele II, Rome
ItNLNa	Biblioteca nazionale Vittorio Emanuele III, Naples
ItRoSM	Biblioteca di storia moderna e contemporanea, Rome
JaNL	National Diet Library, Tokyo
JE	Collection of the late John Edison, Toronto, now a part of the holdings of the Fisher Rare Book Library, University of Toronto
Jones	Mary Lutz Jones, *A Los Angeles Typesticker: William M. Cheney : A Bibliography of His Printed Work* (Los Angeles: [s.n.], 1981 (Van Nuys, CA: Richard J. Hoffman)
Jong	Dirk de Jong, *Bibliografie van illegale en clandestiene bellettrie*, 2nd edition (Schiedam: Interbook International, 1978)
LLT	Collection of Lloyd Thomas
LT	Collection of Lowell Tuttman
Magee	*Bibliography of the Grabhorn Press 1940–1956 [with a Check-List, 1916–1940]* (San Francisco: Grabhorn, 1957)
Massmann	*The Bibliomidgets of Achille J. St. Onge: A Memorial and a Bibliography* (New Britain, CT: Massmann, 1979)
MC	Private collection, Bel-Air, California
MEW	Private collection
MG	Private collection, London, England
MLW	Private collection, Guildford, Surrey, England
MO	Private collection

MR	Private collection
NeNL	Koninklije Bibliotheek, The Hague
NeRoEU	Erasmus University Library, Rotterdam
NeRoL	Gemeente Bibliotheek, Rotterdam
NeUtU	Bibliotheek der Rijksuniversitet Utrecht
NZA	Auckland Public Library, Auckland
NZCh	Canterbury Public Library, Christchurch
NZChUC	Library, University of Canterbury, Christchurch
NZNL	National Library of New Zealand, Wellington
NZNLTu	Alexander Turnbull Library, National Library of New Zealand, Wellington
O'Brien	Philip O'Brien, *T. E. Lawrence: A Bibliography* (Boston: Hall, 1988)
PC	Unidentified private collection
PMM	*Printing and the Mind of Man*, 2nd revised and enlarged edition (Munich: Karl Pressler, 1983)
PMW	Private collection, Toronto
P.W.E.	Political Warfare Executive
RIC	Collection of the author
RML	Private collection, Contoocook, New Hampshire
RPH	Collection of the late Robert Hastings, Pasadena, California
Schroder	*Catalogue of Books and Manuscripts by Rupert Brooke Edward Marsh & Christopher Hassall Collected, Compiled and Annotated by John Schroder* (Cambridge: Rampant Lion Press, 1970)
SF	Collection of Steve Forbes
Spadoni	Carl Spadoni and Judy Donnelly, *A Bibliography of McClelland and Stewart Imprints, 1909–1985: A Publisher's Legacy* (Toronto: ECW Press, 1994)
SvLU	University Library (Lunds Universitetsbibliotek), Lund
SvNL	Kungliga Biblioteket (Sveriges nationalbibliotek), Stockholm
SwGBPU	Bibliothèque publique et universitaire, Geneva
SwZChL	Sir Winston Churchill Library, Zurich
TaNL	National Central Library, Taipei
TR	Private collection
TR2	Private collection

TuIsU	Beyazit Devlet Kütüphânesi, Istanbul
TuNL	Milli Kütüphane, Ankara
UKBiU	University of Birmingham
UKBL	British Library, London
UKBrU	University of Bristol Library
UKCaU	Cambridge University Library
UKChP	The Churchill Papers housed at the Roskill Library, Churchill College, Cambridge
UKChT	The Chartwell Trust papers housed at the Roskill Library, Churchill College, Cambridge
UKDuU	Durham University
UKFCL	Foreign and Commonwealth Library, London
UKIl	Local Studies and Archive Service, Redbridge Libraries, Central Library, Ilford, Essex
UKIWM	Imperial War Museum Library, London
UKLGh	Guildhall Library, London
UKLHa	Harrow School Archives Room, London
UKLKc	King's College, London
UKLeU	Leeds University
UKLiU	University of Liverpool
UKLo	Collection of the Marquess of Bath, Longleat, Warminster, Wiltshire/Wessex
UKLRcp	Library, Royal College of Physicians, London
UKLse	British Library of Political & Economic Science, London School of Economics
UKLUc	University College London
UKLWa	The Muniment Room & Library, Westminster Abbey, London
UKMa	Central Library, Manchester
UKMaU	John Rylands University Library of Manchester
UKOl	Local Studies Library, Oldham
UKOxB	The Bodleian Library, Oxford University
UKOxStA	St. Antony's College Library, Oxford University
UKScAb	Central Library, Aberdeen

UKScAbU	University of Aberdeen
UKScDu	Central Library, Dundee
UKScGl	Mitchell Library, Glasgow
UKScGlU	University of Glasgow
UKScNL	National Library of Scotland, Edinburgh
UKShU	Sheffield University
UKSoU	University of Southampton
UKWaNL	National Library of Wales, Aberystwyth
USCLU	University Research Library, UCLA, Los Angeles, California
USCLU-C	William Andrews Clark Memorial Library, UCLA, Los Angeles, California
USCPT	California Institute of Technology, Pasadena, California
USCSt	Stanford University Libraries, Stanford, California
USCSt-H	Hoover Institute on War, Revolution & Peace, Stanford, California
USCtY	Yale University Library, New Haven, Connecticut
USCtY-BR	Beinecke Rare Book and Manuscript Library, Yale University, New Haven, Connecticut
USCU-SB	University of California, Santa Barbara
USDeU	University of Delaware, Newark
USDLC	Library of Congress, Washington, DC
USDS	Department of State Library, Washington, DC
USFM	Miami Dade Public Library System, Miami, Florida
USFMU	University of Miami, Coral Gables, Florida
USICL	Loyola University, Chicago
USINS	Milner Library, Illinois State University, Normal
USICarbS	Morris Library, Southern Illinois University at Carbondale
USICRC	Roosevelt University, Chicago
USICSU	Paul and Emily Douglas Library, Chicago State University, Chicago
USIEdS	Lovejoy Library, Southern Illinois University at Edwardsville
USIEN	Northwestern University, Evanston, Illinois
USIMgO	Oakton Community College, Des Plaines, Illinois
USInNd	University of Notre Dame, Notre Dame, Indiana

USIU	University of Illinois Library at Urbana-Champaign
USLNaN	Northwestern State University, Watson Library, Natchitoches, Louisiana
USLNL	Monroe Library, Loyola University, New Orleans, Louisiana
USMB	Boston Public Library, Boston
USMBAt	Boston Athenaeum, Boston
USMBCo	Countway Library of Medicine, Harvard Medical School, Boston
USMdBJ	Johns Hopkins University Library, Baltimore, Maryland
USMdBU	University of Baltimore Library
USMH	Harvard University Libraries, Cambridge, Massachusetts
USMeLB	Bates College Library, Lewiston, Maine
USMi	Michigan State Library, Lansing
USMiKW	Waldo Library, Western Michigan University, Kalamazoo, Michigan
USMiU	University of Michigan Library
USMnCaE	East Central Regional Library, Cambridge, Minnesota
USMnU	Wilson Library, University of Minnesota, Minneapolis, Minnesota
USMoFuWc	Westminster College, Fulton, Missouri
USMWC	Robert Hutching Goddard Library, Clark University, Worcester, Massachusetts
USNBB	Brooklyn Museum Library, Brooklyn, New York
USNbU	University of Nebraska Library, Omaha, Nebraska
USNcD	Perkins/Bostock Library, Duke University, Durham, North Carolina
USNcRS	North Carolina State University, Raleigh, North Carolina
USNcU	University of North Carolina, Chapel Hill, North Carolina
USNhD	Dartmouth College Library, Hanover, New Hampshire
USNjP	Princeton University Library, Princeton, New Jersey
USNN	New York Public Library
USNNC	Columbia University, New York City
USOCoC	Capital University, Columbus, Ohio
USOKentU	Kent State University, Kent, Ohio
USOrU	University of Oregon Library, Eugene, Oregon
USOU	Ohio State University, Columbus, Ohio

USPPT	Temple University, Philadelphia, Pennsylvania
USScU	University of South Carolina, Columbia
USTU	University of Tennessee at Knoxville
USTxU	University of Texas at Austin
USULA	Merrill Library, Utah State Library, Logan, Utah
USViU	Alderman Library, University of Virginia, Charlottesville
USWaT	Tacoma Public Library, Tacoma, Washington
USWaU	Allen Library, University of Washington Libraries, Seattle
USWM	Milwaukee Public Library
VF	Collection of Valda Forbes
WDF	Private collection, Montreal, Quebec
White	Arthur S. White, *A Bibliography of Regimental Histories of the British Army*, 2nd edition (London: London Stock Exchange, 1988)
WHJ	Private collection, Omaha, Nebraska
Woods	*A Bibliography of the Works of Sir Winston Churchill KG, OM, CH* by Frederick Woods, 2nd revised edition (Godalming, Surrey: St Paul's Bibliographies, [1979])
ZANL	National Library of South Africa, Cape Town
ZAPrU	University of Pretoria
ZACtU	University of Cape Town

ISCC-NBS COLOR-NAME CHARTS ILLUSTRATED WITH CENTROID COLORS

Those who wish to be able to relate the names of the colours used in the text of the bibliography to the colour chips on the *ISCC-NBS Color-Name Charts Illustrated with Centroid Colors* (the Centroid Color Charts) may consult the following alphabetical list of all those colours referred to in the text; the Centroid colour reference number is given in parentheses. In the few cases in which I have "adopted" a colour that is not in the Centroid Color Charts, that information is provided in brackets following the colour name.

black (267)
blackish blue (188)
blackish green (152)
blackish purple (230)
blackish red (21)
bluish grey (191)
brilliant blue (177)
brilliant green (140)
brilliant greenish blue (168)
brilliant greenish yellow (98)
brilliant orange yellow (67)
brilliant purplish blue (195)
brilliant yellow (83)
brilliant yellow green (116)
bronze [no such Centroid colour]
brownish black (65)
brownish grey (64)
brownish orange (54)
copper [no such Centroid colour]
dark blue (183)
dark bluish green (165)
dark bluish grey (192)
dark brown (59)
dark green (146)
dark greenish blue (174)
dark greenish yellow (103)
dark grey (266)
dark greyish blue (187)
dark greyish brown (62)
dark greyish green (151)
dark greyish olive (111)
dark greyish purple (229)
dark greyish red (20)
dark greyish reddish brown (47)

dark greyish yellow (91)
dark greyish yellowish brown (81)
dark olive (108)
dark olive green (126)
dark orange red [no such Centroid colour]
dark orange yellow (72)
dark pink (6)
dark purple (224)
dark purplish blue (201)
dark purplish grey (234)
dark purplish pink (251)
dark purplish red (259)
dark red (16)
dark reddish brown (44)
dark reddish grey (23)
dark reddish orange (38)
dark reddish purple (242)
dark violet (212)
dark yellow (88)
dark yellowish brown (78)
dark yellowish green (137)
dark yellowish pink (30)
deep blue (179)
deep bluish green (161)
deep brown (56)
deep green (142)
deep greenish yellow (100)
deep orange (51)
deep orange red [no such Centroid colour]
deep orange yellow (69)
deep pink (3)
deep purple (219)

deep purplish blue (197)
deep purplish pink (248)
deep purplish red (256)
deep red (13)
deep reddish brown (41)
deep reddish orange (36)
deep reddish purple (238)
deep violet (208)
deep yellow (85)
deep yellow green (118)
deep yellowish brown (75)
deep yellowish green (132)
deep yellowish pink (27)
gold [no such Centroid colour]
greenish grey (155)
greyish blue (186)
greyish brown (61)
greyish green (150)
greyish greenish yellow (105)
greyish olive green (127)
greyish pink (8)
greyish purple (228)
greyish purplish blue (204)
greyish purplish red (262)
greyish red (19)
greyish reddish brown (46)
greyish reddish orange (39)
greyish reddish purple (245)
greyish yellow (90)
greyish yellow green (122)
greyish yellowish brown (80)
greyish yellowish pink (32)
light blue (181)
light bluish green (163)
light bluish grey (190)
light brown (57)
light brownish grey (63)
light greenish blue (172)
light greenish grey (154)
light greenish yellow (101)
light grey (264)
light greyish brown (60)
light greyish olive (109)
light greyish purplish red (261)
light greyish red (18)
light greyish reddish orange (39)
light greyish yellowish brown (79)

light olive (106)
light olive grey (112)
light orange (52)
light orange red [no such Centroid
  colour]
light orange yellow (70)
light purplish blue (199)
light reddish brown (42)
light reddish purple (240)
light yellow (86)
light yellow green (119)
light yellowish brown (76)
light yellowish green (135)
light yellowish pink (28)
medium grey (265)
moderate blue (182)
moderate bluish green (164)
moderate brown (58)
moderate green (145)
moderate greenish blue (173)
moderate greenish yellow (102)
moderate olive (107)
moderate olive brown (95)
moderate olive green (125)
moderate orange (53)
moderate orange yellow (71)
moderate pink (5)
moderate purple (223)
moderate purplish blue (200)
moderate purplish red (258)
moderate red (15)
moderate reddish brown (43)
moderate reddish orange (37)
moderate reddish purple (241)
moderate violet (211)
moderate yellow (87)
moderate yellow green (120)
moderate yellowish brown (77)
moderate yellowish green (136)
moderate yellowish pink (29)
olive grey (113)
orange red [no such Centroid colour]
pale blue (185)
pale green (149)
pale greenish yellow (104)
pale orange yellow (73)
pale purple (227)

pale purplish blue (203)
pale purplish pink (252)
pale reddish purple (244)
pale yellow (89)
pale yellow green (121)
pale yellowish pink (31)
pinkish grey (10)
reddish black (24)
reddish grey (22)
reddish purple (237)
silver [no such Centroid colour]
strong blue (178)
strong bluish green (160)
strong greenish blue (169)
strong orange (50)
strong orange yellow (68)
strong purplish blue (196)
strong purplish pink (247)
strong purplish red (255)
strong red (12)
strong reddish brown (40)
strong reddish orange (35)
strong reddish purple (237)
strong violet (207)
strong yellow (84)
strong yellowish brown (74)
strong yellowish green (131)
strong yellowish pink (26)
very dark bluish green (166)

very dark green (147)
very dark greenish blue (175)
very dark purplish red (260)
very dark red (17)
very dark yellowish green (138)
very deep purple (220)
very deep red (14)
very light blue (180)
very light green (143)
very light greenish blue (171)
very light purplish blue (198)
very pale purplish blue (202)
very pale violet (213)
vivid blue (176)
vivid green (139)
vivid greenish blue (167)
vivid greenish yellow (97)
vivid orange (48)
vivid orange yellow (166)
vivid purplish blue (194)
vivid purplish red (254)
vivid red (11)
vivid reddish orange (34)
vivid yellow (82)
vivid yellowish green (129)
vivid yellowish pink (25)
white (263)
yellowish grey (93)
yellowish white (92)

SECTION B

Contributions to Books, Pamphlets, Leaflets and Portfolios

This section contains titles in which a Churchill contribution in the form of a foreword, preface, introduction, chapter, appendix, epilogue, or innominate division of the work (including works in which a letter is employed as any of the foregoing) appears as part of a book, pamphlet, leaflet or unbound portfolio written, edited or compiled by someone else. The titles are arranged chronologically. Contributions previously unpublished are so identified; references to previous appearances in periodical, volume, pamphlet or leaflet form are provided. All British, American, Canadian and Australian editions, issues and states are described and subsequent printings are noted.

NATIONAL REFORM UNION PUBLICATIONS. | [17.6-mm rule] | [deep reddish orange] THE WAR | AGAINST THE | DUTCH REPUBLICS | IN SOUTH AFRICA | ITS ORIGIN, PROGRESS, AND RESULTS, | [black] BY | H. J. OGDEN. | [ranged left] ANNOTATED WITH .... | [centred] Extracts from Books, Newspapers, Pamphlets, | AND | OTHER LEADERS OF PUBLIC OPINION. | [50.3-mm thick–thin rule] | [deep reddish orange] *"Give me facts, feed me on facts."* | [ranged right] CARLYLE. | [black, centred] Price = ONE SHILLING *Net.* | [17.6-mm rule] | Printed by Taylor, Garnett, Evans, & Co., Ltd., Manchester, Reddish, and London. | Published by the National Reform Union, Haworth's Buildings, 5, Cross Street, Manchester.

PUBLICATION: Manchester: National Reform Union, August 1901. Price 1*s*.

PAGINATION: 344.

CONTRIBUTIONS: Article bearing date-line of 20 November 1899 in the *Morning Post*, on Boer treatment of the wounded: pp. 149–50; statement of 18 February 1901[1] in the House of Commons: p. 199; telegram to the *Manchester Guardian* of 2 April 1900: p. 208; and extract from address of 17 August 1900 at the Guildhall, Plymouth: p. 297.

This is the first volume appearance of each of the pieces and the only volume appearance of the telegram to the *Manchester Guardian*.[2] The *Morning Post* letter was subsequently published in Frederick Woods, ed., *Young Winston's Wars* (**A282**), at pp. 173–7; the maiden speech in Rhodes James, Vol. I, at pp. 65–70, under the title 'The Maiden Speech', and in David Cannadine, ed., *Blood, Toil, Tears and Sweat* (**A290**), at pp. 20–7, under the title '"A Certain Splendid Memory"'; and the Guildhall address in Rhodes James, Vol. I, pp. 56–8, under the title 'Army Reform'.

NOTE: Copies were originally issued in moderate red paper-covered boards with a cloth spine reading vertically up: 'THE WAR AGAINST THE DUTCH REPUBLICS.—H. J. OGDEN'. Since the binding was perishable, such copies are very scarce. Always uncommon, copies may also be seen in various binders' cloths with the more durable paper cover title pasted onto the front. The surface of the paper label is 246 × 165 mm and the back is covered by a blank label of the same size and colour.

LOCATIONS: RIC, UKMaU, USMH, ZANL

---

1. Incorrectly referred to by Ogden as *19* February. The 18th was, of course, the date of Churchill's maiden speech in the House of Commons and the lines quoted include the famous "If I were a Boer fighting in the field—and if I were a Boer, I hope I should be fighting in the field" (presented by Ogden in the third person, in the old style of Hansard). The maiden speech is found in *H. C. Debates*, 1 Edw. VII, 4th Series, Vol. LXXXIX, cols. 407–15.

2. For the time being, it is in fact the *only* known appearance of the telegram in any form. I have made several attempts to locate Churchill's telegram to the *Manchester Guardian* in the newspaper itself, whether before, on or after the 2 April date. Even with the help of the keepers of the *Guardian* archives, the item has not been located in its periodical appearance and cannot, at present, be cross-referenced to Section C.

B2   NATIONAL PHYSICAL TRAINING   1904

NATIONAL | PHYSICAL TRAINING | AN OPEN DEBATE | EDITED BY | J. B. ATKINS | LONDON | ISBISTER & COMPANY | 15 & 16 TAVISTOCK STREET COVENT GARDEN | 1904

PUBLICATION: London: Isbister, June 1904. Price 2s. 6d.

PAGINATION: xvi, 238, 2-page catalogue.

CONTRIBUTION: 'Good Feeding a Necessary Antecedent to All Physical Training' (Chapter IX): pp. 70–3. Only appearance in volume form.

The volume consists of papers and reports of conversations which originally appeared in the *Manchester Guardian* and are reprinted with its permission. According to the editor, "Only a few alterations and additions have been made since." I have been unable to locate the original periodical appearance.

LOCATIONS: RIC, SF, UKBL, UKScNL, USMBCo, USMH, USViU

REFERENCE: Woods D(b)23/2.

B3   COMING MEN ON COMING QUESTIONS   1905

COMING MEN | ON | COMING QUESTIONS. | EDITED BY W. T. STEAD. | "REVIEW OF REVIEWS" OFFICE, | 3, WHITEFRIARS STREET, LONDON, E.C.

PUBLICATION: London: *Review of Reviews,* 1905.

PAGINATION: viii, 476, 25 leaves of plates.

CONTRIBUTION: 'Why I Am a Free Trader': pp. 6–22. First published separately as **A15**.

NOTE: Page 372 is erroneously numbered '72'.

ANNOTATIONS: Some notes on the publication of the series of 26 parts which constitute the volume and the intentions of its compiler, W. T. Stead, the Editor of the *Review of Reviews,* can be found at **A15**. In the April 1905 issue of his magazine, Stead described the composite volume as a "Handbook for the General Election and the next Parliament". The projected volume would in part be "probably from the pen of the Editor [but] the bulk of it [would be] contributed articles on Coming Questions by the Coming Men who after the next Election will be the leading factors in the new Parliament which will control the destinies of the British Empire."

LOCATIONS: CaOHM, FBW, RPH, SF, USMH

REFERENCE: Woods B2.

B4   THE BRAVEST DEED I EVER SAW   1905

Copies in different binding cases within each printing have been noted. I have been unable to assign priority to any of these on the basis of information currently available.

B4.1.a   First edition, first printing, very dark greenish blue cloth binding (1905)

THE BRAVEST DEED | I EVER SAW [two leaf decorations] | STORIES OF PERSONAL EXPERIENCE | AS TOLD BY | [22 names in 8 lines], And Others | EDITED BY | ALFRED H. MILES | *ILLUSTRATED BY VERNON PEARCE* | LONDON | HUTCHINSON & CO. | 34 PATERNOSTER ROW

PUBLICATION: London: Hutchinson, November 1905. Price 5*s*. There were no fewer than four printings of this edition; however, I have unearthed no information which permits me to date the later printings with any certainty.

PAGINATION: 364, [4], 8 leaves of plates.

CONTRIBUTION: 'The Doctor and the Soldier': pp. 162–4. Originally published in *V.C.* on 16 July 1903 (**C223**). The entire chapter containing 'The Doctor and the Soldier' continues to p. 170, Churchill's contribution being limited to the first 3 pages. This is the only appearance of the essay in volume form.

BINDING: The volume is bound in very dark greenish blue unembossed calico-texture cloth. The title of the volume is stamped in gilt and, ranged right beneath it, against a solid light bluish grey sky, there is a picture of a soldier with sabre drawn, mounted on his steed, raising aloft the standard of his fallen comrade, who, in a solid light bluish grey uniform, lies next to a dismantled cannon. Ranged left is a waving standard bearing the names of 13 of the 22 contributors, stamped in gilt. The edges are gilt all around.

LOCATIONS: FBW, USIU, USNhD

REFERENCE: Woods B1.

B4.1.b   First edition, first printing, deep red cloth binding (1905)

BINDING: The volume is bound in deep red unembossed calico-texture cloth. The title of the volume is stamped in gilt and the sky is a blackish blue, fading to pale blue; the soldier's uniform is blackish blue with light yellow stripes.

LOCATIONS: RIC, RPH

B4.1.c   First edition, second printing (1905?)

All second-printing copies examined were bound in very dark green cloth. The title is stamped in gilt and the names of the contributors are in black. The uniform of the fallen soldier and the sky behind the mounted soldier are a solid bluish grey. The stripes on the uniform are white. The colours of the sky are not graduated. The edges are gilt all around.

LOCATION: USDLC

B4.1.d   First edition, third printing (1905?)

The third printing is distinguished only by the addition of the words '𝕿𝖍𝖎𝖗𝖉 𝕰𝖉𝖎𝖙𝖎𝖔𝖓' on the line following the name of the editor on the title page. All copies examined bear the Hutchinson imprint.

I have examined three binding variants of the third printing, all in unembossed calico-texture cloth.

> **BINDING VARIANT A:** Copies are bound in very dark greenish blue cloth. The title and the names of the contributors are stamped in gilt and the fallen soldier's uniform and the sky are a solid light bluish grey. The colours of the sky are not graduated. The edges are gilt all around. On one copy examined, the back bears the words '𝕯𝖔𝖑𝖑𝖆𝖗 𝕴𝖓𝖘𝖙𝖎𝖙𝖚𝖙𝖎𝖔𝖓', stamped in gilt, within a top-opening wreath.

BINDING VARIANT B: Copies are bound in moderate greenish blue cloth. The title is stamped in gilt and the names of the contributors are in black. The uniform of the fallen soldier and the sky behind the mounted soldier are a solid medium grey. The stripes on the uniform are white. The colours of the sky are not graduated. The edges are not gilt.

BINDING VARIANT C: Copies are bound in moderate greenish blue cloth. The title and the names of the contributors are stamped in gilt and the fallen soldier's uniform is vivid orange with vivid yellow stripes. The sky is blackish blue fading to pale blue. The edges are gilt all around.

LOCATIONS: RIC (binding variants a, b and c), USMoFuWc (binding variant b)

B4.1.e   First edition, fourth printing (1905?)

The fourth printing is distinguished only by the addition of the words '𝔉ourth 𝔈dition' following the name of the editor. The only copy examined bears the Hutchinson imprint and is bound in variant binding (b) described above.

LOCATION: RIC

B4.2   Canadian issue of British sheets (1905?)

A Canadian issue of the British sheets was published by Copp, Clark in Toronto. The title page is a *cancellans*:

THE BRAVEST DEED | I EVER SAW [two leaf decorations] | STORIES OF PERSONAL EXPERIENCE | AS TOLD BY | [22 names in 8 lines], And Others | EDITED BY | ALFRED H. MILES | 𝔖econd 𝔈dition | *ILLUSTRATED BY VERNON PEARCE* | THE COPP, CLARK COMPANY, LIMITED | TORONTO

NOTES: The printer's imprint on the copyright page is reduced to: 'PRINTED IN GREAT BRITAIN'. Although described as the 'Second Edition', there have been no textual changes noted, other than on the title page. Copies have been noted bound in the deep red cloth described above and in binding variant (a) (but without the back cover stamp). The edges are gilt all around. Following the names of the 13 contributors listed on the spine, the name of the Canadian publisher is given thus: 'The Copp, Clark | Company, Ltd.'

LOCATIONS: CaOONL, CaOTTC, RIC

B5   FREE TRADE LEAGUE   1908

[Dropped-head title only] FREE TRADE LEAGUE. | [22.9-mm French rule]
PAGINATION: 2. Leaflet.

CONTRIBUTION: 6-line letter of 10 April 1908 from Churchill at the Colonial Office: p. 1.

LOCATION: RIC

B6   THE GOSPEL OF SOCIALISM   [1908]

THE GOSPEL | OF | SOCIALISM. | BY | HECTOR MACPHERSON. | *WITH PREFACE BY* | THE RIGHT HON. WINSTON S. CHURCHILL, M.P. | [37.8-mm double rule] | JOHN LENG & CO., LTD., DUNDEE AND LONDON.

PUBLICATION: Dundee: Leng, [1908].[3]

PAGINATION: 32. Pamphlet in deep yellowish pink and black on white paper wrappers; thickness: 0.12 mm.

CONTRIBUTION: Preface, entitled 'A FOREWORD ON SOCIALISM.', signed in facsimile, 'Winston S. Churchill': p. 3.[4] The 453-word Preface closely resembles a portion of Churchill's speech of 14 May 1908 in Kinnaird Hall, Dundee. The first lengthy (359-word) paragraph differs from the three comparable paragraphs of the speech as published in *Liberalism and the Social Problem* (**A29**).[5] The principal difference consists in the elimination of references to the election; however, there are other minor editorial emendations. The second paragraph of the Preface is entirely new. Note also that the text of the MacPherson pamphlet was first published in August 1908 in the *Edinburgh Evening News*. An earlier (shorter) version of the pamphlet, encompassing editorials published in that newspaper in August 1906, but without the Churchill preface, was Pamphlet No. 9 of the Young Scots Publication Department.

LOCATIONS: CaOTTC, LLT, RIC, UKScDu, USIU, USMH, USMiU

REFERENCE: Woods B3.

B7   LETTERS ADDRESSED TO A. P. WATT   1909

LETTERS | ADDRESSED | [vivid reddish orange, artistic acorn device facing horizontally left; black] TO | [vivid reddish orange, artistic acorn device facing horizontally right] | [black] A • P • WATT | [vivid reddish orange, artistic acorn device, vertical] | [black] LONDON [vivid reddish orange, small artistic acorn device facing horizontally right; black] A. P. WATT | & SON: HASTINGS HOVSE [*sic*] | NORFOLK ST: STRAND 1909

PUBLICATION: London: A. P. Watt, 1909.

PAGINATION: [2], xxvi, [4], 204, plus card wrappers.

CONTRIBUTION: Letter of 20 February 1901 from Churchill's Mount Street address: p. 43.

NOTE: Apparently, the well-known agent A. P. Watt[6] published a volume of testimonial letters from the firm's clients frequently, if not annually. I have had the opportunity to examine several of these volumes;[7] however, none other than that of 1909 contained the 1901 letter from Churchill (or a letter from him of any other date). Although these

---

3. It is clear that the pamphlet cannot have been published before August 1908; however, the precise date of publication remains somewhat speculative. Neither the Central Library, Dundee (which holds some of Leng's personal papers and a copy of *The Gospel of Socialism*), nor the National Library of Scotland has any information regarding the publication date of the pamphlet. Note that Sir John Leng was himself the publisher and editor of the *Dundee Advertiser* from 1851 until 1905 and sat as a Liberal M.P. for Dundee from 1888 to 1905.

4. Woods (p. 148) incorrectly describes the pamphlet as "containing a 1½p. Preface".

5. The paragraphs run from p. 154.7 to p. 156.4 of *Liberalism and the Social Problem* and contain 395 words. The speech is there entitled 'The Dundee Election'.

6. Alexander Pollock Watt (1837–1914) had arranged for the publication of the *Story of the Malakand Field Force* by Longmans.

7. No library of which the author is aware, including the British Library, the National Library of Scotland and A. P. Watt's own London office archives, holds more than a few of the volumes, none of which includes the Churchill letter.

volumes of client letters to Watt are extremely uncommon, it is possible that another such volume, even an earlier volume or volumes (given the date of the Churchill letter), may yet be discovered which contains this very Churchill missive. This is the more so true since two of the 1909 volumes that I have examined contained a leaf which reads in part: 'This volume contains letters, not printed | in former editions, from the following | Authors:– | [there follows a list of 26 authors, which does *not* include Churchill]'.[8]

LOCATIONS: CaOONL, RIC, USNhD, USNN

B8 LAKE VICTORIA TO KHARTOUM 1909

B8.1 First edition, British issue (1909)

[Deep reddish orange] LAKE VICTORIA | TO KHARTOUM | [black] WITH RIFLE & CAMERA | BY CAPTAIN F. A. DICKINSON | D.C.L.I., F.R.G.S., WITH AN INTRODUCTION | [strong reddish orange] BY THE RT. HON. WINSTON CHURCHILL | [black] AND NUMEROUS ILLUSTRATIONS FROM | PHOTOGRAPHS TAKEN BY THE AUTHOR | [strong reddish orange] LONDON JOHN LANE THE BODLEY HEAD | [black] NEW YORK JOHN LANE COMPANY MCMX

PUBLICATION: London: John Lane The Bodley Head, 1910 [November 1909]. Price 12*s*. 6*d*.

PAGINATION: xx, 334, [22], 49 leaves of plates.

CONTRIBUTION: 'INTRODUCTION': pp. v–vii.

NOTE: The British issue is distinguished by its orange red unembossed calico-texture cloth binding, the reference to the Churchill Introduction on the front and spine and the British publisher's imprint on the spine, 'THE BODLEY HEAD'.

LOCATIONS: CaOTTC, RPH, UKBL, USMH, USMoFuWc

REFERENCE: Woods B4.

B8.2 American issue of British sheets (1910)

As the first edition, except that the binding is a dark red ribbed-grain or embossed calico-texture cloth with no reference to the Churchill Introduction on the front or spine and with the American publisher's imprint on the spine, 'JOHN LANE | COMPANY'.

LOCATIONS: RIC, USMoFuWc

B9 LETTER TO ELECTORS 1910

There are at least two separate editions of the publication; on the basis of information currently available, I am unable to assign priority.

B9.1 *Morning Leader* edition (1910)

[Cover title:] [ranged upper right] *Price One Penny.* | MR. LLOYD-GEORGE'S | Great Mile-End Speech. | [32.2-mm rule] | CARTOONS FROM THE "MORNING LEADER." | [32.2-mm rule] | Mr. Winston Churchill's Letter to Electors. | [cartoon in

---

8. In the National Library of Canada volume, the leaf has been tipped in facing p. xxvi; in the New York Public Library volume, the leaf is laid in.

thick (2.4-mm) single-rule box, enclosing 143.3 × 119.5 mm] | [below the box] IN THE GRIP OF THE PEOPLE.

PUBLICATION: London: *Morning Leader*, 1910.

PAGINATION: [*12*]. Pamphlet in self-wrappers.

CONTRIBUTION: ' "Veto—Utter, Blank, Sullen Veto!" ', Churchill's letter of 14 November 1910: pp. 8–10.

ANNOTATIONS: Faced with continuous vetoes by the Tory-dominated House of Lords, Asquith, the Liberal Prime Minister of the day, was forced to ask the King to grant a dissolution of Parliament, in order to make an election issue out of reform of the Lords. This election pamphlet is not a subtle document.

The text states clearly that the Churchill letter was also *separately* issued as a 4-page folded leaflet[9] (supplied at 3*s*. 6*d*. for 1000 copies carriage paid and at 3*s*. for lots of 5000 copies, carriage forward) but I have not located a single copy to examine[10] nor have I ever seen any reference to the separate publication in any library or union catalogue, auction record or dealer catalogue.

LOCATION: USNN (microform)

B9.2 *Sheffield Independent* edition (1910)

There is a separate edition published by the *Sheffield Independent Press* which includes Churchill's letter under the headline, taken from the text, ' "Veto – Utter, Blank, Sullen Veto!" ' on 2 pages. I have been unable to locate a copy.

B10 HOME RULE IN A NUTSHELL 1912

B10.1 Third edition, only printing (1912)

HOME RULE IN A | NUTSHELL. | A POCKET BOOK FOR SPEAKERS AND | ELECTORS. | *CONTAINING A BRIEF EXPOSITION OF THE | ARGUMENTS FOR HOME RULE, AND ANSWERS | TO THE OBJECTIONS RAISED.* | :: :: :: | BY | JEREMIAH MacVEAGH, M.P. | WITH INTRODUCTION BY | RT. HON. WINSTON S. CHURCHILL, M.P., | *First Lord of the Admiralty* | [6.1-mm rule] | *THIRD IMPRESSION.* | [6.1-mm rule] | 𝔏𝔬𝔫𝔡𝔬𝔫: | THE DAILY CHRONICLE, Fleet Street. | THE IRISH PRESS AGENCY, 2 Great Smith Street. | HOME RULE COUNCIL, Great Smith Street. | 𝔇𝔲𝔟𝔩𝔦𝔫: | 𝔖𝔈𝔄𝔏𝔜, 𝔅𝔯𝔶𝔢𝔯𝔰 & 𝔚𝔞𝔩𝔨𝔢𝔯, 86 𝔐𝔦𝔡𝔡𝔩𝔢 𝔄𝔟𝔟𝔢𝔶 𝔖𝔱𝔯𝔢𝔢𝔱.

PUBLICATION: London: *Daily Chronicle*, 9 January 1912. Price 1*d*.[11]

PAGINATION: xii, 92. Pamphlet in paper wrappers. Sewn.

---

9. Presumably entitled *Mr. Winston Churchill's Letter*, although the title may have been selected from either the title or sub-title on p. 8: ' "Veto—Utter, Blank, Sullen Veto!" | [26.1-mm thin–thick rule] | MR. WINSTON CHURCHILL'S CALL TO ARMS. | [26.1-mm thick–thin rule] | Home Office, London, S.W., 14th November, 1910.'

10. Any such pamphlet would, of course, be a Section A item.

11. Note that the first edition (pp. x, 86), without the Churchill Introduction, was published in November 1911. The price of the first edition, according to the *English Catalogue of Books*, was 7*d*. cased or 3*d*. in wrappers. A total of 67,000 copies of the first and second editions had been sold by the date of publication of the third edition.

CONTRIBUTION: Contrary to Woods,[12] it is not the fourth edition which first carries the Churchill Introduction. It is the third edition which does so: pp. iii–vi.[13] It was first published (in part) in *The Times* of 8 January 1912 and the *Manchester Guardian* of the same date (see **C230a** and **C230b** respectively), and subsequently published in the *Collected Essays*, Vol. II, at pp. 40–2.

NOTE: The pamphlet (135.8 × 101.5 mm) is small. It reads [A]⁴ B–D¹⁶, each signature being gathered within the preceding one.

ANNOTATIONS: The new edition of the book was advertised in the *Daily Chronicle* of 9 January 1912 (at p. 5) and its purchase was urged by the newspaper in the following terms: "Every elector in the kingdom should read this book. It presents a bird's-eye view of the case for Home Rule."

LOCATIONS: CaOTMCL, RIC, USNhD

B10.2   Fourth edition, only printing (1912)

HOME RULE IN A | NUTSHELL. | A POCKET BOOK FOR SPEAKERS AND | ELECTORS. | *CONTAINING A BRIEF EXPOSITION OF THE | ARGUMENTS FOR HOME RULE, AND ANSWERS | TO THE OBJECTIONS RAISED.* | :: :: :: | BY | JEREMIAH MacVEAGH, M.P. | WITH INTRODUCTION BY | RT. HON. WINSTON S. CHURCHILL, M.P., | *First Lord of the Admiralty* | [6.4-mm rule] | *FOURTH EDITION, REVISED, ENLARGED AND RESET.* | [6.4-mm rule] | 𝔏𝔬𝔫𝔡𝔬𝔫: | THE DAILY CHRONICLE, Fleet Street. | THE IRISH PRESS AGENCY, 2 Great Smith Street. | HOME RULE COUNCIL, Great Smith Street. | 𝔇𝔲𝔟𝔩𝔦𝔫: | 𝔖𝔢𝔞𝔩𝔶, 𝔅𝔯𝔶𝔢𝔯𝔰 & 𝔚𝔞𝔩𝔨𝔢𝔯, 86 𝔐𝔦𝔡𝔡𝔩𝔢 𝔄𝔟𝔟𝔢𝔶 𝔖𝔱𝔯𝔢𝔢𝔱.

PUBLICATION: London: *Daily Chronicle*, 1912.

PAGINATION: xii, 84.

CONTRIBUTION: Introduction: pp. iii–vii.

LOCATIONS: MLW, UKBL, USNhD

REFERENCE: Woods B5.

B11   STATEMENT SHOWING THE PRESENT AND NEW RATES OF PAY FOR THE ROYAL NAVY AND ROYAL MARINES   1912

ROYAL NAVY (PAY). | [29.5-mm thin–thick rule] | STATEMENT | SHOWING THE | PRESENT AND NEW RATES OF PAY | FOR THE | ROYAL NAVY AND ROYAL MARINES. | [118.5-mm double rule] | 𝔓𝔯𝔢𝔰𝔢𝔫𝔱𝔢𝔡 𝔱𝔬 𝔓𝔞𝔯𝔩𝔦𝔞𝔪𝔢𝔫𝔱 𝔟𝔶 ℭ𝔬𝔪𝔪𝔞𝔫𝔡 𝔬𝔣 𝔥𝔦𝔰 𝔐𝔞𝔧𝔢𝔰𝔱𝔶. | [118.5-mm double rule] | [royal arms, 47.2 × 40.9 mm] | LONDON : | PUBLISHED BY HIS MAJESTY'S STATIONERY OFFICE. | To be purchased,

---

12. Woods states, at p. 149: "The preceding editions [*i.e.* those prior to the *fourth*] do not contain Churchill's Introduction."

13. While I have been unable to locate a second edition of the work in order to ensure that the Churchill Introduction is not to be found there (it is clearly *not* included in the first edition, which I have examined), I am confident that the Introduction *first* appeared in the third edition. See the note to this effect in the *Manchester Guardian* of 4 January 1912, at p. 6.

either directly or through any Bookseller, from | WYMAN AND SONS, LTD., FETTER LANE, E.C., 32, ABINGDON STREET, LONDON, S.W. ; or | H.M. STATIONERY OFFICE (SCOTTISH BRANCH), 23, FORTH STREET, EDINBURGH ; or | E. PONSONBY, LTD., 116, GRAFTON STREET, DUBLIN ; or from the Agencies in the British Colonies and Dependencies, | the United States of America, the Continent of Europe and Abroad of | T. FISHER UNWIN, LONDON, W.C. | [29-mm rule] | PRINTED BY | EYRE AND SPOTTISWOODE, LTD., EAST HARDING STREET, E.C., | PRINTERS TO THE KING'S MOST EXCELLENT MAJESTY. | 1912. | [ranged lower left] [Cd. 6118.] [*sic*, immediately preceding brackets original] [centred] *Price* 1½*d.*

PUBLICATION: London: HMSO, December 1912, 3000 copies. Price 1½*d.*

PAGINATION: 10. Pamphlet in self-wrappers.

CONTRIBUTION: Introduction, without title, of 4 December 1912 (signed 'W.S.C.'): p. 2.

LOCATIONS: CaQMM, UKBL

B12   THE NAVAL ANNUAL, 1912   1912

THE | NAVAL ANNUAL, | 1912. | [39.6-mm rule] | EDITED BY | VISCOUNT HYTHE, D.C.L., A.I.N.A., | *Honorary Fellow of Balliol ; Commander of the Order of the Crown of Italy.* | [39.6-mm rule] | PART I.—EARL BRASSEY, G.C.B. ; SIR WILLIAM H. WHITE, K.C.B. ; | Commander C. N. ROBINSON, R.N. ; JOHN LEYLAND ; | ALEXANDER RICHARDSON ; and the EDITOR. | PART II.—List of Ships : Commander C. N. ROBINSON, R.N. and | JOHN LEYLAND. | Plans of Ships : S. W. BARNABY, M.I.N.A. | PART III.—Armour and Ordnance: Commander C. N. ROBINSON, | R.N. | PART IV.—FIRST LORD'S MEMORANDUM, AND SPEECH ON INTRO- | DUCTION OF NAVY ESTIMATES; BRITISH AND FOREIGN | ESTIMATES. | 1912. | J. GRIFFIN AND CO., 2, THE HARD, PORTSMOUTH. | (BOOKSELLERS TO HER LATE MAJESTY QUEEN VICTORIA.) | *Foreign Agents:* | PARIS : BOYVEAU & CHEVILLET, 22, RUE DE LA BANQUE. | NEW YORK : D. VAN NOSTRAND COMPANY. BERLIN : W. H. KÜHL. | HONG KONG, SHANGHAI, AND YOKOHAMA : KELLY, WALSH & CO. | TOKYO & OSAKA : MARUZEN-KABUSHIKI-KAISHA. | TOKYO : THE METHODIST PUBLISHING COMPANY. | BUENOS AYRES [*sic*] : MITCHELL'S BOOK STORES.

PUBLICATION: Portsmouth: Griffin, May 1912. Price 12*s.* 6*d.*

PAGINATION: vii, [1], 483, [1], 82 leaves of plates, 1 diagram.

CONTRIBUTIONS: 'First Lord's Statement [of 4 March 1912] explanatory of the Navy Estimates, 1912–13': pp. 367–84; 'First Lord's Memo on Naval War Staff': pp. 385–90; minute by First Lord on the appointment of an additional Civil Lord: pp. 391–2; 'First Lord's Speech of 18 March 1912': pp. 412–34.

LOCATIONS: CaOONMC, USMH

B13   THE NAVAL ANNUAL, 1913   1913

B13.1   First edition, only printing (1913)

THE | NAVAL ANNUAL, | 1913. | EDITED BY | VISCOUNT HYTHE, D.C.L., A.I.N.A., | *Honorary Fellow of Balliol; Commander of the Order of the Crown of Italy*. | 1913. | J. GRIFFIN AND CO., | 2, THE HARD, PORTSMOUTH. | (BOOKSELLERS TO HER LATE MAJESTY QUEEN VICTORIA.) | *Foreign Agents:* | PARIS : BOYVEAU & CHEVILLET, 22, RUE DE LA BANQUE. | NEW YORK : D. VAN NOSTRAND COMPANY. BERLIN : W. H. KÜHL. | HONG KONG, SHANGHAI, AND YOKOHAMA : KELLY, WALSH & CO. | TOKYO & OSAKA : MARUZEN–KABUSHIKI–KAISHA. | TOKYO   :   THE   METHODIST PUBLISHING COMPANY. | BUENOS AYRES [*sic*] : MITCHELL'S BOOK STORES.

PUBLICATION: Portsmouth: Griffin, May 1913. Price 12*s*. 6*d*.

PAGINATION: vii, [1], 520, 90 leaves of plates, 1 diagram.

CONTRIBUTIONS: 'First Lord's Statement [of 8 March 1913] explanatory of Navy Estimates, 1913–14': pp. 417–37; 'Memorandum by the First Lord on the Redistribution of Admiralty Business': pp. 442–5; 'Memorandum by the First Lord on Revised Financial Procedure at the Admiralty': pp. 445–7.

LOCATIONS: CaOONMC, UKIWM, USMH

B13.2   Second issue, photo-reproduced from the first issue (1970)

THE | NAVAL ANNUAL | 1913 | Edited by Viscount Hythe | A Reprint | [publisher's device, 18.8 × 16.8 mm] | DAVID & CHARLES REPRINTS

PUBLICATION: Newton Abbot, Devon: David & Charles Reprints, 1970. Price 105*s*. (£5. 5*s*.).

PAGINATION: [4], viii, 520, 5 leaves of plates, 1 diagram.

LOCATIONS: RIC (dj), RPH (dj)

B14   THE NAVAL ANNUAL, 1914   1914

THE | NAVAL ANNUAL, | 1914. | EDITED BY | VISCOUNT HYTHE, D.C.L., A.I.N.A., | *Honorary Fellow of Balliol; Commander of the Order of the Crown of Italy*, | AND | JOHN LEYLAND. | 1914. | LONDON : | WILLIAM CLOWES AND SONS, LIMITED, | 31, HAYMARKET, S.W. | *Foreign Agents:* | PARIS : BOYVEAU & CHEVILLET, 22, RUE DE LA BANQUE. | NEW YORK : D. VAN NOSTRAND COMPANY. BERLIN : W. H. KÜHL. | HONG KONG, SHANGHAI, AND YOKOHAMA : KELLY, WALSH & CO. | TOKYO & OSAKA : MARUZEN–KABUSHIKI–KAISHA. | TOKYO   :   THE   METHODIST PUBLISHING COMPANY. | BUENOS AYRES [*sic*] : MITCHELL'S BOOK STORES.

PUBLICATION: London: Clowes, June 1914. Price 12*s*. 6*d*.

PAGINATION: vii, [1], 456, 4 leaves of plates, 1 diagram.

CONTRIBUTION: 'First Lord's Statement Explanatory of Navy Estimates, 1914–15': pp. 397–8, followed by the statement of the work done by the Department in the year, which runs from p. 399 to p. 418.

LOCATIONS: RIC, USMH

B15   KING ALBERT'S BOOK   1914

B15.1.a   First edition, British issue (1914)

[Light bluish green] KING ALBERT'S | BOOK | [dark olive] A TRIBUTE TO THE BELGIAN | KING AND PEOPLE FROM | REPRESENTATIVE MEN AND | WOMEN THROUGHOUT THE | WORLD | [light bluish green, royal arms] | [dark olive] THE DAILY TELEGRAPH | IN CONJUNCTION WITH | THE DAILY SKETCH THE GLASGOW HERALD | AND HODDER AND STOUGHTON

PUBLICATION: London: *Daily Telegraph et al.*, December 1914. Price 3*s*. Originally issued with a label from the compiler of the book, the English novelist Hall Caine, which reads:

> If the purchaser of this book will sign the above Birthday salutation and forward it to Mr. Hall Caine at the office of The Daily Telegraph, Fleet Street, London, E.C., it will be inserted in a large Birthday volume, which will be Mr. Hall Caine's honour and pleasure to present, in conjunction with the proprietors of The Daily Telegraph, to the King of the Belgians.

PAGINATION AND BINDING: 188, 26 leaves of plates. Printed in blackish green on yellowish white unembossed calico-texture cloth.

CONTRIBUTION: Churchill's tribute to the Belgian people, signed in facsimile: p. 28.

LOCATIONS: CaOONMC, CaOTTC, RIC (dj), RPH, UKBL, USMH

REFERENCE: Woods B6.

B15.1.b   British edition, variant binding (1914)

Copies are known bound in quarter moderate reddish brown patterned-sand-grain cloth and greyish yellow paper-covered boards.

LOCATION: RIC

B15.1.c   The Canadian appearance (1914?)

There is also a Canadian appearance of the British volume, distinguishable only by the dust jacket, which reads at the head of the front, 'ILLUSTRATED CANADIAN EDITION' (there is no comparable information at the head of the British dust jacket), provides the Canadian price of '$1.25' in lieu of the British '3/-net' and the Canadian address of Hodder & Stoughton, namely, 17 Wilton Avenue, Toronto (in lieu of the British publication imprint) at the foot. Moreover, the back of the Canadian jacket is blank, while the back of the British jacket replicates the front.

LOCATIONS: FBW (dj), RIC (dj)

B15.2   French-language edition (1914?)

[Light bluish green] KING ALBERT'S | BOOK | [dark olive] HOMMAGE D'ADMIRATION AU | ROI ET AU PEUPLE BELGE DE | LA PART DES PRINCIPAUX RE- | PRÉSENTANTS DES NATIONS | DE L'UNIVERS | [light bluish green, royal arms] | [dark olive] LE DAILY TELEGRAPH | CONJOINTEMENT AVEC | LE DAILY SKETCH LE GLASGOW HERALD | ET HODDER ET STOUGHTON

PUBLICATION: London: *Daily Telegraph et al.*, 1914?

PAGINATION: 188, 26 leaves of plates.

CONTRIBUTION: Churchill's tribute to the Belgian people, signed in facsimile: p. 25.

LOCATION: RIC

B15.3   American issue of British sheets (1914?)

[Light bluish green] KING ALBERT'S | BOOK | [dark olive] A TRIBUTE TO THE BELGIAN | KING AND PEOPLE FROM | REPRESENTATIVE MEN AND | WOMEN THROUGHOUT THE | WORLD | [light bluish green, royal arms] | [dark olive] NEW YORK | HEARST'S INTERNATIONAL LIBRARY CO

PUBLICATION: New York: Hearst, 1914?

NOTE: The title page is a *cancellans*.

LOCATIONS: CaOONMC, RIC, USMH

B16   BRASSEY'S NAVAL ANNUAL, 1915   1915

BRASSEY'S | NAVAL ANNUAL, | 1915. | CONDUCTED BY | EARL BRASSEY, G.C.B., D.C.L. | EDITED BY JOHN LEYLAND. | WAR EDITION. | 1915. | LONDON : | WILLIAM CLOWES AND SONS, LIMITED, | 31, HAYMARKET, S.W. | *And sold by all* | ENGLISH AND FOREIGN BOOKSELLERS AND AGENTS.

PUBLICATION: London: Clowes, June 1915. Price 10*s*.

PAGINATION: vii, [1], 264, 4 leaves of plates, 10 pages of advertisements.

CONTRIBUTIONS: 'First Lord's Statement of 27 November 1914': pp. 218–24; 'First Lord's Speech on the Navy Estimates of 15 February 1915': pp. 224–37.

LOCATION: USMH

B17   HISTORY OF THE WORLD WAR   1917–20

Published as a five-volume set during and after the conclusion of the Great War. Only Volume I includes a Churchill contribution.

Volume I

[Full colour, within a single-rule frame, enclosing 196.1 × 127.1 mm, a circular decorative device, on which are distributed the arms of eight of the nine principal protagonist nations, and within which, black] HISTORY | OF THE | WORLD | WAR | FRANK H. SIMONDS | [below the arms of Japan and below the circular device] VOL. ONE |

[full colour, the arms of the United States] | Published for | THE REVIEW OF REVIEWS COMPANY | by | DOUBLEDAY PAGE & COMPANY | GARDEN CITY NEW YORK

PUBLICATION: New York: Doubleday Page, 1917.

PAGINATION: li, [1], 394 (including 100 leaves of plates, all of which are numbered).

CONTRIBUTION: 'How the Navy Saved England': pp. 356–60. First published in the *Sunday Pictorial* (see **C231a.3**, where it is titled "The Great Amphibian") and the *New York Tribune* (see **C231b.3**, where it is titled 'Churchill Tells How Navy Saved England'), the latter being the copyright source of this appearance. I expect that *"The Great Amphibian"* (**A47**), which is the only separate publication of this article, also constitutes the first volume appearance; however, this conclusion is necessarily conjectural. The *History of the World War* is, therefore, either the first or second volume appearance of the article.

LOCATION: RIC

B18   HARRY BUTTERS, R.F.A.   1918

B18.1   First edition (1918)

HARRY BUTTERS | [ranged right] R.F.A. | [centred] "AN AMERICAN CITIZEN" | *Life and War Letters* | EDITED BY MRS. DENIS O'SULLIVAN | WITH TWELVE PHOTOGRAPHS | *The Brief Record of a California Boy* | *Who Gave His Life for England* | NEW YORK: JOHN LANE COMPANY | LONDON: JOHN LANE, THE BODLEY HEAD | MCMXVIII

PUBLICATION: New York and London: John Lane, 1918.

PAGINATION: 297, [7], 12 leaves of plates.

CONTRIBUTION: Under the overall heading 'COLONEL WINSTON CHURCHILL'S LETTER', a sub-heading entitled 'A MEETING AT THE FRONT' (which is also the sub-title of the original letter of tribute in the *Observer*): pp. 22–3.[14]

LOCATIONS: RIC, UKBL, USInNd, USMH, USCtY

B18.2   Canadian issue from American plates (1918)

HARRY BUTTERS | [ranged right] R.F.A. | [centred] "AN AMERICAN CITIZEN" | *Life and War Letters* | EDITED BY MRS. DENIS O'SULLIVAN | WITH TWELVE PHOTOGRAPHS | *The Brief Record of a California Boy* | *Who Gave His Life for England* | TORONTO | McCLELLAND, GOODCHILD, STEWART, LIMITED | MCMXVIII

PUBLICATION: Toronto: McClelland, Goodchild & Stewart, 1918.

---

14. The letter, a tribute to Butters, was first published in the *Observer* of 10 September 1916 (**G254**). Churchill also mentioned Butters in a letter of 15 September 1916 to Sir Archibald Sinclair, shortly after Butters's death in action on 31 August (see Gilbert, *WSC*, Vol. IV, *C.V.* 1, at p. 27 and the note below, which contains an excerpt from the *Observer* letter). An exchange of correspondence between Sheila Bray, Butters's sister, and Churchill can be found *ibid.*, Vol. V, *C.V.* 2, at pp. 74 and 90–1. A lengthy extract from that letter can be found in *n.* 1 on p. 74.

PAGINATION: 297, [7], 12 leaves of plates. While the volume does not appear to have been re-set, the order of the leaves of the first two signatures has been altered, affecting, among other things, the location of the Churchill letter.

CONTRIBUTION: 'COLONEL WINSTON CHURCHILL'S LETTER', entitled 'A MEETING AT THE FRONT': pp. 26–7.

LOCATIONS: CaOHM, RIC

REFERENCE: Spadoni 374A.

B19 THE GREAT WAR 1914–1918   1919

THE GREAT WAR | 1914–1918. | [decorative device] | ULSTER GREETS | HER | BRAVE AND FAITHFUL SONS | AND | REMEMBERS HER GLORIOUS DEAD. | [decorative device] | Belfast: | Printed by W. & G. Baird, Limited, Royal Avenue. | 1919.

PUBLICATION: Belfast: Citizens' Committee to the Ulster Service Men, 9 August 1919; presented on behalf of the Citizens' Committee to the Ulster Service Men, as a Souvenir of Peace Day, City Hall, Belfast.

PAGINATION: 125, [1].

CONTRIBUTION: 'Greetings.', undated, but signed by Winston S. Churchill as Secretary of State for War: p. 125.

LOCATIONS: RIC, USIU

B20 PERMANENT ORGANIZATION OF
THE ROYAL AIR FORCE   1919

ROYAL AIR FORCE. | PERMANENT ORGANIZATION OF THE ROYAL | AIR FORCE. | [46.2-mm rule] | Note by the Secretary of State for Air on a Scheme Outlined | by the Chief of the Air Staff. | [155.7-mm double rule] | *Presented to Parliament by Command of His Majesty.* | [155.7-mm double rule] | [royal arms, 48.3 × 40.2 mm] | LONDON : | PUBLISHED BY HIS MAJESTY'S STATIONERY OFFICE. | [50-mm rule] | To be purchased through any Bookseller or directly from | H.M. STATIONERY OFFICE at the following addresses : | IMPERIAL HOUSE, KINGSWAY, LONDON, W.C.2, and 28, ABINGDON STREET, LONDON, S.W.1 | 37, PETER STREET, MANCHESTER ; 1, ST. ANDREW'S CRESCENT, CARDIFF ; | 23, FORTH STREET, EDINBURGH ; | or from E. PONSONBY, LTD., 116, GRAFTON STREET, DUBLIN. | [24.6-mm rule] | 1919. | *Price 1d. Net.* | [ranged left] [Cmd. 467.] [*sic,* immediately preceding brackets original]

PUBLICATION: London: HMSO, December 1919. Price 1*d.*

PAGINATION: 8. Pamphlet in self-wrappers.

CONTRIBUTION: Introductory 'Note by the Secretary of State for War' of 11 December 1919: p. 2.

LOCATIONS: RIC, UKScNL

B21 MEMORANDUM OF THE SECRETARY OF STATE FOR WAR RELATING TO THE ARMY ESTIMATES FOR 1920–21   1920

ARMY. | MEMORANDUM OF THE SECRETARY OF STATE FOR WAR | RELATING TO THE ARMY ESTIMATES FOR 1920–21. | [44.4-mm rule] | Details of the work of the various Departments | of the War Office in connection with the | reconstruction of the Army since the Armistice, | 11th November, 1918. | [44.4-mm rule] | Issued in Amplification of the Speech of the Secretary of State | introducing the Army Estimates for 1920–21. | [158.5-mm double rule] | *Presented to Parliament by Command of His Majesty.* | [158.5-mm double rule] | [royal arms, 48.1 × 40.7 mm] | LONDON : | PUBLISHED BY HIS MAJESTY'S STATIONERY OFFICE. | [50.3-mm rule] | To be purchased through any Bookseller or directly from | H.M. STATIONERY OFFICE at the following addresses : | IMPERIAL HOUSE, KINGSWAY, LONDON, W.C.2, and 28, ABINGDON STREET, LONDON, S.W.1 | 37, PETER STREET, MANCHESTER ; 1, ST. ANDREW'S CRESCENT, CARDIFF ; | 23, FORTH STREET, EDINBURGH ; | or from E. PONSONBY, LTD., 116, GRAFTON STREET, DUBLIN. | [24.9-mm rule] | 1920. | *Price 3d. net.* | [ranged left] [Cmd. 565] [*sic*, immediately preceding brackets original]

PUBLICATION: London: HMSO, February? 1920. Price 3*d.*

PAGINATION: 20. Pamphlet in self-wrappers. Side wire-stitched.

CONTRIBUTION: Foreword of 21 February 1920 from Churchill at the War Office: p. 2.

LOCATIONS: CaOONL, RIC, UKScNL

B22   NAVAL OPERATIONS   1920

B22.1   First edition (1920)

Five volumes in nine parts. There is a Churchill contribution only in Volume I.

Volume I

HISTORY OF THE GREAT WAR | BASED ON OFFICIAL DOCUMENTS | BY DIRECTION OF THE HISTORICAL SECTION OF THE | COMMITTEE OF IMPERIAL DEFENCE | NAVAL OPERATIONS | Vol. I | TO THE BATTLE OF THE FALKLANDS | DECEMBER 1914 | BY | SIR JULIAN S. CORBETT | LONGMANS, GREEN AND CO. | 39 PATERNOSTER ROW, LONDON | FOURTH AVENUE & 30TH STREET, NEW YORK | BOMBAY, CALCUTTA, AND MADRAS | 1920

PUBLICATION: London: Longmans, Green, March 1920. Price 17*s.* 6*d.*

PAGINATION: [2], xiv, 470, [2], 13 maps (5 folding).

CONTRIBUTIONS: Minute of 18 September 1914: p. 441; minute of 12 October 1914: p. 442.

NOTE: Churchill insisted on the inclusion of these two minutes and thus held up the publication of this volume for a year.[15]

---

15. For an account of this saga, see Donald M. Schurman, *Julian S. Corbett, 1854–1922*, London: Royal Historical Society, 1981 (**F251/1**).

LOCATIONS: CaOONMC, USMH

B22.2   Battery Press issue, photo-reproduced from the first edition (1997)

HISTORY OF THE GREAT WAR | BASED ON OFFICIAL DOCUMENTS | BY DIRECTION OF THE HISTORICAL SECTION OF THE | COMMITTEE OF IMPERIAL DEFENCE | NAVAL OPERATIONS | Vol. I | TO THE BATTLE OF THE FALKLANDS | DECEMBER 1914 | BY | SIR JULIAN S. CORBETT | THE IMPERIAL WAR MUSEUM | Department of Printed Books | [29.4-mm rule] | In Association With | THE BATTERY PRESS, INC. | Nashville

PUBLICATION: London: Imperial War Museum; Nashville: Battery Press, 1997. Price $49.95.

PAGINATION: [4], 13 pages numbered vii–xix, [1], 470, [4].

LOCATION: UKBL

B22.3   Naval & Military Press issue, photo-reproduced from the first edition, cased (2003)

NAVAL OPERATIONS | History of the Great War | Based on Official Documents | Vol. I | by | SIR JULIAN S. CORBETT | The Naval & Military Press Ltd | in association with | The Imperial War Museum | Department of Printed Books

PUBLICATION: Uckfield: Naval and Military Press; London: Imperial War Museum, 2003. Price £30.00.

No copies examined.

B22.4   Naval & Military Press issue, photo-reproduced from the first edition, paperback (2003)

NAVAL OPERATIONS | History of the Great War | Based on Official Documents | Vol. I | by | SIR JULIAN S. CORBETT | The Naval & Military Press Ltd | in association with | The Imperial War Museum | Department of Printed Books

PUBLICATION: Uckfield: Naval and Military Press; London: Imperial War Museum, 2003. Price £18.00.

No copies examined.

B23   WITH A BRISTOL FIGHTER SQUADRON   1920

B23.1   First edition (1920)

[All of the following within a single-rule box, enclosing 134.3 × 79.1 mm] With a Bristol | Fighter Squadron | By | WALTER NOBLE, D.F.C. | late R.F.C. and R.A.F. | With an Introduction by the | RIGHT HON. WINSTON CHURCHILL, M.P. | LONDON: ANDREW MELROSE, LTD | 3 YORK STREET, COVENT GARDEN, W.C [*sic*, no point] | 1920

PUBLICATION: London: Andrew Melrose, May 1920. Price 3*s*. 6*d*.

PAGINATION: 186, [6], 5 leaves of plates.

CONTRIBUTION: 'INTRODUCTION' dated 27 October 1919 and signed in facsimile: pp. 5–6.

NOTE: The front of the dust jacket also contains a boxed 20-line extract from the 'INTRODUCTION', signed in facsimile.

LOCATIONS: MLW (dj), RPH

REFERENCE: Woods B7.

B23.2   Second edition (1977)

With a Bristol | Fighter Squadron | Walter Noble D.F.C. *| With an Introduction by |* Winston S. Churchill | [publisher's device, 9.2 × 12.9 mm] | CEDRIC CHIVERS | PORTWAY | BATH

PUBLICATION: Bath: Cedric Chivers, 1977. Price £5.60; to Library Association members £4.20.

PAGINATION: viii, 198.

CONTRIBUTION: 'INTRODUCTION': pp. vii–viii. An excerpt from the Introduction is cited at p. i of this edition.

NOTE: The Cedric Chivers edition is a large-type edition.

LOCATIONS: CaAE, CaAEU, RIC (dj), UKBL

B24   THE EVACUATION OF NORTH RUSSIA, 1919   1920

<u>ARMY.</u> | THE   EVACUATION | OF | NORTH   RUSSIA, | 1919. | [157.5-mm double rule] | *Presented to Parliament by Command of His Majesty.* | [157.5-mm double rule] | [publisher's device, 47.5 × 40.2 mm] | LONDON : | PUBLISHED BY HIS MAJESTY'S STATIONERY OFFICE. | [49.8-mm rule] | To be purchased through any Bookseller or directly from | H.M. STATIONERY OFFICE at the following addresses : | IMPERIAL HOUSE, KINGSWAY, LONDON, W.C.2, and 28, ABINGDON STREET, LONDON, S.W.1 ; | 37, PETER STREET, MANCHESTER ; 1, ST. ANDREW'S CRESCENT, CARDIFF ; | 23, FORTH STREET, EDINBURGH ; | or from E. PONSONBY, LTD., 116, GRAFTON STREET, DUBLIN. | [25-mm rule] | 1920. | *Price* 1*s.* 6*d. net.* | [ranged left] [Cmd. 818.] [*sic*, immediately preceding brackets original]

PUBLICATION: London: HMSO, July 1920, 2000 copies. Price 1*s.* 6*d.*

PAGINATION: 45, [1], 2 maps (folding), plus light blue paper wrappers.

CONTRIBUTIONS: Foreword to the Blue Book, under the title 'Memorandum by the Secretary of State for War' dated 15 July 1920: p. 3. There is also an extract from Churchill's speech on Army Estimates in the House of Commons on 29 July 1919: pp. 3–4.

LOCATION: RIC

B25   THE 4TH (QUEEN'S OWN) HUSSARS IN THE
GREAT WAR   1920

THE | 4th (QUEEN'S OWN) HUSSARS | IN THE GREAT WAR | BY | CAPTAIN H. K. D. EVANS, M.C. | AND CHAPTERS IX AND X BY | MAJOR N. O. LAING, D.S.O. | WITH A FOREWORD BY | RIGHT HON. WINSTON CHURCHILL, P.C. | PRINTED FOR THE REGIMENTAL COMMITTEE | BY | GALE & POLDEN LIMITED | WELLINGTON WORKS, ALDERSHOT | 1920

PUBLICATION: Aldershot: Regimental Committee, 1920.

PAGINATION: xv, [1], 198, [2], 7 leaves of plates, 7 maps (5 folding).

CONTRIBUTION: 'FOREWORD' of 31 August 1920: pp. vii–viii.

LOCATIONS: FBW, DAT, RIC, UKBL, USMH

REFERENCES: Woods B8; White, p. 17.

B26 PICTURES OF MOROCCO, THE RIVIERA AND OTHER SCENES BY SIR JOHN LAVERY, R.A. 1921

B26.1.a First edition, first? printing (1921)

[Cover title:] [ranged upper left] *UNDER REVISION*] [*sic*, immediately preceding bracket original] | [centred] PICTURES | OF | MOROCCO, THE RIVIERA | AND OTHER SCENES | BY | SIR JOHN LAVERY, R.A. | [6.8-mm rule] | PORTRAIT AND CHILD STUDIES | BY | LADY LAVERY | [6.8-mm rule] *FOREWORD* | BY THE | RIGHT HON. WINSTON S. CHURCHILL, P.C., M.P. | [25.3-mm rule] | ALPINE CLUB GALLERY | MILL STREET, CONDUIT STREET, W. | Catalogue, including admission, 1/6

PUBLICATION: London: Chenil Galleries, 1921.

PAGINATION: 12. Pamphlet in card wrappers, sewn.

CONTRIBUTION: 'FOREWORD': pp. 3–5.

NOTE: Having examined only three copies of the catalogue in all, none of which was designated first or second printing, I conjecturally assign the designation of first printing to the copies above described.

LOCATIONS: CaOTTC, MLW

REFERENCE: Woods B8/1.

B26.1.b First edition, second printing (1921)

No copies examined.

B26.1.c First edition, third printing (1921)

As the first printing, except that the words '*THIRD REVISION*' replace '*UNDER REVISION*' on the cover title.

LOCATION: RIC

B27 BRITISH JEWRY BOOK OF HONOUR 1922

B27.1 First edition (1922)

British Jewry | Book of Honour | [Star of David] | EDITED BY | REV. MICHAEL ADLER | D.S.O., S.C.F., B.A. | ORGANISER | MAX R. G. FREEMAN | LONDON | CAXTON PUBLISHING COMPANY, LIMITED | CLUN HOUSE, SURREY STREET, W.C. | 1922

PUBLICATION: London: Caxton, February 1922. Price 105*s*. (£5. 5*s*.). There were 3000 copies of this edition, numbered and signed (by J. Malcolm, the Joint Managing Director of the publishing house).

PAGINATION: [2], xix, [1], 636, followed by 364 numbered leaves of plates, [2]; 2 leaves of plates and 1 map.

CONTRIBUTION: Churchill's 'contribution of a message to the volume', dated 6 March 1920, is the last of 11 such letters and is signed by him as Secretary of State for War: p. xix.

LOCATIONS: CaOONL, MLW, RIC, UKBL, UKScNL, USMH

B27.2 Second issue, photo-reproduced from first-edition sheets (1997)

British Jewry | Book of Honour | [Star of David] | EDITED BY | REV. MICHAEL ADLER | D.S.O., S.C.F., B.A. | ORGANISER | MAX R. G. FREEMAN | [publisher's device, 30.2 × 21.1 mm] | SELOUS BOOKS Ltd. | 40 Station Road, Aldershot, Hampshire, | GU11 1HT Great Britain. | 1997

PUBLICATION: Aldershot: Selous, 1997.

PAGINATION: xix, [1], 636, followed by 364 numbered leaves of plates, [2]; 2 leaves of plates and 1 map.

LOCATION: RIC

B28 THE JEWISH NATIONAL HOME AND ITS CRITICS   1922

[Cover title:] [all of the following within a double-rule box[16]] The Jewish National | Home and its Critics | [medium rule] | THE OXFORD SPEECHES | Sir Alfred Mond and Dr. Ch. Weizmann. | [medium rule] | A REPLY BY THE SECRETARY | OF STATE FOR THE COLONIES | TO THE ARAB DELEGATION. | [medium rule] | PUBLISHED BY THE | ZIONIST ORGANISATION, | 77, GREAT RUSSELL STREET, | LONDON, W.C.1.

PUBLICATION: London: Zionist Organisation, 1922.

PAGINATION: 16. Pamphlet in self-wrappers.

CONTRIBUTION: There is a divisional half-title at p. 13, after which Churchill's statement appears at pp. 14–16.

LOCATION: USNN (microform)

ANNOTATIONS: A public meeting was held on 25 February 1922 in the Town Hall at Oxford under the auspices of the Oxford University Zionist Society. Chaired by the Reverend Dr A. J. Carlyle, the meeting was addressed by Sir Alfred Mond, later 1st Baron Melchett of Lanford, and Dr Chaim Weizmann, later the first President of the State of Israel. The addresses were followed by the 'Official Statement' of the Secretary of State for the Colonies on 'The Palestine Constitution', which was entitled 'Reply to the Arab Delegation'.

---

16. The original paper copy having, regrettably, been destroyed by the New York Public Library, only the microform copy remains. In the circumstances, it is not possible for me to provide rule and box measurements as I do elsewhere in this work.

B29   MARK SYKES: HIS LIFE AND LETTERS   1923

B29.1   First edition (1923)

MARK SYKES: His Life | and Letters [leaf decoration] *By* SHANE LESLIE | *With an Introduction by* [two leaf decorations] | THE RIGHT HON. WINSTON CHURCHILL | *With Portrait* | *and Thirty Cartoons* | *by Mark Sykes* | CASSELL AND COMPANY, LTD | London, New York, Toronto and Melbourne | 1923

PUBLICATION: London: Cassell, April 1923. Price 16s. There was a second printing in May 1923.

PAGINATION: xi, [1], 308, 17 leaves of plates.

CONTRIBUTIONS: 'INTRODUCTION': pp. v–viii; and letter of 26 September 1914, apparently to Sykes: p. 234.

LOCATIONS: CaOTTC (1st and 2nd printings), RIC, RPH, UKBL, USMH, USMoFuWc

REFERENCES: Woods B9; O'Brien F0635.

B29.2   American issue of British sheets (1923)

MARK SYKES: His Life | and Letters [leaf decoration] *By* SHANE LESLIE | *With an Introduction by* [two leaf decorations] | THE RIGHT HON. WINSTON CHURCHILL | *With Portrait* | *and Thirty Cartoons* | *by Mark Sykes* | NEW YORK | CHARLES SCRIBNER'S SONS | 1923

PUBLICATION: New York: Scribner, 1923.

LOCATION: CaOTMCL

B30   THE ROYAL NAVAL DIVISION   1923

B30.1   First edition (1923)

THE ROYAL :: :: | NAVAL DIVISION | By Douglas Jerrold | With an Introduction by the Right | Hon. Winston S. Churchill :: :: | [89-mm thin–thick rule] | *LONDON : HUTCHINSON & CO. | PATERNOSTER ROW | 1923*

PUBLICATION: London: Hutchinson, June 1923. Price 21s.

PAGINATION: xix, [1], 368, 24 leaves of plates, 8 maps (folding).

CONTRIBUTIONS: 'INTRODUCTION' dated April 1923: pp. xi–xix. (A brief excerpt from the Introduction is also found on the front flap of the dust jacket.) Message to the Division on its return from Antwerp: pp. 40–1; a tribute to Rupert Brooke, originally published in *The Times* of 26 April 1915 (**G245**), appears for the first time in volume form at p. 78. The Introduction was subsequently published in the *Collected Essays*, Vol. I, at pp. 249–55.

LOCATIONS: FBW, FrNL, RIC, RPH, UKBL, USMH

REFERENCES: Woods B10; Schroder 246.

B30.2   Second edition (1927)

THE ROYAL :: :: | NAVAL DIVISION | By Douglas Jerrold | With an Introduction by the Right | Hon. Winston S. Churchill :: :: | [70-mm thin–thick rule] | HUTCHINSON & CO. (Publishers) LTD. | PATERNOSTER ROW, LONDON, E.C.

PUBLICATION: London: Hutchinson, October 1927. Price 7s. 6d.

PAGINATION: [2], xx, 360, [2], 32-page catalogue.

CONTRIBUTION: The Churchill 'Introduction' is in the same location; however, there is a new author's 'Preface to the Second Edition' dated September 1927: pp. v–viii.

LOCATIONS: CJZ, RIC (dj), UKBL

B30/1 AMERICA: GREAT CRISES IN OUR HISTORY TOLD BY ITS MAKERS   1925

[All of the following within a decorative frame, enclosing 165 × 110 mm] AMERICA | Great Crises In Our History | Told by Its Makers | A LIBRARY OF ORIGINAL SOURCES | Volume XI | The Great War | 1914–1916 | ISSUED BY | AMERICANIZATION DEPARTMENT | [publisher's device, 19.2 × 19.2 mm] | VETERANS OF FOREIGN WARS | OF THE | UNITED STATES | CHICAGO, U.S.A.

PUBLICATION: Chicago: Veterans of Foreign Wars, 1925. Published in 12 volumes; only Volume XI includes a Churchill contribution.

PAGINATION: 318, 3 leaves of plates.

CONTRIBUTION: 'The Grand Fleet Goes to Sea': pp. 53–67. Excerpted from the American edition of *The World Crisis*.

LOCATIONS: RIC, USMH

B31   A SOUVENIR OF THE GENERAL STRIKE   [1926]

[Cover title, on greyish yellowish brown paper wrappers:] [all of the following within a brilliant greenish blue single-rule box, enclosing 245 × 179.3 mm; dark purplish blue] The British Gazette | COMPLETE REPRODUCTION IN MINIATURE | [brilliant greenish blue, 120.9-mm thin–thick rule] | [dark purplish blue] A SOUVENIR | OF THE | GENERAL STRIKE | Reproduced from the "Luton News" and associated journals, | which, following the general permission to newspapers to | reproduce from the "British Gazette," photographically | made facsimile blocks of the third day's issue in miniature | and thereafter, day by day, REPRODUCED ALL FOUR | pages of the "Gazette" ON ONE of its news pages. | [brilliant greenish blue, 120.9-mm thin–thick rule] | [ranged lower left, dark purplish blue] PUBLISHED BY PERMISSION | OF THE CONTROLLER OF | H.M. STATIONERY OFFICE. | [ranged lower right and opposite the previous 3 lines] 6^D [with two points ranged horizontally beneath the D]

PUBLICATION: Luton: Gibbs, Bamforth, [1926].

NOTE: All eight issues of the *British Gazette* (**C307**) are reproduced herein (having been reduced photographically to 275 × 215.5 mm). Those labelled pages 2 and 3 of the 6 May issue are in fact pages 2 and 3 of the 7 May issue. Those labelled pages 2 and 3 of the 7 May issue are in fact pages 2 and 3 of the 8 May issue; they are also reproduced in the proper location in that issue. Page 2 of the 10 May issue is unknown to me. The 11 and 13 May issues reproduced are the first editions, not the 3 a.m. editions.

LOCATION: RIC

B32 SELECTED ARTICLES ON WAR—CAUSE AND CURE 1926

THE HANDBOOK SERIES | SELECTED ARTICLES ON | WAR—CAUSE AND CURE | Compiled by | JULIA E. JOHNSEN | NEW YORK | THE H. W. WILSON COMPANY | LONDON: SIR ISAAC PITMAN & SONS, LTD. | 1926

PUBLICATION: New York: Wilson, October 1926. Price $2.40.

PAGINATION: lxiv, 350, [2].

CONTRIBUTION: 'Shall We Commit Suicide?': pp. 96–101. First published in periodical form in *Nash's—Pall Mall* of September 1924 (see **C296a**) and separately in volume form under the same title (see **A74**), and collected subsequently in full in *Modern Eloquence* (see **B34**) and in abridged form in *Education for Peace* (New York: Committee of Reference and Counsel of the Foreign Missions Conference of North America, 1926).

LOCATIONS: RIC (dj), USMH

B33 BASIC PRINCIPLES OF AIR WARFARE 1927

BASIC PRINCIPLES OF | AIR WARFARE | (*THE INFLUENCE OF AIR POWER | ON SEA AND LAND STRATEGY*) | By | SQUADRON-LEADER | Aldershot : | GALE & POLDEN, LTD., WELLINGTON WORKS. | ALSO AT LONDON AND PORTSMOUTH. | 1927 | [20.1-mm rule] | *Price – SEVEN SHILLINGS & SIXPENCE Nett.*

PUBLICATION: Aldershot: Gale & Polden, 1927. Price 7*s*. 6*d*.

PAGINATION: xii, 147, [1].

CONTRIBUTION: Appendix I, 'Memorandum by Mr. Winston Churchill of October 21st, 1917': pp. 137–41. Previously published in Appendix V of Part II of *The World Crisis, 1916–1918*.

LOCATIONS: CaOOND, UKBL, UKIWM, USMH

B34 MODERN ELOQUENCE 1927

The principal set is 12 volumes long; however, there was a set of three supplementary volumes (under the same general title), which includes one article by Churchill. (There is an address by Churchill in Volume VII of the principal set, given under **D47**.)

Supplementary Volume I

[All of the following within a double-rule box, enclosing 161.8 × 94.2 mm] MODERN ELOQUENCE | FOUNDED BY THOMAS B. REED | SUPPLEMENTARY VOLUMES | [94.2-mm double rule] | ASHLEY H. THORNDIKE, EDITOR | *Professor of English, Columbia University* | [8.1-mm rule] | ADVISORY EDITORIAL BOARD | BRANDER MATTHEWS, CHAIRMAN | *Professor, Dramatic Literature, Columbia University* | SIR ROBERT LAIRD BORDEN | *Formerly Prime Minister of Canada* | NICHOLAS MURRAY BUTLER | *President, Columbia University* | JOHN W. DAVIS | *Formerly U.S. Ambassador to England* | HENRY CABOT LODGE | *Senator from Massachusetts* | ELIHU ROOT | *Formerly Secretary of State, Secretary of War, Senator* | OSCAR S. STRAUS | *Formerly Secretary of Commerce, Ambassador to Turkey* | AUGUSTUS THOMAS | *Playright* [*sic*], *Chairman, Producing Managers' Association* | HENRY VAN DYKE | *Professor of English Literature, Princeton University* | *Formerly U.S. Minister to the Netherlands* | [94.2-mm double rule] | MODERN ELOQUENCE CORPORATION | NEW YORK

PUBLICATION: New York: Modern Eloquence Corporation, 1927.

PAGINATION: viii, 421 [numbered 9–429], [3], 6 leaves of plates.

CONTRIBUTION: 'Shall We Commit Suicide?': pp. 191–8. First published in periodical form in *Nash's—Pall Mall* of September 1924 (see **C296a**) and separately in volume form under the same title (see **A74**) and collected in *Selected Articles on War—Cause and Cure* (**B32**).

LOCATIONS: RIC, USMH

B35   LITERARY TREASURES OF 1926   1927?

[All of the following within an interlocking decorative frame, enclosing 145.7 × 85.6 mm; deep reddish orange] LITERARY | TREASURES | OF 1926 | [black, publisher's device, 15.4 mm square] | *Published   By* | Hearst's International- | Cosmopolitan Magazine | *for private distribution only*

PUBLICATION: No city indicated [New York?]: International Magazine Company, no date indicated [1927?].

PAGINATION: viii, [2], 316, [2].

CONTRIBUTION: First volume appearance of 'The Tiger and the Bulldog': pp. 225–7. First published in periodical form in the August 1926 issue of *Cosmopolitan* (**C308a**).

LOCATIONS: CaOTTC, RIC, RPH, UKOxB, USMH

B36   THE SECRET BATTLE   1928

The first (British) edition, without the Churchill Introduction, was published on 29 May 1919 by Methuen and reprinted in January 1924.[17] The first American edition was published by Knopf in 1920. The Churchill contribution is not found before the third British edition and the second American edition of the book, but is present in all subsequent British and American editions, issues and printings, up to and including the 1989 Methuen Centenary issue; it is no longer present in the 2001 House of Stratus paperback.

B36.1   Third (British) edition (1928)

THE | SECRET BATTLE | BY | A. P. HERBERT | WITH AN INTRODUCTION | BY THE RIGHT HON. | WINSTON S. CHURCHILL | [publisher's device, 19.1 × 16.8 mm] | METHUEN & CO. LTD | 36 ESSEX STREET W.C. | LONDON

---

17. It is worthy of note that it was printed by T. and A. Constable, Printers to His Majesty at the Edinburgh University Press, and that its pagination was [4], 244, with a 32-page catalogue. Although I have been unable to locate a copy of the 1924 printing, I assume that it was a second printing of the first edition. The so-called third 'edition' was reset and printed by Jarrold & Sons, Norwich. It was this setting of type that served all subsequent appearances in England and the United States until the new Oxford paperback edition of 1982. Note also that the original American appearance of the work by Knopf, which credits no printer by name, was 132 leaves, beginning with two unnumbered leaves: [4], 7–266.

PUBLICATION: London: Methuen, March 1928. Price 3s. 6d. The fourth printing (publisher-styled "edition") was published in July 1929, the fifth in March 1930, and the sixth in 1931.

PAGINATION: viii, 216, [8].

CONTRIBUTION: 'INTRODUCTION': pp. v–viii. Subsequently collected in the *Collected Essays*, Vol. I, at pp. 273–4.

ANNOTATIONS: Herbert wrote to Churchill on 2 January 1928, asking him to write an introduction to the volume.[18] Churchill responded affirmatively on 6 January and proofs of the Introduction were ready by 13 February.[19]

LOCATIONS: CaOTTC, IeDTc, RIC (3rd, 4th and 5th printings), RPH, UKBL (3rd, 4th and 5th printings), UKOxB, USIU

REFERENCE: Woods B11.

B36.2   Minerva issue (n.d.)

[Above a moderate yellow boxed illustration of the goddess Minerva, standing, and an unknown seated god] THE MINERVA EDITION | [within the box but above the figures, deep bluish green] THE | SECRET BATTLE | By A. P. HERBERT | [below the box, moderate yellow] THE LIBRARY PRESS L^(TD) | 83. [*sic*] Southwark Street . London S.E [*sic*, no point] 1

PUBLICATION: London: Library Press, n.d. Price 6s.

NOTE: I have been unable to assign a publishing date to this issue of the volume in the Minerva Editions of Modern Authors. While the British Library dates the series '[1926–]', the Churchill Introduction was not available before February 1928, so the Library Press issue cannot be earlier. While it is possible that the undated Library Press issue pre-dated the Methuen edition or was issued simultaneously with it, I have no information substantiating that conjecture and the Methuen third edition, which is indicated as *March* 1928, clearly appeared within weeks of the availability of the Churchill Introduction. The fourth, fifth, sixth and seventh printings by Methuen are dated 1929, 1930, 1931 and 1936 respectively and there are no clues with respect to the Library Press. Accordingly, while it is possible that the Minerva issue is the first with the Churchill Introduction, I conservatively assign it second-issue status.

LOCATIONS: CaOTTC, RIC, UKBL

B36.3   Gateway Library issue (1931)

THE | SECRET BATTLE | BY | A. P. HERBERT | WITH AN INTRODUCTION | BY THE RIGHT HON. | WINSTON S. CHURCHILL | SIXTH EDITION | [publisher's device, 19.1 × 16.8 mm] | METHUEN & CO. LTD | 36 ESSEX STREET W.C. | LONDON

PUBLICATION: London: Methuen, 1931. The reference to the Gateway Library can be found on the half-title and on p. 217.

LOCATION: UKScAbU

---

18. Herbert's request is CHAR 8/216/7–8. Churchill's reply and the Herbert thank-you can all be found in CHAR 8/216.

19. The proofs are CHAR 8/216/63–6.

B36.4   Fountain Library issue (1936)

THE FOUNTAIN LIBRARY | [71-mm swelled rule] | THE SECRET BATTLE | *BY* | A. P. HERBERT | WITH AN INTRODUCTION | BY THE RIGHT HON. | WINSTON S. CHURCHILL | [71.6-mm swelled rule] | METHUEN & CO. LTD. LONDON

PUBLICATION: London: Methuen, April 1936. Publisher-styled seventh edition. Price 2s. 6d. There was a publisher-styled eighth "edition" in 1945.

PAGINATION: viii, 216.

LOCATIONS: RIC (dj), UKBL, UKOxB (8th printing)

B36.5   New Methuen issue (1949)

A. P. Herbert | [62.4-mm swelled rule] | THE | SECRET BATTLE | WITH AN INTRODUCTION | BY THE RIGHT HON. | WINSTON S. CHURCHILL | [publisher's device, 19.1 × 16.8 mm] | METHUEN & CO. LTD. LONDON | *36 Essex Street, Strand, W.C.2*

PUBLICATION: 1949. Publisher-styled ninth edition. Price 6s.

NOTE: Although the page size has been increased from 169.5 × 105.8 mm to 183.9 × 123.4 mm, the size of the block of type is unaltered.

LOCATIONS: RIC (dj), UKBL

B36.6.a   Chatto & Windus issue (1969)

THE | SECRET BATTLE | [32.3-mm decorative rule] | A. P. Herbert | *With an Introduction by* | SIR WINSTON CHURCHILL | [publisher's device, 13.5 × 9.2 mm] | CHATTO & WINDUS | LONDON

PUBLICATION: London: Chatto & Windus, 1969. Price '21s. (£1.05)', anticipating the 1971 decimalization. There is a notice on the copyright page that reads '*This edition first published 1969*'.

PAGINATION: viii, 216.

LOCATION: RIC (dj)

B36.6.b   Chatto & Windus issue, second? printing (1970)

Also known in an issue that is identical to **B36.6.a**, except that the notice on the copyright page reads '*This edition first published 1970*'.

LOCATIONS: FrNL, RIC (dj), UKBL, UKScNL, USDLC

B36.7   Hutchinson issue (1976)

A. P. Herbert | [68.4-mm swelled rule] | THE | SECRET BATTLE | WITH AN INTRODUCTION | BY THE RIGHT HON. | WINSTON S. CHURCHILL | HUTCHINSON OF LONDON

PUBLICATION: London: Hutchinson, 1976.

PAGINATION: viii, 216.

CONTRIBUTION: The Introduction is in the same location as before.

LOCATIONS: UKBL, UKScNL, USDLC, USMH

B36.8 First American edition (with the Churchill introduction) (1981)

A. P. HERBERT | [92.3-mm swelled rule] | THE | SECRET BATTLE | WITH AN INTRODUCTION | BY THE RIGHT HON. | WINSTON S. CHURCHILL | ATHENEUM NEW YORK | *1981*

PUBLICATION: New York: Atheneum, 1981. Price $9.95.

PAGINATION: viii, 216.

CONTRIBUTION: The Introduction is in the same location as before.

LOCATIONS: RIC (dj), USDLC

B36.9 Oxford University Press paperback edition (1982)

A. P. HERBERT | *The Secret Battle* | [24.4-mm decorative swelled rule] | *With a Preface by* | WINSTON S. CHURCHILL | *and an Introduction by* | JOHN TERRAINE | Oxford Melbourne Delhi | OXFORD UNIVERSITY PRESS | 1982

PUBLICATION: Oxford: Oxford University Press, 1982. Price £2.50.

PAGINATION: [2], xv, [1], 130, 10-page catalogue, [2].

CONTRIBUTION: Introduction: pp. vii–viii.

LOCATIONS: RIC, UKBL, UKScNL

B36.10 Methuen Centenary issue (1989)

[All of the following within a thick–thin rule box, enclosing 156.2 × 94.3 mm] | THE | SECRET BATTLE | BY | A. P. HERBERT | WITH AN INTRODUCTION | BY THE RIGHT HON. | WINSTON S. CHURCHILL | METHUEN LONDON | [in the centre of the bottom thick–thin rule frame] *A Methuen Centenary Edition*

PUBLICATION: London: Methuen, 1989. Price £9.99.

PAGINATION: viii, 216.

CONTRIBUTION: The Introduction is in the same location as before.

LOCATIONS: RIC (dj), UKOxB, UKScNL

B37 BUILDING SOCIETIES   1929

BUILDING SOCIETIES | THEIR ORIGIN, METHODS, AND | PRINCIPLES | By | LEONARD G. HODGSON | A.K.C., F.C.I.S. | [publisher's device, 25.6 × 16.5 mm] | London | John Long, Limited | 34, 35 & 36 Paternoster Row | [*All Rights Reserved*] [*sic*, immediately preceding brackets original]

PUBLICATION: London: John Long, May 1929. Price 5*s*.

PAGINATION: 224.

CONTRIBUTION: Letter of 19 March 1929 to the National Association of Building Societies, entitled 'A TRIBUTE BY THE RIGHT HON. WINSTON CHURCHILL, M.P.': pp. 5–6.

LOCATIONS: CaAEU, CaOOCM, CaOTMCL, RIC, UKBL

REFERENCE: Woods B12/1.

B38   THE LEGION BOOK   1929

B38.1   First edition, first (limited) issue (1929)

THE | LEGION | BOOK | [76-mm swelled rule] | EDITED BY | CAPTAIN H. COTTON MINCHIN | [76-mm swelled rule] | [engraving by Clifford Webb of a poppy on a recessed stamp, 77.8 mm square] | LONDON | PRIVATELY PRINTED | 1929

PUBLICATION: London: Privately printed, 1929.

NOTE: Published in a limited edition of 600 copies, of which 500, signed by the editor, were for sale at a price of 5 guineas. The first 100 copies were reserved for H.R.H. the Prince of Wales, sponsor of the volume, in his gift. Each of these reserved copies was signed by all of the contributors; the remaining limited-edition copies were signed only by the Editor, H. Cotton Minchin. Exceptionally, the copy in the Mortlake Collection at the University of Illinois at Urbana-Champaign is also signed by 19 of the contributors. Mr Seymour Stein, the subscriber of this presentation copy, set out to obtain the signatures of each of the surviving contributors on the half-title of his copy, until the Controller, Admiral Sir Lionel Halsey, was able to insist that Mr Stein should cease from soliciting them.

PAGINATION: [6], xiv, 242, [2], [9 unnumbered collotype plates], [2], 10 leaves of plates.

CONTRIBUTION: 'EARL HAIG': pp. 21–2.

LOCATIONS: FBW, RPH, UKBL, USIU, USMH

REFERENCE: Woods B12(a).

B38.2   First edition, second (trade) issue (1929)

THE LEGION BOOK | EDITED BY CAPTAIN H. COTTON MINCHIN | [130.3-mm rule] | CASSELL AND COMPANY LTD. | LA BELLE SAUVAGE, LONDON, E.C.4

PUBLICATION: October 1929; there were at least nine impressions: the first in September 1929,[20] two in October, two in November, one in December, one in January 1930, one in February and one in July. Price 21*s*.

PAGINATION: [11], [1], 234, [2], 12 leaves of plates.

CONTRIBUTION: 'EARL HAIG': pp. 21–2.

NOTE: Complete copies with dust jackets should have a light yellow wrapper band, reading: within a decorative frame (4.7-mm) box, enclosing 53.5 × 187.9 mm, 'By the wish of H.M. The King | all proceeds go to the British Legion as Thankoffering | for His Majesty's Recovery'. As some of the advertising for the volume explained: "It was primarily published as a practical appreciation of the British Legion and what it is doing for ex-Service men and their families. The Prince of Wales has taken a personal interest in the preparation of it, and when he showed it to the King, His Majesty suggested that the proceeds should be given to the British Legion as a thank-offering for his recovery."[21]

---

20. As indicated by the publisher on the title-page verso.
21. *Nash's—Pall Mall*, December 1929, p. 123.

LOCATIONS: CaOTTC (7th printing), RIC (dj and 7th printing), RPH (without dj but with wrapper band), UKBL, USMH

REFERENCE: Woods B12(b).

B38.3 American edition, only printing (1929)

[Vivid reddish orange] LEGION | [black] THE BOOK OF THE BRITISH LEGION | BY BRITAIN'S FOREMOST | WRITERS IN PROSE | AND VERSE | [vivid reddish orange, publisher's device, 26.7 mm in diameter] | [black] *ILLUSTRATIONS FROM PHOTOGRAPHS* | [113.7-mm rule] | DOUBLEDAY, DORAN & COMPANY, INC. | GARDEN CITY, NEW YORK | *MCMXXIX*

PUBLICATION: Garden City: Doubleday, Doran, 1929.

PAGINATION: [2], xi, [1], 290, [2], 8 leaves of plates.

CONTRIBUTION: 'EARL HAIG': pp. 27–8.

LOCATIONS: CaOTTC (dj), RIC (dj), RPH, USDLC, USMH

B39   THE HUNDRED BEST ENGLISH ESSAYS   1929

THE HUNDRED BEST | ENGLISH ESSAYS | SELECTED AND EDITED, WITH | AN INTRODUCTORY ESSAY, BY | THE RT. HON. THE EARL OF BIRKENHEAD, | P.C., D.L. | [publisher's device, 19.7 × 12.9 mm] | CASSELL AND COMPANY, LTD. | LONDON, TORONTO, MELBOURNE AND SYDNEY

PUBLICATION: London: Cassell, November 1929. Price 8*s.* 6*d.*; in half-leather 15*s.* There were second, third and fourth printings (designated "Editions" by the publisher) published respectively in May 1931, January 1947 and February 1950.

PAGINATION: [2], xxii, 924.

CONTRIBUTION: 'Painting as a Pastime': pp. 849–61. This is the first volume appearance of the article, which was first published in periodical form in the *Strand Magazine* in two parts in December 1921 and January 1922 (**C267a.1** and **C267a.2**). The piece was subsequently collected in *Thoughts and Adventures* (**A95**) and later published separately as *Painting as a Pastime* (**A242**).

LOCATIONS: CaQMM (4th printing), MLW, RIC (1st and 3rd printings), RPH, UKBL, USMH

REFERENCE: Woods D(a)2.

B40   WALL STREET   1930

B40.1 First (French) edition (1930)

BIBLIOTHÈQUE POLITIQUE ET ÉCONOMIQUE | [98.6-mm rule] | ROBERT IRVING WARSHOW | [17.6-mm rule] | WALL STREET | HISTOIRE DE LA BOURSE DE NEW-YORK | DES ORIGINES A 1930 | [16.8-mm rule] | ÉDITION FRANÇAISE PAR PIERRE COSTE | ATTACHÉ AU SERVICE DES ÉTUDES DE LA BANQUE DE FRANCE | [18.1-mm rule] | *PRÉFACE DE WINSTON S. CHURCHILL* | EX-CHANCELIER DE L'ÉCHIQUIER | *Avec 8 photographies et 4 graphiques* | [oval publisher's device, 25.7 × 20.1 mm] | PAYOT, PARIS | 106, BOULEVARD ST-GERMAIN | [3-mm rule] | 1930 | *Tous droits réservés*

PUBLICATION: Paris: Payot, January 1930. Price 25 francs.

PAGINATION: [6], VIII, 230 [numbered from (7) to (236)], 2-page catalogue, [2], 1 graph (folding), 8 leaves of plates.

CONTRIBUTION: '*PRÉFACE DE L'ÉDITION FRANÇAISE*': pp. I–VI. The work is a translation of Robert I. Warshow's *The Story of Wall Street* (New York: Greenberg, 1929), the first edition of which was published in September. Neither the American[22] nor the British edition[23] includes the Churchill Preface. The French publisher was the first to suggest that Churchill's article on the stock market crash in the newspaper series on his impressions of America and Canada (**C330**) would be appropriate as the preface to the Warshow book.[24] Curtis Brown, Churchill's literary agent, reported that, "so far as they [*Le Figaro* and the translator] are concerned they will have no objection to the article being used in this way. It now only remains for Mr. Churchill to give his consent, and we shall be glad if you will kindly consult him about this point and let us know what he says. We shall, of course, obtain a small nominal fee from MM. Payot."[25] It appears that only the French and Brazilian (Portuguese) translations of Warshow's work do contain this preface. The article was first published in the *Washington Post* (**C330a.4**).

LOCATIONS: CaQMBM, FrNL, ItNL, RIC, RPH, USMH

B40.2 Brazilian edition (1944)

ROBERT IRVING WARSHOW | [99-mm rule] | WALL STREET | HISTÓRIA DA BOLSA DE NOVA YORK | DESDE SUAS ORIGENS ATÉ 1930. | PREFÁCIO DE | WINSTON S. CHURCHILL | Ex-chanceler do Tribunal do Tesouro da Inglaterra. | PREFÁCIO E HISTÓRICO DO *CRACK* DE 1929 POR | PIERRE COSTE | Adido ao Serviço de Estudos de Banco de França. | COM DOIS GRÁFICOS DEMOSTRATIVOS | [ranged right] Tradução de | C. FONSECA | [centred] | [99-mm rule] | EDIÇÕES CULTURA BRASILEIRA | RUA 7 DE ABRIL, 21 — TELEFONE: 4-1860 | S. PAULO

PUBLICATION: São Paulo: Edições Cultura Brasileira, 1944.

CONTRIBUTION: 'PREFÁCIO DE WINSTON S. CHURCHILL': pp. 7–14.

LOCATION: FrPaBp, RIC

B41 LIAISON, 1914   1930

B41.1 First edition, British issue, first printing (1930)

LIAISON, 1914 | A Narrative of the Great Retreat | by | Brigadier-General E. L. SPEARS | C.B., C.B.E., M.C. | (*Late 11th Hussars*) | With fourteen maps & two sketches by | Lt.-Col. SIR MORGAN CROFTON | BART., D.S.O. | (*Late 2nd Life Guards*) | [publisher's device, 20.4 × 17.3 mm] | LONDON | WILLIAM HEINEMANN LTD

---

22. The second printing occurred in June 1930 and the third in January 1931.
23. Published by Grant Richards, London, 1931.
24. The articles had been purchased for French serialization by *Le Figaro*. Payot cleared the French rights with the newspaper and the translator of the preface.
25. Letter of 20 December 1929 from Jean Watson, Manager of the Foreign Department, Curtis Brown Ltd., 6 Henrietta Street, Covent Garden, London, to Miss Josephine Cummings of 62 Onslow Gardens, London (CHAR 8/227/121).

PUBLICATION: London: Heinemann, September 1930. Price 25s. There were at least six impressions: the second and third in October and the fourth in December 1930; the fifth in January 1931, and the sixth in December 1932.

PAGINATION: xxix, [1], 597, [1], 33 leaves of plates, 14 maps (folding).

CONTRIBUTION: 'PREFACE': pp. vii–ix. Subsequently published in the *Collected Essays*, Vol. I, at pp. 275–6.

TRANSLATION

French: *En liaison, 1914*, Paris: Presses de la Cité, 1967.

LOCATIONS: CJZ (1st and 5th printings), FrNL (French edition), RIC, RPH, USMH

REFERENCE: Woods B13.

B41.2   American issue of British sheets (1931)

LIAISON, 1914 | A Narrative of the Great Retreat | by | Brigadier-General E. L [*sic*, no point] SPEARS | C.B., C.B.E., M.C. | (*Late 11th Hussars*) | With fourteen maps & two sketches by | Lt.-Col. SIR MORGAN CROFTON | BART., D.S.O. | (*Late 2nd Life Guards*) | GARDEN CITY NEW YORK | DOUBLEDAY, DORAN & COMPANY, INC [*sic*, no point] | 1931

PUBLICATION: New York: Doubleday Doran, 1931.

LOCATIONS: RIC, USMH

B41.3   Second edition, British issue (1968)

LIAISON 1914 | *A NARRATIVE OF THE* | *GREAT RETREAT* | by | Major-General | Sir Edward Spears | EYRE & SPOTTISWOODE | LONDON

PUBLICATION: London: Eyre & Spottiswoode, April 1968. Price 105s. (£5. 5s.).

PAGINATION: xxxv, [1], 588, 15 leaves of plates.

CONTRIBUTION: '*Foreword to the First Edition*': pp. vii–ix.

NOTE: The second edition contains a new Author's Preface and a new Chapter XVI "containing material concerning events on the left of the front on the eve of the Battle of the Marne, which was not available to me when I wrote the book".

LOCATIONS: FrNL, RIC, UKBL, USMH

B41.4   American issue of British second-edition sheets (1968)

LIAISON 1914 | *A NARRATIVE OF THE* | *GREAT RETREAT* | by | Major-General | Sir Edward Spears | WITH A FOREWORD BY | WINSTON S. CHURCHILL | [publisher's device, 8.0 × 7.9 mm] | STEIN AND DAY / *Publishers* / New York

PUBLICATION: New York: Stein & Day, 1968. Price $15.00.

PAGINATION: xxxv, [1], 588, 15 leaves of plates.

LOCATIONS: CaOONMC (dj), RIC (dj)

B41.5   Second edition, second British issue (1999)

LIAISON 1914 | *A Narrative of the Great Retreat* | Major-General Sir Edward Spears | Cassell | LONDON

PUBLICATION: London: Cassell, 1999. Price £25.00.

PAGINATION: xxxv, [1], 588, 8 leaves of plates.

LOCATIONS: RIC (dj), UKBL, USMH

B42 DICTATORSHIP ON ITS TRIAL 1930

B42.1 First edition (1930)

DICTATORSHIP | ON ITS TRIAL | BY EMINENT LEADERS | OF MODERN THOUGHT | EDITED BY | OTTO FORST DE BATTAGLIA | TRANSLATED BY | HUNTLEY PATERSON | WITH AN INTRODUCTION BY | THE RIGHT HON. WINSTON S. CHURCHILL C.H. | [publisher's device, 28.4 × 19.3 mm] | GEORGE G. HARRAP & CO. LTD. | LONDON BOMBAY SYDNEY

PUBLICATION: London: Harrap, November 1930. Price 18*s*.

PAGINATION: 390, [2], 16 leaves of plates.

CONTRIBUTION: 'INTRODUCTION': pp. 7–10. Subsequently published in the *Collected Essays*, Vol. II, at pp. 206–8.

LOCATIONS: CaOTTC, RIC (dj), RPH (dj), UKBL, USMH

REFERENCE: Woods B14.

B42.2 American edition (1931)

DICTATORSHIP | ON TRIAL | [95.5-mm rule] | BY EMINENT LEADERS | OF MODERN THOUGHT | [95.5-mm rule] | *Edited by Otto Forst de Battaglia* | TRANSLATED BY HUNTLEY PATERSON | *With an Introduction by* | THE RIGHT HON. WINSTON S. CHURCHILL, C.H. | [publisher's device, 13.4 × 14 mm] | HARCOURT, BRACE AND COMPANY | NEW YORK

PUBLICATION: New York: Harcourt, Brace, 1931.

PAGINATION: 390, [2], 16 leaves of plates.

CONTRIBUTION: As in the first edition.

LOCATIONS: CaOONL, USDLC

B42.3 Books for Libraries issue, photo-reproduced from the first edition (1970)

DICTATORSHIP | ON ITS TRIAL | BY EMINENT LEADERS | OF MODERN THOUGHT | EDITED BY | OTTO FORST DE BATTAGLIA | TRANSLATED BY | HUNTLEY PATERSON | WITH AN INTRODUCTION BY | THE RIGHT HON. WINSTON S. CHURCHILL C.H. | *Essay Index Reprint Series* | [publisher's device, 9.6 × 8 mm] | [opposite the publisher's device, in 2 lines] BOOKS FOR LIBRARIES PRESS | FREEPORT, NEW YORK

PUBLICATION: Freeport (NY): Books for Libraries Press, 1970.

PAGINATION: 424, being numbered 1–390, [4]; 15 of the 16 leaves of plates are unnumbered but printed as part of the 14 signatures [the volume is gathered as thirteen 16s and one 4].

CONTRIBUTION: As in the first edition.

LOCATION: RIC

B43   IF IT HAD HAPPENED OTHERWISE   1931

B43.1.a First edition, first printing (1931)

IF | IT   HAD   HAPPENED   OTHERWISE | LAPSES   INTO   IMAGINARY
HISTORY | BY | WINSTON   CHURCHILL RONALD   KNOX | EMIL
LUDWIG   H. A. L. FISHER | ANDRÉ MAUROIS   J. C. SQUIRE | G. K.
CHESTERTON   HILAIRE   BELLOC | HAROLD   NICOLSON   PHILIP
GUEDALLA | MILTON WALDMAN | Edited by J. C. SQUIRE | LONGMANS,
GREEN AND CO. | LONDON ◆ NEW YORK ◆ TORONTO | 1931

PUBLICATION: London: Longmans, Green, February 1931. Price 21*s*.

PAGINATION AND BINDING: vii, [1], 290, [2]. Bound in moderate reddish brown
unembossed calico-texture cloth, stamped in gilt.

CONTRIBUTION: 'IF LEE HAD NOT WON THE BATTLE OF GETTYSBURG':
pp. 175–96. First published in *Scribner's Magazine* in December 1930 (**C334**). Collected
in the *Complete Essays*, Vol. IV, pp. 73–84. The article was only separately published in
a German-language edition, *Wenn Lee die Schlacht von Gettysburg nicht gewonnen hätte*
(**A294**).

LOCATIONS: CaOTTC, CJZ, FBW (dj), RIC, RPH, UKBL

REFERENCE: Woods B18.

B43.1.b   First edition, first printing, variant binding (1931)

Bound in moderate bluish green embossed calico-texture cloth without blind rules on the
front and without gilt rules on the spine. The page size has been reduced from 235 ×
151.2 mm to 217 × 140.7 mm.

LOCATION: CJZ

B43.1.c   First edition, second printing ("cheap edition") (1932)

There was a "reissue" in September 1932, whose title page is distinguished only by the
change of date to 1932.

LOCATION: RIC

B43.2   American edition (1931)

[Cutting through the middle of the top rule of a single-rule strong reddish brown box,
enclosing 115.7 × 91.5 mm, a strong reddish brown swash word, itself roughly bisected
by the top rule] If | [the whole of the following within the single-rule box, black] or
History Rewritten | BY | PHILIP GUEDALLA | G. K. CHESTERTON | HENDRIK
WILLEM VAN LOON | ANDRÉ MAUROIS | HILAIRE BELLOC | H. A. L.
FISHER | HAROLD   NICOLSON | WINSTON   CHURCHILL | MILTON
WALDMAN | EMIL LUDWIG | J. C. SQUIRE | NEW YORK The Viking Press
MCMXXXI

PUBLICATION: New York: Viking, 1931. Price $3.00.

PAGINATION: ix, [1], 379, [3].

CONTRIBUTION: The divisional half-title is at p. 257 and the résumé of the chapter at
p. 259. 'IF LEE HAD NOT WON THE BATTLE OF GETTYSBURG': pp. 260–84.

NOTE: Copies are known in half moderate reddish brown unembossed calico-texture cloth with yellowish white embossed calico-texture spine, stamped in gilt on a blackish red painted label, or in moderate yellow unembossed calico-texture cloth, stamped in gilt on a blackish red painted label.

LOCATIONS: RIC (dj), USMH

B43.3   Second American issue (1964)

[Cutting through the middle of the top rule of a single-rule box, enclosing 115.7 × 91.5 mm, a swash word, itself roughly bisected by the top rule] If | [the whole of the following within the single-rule box] or History Rewritten | BY | PHILIP GUEDALLA | G. K. CHESTERTON | HENDRIK WILLEM VAN LOON | ANDRÉ MAUROIS | HILAIRE BELLOC | H. A. L. FISHER | HAROLD NICOLSON | WINSTON CHURCHILL | MILTON   WALDMAN | EMIL   LUDWIG | J.   C.   SQUIRE | KENNIKAT PRESS, INC./PORT WASHINGTON, N.Y.

PUBLICATION: Port Washington (NY): Kennikat, 1964.

LOCATION: RIC

B43.4   Second British edition (1972)

IF | IT HAD HAPPENED OTHERWISE | *by* | WINSTON CHURCHILL   J. C. SQUIRE | EMIL LUDWIG   HILAIRE BELLOC | ANDRÉ MAUROIS   PHILIP GUEDALLA | G.   K.   CHESTERTON   MILTON   WALDMAN | HAROLD NICOLSON   CHARLES PETRIE | RONALD KNOX   G. M. TREVELYAN | H. A. L. FISHER   A. J. P. TAYLOR | *EDITED BY J. C. SQUIRE* | *Introduction by* | SIR JOHN WHEELER-BENNETT, K.C.V.O., C.M.G., O.B.E. | [publisher's device, 12 × 9.8 mm] | SIDGWICK & JACKSON | LONDON

PUBLICATION: London: Sidgwick & Jackson, March 1972. Price £3.25.

PAGINATION: xiii, [1], 320, [2].

CONTRIBUTION: As in the first edition.

LOCATIONS: RIC (dj), UKBL, USMH

B44   THE FIVE HUNDRED BEST ENGLISH LETTERS 1931

THE | *FIVE HUNDRED* | *BEST ENGLISH LETTERS* | Selected and Edited, | with an Introduction, | by | THE FIRST EARL OF | BIRKENHEAD | [publisher's device, 19.5 × 12.8 mm] | CASSELL   AND   COMPANY   LIMITED | LONDON, TORONTO, MELBOURNE | AND SYDNEY

PUBLICATION: London: Cassell, April 1931. Price 8*s.* 6*d.* A cheap edition was published May 1936, price 3*s.* 6*d.*

PAGINATION: xxvii, [1], 960.

CONTRIBUTION: Churchill's letter to his American novelist namesake: pp. 919–20. Previously published in the *News Chronicle* of 16 September 1930 (**C341.15**) and in *My Early Life* (**A91**), and subsequently in R. Churchill, *WSC*, Vol. I, *C.V.* 2, at p. 1026.

LOCATIONS: CaOONL, CaOTTC, CaQMM, MLW (dj), RIC (dj), RPH

REFERENCES: Woods D(b)44/1; Schroder 219.

B45   A CATALOGUE OF BOOKS   1931

[Ranged left] Catalogue 36 [ranged right] May, 1931 | [centred] A | CATALOGUE OF BOOKS | SELECTED FROM THE LIBRARY OF | THE LATE EARL OF BIRKENHEAD | WITH AN INTRODUCTION BY | THE RIGHT HON. WINSTON CHURCHILL, M.P. | ELKIN MATHEWS LTD. | 33 Conduit Street, | London, W.1 | *Cables: Guinpen, London. Telephone: Regent* 2936

PUBLICATION: London: Elkin Mathews, 1931.

PAGINATION: 43, [5]. Pamphlet in self-wrappers.

CONTRIBUTION: 'INTRODUCTION' dated April 1931: p. 5.

NOTE: The sale of the "Major Portion of the Birkenhead Library" was conducted by Hampton & Sons, 32 Grosvenor Gardens, London, S.W., from 8 to 12 December 1931. It was advertised as containing "Fine examples of the Bibliopegistic art by eminent 18th Century and modern French and English craftsmen". It included Madame de Pompadour's own copy of Homer, "in all upwards of 10,000 volumes each with *ex libris* of the late Earl". The auction catalogue itself is 76 pages in card wrappers.

LOCATIONS: FBW, MLW, RIC

REFERENCE: Woods B15.

B46   WILDERNESS TRAILS IN THREE
     CONTINENTS   1931

B46.1   First edition (1931)

WILDERNESS TRAILS IN | THREE CONTINENTS | *AN ACCOUNT OF TRAVEL, BIG GAME HUNT-* | *ING AND EXPLORATION IN INDIA, BURMA,* | *CHINA, EAST AFRICA AND LABRADOR* | BY | LIONEL A. D. LESLIE, F.R.G.S. | *WITH A FOREWORD BY* | THE RT. HON. WINSTON S. CHURCHILL, P.C. | *ILLUSTRATED* | HEATH CRANTON LIMITED | 6 FLEET LANE LONDON E.C.4 | 1931

PUBLICATION: London: Heath Cranton, June 1931. Price 10*s.* 6*d.*

PAGINATION: xvi, 223, [1], 24 leaves of plates.

CONTRIBUTION: 'FOREWORD' dated 24 April 1931: p. vii.

LOCATIONS: CaOTTC, RIC (dj), RPH, UKBL, USMH

REFERENCE: Woods B16.

B46.2   Second edition (1944)

[Within a framed line drawing of a castle and town in a wilderness setting, 136 × 92 mm; against a blank rectangle, ranged right, and enclosing 99.5 × 50.6 mm] WILDERNESS TRAILS | IN | THREE CONTINENTS | *BY* | LIONEL A. D. LESLIE | [ranged right] F.R.G.S. | [below the line drawing] MELLIFONT PRESS LIMITED | [ranged left] *1, Furnival Street* [ranged right] *London, E.C.4*

PUBLICATION: London: Mellifont, 1944.

PAGINATION: 96, plus very deep purple on strong reddish orange and white patterned paper wrappers.

CONTRIBUTION: The Foreword is on p. 2, the title-page verso.

LOCATION: UKBL

B47   THE MAHDI OF ALLAH   1931

B47.1   First (British) edition (1931)

THE MAHDI OF ALLAH | THE STORY OF THE DERVISH | MOHAMMED AHMED | *by* | RICHARD A. BERMANN | *With an Introduction by* | THE RT. HON. WINSTON S. CHURCHILL, | P.C., C.H., M.P. | PUTNAM | [86-mm swelled rule] | LONDON & NEW YORK

PUBLICATION: London: Putnam, September 1931. Price 16*s.* Translated by Robin John from the German first edition, *Die Derwischtrommel* (Berlin: Volksverband der Bücherfreunde Wegweiser-Verlag, 1931).[26] The Churchill Introduction is not present in the German edition.

PAGINATION: xv, [1], 318, [2], 15 leaves of plates.

CONTRIBUTION: 'INTRODUCTION' dated 14 March 1931: pp. xi–xiv.

NOTE 1: The British edition should contain a slip tipped onto p. v which reads, in vivid reddish orange boldface type,

> To avoid the possibility of causing | offence to Mohammedan readers, | the Publishers desire to state that | the claim of the Dervish Mohammed | Ahmed to the sublime title of "The | Mahdi of Allah" is not recognised | by the author of this book, nor by | any of those associated with its | English presentation.[27]

NOTE 2: An excerpt from the 'INTRODUCTION' is quoted on the front flap of the dust jacket.

LOCATIONS: CaOTTC, FrNL, RIC (dj), RPH (dj), UKBL, USMH

REFERENCE: Woods B17.

B47.2   American issue from British plates (1932)

THE MAHDI OF ALLAH | THE STORY OF THE DERVISH | MOHAMMED AHMED | *by* | RICHARD A. BERMANN | *With an Introduction by* | THE RT. HON. WINSTON S. CHURCHILL, | P.C., C.H., M.P. | THE MACMILLAN COMPANY | [86-mm swelled rule] | NEW YORK 1932

PUBLICATION: New York: Macmillan, March 1932.

PAGINATION: xv, [1], 318, [2], 15 leaves of plates.

---

26. Published under the pseudonym Arnold Höllriegel. See *Richard A. Bermann alias Arnold Hollriegel: Osterreicher – Demokrat – Weltburger* (Munich: Saur, 1995).

27. The same text appears, in black, on the front of the dust jacket.

NOTE: The identical warning to readers which is tipped onto p. v of the British edition is included in the text of the American edition on p. vi.

LOCATIONS: RIC, USMH

B48   4TH THE QUEEN'S ROYAL REGIMENT   1931

4th THE QUEEN'S ROYAL REGIMENT | AN UNOFFICIAL WAR HISTORY | With chapters on the 2/5th Battalion | *By* | CAPTAIN RONALD BANNERMAN, M.C. | [27.2-mm rule] | *With Illustrations* | [27.2-mm rule] | CROYDON | H. R. GRUBB LTD., POPLAR WALK | 1931 | (*All rights reserved*)

PUBLICATION: Croydon, Grubb, August 1931. Price 5*s*. There was also a second printing in December 1931.

PAGINATION: [*12*], 106, [2], 11 leaves of plates.

CONTRIBUTION: 'FOREWORD' dated 23 July 1931: p. iii. There is a further brief comment by Churchill on p. vi.

NOTE: There is also a deluxe leather-bound edition, with gilt edges all around and marbled endpapers.

LOCATIONS: CaOTTC, MLW, RPH, UKBL, USMH

REFERENCES: Woods B18/1; White, p. 216.

B49   THE CHARTERED SURVEYOR   1932

B49.1   First edition, only printing (1932)

THE | CHARTERED SURVEYOR | *HIS TRAINING & HIS WORK* | With a Foreword | by | THE RT. HON. | WINSTON CHURCHILL | M.P. | [seal of the Chartered Surveyors' Institution, 37.6 mm in diameter] | PUBLISHED BY THE | CHARTERED SURVEYORS' INSTITUTION | 12 GREAT GEORGE STREET | WESTMINSTER | SW

PUBLICATION: London: Chartered Surveyors' Institution, 1932. Included with the March 1932 issue of *The Chartered Surveyor*. Additional copies were available to members for 1*s*. As the Institution explained in its note accompanying the volume, "Copies of this booklet [we]re being issued to public authorities, leading banks and insurance companies, solicitors and others." Otherwise, "published" May 1932, according to *Whitaker's Book List*. Price 2*s*. 6*d*.

PAGINATION: [*2*], 28, [2].

CONTRIBUTION: 'FOREWORD': pp. 7–10.

LOCATIONS: CaOTTC, FBW, RIC, RPH, UKBL

REFERENCE: Woods B19.

B49.2   Second edition, only printing (1955)

THE | CHARTERED SURVEYOR | *HIS TRAINING & HIS WORK* | With a Foreword | by | THE RT. HON. | SIR WINSTON CHURCHILL | KG, OM, CH, MP | [Royal Institution of Chartered Surveyors' arms, 25.1 × 24.8 mm] | PUBLISHED BY | THE ROYAL INSTITUTION OF CHARTERED SURVEYORS | 12 GREAT GEORGE STREET | WESTMINSTER | SW1

PUBLICATION: London: Royal Institution of Chartered Surveyors, November? 1955. Price to members 5*s.*, post free.

PAGINATION: 36.

CONTRIBUTION: 'FOREWORD TO THE FIRST EDITION': pp. 7–10.

NOTE: A reference to the publication of the second edition can be found in the Institution's periodical, *The Chartered Surveyor*, November 1955, at p. 238. A 192-word extract from the Foreword suitable "for display in [members'] offices", measuring 12 × 6 inches and printed in black ink on Basingwerk parchment, was published at that time by the Institution and made available to members for 1*s.* 6*d.*

LOCATIONS: CaOTTC, RIC, UKBL

B50   I WAS A SPY!   1932

B50.1   First edition (1932)

I WAS A SPY! | By | MARTHE McKENNA | JARROLDS *Publishers* LONDON | *Limited* 34 *Paternoster Row*, E.C.4. | MCMXXXII

PUBLICATION: London: Jarrolds, October 1932.[28] Price 12*s.* 6*d.* There are five impressions of the first edition noted by the publisher, three in September and two in December 1932.

PAGINATION: 288, 17 leaves of plates.

CONTRIBUTION: 'FOREWORD': pp. 5–6.

NOTE: Marthe McKenna's subsequent book, *Spies I Knew*, published in 1933 (when *I Was a Spy!* was in its 15th overall impression, including both the first and cheaper editions), includes an excerpt from the 'FOREWORD' to this work on the back of the dust jacket. A brief quotation from that 'FOREWORD' and comment upon it by the author constitute the opening remarks of the first chapter of *Spies I Knew*.

TRANSLATIONS

French: *Souvenirs d'une espionne*, Paris: Payot, March 1933.

Icelandic: *Ég var njósnari*, Reykjavik: Leiftur, 1941.

LOCATIONS: UKBL, USDLC, USMH

REFERENCE: Woods B20.

B50.2   American issue from British plates (1933)

I WAS A SPY! | BY | *MARTHE McKENNA* | WITH A FOREWORD BY | THE RT. HON. WINSTON S. CHURCHILL | ILLUSTRATED WITH PHOTOGRAPHS | [publisher's device, 16.1 × 10.5 mm] | *1933* | *NEW YORK* | *ROBERT M. McBRIDE & COMPANY*

PUBLICATION: New York: McBride, February 1933. There was a second impression in March, third and fourth impressions in intervening months and a fifth in September 1933.

PAGINATION: 288, 17 leaves of plates.

---

28. The accession date of the Library of Congress copy is 25 October 1932.

CONTRIBUTION: '*FOREWORD*': pp. 5–6.

LOCATIONS: RIC, USMH

B50.3   First "cheap" issue (1933)

I WAS A SPY! | By | MARTHE McKENNA | Foreword by | THE RT. HON. WINSTON S. CHURCHILL | P.C., C.H., M.P. | (*Secretary of State for War, 1918–1921*) | CHEAPER EDITION | JARROLDS *Publishers* LONDON | *Limited* 34 *Paternoster Row*, E.C.4. | MCMXXXIII

PUBLICATION: London: Jarrolds, September 1933. The self-described 'CHEAPER EDITION'. Price 5*s*. There were at least thirteen impressions of the Cheaper Edition, that of September 1933, one in October, four in November, three in December, two in January 1934 and two in December.

NOTE: The dust jacket includes a 28-word excerpt from the Foreword on the front and a 111-word excerpt on the back.

LOCATIONS: CJZ (12th cheaper printing, dj), RIC (13th cheaper printing, dj), RPH (13th cheaper printing)

B50.4   Second British edition (1939)

I WAS A SPY! | BY | MARTHE McKENNA | FOREWORD BY | THE RT. HON. WINSTON S. CHURCHILL | P.C., C.H., M.P. | (*Secretary of State for War,* 1918–1921) | THE QUEENSWAY LIBRARY | 66–66A GREAT QUEEN ST., LONDON, W.C.2

PUBLICATION: London: Queensway Library, May 1939. Price 6*d*. Issued in wrappers February 1940. Price 6*d*.

PAGINATION: 314, [2]. Note, however, that the first leaf of the first signature and the last leaf of the last signature serve as the front and back pastedowns.

CONTRIBUTION: 'FOREWORD': pp. 7–10.

NOTE: In this re-set volume, the page size is reduced to 187 × 126 mm. The sheets bulk 30.2 mm. The volume is bound in deep red embossed linen-grain cloth, stamped in gilt. The dust jacket includes an 28-word 4-line excerpt from the Foreword.

LOCATIONS: RIC (dj), UKBL, USIU

B51   FREDERICK EDWIN, EARL OF BIRKENHEAD: THE FIRST PHASE   1933

B51.1   First edition, first issue (1933)

FREDERICK EDWIN | EARL OF | BIRKENHEAD | *THE FIRST PHASE* | By | HIS SON | THE EARL OF BIRKENHEAD | FOREWORD BY | The Rt. Hon. WINSTON S. CHURCHILL, C.H. | [publisher's device, 18.9 mm in diameter] | THORNTON BUTTERWORTH, LIMITED | 15 BEDFORD STREET, LONDON, W.C.2

PUBLICATION: London: Thornton Butterworth, May 1933. Price 21*s*. There was a second volume, not designated Volume *II*, to this biography. Of the two volumes, it is only the first which includes a Churchill foreword. David Lloyd George wrote the Foreword to the second volume. Since that volume, *Frederick Edwin, Earl of Birkenhead:*

The Last Phase, does, however, contain other first-appearance Churchill material, it is included in Section F (**F47**).

PAGINATION: 320, 20 leaves of plates.

CONTRIBUTIONS: 'FOREWORD': pp. 11–16. First published in the *Daily Telegraph* as the first instalment of the serialization of the volume on 6 April 1933 (**C399**). The volume also includes a letter of 1 August 1914 to F. E. Smith, expressing Churchill's gratitude at the position taken informally the evening before by members of the Unionist party regarding the anticipated invasion of Belgium by the Germans: p. 310. A brief (21-word) excerpt from the 'FOREWORD' appears on the front and back of the dust jacket.

NOTE: All copies should possess an errata slip tipped onto p. 9.

ANNOTATIONS: On 11 February 1933, Churchill advised Thornton Butterworth, who published the volume, that he had spent two hours with Birkenhead the day before "and suggested to him a considerable reshaping of the book to bring it in closer accordance with sequence and chronology". He also reported that he had already written the intro-duction, which he had given to Birkenhead at that time.[29]

LOCATIONS: CaOTTC, RIC (dj), RPH (dj), UKBL, USMH

REFERENCE: Woods B21.

B51.2   First edition, second issue (1936)

FREDERICK EDWIN | EARL OF BIRKENHEAD | *THE FIRST PHASE* | BY | HIS SON | [dark greenish blue] KEYSTONE | [publisher's device, 26.4 × 22.1 mm] | LIBRARY | [black] | LONDON | Thornton Butterworth Ltd

PUBLICATION: London: Thornton Butterworth, March 1936. Re-issued in Thornton Butterworth's Keystone Library. Price 5*s.*

LOCATIONS: RIC, USMWC

B51.3   First edition, third issue (1940?)

FREDERICK EDWIN | EARL OF BIRKENHEAD | THE FIRST PHASE | BY | HIS   SON | KEYSTONE | [publisher's   device,   26.4 × 22.1 mm] | LIBRARY | LONDON | Thornton Butterworth Ltd.

PUBLICATION: London: [Eyre & Spottiswoode], [1940?].

NOTE: The volume itself bears no indication of the involvement of Eyre & Spottiswoode, the name of Thornton Butterworth Ltd. being retained on the title page. Only the dust jacket, which still shows the book as a publication in the Keystone Library, substitutes Eyre & Spottiswoode for Thornton Butterworth. Copies without dust jackets will, however, be distinguishable as third-issue copies by the changes noted on the title-page transcriptions.

When Thornton Butterworth Ltd. was wound up on 6 September 1940, Thornton Butterworth himself attempted to purchase the stocks and copyrights held by the liquidator in the stead of the bankrupt firm. His offer could not match that of Eyre & Spottiswoode, which acquired all of the stocks and copyrights of the insolvent enterprise, save those titles written by Winston Churchill. Thus, rights in the Birkenhead biography

---

29. Gilbert, *WSC*, Vol. V, *C.V.* 2, p. 525.

fell to Eyre & Spottiswoode at some date after 6 September. I conjecture that it was reissued by its new publisher either late in 1940 or early in 1941.

LOCATION: RIC (dj)

B52   MODERN ENGLISH PROSE   1933

MODERN ENGLISH PROSE | Selected and Edited by | GUY BOAS, M.A. | *Headmaster of Sloane School, formerly* | *Senior English Master, St. Paul's School* | MACMILLAN AND CO., LIMITED | ST. MARTIN'S STREET, LONDON | 1933

PUBLICATION: London: Macmillan, October 1933. Price 2s. 6d.

PAGINATION: xv, [1], 260.

CONTRIBUTION: 'Lenin', excerpted from *The Aftermath*: pp. 62–6.

LOCATIONS: CaMWU, RIC, UKBL

B53   THE NEW "EXAMEN"   1934

B53.1   Limited edition (1934)

THE NEW | "EXAMEN" | By | JOHN PAGET | *With a Critical Introduction by* | *the Right Honourable* | WINSTON S. CHURCHILL | C.H., M.P. | THE HAWORTH PRESS | 1934

PUBLICATION: Manchester?: The Haworth Press, 1934.

PRINTING AND BINDING: The Deluxe Limited Edition was printed on hand-made water-marked laid paper (vertical chain lines 38.4 mm apart) with deckle edges retained and bound in full chestnut niger morocco by Sangorski & Sutcliffe, the limitation statement (colophon), on p. 4, of all copies having been signed by Churchill. "This Edition is printed on English Hand-made paper by | Sherratt & Hughes at the St. Ann's Press, Manchester, | and is bound in the olden style in Native-dyed Niger | Morocco by Sangorski & Sutcliffe; each copy is | signed and numbered, this being | No.   ". The sheets bulk 24.0 mm.

PAGINATION: [4], xv, [1], 236, [4].

CONTRIBUTION: 'INTRODUCTION': pp. ix–xv.

NOTE: John Paget's *Examen* was first issued in 1861. It is, of course, only this republication which attracted a Churchill Introduction.

ANNOTATIONS: Churchill much admired Paget's *Paradoxes and Puzzles*, which provided "the most effective vindication of the Duke of Marlborough in regard to the Brest Expedition charge that I have yet seen".[30] Churchill borrowed Lord Rosebery's copy of the original *Examen*, which he returned on 4 December 1924 with a note saying that he had, by advertising, obtained a copy of his own, adding, "I am very glad indeed to possess such a little known and deeply interesting book."[31] He said, in a later letter to Robert Birley,[32] that "several of the essays are fully equal to Macaulay's essays, and apparently

---

30. Letter of 22 August 1924 to Clementine (Gilbert, *WSC*, Vol. V, *C.V.* 1, pp. 179–81, at p. 180, and *Speaking for Themselves*, p. 285).
31. Letter of 4 December 1934 to Lord Rosebery (Gilbert, *ibid.*, pp. 290–1, at p. 290).
32. Then Assistant Master at Eton College, later (1949–63) Head Master there.

backed by an immense amount of literary knowledge and authorities. It is remarkable that they did not make a greater impression."[33]

LOCATIONS: PMW, UKLo

B53.2   Second (trade) edition (1934)

PUBLICATION: February 1934. Price 10s. 6d.

PAGINATION: xv, [1], 236, [4].

ANNOTATION: Churchill sent a copy of the volume to Stanley Baldwin with the following letter in which his deeply held critical perspective on Macaulay was expressed:

> I send you herewith Paget's Examen resurrected by my exertions. I think you sh[oul]d keep it in y[ou]r Library alongside of Macaulay, to which it is a necessary corrective and counterpart.[34]

LOCATIONS: CaOTTC, FBW (dj), RIC (dj), RPH (dj), UKBL, UKLo, USMH
REFERENCE: Woods B22.

B54   THE EMPLOYMENT EXCHANGE SERVICE OF GREAT BRITAIN   1934

B54.1   First (American) edition (1934)

[All of the following within a double-rule box, enclosing 184.3 × 109.2 mm] THE EMPLOYMENT EXCHANGE | SERVICE OF GREAT BRITAIN | *AN OUTLINE OF THE ADMINIS-* | *TRATION OF PLACING AND* | *UNEMPLOYMENT INSURANCE* | BY | T.   S.   CHEGWIDDEN | AND | G.   MYRDDIN-EVANS | WITH FOREWORD BY | THE RT. HON. WINSTON S. CHURCHILL, C.H., M.P. | [76.7-mm swelled rule] | INDUSTRIAL RELATIONS COUNSELORS | INCORPORATED | NEW YORK : : : : : : 1934

PUBLICATION: New York: Industrial Relations Counselors, 1934.

PAGINATION: xv, [1], 310, 2 leaves of plates (one numbered), 1 map (folding).

CONTRIBUTION: 'FOREWORD' of 24 January 1934, from Chartwell: pp. vii–viii.

LOCATIONS: FBW, RIC, RPH, USDLC, USMH
REFERENCE: Woods B25/1.

B54.2   British issue of American sheets (1934)

THE | EMPLOYMENT EXCHANGE SERVICE | OF GREAT BRITAIN | AN OUTLINE OF THE ADMINISTRATION OF | PLACING AND UNEMPLOYMENT INSURANCE | BY | T.   S.   CHEGWIDDEN | AND | G. MYRDDIN-EVANS | WITH FOREWORD BY | THE RT. HON. WINSTON S. CHURCHILL, C.H., M.P. | MACMILLAN AND CO., LIMITED | ST. MARTIN'S STREET, LONDON | 1934

PUBLICATION: London: Macmillan, October 1934. Price 14s.

---

33. Gilbert, *WSC*, Vol. V, *C.V.* 1, p. 1294.
34. *Ibid.*, *C.V.* 2, pp. 735–6, at p. 735.

LOCATIONS: CaOTTC, MLW, UKBL, UKScGlU

B55   SIX STORIES FROM SHAKESPEARE   1934

[All of the following within a single-rule box, enclosing 148.3 × 97.7 mm] SIX
STORIES | FROM | SHAKESPEARE | *Retold*   *by* | JOHN   BUCHAN | HUGH
WALPOLE | CLEMENCE   DANE | FRANCIS   BRETT   YOUNG | Rt.   Hon.
WINSTON CHURCHILL | Rt. Hon. VISCOUNT SNOWDEN | *Illustrations by* |
FORTUNINO   MATANIA | LONDON | GEORGE   NEWNES   LIMITED |
Southampton Street, Strand, W.C.2

PUBLICATION: London: George Newnes, October 1934. Price 7*s.* 6*d.*

PAGINATION: 179, [1], 8 leaves of plates. (Note that, through p. vii, lower-case roman
numerals are used for the pagination.)

CONTRIBUTION: 'JULIUS CÆSAR': pp. 41–63 (preceded by its divisional half-title at
p. 39). First published in the *Strand Magazine* of November 1933 (**C410**).

NOTE: In the words of the publisher, "This book is the result of an interesting experiment
in which six of the foremost writers of the day undertook to rewrite six of Shakespeare's
most popular plays as short stories."

LOCATIONS: CaMWU, CaOTTC, RIC (dj), RPH (dj), UKBL, USDLC

REFERENCES: Woods B24; Blanchard C92.

B56   A FRENCHMAN IN KHAKI   1934

B56.1   First edition (1934)

A FRENCHMAN IN | KHAKI | *By* | PAUL MAZE | D.C.M., M.M. *with bar,* C. de
G. | *With a Preface by* | The Rt. Hon. WINSTON CHURCHILL | P.C., C.H., M.P. |
[publisher's device, 18.3 × 18.1 mm on a 70.7-mm rule] | [ranged left] LONDON & |
TORONTO | [opposite the city names, a right brace; ranged right of its centre] WILLIAM
HEINEMANN, LTD.

PUBLICATION: London: Heinemann, October 1934. Price 12*s.* 6*d.* Reprinted November
1934.

PAGINATION: [*16*], 353, [3], 7 leaves of plates.

CONTRIBUTION: 'INTRODUCTION' dated 22 August 1934: pp. xiii–xv. The
front and back flaps of the dust jacket contain 24 and 27 lines, respectively, of the
Introduction.

ANNOTATIONS: On 11 August, Churchill advised Maze: "I am in the throes of proof
corrections, and am working against time. I have not found it possible to write your
introduction yet, but if you can wait another fortnight, I will certainly do so."[35] He was
as good as his word; the Introduction was dated 22 August. On 6 September, Maze wrote
Churchill a letter of appreciation and sent one of his own paintings "with my affection".[36]

LOCATIONS: CaOTTC, RIC (2nd printing; dj), RPH, UKBL, USIU (2nd printing)

---

35. *Ibid.*, p. 845.

36. *Ibid.*, p. 867.

REFERENCE: Woods B25.

B56.2   First edition, second issue (1936)

Cheap edition published November 1936. Price 5*s*.

LOCATION: RIC (dj)

B57   MY LIFE OF REVOLT   1935

[All of the following within overlapping vertical and horizontal boxes] My Life of |
REVOLT | BY | DAVID KIRKWOOD | M.P. J.P. | WITH FOREWORDS BY
THE RT. HON. | WINSTON S. CHURCHILL C.H. M.P. | AND THE RT. HON.
| GEORGE LANSBURY M.P. | [publisher's device, 25.5 × 13.7 mm] | GEORGE G.
HARRAP & CO. LTD. | LONDON BOMBAY SYDNEY

PUBLICATION: London: Harrap, November 1935. Price 10*s*. 6*d*. There was a second
printing in the same month and a cheap edition in September 1936, price 5*s*.

PAGINATION: xi, [1], 270, [2], 10 leaves of plates.

CONTRIBUTION: '*FOREWORD*': pp. v–vi.

LOCATIONS: CaOTTC (dj), RIC (dj), RPH, UKBL

REFERENCE: Woods B26.

B58   ALL CLEAR AFT   1936

ALL CLEAR AFT | *Episodes at Sea* | *by* | [10 names appearing in two columns, the first
five in 6 lines in the left-hand column] "BARTIMEUS" | VICE-ADMIRAL
GORDON | CAMPBELL, V.C., D.S.O. | C. FOX SMITH | ADMIRAL R. A.
HOPWOOD, C.B. | ERIC KEOWN | [the next five in 5 lines in the right-hand
column] BASIL LUBBOCK | F. DOROTHY SENIOR | "SINBAD" | "TAFFRAIL"
| W.   TOWNEND | *Illustrations   by   Charles   Grave* | PUBLISHED   FOR | THE
SEAMEN'S HOSPITAL SOCIETY | *by* | CASSELL AND COMPANY LIMITED |
London, Toronto, Melbourne and Sydney

PUBLICATION: London: Seamen's Hospital and Cassell, February 1936. Price 3*s*. 6*d*.

PAGINATION: x, 245, [1].

CONTRIBUTION: 'FOREWORD' dated 25 December 1935 and signed in facsimile:
p. ix.

LOCATIONS: CaOTTC (dj), RIC (dj), RPH (dj), UKBL

REFERENCE: Woods B27.

B59   FIFTY TRUE STORIES STRANGER THAN
FICTION   1936

FIFTY | TRUE STORIES | *STRANGER THAN* | FICTION | [publisher's device,
36.1 × 25.9 mm] | ODHAMS PRESS LTD. | LONG ACRE, LONDON, W.C.2

PUBLICATION: London: Odhams, 1936. Reprinted at least once, in 1948.

PAGINATION: 767, [1].

CONTRIBUTION: 'My Escape from the Boers', excerpted from *My Early Life* (**A91**): pp. 26–38.

LOCATIONS: CaOTTC, RIC (dj), UKBL

REFERENCE: Woods D(a)3.

B59/1 ADVENTURES AND ENCOUNTERS   1936

[All of the following within a single decorative-rule box, enclosing 134.4 × 81.3 mm] ADVENTURES AND | ENCOUNTERS | SELECTED BY | E. W. PARKER, M.C. | AND | A. R. MOON, M.A. | LONGMANS, GREEN AND CO. | LONDON • NEW YORK • TORONTO

PUBLICATION: London: Longmans, Green, 1936.

PAGINATION: 192.

CONTRIBUTION: 'My Escape from the Boers', excerpted from *My Early Life* (**A91**): pp. 46–62.

LOCATIONS: RIC, UKBL

B60   QUEST AND CONQUEST   1936

B60.1 First edition (1936)

QUEST AND CONQUEST | AN ANTHOLOGY OF | PERSONAL ADVENTURES | Compiled by | E. V. ODLE | MACMILLAN AND CO. LIMITED | ST. MARTIN'S STREET, LONDON | 1936

PUBLICATION: London: Macmillan, November 1936. Price 2*s.* 6*d.* There were subsequent printings in 1937, 1939 and 1941 (two). Price in 1941, 3*s.* 6*d.*

PAGINATION: xv, [1], 231, [1].

CONTRIBUTION: 'The Armoured Train', excerpted from *My Early Life* (**A91**): pp. 67–77.

LOCATIONS: RIC (dj), UKBL (5th printing), UKScNL

B60.2 Canadian issue from British plates (1937)

There were at least six printings of the Canadian issue, the first in 1937, another in 1939, two in 1941, one in 1946 and one in 1947. I have not located a copy of the first printing to examine.

B60.2.f Canadian issue from British plates, sixth printing (1947)

QUEST AND CONQUEST | AN ANTHOLOGY OF | PERSONAL ADVENTURES | Compiled by | E. V. ODLE | TORONTO | THE MACMILLAN COMPANY | OF CANADA LIMITED | 1947

PUBLICATION: Toronto: Macmillan, 1947.

PAGINATION: xv, [1], 235, [5].

LOCATION: CaOONL

B61   T. E. LAWRENCE BY HIS FRIENDS   1937

B61.1   First edition (1937)

T. E. LAWRENCE | BY HIS FRIENDS | EDITED BY | A. W. LAWRENCE | [publisher's device, 16 mm in diameter] | JONATHAN CAPE | THIRTY BEDFORD SQUARE | LONDON

PUBLICATION: London: Jonathan Cape, May 1937. Price 15*s*. The second impression was published in June and the third in September 1937; the fourth in January 1938; and the fifth in May 1939.[37]

PAGINATION: 595, [1], 8 leaves of plates.

CONTRIBUTION: Churchill's chapter (untitled): pp. 193–202. It was first published in the *News of the World* on 26 May 1935 (**C472a**) and subsequently, with additions, in *Great Contemporaries* (**A105**).

LOCATIONS: CaOTTC (dj), MLW (dj), RIC, RPH (dj), UKBL, USMH

REFERENCES: Woods B29; O'Brien E107.

B61.2   Second (American) edition (1937)

T. E. Lawrence | BY HIS FRIENDS | EDITED BY A. W. LAWRENCE | [publisher's device, 23.9 × 32.2 mm] | Doubleday, Doran & Company, Inc. | GARDEN CITY 1937 NEW YORK

PUBLICATION: New York: Doubleday, Doran, 1937. Price $4.00.

PAGINATION: xiv, 538, 8 leaves of plates.

CONTRIBUTION: Churchill's chapter (untitled): pp. 166–74.

LOCATIONS: RIC (dj), RML, USMH

REFERENCE: O'Brien E109.

B61.3   First abridged edition (1954)

T. E. LAWRENCE | BY HIS FRIENDS | EDITED BY | A. W. LAWRENCE | [publisher's device, 15.8 mm in diameter] | JONATHAN CAPE | THIRTY BEDFORD SQUARE | LONDON

PUBLICATION: London: Jonathan Cape, 11 October 1954. Price 16*s*.

PAGINATION: 319, [1].

CONTRIBUTION: Churchill's chapter (untitled): pp. 156–65.

NOTE: The prospectus for the volume has a Churchill quotation on the first page and the dust jacket includes a 78-word excerpt from the Churchill chapter on the front flap.

REFERENCE: O'Brien E108.

LOCATIONS: RIC (dj), UKBL, USMH

---

37. It is not clear why the publisher notes only the first three printings on the title-page verso of the British abridged edition (1954).

B61.4   Second American issue from second (American) edition sheets (1980)

T. E. Lawrence | BY HIS FRIENDS | EDITED BY A. W. LAWRENCE | [publisher's device, 12.7 × 9.7 mm] | GORDIAN PRESS | NEW YORK | 1980

PUBLICATION: New York: Gordian Press, 1980.

PAGINATION: [2], xiii, [1], 538. The plates of the second (American) edition have now been printed as a part of the letterpress sheets and are gathered within the 16s as unnumbered sheets.

LOCATION: RIC

B62   THE WAR IN THE AIR   1937

B62.1   First edition (1937)

THE WAR IN THE AIR | Being the Story of | The part played in the Great War | by the Royal Air Force | APPENDICES | BY | H. A. JONES | OXFORD | AT THE CLARENDON PRESS | 1937

PUBLICATION: Oxford: Oxford University Press, July 1937.

PAGINATION: vii, [1], 174, 8 tables (folding).

CONTRIBUTION: Appendix IV, 'Munitions Possibilities of 1918', extract from a paper by Churchill as Minister of Munitions, dated 21 October 1917: pp. 18–21.

NOTE: Of the lengthy set, this is the volume of Appendices.

LOCATIONS: CaOONMC, UKBL, UKIWM

B62.2   Second issue, photo-reproduced from the first edition (1997)

THE WAR IN THE AIR | Being the Story of | The part played in the Great War | by the Royal Air Force | APPENDICES | BY | H. A. JONES | THE IMPERIAL WAR MUSEUM | Department of Printed Books | [29.4-mm rule] | In Association With | THE BATTERY PRESS | Nashville

PUBLICATION: London: Imperial War Museum; Nashville: Battery Press, 1997. Published jointly by the Battery Press, 600 copies, price $39.95, and the Imperial War Museum, 100 copies, price £27.00.

PAGINATION: v, [1], 173, [9], 1 table (folding).[38]

CONTRIBUTION: As **B62.1**.

LOCATION: RIC

B63   ALARMS & EXCURSIONS   1938

ALARMS & EXCURSIONS | *REMINISCENCES OF A SOLDIER* | by | LIEUT-GEN. SIR TOM BRIDGES | K.C.B., K.C.M.G., D.S.O., LL.D. | *With a Foreword by* | THE RT. HON. WINSTON S. CHURCHILL | P.C., C.H., M.P. | WITH FRONTISPIECE PORTRAIT | LONGMANS GREEN AND CO. | LONDON ◊ NEW YORK ◊ TORONTO

---

38. A single large folded sheet consisting of the tables contained in Appendices XVI, XVII, XXVII, XL and XLI, inserted in a pocket on the back pastedown.

PUBLICATION: London: Longmans, Green, March 1938. Price 12*s.* 6*d.* There was also a "Cheap edition" published November 1939, price 5*s.*

PAGINATION: [*2*], ix, [1], 362, 1 leaf of plates.

CONTRIBUTION: 'FOREWORD' dated 31 January 1938: pp. v–vii.

ANNOTATIONS: Bridges thanked Churchill "for that *excellent* preface to my book, it made the sale".[39]

LOCATIONS: CaOONMC, CaOTTC, MLW (dj), RIC, RPH (dj), UKBL, USMH

REFERENCE: Woods B30.

B64   GUARD FROM THE YARD   1938

[101.3-mm swelled rule] | GUARD FROM | THE YARD | *by* | Ex-Detective-Inspector W. H. THOMPSON | [101.3-mm swelled rule] | *With a Foreword by* | The Rt. Hon. WINSTON CHURCHILL, M.P. | 15 *Illustrations* | JARROLDS *Publishers* LONDON *Limited* | *Paternoster House, Paternoster Row, E.C.4* | *(Founded* 1770) | MCMXXXVIII

PUBLICATION: London: Jarrolds, November 1938. Price 12*s.* 6*d.*

PAGINATION: 255, [1] [the prelims, through p. xii, are paginated in lower-case roman numerals], 8 leaves of plates.

CONTRIBUTION: 'FOREWORD' signed in facsimile: pp. vii–viii.

NOTE: Copies are also known stamped in black on dark reddish orange embossed calico-texture cloth, and in red cloth, stamped in gilt (I did not have the Centroid Color Chart with me when I examined this copy). There also exists a black on brownish orange remainder binding.

LOCATIONS: CaOTTC, FBW (dj), MLW, RIC, RPH (dark reddish orange cloth), UKBL

REFERENCE: Woods B31.

B65   ADVENTURES ASHORE & AFLOAT   1939

B65.1   First edition (1939)

ADVENTURES | ASHORE & AFLOAT | *By* | ADMIRAL OF THE FLEET | SIR ROGER KEYES Bart. | G.C.B. K.C.V.O. C.M.G. D.S.O. | LL.D. D.C.L. M.P. | HON. COLONEL COMMANDANT ROYAL MARINES | *With a Foreword by* | THE RIGHT HON. WINSTON S. CHURCHILL | C.H. M.P. | [publisher's device, 29.3 × 18.4 mm] | GEORGE G. HARRAP & CO. LTD. | LONDON TORONTO BOMBAY SYDNEY

PUBLICATION: London: Harrap, May 1939. Price 18*s.* There was also a "Cheap edition" published June 1941, price 7*s.* 6*d.*

PAGINATION: [*4*], 373, [3], 23 leaves of plates.

CONTRIBUTION: 'FOREWORD' dated 9 March 1939 and signed in facsimile: pp. 5–6.

LOCATIONS: CaOTTC, MLW, RIC (dj), RPH, UKBL, USIU, USMH

REFERENCE: Woods B32.

---

39. Letter of 1 June 1938 (Gilbert, *WSC*, Vol. V, *C.V.* 3, p. 1051).

B65.2 **White Lion issue, photo-reproduced from first-edition sheets (1973)**

SIR ROGER KEYES | *Adventures* | *Ashore and Afloat* | with a Foreword by | Winston S. Churchill | [publisher's device, 13.1 × 18.0 mm] | WHITE LION PUBLISHERS | London and New York

PUBLICATION: London: White Lion, July 1973. Price £3.25.

PAGINATION: [6], 373, [3], 23 leaves of plates. The page size has been reduced to 205.5 × 134.7 mm.

LOCATIONS: RIC (dj), UKBL

B66   I WAS THERE! 1939

Published September 1939, in four volumes. Price £3.6s.6d., or 2s. down and 17 monthly payments of 4s. each. The only Churchill contribution is in Volume I.

Volume I

[157.7-mm triple rule] | 'I WAS THERE!' | THE HUMAN STORY OF | THE GREAT WAR OF 1914—1918 | Edited by | SIR JOHN HAMMERTON | [within and at one point overlapping beyond a single-rule frame, otherwise enclosing 42.4 × 72.5 mm, a half-tone photograph of a cannon firing] | VOLUME ONE | Pages 1—496 | LONDON | THE WAVERLY BOOK COMPANY LTD | [157.7-mm triple rule]

PUBLICATION: London: Waverly Book Company, 1939.

PAGINATION: viii, 496.

CONTRIBUTION: 'The Clock Ticks at the Admiralty': pp. 14—16 (in Part 1 of the 51 individually published parts). Reprinted from *The World Crisis* (**A69**).

NOTE: The prospectus for the series was hardly understated:

> No greater human document has been completed throughout the ages. It records in permanent form the most vivid, poignant, and human experiences of those who took part in those world-shaking events. Thrilling personal narratives of stirring deeds, human suffering and endurance, triumph and disaster, bring to life with startling realism the most dramatic and significant episodes wherever Britain fought in the last Great War.

Churchill's contribution is listed first among the 16 listed contributions under the heading: 'Some of the Hundreds of Thrilling Narratives'.

LOCATIONS: RIC, USICarbS, USIU, USMH, USViU

REFERENCE: Woods D(a)4.

B67   PRELUDE TO VICTORY 1939

PRELUDE | TO VICTORY | By | Brigadier-General | E. L. SPEARS | C.B., C.B.E., M.C. | *With an Introduction by* | The Rt. Hon. | WINSTON S. CHURCHILL | P.C., M.P. | [publisher's device, 16.3 mm in diameter] | JONATHAN CAPE | THIRTY BEDFORD SQUARE | LONDON

PUBLICATION: London: Jonathan Cape, November 1939. Price 18s. There was a second printing in January 1940.

PAGINATION: 640, 31 leaves of plates, 5 maps (all folding).

CONTRIBUTION: 'INTRODUCTION': pp. 11–13. Subsequently published in the *Collected Essays*, Vol. I, at pp. 489–91.

NOTE: The dust jacket of the second printing differs from that of the first in the following respects: The spine bears the words '2nd printing' above the publisher's device; the blurb on the front flap is replaced by a review from the *New Statesman and Nation*; the back flap, which had been blank, now contains reviews from *The Spectator* and the *Manchester Evening News*; and the back, which had also been blank, now contains reviews from *The Listener* and the *Daily Telegraph*.

ANNOTATIONS: On 20 July 1939, Churchill wrote to Spears of his enthusiastic reaction to the book:

> I have just finished the book. I think it a great work, and one of the finest I have read in the literature of the War. ... Your book ought certainly to be read by all British and French field officers and upwards—especially upwards![40]

TRANSLATION

French: *Prélude à la victoire*, Paris: Presses de la Cité, 1968.

LOCATIONS: CaOTTC (dj), FrNL (French edition), RIC (dj), RPH, UKBL, USMH

REFERENCE: Woods B33.

B68   MY FIGHT TO REARM BRITAIN   1939

MY FIGHT TO | REARM BRITAIN | BY | VISCOUNT ROTHERMERE | *With an Introduction by* | THE RIGHT HON. | WINSTON S. CHURCHILL, C.H., M.P. | MCMXXXIX | EYRE AND SPOTTISWOODE | LONDON

PUBLICATION: London: Eyre & Spottiswoode, December 1939. Price 5s.

PAGINATION: xi, [1], 190, [2], 8 leaves of plates.

CONTRIBUTION: Introduction, in the form of a letter dated 4 December 1939 to Lord Rothermere from the Admiralty: pp. vii–viii. A 33-word excerpt from this Introduction is found on the front flap of the dust jacket.

LOCATIONS: RIC (dj), RPH, UKBL, UKLo (dj), USMH

REFERENCE: Woods B32/1.

B68/1 THE B.B. & C.I. ANNUAL, 1939   1939?

An annual publication of the Bombay Baroda and Central India Railway in magazine format. There is no title page.

PUBLICATION: Bombay: G. de P. Leeper, Publicity and Advertising Superintendent, B.B. & C.I. Railway, Bombay, 1939?

PAGINATION: 124, plus wrappers.

CONTRIBUTION: Undated foreword in the form of a facsimile typed letter on Chartwell letterhead, signed 'W. Churchill': p. 19.

LOCATION: RIC

---

40. CHAR 2/367/59.

B69   POLAND AND SCOTLAND   1940

[Cover title:] [in two sectors, side by side, each against a white background, 146.5 ×
85.9 mm; on the left, gold, the Polish eagle; on the right, vivid reddish orange, the British
lion] | [against a black background, 81.7 × 171 mm, white] POLAND AND
SCOTLAND

PUBLICATION: London: HMSO, September? 1940.

PAGINATION: 12, in self-wrappers.

CONTRIBUTION: Letter of 3 September 1940 from Churchill welcoming "every Polish
soldier, sailor or airman", in facsimile: p. 2 (in English) and p. 3 (in Polish).

LOCATIONS: RIC, UKBL, UKOxB

B70   WORKING AFTER THE SIREN   1940

[Dropped-head title only, deep purplish blue] ISSUED BY THE MINISTRY [royal
arms, 21.8 × 25.2 mm] OF HOME SECURITY | WORKING | AFTER THE SIREN
| [within a single-rule box, enclosing 92.5 × 118.7 mm] MESSAGE BY THE PRIME
MINISTER [16 lines of text] | 10*th September*, 1940. [facsimile signature] Winston S.
Churchill | [text of the Ministry's new advice on working after an air-raid siren]

PUBLICATION: London: Ministry of Home Security, September 1940, 2 million copies.
Price 1*d*.

PAGINATION: 2. Leaflet.

CONTRIBUTION: 'MESSAGE BY THE PRIME MINISTER' of 10 September 1940 in
16 lines: p. 1.

LOCATIONS: RIC, UKLse

B71   THE WAR SPEECHES OF WILLIAM PITT THE
YOUNGER   1940

THE | WAR SPEECHES | OF | WILLIAM PITT | THE YOUNGER | SELECTED
BY | R. COUPLAND | WITH A FOREWORD BY | THE RIGHT HON. |
WINSTON S. CHURCHILL | THIRD EDITION | OXFORD | AT THE
CLARENDON PRESS | 1940

PUBLICATION: Oxford: Clarendon Press, 1940. First published in 1915, with a second
edition in 1916. Churchill's Foreword does not appear until the third and last edition,
published December 1940. Price 5*s*.

PAGINATION: xlviii, 360.

CONTRIBUTION: 'FOREWORD' dated October 1940: pp. v–vi. Subsequently published
in the *Collected Essays*, Vol. I, at p. 492.

NOTE: A 121-word excerpt from the Foreword is included on the front flap of the dust
jacket.

LOCATIONS: CaACU, CaOOCC, CaOTTC, RIC (dj), RPH (dj), UKBL, UKCaU,
UKOxB

REFERENCE: Woods B34.

B72   MEMOIRS OF A FIGHTING LIFE   1940

MEMOIRS | OF | A FIGHTING LIFE | *By* | RT. HON. JOSIAH C. WEDGWOOD | D.S.O., M.P. | *Foreword by* | THE RT. HON. WINSTON CHURCHILL, M.P. | *With* 15 *Illustrations* | HUTCHINSON & CO. (Publishers) LTD. | LONDON AND MELBOURNE

PUBLICATION: London: Hutchinson, December 1940. Price 18*s*.

PAGINATION: 256, 15 leaves of plates, 24-page catalogue.

CONTRIBUTION: 'FOREWORD' dated 20 October 1940: p. 5.

LOCATIONS: CaOHM, RPH, UKBL, USMH, USNN, USNNC

REFERENCE: Woods B35.

B73   I WAS WINSTON CHURCHILL'S PRIVATE
    SECRETARY   1941

B73.1.a   First edition, first printing (1941)

I   WAS | WINSTON | CHURCHILL'S | PRIVATE | SECRETARY | WILFRID FUNK, INC. | PUBLISHERS NEW YORK

PUBLICATION: New York: Wilfrid Funk, April 1941. Price $2.00.

PAGINATION: xii, 221, [7].

CONTRIBUTION: Undated letter of recommendation for the author, reproduced in facsimile as a foreword: p. ix. There is a 16-word excerpt from the letter reproduced on the front flap of the dust jacket.

NOTE: Parts of this book were later serialized in *The Gregg Writer*, beginning with 'I Meet the Man', in the issue of November 1941, Vol. XLIV, No. 3, at pp. 143–7.

TRANSLATION

Swedish: *Jag var Churchills sekreterare*, Stockholm: no publisher indicated, 1941.

LOCATIONS: CaOTTC, CaOTU, RIC, USMH

REFERENCE: Woods D(b)54.

B73.1.b   First edition, second printing (1941)

Unusually, the first-edition title page did not include the name of the author; it has now been altered to do so.

I WAS | WINSTON | CHURCHILL'S | PRIVATE | SECRETARY | by | PHYLLIS MOIR | WILFRID FUNK, INC. | PUBLISHERS   NEW YORK

PUBLICATION: April 1941.

LOCATIONS: RIC (dj), UKBL

B73.1.c   First edition, third printing (1941)

PUBLICATION: May 1941.

LOCATION: RIC (dj)

B73.2   Australian edition (1941)

I WAS | WINSTON | CHURCHILL'S | PRIVATE | SECRETARY | ANGUS AND ROBERTSON LTD | SYDNEY :: LONDON | 1941

PUBLICATION: Sydney: Angus and Robertson, published 1941 in Sydney and January 1942 in London. Price 6*s*.

PAGINATION: xiv, 186, 1 leaf of plates.

NOTE: The volume was set up, printed and bound in Australia; however, the facsimile letter of introduction is in the same location as in the American edition. The plate is the signed Cecil Beaton photograph of Churchill at his desk, cigar in hand, which serves as the frontispiece. The name of the author is left off the title page of this edition, as in the first edition.

LOCATIONS: AuNL, RIC

B74   HIGHROAD TO ADVENTURE   1941

Highroad to Adventure | *An Anthology* | [108.7-mm crenellated rule] | *Edited by* | EARL P. HANSON | *With Introductory Notes by the Editor* | [108.7-mm crenellated rule] | NATIONAL TRAVEL CLUB | *New York*

PUBLICATION: New York: National Travel Club, 1941.

PAGINATION: ix, [1], 591, [7].

CONTRIBUTION: 'Escape from the Boers': pp. 5–29. Taken from *A Roving Commission* (**A91.2**).

LOCATION: RIC (dj)

B75   KHAKI AND GOWN   1941

B75.1   First edition (1941)

KHAKI   AND   GOWN | *An   Autobiography* | *By* | FIELD-MARSHAL   LORD BIRDWOOD | OF ANZAC AND TOTNES | G.C.B., G.C.S.I., G.C.M.G., G.C.V.O., C.I.E., D.S.O., | LL.D., D.C.L., D.Litt., M.A. | *With a Foreword by* | THE RT. HON. WINSTON CHURCHILL, C.H., P.C. | [5-line epigraph from *Tristram Shandy*] | WARD, LOCK & CO., LIMITED | LONDON AND MELBOURNE

PUBLICATION: London: Ward, Lock, December 1941. Price 18*s*. The book was reprinted in 1942.

PAGINATION: 456, 16 leaves of plates, 5 maps (4 folding).

CONTRIBUTION: 'FOREWORD', signed in facsimile: pp. 7–8.

LOCATIONS: CaOONMC, CaOTTC, RIC (dj), RPH, UKBL, USMH

REFERENCE: Woods B36.

B75.2   American issue from British plates (1957)

KHAKI   and   GOWN | An   Autobiography | *By* | Field-Marshal   Lord   Birdwood | *of Anzac and Totnes* | *With a Foreword By* | SIR WINSTON CHURCHILL | ROBERT SPELLER & SONS | PUBLISHERS NEW YORK 36 | 1957

PUBLICATION: New York: Speller, 1957. Price $6.00.

PAGINATION: 456, 17 leaves of plates.[41]

NOTE: There is a 124-word excerpt from the Churchill Foreword on the front flap of the dust jacket.

LOCATIONS: CJZ (dj), RIC (dj), USMH

B76   BEATING THE INVADER   1941

Three English-language issues have been noted; all indications are that they were issued simultaneously, although possibly for different purposes and in different locations in England.

B76.1   First edition, first issue (1941)

[Dropped-head title:] *Issued by the Ministry of Information* [royal arms, 18.8 × 21.1 mm] *in co-operation with the War Office | and the Ministry of Home Security |* [188-mm swelled rule] | Beating the INVADER | A MESSAGE FROM THE PRIME MINISTER

PUBLICATION: London: Ministry of Information, May 1941; 14,050,800 copies (first and second issues).

PAGINATION: 2. Leaflet.

CONTRIBUTION: 'A Message from the Prime Minister': p. 1.

NOTE: A final copy of the leaflet was provided to the Prime Minister by John Peck[42] on 23 May, no doubt very shortly after its distribution but no precise date of publication is found in the file. The British Library received its copy on 28 May 1941.

ANNOTATIONS: This leaflet appears to have been considered by Woods as being *entirely* of Churchill's hand.[43] National Archives documents, however, show clearly that the leaflet was prepared by the Ministry of Information and forwarded to the Prime Minister by Duff Cooper on 7 March 1941 with a request that he provide an introduction: "Would you consider writing such an introduction yourself? It would of course give the leaflet far greater authority and would induce many people to read and to keep it who might otherwise neglect to do so."[44] Churchill quickly (on the 10th) provided his comments on the draft leaflet and suggestions of material which could be included in his introduction. It had been initially thought by the War Cabinet that the text could be released in the Sunday newspapers on 16 March but that never took place. Churchill dictated his introduction on 25 March and it was sent over by John Peck to the M.O.I. that day. Proofs of the leaflet went back and forth[45] while further thought was given to the leaflet's fate. Churchill noted that, since the leaflet was planned, circumstances had

---

41. The added plate is a photograph of 'Lord Kitchener Inspecting Anzac From Russell's Top', with General Birdwood beside him on 13 November 1915. It faces p. 280.

42. Then Assistant Private Secretary to the Prime Minister, a position he held from 1940 to 1945. He later joined the Foreign Service (in 1946) and served in the 1960s and 1970s as Ambassador to Senegal, Mauritania and Ireland. His memoirs, *Dublin from Downing Street*, were published in Dublin by Gill and Macmillan in 1978.

43. It was **A69** in the Woods bibliography.

44. PREM 3/236.

45. A proof copy with corrections in Churchill's hand survives (*ibid.*).

changed and other events had distracted people's minds from invasion. He thought that, if the leaflet were issued now, it would not have anything like the original intended effect. Among the actions considered were the following: issue it as planned; postpone its publication until a more suitable moment; or distribute it on a limited basis. Churchill recommended the third course but the final decision—to distribute the leaflet to all householders—was not made until the War Cabinet meeting of 24 April and resulted in the printing of more than 14 million copies. The huge print run might leave one with the impression that the leaflet would be commonly found today. It was, however, only a *leaflet* anticipating an event that never came to pass. In the event, few copies have survived.[46]

TRANSLATION
Welsh: *Trechu'r Goresgynnydd*, London: Ministry of Information, May 1941, 160,400 copies.

LOCATIONS: CaOTTC, RIC, UKBL (English and Welsh editions), USIU

REFERENCE: Woods A69.

B76.2   First edition, second issue (1941)

The only difference noted between the first and second issues is that the second issue was co-published by the Ministry of Public Security. There is currently no method of determining the difference, if any, in quantities of production of the first and second issues. The British Library received its copy on 28 May 1941.

LOCATION: UKBL

B76.3   First edition, third issue (1941)

As the first issue, except that the following notice appears ranged upper left: vivid red, 'IMPORTANT NOTICE | This leaflet is being distributed throughout the | country. If invasion comes it applies in this town | as elsewhere, but <u>before</u> invasion comes those | who are not engaged on useful work should leave | this town—see special posters and leaflets.'

PUBLICATION: London: Ministry of Information, May 1941; 250,000 copies.

NOTE: The British Library received its copy on 28 May 1941.

LOCATIONS: CJZ, UKBL

B77   JEAN   1941

B77.1   First edition, first issue (1941)

JEAN | [88.1-mm rule] | A MEMOIR | BY | IAN HAMILTON | [Hamilton family arms,   44.5 × 44.6 mm] | [88.1-mm   rule] | PRIVATELY   PRINTED | LONDON MCMXLI

PUBLICATION: London: privately published [printed by Adprint Limited], 1941.

---

46. The leaflet is far less common than the famous 20 August 1940 tribute to "the few" (see **A131**), of which only 300,000 copies were published. However ephemeral such items are, the relative durability of that card-wrapped pamphlet and the importance of the address have resulted in its ready availability, compared to this leaflet.

PAGINATION: [*8*], 71, [1], 14 leaves of plates.

CONTRIBUTION: Letter of sympathy of 25 February 1941 to Sir Ian Hamilton on the death of his wife, Jean, reproduced in facsimile: pp. 41–2 and in type, p. 43.

LOCATIONS: RIC (dj), UKBL, UKScNL, USMH

B77.2 First edition, second (trade) issue (1942)

JEAN | [88.1-mm rule] | A MEMOIR | BY | IAN HAMILTON | [Hamilton family arms, 44.5 × 44.6 mm] | [88.1-mm rule] | FABER AND FABER LTD | 24 RUSSELL SQUARE | LONDON

PUBLICATION: London: Faber & Faber, July 1942. Price 12*s.* 6*d.*

LOCATIONS: CaOTTC (dj), RIC (dj), UKScNL

REFERENCE: Woods D(b)55/3.

B78   THE SIXTH COLUMN INSIDE THE NAZI-OCCUPIED COUNTRIES   1942

[96.4-mm double rule] THE | SIXTH COLUMN | [96.4-mm rule] | INSIDE THE | NAZI-OCCUPIED COUNTRIES | [96.4-mm double rule] | [oval publisher's device, 21.2 × 18.6 mm] | [96.4-mm rule] | ALLIANCE BOOK CORPORATION | NEW YORK | [96.4-mm double rule]

PUBLICATION: New York: Alliance Book Corporation, 1942.

PAGINATION: xii, 314, [2].

CONTRIBUTION: Introduction, entitled 'Our Efforts Will Not Be in Vain': pp. vii–xi.

NOTE: There is also a 7-word quotation from Churchill's Introduction on the front of the dust jacket.

LOCATIONS: CJZ (dj), RIC (dj), USDLC, USMH

REFERENCE: Woods D(b)55/2.

B79   RONALD CARTLAND   1942

B79.1 First edition (1942)

RONALD CARTLAND | BY | *His Sister* | BARBARA CARTLAND | *With a Preface by* | RT. HON. WINSTON S. CHURCHILL. M.P. | [publisher's device, 18.7 × 26.2 mm] | *Collins Publishers* | 48 PALL MALL LONDON | 1942

PUBLICATION: London: Collins, April 1942. Price 12*s.* 6*d.*

PAGINATION: 264, 1 leaf of plates.

CONTRIBUTIONS: 'PREFACE', dated 7 November 1941: p. 23. The volume also includes the following first-appearance items: message to Captain Peto, the Conservative candidate in the King's Norton Division of Birmingham by-election: p. 10; and letter of condolence to Cartland's mother: p. 11. The message to Captain Peto was, however, first published in *The Times* of 6 May 1941 (**G543a**).

LOCATIONS: CaOTTC (dj), RIC (dj), RPH (dj), UKBL, USMH

REFERENCE: Woods B37.

B79.2.a Second edition, first printing (1945)

RONALD CARTLAND | BY | *His Sister* | BARBARA CARTLAND | *With a Preface by* | RT. HON. WINSTON S. CHURCHILL. M.P. | *Ninth Thousand* | HUTCHINSON & CO. (Publishers), LTD. | LONDON : NEW YORK : MELBOURNE : SYDNEY

PUBLICATION: London: Hutchinson, n.d. [January 1945]. Price 10*s*. 6*d*.

PAGINATION: 160, 1 leaf of plates.

CONTRIBUTIONS: Churchill's 'PREFACE' is at p. 15 and the messages are at p. 9.

NOTES: This cheap edition was undoubtedly published by Hutchinson to meet war economy standards, particularly relevant in the case of a popular work. Paper rationing would have militated against the reprinting of a 264-page volume; hence its resetting at 160 pp. Note that the sheets are each 0.15 mm thick and bulk 12.3 mm. The binding is strong red embossed calico-texture cloth, stamped in gilt.

LOCATIONS: CJZ (dj), RIC, UKBL

REFERENCE: O'Brien F0188.

B79.2.b Second edition, second? printing (1945?)

RONALD CARTLAND | BY | *His Sister* | BARBARA CARTLAND | *With a Preface by* | RT. HON. WINSTON S. CHURCHILL. M.P. | THE NATIONAL BOOK ASSOCIATION | HUTCHINSON & CO. (Publishers), LTD. | BOUVERIE HOUSE | 154 FLEET STREET, LONDON, E.C.4

PUBLICATION: London: National Book Association and Hutchinson, n.d.

NOTE: The sheets are each 0.14 mm and bulk 10.3 mm. The binding is black on light bluish green embossed calico-texture cloth.

LOCATION: RIC

B79.3 Second issue from first-edition sheets (1980)

My Brother, Ronald | by | Barbara Cartland | *Preface by* | SIR WINSTON CHURCHILL | *Foreword by* | SIR ARTHUR BRYANT | [publisher's device, 7.7 × 6.7 mm] | SHELDON PRESS | LONDON

PUBLICATION: London: Sheldon Press, 1980. Price £4.95.

PAGINATION: 264, [8], 4 leaves of plates.

CONTRIBUTIONS: The Preface: p. 21; the messages are at pp. 9 and 10.

LOCATION: RIC

B80   THE USE OF AIR POWER   1942

B80.1 First edition (1942)

THE USE OF AIR POWER | By | Flight-Lieut. V. E. R. BLUNT | [ranged right] M.A., LL.B. | [centred, decorative device, 8.3 mm in diameter] | THORSONS PUBLISHERS LTD. | 91 ST. MARTIN'S LANE, | LONDON, W.C.2

PUBLICATION: London: Thorsons, October 1942. Price 8*s*. 6*d*.

PAGINATION: 169, [1].

CONTRIBUTION: Appendix C, 'Extracts from a Paper by Winston S. Churchill, Minister of Munitions, Dated October 21ˢᵗ, 1917': pp. 165–9.

LOCATIONS: CaOOND, RIC, UKBL, USMH

B80.2.a   First American edition, first printing (1943)

Flight-Lieut. V. E. R. Blunt, R.A.F. | THE USE OF | AIR POWER | [8.2-mm fancy curved rule] | COMMENT | By Winston Churchill | First American Edition | [8.2-mm fancy curved rule] | Military Service Publishing Company | Harrisburg, Pennsylvania | 1943

PUBLICATION: Harrisburg (PA): Military Service Publishing, 1943. Price $1.00.

PAGINATION: xiii, [1], 162, 1 leaf of plates.

CONTRIBUTION: The Churchill article appears as an introduction, under the heading 'Comment', at pp. (v)–(ix) [*sic*, parentheses original].

LOCATION: UKIWM

B80.2.b   First American edition, second printing (1943)

PUBLICATION: December 1943.

LOCATIONS: RIC (dj), USNNC

B81   MEN AT WAR   1942

B81.1   First edition (1942)

MEN AT WAR | *The Best War Stories* | *of All Time* | EDITED | *with an Introduction* | BY | ERNEST HEMINGWAY | *Based on a plan by William Kozlenko* | CROWN PUBLISHERS | NEW YORK

PUBLICATION: New York: Crown Publishers, 22 October 1942. There were no fewer than five printings but I have been unable to find any characteristics which enable me to distinguish one from the other, except for the designations to that effect on the dust jackets.

PAGINATION: xxxii, 1072.

CONTRIBUTION: 'The Cavalry Charge at Omdurman', excerpted from *My Early Life* (**A91**): pp. 813–21.

LOCATIONS: RIC, UKBL, USDLC, USMH

REFERENCES: Woods D(a)11; Hanneman A19a; O'Brien D0016.

B81.2   First paperback edition (1952)

[All of the following within a decorative-rule box, enclosing 64 × 61.4 mm] MEN | AT | WAR | Edited by, and with a | special introduction by | ERNEST HEMINGWAY | [below the box] Based on a plan by William Kozlenko | [publisher's device, being a line drawing of Shakespeare's head, 18.9 × 13.4 mm] | All stories complete and unabridged as | they appeared in the original edition. | AVON PUBLISHING CO., INC. | 575 Madison Avenue, New York 22, N.Y. | [89.3-mm decorative rule]

PUBLICATION: New York: Avon, June 1952. Price 50¢.

PAGINATION: 640 [numbered i–xviii, 19–640].

CONTRIBUTION: 'The Cavalry Charge at Omdurman': pp. 506–17.

LOCATION: RIC

REFERENCE: Hanneman A19b.

B81.3 New Crown Publishers issue (1955)

MEN AT WAR | The Best War Stories | of All Time | EDITED | with an Introduction | BY | ERNEST HEMINGWAY | *Based on a plan by William Kozlenko* | New Complete Edition | CROWN PUBLISHERS, INC. | NEW YORK

PUBLICATION: New York: Crown Publishers, 5 May 1955. Price $4.95.

REFERENCE: Hanneman A19c.

LOCATION: USMH

B81.4 Bramhall House issue (1955)

MEN AT WAR | The Best War Stories | of All Time | EDITED | with an Introduction | BY | ERNEST HEMINGWAY | *Based on a plan by William Kozlenko* | New Complete Edition | BRAMHALL HOUSE | NEW YORK

PUBLICATION: New York: Bramhall House, 1955.

REFERENCE: Hanneman A19d.

LOCATIONS: CaOTY, CaQMU

B81.5 Second paperback edition (1958)

MEN | AT | WAR | EDITED | *with an Introduction* | BY | ERNEST HEMINGWAY | *Based on a plan by William Kozlenko* | [publisher's device, 12.4 × 11.7 mm] | BERKLEY PUBLISHING CORP. | 145 West 57th Street • New York 19, N.Y.

PUBLICATION: New York: Berkley, June 1958. Price 75¢. There have been no fewer than five printings of this edition, the second in July 1960 and the fifth in April 1963.

PAGINATION: [4], 508.

CONTRIBUTION: 'The Cavalry Charge at Omdurman': pp. 402–12.

LOCATIONS: CaAEU, CaMWU, RIC (1st and 5th printings), USMH

REFERENCE: Hanneman A19e.

B81.6 Second Bramhall House issue (1979)

MEN AT WAR | *The Best War Stories* | *of All Time* | EDITED | *with an Introduction* | BY | ERNEST HEMINGWAY | *Based on a plan by William Kozlenko* | BRAMHALL HOUSE | NEW YORK

PUBLICATION: New York: Bramhall House, 1979.

PAGINATION: xxviii, 1072, [2].

CONTRIBUTION: 'The Cavalry Charge at Omdurman': pp. 813–21.

LOCATIONS: CaOGU, RIC (dj), RPH (dj), USDLC

B81.7 Wings Books issue (1991)

MEN | AT [line drawing of soldiers with fixed bayonets advancing towards a barbed-wire obstruction, 17 × 58.7 mm] | WAR | THE BEST WAR STORIES | OF ALL

TIME | EDITED WITH AN INTRODUCTION BY | ERNEST | HEMINGWAY | Based on a plan by William Kozlenko | WINGS BOOKS | NEW YORK

PUBLICATION: New York: Wings Books, 1991.

PAGINATION: xxviii, 1072, [4].

CONTRIBUTION: 'The Cavalry Charge at Omdurman': pp. 813–21.

LOCATIONS: CaOOC, CaOL, RIC (dj)

B82   TESTAMENT TO DEMOCRACY   1943

TESTAMENT TO DEMOCRACY | By | THE RT. HON. LORD WEDGWOOD | Foreword by | THE RT. HON. WINSTON CHURCHILL, M.P. | Preface and Additional Footnotes by | MOSES SCHONFELD | WITH 10 ILLUSTRATIONS | GRAPHICS COURTESY PICK-S | Published under the auspices of | AMERICAN CHAPTER | RELIGIOUS EMERGENCY COUNCIL OF GREAT BRITAIN | NEW YORK

PUBLICATION: New York: Ad Press, 1943.

PAGINATION: xx, 357, [7].

CONTRIBUTION: Churchill's Foreword to *Memoirs of a Fighting Life* (**B72**) is republished here as a Foreword: p. ix. There is also a British edition of the work (London: Hutchison, 1942), which does not contain the Foreword.

NOTE: There are small differences of punctuation and paragraphing between this version of the Foreword and that in Wedgwood's autobiography.

LOCATIONS: RIC (dj), RPH (dj), USMH

B83   A SOLDIER'S READER   1943

[Within a thin–thick–thin rule box, enclosing 46.3 × 84 mm] A | SOLDIER'S | READER | [below the box] *A VOLUME CONTAINING FOUR HUNDRED | THOUSAND WORDS OF SELECT LITERARY | ENTERTAINMENT FOR THE AMERICAN | SOLDIER ON THE GROUND OR IN THE AIR | EDITED BY GEORGE MACY FOR* | [publisher's device, 40.6 × 38.7 mm] | THE HERITAGE PRESS, NEW YORK

PUBLICATION: New York: Heritage Press, 1943. Price $2.95.

PAGINATION: xv, [1], 751, [1].

CONTRIBUTION: 'If Lee Had Not Won the Battle of Gettysburg': pp. 421–35 (the first page being an introduction to the piece).

NOTE: One of the dust jackets I have examined bears the title 'Reader's Treasury' rather than 'A Soldier's Reader'.

LOCATION: RIC (dj)

B84   THE EPIC OF MALTA   1943

B84.1   First edition (1943)

𝕿𝖍𝖊 | 𝕰𝖕𝖎𝖈 𝖔𝖋 𝕸𝖆𝖑𝖙𝖆 | [chart of Malta, 51 × 76.1 mm] | *Foreword by* | THE RIGHT HON. WINSTON S. CHURCHILL, C.H., M.P. | [list of contents in 5 lines] | ★ | *The world acknowledges the immeasurable debt which the cause of Freedom | owes to the gallantry and dogged determination of the men, women and | children of Malta. This book is published as a small token of | admiration and gratitude, and the entire proceeds of its | sale will be devoted to the Malta Relief Fund* | ODHAMS PRESS LIMITED | LONG ACRE, LONDON, WC2

PUBLICATION: London: Odhams, March 1943. Price 3s. 6d.

PAGINATION: 128.

CONTRIBUTION: Message, in the form of an undated facsimile letter: p. 3.

LOCATIONS: CaOTTC (dj), RIC (dj), RPH (dj), UKBL, USMH

REFERENCE: Woods B38.

B84.2   Second issue (1990)

FACSIMILE EDITION | THE | EPIC OF MALTA | A pictorial survey of Malta during the Second World War | with an introduction by | Professor Henry Frendo | MELITENSIA EDITIONS | VALETTA PUBLISHING | MALTA | 1990

PUBLICATION: Valetta: Valetta Publishing, 1990.

PAGINATION: [2], vi, 128.

LOCATION: RIC (dj)

B85   ARTISTS AID CHINA EXHIBITION FOR LADY CRIPPS' UNITED AID TO CHINA FUND   1943

ARTISTS AID CHINA EXHIBITION | FOR LADY CRIPPS' UNITED AID TO CHINA FUND | MARCH 31st – MAY 25th | [moderate green and black, drawing of oriental lady with child in her arms] | [moderate green] Steadfast to the end, they could not | be daunted. | [ranged right] Ch'ü Yüan (300 B.C.) | [black, centred] THE WALLACE COLLECTION | HERTFORD HOUSE | (By courtesy of the Trustees and the Ministry of Works and Buildings) | [ranged right] PRICE: ONE | SHILLING

PUBLICATION: London: Central Institute of Art and Design, March? 1943. Price 1s.

PAGINATION: 20 pp. plus paper wrappers.

CONTRIBUTION: 'FOREWORD': p. 1.

LOCATION: CaOTTC

REFERENCE: Woods B38/1.

B86   GENERAL SIKORSKI   1943

GENERAL | SIKORSKI | BY | F.   C.   ANSTRUTHER | with   Foreword   by | CAPTAIN ALAN GRAHAM, M.P. | and | MR. CHURCHILL'S TRIBUTE | at the end | *2nd Revised Edition* | *Copyright 1943* | "ATLANTIS" Publishing Co., Ltd., | 40, Gerrard Road, Harrow, Middlesex, 1943

PUBLICATION: London: "Atlantis" Publishing, August? 1943. Price 1*s*. 3*d*.

PAGINATION: 32. Pamphlet in paper wrappers.

CONTRIBUTION: 'MR. CHURCHILL'S TRIBUTE TO GENERAL | SIKORSKI' (address in the House of Commons on 6 July 1943): pp. 31–2. Subsequently published in Rhodes James, Vol. VII, at pp. 6803–4, under the title 'General Sikorski's Death'.

NOTE: The first edition of the pamphlet (24 pp. plus paper wrappers) having been published while Sikorski was still alive,[47] the Churchill tribute is not present.[48] I am unable, on the basis of information currently available, to establish publication priority between **B86** and **B87**.

LOCATIONS: CaOOU, RIC, USDLC

B87 TRIBUTE TO GENERAL SIKORSKI   1943

[Cover title:] [white on a black rounded-edge rectangular background] TRIBUTE | [nearly full height of page, half-tone waist-up photograph of General Sikorski against a white background] | [ranged left] TO GENERAL | [centred, in black-on-white outline letters on a black background] SIKORSKI

PUBLICATION: London: Polish Ministry of Information, 1943.

PAGINATION: [*36*]. Pamphlet in self-wrappers.

CONTRIBUTION: *'Mr. Churchill's Tribute to General Sikorski'*: pp. 2–7. Note that the tribute in the House of Commons is here misdated as 7 July 1943.

LOCATIONS: RIC, UKBL, USMH

B88 THE LITTLE SHIPS   1943

THE LITTLE SHIPS | [103-mm rule] | BY | GORDON HOLMAN | *Author of* | *"Commando Attack"* | London : HODDER & STOUGHTON Limited

PUBLICATION: London: Hodder & Stoughton, October 1943. Price 7*s*. 6*d*. Reprinted December 1943 and March 1944.

PAGINATION: 164, 9 leaves of plates.

CONTRIBUTION: 'The Prime Minister's Message'[49] to all light coastal forces at home and abroad: p. 8. Note also that there is a Churchill speech extract at the start of each of the twelve chapters.

LOCATIONS: RIC (dj), RIC (3rd printing), UKBL, UKScNL, USMH, USNN

---

47. He and his daughter were killed on 5 July 1943 in a Liberator taking off from Gibraltar. Churchill was badly shaken by the news. See Gilbert, *WSC*, Vol. VII, p. 426.

48. The only copy of the first edition I have been able to examine is in the collection of the National Library of Scotland.

49. The volume actually identifies this as a *June* message. This no doubt results from the fact that the first publication of the message was in *The Times* of 28 June 1943 (**G718a**). Ultimately, the *facsimile* appearance of the message in *The Battle of the Narrow Seas* (**B98**) conclusively establishes that the date of the letter was 30 May.

B89   THE NAVY LEAGUE YEAR BOOK AND DIARY (JUBILEE ISSUE)   1944

[Navy League device centred within a double wavy rule] | THE NAVY LEAGUE | Year Book | AND DIARY | JUBILEE ISSUE | [125.7-mm rule] | PUBLISHED BY THE NAVY LEAGUE | PRINTED BY GALE & POLDEN LTD ALDERSHOT | MCMXLIV

PUBLICATION: Aldershot: Navy League, 1944. Price 7s. 6d.

PAGINATION: 240.

CONTRIBUTION: Undated letter of congratulations from Churchill, reproduced in facsimile: p. 4. First published in *The Times* of 18 December 1944 (**G815**).

LOCATIONS: RIC, UKBL

B90   WELCOME   1944

[No title page; dropped-head title only:] ★ WELCOME ★

PUBLICATION: March 1944.

PAGINATION: [4].

CONTRIBUTION: 16-line message of welcome to American soldiers gathering in Britain, signed in facsimile: p. 1.

LOCATION: RIC

B90/1 SALUTE THE SOLDIER   [1944]

[Cover title:] [against a strong red background, 163.9 × 137.5 mm, of six photographs of soldiers, black, a centred photograph of *The Soldier*, a statue by Sir William Reid Dick, above which] WAR SAVINGS SPECIAL ISSUE | [ranged left] VOL. 4; [ranged right] No. 7 | [below the foot of the statue, against a dark grey background, 38.4 × 137.5 mm, a strong red background with rounded ends, within which, white] "The Soldier," a statue specially designed for Salute the | Soldier Weeks by Sir William Reid Dick, K.C.V.O., R.A. | [below the strong red background, white] SALUTE THE SOLDIER

PUBLICATION: London: HMSO, [1944]. Published during the Salute the Soldier Weeks in May and June 1944 around the country.

PAGINATION: 16. Pamphlet in self-wrappers.

CONTRIBUTION: A message 'FROM THE PRIME MINISTER' wishing 'the "Salute the Soldier" campaign every success', in the form of a facsimile letter on 10 Downing Street stationery signed by 'Winston S. Churchill': back cover (p. 16).

NOTE: The pamphlet may not have survived in significant numbers since the publisher invited its destruction:

> Many Group Secretaries will find this reproduction useful for their notice board or indicator. Before putting it up, trim off this wording below the line.

The message was also available in the form of a 15″ × 20″ poster (W.F.P. 361).

LOCATION: RIC

B91   LOYALTY AND SERVICE   1944?

[Cover title:] [ranged upper left] Loyalty | and | Service | [moderate blue] YEAR BOOK | AND | SOUVENIR | [black] 1944–45 | [ranged right from the level of the word 'Service' down; moderate blue and strong reddish orange, drawing of a crown] | [moderate blue] Forward to Victory | Security and Peace | [strong reddish orange, depiction of a lion rampant facing left] | [moderate blue, three parallel vertical lines 28 mm long] | [black] Published for the | Sydney Frankenburg | Branch of the | [ranged lower left] Price 6d. [ranged lower right] British Legion

PUBLICATION: Manchester: Edgar Publishing for the Sydney Frankenburg Branch of the British Legion, n.d.

PAGINATION: [*16*] plus card wrappers.

CONTRIBUTIONS: Under the title 'From War to Lasting Peace', an excerpt from Churchill's address at Quebec serves as an Introduction at p. 1. There are further excerpts from unidentified speeches of Churchill's at pp. 15 and 16. The date of publication would appear to be June or July 1944. The broadcast of 31 August 1943 from Quebec was collected in *Onwards to Victory* (**A194**), at pp. 173–80, under the title 'The Call for a Three-Power Talk', and in Rhodes James, Vol. VII, at pp. 6816–22, under the title 'The Quebec Conference'. The speech extract at p. 15 was taken from Churchill's speech at the Harvard Commencement on 6 September 1943; it was separately published (**A186**) and subsequently collected in *Onwards to Victory*, at pp. 181–6, and in Rhodes James, Vol. VII, at pp. 6823–7, in both cases under the title 'Anglo-American Unity'.

LOCATION: RIC

B92   "NOT IN VAIN"   [1944]

[All of the following within a double-rule frame, the outer frame deep red, enclosing 202 × 157.2 mm, the inner frame light bluish green, enclosing 194 × 151 mm; black, the Division arms, 33.6 × 57.4 mm] 3rd   BATTALION | THE   PARACHUTE REGIMENT | [59.1-mm rule] | 1st BRITISH AIRBORNE DIVISION | "NOT IN VAIN" | 17th–25th September, 1944

PUBLICATION: No location, publisher or date indicated.

PAGINATION: [*20*], 1 tipped-in photograph.

CONTRIBUTION: 'The Prime Minister's Tribute', excerpt from speech of 28 September 1944 in the House of Commons: p. 7.

NOTE: While the volume is undated, the copy which I have examined bears a donor inscription of September 1944, which is consistent with the purpose of the volume and the commemorated events.

ANNOTATIONS: The volume contains tributes to the First Airborne Division, which parachuted into Arnhem and contributed to the capture of the Nijmegen bridges and the advance of the Allied Forces to the Rhine. The excerpt from Churchill's tribute is the first, and it is followed by letters from Eisenhower, Montgomery and others.

LOCATION: RIC

B93   PEACE IS A PROCESS   1944

Peace Is a Process | Selected Articles from *The Rotarian Magazine* | Charting Postwar Opportunities Created | By New Forces in World Affairs | *Edited by* | LELAND D. CASE | Editor, *The Rotarian* Magazine | *Foreword by* | RICHARD H. WELLS | *President, Rotary International* | PUBLISHED BY ROTARY INTERNATIONAL | [ranged left] *35 East Wicker Drive* [ranged right] *Chicago 1, Illinois, U.S.A.*

PUBLICATION: Chicago: Rotary International, November 1944. Price 25¢.

PAGINATION: 128.

CONTRIBUTION: 'Aviation: Man's Bane or Boon?': pp. 9–12. First published in *Rotarian* (**C653**).

LOCATIONS: RIC, USMH

B94   RUPERT BROOKE: TWO SONNETS   1945

[Ranged left] Rupert Brooke | [ranged right, moderate blue] *Two Sonnets* | [black] ★ | With a memoir | of | WINSTON S. CHURCHILL

PUBLICATION: In occupied Holland: Vliegend Verzet, 1945.

PAGINATION: [8]. Pamphlet in patterned moderate blue and very light blue paper wrappers.

CONTRIBUTION: Letter to *The Times* on the death of Brooke: p. 7. The letter was published first in *The Times* of 26 April 1915 (**G245**) and, in volume form, for the first time in Douglas Jerrold's *Royal Naval Division* (**B30**) and subsequently in the *Collected Essays*, Vol. III, at p. 18, under the title 'Rupert Brooke'.

NOTE: This pamphlet was published in a limited and numbered first edition of 100 copies 'somewhere in occupied Holland', on the Ides of March 1945. A second such edition was published in April. In the words of the beleaguered publishers, appearing in the Colophon, at p. 8: '*We give this reprint somewhere in occupied Holland, in consequence of the war circumstances without the use of stream, in honour of our British Allies on the Ides of March 1945.*' In the second edition, the awkward and incorrectly rendered translation of the Dutch expression as '*without the use of stream*' was revised to the still slightly awkward, but correct, phrase '*without using electrical current*'.

LOCATIONS: NeNL, RIC, RML (1st edition), USDLC (2nd edition)

REFERENCE: Jong 120 (1st edition) and 121 (2nd edition).

B95   PARLIAMENTARY GENERAL ELECTION, 1945   1945

[Cover title:] [printed strong purplish blue] PARLIAMENTARY GENERAL ELECTION, 1945 | Polling Day — Thursday, July 5th | [41.6-mm rule] | MONMOUTH DIVISION. | [151.3-mm thin–thick rule] | [ranged left in 2 lines] *A VOTE FOR | PYM* | [ranged right in 2 lines opposite] *PUTS CHURCHILL | IN* | [ranged left, a half-tone head-and-shoulders photograph of Leslie Pym, 50.7 × 36.6 mm; ranged right, the Stoneman head-and-shoulders photograph of Churchill, 49.8 × 36.4 mm] | [151.3-mm thick–thin rule] | FOR FREEDOM — HOMES — WORK | AND SECURITY | VOTE FOR PYM | THE NATIONAL CONSERVATIVE AND UNIONIST CANDIDATE | [151.6-mm rule] | Printed and Published by Seargeant Brothers Limited, Usk Vale Works, Abergavenny

PUBLICATION: Abergavenny: Seargeant Brothers, 1945.

PAGINATION: [4].

CONTRIBUTION: 'Mr. WINSTON CHURCHILL'S MESSAGE TO <u>YOU</u>.': p. 4.

LOCATION: USIU

B96 ELECTION ADDRESS: GENERAL ELECTION (1945)   1945

[Cover title:] [ranged slightly left of centre, a half-tone photograph of Lieut.-Commander William Garthwaite, 89.9 × 60.3 mm; ranged right and opposite the photograph in 5 lines] VOTE FOR | GARTHWAITE. | [27-mm rule] | THE NATIONAL | GOVERNMENT | CANDIDATE. | [centred, against a half-tone background of the Houses of Parliament, reversed type] ELECTION ADDRESS | *General Election*

PUBLICATION: Willenhall: Matthew Foy, 27 June 1945.

PAGINATION: [4].

CONTRIBUTION: 'A Personal Message from the Prime Minister to You', dated 15 June 1945: p. 4.

LOCATION: RIC

B97 TIME TO BE YOUNG   1945

B97.1 First edition (1945)

[Ranged left] *TIME TO BE YOUNG* | *GREAT STORIES OF THE GROWING YEARS* | *EDITED BY WHIT BURNETT* | *PHILADELPHIA AND NEW YORK* | [ranged right opposite the previous line, publisher's device, 20.8 × 13.9 mm] | [ranged left] *J. B. LIPPINCOTT COMPANY*

PUBLICATION: Philadelphia: Lippincott, 1945.

PAGINATION: xix, [1], 440, [4].

CONTRIBUTION: 'Examinations at Harrow', reprinted from *A Roving Commission* (**A91.2**): pp. 293–301.

LOCATIONS: CaOONL, RIC, USMH

REFERENCE: Woods D(a)13.

B97.2 Armed Services issue (1945)

[All of the following within a double-rule box, enclosing 83.4 × 130.3 mm; set in two columns separated by a 71.8-mm vertical rule; on the left] PUBLISHED BY ARRANGEMENT WITH | J. B. LIPPINCOTT COMPANY, | PHILADELPHIA | *A Story Press Book* | *Note: Due to limitations of space,* | *it has been necessary to eliminate* | *some of the material contained in* | *the original edition of this book.* | COPYRIGHT, 1945, BY WHIT BURNETT | *Manufactured in the United States of America* | [on the right] TIME | *to be* YOUNG | edited by | WHIT BURNETT | *Editions for the Armed Services, Inc.* | A NON-PROFIT ORGANIZATION ESTABLISHED BY | THE COUNCIL ON BOOKS IN WARTIME, NEW YORK | [below the double-rule box, ranged left] 848

PUBLICATION: New York: Editions for the Armed Services, 1945.

PAGINATION: 384.

CONTRIBUTION: 'Examinations at Harrow': pp. 313–25.

LOCATION: RIC

B98   THE BATTLE OF THE NARROW SEAS   1945

B98.1   First edition (1945)

[146.3-mm decorative rule, 5.2 mm thick, in the repeating pattern of a ship cutting through a wave] | THE BATTLE | OF THE | NARROW SEAS | A History of the Light Coastal Forces in the Channel | and North Sea, 1939–1945 | by | LIEUTENANT-COMMANDER PETER SCOTT | M.B.E., D.S.C. & Bar, R.N.V.R. | [line-cut of a boat cutting through the sea, 35.8 × 125.6 mm] | LONDON: COUNTRY LIFE LIMITED | 2–10 TAVISTOCK STREET, COVENT GARDEN, W.C.2 | [146.3-mm decorative rule]

PUBLICATION: London: Country Life, November 1945. Price 15s. There was also a second impression.

PAGINATION: xii, 228, 32 leaves of plates.

CONTRIBUTION: Letter of 30 May 1943, reproduced in facsimile: p. x. The letter was first published in *The Times* of 28 June 1943 (**G718a**) and first appeared in volume form in *The Little Ships* (**B88**).

LOCATIONS: RIC, RPH (dj), UKBL, USMH

REFERENCE: Woods D(b)64.

B98.2   American issue from British plates (1946)

[146.3-mm decorative rule, 5.2 mm thick, in the repeating pattern of a ship cutting through a wave] | THE BATTLE | OF THE | NARROW SEAS | A History of the Light Coastal Forces in the Channel | and North Sea, 1939–1945 | by | LIEUTENANT-COMMANDER PETER SCOTT | M.B.E., D.S.C. & Bar, R.N.V.R. | [line-cut of a boat cutting through the sea, 35.8 × 125.6 mm] | NEW YORK | CHARLES SCRIBNER'S SONS | 1946 | [146.3-mm decorative rule]

PUBLICATION: New York: Scribner's, 1946. Price $7.50.

LOCATION: RIC (dj)

B98.3   Second British issue from first-edition plates (1974)

THE BATTLE | OF THE | NARROW SEAS | A History of the Light Coastal Forces in the | Channel and North Sea, 1939–1945 | by | LIEUTENANT-COMMANDER PETER SCOTT | M.B.E., D.S.C. & Bar, R.N.V.R. | [publisher's device, 12.6 × 18.4 mm] | WHITE LION PUBLISHERS | London New York Sydney Toronto

PUBLICATION: London: White Lion, October 1974. Price £4.25.

PAGINATION: xii, 228, 24 leaves of plates. Note that the plates are now gathered in three 8-leaf signatures, between pp. 68–9, 132–3 and 196–7; although the index of the individual plates from the first British issue is still present at pp. viii–ix, it bears incorrect page references (which correspond to the placement of the plates in the first issue).

LOCATIONS: RIC (dj), UKBL

B99   ROOSEVELT: A FIRST APPRAISAL BY THOSE WHO KNEW HIM   1946

[Cover title:] [ranged upper left, a solid black rectangle, 50.8 × 113.5 mm, within which, white] ROOSEVELT | A FIRST APPRAISAL BY THOSE WHO KNEW HIM | [below the rectangle, centred, black, head-and-shoulders line drawing of Roosevelt, 180 × 167 mm] | [ranged right, a solid black rectangle, 7.7 × 135.2 mm, within which, white] The New Republic   In two Parts • Part two   April 15, 1946

PUBLICATION: New York: New Republic, 1946.

PAGINATION: 40, numbered pp. 521–60.

CONTRIBUTION: Facsimile of a telegram to the Managing Editor of *The New Republic*: p. 522. Subsequently collected in *The New Republic Reader* (**B207**).

LOCATIONS: CaOTTC, RIC

REFERENCE: Woods D(b)69/3.

B100   R.A.A.F. OVER EUROPE   1946

R.A.A.F. | Over Europe | Edited by | FRANK JOHNSON | Introduction by the Rt. Hon. | WINSTON S. CHURCHILL P.C., M.P. | Foreword by | Air Vice-Marshal H. N. Wrigley | C.B.E., D.F.C., A.F.C. (Air Officer Commanding R.A.A.F. Overseas H.Q. 1942–46) | Published in conjunction with Frank Johnson | by | EYRE & SPOTTISWOODE | LONDON

PUBLICATION: London: Eyre & Spottiswoode, November 1946. Price 10s. 6d.

PAGINATION: x, 90, 55 leaves of plates.

CONTRIBUTION: 'FOREWORD': p. ix.

NOTE: The copies I have examined with dust jackets indicated the 10s. 6d. price by a sticker placed over an originally printed '12/6 net' price on the front flap.

LOCATIONS: CaOTTC, RIC (dj), RPH, UKBL, USIU, USMH

REFERENCE: Woods B39.

B101   GETTING THE MOST OUT OF LIFE   1946

[All of the following within a strong reddish brown triple-rule frame, enclosing 144.7 × 100.1 mm; black] GETTING THE | MOST | OUT OF LIFE | *An Anthology | from* | The Reader's Digest | [strong reddish brown, decorative device, 15.9 × 26.9 mm; black] THE READER'S DIGEST ASSOCIATION, INC. | Pleasantville, New York

PUBLICATION: Pleasantville (NY): Reader's Digest, 1946.

PAGINATION: [6], 250.

CONTRIBUTION: 'My Adventures with a Paint Brush': pp. 246–50. Condensed from *Amid These Storms* (**A95.2**); first published in this condensed form in *Reader's Digest* of June 1933 (**C267b**). Subsequently collected in *The Reader's Digest 40th Anniversary Treasury* (**B172**), under the title 'Painting as a Pastime', and in *How to Live with Life* (**B181/1**), under the title 'My Adventures with a Paintbrush'.

LOCATIONS: CaMWU, CaOONL, RIC, USDLC

B102 THE CHURCHILL APPEAL   1946

[Arms of the University of Bristol, 18.8 × 15.9 mm] | UNIVERSITY OF BRISTOL | *This description of the University's work and | future is published in connection with the Appeal | made on behalf of the University to commemorate | the Chancellorship of Mr. Winston Churchill | and his services to the country | and to humanity* | 1946

PUBLICATION: Bristol: no publisher indicated (Bristol University?), 1946.

PAGINATION: 20 pp. plus dark greyish red paper wrappers, 2 leaves of plates, 1 facsimile (folding).

CONTRIBUTION: Folded undated holograph letter, reproduced in very dark greenish blue facsimile, bound into the booklet: facing p. 3.

NOTE: This was the first publication associated with the University of Bristol to contain a Churchill letter. He served as Chancellor of the University from 13 December 1929 until his death on 24 January 1965.[50]

LOCATIONS: RIC, UKBrU

B103 THE 6TH BATTALION ROYAL SCOTS FUSILIERS   1946?

The 6th Battalion | Royal Scots Fusiliers | 1939–46 | [publisher's device, 29.7 × 24.9 mm] | [40.7-mm rule] | Printed by T. M. Gemmell & Son, Ltd., 100 High Street, Ayr. | [ranged lower left] A

PUBLICATION: Ayr?: Royal Scots Fusiliers?, n.d. [1946?][51]

PAGINATION: 160, 4 leaves of plates, 1 map (folding).

CONTRIBUTION: 'FOREWORD': p. 3.

LOCATIONS: RIC, UKScGl

REFERENCE: White, p. 279.

B104 JAMES MAXTON   1947

JAMES MAXTON | *"Write me as one who loved | his fellow-men"* | AN APPRECIATION | WITH A NUMBER OF TRIBUTES

PUBLICATION: London: Independent Labour Party, 1947.

PAGINATION: 32. Pamphlet in card wrappers.

---

50. Details regarding his installation as Chancellor can be found in *The Nonesuch*, the official organ of the Union of the University of Bristol, No. 56, Spring 1930, at pp. 53–5. For other publications related to Churchill and the university, see *Grotesques at Wills Hall* (**B124**) and *A History of Wills Hall* (**F298/1**).

51. While the publication date is conjectural, Major (Retd) W. Shaw, MBE, Assistant Regimental Secretary of the Royal Highland Fusiliers, informed me that, while their own library copy bears no accession information which is helpful in the dating process: "I am assured by members of the battalion that they all received a copy of the book prior to the Battalion being disbanded in 1946." I should add that the accession date on the Mitchell Library copy (1981) is clearly of no assistance in this regard.

CONTRIBUTION: Tribute: p. 20.

ANNOTATION: That Churchill should have written a tribute to James Maxton might seem unexpected, given the divergence of their political views. Born in 1885 in Pollokshaws near Glasgow, Maxton was a schoolteacher from 1905 until 1916, when his political activism resulted in his dismissal by the School Board. A member of the Independent Labour Party (ILP) from 1906 and a vocal opponent of the First World War, in 1916 he was arrested, charged and convicted under the Defence of the Realm Act for a seditious speech made on Glasgow Green. After serving his term in prison, he first stood unsuccessfully for Bridgeton in the 1918 election, but gained the seat in 1922 and held it until his death in 1946. Maxton was not included in the first Labour Cabinet (in 1924) and, from 1925, was accepted as the leader of the left-wing forces in the Labour Party, along with the other "Red Clydesider" Glasgow MPs. He served as Chairman of the ILP (1926–31) before its break with the Labour Party in 1932 and again after the rupture (1934–39). An ardent international Socialist, he spoke out against conscription and the rush into "the horror of world-wide war" on the eve of Britain's declaration of war. Although ill, he stood for Bridgeton in the 1945 General Election and appeared in the House of Commons for the last time on 6 December 1945. He neither served nor ever sought a post in Cabinet but was much loved by his fellow MPs. In his tribute, Churchill referred to him as "a warm-hearted and chivalrous man", whom he had often thought of as the " 'greatest gentleman in the House of Commons'. Our free Parliament gives opportunities for such figures to live and shine even though they may never hold or wish to hold any public office or become the leaders of large Parties."

LOCATIONS: CaOTTC, RIC, RPH, UKBL, UKLse, UKScNL

REFERENCE: Woods B40.

B105   IT HAPPENED HERE   1948

B105.1   First edition (1948)

It Happened Here ... | [ranged left, in a single-rule box, enclosing 152 × 75.9 mm, information, in 29 lines, on casualties and destruction in the Borough of Wanstead & Woodford] | [ranged right of the box] The Story | of | Civil Defence | in | Wanstead | and | Woodford | [black dot of 2.3-mm diameter] | 1939–1945 | [black dot of 4.4-mm diameter] | [arms of the Borough Council centred between the following words; ranged left of the arms] Borough | Council | of | [ranged right of the arms] Wanstead | and | Woodford | [below the box and the words ranged right of it, centred] Price seven shillings and sixpence

PUBLICATION: [Woodford]: Borough Council of Wanstead & Woodford, 1948. Compiled by Stanley Tiquet. Price 7s. 6d.

PAGINATION: [4], 84, 5 leaves of plates, 1 map (folding).

CONTRIBUTION: Facsimile letter from Churchill dated 20 May 1947, praising the Civil Defence Organisation of the Borough: p. 3.

LOCATIONS: RIC, RPH, UKBL

B105.2   Second issue, photo-reproduced from the first edition (1994)

PAGINATION: [10], 84, [2], 1 map (folding).

CONTRIBUTION: As in the first edition.

LOCATIONS: UKIl, RIC

B106 THE TIMES BROADSHEETS   1948

THE [publisher's device, 7.1 × 21.1 mm] TIMES | BROADSHEETS | 264 Passages from English Literature | chosen by *The Times* and brought | together in one volume | With an introduction by | THE EDITOR of *THE TIMES* | HODDER & STOUGHTON | ST. PAUL'S HOUSE, LONDON, E.C.4

PUBLICATION: London: Hodder & Stoughton, October 1948.

PAGINATION: xxiv, 526, [2].

CONTRIBUTIONS: Chapter 1, 'The Last Days of Marlborough': pp. 1–2; Chapter 113, 'Subaltern's Reading': pp. 220–2. Both chapters were first separately published under those titles as **A189** and **A210**.

LOCATIONS: RIC, UKBL, UKCaU, UKOxB, USMB, USMH

B107 LIFE OF LORD LLOYD   1948

LIFE OF | LORD LLOYD | BY | COLIN FORBES ADAM | With a Foreword by | THE RT. HON. WINSTON S. CHURCHILL, O.M. | LONDON | MACMILLAN & CO. LTD | 1948

PUBLICATION: London: Macmillan, October 1948. Price 21*s*.

PAGINATION: x, 318, 8 leaves of plates.

CONTRIBUTION: 'FOREWORD': pp. v–vi.

LOCATIONS: CaOTU, CaQMM, CaOTTC, RIC (dj; proof), RPH (dj), UKBL, USMH

REFERENCES: Woods B41; O'Brien F0004.

B108 FORWARD FROM VICTORY   1948

FORWARD *from* VICTORY | *Speeches and Addresses* | *by* | FIELD MARSHAL | THE VISCOUNT MONTGOMERY | OF ALAMEIN | K.G., G.C.B., D.S.O. | *Foreword by* | THE RT. HON. | WINSTON S. CHURCHILL | O.M., C.H., M.P. | HUTCHINSON & CO. (Publishers) LTD | *London   New York   Melbourne   Sydney   Cape Town*

PUBLICATION: London: Hutchinson, October 1948. Price 15*s*. Known in both an embossed moderate pink and moderate red calico-texture cloth and an unembossed strong red calico-texture cloth.

PAGINATION: [*2*], xvi, [2], 266 [numbered 19–284], [2], 1 leaf of plates.

CONTRIBUTION: 'FOREWORD', in the form of a facsimile typewritten letter and signature, dated 17 July 1948: p. ix.

LOCATIONS: CaOTTC, RIC (embossed and unembossed cloths; dj), RPH, UKBL, USMH

REFERENCE: Woods B42.

B109 EUROPE UNITES   1949

EUROPE UNITES | The story of the campaign for | European Unity, including a | full report of the | Congress of Europe, | held at The Hague, | May, 1948 | HOLLIS & CARTER | LONDON

PUBLICATION: London: Hollis & Carter, March 1949. Price 3s. 6d.

PAGINATION: viii, 95, [1], 24 leaves of plates [numbered 97–120], plus 1 additional unnumbered leaf of plates.

CONTRIBUTION: 'FOREWORD' of December 1948, signed in facsimile: p. viii.

LOCATIONS: CaOTTC, RIC, UKBL, UKOxB, USMH

REFERENCE: Woods B43.

B110   A CONSTRUCTIVE POLICY FOR BRITAIN   1949

[Cover title:] [all of the following within a thick–thin rule box, enclosing 179.8 × 104.4 mm] A | CONSTRUCTIVE | POLICY | FOR BRITAIN | AN ADDRESS | by | LORD ROSEBERY | (President of the National Liberal Council) | AND | A MESSAGE FROM MR. CHURCHILL | on co-operation in constituencies under the | Woolton–Teviot Agreement | [25.3-mm fancy swelled rule] | PRICE TWOPENCE

PUBLICATION: London: National Liberal Organisation and the Conservative and Unionist Central Office, June? 1949. Price 2d.

PAGINATION: 12. Pamphlet in light blue paper wrappers.

CONTRIBUTION: 'MR. CHURCHILL'S MESSAGE', a message to Lord Rosebery, who chaired the week-end Conference of the National Liberal Council at Bournemouth on 21 May 1949: p. 1.

LOCATIONS: UKBL, UKScNL

REFERENCE: Woods B45.

B111   THE RIGHT ROAD FOR BRITAIN   1949

THE | RIGHT ROAD | FOR BRITAIN | *The Conservative* | *Party's Statement* | *of Policy* | *Foreword* | *by* | The Rt. Hon. WINSTON S. CHURCHILL | O.M., C.H., M.P. | July, 1949 | CONSERVATIVE AND UNIONIST | CENTRAL OFFICE

PUBLICATION: London: Conservative Party, July 1949. Price 6d.

PAGINATION: 68, plus paper wrappers.

CONTRIBUTION: 'FOREWORD', in the form of a letter signed in facsimile: p. 5.

NOTE: This is Conservative Party pamphlet No. 3969 and ought not to be confused with pamphlet No. 3975, which bears the same title but is a "popular" illustrated version, without the Churchill foreword. The latter sold for 1d. Note also that this pamphlet appears on the cover of the 25 February 1950 issue of *Illustrated*.[52]

LOCATIONS: CaOTTC, CaOTUTF, RIC, RPH, UKBL, UKOxB

REFERENCE: Woods B46.

---

52. On the verge of the election. Within are interesting pieces on past elections by Dennis Bardens ('Focus on Elections', which includes among the photographs one of Diana Churchill in a pram, being followed by a detective to protect her from the suffragettes in the course of the December 1910 election), on the present election by Hugh Massingham ('Number 10—Cigar or Pipe?') and on the contest in Devonport by Lord Kinross ('The Siege of Devonport', a seat which was fought by Michael Foot and Randolph Churchill).

B112   THE LIFE AND DEATH OF A PAY PACKET   1949

[Cover title:] [against a multicoloured background of currency being enveloped in flames, the wording ranged lower right] *The life and death | of a pay packet—*

PUBLICATION: London: Conservative Party, 1949. Conservative Party pamphlet No. 3282.

PAGINATION: [*8*]. Pamphlet in self-wrappers.

CONTRIBUTION: 'THE RIGHT ROAD FOR BRITAIN', signed in facsimile: p. 8. First published in *The Right Road for Britain* (**B111**).

LOCATIONS: UKOxB, UKScNL

REFERENCE: Woods D(b)73.

B113   THE HORSE-LOVERS' ANTHOLOGY   1949

THE   HORSE-LOVERS' | ANTHOLOGY | *Edited   by* | SHIRLEY   FULKNER-HORNE | Author of *Mexican Saddle,* | *Green Trail,* etc. | H. F. & G. WITHERBY LTD. | 5 WARWICK COURT, LONDON, W.C.1

PUBLICATION: London: Witherby, November 1949. Price 9*s.* 6*d.*

PAGINATION: xii, 315, [1].

CONTRIBUTION: 'From the Battle of Blenheim': pp. 20–1.

LOCATIONS: RIC (dj), UKBL, UKOxB, UKScNL, USDLC

B114   A TREASURY OF GREAT REPORTING   1949

B114.1   First edition (1949)

[All of the following within a strong purplish red single-rule box, enclosing 184.5 × 112.9 mm; black] A TREASURY OF | [strong purplish red] GREAT | REPORTING | [black] "Literature under Pressure" | from the Sixteenth Century | to Our Own Time | Edited by | [strong purplish red] Louis L. Snyder | [black] ASSOCIATE PROFESSOR OF HISTORY | THE COLLEGE OF THE CITY OF NEW YORK | AND | [strong purplish red] Richard B. Morris | [black] PROFESSOR OF HISTORY, COLUMBIA UNIVERSITY | [strong purplish red] 1949 | [black] SIMON AND SCHUSTER • NEW YORK

PUBLICATION: New York: Simon & Schuster, 1949.

PAGINATION: xlv, [1], 786, 16 leaves of plates.

CONTRIBUTION: 'How I Escaped from Pretoria': pp. 250–1. As published in *Pearson's Illustrated War News*, 30 December 1899 (**C83d**).

LOCATIONS: CaOLU, RIC, USDLC, USIU

B114.2   Second edition (1962?)

[All of the following within a single-rule box, enclosing 171 × 104.5 mm] A TREASURY OF | GREAT | REPORTING | "Literature under Pressure" | from the Sixteenth Century | to Our Own Time | Edited by | Louis L. Snyder | PROFESSOR OF HISTORY | THE CITY UNIVERSITY OF NEW YORK | AND | Richard B.

Morris | GOUVERNEUR MORRIS PROFESSOR OF HISTORY COLUMBIA UNIVERSITY | 2nd Edition, Revised and Enlarged | Simon and Schuster • New York

PUBLICATION: New York: Simon & Schuster, 1962. Published as an Essandess Paperback. Price $2.75.

PAGINATION: xxxv, [1], 796.

CONTRIBUTION: As in the first edition.

LOCATIONS: CaOLU, CaOONL, USDLC, USIU (4th printing; card wrappers)

B115 ATOMIC ENERGY YEAR BOOK   1949

B115.1   First edition (1949)

ATOMIC | ENERGY | YEAR BOOK | Edited by | JOHN TUTIN, D.Sc. | [publisher's device, 15.6 × 11.1 mm] | TEMPLE PRESS LIMITED | Bowling Green Lane, London, E.C.1

PUBLICATION: London: Temple Press, May 1949. Price 21s.

PAGINATION: xii, 243 [numbered 1–237, xiv–xx].

CONTRIBUTION: 'A Statement on Atomic Energy': p. ix. Previously published in *Statements Relating to the Atomic Bomb* (**F66**).

LOCATION: UKScNL

B115.2   American issue of British sheets (1949)

ATOMIC | ENERGY | YEAR   BOOK | Edited   by | JOHN   TUTIN,   D.Sc. | PRENTICE-HALL, INC. | 70 Fifth Avenue, New York 11, U.S.A.

PUBLICATION: New York: Prentice-Hall, 1949. Price $3.85.

LOCATIONS: RIC (dj), USDLC, USMH

B116 EUROPEAN MOVEMENT AND THE COUNCIL
OF EUROPE   1949

EUROPEAN MOVEMENT | AND | THE COUNCIL OF EUROPE | [25.6-mm swelled rule] | *With Forewords by* | WINSTON S. CHURCHILL | and | PAUL-HENRI SPAAK | *Published   on   behalf   of* | THE   EUROPEAN   MOVEMENT | *by* | HUTCHINSON & CO. (Publishers) LTD. | *London   New York   Melbourne   Sydney   Cape Town*

PUBLICATION: London: Hutchinson, July 1949. Price 10s. 6d.

PAGINATION: vi, 198 [numbered 7–204], 8 leaves of plates.

CONTRIBUTION: 'FOREWORD', signed in facsimile: pp. 11–12.

NOTE: Churchill was one of four presidents of honour of the European Movement.

LOCATIONS: CaOTTC, RIC, RPH, UKBL, USMH

REFERENCE: Woods B44.

B117   THIS IS THE ROAD   1950

[Cover title:] [white on moderate blue] THIS | IS THE | ROAD | *The Conservative and | Unionist Party's Policy* | GENERAL ELECTION | 1950

PUBLICATION: London: Conservative Central Office, 1950. Conservative Party pamphlet 4012.

PAGINATION: 24. Pamphlet in paper wrappers.

CONTRIBUTION: 'INTRODUCTION BY THE LEADER OF THE PARTY' of 19 January 1950, signed in facsimile: p. 1. Churchill was also involved in the drafting of the manifesto itself. An account of the drafting of some parts is given in Lord Butler's memoirs, *The Art of the Possible* (**F220**), at p. 152.

LOCATIONS: CaOTUTF, RIC, RPH, UKBrU

REFERENCE: Woods B48.

B118   THEN AND NOW   [1950]

There is no title page. The first page, entitled 'Then and Now', consists of advertisements and the following Conservative and Unionist statement: 'These advertisements appeared in the | daily newspapers in 1945. See for | yourself how prices have risen since | the Socialists came into office.'

PUBLICATION: London: Conservative and Unionist Central Office, [1950].

PAGINATION: [4].

CONTRIBUTION: Under the heading 'UNITED FOR LIBERTY | *Liberal and Conservative Leaders Fight for Freedom*' there are statements from Churchill and Viscount Samuel: p. 4.

LOCATION: RIC

B119   ROYAL LIVER FRIENDLY SOCIETY   1950

Royal Liver Friendly Society | THIS BROCHURE HAS BEEN PREPARED | TO COMMEMORATE THE CENTENARY OF | THE SOCIETY | 1850–1950 | ROYAL LIVER BUILDING | LIVERPOOL, 3

PUBLICATION: Liverpool: Royal Liver Society, 1950.

PAGINATION: 36.

CONTRIBUTION: '*Foreword*', dated March 1950, signed in facsimile: p. 3.

NOTE: Complete copies will be wrapped in a clear patterned cellophane jacket and inserted in a patterned envelope bearing the centenary device and name of the Society.

LOCATIONS: UKBL, UKBrU, USNhD

B120   MAYHEW'S ELECTION ADDRESS   1950

[Cover title:] [vivid purplish blue] EAST HAM NORTH | [159.2-mm rule] | PARLIAMENTARY ELECTION | POLLING DAY : THURSDAY, FEBRUARY 23, 1950 | [159.2-mm rule] | [photograph of John Mayhew, 125.8 × 85.3 mm, between

several summary lines of election blurb on either side] | MAYHEW'S | ELECTION
ADDRESS | [159.2-mm rule]

PUBLICATION: London: Maurice J. Hill, February 1950.

PAGINATION: 4. Folded leaflet.

CONTRIBUTION: Letter of 3 February 1950 to the electors of the East Ham North
Constituency: p. 3.

LOCATION: RIC

B121   OUR GREATEST HARVEST   1950

Our Greatest | *Harvest* | SELECTED | SPEECHES OF | *John G. Winant* | 1941—1946 |
HODDER & STOUGHTON

PUBLICATION: London: Hodder & Stoughton, April 1950. Price 12*s.* 6*d.*

PAGINATION: xi, [1], 228.

CONTRIBUTION: 'FOREWORD' dated 29 December 1949: p. v. Four of the five
sentences from the 'Foreword' are also printed on the front flap of the dust jacket.

LOCATIONS: CaOTTC, RIC (dj), RPH (dj), UKBL

REFERENCE: Woods B46/1.

B122   HAPPY ODYSSEY   1950

B122.1   First edition (1950)

HAPPY ODYSSEY | *The Memoirs of* | Lieutenant-General | SIR ADRIAN CARTON
DE WIART | V.C., K.B.E., C.B., C.M.G., D.S.O. | *With a Foreword by* | the Rt. Hon.
| WINSTON S. CHURCHILL | O.M. | [publisher's device, 16.2 mm in diameter] |
JONATHAN CAPE | THIRTY BEDFORD SQUARE | LONDON

PUBLICATION: London: Jonathan Cape, July 1950. Price 12*s.* 6*d.* There were second and
third printings in August 1950, a fourth later in the year, and a fifth in 1951.

PAGINATION: 287, [1], 1 leaf of plates.

CONTRIBUTION: 'FOREWORD': p. 7.

LOCATIONS: CaOONMC (5th printing; dj), CaOTTC (dj), RIC (dj; proof), RPH (dj),
UKBL, USMH

REFERENCE: Woods B47.

B122.2   First paperback edition (1955)

HAPPY ODYSSEY | *The Memoirs of* | LIEUTENANT-GENERAL | SIR ADRIAN
CARTON DE WIART | V.C. K.B.E. C.B. C.M.G. D.S.O. | [publisher's device,
13.1 mm in diameter] | *With a Foreword by The Rt. Hon.* | SIR WINSTON S.
CHURCHILL | K.G. O.M. C.H. | COMPLETE AND UNABRIDGED | PAN
BOOKS LTD: | LONDON

PUBLICATION: London: Pan, 1955. Price 2*s.*

PAGINATION: 224.

CONTRIBUTION: 'FOREWORD': p. 7.

LOCATION: RIC

B123 HANDBOOK AND TRADE DIRECTORY 1950   1950

[Cover title:] [single rule running the width of the cover] | WANSTEAD & WOODFORD | CHAMBER OF COMMERCE | [borough arms, 60.5 × 62.3 mm] | HANDBOOK AND | TRADE DIRECTORY | 1950 | [thin–thick rule running the width of the cover]

PUBLICATION: Hornsey: March Publicity, 1950.

CONTRIBUTION: Undated message of good wishes to the Chamber of Commerce (of which Churchill was patron), signed in facsimile: p. 5.

LOCATION: UKIl

B124 GROTESQUES AT WILLS HALL   1950

There is no title page. The front wrapper is printed very dark purplish red on yellowish grey card wrappers; thickness: 0.39 mm, with a line drawing of the gargoyle, or grotesque, of the Navigator in the upper centre.[53] The title is ranged along the bottom.

PUBLICATION: Bristol: Wills Hall Association, 1950.

PAGINATION: [4], 20, 1 facsimile.

CONTRIBUTION: Letter of 23 November 1950 from Chartwell, reproduced in facsimile as the 'FOREWORD': p. 1.

NOTE: The booklet was originally issued with a separate light yellowish brown band 63.9 mm high, on the front of which were the words: '*With Foreword by* | WINSTON CHURCHILL | 5/-'.

LOCATIONS: CaOTTC, RIC, RPH (with band), UKBL, UKBrU

REFERENCE: Woods B48/1.

B125 THE *EAGLE* BOOK OF ADVENTURE STORIES   1950

THE *EAGLE* BOOK OF | ADVENTURE | STORIES | *by* | WINSTON S. CHURCHILL | H. G. WELLS | LESLIE CHARTERIS | FRANK C. ROBERTSON | BERNARD NEWMAN | W. E. JOHNS | ARTHUR CONAN DOYLE | R. L. STEVENSON | RAFAEL SABATINI | JOHN BUCHAN | E. W. HORNUNG | [device of an eagle in flight, 29.4 × 22.7 mm] | [68.9-mm rule] | HULTON PRESS LTD: 43–44 SHOE LANE, | LONDON, E.C.4

PUBLICATION: London: Hulton Press, December 1950. Price 3*s*. The book was reissued in September 1951, price 5*s*.

PAGINATION: v, [1], 242.

CONTRIBUTION: 'The Battle of Sidney Street': pp. 1–9. Previously published in *Thoughts and Adventures* (**A95**), at pp. 65–72.

---

53. Photographs of the grotesques may be found at pp. 15–16 of M. J. Crossley Evans and A. Sulston's *A History of Wills Hall* (Bristol: University of Bristol Press, 1994). Construction of Wills Hall began in 1925. It was ready for occupancy on 4 October 1929 and was officially opened on 14 December 1929, the day following Churchill's installation as the third Chancellor of the University.

LOCATIONS: CaOTTC, RIC, UKBL (1st edition and reissue), UKCaU (reissue), USDLC
REFERENCE: Woods D(a)16.

B126   BRITAIN STRONG AND FREE   1951

A STATEMENT OF CONSERVATIVE | AND UNIONIST POLICY | ★ | BRITAIN | Strong and | Free | October, 1951 | CONSERVATIVE AND UNIONIST | CENTRAL OFFICE

PUBLICATION: London: Conservative Central Office, 1951.

PAGINATION: 36. Pamphlet in paper wrappers.

CONTRIBUTION: Introductory note signed in facsimile: p. 2.

LOCATIONS: CaOTUTF, RIC, RPH, USMiU

REFERENCE: Woods B49.

B127   EVE OF POLL MESSAGE TO SIR WALDRON
SMITHERS   1951

I have been unable to locate a copy of the work.

PUBLICATION: Orpington (Kent): Charles Knight (Election Agent), 1951.

CONTRIBUTION: Letter to Smithers: p. 2.

REFERENCE: Woods D(b)80.

B128   FIFTY YEARS OF POPULAR MECHANICS   1951

[All of the following against a moderate reddish brown background; white] *Fifty Years of* | POPULAR | MECHANICS | *1902–1952* | *An album of American progress containing the* | *most fascinating articles, predictions, pictures* | *and inventions that have appeared since the first issue of Popular Mechanics* | EDITED BY | *Edward L. Throm.* | [black and white, publisher's device, 25.9 × 29.9 mm] | [white] SIMON AND SCHUSTER | *New York*

PUBLICATION: New York: Simon & Schuster, 1951. Price $5.00. There was a second printing.

PAGINATION: xi, [1], 308.

CONTRIBUTION: 'Fifty Years Hence', reproduced in facsimile: pp. 208–15.

LOCATIONS: CaOOCC, RIC (dj), USDLC, USMH

B129   FAMOUS BRITISH GENERALS   1951

[Deep reddish orange] FAMOUS | BRITISH GENERALS | [black] *Edited by Barrett Parker* | [deep reddish orange, line drawing of crossed antique rifles, helmets and boots] | [black] CONTRIBUTORS | THE HON. SIR JOHN FORTESCUE • MAJOR-GENERAL J. F. C. FULLER | CAPTAIN B. H. LIDDELL HART • SIR GEORGE ARTHUR | THE RT. HON. WINSTON S. CHURCHILL • MAJOR H. A. DE WEERD | CAPTAIN CYRIL FALLS | [triple rule, thin–thick–thin, 95.9 mm] | [deep reddish orange] LONDON | NICHOLSON & WATSON

PUBLICATION: London: Nicholson & Watson, November 1951. Price 12s. 6d.

PAGINATION: xiv, 242, 9 leaves of plates.

CONTRIBUTION: 'Haig': pp. 107–18.

LOCATIONS: CaOTTC (dj), RIC (dj), RPH (dj), UKBL, USDLC, USMH, USNhD (dj)

B129/1 PROUD HERITAGE: A PORTRAIT OF GREATNESS   [1951]

[Cover title:] [against a very deep red background, over which gilt borders, head and foot, and gilt horizontal rules, a representation of a coat of arms, below which a (very) light yellowish brown shield, gilt-trimmed, within which, very deep red] 𝕻𝖗𝖔𝖚𝖉 | 𝕳𝖊𝖗𝖎𝖙𝖆𝖌𝖊 | [below which, against a (very) light yellowish brown rectangular background, very deep red] 𝔄 𝕻𝖔𝖗𝖙𝖗𝖆𝖎𝖙 𝖔𝖋 𝕲𝖗𝖊𝖆𝖙𝖓𝖊𝖘𝖘

PUBLICATION: London: John Dron, [1951].

PAGINATION: [*106*].

CONTRIBUTION: 'Epilogue', being an excerpt from *My Early Life* (**A91**): p. 105.

LOCATIONS: RIC, UKBL

B130 ANDREW RAE DUNCAN   1952

ANDREW RAE DUNCAN | 3rd June 1884 – 30th March 1952

PUBLICATION: London?: privately printed for his friends by the British Iron and Steel Federation, 1952.

PAGINATION: [*6*], 29, [3], 1 leaf of plates.

CONTRIBUTION: The Prime Minister's tribute: p. 1.

LOCATIONS: CaOTTC, RIC, UKBL, UKScNL

REFERENCE: Woods B49/1.

B131 THE LIFE AND TIMES OF KING GEORGE VI   1952

B131.1   First edition, British issue (1952)

THE | LIFE AND TIMES OF | KING GEORGE VI | 1895–1952 | *Contents* | KING GEORGE VI: AN APPRECIATION *p.* 5 | TRIBUTE BY THE PRIME MINISTER *p.* 13 | THE EARLY YEARS *p.* 19 | THE FIRST YEARS ON THE THRONE *p.* 57 | THE WAR YEARS *p.* 91 | THE LAST YEARS *p.* 121 | [publisher's device, 23.8 × 12.7 mm] | ODHAMS PRESS LIMITED | LONG ACRE, LONDON

PUBLICATION: London: Odhams, 29 April 1952. Price 10*s*. 6*d*.

PAGINATION: 160.

CONTRIBUTIONS: 'Tribute by the Prime Minister': pp. 13–15, being his broadcast address of 7 February, reproduced from *The Times* and previously separately published (**A262**). The volume also includes the text of the inscription on the official wreath, signed by the Prime Minister: p. 159. This is the first published appearance of the inscription; however, Churchill's address was previously separately published as noted and subsequently in Rhodes James, Vol. VIII, at pp. 8336–8, under the title 'King George VI'.

NOTE: Copies are known in pale yellow embossed calico-texture cloth; in very deep red crackle-grain cloth; and in black cloth with a more elaborate decoratively patterned and blind-stamped front cover, stamped in gilt, with moderate reddish brown and gilt painted labels on the spine, all edges stained deep purplish pink.

LOCATIONS: CaOTTC (very deep red (dj) and black cloth copies), RIC (pale yellow, very deep red and black cloth copies), RPH (dj), UKBL, USDLC

REFERENCE: Woods B49/2.

B131.2   Australian issue (1952?)

THE | LIFE AND TIMES OF | KING GEORGE VI | 1895–1952 | A COLOR-GRAVURE PUBLICATION

PUBLICATION: Melbourne: Colorgravure Publications (The Herald & Weekly Times Ltd.), 1952?.

LOCATIONS: AuNL, RIC (dj)

B132   BRITAIN'S HOMAGE TO 28,000 AMERICAN DEAD   1952

BRITAIN'S HOMAGE | TO 28,000 | AMERICAN DEAD | [rendering of the Great Seal of the United States, 57.7 mm in diameter] | LONDON | THE [publisher's device, 7.6 × 22 mm] TIMES | 1952

PUBLICATION: London: *The Times*, 1952.

PAGINATION: xiii, [1], 69, [1], 14 leaves of plates.

NOTE: The volume was presented, not sold. Copies were sent to the next-of-kin of members of the American armed forces stationed in Britain or operating from British bases who died during the Second World War. Save for several hundred copies (about 1% of those published), each volume was individually inscribed on the front cover, in gilt, "IN MEMORY OF | [name of the deceased]". By February 1955, *The Times* had dispatched 71,069 "inscribed" copies of the volume and 716 plain copies. The cost of producing the volume was borne by *The Times* Publishing Company and the Dulverton Trust. There was also a second printing.

CONTRIBUTION: Message (undated) in facsimile: p. xi. First published in *The Times* of 21 November 1952 (**G1070**).

LOCATIONS: CaOTTC, RIC (dj), RPH, UKBL, USDLC

B133   BRITAIN AND EUROPE   1952

[Cover title:] [against a vivid yellowish green background, black] Britain | and Europe | [in a white rectangular box] SPECIAL ISSUE | Published by | EUROPEAN AND ATLANTIC DIGEST | in co-operation with | THE UNITED EUROPE MOVEMENT | [below the box] MAY, 1952

PUBLICATION: London: European and Atlantic Digest and The United Europe Movement, May 1952. Price 1s.

PAGINATION: 32. Pamphlet.

CONTRIBUTION: Undated message from Churchill as Founder and Chairman of the United Europe Movement: back inside wrapper.

LOCATION: RIC

B134 THE RICHES OF CHRISTMAS   1952

[Within a dark purplish red wreath, black] THE RICHES | OF CHRISTMAS | [below the wreath] *Edited by* | HANNEN FOSS | LONDON | BLANDFORD PRESS

PUBLICATION: London: Blandford Press, October 1952. Price 15*s*.

PAGINATION: 204.

CONTRIBUTION: Chapter entitled 'Christmas at the White House': pp. 65–6. Excerpted from *The Second World War* (**A240**), Volume III.

LOCATIONS: CaOOP, RIC (dj), UKBL, USDLC, USMH

B135 RED COAT   1952

RED | COAT | AN ANTHOLOGY OF THE BRITISH | SOLDIER DURING THE LAST | THREE HUNDRED YEARS | *by* | E. W. SHEPPARD | LONDON | THE BATCHWORTH PRESS

PUBLICATION: London: Batchworth, 1952. Price 20*s*.

PAGINATION: xiii, [1], 245, [1], 13 leaves of plates.

CONTRIBUTION: 'Cavalry Charge at Omdurman': pp. 85–91.

LOCATIONS: CaOONL, RIC (dj), UKBL, USMH

B136 HERBERT HASELTINE: EXHIBITION OF
SCULPTURE   1953

HERBERT HASELTINE | EXHIBITION | OF SCULPTURE | THURSDAY MAY 28TH | to | SATURDAY JUNE 27TH | 1953 | FRANK PARTRIDGE 144–146 NEW BOND STREET LONDON W.1 | *The proceeds from the sale of Catalogues will be given to* | *the King George VI Memorial Fund*

PUBLICATION: London: Frank Partridge, 1953.

PAGINATION: 42, plus card wrappers.

CONTRIBUTION: '*Foreword*', dated 6 February 1953, in the form of a facsimile letter from 10 Downing Street: p. 3. See also the Preface to the 1955 Galerie Jansen exhibition (**B151**).

LOCATIONS: RIC, RPH, USMH, USNBB

B137 EDDIE MARSH   1953

Eddie Marsh | SKETCHES FOR A COMPOSITE LITERARY PORTRAIT OF | SIR EDWARD MARSH, K.C.V.O., C.B., C.M.G. | *Compiled by* | CHRISTOPHER HASSALL | *and* | DENIS MATHEWS | *Published by* LUND HUMPHRIES *for the* | CONTEMPORARY ART SOCIETY | *The Tate Gallery, London SW1*

PUBLICATION: London: Lund Humphries and the Contemporary Art Society, 5 May 1953. Price 7*s*. 6*d*. Special price to members of the Contemporary Art Society: 5*s*.

PAGINATION: 52, plus card wrappers, 6 leaves of plates, 1 facsimile.

CONTRIBUTION: 'FOREWORD', signed in facsimile: p. 9.

LOCATIONS: RIC, RPH, UKBL, USMH

REFERENCES: Woods B51; Schroder 416.

B138   OFFICIAL SOUVENIR PROGRAMME   1953

[Cover title:] [white on very deep purple background] BOROUGH OF WANSTEAD & WOODFORD | **Coronation** | 1953 | [framed oval photograph of the Queen surmounted by a crown] | OFFICIAL | *Souvenir Programme* | SIXPENCE

PUBLICATION: Chatham?: no publisher indicated [Borough Council of Wanstead & Woodford?], May? 1953. Price 6*d*.

PAGINATION: 40, plus paper wrappers.

CONTRIBUTION: 'A Message from The Prime Minister', in the form of a facsimile letter: p. 3.

LOCATION: UKIl

B139   THE QUEEN'S CORONATION BROADCAST   1953

[Deep blue] *THE QUEEN'S* | [black] MESSAGE | BROADCAST ON | [deep blue] *Coronation Day* | [black] 2 JUNE 1953 | INTRODUCED | BY | *The Rt. Honourable* | *Sir Winston Churchill* | THE HAND & FLOWER | PRESS

PUBLICATION: Aldington, Kent: Hand & Flower Press, 30 June 1953, 500 numbered copies, printed on hand-made Barcham Green paper and set by hand in 8 pt Perpetua by Alex Waddington at his Peregrine Press in Egerton, Kent, to the design of the Hand & Flower Press in Aldington, Kent, and bound by Sangorski & Sutcliffe. The endpapers were made by the boys of Ashford (Kent) North County Secondary School, at which Alex Waddington was a master. Price 1 guinea.

PAGINATION: [*24*].

CONTRIBUTION: Churchill's broadcast introduction to the Queen's Coronation Day Broadcast: p. 5. It was subsequently published in Rhodes James, Vol. VIII, at p. 8487, under the title 'The Coronation of Queen Elizabeth II'.

ANNOTATIONS: Proceeds of the sale of the book went to the Royal National Life-Boat Institution.

LOCATION: RIC

REFERENCE: Woods B50.

B140   SCIENCE AND FRUIT   1953

SCIENCE *and* FRUIT | *Edited by* | T. WALLACE, C.B.E., F.R.S. | AND | R. W. MARSH, M.A. | *Commemorating* | the Jubilee of the | Long Ashton Research Station | *1903–1953* | UNIVERSITY OF BRISTOL | 1953

PUBLICATION: Bristol: University of Bristol, July 1953. Price 30*s.* / $4.50.

PAGINATION: xiv, 308, [2].

CONTRIBUTION: '*Foreword by the Chancellor*', signed in facsimile: p. v.

LOCATIONS: CaAEGA, CaOTTC (dj), RIC (dj), RPH (dj), UKBL

REFERENCE: Woods B52/1.

B141   AN IDEA CONQUERS THE WORLD   1953

B141.1   First (British) edition (1953)

An Idea | Conquers the World | [49.7-mm rule] | COUNT | COUDENHOVE-KALERGI | With a Preface by | The Rt. Hon. | Sir Winston S. Churchill | HUTCHINSON | Stratford Place | London

PUBLICATION: London: Hutchinson, 27 July 1953. Price 21*s*.

PAGINATION: x, 310, 1 leaf of plates.

CONTRIBUTION: 'INTRODUCTION': pp. ix–x.

LOCATIONS: CaOTTC (dj), RIC (dj), RPH (dj), UKBL, USMH

REFERENCE: Woods B52.

B141.2   American issue of British sheets (1953)

An Idea | Conquers the World | [49.7-mm rule] | COUNT | COUDENHOVE-KALERGI | With a Preface by | The Rt. Hon. | Sir Winston S. Churchill | [publisher's device, 16.9 × 14.9 mm] | ROY PUBLISHERS • NEW YORK

PUBLICATION: New York: Roy, 1953. Price $5.00.

LOCATIONS: RIC (dj), USMoFuWc

B142   THE ESCAPERS   1953

B142.1   First edition (1953)

THE | ESCAPERS | [58.7-mm decorative swelled rule] | *A Chronicle of Escape in Many Wars | with Eighteen First-hand Accounts | arranged and introduced | by* | ERIC WILLIAMS | COLLINS | *with* | EYRE & SPOTTISWOODE 1953

PUBLICATION: London: Collins and Eyre & Spottiswoode, September 1953. Price 16*s*. There was a second printing in the same month and a third in October. By the date of the fourth printing, in November, the price had been lowered to 10*s*. 6*d*. and the work was designated the "First Cheap Edition".

PAGINATION: x, 422 (numbered 11–432).

CONTRIBUTION: Chapter eight (pp. 150–62) is Churchill's story of his escape from the Boers. It consists of an introduction to the tale, including some of Churchill's own words, followed by a lengthy excerpt at pp. 152–62. It is taken from Chapter XXI, 'I Escape from the Boers—I', of *My Early Life* (**A91**), pp. 284–99.

NOTE: Second-impression dust jackets are so indicated by a line reading '*SECOND IMPRESSION*', the top of which begins 5.3 mm below the blurb and the bottom of which is 17.2 mm from the foot of the front flap.

LOCATIONS: RIC (dj; 2nd printing, dj; cheap edition, dj), USIU, USMH

B142.2   American edition (1954)

[Title across two pages; on the left-hand page] The Book of [on the right-hand page] FAMOUS | ESCAPES | *A CHRONICLE OF ESCAPE* | *IN MANY WARS WITH* | *EIGHTEEN FIRST-HAND* | *ACCOUNTS ARRANGED* | *AND INTRODUCED* BY | ERIC WILLIAMS | [on the left-hand page opposite the author's name and below]

Other Books by Eric Williams | *The Tunnel* (COWARD-MC CANN) | *The Wooden Horse* | (HARPER & BROTHERS) | [76.7-mm rule; publisher's device, 18.5 × 15 mm; 5.1-mm rule; on the right-hand page, 100.8-mm rule] | W • W • NORTON & COMPANY • INC • *New York*

PUBLICATION: New York: Norton, 1954.

PAGINATION: 453, [3].

CONTRIBUTION: Untitled chapter under the broader heading 'The Boer War, 1899–1902': pp. 161–74.

LOCATIONS: RIC (dj), USMH

B143   MARK TWAIN AND DWIGHT D. EISENHOWER 1953

Mark Twain and Dwight D. Eisenhower | *by* | CYRIL CLEMENS | *foreword by* | WINSTON S. CHURCHILL | Knight of Mark Twain | Mark Twain Gold Medal, 1943 | INTERNATIONAL MARK TWAIN SOCIETY | Webster Groves, Missouri | 1953 | T. Werner Laurie, Limited | London, England

PUBLICATION: London: T. Werner Laurie, 1953.

PAGINATION: 28. Pamphlet in glossy paper wrappers.

CONTRIBUTIONS: 'FOREWORD': pp. 9–10. At p. 26, there is also a brief quotation of some Churchillian advice to Eisenhower on public speaking.

ANNOTATIONS: The International Mark Twain Society, the creation of Cyril Clemens, appears to have been a one-person venture although Clemens managed to attract internationally known individuals to his letterhead. In 1936, the Honorary President of the Society was Benito Mussolini. In a 1936 interview with the *New Yorker*, the author wrote that Clemens "isn't disturbed by the apparent discrepancy between Sig. Mussolini's aims and the Society's aims. 'We think of Mussolini only as a lover of Mark Twain,' he told us."[54] In 1939, the *Saturday Review of Literature* reported that the Society had not had a meeting since 1927;[55] "It has no constitution, no by-laws, no dues and perhaps more vice-presidents than all the National Banks in the country."[56] One of the individuals gracing the top of the letterhead (at least in the early 1940s) was Churchill.[57] Lee Meriwether, at one time the President of the Mark Twain Memorial Association, explained that he had written to ex-Presidents Truman and Hoover, Churchill and other "Honorary" Vice-Presidents of the Society, every one of whom replied that their names had been used on the letterhead without their consent.[58] In fact, Cyril Clemens had tried to attract Churchill to become Honorary President of the Society as early as 1927. On 30 March, Eddie Marsh sent the following query to Charles Kingsley at Scribner's:

---

54. Vol. 12, No. 16, 6 June 1936, pp. 10–11.

55. Bunker Blaise, 'The Mark Twain Society', *Saturday Review of Literature*, Vol. XX, 15 July 1939, pp. 11–12.

56. *Ibid.*

57. For Cyril Clemens's recounting of the relationship between Churchill and Mark Twain, see 'Winston Churchill and Mark Twain: An International Friendship', *Slant*, Winter 1945–46, Vol. II, No. 3, pp. 5–6.

58. 'Our Struggle with the Internal Revenue Bureau', Vol. XXX, Fall–Summer 1957, at p. 2.

Mr Churchill has received a letter from Mr Cyril Clemens, of Webster Groves, Mo, President of the "Mark Twain Society", offering him the honorary presidency of the Society "in recognition of his book". He presumes that this is Mark Twain's son, & that the Society is of good standing, but he wants to be quite sure before accepting that it is all right, & he thinks you are likely to be able to advise him; & if so he w[oul]d be very much obliged if you would.

He presumes that the post is purely honorary & that he w[oul]d not be expected to pay any subscription.[59]

Kingsley replied the following day.

I am afraid I have no direct knowledge of the Mark Twain Society about which you inquire, beyond having seen in two or three literary papers a statement to the effect that such a society had been organized, and inviting application for membership from those who were enthusiastic admirers of Mark Twain. These notices were in the form of a letter signed by Mr Cyril Clemens, who is probably a nephew or cousin of Mark Twain's, as the latter's children were both girls.

Cyril Clemens and Mark Twain (Samuel Clemens) were, in fact, third cousins, twice removed,[60] although they only met once, in the summer of 1909, towards the end of Twain's life.[61] The relationship between Clemens and the Mark Twain literary executors appears to have been largely adversarial, resulting ultimately in court proceedings that prohibited Clemens from publishing what he alleged was the "only official edition of Mark Twain's letters".[62]

LOCATIONS: CJZ, RIC, UKBL, USMH

REFERENCE: Woods B52/2.

B144   YOUTH'S COMPANION   1954

[Title across two pages] [on the left-hand page] YOUTH'S [on the right-hand page] COMPANION | [on the left-hand page, line drawing of a young man in American Colonial dress with a sack on a stick over his shoulder, stepping left; opposite the line drawing, on the right-hand page] EDITED BY LOVELL THOMPSON | WITH THREE FORMER COMPANION | EDITORS, M. A. DeWOLFE HOWE, | ARTHUR STANWOOD PIER, AND | HARFORD POWEL | ☆ [publisher's device, 19.1 × 8.9 mm] ☆ | *with illustrations* | HOUGHTON MIFFLIN COMPANY BOSTON | 𝕿𝖍𝖊 𝕽𝖎𝖛𝖊𝖗𝖘𝖎𝖉𝖊 𝕻𝖗𝖊𝖘𝖘 𝕮𝖆𝖒𝖇𝖗𝖎𝖉𝖌𝖊 | 1954

PUBLICATION: Boston: Houghton Mifflin, 1954.

PAGINATION: xii, 1140, 8 leaves of facsimiles.

---

59. Marsh's and Kingsley's letters are found in the Scribner Archives, Box 31, Folder 2.
60. See Isabelle Budd, 'The Relation of Mark Twain to Cyril Clemens', *Mark Twain Journal*, Vol. 23, No. 2, Fall 1985, p. 2, and the authorities cited there.
61. Don Crinklaw, 'The Twain Cousin', *Saint Louisan*, Vol. VII, No. 6, June 1975, p. 42.
62. Isabelle Budd, *loc. cit.* In general, see Thomas A. Tenney, *Mark Twain: A Reference Guide* (Boston: Hall, 1977).

CONTRIBUTION: 'On the Flank of the Army': pp. 263–73. This is the only volume appearance of the article, which was first published in *Youth's Companion* of 18 December 1902 (**C222a**).

LOCATIONS: CaOTMCL, RIC (dj), USDLC, USMH

REFERENCE: Woods D(a)19/1.

B145 THE HOME LETTERS OF T. E. LAWRENCE AND HIS BROTHERS   1954

B145.1 First edition (1954)

THE HOME | LETTERS OF | T. E. LAWRENCE | AND HIS | BROTHERS | [large outline letter in deep reddish orange, 26.8 × 24.5 mm] L | [black] BASIL BLACKWELL | OXFORD | 1954

PUBLICATION: London: Basil Blackwell, 17 May 1954. Price £3. 3s. Advance proof copies are known.

PAGINATION: xvi, 731, [1], 20 leaves of plates.

CONTRIBUTIONS: Letter of 4 March 1954, giving Mrs Lawrence permission to reproduce his speech at the unveiling of the memorial at Lawrence's old school in Oxford, reproduced in facsimile: p. xii. The allocution itself, reprinted, appears at pp. xiii–xvi.

NOTE: Complete copies will have the light orange yellow wrapper band (37.3 × 506.2 mm) which reads: over the spine, '*RECOMMENDED* | *BY THE* | *BOOK SOCIETY*'; over the front, '*RECOMMENDED* | *BY THE BOOK SOCIETY* '; and, over the front flap, reading vertically up, '*The Home Letters* | *of T. E. Lawrence* | *and his brothers*'.

LOCATIONS: CaOTTC (dj), RIC (dj with band), RPH (dj), UKBL, USMH

REFERENCES: Woods B53; O'Brien A246.

B145.2.a American edition, first state (1954)

THE HOME | LETTERS OF | T. E. LAWRENCE | AND HIS | BROTHERS | [large outline letter in deep reddish orange, 26.8 × 24.5 mm] L | [black] THE MACMILLAN COMPANY | NEW YORK | 1954

PUBLICATION: New York: Macmillan, May 1954. Price $10.00.

PAGINATION: xvi, 731, [1], 20 leaves of plates [one of which is numbered].

NOTE: In the first state, the title page is a *cancellans*. In the second state, the title page is an integral part of the first gathering. Also, the only first-state copy I have examined had a British dust jacket. I do not consider this mismatched; there is no reason to expect that new dust jackets would have been ready at a time when the first signature itself had not been integrally reprinted.

LOCATIONS: CJZ, USMH

REFERENCE: O'Brien A247.

B145.2.b American edition, second state (1954)

LOCATION: RPH

B146   MEMO TO CONTRIBUTORS TO WINSTON CHURCHILL 80TH BIRTHDAY PRESENTATION FUND   1954?

[Dropped-head title only:] *Memo to Contributors to* | WINSTON CHURCHILL 80TH BIRTHDAY | PRESENTATION FUND | MAIN OFFICE : 156 CHARING CROSS ROAD, LONDON, W.C.2

PUBLICATION: London: Winston Churchill 80th Birthday Presentation Fund?, 1954?.

PAGINATION: [2]. A small (183 × 121 mm) leaflet sent as a memorandum to contributors to Sir Winston's Birthday Fund.

CONTRIBUTION: Undated reply to Lord Moynihan, Honorary Treasurer of the Birthday Fund: pp. 1–2.

NOTE: The Executive Committee of the Winston Churchill 80th Birthday Presentation Fund was made up of Lord Moynihan, as Honorary Treasurer, Edward Martell, Chairman, Malcolm Dunbar, and Brian Goddard, Secretary. This leaflet includes the letter to Sir Winston from the members of the Executive Committee of the Birthday Fund which accompanied their cheque for £150,000 and Churchill's reply acknowledging the gift and forming, with some or all of the proceeds, The Winston Churchill Birthday Trust. The leaflet was sent to those who had contributed to the Birthday Fund. *Cf.* **B148**, which was a document of solicitation of funds.

LOCATION: RIC

B147   THE NAVY YEAR BOOK AND DIARY 1955   1954

[Wavy rules with Navy League device in the centre, 26.3 mm in diameter] | THE NAVY Year Book | AND DIARY | 1955 | DIAMOND JUBILEE NUMBER | [125.3-mm rule] | PUBLISHED *by* THE NAVY LEAGUE | MCMLIV

PUBLICATION: London: The Navy League, December 1954.

PAGINATION: 268, plus diary of 64 pp.

CONTRIBUTION: Facsimile letter of congratulations: p. 2.

LOCATIONS: RIC (dj), UKLo, USMBAt

REFERENCE: Woods B53/1.

B148   THE PEOPLE'S TRIBUTE   1955

[Cover title:] [printed deep purplish blue] WINSTON CHURCHILL BIRTHDAY TRUST | TRUSTEES | [names of the five trustees and the names and addresses of the auditor, solicitors and bankers in 11 lines] | 156 CHARING CROSS ROAD, LONDON, W.C.2 | Telephone: COVent Garden 1051 | [24.8-mm French rule] | THE PEOPLE'S TRIBUTE | [half-tone photograph of Churchill, seated] | NOT AN APPEAL – AN OPPORTUNITY

PUBLICATION: London: Winston Churchill Birthday Trust, February 1955.

PAGINATION: [4]. Leaflet, folded (241.2 × 174.5 mm).

CONTRIBUTION: The undated letter to Lord Moynihan: pp. 3–4.

NOTE: Unlike **B146**, which was a memorandum acknowledging a contribution to the Birthday Fund, this folded leaflet announces the details of the formation of the Winston Churchill Birthday Trust, whose trustees included Lord Moynihan and Edward Martell of the Birthday Fund but added Viscount Leathers, as Chairman, John Colville and Anthony Moir. The folded leaflet also includes a contribution form on p. 4. Related documents without an original Churchill contribution which may be found accompanying it include a letter of solicitation of November 1954, a separate contribution form printed deep purplish blue, and a receipt. There may also be a facsimile holograph letter of thanks from Churchill on 10 Downing Street headed paper, which reads: 'I am deeply touched by | your kind contribution to | my birthday present & | grateful for your good | wishes. | Winston S. Churchill'. I date this conjecturally as February 1955 since it was enclosed with the letter which Moynihan sent to contributors on that date, the text of which is, in pertinent part:

> I feel that I should inform you that the Fund is now closing. To date over a quarter of a million people and Companies have contributed from all parts of the world. Details of the Trust which Sir Winston has set up are given in the enclosed leaflet.

This folded leaflet ought not to be confused with one of similar title and appearance, printed black, but headed 'WINSTON CHURCHILL 80th BIRTHDAY | PRESENTATION FUND'. That was the original pre-November solicitation of donations, which includes no Churchill contribution.

LOCATIONS: FBW, RIC

B149   APRIL 29, 1945–APRIL 29, 1955   1955

[Dropped-head title only:] APRIL 29, 1945–APRIL 29, 1955

PUBLICATION: London: no publisher indicated (HMSO?), 29 April 1955, 50,000 copies.

PAGINATION: 2. Leaflet.

CONTRIBUTION: Message from Churchill to the Dutch Prime Minister: p. 1. Churchill's is one of five messages from British leaders to Dutch leaders.

NOTE: At the end of the Second World War, between 29 April and 8 May 1945, Royal Air Force Bomber Command Lancasters and Mosquitoes dropped 6685 tons of food supplies to the starving people of the Netherlands. To commemorate that event and to open Holland's nationwide Liberation festivities, these goodwill leaflets were dropped over The Hague by Lincolns of that Command on 29 April 1955, together with 1,250,000 tulips.

LOCATIONS: FBW, RIC

REFERENCE: Woods D(b)97/1.

B150   ROAD SAFETY INFORMATION HANDBOOK   1955

Wanstead & Woodford | [136.3-mm rule] | ROAD SAFETY | [136.3-mm rule] | INFORMATION HANDBOOK | [ranged left, with an extended 'f'] for [ranged right opposite that word] • Motorists | • Motorcyclists | • Pedestrians | • Cyclists | [centred and below the foregoing] Contents | [list of contents in 15 lines] | ISSUED BY THE BOROUGH OF WANSTEAD & WOODFORD | ROAD SAFETY COUNCIL |

Cover photo: Henry Ford & Son Ltd. (Cork) | [136.3-mm rule] | [ranged left, publisher's device] | [ranged right opposite the publisher's device] *Published by* | BATISTE PUBLICATIONS LTD. | 20 Bedford St., London W.C.2 | [page] 5

PUBLICATION: London: Batiste Publications (for the Borough of Wanstead & Woodford Road Safety Council), 1955.

NOTE: The entry is based on a photocopy only. I have been unable to locate a copy of the original pamphlet.

CONTRIBUTION: Facsimile letter of January 1955 on 10 Downing Street stationery, with a photograph of the Prime Minister ranged upper right: p. 7.

B151   HERBERT HASELTINE: EXPOSITION DE SCULPTURES   1955

HERBERT   HASELTINE | EXPOSITION | DE   SCULPTURES | *Sous   le   Haut Patronage de* | *LL. EE. les Ambassadeurs de Grande-Bretagne* | *et des Etats-Unis* | *et de M. Jacques Jaujard,* | *Directeur Général des Arts et des Lettres* | *à partir du jeudi 9 juin 1955* | à la Galerie JANSEN et Cie, 9, rue Royale, Paris | Une œuvre de l'artiste | sera mise en tombola au profit de la Croix-rouge française

PUBLICATION: Paris, S.F.R., June? 1955.

PAGINATION: [*48*].

CONTRIBUTION: '[Préface]', being a letter of 11 May 1955 on 28 Hyde Park Gate stationery in facsimile: pp. 5–6 (and translated into French at p. 7). While the text of the letter is very similar to that which constitutes the Preface to the 1953 Frank Partridge exhibition (**B136**), it is clearly a different letter, written at a later date and on 28 Hyde Park Gate rather than 10 Downing Street stationery.

LOCATIONS: RIC, USMH

B152   THE NEW HILTON BEDSIDE BOOK   1955

[Ranged upper right in a single-rule box, enclosing 7.4 × 39.1 mm] VOLUME THREE | [to the left of but principally below the box] THE | *Hilton* | BEDSIDE BOOK | [ranged right] A TREASURY OF *Entertaining Reading* | SELECTED EXCLUSIVELY | FOR THE GUESTS OF THE *Hilton Hotels* | PUBLISHED BY *Hilton Hotels Corporation*

PUBLICATION: Chicago: Hilton Hotels, 1955

PAGINATION: [*2*], 249, [*5*].

CONTRIBUTION: 'Escape from Pretoria': pp. 13–31. It includes all of the text of the first of the chapters ('I Escape from the Boers—I') and some of the second ('I Escape from the Boers—II') from *A Roving Commission* (**A91.2**), pp. 268–96.

LOCATION: RIC

B153   A TREASURY OF THE ESSAY   1955?

B153.1   Grolier issue (1955?)

A | *Treasury* | OF THE *Essay* | FROM MONTAIGNE TO E. B. WHITE | *Edited by* | HOMER C. COMBS | *Associate Professor of English* | *Washington University* | [79.4-mm rule] | [publisher's device] Grolier | INCORPORATED | NEW YORK

PUBLICATION: New York: Grolier, 1955? The volume was reprinted in 1973.

PAGINATION: 528.

CONTRIBUTION: 'Painting as a Pastime': pp. 414–28.

LOCATION: RIC

B153.2   Spencer Press issue (1955?)

A | *Treasury* | OF THE *Essay* | FROM MONTAIGNE TO E. B. WHITE | *Edited by* | HOMER C. COMBS | *Associate Professor of English* | *Washington University* | [79.4-mm rule] | *Chicago* | SPENCER PRESS, *Inc.*

PUBLICATION: Chicago: Spencer Press, 1955?

LOCATIONS: CaAEU, CaOOU, RIC, USDLC

B154   JOHN PHILIPOT'S ROLL OF THE CONSTABLES OF DOVER CASTLE AND LORD WARDENS OF THE CINQUE PORTS 1627   1956

JOHN PHILIPOT'S ROLL | OF THE | CONSTABLES OF DOVER CASTLE | AND LORD WARDENS | OF THE CINQUE PORTS | 1627 | With a Foreword by | SIR WINSTON CHURCHILL, K.G., P.C., O.M., C.H. | Introduction and Notes by | FRANCIS W. STEER, F.S.A. | *County Archivist* | *East and West Sussex* | LONDON | G. BELL AND SONS, LTD | 1956

PUBLICATION: London: G. Bell, 21 March 1956. Price 21*s*. While there appears to have been but a single printing, the volume is found in two distinct bindings: one is stamped in gilt on strong purplish blue embossed calico-texture cloth; the other is in dark purplish blue on light purplish blue embossed calico-texture cloth.

PAGINATION: 31, [1], 2 leaves of plates and 8 leaves of the emblazoned Roll of the Constables of Dover Castle and the Lord Wardens of the Cinque Ports.

CONTRIBUTION: Undated letter regarding George Villiers and the Lord Wardens, reproduced in facsimile: p. 5.

LOCATIONS: RIC (dj), RPH (dj), UKBL, USMH

REFERENCE: Woods B54.

B154/1 MEN AT WAR   1957

MEN AT WAR | *The Best War Stories of* | *All Time* | *Edited and Selected by* | FRED URQUHART | [publisher's device, 20.6 mm in diameter] | ARCO PUBLICATIONS: LONDON | 1957

PUBLICATION: London: Arco, 15 May 1957, 10,000 copies. Price 16*s*.

PAGINATION: 615, [1].

CONTRIBUTION: 'The London Blitz, 1940': pp. 391–7. This chapter of the work is taken from Chapter XVII of *The Second World War* (**A240**), pp. 301–15, the excerpted portion ending at p. 308.

LOCATIONS: CaOTMCL, RIC (dj), UKBL, USMH

B155 SIERRA LEONE   1957

SIERRA LEONE | *A Modern Portrait* | BY | ROY LEWIS | LONDON | HER MAJESTY'S STATIONERY OFFICE | 1954

PUBLICATION: London: HMSO, 1957, 16,00 copies. Price 25*s*. The Churchill Foreword is not present in the first edition of *Sierra Leone*, which was published in 1954. It first appears in the second printing of 1957 and again in the third printing of 1958.

PAGINATION: xi, [1], 264, 17 leaves of plates, 1 map (folding).

CONTRIBUTION: 'FOREWORD', of September 1956 to the Corona Library, signed in facsimile: p. vii.

NOTE: The series of volumes on various British colonial territories began with *Hong Kong*, by Harold Ingrams, published in 1952. Its Foreword was by the Rt Hon. Oliver Lyttleton, then Secretary of State for the Colonies. There is no Foreword at all in the first edition of the second volume, *Sierra Leone*, published in 1954, or in the third volume, *Nyasaland*, by Frank Debenham, published in 1955; however, the Churchill Foreword, which appears first in the second printing of this volume, was repeated unaltered in almost all the remaining volumes in the Corona Library, *i.e.*, *British Guiana* (**B156**), *Jamaica* (**B157**), *Uganda* (**B167**), *North Borneo* (**B171**), *Fiji* (**B176**), *Swaziland* (**B182**), *Basutoland* (**B184**), *Bechuanaland* (**B186**) and *British Honduras* (**B190**). It was not included in *Western Pacific Islands*, the final volume in the series.

LOCATIONS: CaOONL, RIC (1st, 2nd and 3rd printings; djs), UKBL, UKOxB, UKScNL

B156 BRITISH GUIANA   1957

BRITISH GUIANA | *The Land of Six Peoples* | BY | MICHAEL SWAN | LONDON | HER MAJESTY'S STATIONERY OFFICE | 1957

PUBLICATION: London: HMSO (for the Colonial Office), 24 May 1957, 28,000 copies. Price 25*s*.

PAGINATION: xv, [1], 236, 17 leaves of plates, 1 map (folding).

CONTRIBUTION: 'FOREWORD', of September 1956 to the Corona Library, signed in facsimile: p. vii. For other appearances, see 'Note' under **B155**.

LOCATIONS: RIC (dj), RPH (dj), UKBL, USMH

REFERENCE: Woods B55.

B157 JAMAICA   1957

JAMAICA | *An Island Mosaic* | BY | PETER ABRAHAMS | LONDON | HER MAJESTY'S STATIONERY OFFICE | 1957

PUBLICATION: London: HMSO (for the Colonial Office), 29 November 1957, 28,000 copies. Price 25*s*. There was a second printing in 1958.

PAGINATION: xv, [1], 288, 13 leaves of plates, 1 map (folding).

CONTRIBUTION: 'FOREWORD', of September 1956 to the Corona Library, signed in facsimile: p. vii. For other appearances, see 'Note' under **B155**.

LOCATIONS: CaOTTC (dj), RIC (1st and 2nd printings; djs), RPH (dj), UKBL, UKOxB, UKScNL, USMH

REFERENCE: Woods B56.

B158   MARK TWAIN JEST BOOK   1957

There have been three editions of the *Mark Twain Jest Book*.[63] The Churchill letter present in the first one was removed from the second edition (published in 1963) and restored in the third.[64]

B158.1   First edition (1957)

MARK TWAIN JEST BOOK | Edited by | CYRIL CLEMENS | foreword by | CARL SANDBURG | Mark Twain is the only American writer who is also an | American hero, known to many men and women who have bare- | ly read his books. He created many characters, but none of them | is greater than he is himself. | Carl Van Doren to Cyril Clemens | Mark Twain Journal | Kirkwood 22, Missouri

PUBLICATION: Kirkwood (MO): Mark Twain Journal, 1957.

PAGINATION: [2], 32, [2]. Pamphlet in card wrappers.

CONTRIBUTION: While the Sandburg contribution is designated as the Foreword, the Churchill letter of 25 October 1943 to Cyril Clemens, in facsimile, thanking the International Mark Twain Society for its award to him of a Gold Medal, is included in a prefatory position: p. 3. The letter was first published in periodical form in *Slant* of Winter 1945–46 (**G885**).

LOCATIONS: RIC, UKBL, UKScNL, USMH

B158.2   Third edition (1965)

[Ranged left] Mark Twain's | [ranged right] Jest Book | [centred] Edited by | *Cyril Clemens* | <u>Foreword by</u> | <u>Carl Sandburg</u> | Mark Twain is the only American writer who is also | an American hero, known to many men and women who | have barely read his books. He created many charac- | ters, but none of them is greater than himself. | [ranged right] Carl Van Doren to Cyril Clemens | [centred] Mark Twain Journal | Kirkwood, Missouri 63122

PUBLICATION: Kirkwood (MO): Mark Twain Journal, 1965. Described as a third edition with new material.

PAGINATION: [8], 28, plus card wrappers.

CONTRIBUTION: Letter of 25 October 1943, in facsimile: p. 6.

NOTE: For a discussion of Cyril Clemens, his relationship to Mark Twain and Churchill's "role" in the International Mark Twain Society, see the 'Annotations' to **B143**.

LOCATIONS: CaOTTC, UKBL, UKScNL, USIU

REFERENCE: Woods D(b)117/9.

---

63. This is the title of the first edition; the second and third editions bear the slightly varied title *Mark Twain's Jest Book*.

64. The only second-edition copy I have examined is held by the National Library of Scotland.

B159 THE HISTORY OF THE HUDSON'S BAY COMPANY, 1670–1870 1958

The Hudson's Bay Record Society edition was published in two volumes. The Canadian and American trade issues were published in three volumes from first-edition sheets (Volume I from sheets of Volume I of the first edition and Volumes II and III from sheets of Volume II). In each case, it is only the first volume which contains the Churchill 'FOREWORD'.

Volume I

B159.1   First edition, only printing (1958)

THE HISTORY OF THE | HUDSON'S BAY COMPANY | 1670–1870 | Volume I: 1670–1763 | BY | E. E. RICH, M.A. | *Master of St. Catharine's College, Cambridge* | *Vere Harmsworth Professor of Imperial and Naval History* | WITH A FOREWORD BY THE RIGHT HONOURABLE | SIR WINSTON CHURCHILL, K.G., O.M., C.H., F.R.S., M.P. | *Grand Seigneur of the Company of Adventurers of England* | *trading into Hudson's Bay* | LONDON | THE HUDSON'S BAY RECORD SOCIETY | 1958

PUBLICATION: London: Hudson's Bay Record Society, 1958. Published as Volume XXI of the Hudson's Bay Record Society publications.

PAGINATION: xvi, 687, [1], xv, [1], 3 leaves of plates, 1 map (folding).

CONTRIBUTION: Foreword, in the form of a letter from Chartwell of September 1957, signed in facsimile: p. ix.

NOTES: The deckle edges have been retained.

  The second volume (Volume XXII of the Hudson's Bay Record Society publications), published in 1959, covers the period from 1763 to 1870. The title page of that volume makes no reference to the Churchill Foreword.

LOCATIONS: CaOONL, CaOTTC, RIC, RPH, UKBL, USMH

REFERENCE: Woods B57/1.

B159.2   Canadian (first trade) issue of British sheets (1960)

HUDSON'S BAY COMPANY | 1670 – 1870 | Volume I: 1670–1763 | BY | E. E. RICH, M.A. | *Master of St. Catharine's College, Cambridge* | *Vere Harmsworth Professor of Imperial and Naval History* | WITH A FOREWORD BY THE RIGHT HONOURABLE | SIR WINSTON CHURCHILL, K.G., O.M., C.H., F.R.S., M.P. | *Grand Seigneur of the Company of Adventurers of England* | *trading into Hudson's Bay* | [publisher's device, 15.2 × 23.3 mm] | TORONTO | McCLELLAND AND STEWART LIMITED | 1960

PUBLICATION: Toronto: McClelland and Stewart, 1960.

PAGINATION: xiii, [1], 687, [1], 3 leaves of plates, 1 map (folding).

CONTRIBUTION: 'FOREWORD': p. v of the first volume. Note, however, that the text of the Foreword appears on the front of the dust jackets of each of the three volumes, although it is not otherwise mentioned in Volumes II and III.

NOTE: All page edges are trimmed. The volumes were issued in a slipcase, but I have been unable to examine a copy.

LOCATIONS: CaAEU, CaOOCC, CaOTU, CaQMM, RIC (dj)

REFERENCE: Spadoni 1558.

B159.3 American issue of British sheets (1961)

HUDSON'S BAY COMPANY | 1670 – 1870 | Volume I: 1670–1763 | BY | E. E. RICH, M.A. | *Master of St. Catharine's College, Cambridge* | *Vere Harmsworth Professor of Imperial and Naval History* | WITH A FOREWORD BY THE RIGHT HONOURABLE | SIR WINSTON CHURCHILL, K.G., O.M., C.H., F.R.S., M.P. | *Grand Seigneur of the Company of Adventurers of England* | *trading into Hudson's Bay* | THE MACMILLAN COMPANY | NEW YORK

PUBLICATION: New York: Macmillan, 1961.

NOTE: The American issue was published in three volumes in dust jackets and boxed. The Macmillan box is dark blue on pebble-grained paper-covered board with the emblem of the Hudson Bay Company on the right side, stamped in gilt. Otherwise, it is as the Canadian issue. The American issue was also sold as a trade edition in the United Kingdom from 27 March 1961 at £12. 5s.

LOCATIONS: RIC (dj and slipcase), UKBL, USMH

B160 BRENDAN BRACKEN   1958

[Moderate blue] BRENDAN | BRACKEN | [black] 1901–1958 | [12.9-mm thin–thick rule] | PORTRAITS | AND | APPRECIATIONS | LONDON | 1958

PUBLICATION: London: No publisher indicated, 1958.

PAGINATION: [8], 82, 1 leaf of plates.

CONTRIBUTION: Churchill's appreciation (untitled), signed in facsimile: p. vii.

LOCATIONS: CaOTTC, CaOTU, FBW, RIC, RPH, UKBL

REFERENCE: Woods B57/2.

B160/1 [THE VICTORY EX-SERVICES CLUB]   1958

No title page.

PUBLICATION: London: Victory Ex-Services Club, 1958.

PAGINATION: 8. Pamphlet in self-wrappers.

CONTRIBUTION: Message from Churchill to the Victory Club for ex-Service men and women: p. 1. There is also a box on p. 7, enclosing a photograph of Churchill, the words "Giving All Daring All Enduring All", described as 'MR Churchill's famous words after Dunkirk 1940', and his facsimile signature.

LOCATION: CB

B160/2 HASTINGS' REGENCY CRESCENT   1958?

OLD HASTINGS PRESERVATION SOCIETY | PELHAM CRESCENT APPEAL | President of the Old Hastings Preservation Society: Rear-Admiral H. E. Dannreuther, D.S.O. | Chairman of Appeal Committee: Councillor Roger Frewen | Hastings' | Regency Crescent | £4,000 | NEEDED TO SAVE THIS ARCHITECTURAL GEM

| [within a single-rule box, enclosing 73.9 × 125.9 mm, '*Message from the Right Worshipful The Mayor*']

PUBLICATION: Hastings: Old Hastings Preservation Society, 1958?

PAGINATION: [4].

CONTRIBUTION: Message from Sir Winston Churchill (as Lord Warden of the Cinque Ports) to the Old Hastings Preservation Society: p. 4.

NOTE: Although the document is undated, the general appeal to the public was launched in July 1958; its financial target was £4000, which sum was intended to supplement the grant of £3250 from the Ministry of Works, which was promised in February 1958, and the sum committed by the Borough Council in April 1958. R. H. Bryant, whose name is noted in the box on p. 1, was Mayor of Hastings from 1958 to 1959.

LOCATION: RIC

B161 ADVENTURE IN OIL   1959

Adventure in Oil | THE STORY OF BRITISH PETROLEUM | [96.4-mm rule] | BY | HENRY LONGHURST | WITH A FOREWORD BY | The Rt. Hon. Sir Winston Churchill | SIDGWICK AND JACKSON | LONDON

PUBLICATION: London: Sidgwick & Jackson, 14 April 1959. Price 21*s*.

PAGINATION: 286, [2], 25 leaves of plates.

CONTRIBUTION: Undated facsimile letter: p. 5.

LOCATIONS: CaOTTC (dj), RIC (dj), TuNL, UKBL, USMH

REFERENCE: Woods B58.

B162 BATTLE OF BRITAIN SOUVENIR
BROCHURE   [1959]

[Cover title:] [against a full-colour background of a distant dogfight over an English countryside in the foreground; orange red] BATTLE OF BRITAIN | [below the illustration, against a solid moderate reddish brown background; light greenish yellow] SOUVENIR BROCHURE

PUBLICATION: London: Royal Air Forces Association, [1959]. Published, it appears, by the Royal Air Forces Association immediately prior to or in conjunction with the Battle of Britain Exhibition of 14–20 September 1959 at the Horse Guards Parade and Air Ministry, Whitehall, London.

PAGINATION: 24, plus 16-page programme in the centre of the magazine, plus paper wrappers. Wire-stitched.

CONTRIBUTION: Undated facsimile letter with signature and, ranged upper left, a photograph of Churchill: p. 1.

LOCATION: RIC

B163   4TH HUSSAR   1959

4TH HUSSAR | THE STORY OF | THE 4TH QUEEN'S OWN HUSSARS | 1685–1958 | BY | DAVID SCOTT DANIELL | WITH A FOREWORD BY | SIR WINSTON CHURCHILL | *Colonel of the Regiment* | ALDERSHOT | GALE & POLDEN LTD. | 1959

PUBLICATION: Aldershot: Gale & Polden, 30 September 1959. Price 42*s*.

PAGINATION: xv, [1], 416, 14 leaves of plates, 15 maps (all folding).

CONTRIBUTIONS: 'FOREWORD', signed in facsimile and dated September 1957: p. vii. The volume also includes an excerpt from a 1936 speech in the 4th Hussars' Sergeants' Mess: p. 291; an address of 1 February 1943 to the parade of the 4th Hussars at Kokkini Trimithia (near Nicosia): pp. 345–6; a brief comment of 3 December in Egypt re the Africa Star ribbon: p. 350; message of early January to General McReery following the battle of Senio Pocket: p. 374; message of about 19 August 1948 to the 4th Hussars, then setting out for service in Malaysia: p. 394; and message of 24 October 1958 upon the amalgamation of the 4th Hussars and the 8th King's Royal Irish Hussars: pp. 405–6. There are also numerous lengthy excerpts from *My Early Life* (**A91**), *The World Crisis* (**A69**) and *The Second World War* (**A240**) cited *passim*. While the address of 1 February 1943 was previously collected in *Onwards to Victory* (**A194**), at p. 5, and later in Rhodes James, Vol. VII, at p. 6735, the version of the speech published in *4th Hussar* differs somewhat from those appearances.[65]

LOCATIONS: CaOHM, RIC (dj), RPH (dj), UKBL, USMH

REFERENCES: Woods B58/1; White, p. 17.

B164   THE IMPACT OF AIR POWER   1959

THE IMPACT | OF AIR POWER | NATIONAL SECURITY AND WORLD POLITICS | [88.9-mm swelled rule] | *by* | EUGENE M. EMME | *Officer of Civil and Defense Mobilization* | *Former Professor of International Politics* | *Air University* | [publisher's device, 16.8 × 22.6 mm] | D. VAN NOSTRAND COMPANY, INC. | PRINCETON, NEW JERSEY | [ranged left] TORONTO [ranged right] LONDON | [centred] NEW YORK

PUBLICATION: Princeton: Van Nostrand, 1959. Price $12.50.

PAGINATION: xiv, 914.

CONTRIBUTIONS: 'Air Defense Memoranda of 1914', being the memoranda of 1 and 5 September and 2 October 1914: pp. 27–9; 'The Possibilities of an Air Offensive in 1918', Section IV of the memorandum of 21 October 1917: pp. 37–40; 'The German

---

65. Churchill became a 4th Hussar in 1895 and a Colonel of the Regiment on 22 October 1941. Aspects of his long association with the Regiment, which continued until its amalgamation with the 8th King's Royal Irish Hussars in 1958, are documented in *My Early Life*, *The Second World War* and *4th Hussar*, among other places. What is less known, perhaps, is the following 1925 entry in the Regimental Betting Book: "Lt.-Col. H. Nugent-Head, M.C., bets General Cassels 200 rupees that Winston Churchill will one day be Prime Minister of England" ('Warrior's Night Out', *Illustrated*, 26 June 1954, p. 20).

Aerial Menace', excerpt from speech of 20 July 1934: pp. 53–4; 'Their Finest Hour', a brief excerpt from the speech of 18 June 1940: pp. 77–8; 'So Much Owed by So Many to So Few', a brief excerpt from the speech of 20 August 1940: pp. 78–9; 'The Advent of Air Power', speech of 31 March 1949 at the Massachusetts Institute of Technology: pp. 86–94; and 'The Balance of Terror', the speech of 1 March 1955 in the House of Commons: pp. 754–64.

LOCATIONS: CaOGU, CaOONL, CaOTMCL, RIC (dj), USDLC

B165   A CAVALCADE OF COLLIER'S   1959

A | Cavalcade   of | Collier's | *Edited   by* | Kenneth   McArdle | A.   S.   BARNES   & COMPANY, INC. • NEW YORK

PUBLICATION: New York: Barnes, 1959. Price $10.00.

PAGINATION: xviii, 574, 4 leaves of plates.

CONTRIBUTION: 'What Americans Think about the Boer War': pp. 32–6. First published in *Collier's Weekly* of 26 January 1901 (**C218**). This is the only volume appearance of the article.

LOCATIONS: CaAEU, CaOOCC, RIC (dj), USDLC, USMH

B166   ACTION THIS DAY   1960

ACTION | THIS DAY | A WAR MEMOIR | *by* | ADMIRAL OF THE FLEET | SIR PHILIP VIAN | G.C.B., K.B.E., D.S.O. | FREDERICK MULLER LIMITED | LONDON

PUBLICATION: London: Muller, 14 March 1960. Price 21*s*.

PAGINATION: 223, [1], 6 leaves of plates, 1 facsimile.

CONTRIBUTION: Includes a photograph of a minute of March 1942 from Churchill to Vian as the frontispiece.

LOCATIONS: RIC (dj), UKBL, UKScNL, USMH

B167   UGANDA   1960

UGANDA | *A Crisis of Nationhood* | BY | HAROLD INGRAMS | *LONDON* | HER MAJESTY'S STATIONERY OFFICE | 1960

PUBLICATION: London: HMSO, 24 June 1960. Price £1. 10*s*. 0*d*. There was a second printing in 1961.

PAGINATION: xvi, 366, [2], 18 leaves of plates, 2 maps (folding).

CONTRIBUTION: 'FOREWORD', of September 1956 to the Corona Library, signed in facsimile, 'Winston S. Churchill': p. vii. Note that the facsimile signature is not present in the second printing. For other appearances, see 'Note' under **B155**.

LOCATIONS: CaNSH, CaOTMCL (1st and 2nd printings), RIC (dj), RPH (2nd printing; dj), UKBL, UKOxB, UKScNL, USMH

REFERENCE: Woods B59.

B168 THE MEMOIRS OF GENERAL THE LORD ISMAY   1960

B168.1 First edition, only printing (1960)

THE MEMOIRS OF | GENERAL THE LORD | ISMAY | K.G., P.C., G.C.B., C.H., D.S.O. | [publisher's device, 11.7 × 12.3 mm] | HEINEMANN | LONDON MELBOURNE TORONTO

PUBLICATION: London: Heinemann, 26 September 1960. Price 42*s*.

PAGINATION: xiii, [1], 486, [4], 1 leaf of plates, 1 diagram (folding).

CONTRIBUTIONS: Letter of tribute of April 1960, reproduced in facsimile: p. xi. It should also be noted that there are numerous snippets of Churchill conversations, monologues and comments cited *passim*.

NOTE: All copies should possess an errata slip tipped onto p. v.

LOCATIONS: CaOONL, CaOONMC (dj), CaOTTC (dj), RIC (dj), UKBL

REFERENCE: Woods B60.

B168.2 American edition (1960)

The | MEMOIRS | of | General Lord | ISMAY | 19 [publisher's device, 15.4 × 21.6 mm] 60 | NEW YORK : THE VIKING PRESS

PUBLICATION: New York: Viking, 1960.

PAGINATION: [*xvi*], 488, [2], 1 plate, 1 diagram (folding).

CONTRIBUTIONS: As in the first edition (although the volume has been re-set).

NOTE: There is no errata slip in the volume; moreover, the correction called for has not been made on p. 396.

LOCATIONS: CaOHM, CaOTY, RIC, USMH

B168.3 Greenwood Press issue, photo-reproduced from the American edition (1974)

The | MEMOIRS | of | General Lord | ISMAY | [publisher's device, 14.3 × 12 mm] | GREENWOOD PRESS, PUBLISHERS | WESTPORT, CONNECTICUT

PUBLICATION: Westport (CT): Greenwood Press, 1974.

PAGINATION: xv, [1], 488, 1 diagram (folding).

LOCATIONS: CaNSWA, USDLC

B169 GREAT READING FROM LIFE   [1960]

B169.1 First edition (1960)

great | reading | from | [white reversed-out lettering against a deep red rectangle, 22.6 × 44 mm] LIFE | [below the rectangle, black] *A Treasury of the Best Stories and Articles* | *Chosen by the Editors* | [ranged left, deep red, publisher's device, 19.4 × 8.6 mm; ranged right of the device in 2 lines, black] HARPER & BROTHERS PUBLISHERS | NEW YORK

PUBLICATION: New York: Harper, [1960].

PAGINATION: xii, 777, [11].

CONTRIBUTIONS: 'The Battle of Britain': pp. 343–57; 'The Norman Conquest': pp. 527–39. 'The Battle of Britain' was first published in the 28 February 1949 issue of *Life* (**C680c.4**) and 'The Norman Conquest' in the 26 March 1956 issue (**C692a.2**). This is the only volume appearance of these articles. Both were previously incorporated in the texts of *The Second World War* (**A240**) and *A History of the English-Speaking Peoples* (**A267**) in different forms.

LOCATIONS: CaAEU, CaMWU, RIC (dj), USDLC

B169.2   British edition (1962)

great | reading | from | [white reversed-out lettering against a deep red rectangle, 22.6 × 44 mm] LIFE | [below the rectangle, black] *A Treasury of the Best Stories and Articles* | *Chosen by the Editors* | [ranged left, publisher's device, 16.1 mm in diameter; ranged right of the device in 2 lines] JONATHAN CAPE | THIRTY BEDFORD SQUARE LONDON

PUBLICATION: London: Jonathan Cape, 5 November 1962. Price 42*s*.

PAGINATION: xii, 729, [3].

CONTRIBUTIONS: 'The Battle of Britain': pp. 297–311; 'The Norman Conquest': pp. 481–93.

LOCATIONS: CaACU, UKBL, USIU (dj)

B169.3   Second American edition (1987)

Great | Reading | from | [white reversed-out lettering on a black rectangle, as the magazine device, 22.9 × 43.7 mm] LIFE | [below the rectangle, black] *A Treasury of the Best Stories and Articles* | *Chosen by the Editors* | BONANZA BOOKS | New York

PUBLICATION: New York: Bonanza Books, 1987.

PAGINATION: [2], xiv, 729, [7].

CONTRIBUTIONS: 'The Battle of Britain': pp. 297–311; 'The Norman Conquest': pp. 481–93.

LOCATIONS: RIC (dj), USDLC

B170   THE PRINCE CONSORT'S LIBRARY, ALDERSHOT, 1860–1960   1960

[Arms of the Prince Consort, 38.7 × 38 mm] | THE | PRINCE CONSORT'S | LIBRARY | [decorative device, 4.2 × 4.1 mm] | ALDERSHOT | [decorative device, 4.2 × 4.1 mm] | 1860—1960

PUBLICATION: Aldershot: Gale & Polden, 1960.

PAGINATION: 40, 1 leaf of plates. Pamphlet in white card wrappers.

CONTRIBUTION: Churchill's letter of September 1960, reproduced in facsimile, as the Foreword: p. 5.

NOTE: The booklet was published to mark the centenary of the Library. The two catalogues of the book display and the museum display, which may accompany the above history of the Prince Consort's Library, do not contain any original material by Churchill.

LOCATIONS: CaOTTC, RIC, RPH, UKBL, USIU

REFERENCE: Woods B62.

B171   NORTH BORNEO   1960

NORTH BORNEO | BY | K. G. TREGONNING | *LONDON* | HER MAJESTY'S STATIONERY OFFICE | 1960

PUBLICATION: London: HMSO, 18 November 1960. Price 30*s*.

PAGINATION: xiii, [1], 274, 17 leaves of plates, 1 map (folding).

CONTRIBUTION: 'FOREWORD', of September 1956 to the Corona Library, signed in facsimile: p. vii. For other appearances, see 'Note' under **B155**.

LOCATIONS: CaOONL, CaOTMCL, CaOTTC, RIC (dj), RPH (dj), UKBL, USMH

REFERENCE: Woods B61.

B172   THE READER'S DIGEST 40TH ANNIVERSARY TREASURY   1961

[All of the following against a very light bluish green background, white, decorative rule] | [black] THE READER'S DIGEST | 40th | ANNIVERSARY TREASURY | [white, decorative rule] | [black] A selection of outstanding articles, | book condensations and humor | published by The Reader's Digest | during its first 40 years, 1922–1961 | [white, decorative device] | [black] THE READER'S DIGEST ASSOCIATION, INC. | Pleasantville, N.Y.

PUBLICATION: Pleasantville (NY): Reader's Digest Association, 1961.

PAGINATION: 576.

CONTRIBUTION: 'Painting as a Pastime': pp. 88–91. First published in *Reader's Digest* of June 1933 (**C267b**) under the title 'My Adventures with a Paint Brush'.

NOTE: Issued without dust jacket in slipcase.

LOCATIONS: CaOONL, RIC

B173   UNIVERSITY OF BRISTOL APPEAL   1962

[Cover title:] [against a moderate reddish brown background occupying the top 150.3 mm of the cover title, white, the arms of the University, 70.6 × 59.2 mm] | [against a white background, occupying the bottom 93.6 mm of the cover title, moderate reddish brown] UNIVERSITY | OF BRISTOL | APPEAL

PUBLICATION: Bristol: University of Bristol, 1962.

PAGINATION: 24. Pamphlet in coated card wrappers; thickness: 0.25 mm.

CONTRIBUTION: Facsimile letter of 3 August 1962 in support of the Appeal: p. 3.

NOTE: A perfectly complete copy should contain two copies each of Forms A through E plus an envelope pre-addressed to The Hon. Treasurer, the University of Bristol Appeal, folded into the sleeve for the purpose on the inside back wrapper. They are all on watermarked ('WT & Co.') white wove paper; thickness: 0.09 mm. Forms A and B were Deeds of Covenant for use by private donors; Forms C and D were Deeds of Covenant for use by a company; and Form E was for use with a 'cheque/Banker's Order/Cash Value' donation. On each form, there was a detachable 'BANKER'S ORDER'.

LOCATIONS: RIC, UKBrU (with forms)

B174 SILVER JUBILEE SOUVENIR PROGRAMME   1962

PUBLICATION: Woodford?: Borough Council of Wanstead & Woodford, 1962.

PAGINATION: 12. Pamphlet in card wrappers.

CONTRIBUTION: 'A Message from The Member of Parliament For The Woodford Division, The Right Hon. Sir Winston S. Churchill, K.G., O.M., C.H., M.P.': p. 3.

NOTE: The entry is based on a report and a photocopy only. I have been unable to locate a copy of the original pamphlet.

B175 ALFRED NOBEL   1962

ALFRED NOBEL | The man and his work | by | ERIK BERGENGREN | *With a supplement on the Nobel Institutions | and the Nobel Prizes | by | Nils K. Ståhle |* TRANSLATED BY ALAN BLAIR | Thomas Nelson and Sons Ltd | London Edinburgh Paris Melbourne Johannesburg | Toronto and New York

PUBLICATION: London: Nelson, 13 September 1962. Price 30*s.* in the UK and $6.50 in Canada and the United States. Note that the first Swedish edition was published in 1960.

PAGINATION: xviii, 222, 7 leaves of plates.

CONTRIBUTION: In the British edition, there is a Foreword by Dag Hammarskjöld on p. v and one by Churchill on p. vii. There is an excerpt from the Churchill Foreword on the front flap of the dust jacket.

LOCATIONS: CaOONL, CaOTTC (dj), MLW, RIC (dj), RPH (dj), UKBL, USMH

B176 FIJI   1963

FIJI | BY | SIR ALAN BURNS G.C. M.G. | [line-block drawing of a Fijian island, 48.1 × 86 mm] | A Fijian Island | *LONDON* | HER MAJESTY'S STATIONERY OFFICE | 1963

PUBLICATION: London: HMSO (for the Colonial Office), 29 April 1963. Price 30*s.*

PAGINATION: xv, [1], 256, 17 leaves of plates, 1 map (folding).

CONTRIBUTION: 'FOREWORD TO THE CORONA LIBRARY', of September 1956: p. vii. For other appearances, see 'Note' under **B155**.

LOCATIONS: CaOONL, CaOTMCL, RIC (dj), RPH (dj), UKBL, USMH

REFERENCE: Woods B63.

B177 SIR WINSTON S. CHURCHILL: HONORARY CITIZEN OF THE UNITED STATES OF AMERICA   1963

SIR WINSTON S. | CHURCHILL | HONORARY CITIZEN OF | THE UNITED STATES | OF AMERICA BY | ACT OF CONGRESS | APRIL 9, 1963 | *Achille J. St. Onge | Worcester, Massachusetts | 1963*

PUBLICATION: Worcester (MA): Achille J. St. Onge, 1963. A miniature (63.2 × 43.5 mm). There was a second printing in 1964, so identified by the change of date on the title page.

PAGINATION: 30, [2].

CONTRIBUTION: Letter to the President of the United States: pp. 25–30.

NOTE: There were 1000 copies printed in Bembo type on 'Old Kentucky Linen' paper by Joh. Enschedé Zonen, Haarlem, The Netherlands. The second printing consisted of 1500 copies.

LOCATIONS: CaACU, CaOTTC, RIC (1st and 2nd printings)

REFERENCE: Massmann 23 (the first edition) and 23a (the 1964 printing).

B178   MODERN ENGLISH PROSE AND POETRY   1963

MODERN | ENGLISH | PROSE | AND | POETRY | [22.9-mm   swelled   rule] | Nelda B. Kubat | *Lansing High School* | *Ludlowville, New York* | James G. Magill | *Head of the Department of English* | *Lincoln High School* | *Manitowoc, Wisconsin* | The Macmillan Company, New York

PUBLICATION: New York: Macmillan, 1963. Price $1.25.

PAGINATION: xii, 369, [3].

CONTRIBUTION: 'Harrow': pp. 223–31. Previously published in *My Early Life* (**A91**).

LOCATIONS: CaOONL, RIC

B179   COMBAT: WORLD WAR I   1964

COMBAT: | World   War   I | [96.6-mm   rule] | Edited   by   DON   CONGDON | Foreword and Afterword by William Manchester | Introduction by Herbert Mitgang | [publisher's device, 19.7 mm in diameter] | A Delacorte Press Book • Distributed by The Dial Press, New York

PUBLICATION: New York: Delacorte Press, 1964. Price $5.95.

PAGINATION: xix, [1], 426, [2].

CONTRIBUTION: 'The Marne': pp. 18–34 (taken from the Scribner's edition of *The World Crisis*; **A69.1**).

LOCATION: RIC (dj)

B180   ONE HUNDRED YEARS   1964

Buckhurst Hill Cricket and Lacrosse | Club | 1864 [club device, 25.9 mm in diameter] 1964 | [message from Charles S. French, Club President, signed in facsimile] | [message from Churchill signed in facsimile] | Editorial [in 14 lines]

PUBLICATION: No place indicated, Buckhurst Hill Cricket and Lacrosse Club, 1964.

PAGINATION: 80, plus card wrappers.

CONTRIBUTION: Message from Churchill (23 words), a Vice-President of the Buckhurst Hill Cricket and Lacrosse Club, to the Club with his good wishes: p. 1.

LOCATIONS: MLW, RIC, RPH, UKBL

B181 WIE DER ENGLÄNDER SICH UND DIE WELT SIEHT 1965

B181.1 First (German) edition (1965)

Wie der | Engländer sich und | die Welt sieht | 49 Meisteressays | herausgegeben und über stezt von | Katherine Feldberg | Vorwort von Hilde Spiel | Nymphenburger Verlagshandlung

PUBLICATION: Munich: Nymphenburger Verlagshandlung, 1965.

PAGINATION: 384.

CONTRIBUTION: 'Moses, der Führer eines Volkes': pp. 81–95. The translation of 'Moses: The Leader of a People', which was first published in the *Sunday Chronicle* of 8 November 1931 (**C370**) and subsequently collected in *Thoughts and Adventures* (**A95**), at pp. 283–94.

LOCATIONS: CaOTU, RIC (dj)

B181.2 Second (American) edition (1970)

Of Men and Manners: | The Englishman | and His | World | *Essays Compiled by Katherine Feldberg* | [publisher's device, 11.8 × 10.4 mm] | UNIVERSITY OF MIAMI PRESS | *Coral Gables, Florida*

PUBLICATION: Coral Gables (FA): University of Miami Press, 1970. Price $10.00.

PAGINATION: xv, [1], 240.

CONTRIBUTION: 'Moses, the Leader of a People': pp. 43–52.

LOCATIONS: CaOOCC, CaQMM, RIC (dj), UKBL, USDLC

B181/1 HOW TO LIVE WITH LIFE 1965

[(Light) greyish olive green] HOW | TO LIVE | WITH | LIFE | [black] *Introductions by Arthur Gordon* | [(light) greyish olive green] THE READER'S DIGEST ASSOCIATION, | PLEASANTVILLE, NEW YORK | THE READER'S DIGEST ASSOCIATION, LTD., | MONTREAL, CANADA

PUBLICATION: Pleasantville (NY): Reader's Digest Association, 1965.

PAGINATION: 576.

CONTRIBUTION: 'My Adventures with a Paintbrush': pp. 332–7. Condensed from *Amid These Storms* (**A95.2**); first published in this condensed form in *Reader's Digest* of June 1933 (**C267b**); and previously collected in *Getting the Most out of Life* (**B101**), under the same title, and subsequently in *The Reader's Digest 40th Anniversary Treasury* (**B172**), under the title 'Painting as a Pastime'.

LOCATIONS: CaOHM, CaOONL, RIC (dj), USDLC

B182   SWAZILAND   1965

SWAZILAND | BY | DUDLEY BARKER | *LONDON* | HER MAJESTY'S STATIONERY OFFICE | 1965

PUBLICATION: London: HMSO (for the Colonial Office), 9 September 1965, 40,000 copies. Price 20*s*.

PAGINATION: xiii, [1], 146, 9 leaves of plates, 1 map (folding).

CONTRIBUTION: 'FOREWORD TO THE CORONA LIBRARY', dated September 1956: p. vii. For other appearances, see 'Note' under **B155**.

LOCATIONS: CaOHM, RIC, RPH (dj), UKBL, USDLC, USMH

REFERENCE: Woods B64.

B183   THE FINE ART OF SPYING   1965

B183.1   First edition (1965)

The | fine | art of [opposite these 3 lines, a line drawing of a person's eye, 21.6 × 31.1 mm] | [below the eye, ranged left] SPYING | Edited by | WALTER B. GIBSON | Illustrated by | CAL SACKS | GROSSET & DUNLAP | Publishers   New York

PUBLICATION: New York: Grosset & Dunlap, 1965. Price $2.95.

PAGINATION: xii, 244.

CONTRIBUTION: 'I Escape from the Boers': pp. 109–25.

LOCATIONS: CaNSH, CaPCU, RIC (dj), USDLC

B183.2   First paperback issue from first-edition plates (1967)

The | fine | art of [opposite these 3 lines, a line drawing of a person's eye, 21.6 × 31.1 mm] | [below the eye, ranged left] SPYING | Edited by | WALTER B. GIBSON | Illustrated by | CAL SACKS | [publisher's device for Tempo Books, 13.6 × 12.8 mm] | GROSSET & DUNLAP | Publishers   New York

PUBLICATION: New York: Tempo Books, April 1967. Price 50¢.

PAGINATION: xi, [1], 244.

LOCATIONS: CaOTMCL, RIC

B184   BASUTOLAND   1966

BASUTOLAND | BY | AUSTIN COATES | *LONDON* | HER MAJESTY'S STATIONERY OFFICE | 1966

PUBLICATION: London: HMSO (for the Colonial Office), 26 January 1966, 40,000 copies. Price 20*s*.

PAGINATION: xiii, [1], 135, [1], 9 leaves of plates, 1 map (folding).

CONTRIBUTION: 'FOREWORD TO THE CORONA LIBRARY', dated September 1956: p. vii. For other appearances, see 'Note' under **B155**.

LOCATIONS: CaOONL, RIC (dj), RPH (dj), UKBL, USDLC, USMH

REFERENCE: Woods B66.

B185 ALFONSO XIII 1966

B185.1 Second edition (1966)

JULIÁN CORTÉS-CAVANILLAS | ALFONSO XIII | *VIDA, CONFESIONES Y MUERTE* | PREFACIO DE | WINSTON S. CHURCHILL | PRÓLOGO DE | J. IGNACIO LUCA DE TENA | [publisher's device, 8.5 × 11.5 mm] | EDITORIAL JUVENTUD, S.A. | PROVENZA, 101 – BARCELONA

PUBLICATION: Barcelona: Juventud, May 1966. Reprinted in June 1973. The first edition of the work, published in Madrid in 1956 and reprinted in 1959 by Prensa Española, does not contain the Churchill Preface.

PAGINATION: 368, 16 leaves of plates.

CONTRIBUTION: Preface, being the chapter on King Alfonso XIII from *Great Contemporaries* (**A105**) (translated into Spanish), used with Churchill's permission, as conveyed by H. T. Sturdee, his Private Secretary, in a letter of 26 January 1951, which is also published here (at p. 5): pp. 7–15.

LOCATIONS: EsNL, FrNL, RIC (2nd printing; dj), UKScNL

B185.2 Third edition (1982)

J. CORTÉS-CAVANILLAS | ALFONSO XIII | VIDA, CONFESIONES Y MUERTE | PREFACIO DE | WINSTON S. CHURCHILL | PRÓLOGO DE | J. IGNACIO LUCA DE TENA | [publisher's device, 9.8 × 12.2 mm] | EDITORIAL JUVENTUD, S.A. | PROVENZA, 101 – BARCELONA

PUBLICATION: Barcelona: Juventud, 1982.

PAGINATION: 478, [2], 12 leaves of plates.

CONTRIBUTION: Preface: pp. 7–17; Sturdee letter: p. 5.

LOCATIONS: CaQMM, EsNL

B185.3 Planeta-DeAgostini issue (1995)

Julián Cortés-Cabanillas | [16.9-mm rule] | ALFONSO XIII | Vida, confesiones | y muerte | PLANETA DᵉAGOSTINI

PUBLICATION: Barcelona: Planeta-DeAgostini, 1995.

LOCATION: EsNL

B186 BECHUANALAND 1966

BECHUANALAND | BY | B. A. YOUNG | *LONDON* | HER MAJESTY'S STATIONERY OFFICE | 1966

PUBLICATION: London: HMSO (for the Commonwealth Office), 16 September 1966. Price 20*s*.

PAGINATION: xv, [1], 128, 9 leaves of plates, 1 map (folding).

CONTRIBUTION: 'FOREWORD TO THE CORONA LIBRARY', dated September 1956: p. vii. For other appearances, see 'Note' under **B155**.

LOCATIONS: CaOONL, RIC (dj), RPH (dj), UKBL, USDLC, USMH

REFERENCE: Woods B65.

B187 WINSTON S. CHURCHILL: YOUTH 1874–1900   1966?

No title page. The sleeve consists of a montage of the July 1900 Spy caricature of Churchill over a background of various facsimile documents included in the portfolio. Ranged lower left, against a moderate to dark blue background, 10.6 × 146.4 mm, white, 'A DOCUMENTS OF HISTORY PORTFOLIO'; ranged right, against a similar background, 152.6 × 168 mm, white, 'WINSTON S. | CHURCHILL | YOUTH • 1874–1900' | within a single-rule frame, enclosing 24.8 × 158 mm, 'BASED UPON RANDOLPH S. CHURCHILL'S BOOK | "WINSTON S. CHURCHILL" ' | below the frame, 'A GINIGER PORTFOLIO | PUBLISHED IN ASSOCIATION WITH | UNIVERSITY MICROFILMS, INC. | A SUBSIDIARY OF XEROX CORPORATION'.

PUBLICATION: New York: University Microfilms, 1966?. The pack contains 16 documents: a 16-page booklet bearing the same title and 15 facsimile documents. Price $3.95.

CONTRIBUTIONS: All in facsimile. Document 7: a 4-page letter, probably written in 1889, to Lady Randolph Churchill, imploring her to visit him at Harrow; Document 10: p. 4 of the *Daily Graphic* of 27 December 1895, being the fourth of Churchill's contributions on the Spanish–American War (**C1.4**); Document 12: Field Despatch, No. 1, of 2 September 1898, from Lieutenant Winston Churchill to the Sirdar, Sir Herbert Kitchener, "near Omdurman". There is also an additional unnumbered Field Despatch from Churchill to his commanding officer, Colonel Martin, detailing some of what he had sent to the Sirdar. There is additional Churchill material quoted in the accompanying pamphlet.

LOCATIONS: CaOTTC, RIC

B188 WINSTON S. CHURCHILL: YOUNG STATESMAN 1900–1914   1967?

No title page. The sleeve consists of a montage of the various facsimile documents included in the portfolio. Ranged lower left, against a dark greyish olive background, 10.6 × 146.4 mm, white, 'A DOCUMENTS OF HISTORY PORTFOLIO'; ranged upper right, against a similar background, 152.6 × 168 mm, white, 'WINSTON S. | CHURCHILL | YOUNG STATESMAN 1900–1914' | within a single-rule frame, enclosing 24.8 × 158 mm, 'BASED UPON RANDOLPH S. CHURCHILL'S BOOK | "WINSTON S. CHURCHILL" ' | below the frame, 'A GINIGER PORTFOLIO | PUBLISHED IN ASSOCIATION WITH | UNIVERSITY MICROFILMS LIBRARY SERVICES | XEROX'.

PUBLICATION: New York: University Microfilms, 1967?. The pack contains 22 documents: a 16-page booklet bearing the same title, 20 facsimile documents and an order form for this portfolio and **B187**. Price $3.95.

CONTRIBUTIONS: All in facsimile. Document 3: letter of 14 February 1901 to Lady Randolph Churchill; Document 6: Churchill's first letter (of 16 April 1908) to Clementine Hozier; Document 7: Churchill's letter to Clementine on the morning following their engagement; Documents 14 and 15: exchange of notes in Cabinet meeting between Churchill and Lloyd George regarding the Naval Estimates. There is additional Churchill material quoted in the accompanying pamphlet.

LOCATIONS: CaOTTC, RIC

B189   THE ARTS OF SPORT AND RECREATION   1967

Compiled and edited by | DEREK STANFORD | [95.3-mm rule] | *The Arts* | *of Sport and Recreation* | [line drawing of a scuba diver and fish, 49.1 × 50.8 mm] | NELSON

PUBLICATION: London: Nelson, May 1967. Price 8*s*.

PAGINATION: x, 230.

CONTRIBUTION: 'Starting at Forty', excerpt from *Painting as a Pastime* (**A242**): pp. 110–19.

LOCATIONS: CaOOCC, RIC, UKBL, USDLC

B190   BRITISH HONDURAS   1968

BRITISH HONDURAS | BY | A. R. GREGG | *LONDON* | HER MAJESTY'S STATIONERY OFFICE | 1968

PUBLICATION: London: HMSO, 1968, 40,000 copies. Price 20*s*.

PAGINATION: xi, [1], 158, [2], 5 leaves of plates, 1 map (folding).

CONTRIBUTION: 'FOREWORD TO THE CORONA LIBRARY', dated Chartwell, September 1956: p. vii. For other appearances, see 'Note' under **B155**.

LOCATIONS: CaOHM, CaOWTL, RIC (dj), UKBL, USDLC, USMH

B191   WINSTON CHURCHILL   1969

No title page. The sleeve flap shows the title 'WINSTON | CHURCHILL' in large outline letters with a brilliant yellow centre, ranged left, and a picture of Churchill in 1918, ranged right, over the background of what appears to be the Churchill entry in *Who's Who*. Below the flap, ranged left, 'compiled by | MARTIN GILBERT | *Jackdaw Publications Founded and distributed by Jonathan Cape* | *Thirty Bedford Square London, W.C.1*'.

PUBLICATION: London: Jonathan Cape, 1969. This is Jackdaw Publication No. 31. It contains 17 documents: a folded leaflet describing the contents of the document pack and facsimile documents numbered 1 to 13, the last of which consists of four broadsheets by Gilbert on different periods of Churchill's life.

CONTRIBUTIONS: All in facsimile. Document 1: 'How I Escaped from Pretoria' (the 30 December 1899 article in *Pearson's Illustrated War News*; **C83d**); Document 2: manuscript letter of 10 April 1908 to Prime Minister H. H. Asquith accepting his offer of the Board of Trade; Document 4: typed note of 12 June 1914 to the Committee of Imperial Defence entitled 'Channel Tunnel'; Document 6: *Beating the Invader* (**B76.1**); Document 8: telegram to the editor of the *New Republic* on the death of President Franklin D. Roosevelt on 12 April 1945 (**B99**); Document 11: extracts from eight speeches given between 1901 and 1941.

This is the only published appearance of Document 4 and the first appearance in volume form of Document 1, of Document 2 in facsimile (see Gilbert, *WSC*, Vol. III, *C.V.* 2, pp. 765–6, for the transcribed text) and of Document 8.

LOCATION: RIC

B192   GREAT UNTOLD STORIES OF FANTASY AND HORROR   1969

GREAT UNTOLD STORIES OF | FANTASY AND HORROR | [ranged right] *Edited by* | ALDEN H. NORTON | *and* SAM MOSKOWITZ | [centred] *With notes by Sam Moskowitz* | [ranged right] ▲ *PYRAMID BOOKS • NEW YORK*

PUBLICATION: New York: Pyramid, October 1969. Price 75¢. There was a second printing in January and a third in November 1970.

PAGINATION: 222. Perfect-bound in card wrappers.

CONTRIBUTION: 'Man Overboard!': pp. 164–7. This is the first volume appearance of Churchill's only short story, which was first published in *Harmsworth Magazine* (**C72a**) and subsequently collected in *The Lucifer Society* (**B195**) and *The Arbor House Treasury of Horror and the Supernatural* (**B203**).

LOCATIONS: CaNBSU, RIC (1st and 3rd printings)

B193   THE LIBERTY YEARS   1969

THE   Liberty | YEARS | 1924–1950 | *AN   ANTHOLOGY* | Edited   and   with Commentary by | ALLEN CHURCHILL | *PRENTICE-HALL, INC. Englewood Cliffs, New Jersey*

PUBLICATION: Englewood Cliffs, NJ: Prentice-Hall, late 1969. Price $15.95.

PAGINATION: [*12*], 435 [numbered 1–427; there are four unnumbered leaves following pages 98, 204, 254 and 378], [1], 6 leaves of plates.

CONTRIBUTION: 'Will Americans and the English Ever Understand Each Other?': pp. 118–21. First published in *Liberty* (**C355**). This is the only volume appearance of the article.

LOCATIONS: CaOH, CaOOU, CaOTY, RIC (dj), USDLC

B194   NOBEL PRIZE LIBRARY   1971

Nobel Prize Library | PUBLISHED UNDER THE SPONSORSHIP OF THE | NOBEL FOUNDATION & THE SWEDISH ACADEMY | [103.2-mm swelled rule] | *Albert Camus* | *Winston Churchill* | [103.2-mm swelled rule] | ALEXIS GREGORY, *New York*, AND | CRM PUBLISHING, *Del Mar, California*

PUBLICATION: New York and Del Mar (CA): Alexis Gregory and CRM Publishing, 1971.

PAGINATION: [*6*], 409, [1], 4 leaves of plates, 4 maps.

CONTRIBUTIONS: Acceptance speech read by Lady Churchill: pp. 183–4; excerpt from *My Early Life* (**A91**, Chapters XXI and XXII, 'I Escape from the Boers'): pp. 185–200; and *The Island Race* (**A275**), pp. 202–390.

LOCATIONS: CaOHM, CaOTTC, CaQMM, RIC, USDLC, USMnCaE

B195   THE LUCIFER SOCIETY   1972

The Lucifer Society | Edited by | PETER HAINING | Foreword by | KINGSLEY AMIS | W. H. ALLEN | LONDON AND NEW YORK | *A Division of Howard and Wyndham Ltd* | 1972

PUBLICATION: London: W. H. Allen, 1972. Price £2.50.

PAGINATION: 256.

CONTRIBUTION: 'Man Overboard': pp. 19–22. First collected in *Great Untold Stories of Fantasy and Horror* (**B192**) and subsequently in *The Arbor House Treasury of Horror and the Supernatural* (**B203**).

LOCATIONS: CaOTMCL, RIC (dj), UKBL, USDLC, USMH

B196   READER'S DIGEST 50TH ANNIVERSARY
   TREASURY   1972

[Strong reddish brown, triangle of decorative devices above a 68-mm rule] | [black] READER'S DIGEST | *50th Anniversary Treasury* | [strong reddish brown, decorative device] | [black] *A selection of the best of 50 years* | *from The Reader's Digest* | [strong reddish brown, a reversed triangle of decorative devices below a 68-mm rule] | [black] THE READER'S DIGEST ASSOCIATION, INC. | PLEASANTVILLE, NEW YORK

PUBLICATION: Pleasantville (NY): Reader's Digest, 1972. There was at least one additional printing.

PAGINATION: 647, [1].

CONTRIBUTION: 'A Troublesome Boy': pp. 448–52. First published in this form in the August 1949 issue of *Reader's Digest* (**C681**).

LOCATIONS: RIC, USDLC

B197   EUROTUNNEL   1973

B197.1   First edition (1973)

[Title spread across 2 pages; dark greenish blue] EUROTUNNEL | [on right-hand page] An Illustrated History of the Channel Tunnel Scheme | Peter Haining | [on left-hand page, depiction of old-fashioned trains passing in a tunnel, 123.9 mm in diameter] | [on right-hand page, publisher's device, 15.9 × 11.5 mm] | NEW ENGLISH LIBRARY

PUBLICATION: London: New English Library, 1973.

PAGINATION: 144.

CONTRIBUTION: 'Why Not a Channel Tunnel?': pp. 98–100. First volume appearance; first published in the *Daily Mail* on 12 February 1936 (**C488**).

LOCATIONS: CaOHM, CaOOM, RIC, UKBL, USDLC, USMH

B197.2   First paperback issue (1989)

EUROTUNNEL | by | Peter Haining | [all of the following within a single-rule box, enclosing 26.5 × 118.9 mm] First published 1973 | Reprinted unabridged in 1989 from the original version | © The Channel Tunnel Group Limited

PUBLICATION: London: Channel Tunnel Group, 1989.

NOTE: A modified black-and-white version of the original title pages is retained at pp. 3–4.

LOCATIONS: CaOLU, RIC, UKBL

B198   ZIONISM: A BASIC READER   1975

ZIONISM | A Basic Reader | Edited by Mordecai S. Chertoff | Herzl Press | New York

PUBLICATION: New York: Herzl Press, 1975. Appears to have been published in two printings, although no copy of a first printing has been reported to me.

PAGINATION: [2], ii, 92.

CONTRIBUTION: 'Fairness to Arab and Jew': pp. 47–8 (taken from Churchill's speech of 23 May 1939 in the House of Commons).

LOCATIONS: CaMWU, CaQMM, RIC, USDLC, USMH

B199   THE FIRST CUCKOO   1976

B199.1   First edition (1976)

THE FIRST | CUCKOO | *A selection of the most witty* | *amusing and memorable letters to* | THE TIMES | 1900–1975 | CHOSEN AND INTRODUCED | BY | KENNETH GREGORY | *London* | TIMES BOOKS | [74.8-mm rule] | GEORGE ALLEN & UNWIN LTD

PUBLICATION: London: Allen and Unwin/Methuen, April 1976. Price £5.50. Reprinted four times, in 1976, 1977, 1978 and 1980.

PAGINATION: 350, [2].

CONTRIBUTION: Letter of 8 July 1902 re flogging under the subject heading 'Sandhurst Punishments': p. 41. First published in *The Times* of 9 July 1902 (**G44**) and subsequently collected in R. Churchill, *WSC*, Vol. II, *C.V.* 2, at pp. 153–4.

NOTE: There are no Churchill contributions to Kenneth Gregory's next selection of letters to *The Times*, entitled *The Second Cuckoo* (London: George Allen & Unwin, 1983, and in paperback, London: Unwin, 1984), or to *The Third Cuckoo* (London: Allen & Unwin, 1985), later published as *The Next to Last Cuckoo* (Pleasantville, NY: Akadine Press, 1997). For the Churchill contribution in *The Last Cuckoo*, see **B205**.

LOCATIONS: CaOOCC (2nd printing), CaQMG, RIC (dj), UKBL, USDLC, USMH

B199.2.a   Canadian issue of British sheets, first printing (1976)

YOUR | OBEDIENT | SERVANT | *A selection of the most witty, amusing* | *and memorable letters to* | THE TIMES OF LONDON | 1900—1975 | *chosen and introduced by Kenneth Gregory* | *with a Foreword by Bernard Levin* | *and a Preface by Geoffrey Woolley* | METHUEN/Two Continents | Toronto New York London Sydney Wellington

PUBLICATION: Agincourt (Ont.): Methuen/Two Continents, 1976. Price $10.00.

PAGINATION: 350, [2].

CONTRIBUTION: As the first edition.

LOCATIONS: CaOHM, CaOONL, CaQMM, RIC (dj)

B199.2.b   Canadian issue from British plates, second printing (1977)

YOUR | OBEDIENT | SERVANT | *A selection of the most witty, amusing* | *and memorable letters to* | THE TIMES OF LONDON | 1900—1975 | *chosen and introduced by Kenneth Gregory* | *with a Foreword by Bernard Levin* | *and a Preface by Geoffrey Woolley* | METHUEN | Toronto New York London Sydney Wellington

PUBLICATION: Agincourt (Ont.): Methuen, 1976. Printed in the United States rather than Great Britain.

NOTE: Distinguished from the first printing by the deletion of 'Two Continents' as co-publisher on the title page and the copyright page, the re-setting of the copyright page in smaller type, the elimination of a New York address for Methuen on the copyright page, the elimination of the New York ISBN and the substitution of a printing line indicating that the current printing was done in the United States rather than Great Britain. Despite the reference to first publication at the top of the copyright page, the publication line omits the '1' and '76', indicating that this was the second printing and was accomplished in 1977.

LOCATION: RIC (dj)

B199.3   Book Club issue from first-edition sheets (1977)

THE FIRST | CUCKOO | *A selection of the most witty* | *amusing amd memorable letters to* | THE TIMES | 1900–1975 | CHOSEN AND INTRODUCED | BY | KENNETH GREGORY | BOOK CLUB ASSOCIATES LONDON

PUBLICATION: London: Book Club Associates, 1977.

LOCATION: RIC (dj)

B199.4   First paperback issue (1978)

[Ranged left] The First | Cuckoo | *A selection of the most witty* | *amusing and memorable letters to* | THE TIMES | since 1900 | CHOSEN AND INTRODUCED BY | KENNETH GREGORY | London | UNWIN PAPERBACKS | Boston   Sydney | in association with TIMES BOOKS

PUBLICATION: London: Unwin Paperbacks, 1978. Price £2.50. Reprinted four times.

PAGINATION: 350, [2].

LOCATIONS: RIC (4th printing), UKBL

B199.5   Second British edition (1981)

THE FIRST | CUCKOO | [publisher's device of *The Times*, 14.2 × 70.8 mm] | *A selection of the most witty,* | *amusing and memorable letters to* | THE TIMES | 1900–1980 | Chosen and introduced | by | KENNETH GREGORY | TIMES BOOKS | [74.8-mm rule] | GEORGE ALLEN & UNWIN LTD

PUBLICATION: London: Times Books/Allen and Unwin, 1981. Price £7.95. There was a second printing in 1982.

PAGINATION: 369, [1].

LOCATIONS: RIC (2nd printing; dj), UKBL, USDLC (2nd printing), USMH

B199.6   Second paperback issue from second-edition plates (1983)

THE FIRST | CUCKOO | [publisher's device of *The Times*, 9 × 71 mm] | *A selection of the most witty,* | *amusing and memorable letters to* | THE TIMES | 1900–1980 | chosen and introduced | by | KENNETH   GREGORY | London | UNWIN   PAPERBACKS | Boston   Sydney | in association with | TIMES BOOKS

PUBLICATION: London: Unwin Paperbacks, 1983. Price £2.95.

PAGINATION: [4], 359, [1], 4-page catalogue.

CONTRIBUTION: Churchill letter: p. 40.

LOCATION: RIC

B199.7   First American issue from first-edition plates (1997)

THE FIRST | CUCKOO | *A selection of the most witty* | *amusing and memorable letters to* | THE TIMES | 1900–1975 | CHOSEN AND INTRODUCED | BY | KENNETH GREGORY | *Chosen and Introduced by Kenneth Gregory* | [publisher's device, 12.3 × 10.5 mm] | The Akadine Press | 1997

PUBLICATION: Pleasantville, NY: Akadine, September 1997. Price $15.95.

PAGINATION: 350, [2].

CONTRIBUTION: Churchill letter: p. 41.

LOCATION: RIC

B200   TRUE STORIES OF GREAT ESCAPES   1977

[All of the following over a (very) light grey background, within a single-rule box, enclosing 199.5 × 121.1 mm] Reader's Digest | TRUE STORIES OF | [strong purplish red] Great Escapes [black, half-tone figure of a man escaping] THE READER'S DIGEST ASSOCIATION, INC. | Pleasantville, New York/Montreal

PUBLICATION: Pleasantville (NY) and Montreal: Reader's Digest, 1977. There was a second printing in 1982.

PAGINATION: 608.

CONTRIBUTION: 'My Escape': pp. 347–62; letter of 11 December 1899 to Minister De Souza: p. 362. This is an excerpt from the condensation of the second American issue of *A Roving Commission* (**A91.5.a**), which ran in *Reader's Digest* (**C658**), at pp. 176–89. The version of the letter is that published in *In Search of South Africa* (with minor differences; see **F78**), not that of *London to Ladysmith*.

LOCATIONS: CaNSH, CaOONL, RIC, USDLC

B201   ADVENTURE STORIES FOR BOYS   1978

Adventure Stories | for Boys | Edited by | John Canning | [publisher's device, 16.3 × 35.4 mm]

PUBLICATION: London: Octopus, September 1978. Price £1.99. Reprinted at least five more times, in 1979, 1980, 1981, 1982 and 1983.

PAGINATION: 400.

CONTRIBUTION: 'I Escape from the Boers': pp. 74–84.

LOCATIONS: CaAEU, RIC (dj), UKBL

B202   THE WORLD'S GREATEST HORSE STORIES   1979

[Within a fancy single-rule box, enclosing 51.2 × 106.3 mm] *The World's Greatest* | *Horse Stories* | Edited by J. N. P. Watson | [below the box, thin–thick 35.3-mm rule] | PADDINGTON | PRESS LTD | [thick–thin 35.3-mm rule] | NEW YORK & LONDON

PUBLICATION: New York: Paddington, 1979.

PAGINATION: 336.

CONTRIBUTIONS: 'An Officer in Riding School': pp. 132–3; 'A Charge by the Lancers': pp. 135–8; and 'India and the Indispensability of the Game': pp. 257–8. Each of the chapters has been excerpted from *My Early Life* (**A91**).

LOCATIONS: CaOL, RIC (dj), UKBL, USDLC

B203   THE ARBOR HOUSE TREASURY OF HORROR
AND THE SUPERNATURAL   1981

B203.1   First edition, first issue (1981)

THE | ARBOR HOUSE TREASURY | OF | HORROR | AND THE | SUPER- | NATURAL | [113.7-mm rule] | Compiled by BILL PRONZINI, | BARRY N. MALZBERG | and MARTIN H. GREENBERG | With an Introduction by STEPHEN KING | [publisher's device, 14.5 × 12.6 mm] | ARBOR HOUSE *New York*

PUBLICATION: New York: Arbor House, 1981. Price $19.95.

PAGINATION: 599, [1].

CONTRIBUTION: 'Man Overboard!': pp. 135–8. First published in periodical form in *Harmsworth Magazine* (**C72a**). Previously collected in volume form in *Great Untold Stories of Fantasy and Horror* (**B192**) and *The Lucifer Society* (**B195**). Subsequently collected in *Demonic, Dangerous and Deadly* (**B204**).

LOCATIONS: CaOL, CaOTMCL, RIC (dj), USDLC

B203.2   Second (Castle) issue (1985)

GREAT TALES OF | HORROR & [a single-rule frame runs horizontally to the left of the word 'HORROR' and to the right of the ampersand, then vertically on both sides to the fifth following line, at which point it runs horizontally from right and left to the words 'Compiled by'] | THE | SUPERNATURAL | *Introduction by* | STEPHEN KING | *Compiled by*

| BILL PRONZINI, BARRY N. MALZBERG | & MARTIN H. GREENBERG | CASTLE

PUBLICATION: New York: Castle, 1985.

PAGINATION: 597, [11]. The change in pagination results from the dropping of Arthur Samuels's 'Mass without Voices' (formerly pp. 548–9).

CONTRIBUTION: 'Man Overboard!': pp. 135–8.

LOCATION: RIC (dj)

B203.3.a   Third (Galahad) issue, first printing (1988)

GREAT TALES OF | HORROR & [a single-rule frame runs horizontally to the left of the word 'HORROR' and to the right of the ampersand, then vertically on both sides to the fifth following line, at which point it runs horizontally from right and left to the words '*Compiled by*'] | THE | SUPERNATURAL | *Introduction by* | STEPHEN KING | *Compiled by* | BILL PRONZINI, BARRY N. MALZBERG | & MARTIN H. GREENBERG | [publisher's device, 17.3 mm in diameter]

PAGINATION: As **B203.2**.

PUBLICATION: New York: Galahad, 1988.

LOCATION: RIC (dj)

B203.3.b   Third (Galahad) issue, second printing (1994)

GREAT TALES OF | HORROR & | THE | SUPERNATURAL | *Introduction by* | STEPHEN KING | *Compiled by* | BILL PRONZINI, BARRY N. MALZBERG | & MARTIN H. GREENBERG | [publisher's device, 17.7 mm in diameter]

PUBLICATION: New York: Galahad Books, 1994.

LOCATION: RIC (dj)

B204   DEMONIC, DANGEROUS AND DEADLY   1983

B204.1   First edition (1983)

[60-mm decorative rule] | DEMONIC, | DANGEROUS | & DEADLY | [60-mm decorative rule] | AN ANTHOLOGY CHOSEN BY | HELEN HOKE | J. M. Dent & Sons Limited | LONDON   MELBOURNE   TORONTO

PUBLICATION: London: Dent, March 1983. Price £6.50.

PAGINATION: xiii, [1], 143, [3].

CONTRIBUTION: 'Man Overboard!': pp. 107–10. First published in periodical form in *Harmsworth Magazine* (**C72a**) and previously collected in volume form in *Great Untold Stories of Fantasy and Horror* (**B192**), *The Lucifer Society* (**B195**) and *The Arbor House Treasury of Horror and the Supernatural* (**B203**).

LOCATIONS: RIC (dj), UKBL

B204.2   American issue (1983)

[60-mm decorative rule] | DEMONIC, | DANGEROUS | & DEADLY | [60-mm decorative rule] | AN ANTHOLOGY BY | HELEN HOKE | LODESTAR BOOKS | E. P. DUTTON   NEW YORK

PUBLICATION: New York: Lodestar/Dutton, 1983.

PAGINATION: xiii, [1], 143, [3].

CONTRIBUTION: 'Man Overboard!': pp. 107–10.

LOCATIONS: CaOGWE, CaOKQ, USDLC

B205 THE LAST CUCKOO 1987

B205.1 First edition (1987)

THE LAST | CUCKOO | [publisher's device, 13.8 × 71.2 mm] | *The very best letters to* | THE TIMES | since 1900 | Chosen and introduced | by | KENNETH GREGORY | UNWIN HYMAN | London   Sydney

PUBLICATION: London: Unwin Hyman, September 1987. Price £10.95.

PAGINATION: viii, 343, [1].

CONTRIBUTION: 'Sandhurst Punishment', letter of 9 July 1902: p. 303.

LOCATIONS: CaOOC, CaQMM, UKBL, UKScNL, USDeU, USMH

B205.2 First paperback issue (1988)

PUBLICATION: London: Unwin Hyman, 1988.

LOCATIONS: CaOL, CaOTU, UKBL

B205.3 First American issue (1996)

THE LAST | CUCKOO | [publisher's device, 14.1 × 71 mm] | THE VERY BEST LETTERS TO | THE TIMES SINCE 1900 | *Chosen and introduced by Kenneth Gregory* | *Foreword by Bernard Levin* | AKADINE

PUBLICATION: Pleasantville, NY: Akadine, February 1996. Price $15.95.

LOCATION: RIC

B206 MASTERPIECES OF TERROR AND THE UNKNOWN 1993

B206.1 First edition (1993)

[Title across two pages] [on the left-hand page] Masterpieces [on the right-hand page] of Terror | and the Unknown | [running across both pages, a thick double rule] | [on the left-hand page, a skull with a small handle to lift off the top, revealing a clock; on the right-hand page] Selected by Marvin Kaye | St. Martin's Press | New York

PUBLICATION: New York: St. Martin's Press, 1993. Price $24.95 ($34.99 in Canada).

PAGINATION: [2], xvii, [1], 573, [7].

CONTRIBUTION: 'Man Overboard': pp. 223–6.

LOCATION: RIC (dj)

B206.2 First edition, second (book club) issue (1993)

[Title across two pages] [on the left-hand page] Masterpieces [on the right-hand page] of Terror | and the Unknown | [running across both pages, a thick double rule] | [on the left-hand page, a skull with a small handle to lift off the top, revealing a clock; on the right-hand page] Selected by Marvin Kaye | [GUILDAMERICA BOOKS publisher's device, 19.1 × 47 mm] | DOUBLEDAY BOOK & MUSIC CLUBS | Garden City, New York

PUBLICATION: Garden City: Guild America Books, 1993.

LOCATIONS: CaBVA, CaNSH, CaOOC, RIC (dj)

B207 THE NEW REPUBLIC READER   1994

B207.1 First edition (1994)

The | *New Republic* | *Reader* | [98.1-mm French rule] | EIGHTY YEARS OF OPINION | AND DEBATE | *Edited by* | DOROTHY WICKENDEN | [publisher's device, 16.4 × 15.8 mm] | A New Republic Book | BasicBooks | *A Division of* HarperCollins *Publishers*

PUBLICATION: New York: New Republic, 1994. Price $28.00.

PAGINATION: ix, [1], 518.

CONTRIBUTION: 'On Roosevelt', cable to the Press Managing Editor of the *New Republic*, in facsimile: p. 60. First published in the *New Republic* of 15 April 1946 (**G889**) and collected in *Roosevelt: A First Appraisal of Those Who Knew Him* (**B99**) and the Jackdaw *Winston Churchill* (**B191**).

LOCATIONS: CaNSH, CaOOC, RIC (dj), UKBL, USDLC, USMH

B207.2 Paperback issue (1995?)

The | *New Republic* | *Reader* | [98.1-mm French rule] | EIGHTY YEARS OF OPINION | AND DEBATE | *Edited by* | DOROTHY WICKENDEN | [publisher's device, 16.4 × 15.8 mm] | A New Republic Book | BasicBooks | *A Division of* HarperCollins *Publishers*

PUBLICATION: 1995? Price $16.00.

PAGINATION: ix, [1], 518.

LOCATION: RIC

B208 ESCAPE: AN ANTHOLOGY   1996

Escape | AN ANTHOLOGY | EDITED AND INTRODUCED BY | MICHAEL MASON | CHATTO & WINDUS | LONDON

PUBLICATION: London: Chatto & Windus, 1996. Price £16.99.

PAGINATION: xi, [1], 366, [6].

CONTRIBUTION: 'Latin Gibberish', excerpt from *London to Ladysmith via Pretoria* (**A4**, pp. 181–9), describing Churchill's escape from the State Model Schools: pp. 148–51.

LOCATIONS: RIC (dj), UKBL

B209 CHURCHILL: THE WAR LEADER   1998

No title page. The sleeve consists of a head-only photograph of Churchill, taken during the war, over a copy of Document 10, and bears the title 'Churchill | The War Leader | 1940–1945'.

PUBLICATION: London: published June 1998 jointly by the Public Record Office, the Imperial War Museum and the Churchill College Archives, 6000 copies. Price £12.99. The document pack contains 15 documents: a 20-page booklet entitled *Churchill: The War Leader, 1940–1945*, which summarizes the period and the documentation chosen, 13 facsimile documents, and a marketing evaluation form for the PRO.

CONTRIBUTIONS: All in facsimile. Document 3: speech of 20 August 1940 (**A131**); Document 7: telegram of 21 August 1942 to Deputy Prime Minister Clement Attlee; Document 10: minute of 28 March 1945 to General Ismay for the Chiefs of Staff on Allied bombing policy; Document 11: telegram of 31 March to General Eisenhower on the desirability of taking Berlin; Document 13: statement of resignation from office of 26 July 1945.

This is the only published appearance of Document 10 in its original form, and the first appearance in volume form of Document 3 from Hansard in facsimile, of Document 7 in facsimile (see *Second World War*, Vol. IV, pp. 465–7, for the transcribed text), of Document 11 in facsimile (see *Second World War*, Vol. VI, pp. 405–6, for the transcribed text), and of Document 13 in facsimile (see *Second World War*, Vol. VI, p. 584, for the transcribed text).

LOCATIONS: CB, RIC, UKBL

B210 PAINTING AS A PASTIME   1998

PAINTING AS A PASTIME | Winston Churchill – his life as a painter | On exhibition at | Sotheby's, 34–35 New Bond Street, London W1A 2AA | 5th–17th January 1998 | Monday to Friday: 9.30 am to 4.30 pm | Weekends: 12 noon to 4 pm | SOTHEBY'S

PUBLICATION: London: Sotheby's, 5 January 1998, 500 copies cased, 3000 in card wrappers. Price £28 cased, £17 in card wrappers.

PAGINATION: 200.

CONTRIBUTIONS: 'The Academy Reveals Britain's Gaiety': pp. 44–5, 47; 'This Year's Royal Academy Is Exhilarating': pp. 47–9; and 'Painting as a Pastime': pp. 51–63. Each was previously published in periodical form and collected in volume form. The Royal Academy articles were published in the *Daily Mail* of 7 May 1932 (**C378**) and 16 May 1934 (**C434**). Both were collected in *The Collected Essays* (**A286**). 'Painting as a Pastime' first appeared in the *Strand Magazine* in December 1921 and January 1922 (**C267a.1** and **C267a.2**) and was collected in *Thoughts and Adventures* (**A95**) subsequently and published separately (**A242**).

LOCATION: RIC

B211 SUDAN: THE RECONQUEST REAPPRAISED   1998

SUDAN | *The Reconquest Reappraised* | Edited by | EDWARD M. SPIERS | *University of Leeds* | [publisher's device] | FRANK CASS | LONDON • PORTLAND, OR

PUBLICATION: London and Portland (OR): Frank Cass, September 1998. Price £37.50 cased and £17.50 as a trade paperback.

PAGINATION: xiv, 269, [5], 4 leaves of plates.

CONTRIBUTIONS: Excerpts from letters to Oliver Borthwick of 10 August 1898 and of 16 September: pp. 224–5, 225; excised paragraphs from published letters to the *Morning*

Post: first letter (of 8 August): p. 226; eighth letter (of 6 September): p. 226; and fifteenth letter (of 20 September): p. 227; facsimile of entire eleventh letter (of 10 September): pp. 230–45.

LOCATIONS: CaOHM, CaOTY (trade paperback), CaQMM, RIC (dj), UKBL, USDLC, USMH

B212   BATTLEFRONT: D-DAY   1999

No title page. The sleeve consists of a montage of documents from the pack in full colour, over which, white, ' *'The hour of your liberation is approaching'* – *General Dwight D. Eisenhower, SHAEF* | BATTLEFRONT: *D-DAY* '.

PUBLICATION: Richmond (Surrey): Public Record Office, May 1999, 5000 copies. Price £9.99. The pack contains 14 documents: a 4-page folded leaflet entitled *Battlefront: D-Day*, which summarizes the events and the documentation chosen, 12 facsimile documents, and a list of military titles available from the PRO.

CONTRIBUTION: In facsimile, Document [10—not numbered; in the order of packing]: telegram of 14 June 1944 from Churchill to President Roosevelt [mistakenly described as 18 June on the back of the sleeve].

LOCATIONS: RIC, UKBL

ADDENDUM TO SECTION B

B1/1   HOW I KILLED THE TIGER   1902

HOW I KILLED | THE TIGER | BEING | AN ACCOUNT OF MY | ENCOUNTER WITH A ROYAL | BENGAL TIGER | WITH AN APPENDIX CONTAINING SOME | GENERAL INFORMATION ABOUT INDIA. | BY | LIEUT.-COLONEL FRANK SHEFFIELD | *Commanding 1st Cadet Battalion The Royal Fusiliers* | *(City of London Regiment).* | [8.4-mm rule] | SECOND EDITION. | [8.4-mm rule] | [the Tudor crown, 23.7 × 23.4 mm] | PRINTED CORONATION YEAR, A.D. 1902. | PUBLISHED FOR THE AUTHOR, TO WHOM ALL COMMUNICATIONS MAY BE | ADDRESSED. | [ranged left] HEAD QUARTERS— | [centred] 1ST CADET BATTALION, THE ROYAL FUSILIERS, | (CITY OF LONDON REGIMENT) | [ranged right] POND STREET, HAMPSTEAD, N.W [*sic*, no point] | [ranged left] *ALL RIGHTS RESERVED*.

PUBLICATION: London: Frank Sheffield, 1902. It is only the second edition which includes the letter from Churchill.

PAGINATION: xi, [1], 114, [2], 26 leaves of plates.

CONTRIBUTION: Letter of 21 October to Lieut.-Col. Sheffield regarding the first edition of the book: p. 106.

LOCATIONS: CaOTU, RIC, UKBL

SECTION C

Articles, Reviews and News Reports from War Zones in Serial Publications

This section contains all articles, reviews and news reports from war zones in newspapers, magazines, and other periodical publications, appearing no less frequently than quarterly. It includes first and subsequent appearances of contributions by Churchill, arranged chronologically on the basis of the first periodical appearance of the Churchill contribution.

LIST OF PERIODICALS CONTAINING CHURCHILL CONTRIBUTIONS

What follows is a list of the periodicals in which a Churchill contribution has been located, together with information regarding the frequency of publication and the name and address of the printer and publisher. This list is not meant to be a history of any or all of the publications and was compiled from information accurate at the time of publication of the Churchill item(s).

Adam International Review
Published by "Adam International Review", 28 Emperor's Gate, London, S.W.7, and printed by Wyndham Printers, Ltd. (T.U.), 3–5 Barrett Street, London, W.1.

Advance
Published quarterly by the Conservative Central Office, Abbey House, 2–8 Victoria Street, London. Printed by the Whitefriars Press Ltd., London and Tonbridge.

Agriculture
The journal of the Ministry of Agriculture. Printed and published monthly by HMSO, Kingsway, London, W.C.2.

American Mercury, The
Published monthly by the American Mercury, Inc., at Concord, NH, with editorial and general offices at 570 Lexington Avenue, New York.

Anglo-Italian Review
Published on the 15th of each month by Constable & Co., Ltd., 10 Orange Street, London, W.C.2. Printed by R. Clay and Sons, Ltd., Brunswick Street, Stamford Street, London, S.E.1, and Bungay, Suffolk.

Anglo-Saxon Review, The
Published quarterly by Mrs George Cornwallis-West, 49 Rupert Street, London, W.

Answers
Printed and published every Saturday by The Amalgamated Press, Ltd., The Fleetway House, Farringdon Street, London, E.C.4.

Argosy (UK)
The British pocket-book format magazine was published monthly by Fleetway Publications Ltd., Fleetway House, Farringdon Street, London.

Argosy (US)
The American magazine was published monthly by Popular Publications, Inc., McCall Street, Dayton 1, OH, with executive and editorial offices at 205 East 42nd Street, New York.

Army and Navy Gazette, The
Published every Saturday at 3 York Street, Covent Garden, London, W.C.

Arts & Decoration
Published monthly by Joseph A. Judd Publishing Company, 50 West 47th Street, New York.

Association of American Colleges Bulletin
Published quarterly in March, May, October and December by the Association of American Colleges, N. Queen Street and McGovern Avenue, Lancaster, PA.

Atlantic, The
Published monthly by The Atlantic Monthly Company at 10 Ferry Street, Concord, NH, with editorial and general offices at 8 Arlington Street, Boston 16.

Atlantic Monthly, The
In 1917, published monthly at 3 Park Street, Boston.

Belfast Chamber of Commerce Journal
Published monthly by the Belfast Chamber of Commerce, 7 Donegall Square West, Belfast.

Berrow's Worcester Journal
Published every Friday by George Williams & Berrow's Ltd., 54 Fleet Street, London, E.C.4.

Britannic Review, The
Published quarterly by The Britannic Publishing Co., Ltd., 15 Dartmouth Street, Westminster, London, S.W.

Bulletin of International News, The
Published by the Information Department of the Royal Institute of International Affairs, Chatham House, 10 St James's Square, London, S.W.1.

Bulletin and Scots Pictorial, The
Published daily at 65 Buchanan Street, Glasgow, C.1, and printed by George Outram and Company, Limited.

Century Magazine, The
Published monthly by The Century Co., 353 Fourth Avenue, New York.

Chartered Surveyor, The
Published monthly by the Royal Institution of Chartered Surveyors, 12 Great George Street, Parliament Square, London.

Chicago Tribune
Published daily as the *Chicago Daily Tribune* and on Sundays as the *Chicago Sunday Tribune*) at the Tribune offices, Tribune Square, Chicago.

Collier's
Published weekly by P. F. Collier & Son Company, Springfield, OH, with executive and editorial offices at 250 Park Avenue, New York. From 1934 to 1939, published by The Crowell Publishing Company, Springfield, and from 1939 to 1947, published by Crowell-Collier Publishing Company, also at Springfield. *Collier's* ceased publication in 1957. The building in Springfield which formerly housed Crowell-Collier was destroyed by fire on 10 May 1999.

Collier's Weekly
Published by P. F. Collier & Son, with editorial and general offices at 521–547 West 13th Street and 518–524 West 14th Street, New York.

Cologne Post, The
Published daily by the Army of the Rhine, 35 Marzellen-Straße, Cologne. The London office of the paper was at 119 Fleet Street, London, E.C.4.

Congressional Digest, The
Published every month, except for July and August, at the Munsey Building, Washington, DC.

Consensus, The
Published quarterly by the National Economic League, 6 Beacon Street, Boston.

Conservative Approach, The
Published monthly by the Conservative and Unionist Association, Abbey House, 2–8 Victoria Street, London, S.W.1, and printed by McCorquodale, London, S.E.

Conspiracy Digest
Published quarterly by Alpine Enterprises, Box 766, Dearborn, MI 48121.

Cosmopolitan
Published monthly by the International Magazine Company, 119 West 40th Street, New York.

Crusader
The "Eighth Army Weekly". Published every Monday from Advance H.Q., Eighth Army.

Current Affairs
Published bi-weekly by the Army Bureau of Current Affairs in the United Kingdom.

Current History
In its origins, published monthly by the New York Times Company, New York. In 1943, published monthly by Events Publishing Co., Inc., 5528 West Oxford Street, Philadelphia. Editorial offices at 299 Madison Avenue, New York.

Daily Chronicle
Printed and published daily except Sunday by United Newspapers, Limited, at the Daily Chronicle Buildings, 80 Fleet Street, London, E.C.

Daily Graphic, The
Published daily except Sunday by E. J. Mansfield, at Milford House, Milford Lane, Strand, London.

Daily Mail, The
Published daily except Sunday by Associated Newspapers, Ltd., at 1 Carmelite House, Carmelite Street, Temple, London, E.C.

Daily Mirror, The
Printed and published by The Daily Mirror Newspapers Ltd., at Geraldine House, Rolls Buildings, Fetter Lane, London, E.C.4.

Daily News
Published daily by News Syndicate Co., Inc., 220 East 42nd Street, New York.

Daily Sketch
Printed and published by the Daily Sketch and Sunday Graphic, Ltd., 200 Gray's Inn Road, London, W.C.1, and Withy Grove, Manchester 4.

Daily Telegraph, The
From 1922 to 1937, published daily except Sunday at 135 Fleet Street, London, E.C.4.

Daily Telegraph & Morning Post, The
From 1 October 1937, the two daily newspapers amalgamated and were published from the *Daily Telegraph* offices at 135 Fleet Street, London, E.C.4.

Dalhousie Review, The
Published quarterly in January, April, July and October by the Review Publishing Company, Halifax, Nova Scotia.

Department of State Bulletin
Published weekly by the Government Printing Office, Washington, DC.

Dundee Advertiser, The
Printed and published daily by John Leng & Co., Limited, Dundee.

Dundee Catholic Herald, The
Published weekly by the Scottish Catholic Printing Co., Ltd., 82 Bell Street, Dundee.

Eastern Daily Press, The
Published by the Norfolk News Company, Limited, 57 London Street, Norwich.

Empire Digest
Published monthly by Empire Information Limited, 47 Wellesley Street, Toronto 5, Ontario.

Empire Review, The
Published monthly by Macmillan and Co., Limited, in London.

Encore
Published monthly by the *Saturday Review of Literature* in the United States.

English Life and the Illustrated Review
Published at St Stephen's House, Westminster, London.

English Race, The
Published quarterly by the Royal Society of St George, 47 Victoria Street, London, S.W.1.

Evening Herald
Printed and published daily except Sunday for the proprietors at 111 Middle Abbey Street, Dublin.

Evening News, The
Published daily except Sunday by Associated Newspapers, Ltd., at Carmelite House, Tallis Street, London, E.C.4.

Evening News, The (Glasgow)
Published daily except Sunday by Associated Scottish Newspapers, Ltd., for J. M. Smith (Lim.), 200 Gray's Inn Road, W.C.

Evening Standard
The *Evening Standard and St. James's Gazette* was printed and published daily except Sunday by the Evening Standard Co., Ltd., 47 Shoe Lane, London, E.C.4.

Everybody's
Printed by Sun Printers Limited, London and Watford, Herts., and published for the proprietors, Everybody's Publications Ltd., by The Amalgamated Press Ltd., Fleetway House, London, E.C.4.

E.S.A.M. Magazine
The official journal of the Ex-Services Association of Malaya. Published intermit-tently by the Association and printed by Rickard Ltd., Singapore.

External Affairs
Issued monthly in English and French by the Department of External Affairs, Ottawa.

Family Herald and Weekly Star
Printed and published weekly on Wednesdays at 241–245 St James Street West by the Montreal Star Company, Limited.

Forethought
The political journal of the Constitutional Club. Published quarterly between December 1946 and November 1948.

France–Grande Bretagne
Published, it appears, bi-monthly, by the Association France–Grande Bretagne, 1 rue d'Astorg, Paris 8ᵉ.

France Illustration Littéraire et Théâtrale
Printed by Imp[rimerie] de Boligny and published monthly by Société Nationale des Entreprises de Presse, Paris.

France Libre, La
Published monthly by Hamish Hamilton Ltd., 90 Great Russell Street, London, W.C.1.

Georgetown Gazette
Printed and published monthly by David J. Clark, 23 Royal Exchange Square and 92 Union Street, Glasgow.

Glasgow Herald
Printed and published daily except Sunday by George Outram & Company Ltd., at 65–69 Buchanan Street and 60 and 68 Mitchell Street, Glasgow.

Graya

A magazine for circulation among the members of Gray's Inn. Published by T. J. F. Hobley, 4 Brick Court, Temple, London, E.C.4, and printed by New Goswell Printing Co. Ltd., 220 Goswell Road, London, E.C.1.

Harmsworth Magazine, The

Published monthly by Harmsworth Bros., Limited, London, E.C.

Harrovian, The

Printed and published monthly (although at irregular intervals) for the proprietors by William Joseph Overhead, High Street, Harrow, Middlesex.

Harvard Alumni Bulletin

Published bi-weekly during the college year by Harvard Bulletin, Inc., for the Harvard Alumni Association, with editorial offices at 18 Plympton Street and business offices at 1400 Massachusetts Avenue, Cambridge, MA.

Headway

Printed for the proprietors, The Focus Publishing Co., Ltd., 19 Devereux Court, London, W.C.2, by St Clements Press Limited, Portugal Street, London, W.C.2, and published for the proprietors by Bernard Jones Publications Ltd., Chansitor House, 27/8 Chancery Lane, London, W.C.2.

Illustrated

Printed by Odhams (Watford) Ltd., St Albans Road, Watford, and published every Wednesday by Odhams Press, Ltd., Long Acre, London, W.C.2.

Illustrated Sunday Herald

Published weekly by London Publishing Co., Ltd., 46–47 Shoe Lane, London, E.C.4.

Illustrated Technion News

Published by Technion Publications, Technion House, 39/41 James Street, Wigmore Street, London, W.1, and printed by Deaner Printers Ltd. (T.U.), 49 Hackney Road, London, E.2.

Inlander, The

"A Literary Magazine by the Students of Michigan University."

International Conciliation

Published monthly, except July and August, by the Carnegie Endowment for International Peace, 405 West 117th Street, New York.

Jewish Chronicle, The

Printed and published weekly by Solomon Davis at 2 Finsbury Square, London, E.C. In 1937, published weekly by the Jewish Chronicle at 47 and 49 Moor Lane, London, E.C.2.

John Bull

Printed and published weekly by Odhams Press Ltd., London, W.C.2.

John O'London's Weekly and the Outline

Published weekly by George Newnes Ltd., 8–11 Southampton Street, London, W.C.2.

Journal of the African Society

Published quarterly by Macmillan & Co., Limited, London, and the Macmillan Co., New York.

Journal of the Institute of Bankers in Ireland

Published monthly by Hely's, Limited, in Dublin.

Journal of the Royal Colonial Institute

Published monthly by the Royal Colonial Institute, Northumberland Avenue, London, W.C.

Journal of the Royal Empire Society
Published monthly by Sir Isaac Pitman and Sons, Limited, Parker Street, Kingsway, London, W.C.2, and printed by McCorquodale & Co., Ltd., London. (Note that the Royal Empire Society was formerly the Royal Colonial Institute.)

Journal of the Royal United Service Institution
In 1901, published monthly by the Royal United Service Institution, Whitehall, London, S.W.1, and, in 1950, published quarterly at the same location.

Ken
Published every other Wednesday by Ken, Inc., 919 N. Michigan Avenue, Chicago.

Kipling Journal
Published quarterly by the Kipling Society and printed by H. F. Lucas & Co., 151 North Road, Southend-on-Sea, Essex.

Lancet, The
Published every Friday at 7 Adam Street, Adelphi, London, W.C.2.

Lecture Recorder and Meeting Reporter, The
Published monthly except during August and September by the Lecture Recorder, 16 Marsham Street, London, S.W.1. Printed by Allen & Donaldson, Ltd., London, S.W.1.

Leeds Chamber of Commerce Journal
Printed and published monthly by Jowett & Sowry Ltd., Albion Street, Leeds.

Liberal Magazine, The
Published by the Liberal Publication Department, 42 Parliament Street, London, S.W.1.

Liberty
Published by Liberty Publishing Corporation, 1926 Broadway, New York. In 1941, published weekly by Macfadden Publications, Incorporated, 205 East 42nd Street, New York. In 1971, co-published quarterly as *Liberty, the Nostalgia Magazine*, by Twenty First Century Communications, Inc. and Liberty Library Corporation, 635 Madison Avenue, New York.

Life
Published weekly by Time Inc., 540 North Michigan Avenue, Chicago 11.

Listener, The
Published every Thursday by the British Broadcasting Corporation, London.

Living Age, The
Published by the Living Age Company, 41 Mount Vernon Street, Boston (the same address as *Atlantic Monthly* and *House Beautiful*). From 1929, published by The Living Age Company at 10 Ferry Street, Concord, NH, with editorial and general offices at 253 Broadway, New York.

London Magazine
Printed and published monthly by the Amalgamated Press, Limited, Fleetway House, Farringdon Street, London, E.C.

Look
Published every other Tuesday by Cowles Magazines, Inc., at 715 Locust Street, Des Moines, IA.

Los Angeles Times, The
Printed and published daily by the Los Angeles Times, 202 West 1st Street, Los Angeles.

Maclean's

Printed and published semi-monthly by Maclean-Hunter Publishing Co., 481 University Avenue, Toronto 2, Ontario.

Macmillan's Magazine

Published monthly by Macmillan and Co., Limited, St Martin's Street, London, W.C., and the Macmillan Company, New York.

Manchester Guardian

Printed and published daily except Sunday by John Russell Scott for Taylor, Garnett, & Co., at the "Guardian" Office, 4 Warren Street, Newmarket Place, Manchester, with editorial offices at 54 Fleet Street, London, E.C.

Mankind

Published every two months by Mankind Publishing Company, 8060 Melrose Avenue, Los Angeles, CA 90046.

Men Only

Published on the 22nd of each month by C. Arthur Pearson, Ltd., in 1936 at Pearson's Buildings, Henrietta Street, London, W.C.2, and in 1938 at Tower House, Southampton Street, Strand, London, W.C.2, and printed by Hazell, Watson & Viney, Ltd., London and Aylesbury.

Ministry of Munitions Journal

Published monthly by the Ministry of Munitions at 10 Princes Street, Westminster, S.W.1, and printed by George Reveirs, Limited, 4 and 5 Greystoke Place, Fetter Lane, London, E.C. Note the title-page admonition (this was strictly a wartime publication) that "Neither the *Journal*, nor any part thereof, may be taken or sent out of the United Kingdom."

Monthly Review, The

Published monthly by George N. Morang & Company Limited, 90 Wellington Street West, Toronto, and John Murray, 50A Albemarle Street, London, W. Printed by Ballantyne Hanson & Co.

Morning Leader, The

In 1900, printed and published daily except Sunday for the proprietors by John Britton Jones, at Stonecutter Street, London, E.C.4. In 1910, printed and published by "The Star" Newspaper Company, Limited, at Stonecutter Street.

Morning Post, The

Printed and published by Edward Eden Peacock daily except Sunday at the Morning Post Offices, 346 Strand and 12 Wellington Street, London, W.C. From 1 October 1937, the *Morning Post*, which had been in operation since 2 November 1772, amalgamated with the *Daily Telegraph* (itself published since 29 June 1855); the combined newspaper was thereafter published from the *Daily Telegraph* offices at 135 Fleet Street, London, E.C.4.

Nash's and Pall Mall Magazine

In 1924, published monthly by the National Magazine Co., Ltd., of 1 Amen Corner, Paternoster Row, London, E.C.4., and printed by Hazell, Watson & Viney Ltd., London and Aylesbury (on the cover *Nash's and Pall Mall Magazine* and on the contents page *Nash's—Pall Mall*). From May 1927, published as *Nash's Magazine* by the National Magazine Co., Ltd., of 153 Queen Victoria Street, London, E.C.4, and printed by Hazell, Watson & Viney Ltd., London and Aylesbury. From October 1929, the title reverted to *Nash's—Pall Mall*.

Natal Mercury
Printed and published daily except Sunday by Robinson & Co., Mercury Buildings, Mercury Lane, Durban, Natal, South Africa.

Natal Witness
Printed and published daily except Sunday by P. Davis & Sons, 254 Longmarket Street, Maritzburg, South Africa.

Nation, The (UK)
The British magazine was published weekly by The Nation Publishing Company, Limited, at 14 Henrietta Street, Covent Garden, London, W.C.

Nation, The (US)
The American magazine was published weekly by The Nation, Inc., at 20 Vesey Street, New York.

National Magazine, The
Conservative Central Office publication. Published and printed for the proprietors by the Amalgamated Press, Ltd. (Printing Works), Sumner Street, London, S.E.1.

Navy, The
The "organ of the Navy League". Published monthly, with editorial offices at 13 Victoria Street, London, S.W.1.

Neptune
Printed monthly in England for The Continental Publishers and Distributors Ltd., 16/17 William IV Street, Charing Cross, London, by LTA Robinson Ltd.

New Commonwealth
Published by the New Commonwealth Society at Thorney House, Smith Square, London, S.W.1.

New Republic
Published weekly by Editorial Publications, Inc., 40 East 49th Street, New York.

New York Times
Published "Every Day in the Year" by the New York Times Company at the Times Building, Times Square, 229 West 43rd Street, New York.

New York Tribune
Published daily in New York.

News Chronicle
Published by the Daily News Ltd. for The News Chronicle Ltd. at Bouverie Street and Salisbury Square, London.

News of the World
Printed and published every Sunday by the News of the World, Limited, 30 Bouverie Street, London, E.C.4.

Nineteenth Century and After, The
Published monthly for the proprietors by Constable & Company Limited, 10 and 12 Orange Street, Leicester Square, London, W.C.2, and printed by the Whitefriars Press Ltd., London and Tonbridge.

North American Review, The
Published monthly by The North American Review Publishing Co., 291 Fifth Avenue, New York.

Northern News, The
Published on Tuesdays and Fridays by Pearce Northern Limited, at 8 Duncan Avenue, Kirkland Lake, Ontario.

Now
Published by the Conservative and Unionist Central Office, Abbey House, 2–8 Victoria Street, London, S.W.1, and printed by Sun Printers Ltd., London and Watford.

Observer, The
Published every Sunday at 12–14 Newton Street, Holborn, London, W.C.

Oldham Chronicle, The
Published daily except Sunday by Hirst & Rennie, Oldham.

Oldham Evening Chronicle, The
Printed and published daily except Sunday for the proprietors, Hirst & Rennie, by John Hirst at their printing works at Union Street, Oldham.

Oldham Standard, The
Printed and published by the Northern Daily & Weekly Newspapers, Ltd., Clegg Street, Oldham.

Omnibook Magazine
Published monthly by Omnibook, Inc., 10 Rockefeller Plaza, New York.

Onward
Published monthly by the Conservative and Unionist Central Office, Abbey House, 2–8 Victoria Street, London, S.W.1, and printed by Sun Printers Limited, London and Watford, Herts.

Outlook, The
Published weekly by The Outlook Company, 381 Fourth Avenue, New York.

Oxford High School Magazine
Published by City of Oxford High School, George Street, Oxford.

Pall Mall Magazine, The
In 1896, published monthly at 18 Charing Cross Road, London, W.C. Printed by Hazell, Watson & Viney Ltd., London and Aylesbury.

Parade
Published monthly by Odhams Press Ltd., at their publishing department, 6 Catherine Street, Strand, London, W.C.2, and printed by Odhams (Watford) Ltd., St Albans Road, Watford, Herts.

Paris Match
Published weekly at 51, rue Pierre-Charron, Paris 8e, and printed by Imprimerie Chaix-Defossés-Néogravure, Paris.

Pearson's Illustrated War News
Published weekly by C. Arthur Pearson, Ltd., Pearson's Weekly Buildings, Henrietta Street, London, W.C.2.

Pearson's Magazine
Published monthly by C. Arthur Pearson, Ltd., at Pearson's Weekly Buildings, Henrietta Street, London, W.C.2. Printed by Newnes & Pearson Printing Co. Ltd., Exmoor Street, Ladbroke Grove, London, W.10.

People's Journal, The
Published every Saturday by John Leng & Co. (Lim.).

Pictorial Magazine
Printed and published every Friday by the Amalgamated Press, Ltd., at Fleetway House, Farringdon Street, London, E.C.4. Formerly published as *Penny Pictorial Magazine* (from 10 June 1899 to 24 June 1922) and later (13 November 1926 to 5 March 1935) as *Pictorial Weekly*.

Pictorial Weekly
See *Pictorial Magazine*.

Picture Post
Printed by The Sun Engraving Co., Ltd., London and Watford, and published weekly by the Hulton Press, Ltd., 43/44 Shoe Lane, London, E.C.4.

Pioneer Mail and Indian Weekly News, The
"Published [weekly] on the night of the despatch for Europe of the Overland Mail via Bombay and Brindisi" at Allahabad. The London office of the publication was at 13a Cockspur Street, Pall Mall, London.

Popular Mechanics Magazine
Published monthly by Popular Mechanics Co., 200 E. Ontario Street, Chicago.

Popular Illustrated
Printed and published for the proprietors (unidentified) by the Amalgamated Press, Ltd. (Printing Works), Sumner Street, London, S.E.1. No frequency of publication is indicated.

Primrose League Gazette
Published nine times per year by The Primrose League, Clutha House, 10 Storey's Gate, London, S.W.1, and printed by the Lavenham Press Ltd., Lavenham, Suffolk.

P.T.O.
Published weekly at 5 Tavistock Street, Covent Garden, London, W.C. In 1939, published monthly by George Newnes, Ltd., at Tower House, Southampton Street, Strand, London, W.C.2, and printed by Hazell, Watson & Viney, Ltd., London and Aylesbury.

Reader's Digest
Published monthly by The Reader's Digest Association, Inc., Pleasantville, NY.

Redbook
Published monthly by the McCall Company, publication offices at McCall Street, Dayton, OH, and editorial offices at 230 Park Avenue, New York.

Reporter's Journal and Shorthand Magazine, The
Published monthly by Sir Isaac Pitman & Sons, 1 Amen Corner, Paternoster Row, London, E.C.

Review of Reviews, The
Published monthly by the Review of Reviews Corporation, 55 Fifth Avenue, New York.

Rotarian, The
Published monthly by Rotary International at 35 E. Wacker Drive, Chicago.

Saturday Evening Post
In 1930, published weekly by The Curtis Publishing Company, Independence Square, Philadelphia.

Saturday Review, The
Published weekly by the Saturday Review, Ltd., 9 King Street, Covent Garden, London, W.C. and printed by Herbert Reiach, Ltd., 43 Belvedere Road, London, S.E.1.

Scouting
Published monthly and bi-monthly May–June and July–August by the Boy Scouts of America, New Brunswick, NJ.

Screen Pictorial
Published monthly by C. Arthur Pearson Ltd., 17 Henrietta Street, London, W.C., and printed by the Sun Engraving Co. Ltd., London and Watford.

Scribner's Magazine
Published monthly by Charles Scribner's Sons, at 597 Fifth Avenue, New York, and at 23 Bedford Square, London, W.C.1.

Sea Stories
Published bi-monthly by Future Publications, Inc., 80 Fifth Avenue, New York 11.

SEAC
The services newspaper of the South East Asia Command. Published daily by courtesy of *The Statesman* in Calcutta.

Shorthand Gazette, The
Published monthly by Sir Isaac Pitman & Sons, Ltd., 1 Amen Corner, London, E.C.

Slant
Published quarterly by Slant Publishing Co., 3944 Olive Street, St. Louis, MO.

Smoker's Companion, The
Published monthly by Companion Publishing Company, Inc., 441 Lexington Avenue, New York, and printed by Charles Francis Press, Inc., Printing Crafts Building, 461 Eighth Avenue, New York.

Spectator, The
Printed by Love & Malcomson (Limited) at Dane Street, High Holborn, London, W.C., and published weekly by John Baker for the "Spectator" (Limited), 1 Wellington Street, Savoy, Strand, London. In 1939, printed by St Clements Press, Ltd., Portugal Street, Kingsway, London, W.C.2, and published by The Spectator, Ltd., 99 Gower Street, London, W.C.1.

Standard & Diggers' News
Printed and published daily except Sunday by Mendelssohn and Bruce, Limited, at their Steam Printing Works, "Standard and Diggers' News" Building, Johannesburg, South Africa.

Star Weekly
Published every Saturday by the Toronto Star Limited at 80 King Street West, Toronto 1.

Straits Times
Printed and published daily except Sunday by Walter Edward Garrett at the Straits

Times Press, Ltd., Cecil and Stanley Streets, Singapore, Straits Settlements.

Strand Magazine, The (UK)
The British edition was published monthly by George Newnes, Ltd., 3 to 12 Southampton Street, Strand, London. In 1946, published by George Newnes, Limited, Tower House, Southampton Street, Strand, London, on the 30th of each month. Printed then by Hazell, Watson & Viney, Ltd., London and Aylesbury.

Strand Magazine, The (US)
The American edition was published monthly by The International News Company, 83 and 85 Duane Street, New York.

Student, The
Published irregularly, at weekly or bi-weekly intervals, by the Students' Representative Council of the University of Edinburgh and printed for them at the Darien Press, Bristo Place, Edinburgh.

Sun, The
Published daily except Sunday at the Sun Buildings, Temple Avenue, London, E.C.

Sunday Chronicle
Printed and published every Sunday by Allied Newspapers Limited, Withy Grove, Manchester.

Sunday Chronicle and Sunday Referee
The name from 1939 of the former *Sunday Chronicle*. Printed and published every Sunday by Allied Newspapers Limited, Withy Grove, Manchester.

Sunday Dispatch
Printed and published weekly by Associated Newspapers, Ltd., at Northcliffe House and Carmelite House, Carmelite Street, London, E.C.4, and

Northcliffe House, Deansgate, Manchester 3.

Sunday Express, The
Printed and published weekly by London Express Newspaper, Ltd., at 8 Shoe Lane, London, E.C.4, and, in 1937, for the Sunday Express Ltd. by London Express Newspaper, Ltd., at Fleet Street, London, E.C.4.

Sunday Mail
Printed and published weekly by Scottish Daily Record and Evening News, Limited, Kemsley House, Glasgow, C.2.

Sunday Pictorial
Printed and published weekly by Sunday Pictorial Newspapers, Ltd., 23–29 Bouverie Street, London, E.C. Self-described as 'The Paper with "The Daily Mirror" Behind It'.

Sunday Times
Printed and published weekly by Allied Newspapers, Ltd., 200 Gray's Inn Road, London, W.C.1.

Times, The
Published daily except Sunday by The Times Publishing Company, Printing House Square, Blackfriars, London, E.C.4.

Tit-Bits
Published weekly on Fridays by George Newnes, Limited, Tower House, Southampton Street, London, W.C.2, and printed by the Newnes & Pearson Printing Co., Ltd., Exmoor Street, London, W.10.

Toronto Daily Star
Printed and published daily except Sunday at 80 King Street West, Toronto.

Tory Challenge
Published monthly by the Conservative and Unionist Central Office, Abbey House, 2–8 Victoria Street, London, S.W.1.

Uniropa
Published by Uniropa Organisation at Station Gates, Broadstairs, Kent (the frequency not indicated).

United Service Magazine, The
Printed and published monthly by William Clowes and Sons, Limited, 13 Charing Cross Road, London.

University of Rochester Library Bulletin, The
Printed by the Robert Hart Printing Co. and published three times a year by the University of Rochester Library at Rochester, New York.

University of the State of New York Bulletin
Published bi-monthly at the University of the State of New York Press, Albany, NY.

V.C., The
"A Weekly Journal of the Brighter Side of Life", published by Isbister & Co., 15 Tavistock Street, Covent Garden, London.

Vital Speeches of the Day
Published semi-monthly by the City News Publishing Co., 33 West 42nd Street, New York.

Vrij Nederland
Published every Saturday (between 1940 and 1945) by the Netherland Publishing Company Limited at 7 Park Lane, London, W.1, and printed by Eyre & Spottiswoode Limited, East Harding Street, London, E.C.4.

War Illustrated, The
Printed and published weekly by the Amalgamated Press, Limited, The

Fleetway House, Farringdon Street, London, E.C.

War Pictures
Published by C. Arthur Pearson Ltd., 17 Henrietta Street, London, W.C., and printed by Horace Cox, Windsor House Printing Works, Breams Buildings, London, E.C.

Washington Post
Printed and published daily by the Washington Post Company, 1150 15th Street, Washington, DC.

Weekly Dispatch, The
Published weekly by the Associated Newspapers, Limited, Carmelite House, London, E.C.4.

Weekly Law Digest
Published weekly by J. Mason Wiegel, 220 Montgomery Street, San Francisco 4.

Weekly News Letter
Published weekly by the Conservative and Unionist Central Office, 32 Smith Square, Westminster, London, S.W.1, and printed by Deverell, Gibson & Hoare, Ltd., 5 Lavington Street, London, S.E.1.

Westminster College Bulletin, The
Published by Westminster College, Fulton, MO.

Westminster Gazette, The
Published daily at Tudor Street, Whitefriars, London, E.C.

Weston-super-Mare Gazette
Printed and published Wednesday and Saturday by The Mendip Press Limited at Wadham Street, Weston-super-Mare, Somerset (now Avon).

Whitefriars Journal
Published irregularly by the Whitefriars Club and issued exclusively to members. As explained in the December 1900 issue,[1] "It was originally intended to issue the 'Journal' regularly, but the Committee did not feel justified in incurring the expense that would be involved ..." Ultimately published three times each in 1900 and 1901, five times in 1902 and once in 1903.[2] Printed by the National Press Agency, Ltd., Whitefriars House, Carmelite Street, London, E.C.

Whitley Bulletin
Published monthly by the Civil Service National Whitley Council (Staff Side) at Parliament Mansions, London, S.W.1, and printed by Stone & Cox Ltd. (T.U.), London and Watford.

Windsor Magazine, The
Published by Ward, Lock & Co., Limited, Warwick House, Salisbury House, London, E.C.

Woodford Times
Incorporating the Wanstead, Woodford, Chigwell, Buckhurst Hill, Chingford, Loughton, Abridge Recorder, Epping & West Essex Times & Star. Noted on inside pages of the newspaper as the "Times & West Essex Star". Printed and published by Essex Publishing Co., Ltd., 68 High Road, Woodford Green, Essex.

World, The
Published daily by The Press Publishing Company, Pulitzer Building, 63 Park Row, New York.

---

1. Issue No. 3, at p. 5.
2. In May, October and December 1900; March, May and December 1901; February, April, May, August and November 1902; and January 1903.

World Digest
Printed in England and published on the first of each month by The Amalgamated Press, Ltd., The Fleetway House, London, E.C.4.

World Press Review
Printed by The Printing and Stationery Services, M.E.F. The weekly paper reprinted for the British and Allied Forces material which had already been published but would not have been available to them on foreign service.

World's Work, The
Published monthly by Doubleday, Page & Co., 34 Union Square East, New York.

Yale Review, The
Published quarterly by the Yale Publishing Association, Inc., 135 Elm Street, New Haven, CN.

Yank
Published weekly by the enlisted men of the United States Army (Branch Office, Information and Education Division, War Dept., 205 East 42nd Street, New York 17). The British edition was published weekly at Britannia House, 17–18 Old Bailey, London, E.C.4, and printed by Odhams (Watford) Ltd.

Yorkshire Observer
Printed and published by Henry Nathaniel Byles, for Wm. Byles & Sons, Ltd., at 10 Piccadilly, Bradford, and 58 Boar Lane, Leeds.

Youth's Companion, The
Published weekly by Perry Mason Company, 201 Columbus Avenue, Boston.

1895

C1.1 Dec. 13 **THE INSURRECTION IN CUBA. / Letters from the Front.—I.**
Daily Graphic, 4
For this and the next four articles on Cuba, Churchill received a total of 25 guineas. Subsequently collected in R. Churchill, *WSC*, Vol. I, *C.V.* 1, pp. 604–7; *Collected Essays*, Vol. I, pp. 3–6; and *War Correspondent*, pp. 3–7.

C1.2 Dec. 17 **THE INSURRECTION IN CUBA. / Letters from the Front.—II.** / Sancti Spiritus, November 23rd.
Daily Graphic, 5
Subsequently collected in R. Churchill, *WSC*, Vol. I, *C.V.* 1, pp. 607–9; *Collected Essays*, Vol. I, pp. 6–7; and *War Correspondent*, pp. 8–10.

C1.3 Dec. 24 **THE INSURRECTION IN CUBA. / Letters from the Front.—III.** / Arroyo, November 27th.
Daily Graphic, 4
Subsequently collected in R. Churchill, *WSC*, Vol. I, *C.V.* 1, pp. 609–11; *Collected Essays*, Vol. I, pp. 8–10; and *War Correspondent*, pp. 11–13.

C1.4 Dec. 27 **THE INSURRECTION IN CUBA. / Letters from the Front.—IV. / The "Battle" of La Reforma.** / Cienfuegos, December 4th.
Daily Graphic, 4
Subsequently collected in R. Churchill, *WSC*, Vol. I, *C.V.* 1, pp. 611–15; *Collected Essays*, Vol. I, pp. 10–13; and *War Correspondent*, pp. 14–18.

1896

C1.5 Jan. 13 **THE CUBAN INSURRECTION. / A Sombre Outlook. / Fifth and Concluding Letter.** / Tampa Bay, December 14, 1895.
Daily Graphic, 4
Subsequently collected in R. Churchill, *WSC*, Vol. I, *C.V.* 1, pp. 615–18; *Collected Essays*, Vol. I, pp. 14–16; and *War Correspondent*, pp. 19–22.

C2   Feb. 15   **THE REVOLT IN CUBA.**
Saturday Review, Vol. LXXXI,[3] No. 2103, 165
Signed Winston L. Churchill. Subsequently collected in
Collected Essays, Vol. I, pp. 17–19.

C3   March 7   **AMERICAN INTERVENTION IN CUBA.**
Saturday Review, Vol. LXXXI, No. 2106, 244–5
Signed Winston S. Churchill. Subsequently collected in
Collected Essays, Vol. I, pp. 20–2.

C4   Aug. 29   **THE REVOLT IN CUBA.**
Saturday Review, Vol. LXXXII, No. 2131, 213–14
Subsequently collected in *Collected Essays*, Vol. I, pp. 23–5.

C5   December   **THE ROYAL MILITARY COLLEGE, SANDHURST.**
Pall Mall Magazine, 593–8
Signed "The Coronet of Horse". Subsequently collected in
R. Churchill, *WSC*, Vol. I, *C.V.* 1, pp. 548–52.

1897

C6   Sept. 9   **LATEST INDIAN INTELLIGENCE. / The Frontier
Risings. / An Afridi Attack Repelled. / Lashkars on the
Samana. / Brush with the Enemy at Doaba. /
[Telegram]** / Malakand, 3rd September.
Pioneer Mail and Indian Weekly News, 13
One of the series of reports "by telegram from our Special
Correspondents". None is signed. Churchill had reported his
new position to his mother on 5 September: "I am at present
correspondent of the *Pioneer*—to which I have to telegraph
300 words a day."[4] For his work as a correspondent to the
Pioneer Mail and Indian Weekly News (which had published
much of Kipling's early writing), Churchill received a total of
£25.[5]

C7   Sept. 9   **[TELEGRAM]** / Later.
Pioneer Mail and Indian Weekly News, 13

C8   Sept. 9   **[TELEGRAM]** / 4th September.
Pioneer Mail and Indian Weekly News, 13

---

3. Noted erroneously in the magazine in arabic numerals as Volume 82.
4. R. Churchill, *WSC*, Vol. I, *C.V.* 2, pp. 784–5, at p. 784.
5. See his letter of 8 February 1898 to his grandmother, Frances, Duchess of Marlborough (*ibid.*,
pp. 876–7, at p. 876).

C9   Sept. 9   **[TELEGRAM]** / 6th September.
Pioneer Mail and Indian Weekly News, 13

C10   Sept. 24   **LATEST INDIAN INTELLIGENCE. / The Frontier Risings. / Severe Fighting in the Watelai Valley. / Heavy Losses among British Officers. / The Attack on the Gulistan Fort. / [Telegram from Sarai of 16th Sept.]** / Inayat Kili [*sic*], 15th September, 2 p.m.
Pioneer Mail and Indian Weekly News, 12
On this and certain subsequent telegrams despatched from the front, the dateline of the report and that of the telegram are divergent, indicating Churchill's need to hold his material until he was able to send it a day or more later.

C11   Sept. 24   **[TELEGRAM]** / Later.
Pioneer Mail and Indian Weekly News, 13

C12   Sept. 24   **[TELEGRAM of 17th September]** / Inayat Kila, 15th September.
Pioneer Mail and Indian Weekly News, 13

C13   Sept. 24   **[TELEGRAM]** / Later.
Pioneer Mail and Indian Weekly News, 13

C14   Sept. 24   **[TELEGRAM of 18th September from Panjkora]** / Inayat Kila, 17th September, 9 a.m.
Pioneer Mail and Indian Weekly News, 13

C15   Sept. 24   **[TELEGRAM]** / Later.
Pioneer Mail and Indian Weekly News, 13

C16   Sept. 24   **[TELEGRAM]** / 18th September, 4–5 p.m.
Pioneer Mail and Indian Weekly News, 13

C17   Sept. 24   **[TELEGRAM of 19th September]** / Inayat Kila, 18th September.
Pioneer Mail and Indian Weekly News, 13

C18   Sept. 24   **[TELEGRAM of 20th September]** / Inayat Kila, 19th September.
Pioneer Mail and Indian Weekly News, 13

C19   Sept. 24   **[TELEGRAM of 22nd September]** / Inayat Kila, 20th September.
Pioneer Mail and Indian Weekly News, 13

C20   Sept. 24   **[TELEGRAM]** / Later.
Pioneer Mail and Indian Weekly News, 13

C21   Sept. 24   **THE   MALAKAND   FIELD   FORCE.** / Simla,   7th
September.
Pioneer Mail and Indian Weekly News, 20–1
Letter to the *Pioneer Mail*.

C22   Oct. 1   **LATEST INDIAN INTELLIGENCE. / The Frontier
Risings. / The Mamunds Still Fighting. / Capture of the
Bedmani Pass. / Mohmand Forts Destroyed.—Jirgahs
Coming In. / [Telegram of 24th September from
Panjkora.]** / Nawagai, 22nd September.
Pioneer Mail and Indian Weekly News, 11

C23   Oct. 1   **[TELEGRAM]** / Nawagai, 21st September.
Pioneer Mail and Indian Weekly News, 11

C24   Oct. 1   **[TELEGRAM]** / Later.
Pioneer Mail and Indian Weekly News, 11

C25   Oct. 1   **WITH   THE   MOHMAND   FIELD   FORCE. / Six
Engagements in Eight Days.** / Inayat Kila, 22nd
September.
Pioneer Mail and Indian Weekly News, 17–18
Letter to the *Pioneer Mail*.

C26   Oct. 6   **ON THE INDIAN FRONTIER** / Malakund [*sic*], Sept. 3
[all abbreviated dates as in original publication].
Daily Telegraph, 7
Subsequently collected in *Young Winston's Wars*, at pp. 3–6,
and *War Correspondent*, pp. 25–9. This and the subsequent
pieces in the *Daily Telegraph* are all indicated as being "By A
YOUNG OFFICER". Churchill was unhappy that the letters
were not signed (although it had been Lord Minto's view that
they should not be: see Lady Randolph Churchill's letter to
Churchill of 7 October 1897[6]). On 25 October 1897, he
wrote to his mother: "I will not conceal my disappointment at
their not being signed. I had written them with the design, a
design which took form as the correspondence advanced, of
bringing my personality before the electorate. I had hoped that
some political advantage might have accrued. This hope
encouraged me to take the very greatest pains with the style
and composition ... I do not think that I have ever written
anything better, or to which I would more willingly have

---

6. *Ibid.*, pp. 808–9, at p. 809.

signed my name."[7] This did not, of course, mean that their author remained anonymous. On 27 January 1898, he received a letter from the Prince of Wales, who acknowledged that he had read "with the greatest possible interest … your letters which appeared in the *Daily Telegraph*".[8] Churchill was paid £5 a column, half of the minimum £10 per column which he had anticipated. In his 21 April 1897 letter to Lady Randolph Churchill, while fixing his mother with the burden of finding him a paper which would "avail themselves of my services", he said, "I should expect to be paid £10 or £15 an article—customary rates for telegrams but would bear my own expenses."[9] On 5 January 1898, he reported, from Bangalore, his having received a cheque for Rs 1238, "about £80 at the current rate of exchange", from the *Daily Telegraph*.[10] In the end, Churchill earned £100 for his letters to the *Daily Telegraph*.[11]

C27	Oct. 7	**THE WAR IN THE INDIAN HIGHLANDS.** / Khar, Sept. 6. *Daily Telegraph*, 11 Subsequently collected in *Young Winston's Wars*, pp. 7–10, and *War Correspondent*, pp. 30–3.
C28	Oct. 8	**THE WAR IN THE INDIAN HIGHLANDS.** / Kotkai, Sept. 9. *Daily Telegraph*, 7 Subsequently collected in *Young Winston's Wars*, pp. 11–14, and *War Correspondent*, pp. 34–7.
C29	Oct. 8	**LATEST INDIAN INTELLIGENCE.** / **The Frontier Risings.** / **Severe Fighting with the Mamunds.** / **[Telegram]** / Inayat Kila, 1st October. *Pioneer Mail and Indian Weekly News*, 13
C30	Oct. 8	**[TELEGRAM of 4th October]** / Inayat Kila, 3rd October. *Pioneer Mail and Indian Weekly News*, 13–14
C31	Oct. 8	**[TELEGRAM]** / Later. *Pioneer Mail and Indian Weekly News*, 14

7. *Ibid.*, pp. 811–13, at p. 811.

8. *Ibid.*, pp. 881–2, at p. 881.

9. *Ibid.*, pp. 754–6, at p. 755.

10. *Ibid.*, pp. 852–5, at p. 853.

11. Letter of 8 February 1898 to Frances, Duchess of Marlborough (*ibid.*, pp. 876–7, at p. 876).

C32   Oct. 8   **[TELEGRAM of 5th October]** / Inayat Kila, 2nd October.
Pioneer Mail and Indian Weekly News, 14

C33   Oct. 9   **THE WAR IN THE INDIAN HIGHLANDS.** / Nawagai,
Sept. 12.
Daily Telegraph, 8
Subsequently collected in *Young Winston's Wars*, pp. 15–18,
and *War Correspondent*, pp. 38–41.

C34   Oct. 14   **WAR IN THE INDIAN HIGHLANDS.** / Camp Inayat
Kili [*sic*], Sept. 17.
Daily Telegraph, 6
Subsequently collected in *Young Winston's Wars*, pp. 19–21,
and *War Correspondent*, pp. 42–4.

C35   Oct. 15   **WAR IN THE INDIAN HIGHLANDS.** / Inayat Kili [*sic*],
Sept. 18.
Daily Telegraph, 5
Subsequently collected in *Young Winston's Wars*, pp. 22–6, and
War Correspondent, pp. 45–8.

C36   Oct. 15   **LATEST INDIAN INTELLIGENCE. / The Frontier
Risings. / Attitude of the Mahmunds. / Movements to
the Front. / The Tochi Operations. / [Telegram
through Panjkora.]** / Inayat Killa [*sic*], 5th October.
Pioneer Mail and Indian Weekly News, 12

C37   Oct. 15   **[TELEGRAM]** / Inayat Killa [*sic*], 6th October.
Pioneer Mail and Indian Weekly News, 12

C38   Oct. 15   **[TELEGRAM]** / Inayat Killa [*sic*], 7th October.
Pioneer Mail and Indian Weekly News, 12

C39   Oct. 15   **[TELEGRAM]** / Inayat Killa [*sic*], 10th October.
Pioneer Mail and Indian Weekly News, 12

C40   Oct. 15   **[TELEGRAM]** / Inayat Killa [*sic*], 12th October.
Pioneer Mail and Indian Weekly News, 12

C41   Oct. 15   **WITH THE MALAKAND FIELD FORCE.** / Inayat Killa
[*sic*], 4th October.
Pioneer Mail and Indian Weekly News, 17
Letter to the *Pioneer Mail*.

C50   Nov. 16   **THE WAR IN THE INDIAN HIGHLANDS.** / Inayati
                        Kila [*sic*], Oct. 8.
                        Daily Telegraph, 7–8
                        Subsequently collected in *Young Winston's Wars*, pp. 49–52,
                        and *War Correspondent*, pp. 70–3.

C51   Nov. 19   **THE WAR IN THE INDIAN HIGHLANDS.** /
                        Nowshera, Oct. 14.
                        Daily Telegraph, 7
                        Subsequently collected in *Young Winston's Wars*, pp. 53–6, and
                        War Correspondent, pp. 74–7.

C52   Dec. 3   **THE WAR IN THE INDIAN HIGHLANDS.** /
                        Nowshera, Oct. 15.
                        Daily Telegraph, 11
                        Subsequently collected in *Young Winston's Wars*, pp. 57–63,
                        and *War Correspondent*, pp. 78–84.

C53   Dec. 6   **THE WAR IN THE INDIAN HIGHLANDS.** /
                        Nowshera, Oct. 16.
                        Daily Telegraph, 10
                        Subsequently collected in *Young Winston's Wars*, pp. 64–6, and
                        War Correspondent, pp. 85–6.

1898

C54   August   **THE ETHICS OF FRONTIER POLICY.**
                        United Service Magazine, Vol. CXXXVIII (Vol. 17, New
                        Series), No. 837, 504–10
                        This article was, in a sense, solicited by the Editor, who, after
                        reading *The Story of the Malakand Field Force*, wrote to
                        Churchill to say that he had "seldom obtained so much
                        pleasure, as well as useful information, from a military
                        work. ... If you would care to write a Political strategical
                        article with reference to the northern Frontier of India I shall
                        be very pleased to insert it in the *U.S. Magazine*. I purposely
                        say 'insert' instead of my more usual term 'consider'."[12]
                        Churchill sent the article to Ian Hamilton in late March or
                        early April 1898, explaining that it had "been evoked by the
                        cordial invitation of the Journal of the U.S. Institution in
                        which it is to appear. I trust you will like it. I have chosen a
                        circuitous, insidious, but none the less effective method of

---

12. Letter of 19 March 1898 (R. Churchill, *WSC*, Vol. I, *C.V.* 2, p. 891).

defending the Forward Policy."[13] Subsequently collected in *Collected Essays*, Vol. I, pp. 30–5.

C55   Aug. 31   **THE SOUDAN CAMPAIGN. / Anglo–Egyptian Force Nearing Khartoum. / Friendlies Engaged. / Dervish Raiders Captured. / The War on the Nile.** / Korosko, August 8.
Morning Post, 5
Described as "the first of a series of letters received by a Correspondent from a friend in the Nile Expeditionary Force". Subsequently collected in *Young Winston's Wars*, pp. 69–74, and *War Correspondent*, pp. 89–93. Churchill was paid £15 a column for these despatches. The manuscript text for this and all but one of the remaining articles in the series are held in the Glenesk–Bathurst Papers, the Brotherton Library, at the University of Leeds. These are the texts as submitted by Churchill and they differ to some extent from the ultimately published versions.

C56   Sept. 2   **THE SOUDAN CAMPAIGN. / Cavalry Skirmish. / Dervish Position Shelled. / The War on the Nile.** / Wady Halfa, August 10.
Morning Post, 5
Subsequently collected in *Young Winston's Wars*, pp. 75–9, and *War Correspondent*, pp. 94–8.

C57   Sept. 23   **THE SOUDAN CAMPAIGN. / The Reconnaissance.** / The British Camp. Sept. 1.
Morning Post, 5

C58   Sept. 23   **THE SOUDAN CAMPAIGN. / The Battle.** / Omdurman, Sept. 2.
Morning Post, 5–6

C59   Sept. 24   **THE SOUDAN CAMPAIGN. / The War on the Nile.** / Atbara, August 15.
Morning Post, 5–6
Indicated as the third in the series of letters received by a correspondent from a friend in the Nile Expeditionary Force. Subsequently collected in *Young Winston's Wars*, pp. 80–4, and *War Correspondent*, pp. 99–103.

---

13. General Sir Ian Hamilton, *Listening for the Drums* (London: Faber and Faber, 1944), at p. 241 (**F62**). The letter is undated but from its substance would appear to have been written late in March or early in April 1898.

| C60 | Sept. 27 | **THE SOUDAN CAMPAIGN. / The War on the Nile.** / Bivouac Magyrich (Near Metemmeh), August 20. |

Morning Post, 5

Indicated as the fourth of the series of letters. Subsequently collected in *Young Winston's Wars*, pp. 85–8, and *War Correspondent*, pp. 104–7.

| C61 | Sept. 28 | **THE SOUDAN CAMPAIGN. / The Abyssinian Natives. / The War on the Nile.** / Camp before Shabluka, August 24. |

Morning Post, 5

Indicated as the fifth of the series of letters. Subsequently collected in *Young Winston's Wars*, pp. 89–92, and *War Correspondent*, pp. 108–11.

| C62 | Sept. 29 | **THE SOUDAN CAMPAIGN. / The Battle of Omdurman.** / Khartoum, Sept. 6. |

Morning Post, 5–6

Indicated as having been "written by a Combatant". Subsequently collected in *Young Winston's Wars*, pp. 104–13, and *War Correspondent*, pp. 123–32.

| C63 | Oct. 3 | **THE SOUDAN CAMPAIGN. / On the Road to Omdurman.** / Camp Wad Habeshi (before Shabluka), August 25. |

Morning Post, 5–6

Subsequently collected in *Young Winston's Wars*, pp. 93–7, and *War Correspondent*, pp. 112–16.

| C64 | Oct. 4 | **THE SOUDAN CAMPAIGN. / The Reconnaissance of Kerreri.** / Khartoum, Sept. 5. |

Morning Post, 5–6

Indicated as being "another letter" received from a correspondent on the war on the Nile. Subsequently collected in *Young Winston's Wars*, pp. 98–103, and *War Correspondent*, pp. 117–22.

| C65 | Oct. 6 | **THE SOUDAN CAMPAIGN. / After the Victory.** / Camp Omdurman, Sept. 9. |

Morning Post, 5

Another letter indicated, with the following one, as having been received "by a Correspondent from a friend in the Soudan Expeditionary Force". Subsequently collected in *Young Winston's Wars*, pp. 120–3, and *War Correspondent*, pp. 139–42.

C66   Oct. 6   **THE SOUDAN CAMPAIGN. / The Battlefield.** / Camp Omdurman, Sept. 10.
Morning Post, 5–6
Subsequently collected in *Young Winston's Wars*, pp. 124–9, and *War Correspondent*, pp. 143–7.

C67   Oct. 7   **THE SOUDAN CAMPAIGN. / Reflections on a Cavalry Charge.** / Camp Omdurman, Sept. 11.
Morning Post, 5–6
A further letter indicated as having been received by a correspondent from a friend in the Soudan Expeditionary Force. Subsequently collected in *Young Winston's Wars*, pp. 130–3, and *War Correspondent*, pp. 148–51.

C68   Oct. 8   **THE SOUDAN CAMPAIGN. / The City of Omdurman.** / Camp Omdurman, Sept. 12.
Morning Post, 5–6
Indicated as the thirteenth of the series of letters received by a correspondent from a friend in the Soudan Expeditionary Force. Subsequently collected in *Young Winston's Wars*, pp. 134–40, and *War Correspondent*, pp. 152–8.

C69   Oct. 11   **THE SOUDAN CAMPAIGN. / Back from Omdurman.** / Atbara Fort, Sept. 16.
Morning Post, 5
Indicated as the fourteenth of the letters received by a correspondent from a friend in the Soudan Expeditionary Force. Subsequently collected in *Young Winston's Wars*, pp. 141–7, and *War Correspondent*, pp. 159–65.

C70   Oct. 13   **THE SOUDAN CAMPAIGN. / Civilisation Once More.** / Assiout, Sept. 20.
Morning Post, 5
Indicated as the last of the series of "interesting letters" written to a correspondent by a friend in the Soudan Expeditionary Force. Subsequently collected in *Young Winston's Wars*, pp. 148–52, and *War Correspondent*, pp. 166–70.

C71   December   **THE FASHODA INCIDENT.**
North American Review, Vol. 167, No. 505, 736–43
On 10 November 1897, Churchill wrote to his mother that "The article on India ... is in a fair way to completion and I hope to make a struggle to finish it this month."[14] Books intervened and he was, of course, unsuccessful in this intention. Subsequently collected in *Collected Essays*, Vol. I, pp. 36–41.

---

14. R. Churchill, *WSC*, Vol. I, *C.V.* 2, pp. 825–6, at p. 825.

1899

C72a January **"MAN OVERBOARD!" / An Episode of the Red Sea**
Harmsworth Magazine, Vol. 1, No. 6, 662–4
Churchill's only published short story, illustrated by Henry
Austin. Subsequently collected in *Great Untold Stories of Fantasy
and Horror* (**B192**), *The Lucifer Society* (**B195**), *The Arbor House
Treasury of Horror and the Supernatural* (**B203**), *Demonic,
Dangerous and Deadly* (**B204**) and the *Collected Essays*, Vol. IV,
pp. 3–5. The story must have been written by March 1898
since Churchill sent it to General Ian Hamilton in late March
or early April 1898 with the following hope: "The story I send
you as it may amuse you for an hour on the voyage."[15]

C72b June **MAN OVERBOARD**
1965 *Argosy* (UK), 14–16

C73 **SAVROLA. / (A Military and Political Romance.)**
A. P. Watt, Churchill's agent, submitted *Affairs of State: A
Political Romance* to Macmillan, who, by their letter of 5
December 1898, agreed to "pay the sum of £100 for the right
to use the story as a serial in Macmillan's Magazine".[16] They
proposed that publication should begin in the April issue.
When they had not heard from Watt that Lady Randolph
Churchill accepted the offer on her son's behalf,[17] they
threatened to withdraw their offer.[18] Watt responded affirmatively the same day, having explained that Lady Randolph had
been out of town. It was at that time proposed that the story
be serialized in six parts "though the editor cannot bind
himself as to this just now".[19] Ultimately, it was published in
eight parts. The proofs were prepared by John Bale, Son &
Danielson, Ltd., Oxford House, 85–89 Great Titchfield
Street, London. The proofs for Chapters I to IX in the
Churchill Archives are dated 10 April 1899; those for Chapters

---

15. *Ibid.*
16. Watt Archives, #11036, Folder 39.16.
17. Churchill was then, of course, in India.
18. "It would not suit us to wait so long as five or six weeks to get an answer by post from the
author himself in India, and unless therefore you are in a position to communicate with him
by telegraph we must ask you to regard our offer as withdrawn, and we will return the
manuscript" (letter of 14 December 1898 from Macmillan to Watt; Watt Archives, #11036,
Folder 39.16).
19. Letter of 23 December (*ibid.*). The Editor was unable to provide the concluding date of the
serialization as late as 24 March 1899. In his letter of that date to Watt, he wrote: "The month
of its conclusion it is of course not easy to determine so exactly; but you will be safe in making
your arrangements for its publication in book form in January, 1900."

X to XIII are dated 23 June 1899; and those for the remainder of the serialization are dated August 1899.

C73a.1	May	**Chapters I–III** *Macmillan's Magazine*, 67–80
C73a.2	June	**Chapters IV–V** *Macmillan's Magazine*, No. 476, 152–60
C73a.3	July	**Chapters VI–VIII** *Macmillan's Magazine*, 226–40
C73a.4	August	**Chapters IX–XI** *Macmillan's Magazine*, 307–20
C73a.5	September	**Chapters XII–XIV** *Macmillan's Magazine*, 388–400
C73a.6	October	**Chapters XV–XVII** *Macmillan's Magazine*, 401–16
C73a.7	November	**Chapters XVIII–XX** *Macmillan's Magazine*, 1–13
C73a.8	December	**Chapters XXI, XXII and Conclusion** *Macmillan's Magazine*, 81–9

C73b	1942	**The First Serialization in the *Sunday Dispatch***
C73b.1	Jan. 4	**SAVROLA** *Sunday Dispatch*, 7
C73b.2	Jan. 11	**SAVROLA** *Sunday Dispatch*, 7
C73b.3	Jan. 18	**SAVROLA** *Sunday Dispatch*, 7
C73b.4	Jan. 25	**SAVROLA** *Sunday Dispatch*, 7
C73b.5	Feb. 1	**SAVROLA** *Sunday Dispatch*, 7
C73b.6	Feb. 8	**SAVROLA** *Sunday Dispatch*, 7

C73b.7	Feb. 15	**SAVROLA** *Sunday Dispatch*, 7
C73b.8	Feb. 22	**SAVROLA** *Sunday Dispatch*, 7
C73b.9	March 1	**SAVROLA** *Sunday Dispatch*, 7

C73c   **1948**   **The French Serialization**

C73c.1	February	**SAVROLA / Roman** inédit de Winston Churchill [Chapters I–VII] *France Illustration Littéraire et Théâtrale*, No. 12, 3–18
C73c.2	March	**SAVROLA / Roman** inédit de Winston Churchill [Chapters VII *cont.*–XVII] *France Illustration Littéraire et Théâtrale*, No. 13, 3–26
C73c.3	April	**SAVROLA / Roman** inédit de Winston Churchill [Chapters XVII *cont.*–XXII] *France Illustration Littéraire et Théâtrale*, No. 14, 3–16

C73d   **1954–5**   **The Second Serialization in the *Sunday Dispatch***

C73d.1	Nov. 28	**SAVROLA** *Sunday Dispatch*, 5
C73d.2	Dec. 5	**SAVROLA** *Sunday Dispatch*, 5
C73d.3	Dec. 12	**SAVROLA** *Sunday Dispatch*, 7
C73d.4	Dec. 19	**SAVROLA** *Sunday Dispatch*, 9
C73d.5	Dec. 26	**SAVROLA** *Sunday Dispatch*, 7
C73d.6	Jan. 2	**SAVROLA** *Sunday Dispatch*, 7
C73d.7	Jan. 9	**SAVROLA / Dictator Shoots at People's Leader** *Sunday Dispatch*, 9

C73d.8   Jan. 16   **SAVROLA / Truce Envoy Is Shot Dead**
                          Sunday Dispatch, 7

C73d.9   Jan. 23   **SAVROLA / The End of a Dictator**
                          Sunday Dispatch, 9

C73d.10   Jan. 30   **SAVROLA / City at Mercy of Fleet—Order for Arrest of Democrat Leader**
                          Sunday Dispatch, 9

C73e   July 16,   **SAVROLA**
               1955   *Star Weekly*, 1–11

C74a   Nov. 16   **"ALL WELL AT LADYSMITH."** / Estcourt, Nov. 10, 9.55 p.m.
                          Morning Post, 5
                          The *Morning Post* of 17 November states that this telegram, which is reprinted there (see **C74b**), appeared on 16 November in the second edition only. I have been unable to examine a copy of the latter.[20] This was, in any case, the first of Churchill's despatches to the *Morning Post* (others of earlier dates were published later; *see* **C78–C82**). The history of this arrangement is as follows. In anticipation of the impending hostilities, Alfred Harmsworth, proprietor of the *Daily Mail*, asked Churchill to serve as their correspondent. He immediately communicated with Oliver Borthwick, later Lord Glenesk, proprietor of the *Morning Post*, and offered his services, as described in his letter of 18 September 1899 to his mother, "for my expenses, copyright of work, and one thousand pounds—for four months from shore to shore—two hundred a month afterwards. He has accepted so that I am at their disposal."[21]

C74b   Nov. 17   **"ALL WELL AT LADYSMITH."** / Estcourt, Nov. 10, 9.55 p.m.
                          Morning Post, 5
                          In order of appearance on p. 5 of the *Morning Post* of the 17th,[22] this is the fourth of the telegrams from Churchill.

---

20. See footnote 22, below.
21. R. Churchill, *WSC*, Vol. I, *C.V.* 2, at p. 1049.
22. The British Library's copy (on microfilm) of the November 17 paper is the *second* (6.25 a.m.) edition. Regrettably, the BL copy of the November 16 paper is the *first* edition, which does *not* contain Churchill's telegram of November 10 at 9.55 p.m., namely, **C74a**, which was his very first despatch to the paper.

C75   Nov. 17   **ESTCOURT ON THE ALERT.** / **Heliographic Humour.** / Estcourt, Nov. 12, 9.30 a.m.
Morning Post, 5
This telegram, the two following and **C74b** all appear under the broad heading 'Mr. Churchill's Despatches'. There are also numerous stories dealing with Churchill's capture in columns 1, 2, 4 and 5.

C76   Nov. 17   **RAILWAY SEVERED.** / Estcourt, Nov. 13, 4.35 p.m.
Morning Post, 5

C77   Nov. 17   **TUGELA CROSSED.** / **Boer Braggadocio.** / Estcourt, Nov. 13, 6.45 p.m.
Morning Post, 5

C78   Nov. 18   **STEAMING SOUTH.** / **Incidents of the Voyage.** / R.M.S. Dunottar Castle, at Sea, Oct. 26.
Morning Post, 7–8
Under the heading 'OUR CAPTURED CORRE-SPONDENT. | MR. WINSTON CHURCHILL'S GALLANTRY.', on p. 5, there appear excerpts from the coverage by *The Times*, *Standard*, *Daily News*, *Daily Telegraph*, *Daily Graphic*, *Daily Mail*, *Spectator*, and eleven other British newspapers.

C79   Nov. 27   **ARRIVAL AND SITUATION.** / **The Man Who Knew.** / Capetown, Nov. 1.
Morning Post, 5–6
Under the broad heading 'War Letters from Winston S. Churchill and E. F. Knight, Our *War Correspondents*'.

C80   Nov. 27   **THE SOUTHERN FRONTIER.** / **A Journey and Many Incidents.** / East London, Nov. 5.
Morning Post, 6
Subsequently collected in *Young Winston's Wars*, pp. 155–9, and *War Correspondent*, pp. 173–7.

C81   Dec. 6   **WITH HEADQUARTERS.** / **To Pietermaritzburg.** / Estcourt, Nov. 6.
Morning Post, 5–6
Under the broad heading 'War Letter from Winston Spencer Churchill, Our *War Correspondent*'. Subsequently collected in *Young Winston's Wars*, pp. 160–3, and *War Correspondent*, pp. 178–81.

C82	Dec. 7	**WITH HEADQUARTERS. / Cruise in the Armoured Train.** / Estcourt, Nov. 9. *Morning Post*, 7–8 Under the broad heading 'War Letter from Winston Spencer Churchill, Our *War Correspondent*'.
C83a	Dec. 27	**THE WAR. / Mr. Winston Churchill. / How He Escaped. / Wandering for Five Days. / Sixty Hours of Misery.** / Lourenço Marques, Dec. 21, 10 p.m. *Morning Post*, 5
C83b	Dec. 28	**"THE STORY OF MY ESCAPE."** / Lourenço Marques, Dec. 21, 10 p.m. *Morning Post*, 5 While the text shows some marked differences from that published in the previous day's second edition, it is essentially the same telegram. The editors state: "The substance of this telegram appeared in our Second Edition yesterday."
C83c	Dec. 28	**HOW I ESCAPED. / Mr. Winston Churchill Tells His Story. / Six Days of Adventure and Misery.** *Daily Mail*, 5
C83d	Dec. 30	**HOW I ESCAPED FROM PRETORIA.** *Pearson's Illustrated War News*, No. 11, 3
C84	Dec. 30	**SOUTH AFRICAN SITUATION. / Boer Expectations. / Big Indemnity. / What Must Be Done. / The Change in Command.** / Durban, Dec. 23, 9.45 p.m. *Morning Post*, 5 The editors advise that the greater part of the telegram appeared in the previous day's second edition, which I have been unable to examine.
C85	Dec. 30	**OPERATIONS IN NATAL. / At Chieveley Camp. / Daily Bombardments.** / Chieveley Camp, Dec. 27, 5.30 p.m. *Morning Post*, 5
C86	Dec. 30	**THE BRITISH PRISONERS. / Life in Pretoria. / Monotonous Inactivity.** / Chieveley Camp, Dec. 27, 2.20 p.m. *Morning Post*, 5

1900

C87 Jan. 1 **OPERATIONS IN NATAL. / With General Buller. / Battle of Search Lights. / Americans and the Volunteers. / Officers Needed.** / Frere Camp, Dec. 30, 1.15 p.m.
Morning Post, 5

C88 Jan. 1 **"WITH HEADQUARTERS." / Fate of the Armoured Train.** / Pretoria, Nov. 19.
Morning Post, 5–6
Under the broad heading 'War Letters from Winston S. Churchill, Our *War Correspondent**'. Subsequently collected in *Young Winston's Wars*, pp. 164–72, and *War Correspondent*, pp. 182–90.

C89a Jan. 1 **PRISONERS OF WAR.**
Morning Post, 6
Letter of 20 November 1899. Subsequently collected in *Young Winston's Wars*, pp. 173–7, and *War Correspondent*, pp. 191–5.

C89b Jan. 2 **MR. WINSTON CHURCHILL'S EXPERIENCES. / A British Prisoner's Sensations. / Generous Tribute to the Boer Forces.**
Manchester Guardian, 6

C90 Jan. 2 **OPERATIONS IN NATAL. / Reinforcements for Buller. / Boers Busy Entrenching. / New Armoured Train.** / Frere Camp, Jan. 1, 12.25 p.m.
Morning Post, 5

C91a Jan. 2 **NICHOLSON'S NEK FIGHT. / Col. Carleton's Surrender. / Captured Officers' Accounts.** / Frere Camp, Dec. 30, 8 p.m.
Morning Post, 5
The surrender at Nicholson's Nek actually occurred on 30 October 1899, on the day of Churchill's first sighting of land from on board the *Dunottar Castle*, just prior to his arrival in Cape Town. He only learned details of the engagement "during his enforced sojourn in Pretoria", from officers who had been taken prisoner in that engagement. This telegram recounts their tale.

C91b Jan. 3 **THE NICHOLSON'S NEK DISASTER. / Mr. Winston Churchill's Account. / Unauthorised Hoisting of the White Flag.**
Manchester Guardian, 3
A part only of the *Morning Post* telegram.

| C92 | Jan. 5 | **OPERATIONS IN NATAL. / Harassing the Boers. /** Frere Camp, Jan. 3, 1.15 p.m. *Morning Post*, 5 |

| C93 | Jan. 6 | **OPERATIONS IN NATAL. / Incidents at Chieveley. /** Chieveley, Jan. 4. *Morning Post*, 5 |

| C94 | Jan. 8 | **OPERATIONS IN NATAL. / The Attack on Ladysmith.** / Frere Camp, Jan. 6, 2.45 p.m. *Morning Post*, 5 |

| C95 | Jan. 9 | **HEAVY FIRING AT LADYSMITH.** / Frere Camp, Jan. 6, 11.50 a.m. *Morning Post*, 5 Note that the superhead 'Operations in Natal' precedes the previous article on p. 5, which is not written by Churchill. |

| C96 | Jan. 9 | **DEMONSTRATION IN RELIEF.** / Frere Camp, Jan. 6, 9.30 p.m. *Morning Post*, 5 |

| C96/1 | Jan. 10 | **THE UITLANDER GRIEVANCES.** *Morning Leader*, 8 Subsequently separately published under the same title (*see* **A2/1**). |

| C97 | Jan. 11 | **OPERATIONS IN NATAL. / The Attack on Ladysmith. / Further Details.** / Frere Camp, Jan. 8, 9.15 a.m. *Morning Post*, 5 |

| C98 | Jan. 11 | **[TELEGRAM]** / Frere Camp, Jan. 8, 12.45 p.m. *Morning Post*, 5 |

| C99 | Jan. 19 | **OPERATIONS IN NATAL. / The Tugela Crossed. / Boer Positions Shelled.** / Spearman's Farm, Jan. 18, 7.15 a.m. *Morning Post*, 5 |

| C100 | Jan. 20 | **OPERATIONS IN NATAL. / General Buller's Advance. / Enemy Unresponsive.** / Spearman's Camp, Jan. 19, 10.10 a.m. *Morning Post*, 5 |

C101   Jan. 22   **OPERATIONS IN NATAL. / The British Advance. /**
Spearman's Camp, Jan. 20, evening.
Morning Post, 5

C102   Jan. 23   **OPERATIONS IN NATAL. / Warren's Advance. /**
Spearman's Camp, Jan. 22, 8 a.m.
Morning Post, 5
Note that the following day's appearance of Churchill's
"graphic description of his escape from Pretoria and of his
subsequent adventures until he reached Delagoa Bay" is antici-
pated in column 3 under the heading 'Mr. Churchill's
Adventures'.

C103   Jan. 23   **THE INVASION OF NATAL. / A Time of Crisis.**
Morning Post, 5–6
Letter from Estcourt of 10 November under the rubric 'War
Letters. | From Our Special Correspondents.*'

C104a   Jan. 24   **HOW I ESCAPED FROM PRETORIA, AND MY
SUBSEQUENT ADVENTURES ON THE ROAD TO
DELAGOA BAY.**
Morning Post, 5–6
Subsequently collected in *Young Winston's Wars*, pp. 178–89,
and *War Correspondent*, pp. 196–206.

C104b   March 3   **HOW I ESCAPED FROM PRETORIA, AND MY
SUBSEQUENT ADVENTURES ON THE ROAD TO
DELAGOA BAY.**
War Pictures, 98–104
Under the superhead, 'The Story of the War', which began
every issue.

C105a   Jan. 26   **THE   WAR. / Warren's   Advance. / The   Recent
Fighting. / Graphic   Description. / Ladysmith   Co-
operating.** / Spearman's Camp, Jan. 23, 10 a.m.
Morning Post, 5
In the second edition. I have been unable to examine a first
edition of the newspaper and do not know whether the
Churchill contribution also appeared there.

C105b   Jan. 27   **OPERATIONS IN NATAL. / Incidents of the
Fighting.** / Spearman's Camp, Jan. 23, 10 a.m.
Morning Post, 5
The re-publication of the telegram of the previous day under
a new heading.

C106a   Jan. 26   **PROGRESS OF THE ADVANCE.** / Spearman's Camp, Jan. 23, 10 p.m.
Morning Post, 5

C106b   Jan. 27   **RECENT OPERATIONS DESCRIBED.** / Spearman's Camp, Jan. 23, 10 p.m.
Morning Post, 5
The re-publication of the telegram of the previous day under a new heading.

C107   Jan. 27   **IN THE BRITISH LINES AGAIN.** / Frere Camp, Natal, Dec. 24.
Morning Post, 5–6
Letter from Frere Camp of 24 December under the rubric 'War Letter from Winston Spencer Churchill'. Subsequently collected in *Young Winston's Wars*, pp. 190–7, and *War Correspondent*, pp. 207–13.

C108   Jan. 29   **OPERATIONS IN NATAL. / The Capture of Spion Kop.** / Spearman's Camp, Jan. 24.
Morning Post, 5

C109   Feb. 1   **OPERATIONS IN NATAL. / Supreme Effort Impending.** / Spearman's Camp, Jan. 28, 9.35 a.m.
Morning Post, 5

C110   Feb. 1   **SPION KOP FIGHTING.** / Spearman's Camp, Jan. 27, 1.10 p.m.
Morning Post, 5
The editor reports that the article appeared in the second edition of the previous day but I have been unable to locate that appearance or the title under which it was published. The editor also notes that this telegram and the two which follow, "though dated January 27, were probably despatched by Mr. Churchill on January 25".

C111   Feb. 1   **BOER LOSSES.** / Spearman's Camp, Jan. 27, 5.50 p.m.
Morning Post, 5
The article is also reported to have appeared in the second edition of the previous day but I have been unable to locate that appearance or the title under which it was published.

C112   Feb. 1   **GLORIOUS DEFENCE.** / Spearman's Camp, Jan. 27, 5.55 p.m.
                          Morning Post, 5
                          This article appeared in the second edition of the previous day but I have been unable to locate that appearance or the title under which it was published.

C113   Feb. 2   **OPERATIONS IN NATAL. / Buller's Task.** / Pietermaritzburg, Jan. 29, 3.40 p.m.
                          Morning Post, 5

C114   Feb. 2   **THE POSITION SURVEYED.** / Pietermaritzburg, Jan. 29, 6.50 p.m.
                          Morning Post, 5

C115   Feb. 3   **OPERATIONS IN NATAL. / Colonel Long's Position.** / Pietermaritzburg, Jan. 31, 9 p.m.
                          Morning Post, 7
                          The following telegram on p. 7, "The 'Maine' at Durban", would appear, by its proximity to this one and the practice of the editors, to be by Churchill as well; however, the dateline is Durban, Jan. 30, 9.30 a.m., and this would scarcely have given Churchill the time to make the 60-mile journey unless he travelled through the night from Pietermaritzburg to Durban, returning later that day or the following one. As Churchill observed elsewhere, "the journey occupies four hours".[23]

C116   Feb. 5   **OPERATIONS IN NATAL. / Spirit of Buller's Force.** / Spearman's Camp, Feb. 3, 9.10 p.m.
                          Morning Post, 5

C117   Feb. 5   **PERSONAL EXPLANATION.** / Spearman's Camp, Feb. 2, 1.20 p.m.
                          Morning Post, 5
                          This interesting telegram provides further insight into the notion circulating at the time that General Joubert had in fact already ordered Churchill's release at the time of his escape. Note also the presence of a large and very detailed map of the theatre of war from Spearman's Hill to Colenso described "as the most accurate yet published in this country".

---

23. *London to Ladysmith via Pretoria* (**A4**), at p. 43.

C118	Feb. 5	**WITH HEADQUARTERS. / Christmas and New Year.** / Chieveley Camp, Jan. 4. *Morning Post*, 5 Letter from Chieveley Camp, of 4 January, under the rubric 'War Letters from Our Special Correspondents'.
C119	Feb. 6	**WITH HEADQUARTERS. / A Military Demonstration and Some Good News.** *Morning Post*, 7–8 Letter from camp before Colenso, of 8 January, under the rubric 'War Letter'.
C120	Feb. 10	**OPERATIONS IN NATAL. / The Tugela Situation.** / Springfield Bridge, Feb. 8, 8.20 p.m. *Morning Post*, 5
C121	Feb. 12	**OPERATIONS IN NATAL. / Review of the Situation.** / Frere Camp, Feb. 9, 10.15 a.m. *Morning Post*, 5
C122	Feb. 12	**INCIDENTS OF THE FIGHTING.** / Frere Camp, Feb. 10, 7.55 p.m. *Morning Post*, 5
C123	Feb. 13	**THE DASH FOR POTGIETER'S FERRY** *Morning Post*, 7–8 Letter from Camp, Spearman's Hill, of 13 January, under the rubric 'War Letters from Our Special Correspondents'. Note that no point follows the title.
C124	Feb. 15	**OPERATIONS IN NATAL. / Dundonald's Engagement.** / Chieveley Camp, Feb. 13, 3.30 p.m. *Morning Post*, 5
C125	Feb. 15	**SKIRMISH AT SPRINGFIELD.** / Chieveley Camp, Feb. 13, 3.35 p.m. *Morning Post*, 5
C126	Feb. 17	**OPERATIONS IN NATAL. / New Appointments.** / Chieveley Camp, Feb. 14, 10 p.m. *Morning Post*, 7
C127	Feb. 17	**THE PASSAGE OF THE TUGELA.** *Morning Post*, 7–8 Letter from Camp Venter Spruit, of 22 January, under the rubric 'War Letters from Winston Spencer Churchill, Our *War Correspondent*'. Subsequently collected in *Young*

Winston's Wars, pp. 198–209, and War Correspondent, pp. 214–25.

C128   Feb. 17   **FIVE DAYS' ACTION AT SPION KOP.**
Morning Post, 8
The second of Churchill's two letters in this issue, this from Cavalry Camp, Venter Spruit, 25 January. Subsequently collected in *Young Winston's Wars*, pp. 210–18, and *War Correspondent*, pp. 226–34.[24]

C129   Feb. 19   **OPERATIONS IN NATAL. / Buller Active.** / Hussar Hill, Feb. 14 / (Via Chieveley Camp, Feb. 18).
Morning Post, 5

C130   Feb. 21   **OPERATIONS IN NATAL. / Buller's Line of Advance.** / Chieveley Camp, Feb. 19, 3.40 p.m.
Morning Post, 7

C131   Feb. 22   **OPERATIONS IN NATAL. / Buller's Turning Movement.** / Chieveley Camp, Feb. 19.
Morning Post, 5

C132   Feb. 22   **STEPS IN THE ADVANCE.** / Chieveley Camp, Feb. 20, 8.10 a.m.
Morning Post, 5

C133   Feb. 22   **DEMANDS OF THE SITUATION.** / Chieveley Camp, Feb. 20, 6.45 p.m.
Morning Post, 5

C134   Feb. 24   **OPERATIONS IN NATAL. / Buller's Advance.** / Chieveley Camp, Feb. 21, 7.35 p.m.
Morning Post, 7

C135   Feb. 27   **OPERATIONS IN NATAL. / Steps Towards Ladysmith.** / Frere Camp, Feb. 25, 8.55 a.m.
Morning Post, 7

C136   Feb. 27   **MAGNIFICENT FIGHTING.** / Colenso Camp, Feb. 25, 11 a.m.
Morning Post, 7

C137   Feb. 27   **SPION KOP DISSOLVING VIEWS.**
Morning Post, 7–8
Letter from Camp Venter Spruit, of 25 January, under the

24. Where it is incorrectly dated 23 January.

rubric 'War Letter from Winston Spencer Churchill, Our *War Correspondent*'. Subsequently collected in *Young Winston's Wars*, pp. 219–29, and *War Correspondent*, pp. 234–44.

C138   March 1   **OPERATIONS IN NATAL. / The Boer Strength.** / Colenso Camp, Feb. 27, 10.15 a.m.
Morning Post, 5

C139   March 1   **USE OF EXPANDING BULLETS.** / Colenso, Feb. 27.
Morning Post, 5
There is an excellent detailed map of the theatre of war in Natal on p. 6 of the 2 March issue of the *Morning Post*.

C140   March 3   **OPERATIONS IN NATAL. / The Relief of Ladysmith.** / Colenso Camp, March 1, 10.25 a.m.
Morning Post, 5

C141   March 3   **THE BATTLE OF PIETERS.** / Colenso Camp, March 1, 10 a.m.
Morning Post, 5

C142   March 3   **SPIRIT OF THE TROOPS.** / Colenso Camp, March 1, 7.15 p.m.
Morning Post, 5

—   March 3   **HOW I ESCAPED FROM PRETORIA** (*War Pictures*; *see* **C104b**)

C143   March 5   **A WEEK'S REST.**
Morning Post, 5
Letter from camp, Spearman's Hill, of 4 February, under the rubric 'War Letter from Winston Spencer Churchill, Our *War Correspondent*'. Subsequently collected in *Young Winston's Wars*, pp. 230–3, and *War Correspondent*, pp. 245–8.

C144   March 6   **OPERATIONS IN NATAL. / Relieved Ladysmith.** / Nelthorpe Camp, March 3, 6.35 p.m.
Morning Post, 7

C145   March 6   **BULLER'S ACHIEVEMENT.** / Colenso Camp, March 3, 7.15 p.m.
Morning Post, 7

C146   March 6   **THE ENTRY INTO LADYSMITH.** / Durban, March 4 (?3rd) [*sic*]
Morning Post, 7

C147 March 7 **OPERATIONS IN NATAL. / The Naval Guns. /** Durban, March 5.
Morning Post, 7

C148.1 March 7 **SIR GEORGE WHITE INTERVIEWED.** / Durban, March 4, 7.30 p.m.
Morning Post, 7
The editors indicate that this instalment of the interview first appeared in the second edition of 6 March but I have been unable to locate a copy of that edition to examine.

C148.2 March 8 **OPERATIONS IN NATAL. / Sir George White's Views.** / Durban, March 6.
Morning Post, 7

C149 March 7 **BRITISH OFFICERS ESCAPE.** / Durban, March 5, 12.30 p.m.
Morning Post, 7
The editors indicate that this telegram appeared in the second edition of the *Morning Post* of 6 March but I have been unable to locate a copy of that edition to examine. Note that the escape reported here by Churchill is that of Captain Haldane and Lieutenant Brockie, the two officers who had tried to escape with him from the Model School in Pretoria.

C150 March 10 **THE COMBAT OF VAAL KRANTZ.**
Morning Post, 7–8
Letter from General Buller's Headquarters, of 9 February, published under the rubric 'War Letters from Our Special Correspondents'.

C151 March 14 **OPERATIONS IN NATAL. / General White's Departure.** / Durban, March 12, 4.55 p.m.
Morning Post, 7

C152 March 14 **CRONJE'S TREATMENT.** / Durban, March 12, 5 p.m.
Morning Post, 7

C153 March 19 **OPERATIONS IN NATAL. / Positions of Forces. /** Ladysmith (Via Pietermaritzburg, March 16).
Morning Post, 5

C154 March 19 **ST. PATRICK'S DAY IN DURBAN.** / Durban, March 17, 6.55 p.m.
Morning Post, 5

C155   March 19   **ON THE TUGELA.**
Morning Post, 5–6
Letter from General Buller's headquarters, of 15 February, under the rubric 'War Letter from Winston Churchill, Our Special Correspondent'. Subsequently collected in *Young Winston's Wars*, pp. 234–9, and *War Correspondent*, pp. 249–53.[25]

C156   March 21   **OPERATIONS IN NATAL. / On Behalf of Buller. /** Pietermaritzburg, March 19, 6.15 p.m.
Morning Post, 7

C157   March 21   **RETURN OF THE "MAINE."** / Pietermaritzburg, March 19.
Morning Post, 7

C158   March 21   **THE LARGE NAVAL GUN.** / Pietermaritzburg, March 19.
Morning Post, 7

C159   March 21   **THE TUGELA BRIDGE.** / Pietermaritzburg, March 19.
Morning Post, 7

C160   March 22   **THE TRANSVAAL. / Treatment of Prisoners. /** Pietermaritzburg, March 21, 4 p.m.
Morning Post, 5
This is an unexpected heading since all of Churchill's previous telegrams had been published under the rubric 'Operations in Natal'.

C161   March 23   **OPERATIONS IN NATAL. / Treatment of Rebels. /** Ladysmith, March 22, Noon.
Morning Post, 5

C162   March 23   **POSTAL DEFECTS.** / Ladysmith, March 22.
Morning Post, 5

C163   March 24   **OPERATIONS IN NATAL. / Boer Defensive Positions.** / Ladysmith, March 22, 4 p.m.
Morning Post, 5

C164   March 24   **THE CENSOR AND CRITICISM.** / Ladysmith, March 22.
Morning Post, 5

---

25. Erroneously dated there as 13 February.

C165   March 26   **OPERATIONS IN NATAL. / Military Considerations.**
                        / Ladysmith, March 24, 2 p.m.
                        Morning Post, 5

C166   March 27   **TREATMENT OF REBELS. / Appeal for Leniency.** /
                        Ladysmith, March 24, 2.5 [*sic*] p.m. / (Delayed by the Censor.)
                        Morning Post, 7

C167   March 27   **SOME SUGGESTIONS.** / Ladysmith, March 25, 5.30 p.m.
                        Morning Post, 7

C168   March 27   **THE VICTORY OF MONTE CRISTO.**
                        Morning Post, 7–8
                        Letter from camp, Cingolo Neck, of 19 February, published
                        under the rubric 'War Letter from Winston Churchill,
                        Our Special Correspondent'. Subsequently collected in
                        Young Winston's Wars, pp. 240–7, and *War Correspondent*,
                        pp. 254–60.

C169   March 31   **TREATMENT OF REBELS.** / Durban, March 30, 4.15
                        p.m.
                        Morning Post, 5

C170   April 7   **THE BATTLE OF PIETERS. / The Passage of the
                        River.**
                        Morning Post, 7
                        Letter of 4 March from the hospital ship *Maine*, under the
                        rubric 'War Letter from Winston Spencer Churchill, Our
                        Special Correspondent'.

C171   April 10   **THE THIRD DAY AT PIETERS. / Attack of the Irish
                        Brigade.**
                        Morning Post, 5–6
                        Letter of 5 March from the hospital ship *Maine*, under the
                        rubric 'War Letter from Winston Spencer Churchill, Our
                        Special Correspondent', including a map of the area of
                        fighting. Subsequently collected in *Young Winston's Wars*,
                        pp. 248–57, and *War Correspondent*, pp. 261–70.

C172   April 11   **THE ANNIVERSARY OF MAJUBA. / Seventh Day's
                        Action at Pieters.**
                        Morning Post, 5
                        Letter of 6 March from the Commandant's Office, Durban,
                        under the rubric 'War Letter from Winston Spencer
                        Churchill, Our Special Correspondent', including a map of
                        fighting in the area. Subsequently collected in *Young Winston's
                        Wars*, pp. 258–65, and *War Correspondent*, pp. 271–7.

C173   April 12   **THE RELIEF OF LADYSMITH.**
Morning Post, 5–6
Letter of 9 March from the Commandant's Office, Durban, under the rubric 'War Letter from Winston Spencer Churchill, Our Special Correspondent'. Subsequently collected in *Young Winston's Wars*, pp. 266–73, and *War Correspondent*, pp. 278–84.

C174   April 14   **THE DUKE OF MARLBOROUGH.** / Bloemfontein, April 13, 1.15 p.m.
Morning Post, 5

C175   April 16   **IN THE ORANGE STATE. / Lord Roberts's Army. /** Bloemfontein, April 13, 6.10 p.m.
Morning Post, 5

C176   April 16   **NEED FOR REMOUNTS.** / Bloemfontein, April 14, 4.10 p.m.
Morning Post, 5

C177   April 16   **THE RELIEF OF LADYSMITH. / After the Siege.**
Morning Post, 5–6
Letter of 10 March from Durban, under the rubric 'War Letter from Winston Spencer Churchill, Our Special Correspondent'. Subsequently collected in *Young Winston's Wars*, pp. 274–87, and *War Correspondent*, pp. 285–97.

C178   April 23   **IN THE ORANGE STATE. / Rundle's Flying Column.** / Oorlogs Poort, April 19, 8 p.m.
Morning Post, 5

C179   April 23   **BOER POSITIONS CAPTURED.** / Wakkerstroom, April 20, 8.45 p.m.
Morning Post, 5

C180   April 23   **ENEMY'S REAR RECONNOITRED.** / Wakkerstroom, April 21, 10 p.m.
Morning Post, 5
Note: There is an interview with Lady Randolph Churchill in the *Morning Post* of the following day under the title 'Return of the "Maine."' on p. 4.

C181   April 25   **COMBINED OPERATIONS.** / Wakkerstroom, April 23, 9 p.m.
Morning Post, 7

C182   May 2   **IN THE ORANGE STATE. / The** Fighting at
                         Thabanchu. / Thabanchu, April 28.
                         Morning Post, 7

C183   May 3   **THE FIGHTING AT THABANCHU.** / Thabanchu,
                         April 29.
                         Morning Post, 7

C184   May 4   **IN THE ORANGE STATE. / The Recent Movements.**
                         / Bloemfontein, May 2, 4.25 p.m.
                         Morning Post, 5

C185   May 10   **HAMILTON'S MARCH TO WINBURG.** / Winburg,
                         May 6, 12.55 p.m.
                         Morning Post, 7

C186   May 11   **IN THE ORANGE STATE. / The** Capture of
                         Winburg. / Winburg, May 7.
                         Morning Post, 5

C187   May 11   **ENEMY'S STORES SEIZED.** / Winburg, May 7, Later.
                         Morning Post, 5

C188   May 11   **ADVANCE TO BLOEMPLAATS.** / Bloemplaats, May 9.
                         Morning Post, 5

C189   May 12   **VENTERSBURG OCCUPIED.** / Ventersburg, May 10.
                         Morning Post, 7

C190   May 14   **A ROVING COMMISSION.**
                         Morning Post, 5–6
                         Letter of 31 March "in the train", under the rubric 'War Letter
                         from Winston Spencer Churchill, Our Special
                         Correspondent'.

C191   May 17   **AT HALF-WAY HOUSE.**
                         Morning Post, 7–8
                         Letter of 16 April from Bloemfontein, under the rubric 'War
                         Letter from Winston Spencer Churchill, Our Special
                         Correspondent'.

C192   May 21   **EXIT GENERAL GATACRE.**
                         Morning Post, 5–6
                         Letter of 13 April from Bloemfontein, under the rubric 'War
                         Letter from Winston Spencer Churchill, Our Special
                         Correspondent'.

C193	May 22	**IN THE ORANGE STATE. / Occupation of Lindley. /** Lindley, May 19, 8.15 a.m. *Morning Post*, 7

C194	May 24	**THE CAPTURE OF HEILBRON.** / Heilbron, May 22. *Morning Post*, 7

C195   May 26   **TWO DAYS WITH BRABAZON.**
Morning Post, 7–8
Letter of 21 April from Dewetsdorp, under the rubric 'War Letter from Winston Spencer Churchill, Our Special Correspondent'.

C196   May 28   **TWO DAYS WITH BRABAZON.**
Morning Post, 5–6
Letter of 22 April from camp before Dewetsdorp, under the rubric 'War Letter from Winston Spencer Churchill, Our Special Correspondent'. Subsequently collected in *Young Winston's Wars*, pp. 288–93, and *War Correspondent*, pp. 298–303.

C197   June 4   **FIRST WIRE.**
Morning Post, 6
Note of 280 words to the war correspondent F. H. Prevost Battersby on the advance of Rundle's column. Undated but censored at Dewetsdorp on 21 April.

C198   June 4   **SECOND WIRE.**
Morning Post, 6
Note of 330 words to Battersby on the same subject. Also undated but censored at Bloemfontein on 21 April.

C199   June 6   **THE TRANSVAAL. / Fighting for Johannesburg. /** Doornkop, May 31. *Morning Post*, 5

C200   June 6   **AWAITING THE SURRENDER.** / Johannesburg, June 1. *Morning Post*, 5

C201   June 11   **ORANGE RIVER COLONY. / Hamilton's Advance North.** / Heilbron, May 22. *Morning Post*, 5

C202	June 18	**THE DEWETSDORP EPISODE.**

THE DEWETSDORP EPISODE.
Morning Post, 5–6
Letter of 1 May from Bloemfontein, under the rubric 'War Letter from Winston Spencer Churchill, Our Special Correspondent'.

C203.1   June 23   **IAN HAMILTON'S MARCH. / First Article.**
Morning Post, 7–8
Letter of 8 May from Winburg, under the rubric 'War Letter from Winston Spencer Churchill, Our Special Correspondent', together with diagrams/maps explaining Hamilton's action at Israel's Poort on April 25 and French's operations around Thabanchu on April 26–7.

C203.2   June 25   **IAN HAMILTON'S MARCH. / Last Article.**
Morning Post, 5–6
Letter of 8 May from Winburg, under the rubric 'War Letter from Winston Spencer Churchill, Our Special Correspondent', together with a rough sketch of the action of Houtnek of 30 April and 1 May. Subsequently collected in *Young Winston's Wars*, pp. 294–302, and *War Correspondent*, pp. 304–12.

C204.1   June 27   **THE TRANSVAAL. / Baden-Powell Interviewed. /** Pretoria, June 19.
Morning Post, 7

C204.2   June 28   **THE TRANSVAAL. / Baden-Powell Interviewed. /** Pretoria, June 19.
Morning Post, 7

C204.3   June 29   **BADEN-POWELL INTERVIEWED. /** Pretoria, June 19.
Morning Post, 5, 3

C205   June 29   **THE CAPTURE OF PRETORIA. /** Pretoria, June 6 / (By post to Capetown).
Morning Post, 5

C206   June 29   **PROTECTING THE RAILWAY. /** Capetown, June 28.
Morning Post, 5

C207.1   June 30   **THE TRANSVAAL. / Operations against Botha. /** Pretoria (delayed) / (via Bloemfontein, June 28).
Morning Post, 7

C207.2   July 2   **OPERATIONS AGAINST BOTHA. /** Bloemfontein, June 29.
Morning Post, 5

C208   July 2   **ORANGE RIVER COLONY. / Lord Methuen's Success.** / Bloemfontein, June 30.
Morning Post, 3

C209   July 3   **BATTLE OF JOHANNESBURG.**
Morning Post, 7–8
Letter of 1 June from Johannesburg, under the rubric 'War Letter from Winston Spencer Churchill, Our *War Correspondent*'.

C210   July 4   **CAPE COLONY. / Publication of Despatches.** / Bloemfontein, July 3 / (Delayed by the Censor).
Morning Post, 7

C211   July 12   **CONCERNING A BOER CONVOY.**
Morning Post, 7–8
Letter of 22 May, delayed in transmission, from Heilbron, under the rubric 'War Letter from Winston Spencer Churchill, Our Special Correspondent'. Subsequently collected in *Young Winston's Wars*, pp. 303–9, and *War Correspondent*, pp. 313–18.[26]

C212   July 17   **THE CAPTURE OF PRETORIA.**
Morning Post, 7–8
Letter of 8 June from Pretoria, under the rubric 'War Letter from Winston Spencer Churchill, Our *War Correspondent*'. Subsequently collected in *Young Winston's Wars*, pp. 310–15, and *War Correspondent*, pp. 319–24.

C213   July 20   **ACTION OF DIAMOND HILLS.**
Morning Post, 5–6
Letter of 14 June from Pretoria, under the rubric 'War Letter from Winston Spencer Churchill, Our *War Correspondent*', together with sketches explaining the operations of 11–13 June and the action of Diamond Hill of 11–12 June. Subsequently collected in *Young Winston's Wars*, pp. 316–28, and *War Correspondent*, pp. 325–37.

C214   July 25   **RAILWAY WAR.**
Morning Post, 5–6
Letter of 28 June from Capetown, under the rubric 'War Letter from Winston Spencer Churchill, Our Special Correspondent'. This is also the final letter from Churchill. In his words: "Here, then, I make my bow to the reader, and bring these letters to their conclusion. They have chronicled as

---

26. Where it is erroneously dated 23 May.

faithfully as lay in my power nearly every exciting adventure or military affair it has been my fortune to share or witness during the last nine months. They have been written amid many difficulties and often adverse conditions, with pen or pencil as the fates decreed, under a waggon, in the shadow of a rock, by the uncertain light of a lantern, or even sitting on the ground in the rain. They had to hurry home without waiting for second thoughts, and spring into print guided by a strange hand; and for these reasons perhaps I may claim some indulgence for their crudities and imperfections." Subsequently collected in *Young Winston's Wars*, pp. 329–41, and *War Correspondent*, pp. 338–50.

C215   Dec. 29   **OFFICERS AND GENTLEMEN**
Saturday Evening Post, Vol. 173, No. 26, 2–3, 18
Subsequently collected in *Collected Essays*, Vol. I, pp. 45–56.

1901

C216a   January   **LORD ROBERTS / The Personality and the Career of Great Britain's Foremost Soldier—The Crucial Incidents in His Record—His Conduct of the War in Africa—His Firm Hold on British Affection**
World's Work, Vol. I, No. 3, 309–18

C216b   July   **LORD ROBERTS.**
Windsor Magazine, Vol. XIV, No. 79, 123–36
Subsequently collected in *Collected Essays*, Vol. III, pp. 3–17.

C217   January   **THE BRITISH OFFICER.**
Pall Mall Magazine, Vol. XXIII, No. 93, 66–75
Note that the article is entitled 'The British Officer in War' on the cover of the January issue.

C218   Jan. 26   **WHAT AMERICANS THINK ABOUT THE BOER WAR**
Collier's Weekly, 3, 17
Subsequently collected in *A Cavalcade of Collier's* (**B165**).

C218/1   February   **SUCCESS IN JOURNALISM.**
Inlander, Vol. XI, No. 5, 169–70
Although the *Inlander* was only a student literary magazine of the University of Michigan, its editor succeeded in obtaining this article when Churchill visited Ann Arbor, Michigan, during his first American speaking tour. At the time of that visit, an enterprising law student named Gustavus Ohlinger also managed to interview Churchill. As a *quid pro quo* to

obtaining the interview, Ohlinger had "promised Churchill not to print anything that would reflect on his parliamentary career, and [he] kept that promise".[27] The interview, which Ohlinger had taken down in shorthand and transcribed at 4:00 a.m. after his return to his room, was kept by him until Churchill's death, at which time he felt that he could publish it without breaking his promise. The interview was thus first published in the spring 1966 issue (Vol. IV, No. 2) of the *Michigan Quarterly Review* and the 24 April 1966 issue of *Detroit*.[28]

C219   March   **BRITISH CAVALRY**
Anglo-Saxon Review, 240–7
Note that the table of contents for the March 1901 volume incorrectly shows the title as 'Cavalry' and the first page number as 239.[29] Subsequently collected in *Collected Essays*, Vol. I, pp. 57–63.

---

27. *Detroit* (the weekly rotogravure section of the *Detroit Free Press*), 24 April 1966, at p. 8.

28. *Ibid.*, pp. 9–10. Since interviews do not form a part of this bibliography, I have not included either publication of that interview here; however, the *Michigan Quarterly Review* appearance is included by Woods as D(b)117/10, although that bibliography does not include interviews either. In a sense, it is only chance that the interview ever saw the light of day, since Ohlinger was himself eighty-nine when it was published in 1966.

29. The review was the creation of Lady Randolph Churchill (by then Mrs George Cornwallis-West). Churchill played some part in helping his mother shape the magazine. Of the early suggestion for the title, *The Arena*, he wrote: "No, I don't like 'The Arena'—it is very commonplace. You want some name that expresses what the Magazine really is—something classical & opulent. It should be a literary Amphitryon. There is probably some good Greek word which expresses this. Alas I am no scholar" (letter of 19 January 1899, R. Churchill, *WSC*, Vol. I, *C.V.* 2, pp. 1003–4). Of the suggestion *The International Quarterly*, he said that it was "much better than the Arena—but very cumbrous and not at all original. You must try and find a title which expresses the *character & special mission* of the Magazine—something exquisite, rich, stately" (letter of 26 January; *ibid.*, pp. 1004–5, at p. 1005). In the next letter, he reiterated his dislike of the name: "There is no idea of elegance about it. It would suggest a very heavy ponderous publication. Not a literary epicure, feast which is what you want" (letter of 2 February; *ibid.*, pp. 1005–6, at p. 1005). He remained most concerned about the title. As he said on 16 February: "A bad name will damn any magazine. ... A bad number doesn't matter. The next may be much better. A bad name sticks always." He added that her suggestion *The Anglo Saxon* "means nothing & has not the slightest relation to the ideas and purpose of the magazine" (*ibid.*, pp. 1008–9, at p. 1008). He was persistent on the point, arguing on 23 February that the title "might do for a v[er]y popular periodical meant to appeal to great masses on either side of the Atlantic. But it is very inappropriate to a Magazine de Luxe" (letter of 23 February; *ibid.*, pp. 1010–11, at p. 1010). He advised again on the title, the motto, the potential market, the publishing price, the acceptable level of profit, and so on, in his letter of 2 March (*ibid.*, pp. 1011–13).

C220   June 17   **ARE WE A MILITARY NATION?**
                       Daily Mail
                       Subsequently collected in *Collected Essays*, Vol. I, pp. 64–7;
                       however, I have been unsuccessful in locating the article in the
                       Daily Mail of that date.

C221   June 18   **THE ONLY WAY.**
                       Daily Mail, 4
                       Subsequently collected in R. Churchill, *WSC*, Vol. II, *C.V.*
                       1, pp. 70–3.

—   July   **LORD ROBERTS.** (*Windsor Magazine*; *see* **C216b**)

1902

C222a   Dec. 18   **ON THE FLANK OF THE ARMY**
                       Youth's Companion, 651–2
                       The publisher of the *Youth's Companion* was extraordinarily
                       enthusiastic about the article. On 17 July 1901 he wrote to
                       Churchill in the following terms: "The more I consider 'On
                       the Flank of the Army' the better I like it, and it seems to me
                       to be equal to Kipling at his best. We are holding it back till
                       next year so that we may have the advantage of giving it
                       prominence in our forthcoming announcement."[30] Churchill
                       was paid $100 per 1000 words "for all serial rights".[31]
                       Subsequently collected in *Youth's Companion* (**B144**) and in
                       Collected Essays, Vol. IV, pp. 6–13.

1903

C222b   March   **ON THE FLANK OF THE ARMY.**
                       Windsor Magazine, 453–60

C223   July 16   **THE BRAVEST DEED I EVER SAW. / The Doctor
                       and the Soldier.**
                       V.C., Vol. I, No. 13, 295
                       Subsequently published in volume form in *The Bravest Deed I
                       Ever Saw* (**B4**) and R. Churchill, *WSC*, Vol. II, p. 64.

C224   November   **SHEFFIELD AND ITS SHADOW**
                       Monthly Review, Vol. 13, No. 2, 17–31
                       The article had initially been solicited for the *Monthly Review*
                       by Henry Newbolt in a letter of 10 October to Churchill:

---

30. CHAR 8/15–16/4.
31. CHAR 8/15–16/5.

"May I hope that the time has now come when this may be possible? The present crisis is certainly one which calls for comment from those who have clear views and know their own minds. I have already published the views of Lord Goschen, Sir A. E. Hicks-Beach, Sir Edward Grey and Lord Hugh Cecil, and I should be very glad to be able to give my public your view of the present situation."[32] Churchill initially turned Newbolt down but was convinced by the latter's letter of 14 October, in which he stated: "You will understand what I mean when I tell you that your article is the only one which I have provided for November on Mr Chamberlain's proposals, and it is now too late to expect anyone else to undertake to fill the gap." Newbolt had apparently taken the risk of announcing the article *before* having Churchill's confirmation. "In the circumstances I should be grateful for the shortest and least laboured contribution which could be held a fulfilment of my undertaking."[33] The article was, of course, provided and Newbolt sent Churchill a cheque with his letter of 31 October.[34] Subsequently collected in *Collected Essays*, Vol. II, pp. 3–12.

1904

C224/1   February   **MR. WINSTON CHURCHILL, M.P., ON "SHORTHAND"**
Reporter's Journal and Shorthand Magazine, Vol. 2, No. 2, 24–5

C225   **A DANGER TO THE EMPIRE. / The Condition of Our Army.**
Although it was originally proposed as a single article, the *Daily Mail* advised Churchill on 14 December that they had decided not to publish a 12-page issue on the Friday "so that we cannot print your article all on one day. Will you therefore kindly divide it into two or three articles of about 1200 words each."[35]

C225.1   Dec. 16   **I.—Who Is to Blame?**
Daily Mail, 4
Subsequently collected in *Collected Essays*, Vol. I, pp. 81–4.

---

32. CHAR 8/17–18/19.
33. CHAR 8/17–18/20.
34. CHAR 8/17–18/24. The amount of the payment is unknown.
35. CHAR 8/19/52.

C225.2   Dec. 17   **II.—Phantom Reforms.**
Daily Mail, 4
Subsequently collected in *Collected Essays*, Vol. I, pp. 84–7.

C225.3   Dec. 19   **III.—Use of the Volunteers.**
Daily Mail, 4
Subsequently collected in *Collected Essays*, Vol. I, pp. 87–90.

1906

C226.1   June 16   **THE CHICAGO SCANDALS. / The Novel Which Is Making History.**
P.T.O., Vol. I, No. 1, 25–6
The first of a two-part article on Upton Sinclair's *The Jungle*, which appeared in the first issue of *P.T.O.* Both parts were subsequently published as a single essay in *Collected Essays*, Vol. II, pp. 16–25.

C226.2   June 23   **THE CHICAGO SCANDALS. / The Novel Which Is Making History.**
P.T.O., Vol. I, No. 2, 65–6

1907

C227a   March 9   **A SMOOTH WAY WITH THE PEERS.**
Nation (UK), Vol. I, No. 2, 65–6
A contribution to the column 'Open Questions'. Subsequently collected in *Collected Essays*, Vol. II, pp. 13–17.

C227b   March 9   **MR. CHURCHILL'S "SMOOTH WAY."**
Manchester Guardian, 9

1908

C228a   **"MY AFRICAN JOURNEY."**
The British serialization. Churchill had begun his negotiations with the *Strand Magazine* before departing for Africa, although it was only after he arrived in East Africa that they were concluded. He was to be paid £150 per article for the originally contemplated five-part serialization in the *Strand* and £30 for the photographs.[36] On 17 November 1907, he wrote to his brother Jack of the successful end of the negotiations: "I

---

36. Geraldine Beare, *Index to the* Strand Magazine, *1891–1950* (Westport, CT: Greenwood Press, 1982), p. xviii.

have received a fine offer from the *Strand Magazine* for five articles for £750, which I propose to accept, as it will definitely liquidate all possible expenses in this journey. There will be another £500 in book form."[37] Writing to his mother six days later, he confirmed that he had accepted the offer from the magazine: "You will be glad to hear that I have accepted the offer of the *Strand Magazine* to write them five articles at £150 a piece, or £750 for the series."[38] Moreover, following the representations of Churchill's literary agent, A. P. Watt,[39] the *Strand* agreed to pay him £150 each for two more articles; although ultimately *nine* were published, Churchill was paid a total of £1050 by the *Strand*.[40]

C228a.1	March	**I.—The Uganda Railway.**
		Strand Magazine (UK), Vol. XXXV, No. 207, 299–306
C228a.2	April	**II.—Around Mount Kenya.**
		Strand Magazine (UK), Vol. XXXV, No. 208, 385–94
C228a.3	May	**III.—The Highlands of East Africa.**
		Strand Magazine (UK), Vol. XXXV, No. 209, 490–6
C228a.4	June	**IV.—The Great Lake.**
		Strand Magazine (UK), Vol. XXXV, No. 210, 680–8
C228a.5	July	**V.—The Kingdom of Uganda.**
		Strand Magazine (UK), Vol. XXXVI, No. 211, 50–6
C228a.6	August	**VI.—Kampala.**
		Strand Magazine (UK), Vol. XXXVI, No. 212, 137–45
C228a.7	September	**VII.—"On Safari."**
		Strand Magazine (UK), Vol. XXXVI, No. 213, 250–8
C228a.8	October	**VIII.—Murchison Falls.**
		Strand Magazine (UK), Vol. XXXVI, No. 214, 374–81
C228a.9	November	**IX.—Hippo Camp.**
		Strand Magazine (UK), Vol. XXXVI, No. 215, 491–8

---

37. R. Churchill, *WSC*, Vol. II, *C.V.* 2, p. 701.
38. *Ibid.*, p. 706.
39. For the report of his meeting with Mr Greenough Smith of the *Strand Magazine*, see Watt's letter of 9 January 1908 to Churchill (CHAR 8/28/3–4).
40. More detailed comments relating to the publication of the book can be found at **A27**.

C228b　　　　　　　**"MY AFRICAN JOURNEY."**
　　　　　　　　　　The American serialization.

C228b.1　April　　**I.—The Uganda Railway.**
　　　　　　　　　　Strand Magazine (US), Vol. XXXV, No. 207, 251–8

C228b.2　May　　　**II.—Around Mount Kenya.**
　　　　　　　　　　Strand Magazine (US), Vol. XXXV, No. 208, 423–32

C228b.3　June　　　**III.—The Highlands of East Africa.**
　　　　　　　　　　Strand Magazine (US), Vol. XXXV, No. 209, 490–6

C228b.4　July　　　**IV.—The Great Lake.**
　　　　　　　　　　Strand Magazine (US), Vol. XXXV, No. 210, 680–8

C228b.5　August　　**V.—The Kingdom of Uganda.**
　　　　　　　　　　Strand Magazine (US), Vol. XXXVI, No. 211, 50–6

C228b.6　September　**VI.—Kampala.**
　　　　　　　　　　Strand Magazine (US), Vol. XXXVI, No. 212, 137–45

C228b.7　October　**VII.—"On Safari."**
　　　　　　　　　　Strand Magazine (US), Vol. XXXVI, No. 213, 248–55

C228b.8　November　**VIII.—Murchison Falls.**
　　　　　　　　　　Strand Magazine (US), Vol. XXXVI, No. 214, 375–82

C228b.9　December　**IX.—Hippo Camp.**
　　　　　　　　　　Strand Magazine (US), Vol. XXXVI, No. 215, 491–8

1909

C229a　July 13　**THE HOUSE OF COMMONS AND ITS BUSINESS.**
　　　　　　　　　　The World, 59–60
　　　　　　　　　　Subsequently collected in *Collected Essays*, Vol. II, pp. 36–9.

C229b　July 13　**MR. CHURCHILL ON THE HOUSE OF COMMONS.**
　　　　　　　　　　The Times, 7
　　　　　　　　　　Reprints one paragraph and part of the conclusion of the previous item.

C229c　July 13　**THE HOUSE OF COMMONS AND ITS BUSINESS. / Article by Mr. Winston Churchill.**
　　　　　　　　　　Manchester Guardian, 8

1912

C230a   Jan. 8   **IMPERIAL SIDE OF HOME RULE. / Mr. Churchill's Plea for Race Reconciliation. / German and American Examples.**
Daily Chronicle, 7
The full text of the Introduction to the new edition of *Home Rule in a Nutshell* by Jeremiah MacVeagh, M.P. (**B10**). Subsequently collected in *Collected Essays*, Vol. II, 40–2.

C230b   Jan. 8   **MR. CHURCHILL AND HOME RULE. / Questions for Great Britain. / What an Enduring Settlement Would Do.**
Manchester Guardian, 8

C230c   Jan. 8   **MR. CHURCHILL AND HOME RULE.**
The Times, 6
Contains a part only of the Introduction.

1916

C231   **FOUR GREAT CHAPTERS OF THE WORLD WAR**
Churchill was paid a considerable amount for these articles. As he wrote to his brother Jack on 15 July 1916: "I get 4 or 5 shillings a word for everything I write: and apparently even at this price the newspaper is the gainer. *Sunday Pictorial* circulation is 448,000 in a single day. This beats all records in journalism."[41] In all, the four articles earned Churchill £1000.

C231a.1   July 9   **No. I.—The Sinister Hypothesis.**
Sunday Pictorial, 5
Signed in facsimile, as are the other articles in this series. Subsequently collected in *Collected Essays*, Vol. I, pp. 91–5.

C231a.2   July 16   **No. II.—The Terrible "It."**
Sunday Pictorial, 5
Subsequently collected in *Collected Essays*, Vol. I, pp. 96–100.

C231a.3   July 23   **No. III.—The Great Amphibian.**
Sunday Pictorial, 5
Subsequently published separately as "*The Great Amphibian*" (**A47**) and collected in *Collected Essays*, Vol. I, pp. 100–4.

---

41. Gilbert, *WSC*, Vol. III, *C.V.* 2, pp. 1530–1, at p. 1530. For this excerpt, see also Vol. III, p. 790.

C231a.4	July 30	**No. IV.—The Slow Fire.**

Sunday Pictorial, 5

Subsequently collected in *Collected Essays*, Vol. I, pp. 104–8.

C231b.1	July 9	**DEMOCRACIES WEAK, CHURCHILL ARGUES / Former Minister Says Politics Kept Britain from Adequate Preparation, and U.S. Will Have Same Difficulty.**

New York Tribune, 1, 3

C231b.2	July 16	**KAISER SOUGHT WAR, CHURCHILL CHARGES / Britain Was Powerless to Stave It Off, He Says— Prosperity Failed to Satisfy Germany.**

New York Tribune, 1, 3

C231b.3	July 23	**CHURCHILL TELLS HOW NAVY SAVED ENGLAND / Vivid Picture of the Night When Telegram, "Commence Hostilities," Was Flashed to Grand Fleet.**

New York Tribune, 1, 8

C231b.4a	July 30	**BRITISH ARMY TURNED TIDE, CHURCHILL SAYS / "Contemptible Handful" Which Saved French Flank in First Battles of War Has Made Kingdom's Military Reputation Undying, He Declares.**

New York Tribune, 1, 4

C231b.4b	October	**THE FACULTY OF WONDER DULLED**

Current History, 111–12

An excerpt from the previous article.

C232a.1	Sept. 30	**THE WAR BY LAND AND SEA**

Collier's, Vol. 58, No. 3, 8–9, 33–4

C232a.2	Nov. 18	**THE MEANING OF VERDUN**

Collier's, Vol. 58, No. 10, 5–7, 22–3

C232b.1	October	**THE WAR BY LAND AND SEA**

London Magazine, Vol. XXXVII, No. 72, 119–29

Subsequently collected in *Collected Essays*, Vol. I, pp. 109–19. Note further that the title is indicated in the table of contents there as 'The War on Land and Sea'.

C232b.2a	Oct. 21	**THE RIGHT VIEW OF VERDUN**

War Illustrated, Vol. 5, No. 114, 238

C232b.2b   November   **THE WAR BY LAND AND SEA**
London Magazine, Vol. XXXVII, No. 73, 235–44
Subsequently collected in *Collected Essays*, Vol. I, pp. 119–30.

C232b.3a   December   **THE WAR BY LAND AND SEA**
London Magazine, Vol. XXXVII, No. 74, 395–404
Subsequently collected in *Collected Essays*, Vol. I, pp. 131–40.

C232b.3b   December   **NEW WAR METHODS AND VICTORY**
Current History, 413–15

C232b.4   January   **THE WAR BY LAND AND SEA**
1917   *London Magazine*, Vol. XXXVII, No. 75, 532–40
Subsequently collected in *Collected Essays*, Vol. I, pp. 140–50.

C232b.5   February   **THE WAR BY LAND AND SEA**
1917   *London Magazine*, 653–60
Subsequently collected in *Collected Essays*, Vol. I, pp. 150–60.

C232b.6   March   **THE WAR BY LAND AND SEA**
1917   *London Magazine*, 58–60, 62–6
Subsequently collected in *Collected Essays*, Vol. I, pp. 160–71.

C233.1   Nov. 19   **ANTWERP: THE STORY OF ITS SIEGE AND FALL / Belgium's Appeal for Help—And How It Was Answered.**
Sunday Pictorial, 5
Subsequently collected in *Collected Essays*, Vol. I, pp. 172–6.

C233.2   Nov. 26   **HOW ANTWERP SAVED THE CHANNEL PORTS / Magnitude of the Peril Which the Allied Cause Escaped.**
Sunday Pictorial, 5–6
Subsequently collected in *Collected Essays*, Vol. I, pp. 177–82.

1917

—   January–   **THE WAR BY LAND AND SEA** (*London Magazine*; *see*
March   **C232b.4–232b.6**)

C234   Jan. 31   **THE WAR BY LAND AND AIR AND SEA**
The Outlook, Vol. 115, No. 5, 196–7
Subsequently collected in *Collected Essays*, Vol. I, pp. 183–8.

C235   March 24   **WHY GERMANY MUST LOSE**
Collier's, Vol. 59, No. 2, 7–8, 34, 36, 40

C236   April 8   **MAN-POWER PROBLEM: WANTED A POLICY /
We Must Put Our Brains into the War.**

Sunday Pictorial, 5

Subsequently collected in *Collected Essays*, Vol. I, pp. 189–92. Lord Beaverbrook states that Churchill was paid £250 per article for these contributions to the *Sunday Pictorial*.[42]

C237   April 22   **GENERAL SMUTS IS NEEDED HERE. / A Minister
with Real War Knowledge.**

Sunday Pictorial, 5

Subsequently collected in *Collected Essays*, Vol. III, pp. 19–22.

C238   May   **REFLECTIONS ON THE STRATEGY OF THE
ALLIES**

Century Magazine, Vol. 94, No. 1, 117–21

C239   May 20   **FINAL CHAPTERS OF THE GREAT WAR. / The
Task Before Us—We Have Got to Hold On.**

Sunday Pictorial, 5

Subsequently collected in *Collected Essays*, Vol. I, pp. 193–6.

C240   May 25   **VALENTINE FLEMING. / An Appreciation.**

The Times, 9

Subsequently collected in *Collected Essays*, Vol. III, pp. 23–4. Fleming was the father of Ian Fleming, the creator of the James Bond novels. See the reference to the son in *n*.1087, at p. 726.

C241   June 10   **THE SUPREME SYMBOLS OF VICTORY. / Need
for a Simpler Definition of Our War Aims.**

Sunday Pictorial, 5

Subsequently collected in *Collected Essays*, Vol. I, pp. 197–200.

C242   June 24   **THE REAL NEED OF THE BRITISH
NAVY. / How to Get at the Enemy—an Aggressive
Policy for Our Vast Surplus Fleets.**

Sunday Pictorial, 5

Subsequently collected in *Collected Essays*, Vol. I, pp. 201–4.

C243   July 8   **RUSSIA—IS IT THE TURNING POINT? / The
Dilemma of the German General Staff—a Lost
Opportunity.**

Sunday Pictorial, 5

Subsequently collected in *Collected Essays*, Vol. I, pp. 205–8.

---

42. *Men and Power 1917–1918* (London: Hutchinson, 1956), pp. 118–19 (see **F129**).

C244	August	**NAVAL ORGANIZATION, AMERICAN AND BRITISH**

Atlantic Monthly, 277–84

C245	Aug. 11	**IRELAND AND WORLD DEMOCRACY** / Evolved from a Talk with T. P. O'Connor

Collier's Weekly, Vol. 59, No. 22, 8, 9, 32

1919

C246 Jan. 12 **THE WHOLE WORLD AT A STANDSTILL. / Urgent Need for Settling the Main Outlines of Peace—Our Unfinished Task.**
Sunday Pictorial, Vol. XXVI, No. 304, 5
Subsequently collected in *Collected Essays*, Vol. I, pp. 209–13.

C247a June 22 **BRITAIN'S FOREIGN POLICY.**
Weekly Dispatch, 6
Signed in facsimile. Subsequently collected in *Collected Essays*, Vol. I, pp. 214–17.

C247b June 22 **CHURCHILL GIVES AIMS OF BRITAIN / Retention of America's Friendship Paramount, He Says—Both Must Aid France. / Must Gain Lasting Peace / Germany to Have Her Chance after Making Amends and Red Terror to Be Crushed.**
New York Times, 8

C247c June 23 **URGES HUN IN LEAGUE. / Churchill Outlines Britain's Policy. / Russia, Shorn of Bolshevism, Also Is Essential to Permanent Organization. / British Secretary of State for War Says Friendship of America Paramount.**
Los Angeles Times, Part 1, 1–2

C248.1 June 29 **1.—OUR ARMAMENTS AFTER THE WAR.**
Weekly Dispatch, 6
Subsequently collected in *Collected Essays*, Vol. I, pp. 218–20.

C248.2 June 29 **2.—The Future of Britain's Finances.**
Weekly Dispatch, 6
A separate article, signed in facsimile, appearing on the same page as the first. Subsequently collected in *Collected Essays*, Vol. I, pp. 221–3.

C249   Sept. 13   **A PROPOSAL FOR A NEW POLITICAL PARTY**
Living Age, Vol. 302 (original numbering) / Vol. 15 (in 8th Series), No. 3923 [on the cover] or 2923 [on p. 5], 641–6
The article is stated to have been reprinted from a report of the speech in the *Daily Telegraph*, which I have not found.

C250   Nov. 9   **THE TRUTH ABOUT THE NAVY. / A Reply to the Sensational Charges Made by Various Naval Authorities.**
Illustrated Sunday Herald, 5, 10.
Subsequently collected in *Collected Essays*, Vol. I, pp. 242–8.

C251   Nov. 16   **COULD LABOUR GOVERN THE COUNTRY? / The Dilemma of "Democracy."**
Illustrated Sunday Herald, 5
Subsequently collected in *Collected Essays*, Vol. II, pp. 43–7.

C252   Nov. 23   **HAVE WE DONE WITH GERMANY? / The Danger of Another Great European Explosion.**
Illustrated Sunday Herald, 5
Subsequently collected in *Collected Essays*, Vol. I, pp. 224–8.

C253   Nov. 30   **WILL AMERICA FAIL US? / Why U.S.A. Hesitates to Ratify the Treaty—and the Consequences**
Illustrated Sunday Herald, 5
B. Buckham, the editor, had suggested that "a powerful and interesting article could be written on America's attitude to European politics in general and to the League of Nations in particular. This seems to be the topic of the moment." Churchill was paid £300 for this article.[43] Subsequently collected in *Collected Essays*, Vol. I, pp. 229–33.

C254   Dec. 7   **THE RIGHT TO STRIKE. / And the Right of the Community to Exist.— / What the State Should Do to Prevent a General Breakdown.**
Illustrated Sunday Herald, 5
Churchill was paid £300 for this article. Subsequently collected in *Collected Essays*, Vol. II, pp. 48–52.

---

43. Letter of 19 November 1919 (CHAR 8/35/3).

1920

C255   Jan. 18   **LABOUR VERSUS THE LABOUR PARTY. / The Attempt to Divide the Nation on a Class Basis.**
Illustrated Sunday Herald, 4
Churchill was paid £250 for this article.[44] It was subsequently published in pamphlet form on the back inside cover of *The Fighting Line* (**A56**) and *Collected Essays*, Vol. II, pp. 53–7.

C256   Jan. 25   **THE RED FEVER: / A Way to Deal with Our Bolshevists: Segregate Them!**
Illustrated Sunday Herald, 5
Churchill was paid £250 for this article. It was subsequently collected in *Collected Essays*, Vol. II, pp. 58–62. On 2 October 1935, Churchill wrote to Lord Beaverbrook in an attempt to trace this article and the one on Kitchener (**C260**) for republication. He could recall neither the article titles nor the name of "the Sunday paper Hulton owned" in which they were published. He also asked for a copy of the article he had written, he thought, for the *Daily Express* on "Wells's book".[45] In fact, the piece on H. G. Wells, entitled 'This Frightful Catastrophe!', was not a review of a book at all but rather of a series of articles Wells had written on his return from Russia.[46] Churchill's retort was published in the *Sunday Express* (**C265**). There is, in the end, no record of any of these three articles having been republished in periodical form.

C257   Feb. 1   **MONARCHY VERSUS AUTOCRACY. / The Moral of the "Willy–Nicky" Correspondence.**
Illustrated Sunday Herald, 5
Churchill was paid £250 for this article. It was subsequently collected in *Collected Essays*, Vol. II, pp. 63–6.

---

44. CHAR 8/35/4.
45. Gilbert, *WSC*, Vol. V, *C.V.* 2, p. 1288. Churchill's query was opportunely put to his old friend, Lord Beaverbrook, who had briefly owned Sir Edward Hulton's newspapers. In 1923, he purchased them and then immediately resold them to Lord Rothermere, retaining the *Evening Standard* for himself. The story of the Express papers was different. Beaverbrook had begun his association with the *Daily Express* in 1911, when he lent its editor, R. D. Blumenthal, £25,000 to assist the paper, which was in severe financial difficulty, being unable even to pay its newsprint bills. Six years later, Beaverbrook assumed financial control of the newspaper and, in 1918, started the *Sunday Express*.
46. Churchill began his piece with the following observation: "When one has written a history of the world from nebula to the Third International and of the human race from protoplasm to Lord Birkenhead in about a twelvemonth, there ought to be no difficulty in becoming an expert on the internal conditions of Russia after a visit of fourteen days."

C258a Feb. 8 **ZIONISM VERSUS BOLSHEVISM. / A Struggle for the Soul of the Jewish People.**
Illustrated Sunday Herald, 5
Churchill was paid £250 for this article. It was subsequently collected in *Collected Essays*, Vol. IV, pp. 26–30.

C258b Spring
1980 **ZIONISM VERSUS BOLSHEVISM / A Struggle for the Soul of the Jewish People.**
Conspiracy Digest, Vol. V, No. 2, 1–2

C259 March 19 **WHY I SUPPORT MR. LLOYD GEORGE. / The Profound Abyss. / "There Must Be a Stable Party to Which Unionists and Liberals Can Belong."**
Evening News, 1, 5
Subsequently collected in *Collected Essays*, Vol. II, pp. 67–9.

C260 April 25 **THE REAL KITCHENER. / Fatal Dilemma of His War Administration.**
Illustrated Sunday Herald, 5
Subsequently collected in *Collected Essays*, Vol. III, pp. 25–9.

C261 May 30 **IS PARLIAMENT PLAYED OUT? / The Lack of New Figures: Press Jealousy: / Revolutionary Dangers.**
Illustrated Sunday Herald, 5
Subsequently collected in *Collected Essays*, Vol. II, pp. 70–4.

C262 June 13 **THE MURDER CAMPAIGN IN IRELAND. / Issues on Which the British Nation Must Stand and Fight.**
Illustrated Sunday Herald, 5
Subsequently collected in *Collected Essays*, Vol. II, pp. 75–8.

C262/1 June 14 **RUSSIA AN ENSLAVED BEDLAM.**
Evening News, 1, 5

C263a July 28 **POLAND: / The Choice That Germany May Have to Face. / Shall the Red Flood of Bolshevism Swamp All Europe? / Poland—Lynch-pin of Peace / The Poison Peril from the East.**
Evening News, 1, 5
Subsequently collected in *Collected Essays*, Vol. I, pp. 234–7, under the title 'The Poison Peril from the East'. The publication of this article led to a critical article in *The Times* of the following day. Churchill wrote to Lord Northcliffe privately to explain the circumstances which had resulted in the publication of the piece in the *Evening News*. He said: "[I]n undertaking to do this, I did not expect to encounter the hostile criticism of the *Times*. I can quite understand that the

Times might not agree with any particular phrase or argument used in an article. . . . Criticism of policy is one thing. Criticism on the propriety of my writing an article for the *Evening News* is another. I confess I feel myself unfairly treated in this respect. No other morning paper that I have read has found it necessary to make any adverse comment, yet the leading paper in your group of papers goes out of its way to attack the propriety of my writing an article which I was strongly pressed to write by another paper in the same group."[47]

C263b	July 29	**POLISH BARRIER TO BOLSHEVISM. / Mr. Churchill States the Issues. / Lynch-pin of the Treaty.**

The Times, 11

Reprints a part of the previous article.

C264	Nov. 4	**"HERE'S ME!" / Mrs. Asquith's Autobiography.**

Daily Mail, 6

Lengthy review (2000–2500 words) of Mrs Asquith's book,[48] for which Churchill was paid £500 for world serial rights.[49] It was, in fact, this review which prompted the book's publisher, Thornton Butterworth, to write to Churchill and offer to publish his subsequent works. In Thornton Butterworth's letter of 9 November to Churchill, he said: "I have been deeply gratified by your most recent admirable review in the *Daily Mail*. I was greatly impressed by the tactful kindness of such criticism as had to be adverse and entire fairmindedness shown to the book throughout. . . . May I add that if at any time you decide to write a new book, I should esteem it a very great favour if you would allow me the privilege of publishing it."[50] Thus began the author–publisher relationship between

---

47. From the archives of *The Times*.

48. When the book, entitled *The Autobiography of Margot Asquith*, was published in October, it aroused considerable reaction in the press; the review in *The Times* predicted that the book would sell not on its merits "but because it is a scandal". As the eldest son of Violet Bonham Carter, herself the step-daughter of Margot Asquith, Mark Bonham Carter later wrote in his introduction to the one-volume abridged edition (London: Eyre & Spottiswoode, 1962), "When it was published the Autobiography caused some embarrassment to her family and friends, and received shocked and critical comment in the press. None the less it won an immediate and widespread success which has been ascribed chiefly to its characteristic indiscretion and to its revelations of high life in society and politics."

49. Letter of 22 October 1920 from the Manager of the Legal Department of the Associated Newspapers, Limited, to Churchill (CHAR 8/38/33). Although Churchill retained "the right to incorporate the review in any book you may subsequently write", he never did and that review, which triggered the Butterworth publishing relationship, has never been collected in volume form.

50. CHAR 8/38/43.

Churchill and Thornton Butterworth, who was Churchill's publisher for *The World Crisis* (**A69**) and all other books, save *Marlborough* (**A97**) and *Arms and the Covenant* (**A107**), from 1923 to 1939.

C265   Dec. 5   **"THIS FRIGHTFUL CATASTROPHE!" — / Mr. Churchill on Bolshevism. / Mr. Wells and Bolshevism. / A Reply.**
Sunday Express, 1, 7
Signed in facsimile. Subsequently collected in *Collected Essays*, Vol. II, pp. 79–84, under the title 'Mr Wells and Bolshevism'. See the note on related matters under **C256**.

1921

C266   December   **A CABINET MINISTER AS ART CRITIC / Winston Churchill on the Art of the Laverys**
Arts & Decoration, Vol. 16, No. 2, 169
Excerpted from the Foreword to *Pictures of Morocco, the Riviera and Other Scenes by Sir John Lavery, R.A.* (**B26**).

C267a.1   December   **PAINTING AS A PASTIME**
Strand Magazine, Vol. LXII, 535–44
On 6 February 1921, Churchill wrote to Clementine that "The *Strand Magazine* accept my terms & will pay £1,000 for two articles with pictures reproduced in colour. As this will not be subject to Income Tax, it is really worth £1,600. So the painting has paid for itself, & a handsome profit over."[51] Both parts were subsequently collected in Birkenhead's *The Hundred Best English Essays* (**B39**), at pp. 849–61, and in *Thoughts and Adventures* (**A95**), at pp. 305–20.

1922

C267a.2   January   **PAINTING AS A PASTIME / Part II.**
Strand Magazine, Vol. LXIII, 13–20

C267b   June 1933   **MY ADVENTURES WITH A PAINT BRUSH**
Reader's Digest, Vol. 23, No. 134, 97–100
Condensed from *Amid These Storms* (**A95.2**). Subsequently collected in *Getting the Most out of Life* (**B101**) and in *The Reader's Digest 40th Anniversary Treasury* (**B172**), in the latter case under the title 'Painting as a Pastime'.

---

51. *Speaking for Themselves*, p. 225.

C267c.1 July 1946 **PAINTING AS A PASTIME**
Strand Magazine, Vol. CXI, No. 667, 44–54
"A specially condensed version of the article", with reproductions of Churchill's paintings on pp. 45–52.

C267c.2 August **WINSTON   CHURCHILL'S   PAINTINGS: A**
1946 **FURTHER SELECTION**
Strand Magazine, Vol. CXI, No. 668, 45–52
Note that seven more Churchill paintings are reproduced here but without any Churchillian text.

C267d Spring **PAINTING AS A PASTIME**
1972 *Saturday Evening Post*, 65–7, 108–10.

1923

C268 **MR. CHURCHILL'S BOOK.**
The serialization of the first volume of *The World Crisis* (**A69**).[52] Churchill was anxious that the serialization should take place in *The Times* and he enlisted Butterworth to make the first contact with the newspaper, rather than his agents, Curtis Brown. This first meeting took place on 2 December 1920.[53] Matters progressed rapidly. Churchill was, however, concerned about being "protected from adverse criticism in [the newspaper's] editorial columns [and being] consistently treated in a spirit of good will and helpfulness".[54] H. Wickham

52. Contrary to the entry in the Woods bibliography, the serialization of the volumes of *The World Crisis* in *The Times* was, in each case, under the rather less descriptive title, 'Mr. Churchill's Book'.

53. Details of that meeting between the book publisher and William Lints Smith, then newly appointed manager of *The Times* (he remained in that position until retiring in 1937), are outlined in Butterworth's letter of 2 December 1920 to Churchill (CHAR 8/38/49–50). As he said, "you may feel assured that my intercession is treated confidentially . . . and, if the idea is accepted, arrangements can easily be made whereby Curtis Brown is brought into it without my appearing in the matter in any way."

54. Either the exact or a paraphrased expression of Churchill's concern as stated in a letter of 11 December 1920 to Sir Campbell Stuart (which I have not seen), taken from a letter of 14 December from H. Wickham Steed, then editor of *The Times*, to Churchill (CHAR 8/38/54). The next quotation in this paragraph is from Wickham Steed's own letter. Wickham Steed himself had been with *The Times* since 1896, as correspondent in Berlin, Rome and Vienna, then foreign editor (from 1914) and editor (following a dispute between Lord Northcliffe and Geoffrey Dawson in January 1919). He remained in that role until soon after the death of Northcliffe and the passage of the paper into the hands of John Jacob Astor, leaving on 1 December 1922, when Dawson again became the editor. Steed was later the editor of the *Review of Reviews*, a lecturer at King's College, London, and a well-known and respected broadcaster on the BBC.

Steed assured the concerned author that "it seems to be self-evident that, when we engage in an enterprise jointly with you, and thereby assume responsibility with you for publication, we should be guilty of gross self-stultification were we to criticize you for associating yourself with us. Earnestly as we endeavour to practise all Christian virtues, including that of humility, our attainments in this direction have not yet reached, even by implication, the point of crying *Confiteor, peccavi* [I confess, I have sinned], in regard to deeds which we, rightly or wrongly, deliberately commit. Therefore, I think you are entitled to assume that consideration for our own consistency, quite apart from the ingrained admiration we have always felt and have sometimes expressed for you, will be a guarantee that we shall not wilfully foul your and our nest."[55] A briefer, more formal and less tongue-in-cheek undertaking to this effect was sent to Churchill on 17 December. The matter was thereby settled and the contract for the "serial publication rights throughout the British Empire except Canada" was concluded on 21 December.[56] *The Times* paid £5000 for the rights, against which they recovered at least £1300 for various Commonwealth rights.[57] This was, according to Thornton Butterworth, the publisher of the volume in the British Empire, "the biggest figure ever offered in this country for serial rights".[58] Churchill had also hoped to

---

55. In a reply of 16 December, Churchill did explain the reason for his letter of 11 December to his literary agent (which gave rise to Wickham Steed's somewhat tongue-in-cheek response quoted above): "I should not have asked for them [the assurances] but for the fact that when I wrote for another of Lord Northcliffe's papers, the *Evening News*, at the earnest request of the Editor, the *Times* scolded me very severely not for what I wrote but for the mere fact of writing at all" (CHAR 8/38/55).

56. CHAR 8/38/59–60. It was agreed that the "complete manuscripts of the two volumes shall together be not less than 150,000 words" and that *The Times* would "publish in serial form not more than 70,000 words of the complete work". While Churchill had the right to co-ordinate the extracts, the decision of the Editor of *The Times* "as to the publication or non-publication of any matter shall be final". The paper was to pay Churchill £2000 on signature of the letter, £500 on delivery of the manuscript of Volume I and £2500 on delivery of Volume II.

57. Serialization rights were sold for Scotland to the *Glasgow Herald* for £500; for Ireland to the *Irish Times* for £150; for India to *The Statesman* (Calcutta) for £150; for South Africa to Argus South African Newspapers for £150; for Australasia to United Cable Service for £300; and for Ceylon to the *Ceylon Observer* for £50. There may have been other sales by *The Times*; however, these are the only ones for which I have been able to locate such information (memorandum of 30 January 1923 from the Manager to the Accountant, *The Times*: Sir Winston Churchill, Managerial File, 1920–28).

58. Letter of 7 January 1921 from Butterworth to Charles Scribner (Scribner Archives, Box 31, Folder 1).

make a serialization deal in the United States but, within two weeks of the start of the British serialization, learned that he would be unsuccessful. This was undoubtedly a relief to Charles Scribner, who had worried about the effect that such a serialization in America would have on the sale of the books "as reading competition between books and periodicals is much greater in this country than in England".[59] Churchill's concern, on the other hand, had been to earn the largest amount from the exploitation of the work. In his letter of 27 January 1923 to Clementine, he said: "We have had a blow over the American serial rights. Owing to the irritation over the Lloyd George episode and the fiasco of the Kaiser's Memoirs, I cannot get a bid of any kind. We have been hoping to make two or three thousand from this source, and it is a great disappointment that it should have dried up so inopportunely. The Scandinavian rights have been sold for £100, which is not bad."[60] Curtis Brown, Churchill's literary agent, announced disappointedly that, in North American terms, they had "only been able to arrange for the appearance of the material in Canada".[61] It was a scant month before publication began that *The Times* completed its selection of the 40,000 words which it was ultimately to run.[62] Following the serialization of the first volume of *The World Crisis*, a significant controversy arose regarding Churchill's publication of official Admiralty telegrams and other official documents. He defended his position in a strong letter of 3 March to the Prime Minister, Andrew Bonar Law, and concluded by saying in a P.S.: "It is only by publishing certain documents and telegrams which I have written myself and for which I bear the prime responsibility, that I can deal with the lies and fictions which have ruled for so long and which I have borne all these years without making any reply, while every other version has been put before the public."[63]

C268a.1	Feb. 8	**How the War Came. / The Fleet at Sea.** *The Times*, 11–12
C268a.2	Feb. 9	**The Decision for War. / Goeben Disclosures.** *The Times*, 11–12

---

59. Letter of 28 January to Butterworth (*ibid.*).
60. Gilbert, *WSC*, Vol. V, *C.V.* 1, pp. 18–20, the portion quoted being from p. 19.
61. Letter of 5 February 1923 from A. W. Barmby, the General Manager of Curtis Brown's New York office, to Charles Scribner (Scribner Archives, Box 31, Folder 1).
62. According to a letter of 9 January 1923 from Barmby (*ibid.*).
63. Gilbert, *WSC*, Vol. V, *C.V.* 1, pp. 32–6, at p. 36. The full correspondence on the issue is included at pp. 30–9.

C268a.3	Feb. 10	**Admirals All. / Lord Fisher and Sir A. Wilson.** *The Times*, 9–10
C268a.4	Feb. 12	**More Admirals. / Lord Beatty and Prince Louis.** *The Times*, 11–12
C268a.5	Feb. 13	**The North Sea Front. / Guarding against Surprise.** *The Times*, 13–14
C268a.6	Feb. 14	**In the Narrow Seas. / The Air Menace.** *The Times*, 13–14
C268a.7	Feb. 15	**Antwerp.—I. / First Efforts at Relief.** *The Times*, 11–12
C268a.8	Feb. 16	**Antwerp.—II. / Organizing the Relief Force.** *The Times*, 11–12
C268a.9	Feb. 17	**Antwerp.—III. / Personal Aspects of the Story.** *The Times*, 11–12
C268a.10	Feb. 19	**From Antwerp to Ypres. / The German Drive.** *The Times*, 13–14
C268a.11	Feb. 20	**The Loss of The Audacious. / Admiralty Changes.** *The Times*, 13–14
C268a.12	Feb. 21	**Coronel and the Falklands.—I. / Cradock's Dispositions.** *The Times*, 13–14
C268a.13	Feb. 22	**Coronel and the Falklands.—II. / A Fateful Action.** *The Times*, 11–12
C268a.14	Feb. 23	**Coronel and the Falklands.—III. / Cradock Avenged.** *The Times*, 13–14
C268a.15	Feb. 24	**German Raids. / Scarborough and Hartlepool.** *The Times*, 11–12
C268a.16	Feb. 26	**German Grip on Turkey. / Initiative Passes to Allies.** *The Times*, 11–12

C268b

THE WORLD CRISIS

The Canadian serialization was published in eight newspapers in the Dominion. In the *Toronto Daily Star*, it was advertised on 10 February as being published "simultaneously with the London Times ... beginning Monday, February 12th", when, in truth, that serialization had already begun four days before. There was no common title to the series. Note also that the use of punctuation in the titles and subtitles that follow was, although inconsistent, as originally published.

C268b.1   Feb. 12   **WINSTON CHURCHILL TURNS TO THE BIBLE FOR MESSAGE OF HOPE WHEN SENT TO THE ADMIRALTY TO PREPARE THE NAVY FOR WAR / Makes Accurate Forecast of the German Army's March Years before Storm. / The Agadir Crisis and Lloyd George / Germany's Request for Explanation of Speech Rejected by Grey. / Visits the Fleet / Who Could Fail to Work for Such a Service, Asks Churchill.**
Toronto Daily Star, 4

C268b.2   Feb. 13   **EIGHTEEN MILES OF WARSHIPS SPEED THROUGH THE NIGHT TO TAKE UP SECRET WAR STATIONS BEFORE THE BLOW FALLS / Winston Churchill Tells How Test Mobilization Prepared Britain for War. / Pumped by Ballin, Who Gets Little. / Naval Officers Secretly Warned of Possibility of Imminent Strife.**
Toronto Daily Star, 4

C268b.3   Feb. 14   **HONORABLE RESTRAINT OF ADMIRALTY SAVED THE GOEBEN, BUT NAVY STOOD READY TO PROTECT FRENCH TRANSPORTS / Cruel Blow Dealt to Sir George Callaghan at War's Outset. / Jellicoe Appointed / Lord Morley Leaves Cabinet to Be Replaced by Kitchener.**
Toronto Daily Star, 4

C268b.4   Feb. 15   **"YOURS-TO-A-CINDER FISHER" THE STORMY PETREL WHOSE RUTHLESSNESS BUILT UP BRITAIN'S NAVY / Officers Who Opposed His Policies Found Professional Careers Ruined. / Sir Arthur Wilson / The Most Selfless Man Winston Churchill Ever Met or Heard Of.**
Toronto Daily Star, 4

C268b.5   Feb. 16   **BEATTY, DOOMED TO RETIREMENT, IS SAVED BY CHURCHILL, "NELSON HAS COME AGAIN" IS ADMIRAL'S TRIBUTE LATER / Is Raised to Power over the Heads of Senior Officers. / Hence Not**

Popular / Approached Questions of Naval Strategy and
Tactics as Soldier Would.
Toronto Daily Star, 4

C268b.6   Feb. 17   BRITAIN COMPELLED TO CHANGE HER NAVAL
STRATEGIC PLANS WHEN GERMANY BECOMES
POTENTIAL FOE INSTEAD OF FRANCE / Front
Shifted from the South to the East Coast and from the
Channel to the North Sea—Close Blockade No Longer
Possible. / Increasingly Hard to Prevent Raids
Toronto Daily Star, 4

C268b.7   Feb. 19   MILLIONS SQUANDERED IN BUILDING BRITISH
ZEPPELINS, CHURCHILL'S AEROPLANE POLICY
REVERSED BY ADMIRALTY / Forerunner of the
Tank Used to Support Advanced Aerial Bases. / A
Blow to the Navy / Three Cruisers Sunk before Revised
Plan Can Be Put into Operation.
Toronto Daily Star, 4

C268b.8   Feb. 20   CHURCHILL   SENT   INTO   BELEAGUERED
ANTWERP, BRITAIN AND FRANCE UNITE TO
PREVENT FALL / Consternation in War Council
When Belgium Decides to Evacuate—Decision Taken
Very Suddenly When Defending Army Finds Itself in
Jeopardy. / Reinforcements Organized for Relief
Toronto Daily Star, 4

C268b.9   Feb. 21   CHURCHILL   SEES   GERMAN   SOLDIERS
CREEPING FORWARD FROM HOUSE TO HOUSE
IN THE SUBURBS OF DOOMED ANTWERP / Finds
Marines Trying to Stem Tide with Machine Gun on
Balcony. / A Critical Period / Defense Prolonged for
Five Momentous Days, and Belgian Army Extricated.
Toronto Daily Star, 4

C268b.10   Feb. 22   CHURCHILL   VOLUNTEERS   TO   COMMAND
BRITISH   FORCES   DEFENDING   ANTWERP /
Kitchener Was Willing, But the Cabinet Does Not
Accept Offer. / Rawlinson Is Sent / Brave Stand Made
by Defenders against the German Hordes.
Toronto Daily Star, 4

C268b.11   Feb. 23   VICTORY OF THE YSER AND EVER-GLORIOUS
YPRES MADE POSSIBLE BY THE DEFENCE OF
ANTWERP / Besieging Army Meets Surprise When
Released by Fall of the City. / No Need for Shame /

Rarely Were More Important Results Achieved by Forces So Limited.
Toronto Daily Star, 4

C268b.12   Feb. 24   **CARPING CRITICISM OF NAVY ENDURED IN FORCED SILENCE, PRINCE LOUIS COMPELLED TO QUIT AND FISHER STEPS IN** / Sinking of the Audacious a Pure Stroke of Luck for Germans. / **Churchill Accused** / **Charged with Wantonly Sending Cruisers to Their Doom—Accomplishments Forgotten.**
Toronto Daily Star, 4

C268b.13   Feb. 26   **HAD ORDERED CRADOCK NOT TO SEPARATE FROM THE CANOPUS, SQUADRON WOULD HAVE BEEN SAFE WITH OLD DREADNOUGHT** / Admiralty Cannot Take Responsibility for Von Spee's Victory at Coronel. / The Truth at Last / Germans Would Not Have Dared to Come within the Range of Heavier Guns.
Toronto Daily Star, 5

C268b.14   Feb. 27   **CRADOCK SEALED HIS FATE IN DECIDING TO FIGHT, COULD STILL HAVE DECLINED UNEQUAL CONTEST** / Less Than Three Hours to Darkness and Safety—Admiralty Still Believed Instructions to Stay with Canopus Were Being Carried Out. / Left One Slow Ship to Take Another.
Toronto Daily Star, 4

C268b.15   Feb. 28   **TERRIBLE APPARITION MEETS THE EYES OF GERMAN ADMIRAL, KNEW THE TRIPOD MASTS IN FALKLAND HARBOR MEANT DEATH** / Warships Cross the Seas to Wipe out Defeat off Coronel. / Well-planned Move / Von Spee Had Expected to Find an Easy Prey.
Toronto Daily Star, 4

C268b.16   March 1   **CHURCHILL JUMPS WITH JOY WHEN NEWS ARRIVES THAT DEFENCELESS CITIES ARE BEING SHELLED** / British Fleet Was out Stationed to Cut off Raiders' Retreat. / Saved by Weather / Hopes of Victory Fade as Visibility Fails—Terrible Message to Keyes.
Toronto Daily Star, 4

C268b.17   March 2   **TURKEY'S BLASTING SECRET WELL KEPT FROM THE ALLIES, CHURCHILL EXPLAINS BOMBARDMENT OF DARDANELLES FORTS / Valuable Data Obtained by Much Criticized Action— The Admiralty's Policy Justified by Future Events—Terrible Strain on Navy During First Few Months. / But at Last Initiative Passes to Allies.**
       Toronto Daily Star, 6

C269   July   **MESOPOTAMIA AND THE NEW GOVERNMENT**
       Empire Review, Vol. XXXVIII, No. 270, 691–8
       Subsequently collected in *Collected Essays*, Vol. II, pp. 85–91.

C270   **MR. CHURCHILL'S BOOK.**
       The serialization of the second volume of *The World Crisis* (**A69**).

C270a.1   Oct. 8   **The Deadlock in the West. / Relief by Sea.**
       The Times, 13–14

C270a.2   Oct. 9   **The Dardanelles. / Decision for Naval Action.**
       The Times, 13–14

C270a.3   Oct. 10   **Fisher and the Dardanelles. / "The Only Rebel."**
       The Times, 11–12

C270a.4   Oct. 11   **Lord Kitchener's Domination. / The Army and the Dardanelles.**
       The Times, 13–14

C270a.5   Oct. 12   **West or East? / Dardanelles Plan Changed.**
       The Times, 13–14

C270a.6   Oct. 13   **Allied Fleet in the Straits. / Pledge to Russia.**
       The Times, 13–14

C270a.7   Oct. 15   **Greece and the Straits. / An Abortive Affair.**
       The Times, 13–14

C270a.8   Oct. 16   **A Turning-point. / Decision to Force the Straits.**
       The Times, 13–14

C270a.9   Oct. 17   **Attack on the Narrows. / Admirals' Veto.**
       The Times, 13–14

C270a.10   Oct. 18   **Changed Plan at the Straits. / The "No" Principle.**
       The Times, 13–14

C270b.3   Oct. 10   **FATEFUL SHOT SAVED GERMANS FROM DESTRUCTION WHEN LION CRIPPLED, AND BEATTY LEFT BEHIND** / Dogger Bank Action Followed at Admiralty by Wireless Reports / Signals Mistaken / All Set in Dardanelles for Long-range Bombardment of Forts
Toronto Daily Star, 4

C270b.4   Oct. 11   **LORD FISHER KICKS OVER THE TRACES; STARTS KNOCKING DARDANELLES PLAN** / "Went the Whole Hog. Totus Porcus," He Later Tells Probers / Sin Not to Stick at It / War Council Shelves Zeebrugge Scheme in Favour of Gallipoli.
Toronto Daily Star, 4

C270b.5   Oct. 12   **KITCHENER TRIES SUPERHUMAN TASK; ATTEMPTS TO RUN WHOLE WAR HIMSELF** / Staff Officers Were Petrified by His Personality and Position / Dominates Cabinet / Winston Agitates for Army Aid at Dardanelles; Is Promised It.
Toronto Daily Star, 4

C270b.6   Oct. 13   **KITCHENER BETWEEN TWO FIRES, PLUNGED INTO PAINFUL INDECISION** / Eastern and Western Policies Divide War Council in Two Camps / 'Winnie' on Warpath / Sailing of Regular Division Canceled at the Last Minute
Toronto Daily Star, 4

C270b.7   Oct. 15   **CHURCHILL'S FAIR WEATHER FRIENDS BEAM BRIGHTLY WHEN ALL GOES WELL** / Naval Guns Rapidly Demolish Outer Forts of the Dardanelles / Temporary Success / Sphinxlike Silence Veils Kitchener's Plans for Army in Drive.
Toronto Daily Star, 4

C270b.8   Oct. 16   **ILL-FATED CZAR, JEALOUS OF GREEKS, KEEPS TINO OUT OF WORLD CONFLICT** / Doesn't Want Christian Rivals to Enter Constantinople First! / Offer 3 Divisions / Sultan Prepares to Flee to Asia Minor, Court and All
Toronto Daily Star, 4

C270b.9   Oct. 17   **CHARGES EFFORTS FLAG WHEN VICTORY IN SIGHT; FISHER OFFERS TO LEAD DARDANELLES DRIVE** / All Set to Launch Gigantic Operations by Land and Sea / But Month Too Late / A

Terrible Moment in Long Struggle to Save Russia from Destruction
Toronto Daily Star, 4

C270b.10   Oct. 18   DISASTROUS NAVAL DRIVE BEGUN UNDER NEW LEADER / Admiral Cardon Knocked out by Illness after First Success / Hamilton on Job / Army on Way to Aid Fleet in Historic Gallipoli Action
Toronto Daily Star, 4

C270b.11   Oct. 19   SPECTACLE OF TERRIBLE MAGNIFICENCE AS WARSHIPS BOMBARD TURK FORTS / Unsuspecting Fleet Wanders into Minefields in Disastrous Action / He Passes the Buck / Admirals Stick in Their Toes—High Words at Council Table
Toronto Daily Star, 4

C270b.12   Oct. 20   HAMILTON LEFT BY ADMIRALS TO FIGHT ALONE AT GALLIPOLI; DECIDE NOT TO RENEW ATTACK ON STRAITS WITH WARSHIPS / Too Much Sentiment Attached to Obsolete Ships by Sailors / Troops Unprepared / 60,000 Men within Striking Distance, but Supplies Scattered
Toronto Daily Star, 4

C270b.13   Oct. 22   FAIR WEATHER FRIENDS DESERT MR. CHURCHILL / Blame Him for Dardanelles Setback—Fisher "Against Scheme from First" / Trouble Galore / Crises Staring Allies in Face from Every Quarter—Vindicated by Coalition
Toronto Daily Star, 4

C270b.14   Oct. 23   LORD FISHER RESIGNS; MEANS IT THIS TIME / Asquith Orders Him in King's Name, to Return to Duty / "Never Explain" / First Sea Lord and Churchill Exchange Series of Breezy Letters
Toronto Daily Star, 4

C270b.15   Oct. 24   AXE FALLS ON "WINNIE" HAS TO QUIT ADMIRALTY / Unconsciously Coaches Balfour to Step into His Shoes / German Fleet Out / Stage All Set for Big Battle When Enemy Speeds Home
Toronto Daily Star, 4

C270b.16   Oct. 25   **WILSON   BACKS   'WINNIE'   AS   WORLD CONDEMNS** / Grizzled Sea-Dog Refuses to Serve under Any Other, Even Balfour / "Disinherited" / First Lord's Action Would Have Vindicated Him, Had the Public Only Known
Toronto Daily Star, 4

C270b.17   Oct. 26   **MR. CHURCHILL BOOSTS USE OF SMOKE SCREENS** / But Frowns on Plans to Develop Poison Gas—Fears German Science / Offered to French / Was Invented by Crimean War Leader—Developed by Grandson, Lord Dundonald
Toronto Daily Star, 4

C270b.18   Oct. 27   **FOUR MILES BETWEEN ALLIES AND VICTORY** / League's Advance at Gallipoli Would Drive Turk from Europe / And What a Result! / Churchill out of Admiralty, but Has Seat of Honor at Council
Toronto Daily Star, 4

C270b.19   Oct. 29   **VICTORY PREVENTED BY CABINET CLEAVAGE** / Premier Asquith Lacked Plenary Authority in May and June, 1915 / As to Dardanelles / Winston Churchill Not Making Reproaches, but Explaining Melancholy Facts
Toronto Daily Star, 4

C270b.20   Oct. 30   **GEN. MONRO PREPARES TO QUIT GALLIPOLI** / He Came, He Saw, He Capitulated—Kitchener Was Thunderstruck / Hamilton Recalled / Would Mean Loss of Half Force, Wires Retiring Leader
Toronto Daily Star, 4

C270b.21   Oct. 31   **KITCHENER   APPROVES   EVACUATION DECISION** / Visits Gallipoli; Has a New Plan to Launch Attack near Alexandretta / Churchill Resigns / Declares Victory within Reach When Troops and Navy Retire
Toronto Daily Star, 4

C270b.22   Nov. 1   **GALLIPOLI EVACUATED WITHOUT LOSS OF LIFE** / Surprised Turks Find Only Empty Trenches, Silent as the Grave / Were in Dire Straits / Wemyss in Naval Bombardment Nearly Cripples Enemy Transport Route
Toronto Daily Star, 4

C270b.23	Nov. 2	**CHURCHILL REVIEWS RESULTS OF THE WAR /** **Russia's Downfall the First of Series of Great Tragedies to Civilization / Traced to Gallipoli / Will Darken the World for Our Children's Children**

Toronto Daily Star, 4

Two interesting articles on the reaction to the series in the United Kingdom appeared in the two following issues of the *Toronto Daily Star*: on Saturday, 3 November, 'Churchill's War Articles Rouse Heated Controversy' and, on Monday, 5 November, 'Back Winston Churchill in His Dardanelles Policy', both at p. 4.

C271	November	**MR. H. G. WELLS AND THE BRITISH EMPIRE**

Empire Review, 1217–23

Of this piece, Churchill wrote to Eddie Marsh: "I have also written an article answering Wells and giving him one or two wipes in the eye. I particularly want you to look through this for me, and I think you will like it in view of the impudent references to you in his book".[64]

C272a.1	December	**MEMORIES OF THE HOUSE OF COMMONS**

Pearson's Magazine, Vol. LVI, No. 336, 503–7

Subsequently collected in *Collected Essays*, Vol. II, pp. 92–100.

C272a.2	January 1924	**MEMORIES OF THE HOUSE OF COMMONS**

Pearson's Magazine, Vol. LVII, No. 337, 3–7

There is also a facsimile excerpt of one page of the manuscript for the article on p. 2. Subsequently collected in *Collected Essays*, Vol. II, pp. 100–8.

C272b	February 1924	**THE TIME WHEN I LOST MY MEMORY AND OTHER INCIDENTS OF MY LIFE IN PARLIAMENT**

Cosmopolitan, Vol. LXXVI, No. 2, 74–5

C273a.1	December	**MY ESCAPE FROM THE BOERS / Now Told in Full for the First Time.**

Strand Magazine, Vol. LXVI, 537–40, 542–4, 546–7

---

64. Letter of 27 September 1923 (Gilbert, *WSC*, Vol. V, *C.V.* 1, p. 61). The reference is to Wells's *Men Like Gods* (London: Cassell, 1923), in which both Eddie Marsh and Churchill, among others, were lampooned.

1924

C273a.2   January   **MY ESCAPE FROM THE BOERS**
Strand Magazine, Vol. LXVII, 14–18, 20–3

C273b   January   **MY ESCAPE FROM THE BOERS**
Cosmopolitan, Vol. LXXVI, No. 1, 30–4, 161–6

C274   January   **LIBERALISM**
English Life and the Illustrated Review, 74–5
Subsequently collected in *Collected Essays*, Vol. II, pp. 109–11.

—   February   **THE TIME WHEN I LOST MY MEMORY AND OTHER INCIDENTS OF MY LIFE IN PARLIAMENT** (*Cosmopolitan; see* **C272b**)

C275a   February   **THE IRISH TREATY**
Nash's—Pall Mall, Vol. LXXII, No. 370, 12–14, 96
Under the superhead 'Dramatic Episodes in My Life. No. 1.'
Subsequently collected in *Thoughts and Adventures* (**A95**), pp. 219–26.

C275b   March   **THE JOKE THAT HELPED TO SETTLE THE IRISH QUESTION / A Dramatic Chapter in the Life of the Rt. Hon. Winston S. Churchill**
Cosmopolitan, Vol. LXXVI, No. 3, 50–1

C276   Feb. 17   **THE COMING CONFLICT: MR. CHURCHILL'S WARNING / Who Has Been Deceived? / The British Public or the Socialist Party? / False Security**
Sunday Chronicle, 2
Subsequently collected in *Collected Essays*, Vol. II, pp. 112–15, under the title 'False Security'.

C277a   March   **WINSTON CHURCHILL DESCRIBES THE BATTLE OF SIDNEY STREET**
Nash's—Pall Mall, Vol. LXXII, No. 371, 16–18, 98
Subsequently collected in *Thoughts and Adventures* (**A95**), pp. 65–72.

C277b   April   **THE BATTLE OF SIDNEY STREET / A Dramatic Chapter in the Life of the Right Hon. Winston S. Churchill**
Cosmopolitan, Vol. LXXVI, No. 4, 84–6

C277c	June 1936	**THE BATTLE OF SIDNEY STREET** *Men Only*, Vol. 2, No. 7, 47–54 Under the superhead 'I REMEMBER—'.

C278	March 2	**THE PERIL OF MODERN POLITICS: MR. CHURCHILL'S WARNING. / Three-Party Confusion. / An Atmosphere of Pretence: "Allies" Who Are Knifing Each Other.** *Sunday Chronicle*, 1 Subsequently collected in *Collected Essays*, Vol. II, pp. 116–19, under the title 'Three-Party Confusion'.

C279	March 22	**WHO RULES BRITAIN?** *John Bull*, Vol. XXXV, No. 929, 13 Subsequently collected in *Collected Essays*, Vol. II, pp. 120–3.

C280	March 30	**THE CASE FOR SINGAPORE. / Abandonment a Long Step towards Imperial Disintegration.** *Sunday Chronicle*, 1 Subsequently collected in *Collected Essays*, Vol. I, pp. 256–9.

—	April	**THE BATTLE OF SIDNEY STREET** (*Cosmopolitan; see* **C277b**)

C281a	April	**"PLUGSTREET" / How the Secret of the Tanks Was "Lost"** *Nash's—Pall Mall*, Vol. LXXIII, No. 372, 18–19, 82–4 Subsequently collected in *Thoughts and Adventures* (**A95**), pp. 113–20.

C281b	May	**THE WORST FRIGHT I EVER HAD / An Episode in the Dramatic Life of the Rt. Hon. Winston S. Churchill** *Cosmopolitan*, Vol. LXXVI, No. 5, 52–3

C282	April	**"THE PARTY GAME"** *English Life and the Illustrated Review*, 258–61 Subsequently collected in *Collected Essays*, Vol. II, pp. 128–32.

C283	April 6	**SOCIALISM UNMASKED / Socialism and Sham. / The Joyless Utopia of Mr. and Mrs. Sidney Webb.** *Sunday Chronicle*, 1 Subsequently collected in *Collected Essays*, Vol. II, pp. 124–7, under the title 'Socialism and Sham'. Note also the interesting reply by Bernard Shaw in the April 13 issue of the *Sunday Chronicle*, pp. 1–2.

C284   May 25   **RAMSAY MACDONALD: THE MAN AND THE POLITICIAN.**
Weekly Dispatch, 8
Subsequently collected in *Collected Essays*, Vol. III, pp. 32–7.

C285a   June   **"IN THE AIR" / The Story of His Experiences in the Years before the War & Some Memories of Gustav Hamel**
Nash's—Pall Mall, Vol. LXXIII, No. 374, 26–7, 82, 84–7
Subsequently collected in *Thoughts and Adventures* (**A95**), pp. 181–98.

C285b   June   **ADVENTURES IN THE AIR**
Cosmopolitan, Vol. LXXVI, No. 6, 66–8

C285c   Sept. 5   **IN THE AIR. / Some Memories of My Early Flying Days.**
Pictorial Magazine, Vol. CVI, No. 1371, 121–4[65]

C286   June 15   **THE DANGERS AHEAD IN EUROPE.**
Weekly Dispatch, 8
Subsequently collected in *Collected Essays*, Vol. I, pp. 238–41.

C287   June 29   **THE FUTURE OF MR. LLOYD GEORGE.**
Weekly Dispatch, 8
Subsequently collected in *Collected Essays*, Vol. II, pp. 133–7.

C288a   July   **"WHY I GAVE UP FLYING" / The Story of Two Almost Fatal Crashes**
Nash's—Pall Mall, Vol. LXXIII, No. 375, 42–3, 114–16

C288b   July   **THE RT. HONORABLE WINSTON S. CHURCHILL RELATES MORE OF HIS PERILS IN THE AIR**
Cosmopolitan, Vol. LXXVII, No. 1, 98–100

C289   July 13   **HOW TO GET THE HOUSES**
Weekly Dispatch, 8
Subsequently collected in *Collected Essays*, Vol. II, pp. 138–42.

C290   July 27   **SHOULD STRATEGISTS VETO THE TUNNEL?**
Weekly Dispatch, 2
Subsequently collected in *Eurotunnel* (**B197**), pp. 98–100, and *Collected Essays*, Vol. I, pp. 260–4.

---

65. Copies of *Pictorial Magazine* (later *Pictorial Weekly*) were, regrettably, among the volumes in the section of the British Library which was destroyed during the Blitz.

C291a August **MY DRAMATIC DAYS WITH THE KAISER IN ALL HIS GLORY**
Cosmopolitan, Vol. LXXVII, No. 2, 90–2
Subsequently collected in *Thoughts and Adventures* (**A95**), pp. 75–83.

C291b October **THE GERMAN SPLENDOUR** / The Magnificence That Was Germany in the Days before the War
Nash's—Pall Mall, Vol. LXXIV, No. 378, 16–17, 80, 82

C291c May 2, 1925 **THE GERMAN SPLENDOUR** / The Magnificence That Was Theirs before the War
Pictorial Weekly, Vol. CIV, No. 1353, 449–53

C292 Aug. 4 **THE BRITISH LION'S SHARE. / "Britain Was Never More Noble Than When She Drew the Sword and Never Stronger Than When She Sheathed It."**
Daily Mail, 5–6
Subsequently collected in *Collected Essays*, Vol. I, pp. 265–72.

C293 Aug. 10 **MR. SNOWDEN'S HOROSCOPE.**
Weekly Dispatch, 6
Subsequently collected in *Collected Essays*, Vol. II, pp. 143–6.

C294 Aug. 31 **LORD BIRKENHEAD: THE MAN & HIS CAREER**
Weekly Dispatch, 6
Subsequently collected in *Collected Essays*, Vol. III, pp. 38–43.

C295a September **MY OWN TRUE SPY STORY BY THE MAN WHO HAS THE BEST RIGHT TO TELL ONE**
Cosmopolitan, Vol. LXXVII, No. 3, 76–7, 108
Subsequently collected in *Thoughts and Adventures* (**A95**), pp. 87–96.

C295b November **MY OWN TRUE SPY STORY / In the Circumstances, What Would You Have Done?**
Nash's—Pall Mall, Vol. LXXIV, No. 379, 26–7, 94–8

C296a September **SHALL WE ALL COMMIT SUICIDE?**
Nash's—Pall Mall, Vol. LXXIII, No. 377, 12–13, 80–1
Subsequently separately published in pamphlet form as *Shall We Commit Suicide?* (**A74**) and collected in *Thoughts and Adventures* (**A95**), pp. 245–52.

C296b Nov. 14 **SHALL WE ALL COMMIT SUICIDE? / The World Menace to Mankind.**
Pictorial Magazine, Vol. CVII, No. 1381, 1–4

C296c	Dec. 3	**SHALL WE COMMIT SUICIDE?** *The Nation* (US), Vol. 119, No. 3100, 608, 610

C296d	February 1925	**RECENT EXPRESSIONS ON WORLD PEACE / I.** **Shall We Commit Suicide?** *Historical Outlook*, Vol. XVI, No. 2, 56–8

—	Sept. 5	**IN THE AIR** (*Pictorial Magazine*; *see* **C285c**)

C297	Sept. 21	**IF WE COULD LOOK INTO THE FUTURE!** *Weekly Dispatch*, 8 Subsequently collected in *Collected Essays*, Vol. II, pp. 147–52.

—	October	**THE GERMAN SPLENDOUR** (*Nash's—Pall Mall*; *see* **C291b**)

C298a	October	**WHEN I RISKED COURT MARTIAL IN SEARCH** **OF WAR** *Cosmopolitan*, Vol. LXXVII, No. 4, 80–1, 112

C298b	December	**THE LURE OF WAR** *Nash's—Pall Mall*, Vol. LXXIV, No. 380, 52–3, 169–72

C299	Oct. 5	**OUR FIRST NEED: STABLE GOVERNMENT** *Weekly Dispatch*, 8 Subsequently collected in *Collected Essays*, Vol. II, pp. 153–5.

—	November	**MY OWN TRUE SPY STORY** (*Nash's—Pall Mall*; *see* **C295b**)

C300a	November	**MY DIFFERENCE WITH KITCHENER** *Cosmopolitan*, Vol. LXXVII, No. 5, 60–1, 135–7

C300b	January 1925	**A DIFFERENCE WITH KITCHENER** *Nash's—Pall Mall*, Vol. LXXIV, No. 381, 46–7, 111–14

C301	Nov. 2	**THE RED PLOT—AND AFTER** *Weekly Dispatch*, 8 Subsequently collected in *Collected Essays*, Vol. II, pp. 156–9.

—	Nov. 14	**SHALL WE ALL COMMIT SUICIDE?** (*Pictorial* *Magazine*; *see* **C296b**)

—	December	**THE LURE OF WAR** (*Nash's—Pall Mall*; *see* **C298b**)

C302	December	**WHEN I WAS YOUNG** *Strand Magazine*, Vol. LXVIII, 604–12

C303a	December	**A HAND-TO-HAND FIGHT WITH DESERT FANATICS** *Cosmopolitan*, Vol. LXXVII, No. 6, 94–5, 152–5

C303b.1	February 1925	**THE EVE OF OMDURMAN** *Nash's—Pall Mall*, Vol. LXXIV, No. 382, 46–7, 124–7 Under the superhead: 'The Rt. Hon. Winston S. Churchill, M.P., on Kitchener's Campaign of 1898'.

C303b.2	March 1925	**OMDURMAN** *Nash's—Pall Mall*, Vol. LXXIV, No. 383, 42–3, 120–2 Under the superhead: 'The Rt. Hon. Winston Churchill's Charge with the Twenty-first Lancers'.

—	Dec. 3	**SHALL WE COMMIT SUICIDE?** (*The Nation* (US); *see* **C296c**)

1925

—	January	**A DIFFERENCE WITH KITCHENER** (*Nash's—Pall Mall*; *see* **C300b**)

C304a	January	**A TRAPPED ARMORED TRAIN** *Cosmopolitan*, 70–2

C304b	April	**HOW THE RT. HON. WINSTON S. CHURCHILL, M.P., AND GENERAL BOTHA FIRST "MET"** *Nash's—Pall Mall*, Vol. LXXV, No. 384, 48–9, 134, 136, 138, 140

—	February	**THE EVE OF OMDURMAN** (*Nash's—Pall Mall*; *see* **C303b.1**)

—	February	**SHALL WE COMMIT SUICIDE?** (*Historical Outlook*; *see* **C296d**)

—	March	**OMDURMAN** (*Nash's—Pall Mall*; *see* **C303b.2**)

C305a	December	**HOBBIES / For Those Whose Work and Pleasure Are One—Each Day Is a Holiday** *Nash's—Pall Mall*, Vol. LXXVI, No. 392, 50–1, 134, 136 Subsequently collected in *Thoughts and Adventures* (**A95**), pp. 297–302.

C305b	February 1926	**WHEN LIFE HARASSES ME I RIDE MY HOBBY** *Cosmopolitan*, Vol. LXXX, No. 2, 80–1

C305c	April 20, 1930	**A MAN'S HOBBIES** *Sunday Chronicle*, No. 2330, 8 The title actually falls within a sentence reading 'Easter, the First Real Holiday of the Year, Is a Good Time to Talk of A MAN'S HOBBIES.'
C305d	March 1961	**"I RIDE MY HOBBY"** *Cosmopolitan*, Vol. 150, No. 3, 52–3

1926

—	February	**WHEN LIFE HARASSES ME I RIDE MY HOBBY** (*Cosmopolitan*; see **C305b**)
C306a	April	**LUCK?** *Cosmopolitan*, Vol. LXXX, No. 4, 19 Subsequently collected in *Thoughts and Adventures* (**A95**), pp. 99–110.
C306b	February 1927	**AT THE FRONT WITH THE GRENADIERS** *Nash's—Pall Mall*, Vol. LXXVIII, No. 405, 10–11, 71–4
C306c	April 6, 1930	**AT THE FRONT WITH THE GUARDS** *Sunday Chronicle*, 10, 12
C307		*The British Gazette* For a detailed account of the saga of the publication of the *British Gazette*, see Gilbert, *WSC*, Vol. V, pp. 146–74. Although Churchill did not actually write an article in every one of the eight issues, he played a major role in the mounting of the enterprise, the solicitation of personnel to publish the newspaper and paper on which to print it, as well as the editorial guidance of its content. The articles he wrote are all unsigned. Issues without Churchill-authored contributions are: **C307.4** (May 8), **C307.5** (May 10), **C307.6a** (May 11), **C307.6b** (May 11, 3 a.m. edition) and **C307.7** (May 12).
C307.1a	May 5	**THE "BRITISH GAZETTE" AND ITS OBJECTS / Reply to Strike Makers' Plan to Paralyse Public Opinion / Real Meaning of the Strike / Conflict between Trade Union Leaders and Parliament.** *British Gazette*, No. 1, 1
C307.1b	May 5	No. 1 (variant issue, pp. 2 and 3 blank)

C307.2	May 6	**NATION CALM AND CONFIDENT** / Gradual Recommencement of the Railway Services. / Good Fuel and Food Supplies. / Volunteers in Large Numbers at All the Centres.

British Gazette, No. 2, 1

C307.3 May 7   **NEGOTIATIONS UNDER MENACE.** / T.U.C.'s Plans for Paralysing the Life of the Nation / Cabinet's Refusal to Be Intimidated. / Mr. J. H. Thomas's Responsibility.
British Gazette, No. 3, 1

VITAL SERVICES IMPROVING. / All Obstacles Being Progressively Surmounted. / Warning against Rumours. / Defeat of the Attempt to Silence the Press. / Result of the Strike Now beyond Doubt. / Official Communique.
British Gazette, No. 3, 1

C307.8a May 13   **THE BIRTH AND LIFE OF THE "BRITISH GAZETTE"** / An Unexampled Achievement in Journalism. / How an Improvident Newspaper Reached a Circulation of 2,209,000.
British Gazette, No. 8, 1-2
The article ends with a bold Churchillian flourish: "The *British Gazette* may have had a short life; but it has fulfilled the purpose of living. It becomes a memory; but it remains a monument."

C307.8b May 13   No. 8 (3 a.m. edition, so indicated on the title line of pp. 2 and 3)

C308a August   **THE TIGER AND THE BULLDOG**
Cosmopolitan, Vol. LXXXI, No. 2, 25

C308b March 1927   **THE BULLDOG AND THE TIGER** / A Day with Clemenceau amid the Bursting Shrapnel of the French Battlefields
Nash's—Pall Mall, Vol. LXXVIII, No. 406, 28–9, 84–8

C309a December   **A GREAT DREAM**
Cosmopolitan, Vol. LXXXI, No. 6, 15

C309b April 1927   **IN DURANCE VILE** / "I certainly hated every minute of my captivity more than I have ever hated any other period in my whole life"
Nash's and Pall Mall Magazine, Vol. LXXIX, No. 407, 12–13, 82, 84

C309c	May 11, 1930	**A WILD PLOT OF MY YOUTH / Here Was Something to Stagger Humanity!** *Sunday Chronicle*, 10

C309/1	Dec. 13	**MR. CHURCHILL AND TRADE UNIONS. / Privileges Abused in the General Strike.** *The Times*, 16 Apparently reprints part of an article, reported to be entitled 'The Challenge of the Constitution' and to have been published in the *West Essex Constitutional* of December. I have been unsuccessful in locating any copies of the periodical in question.

1927

—	February	**AT THE FRONT WITH THE GRENADIERS** (*Nash's—Pall Mall*; *see* **C306b**)
C310		**MR. CHURCHILL'S BOOK.** The serialization of the third volume of *The World Crisis* (**A69**). *The Times* paid £2250 for British Empire serialization rights (excluding Canada). Of this licence fee, they recovered no less than £500 from other licensees.[66]
C310.1	Feb. 7	**I. / The Blood Test. / Another View of Attrition.** *The Times*, 15–16
C310.2	Feb. 8	**II. / Attrition. / A Comparison of Losses.** *The Times*, 15–16
C310.3	Feb. 9	**III. / The Battle of Jutland. / Unequal Stakes.** *The Times*, 15–16
C310.4	Feb. 10	**IV. / Tactics at Jutland. / Scheer's Escape.** *The Times*, 13–14
C310.5	Feb. 11	**V. / The Night of Jutland. / Nobody's Victory.** *The Times*, 15–16
C310.6	Feb. 12	**VI. / Martyrs of the Somme. / The First Tanks.** *The Times*, 13–14

---

66. *The Times* sold the rights for Australia to the Australasian Newspapers Cable Service for £200; for India to *The Statesman* (Calcutta) for £100; for South Africa to Argus South African Newspapers for £150; and for Ceylon to the *Ceylon Observer* for £50 (memo of 20 December 1926, *The Times*: Sir Winston Churchill, Managerial File, 1920–28).

C310.7	Feb. 14	**VII. / The Test of Nivelle. / French Mutinies.** *The Times*, 13–14
C310.8	Feb. 15	**VIII. / The Russian Collapse. / America at War.** *The Times*, 13–14
C310.9	Feb. 16	**IX. / The Man-Power Crisis. / Cabinet and G.H.Q.** *The Times*, 15–16
C310.10	Feb. 21	**X. / Towards Unity of Command. / The New Defences.** *The Times*, 13–14
C310.11	Feb. 22	**XI. / Chief of Staff. / Sir Henry Wilson's Contribution.** *The Times*, 15–16
C310.12	Feb. 23	**XII. / March 21, 1918. / The Barrage Falls.** *The Times*, 13–14
C310.13	Feb. 24	**XIII. / The Fury of "Michael." / Marshal Foch.** *The Times*, 15–16
C310.14	Feb. 25	**XIV. / Battle of the Lys. / "Backs to the Wall."** *The Times*, 15–16
C310.15	Feb. 26	**XV. / Working with America. / Plans for 1919.** *The Times*, 11–12
C310.16	Feb. 28	**XVI. / The Genius of Foch. / Paris or Union.** *The Times*, 13–14
C310.17	March 1	**XVII. / Victory. / The Curtain Falls.** *The Times*, 15–16
—	March	**THE BULLDOG AND THE TIGER** (*Nash's—Pall Mall*; *see* **C307b**)
—	April	**IN DURANCE VILE** (*Nash's and Pall Mall Magazine*; *see* **C308b**)
C310/1	May	**AN ESTIMATE OF WOODROW WILSON** *Smoker's Companion*, Vol. I, No. 3, 42–3 Excerpted from Volume III of *The World Crisis* (**A69.1(III)**).

C311a   July   **CONSISTENCY   IN   POLITICS / A   Foolish Consistency Is the Hobgoblin of Little Minds Adored by Little Statesmen and Philosophers and Divines ...**
Nash's and Pall Mall Magazine, Vol. LXXIX, No. 410, 42–3, 92–4
Subsequently collected in *Thoughts and Adventures* (**A95**), pp. 39–47.

C311b   April 27, 1930   **MEN WHO CHANGE THEIR MINDS**
Sunday Chronicle, No. 2331, 10
The title is found within a sentence which reads "It is very often unfair to accuse them of being turncoats when the MEN WHO CHANGE THEIR MINDS Risk Political Friendships for their Convictions."

C311c   January 1936   **CONSISTENCY IN LEADERSHIP**
Rotarian, 10–14

C312   September   **IN AN INDIAN VALLEY / A Frontier Skirmish Which Nearly Cost Mr. Churchill His Life**
Nash's Magazine, Vol. LXXIX, No. 412, 20–3, 95–7

C313   October   **HOW I PLACATED LORD ROBERTS**
Nash's Magazine, Vol. LXXX, No. 413, 48–51, 121–4

C314   November   **WITH BULLER TO THE CAPE**
Nash's Magazine, Vol. LXXX, No. 414, 44–5, 120–2

1928

C315   August   **HERBERT HENRY ASQUITH / First Earl of Oxford and Asquith**
Nash's Magazine, Vol. LXXXI, No. 423, 24–5, 78, 80

C316a   November   **DOUGLAS HAIG**
Nash's Magazine, Vol. LXXXII, No. 426, 14–16

C316b   November 1929   **HAIG**
Cosmopolitan, Vol. LXXXVII, No. 5, 21
Intended to be "the first of a Group of DRAMAS in Statecraft". Subsequently published, with slight revision, as a part of the series 'Great Men of Our Time' in the *News of the World* (**C486.5**).

C316c   May 4, 1930   **THE TRUTH ABOUT DOUGLAS HAIG.**
Sunday Chronicle, No. 2332, 10

1929

C317   January   **GEORGE CURZON / The Man Who Often Domineered But Never Dominated**
Nash's Magazine, Vol. LXXXII, No. 428, 20–3
This article also served as the basis for 'Curzon: Majestic, But He Never Led' in the 1936 *News of the World* series 'Great Men of Our Time' (**C486.9**).

C318   February   **BORIS SAVINKOV / The Story of a Man Who Was Not without Honour Except in His Own Country**
Nash's Magazine, Vol. LXXXII, No. 429, 26–9

C319   **THE AFTERMATH.**
The serialization of the fourth volume of *The World Crisis* (**A69**).[67] *The Times* contracted to pay £2000 for British Empire serialization rights (excluding Canada),[68] against which they recovered at least £600.[69] *The Toronto Star* paid £105 for the exclusive Canadian syndication rights; however, I have found no indication that the newspaper ever exercised those rights.

C319.1   Feb. 11   **I.—Masters of the World. / Three Men at Their Goal.**
The Times, 13–14

C319.2   Feb. 12   **II.—What Might Have Been. / An Armistice Dream.**
The Times, 15–16

C319.3   Feb. 13   **III.—President Wilson. / A Party Leader.**
The Times, 15–16

C319.4   Feb. 14   **IV.—Phases of Peace. / The Making of the League.**
The Times, 15–16

---

67. There was a last-minute attempt to have the *New York Times* take the serialization but they would not agree to more than $1000 for 6000 words. In Curtis Brown's letter of 28 January 1929, he expresses his disappointment with the offer but said that he "knew from the first how extraordinarily little interest American newspapers now take in the subject" (CHAR 8/227/16).

68. They ultimately paid £2250. Churchill vaguely explained this discrepancy in his letter of 4 April 1930 to Thornton Butterworth: "they were good enough to send me £250 more than the £2,000 contracted for, on account of the full use they made of the material" (Gilbert, *WSC*, Vol. V, *C.V.* 2, pp. 147–8, at p. 147).

69. *The Times* sold the rights for Australia to the Australasian Newspapers Cable Service for £300; for India to *The Statesman* (Calcutta) for £100; for South Africa to Argus South African Newspapers for £150; and for Ceylon to the *Ceylon Observer* for £50 (memo of 2 November 1928, *The Times*: Sir Winston Churchill, Managerial File, 1920–28).

C319.5	Feb. 15	**V.—Making Them Pay. / Rise and Fall in Reparations.** *The Times*, 15–16
C319.6	Feb. 16	**VI.—Completing the Terms. / A Page from Exodus.** *The Times*, 13–14
C319.7	Feb. 18	**VII.—Russia and Lenin. / Grand Repudiator.**[70] *The Times*, 13–14
C319.8	Feb. 19	**VIII.—Ireland and the War. / The Rise of Sinn Fein.** *The Times*, 15–16
C319.9	Feb. 20	**IX.—Emissaries of Ireland. / A Visit to De Valera.** *The Times*, 15–16
C319.10	Feb. 21	**X.—Signing the Treaty. / Mr. Lloyd George and Ireland.** *The Times*, 15–16
C319.11	Feb. 22	**XI.—Two Objects in Ireland. / An Appeal to Hope and Law.** *The Times*, 15–16
C319.12	Feb. 25	**XII.—A Period of Convulsion. / Irish Patriots.** *The Times*, 13–14
C319.13	Feb. 26	**XIII.—Turkey Reborn. / A Man of Destiny.** *The Times*, 17–18
C319.14	Feb. 27	**XIV.—A Greek Tragedy. / Mr. Lloyd George's View.** *The Times*, 15–16
C319.15	March 4	**XV.—Climax at Chanak. / Peace with Honour.** *The Times*, 17–18
C319.16	March 5	**XVI.—Back to 1914. / The Test of War Guilt.** *The Times*, 17–18
C319.17	March 6	**XVII.—A New Era in Prospect. / Locarno and Hope.** *The Times*, 17–181
C320	May 8	**SOCIALIST QUACKERY** *Daily Mail*, 12, 18 Subsequently collected in *Collected Essays*, Vol. II, pp. 160–4.

---

70. See, on the subject of Churchill and Lenin, the note under **C695**.

C321	June 15	**WHY WE LOST** *John Bull*, 9 Odhams, the publishers of *John Bull*, paid Churchill £500 for this article. Subsequently collected in *Collected Essays*, Vol. II, pp. 165–7.
C322	July	**FOCH THE INDOMITABLE** *Nash's Magazine*, Vol. LXXXIII, No. 434, 12–15 Churchill was paid £500 by Hearst's National Magazine Co. for "world's serial rights in article on Marshall Foch".[71]
C323	July	**LORD BIRKENHEAD'S ORATIONS / One Great Conservative Reviews Ten Speeches of a Former Cabinet Associate** *Living Age*, Vol. 336, No. 4343, 353–4
C324a	August	**BERNARD SHAW / Saint, Sage and Clown, Venerable, Profound, Irrepressible—He Is a Link in the Humanities of Peoples—the Greatest Living Master of English Letters in the World** *Nash's Magazine*, Vol. LXXXIII, No. 435, 16–18
C324b	April 13, 1930	**BERNARD SHAW—SAINT, SAGE, AND CLOWN.** *Sunday Chronicle*, No. 2329, 10
C324c	September 1931	**G.B.S. SAGE OR CLOWN?** *Cosmopolitan*, Vol. XCI, No. 3, 25
C324d	Sept. 19, 1937	**G.B.S.** *Sunday Chronicle*, 6 In the series 'Men the World Will Never Forget'. Under the heading, 'He derides the marriage vow and even the sentiment of love itself; yet no one is more happily married.'
C325	Sept. 22	**THE PALESTINE CRISIS. / Sequel to Lord Lloyd's Dismissal. / A Signal to Arab Factions. / Need for British Gendarmerie.** *Sunday Times*, 16 Subsequently collected in *Collected Essays*, Vol. II, pp. 168–71. Reported to have also been published in the *Zionist Record* in New York.[72]

---

71. See statement of 21 May 1929 from Curtis Brown Ltd. (CHAR 8/227/25).

72. Gilbert, *WSC*, Vol. V, *C.V.* 2, p. 86*n*. In Churchill's letter of 19 September to Clementine (pp. 85–8), the report of his "profits of fortune & labour" indicates that he was paid £300 for the article.

| C326 | October | **LORD ROSEBERY** |

Nash's—Pall Mall, Vol. LXXXIV, No. 437, 10–13

| C327 | Oct. 26 | **WILL THE BRITISH EMPIRE LAST?** |

Answers, 3, 5

Churchill was advised of *Answers'* agreement to publish the article while on the Canadian part of his North American tour. The Editor asked Churchill's literary representative, Nancy Pearn, "to pass on his expression of hope that you will deal with the subject in your most challenging fashion". She added that it was "understood that the article will not appear elsewhere prior to publication in *Answers*".[73] Proofs were provided to Josephine Cummings, Churchill's secretary, on 1 October. She corrected "one word" only and returned them to the publisher the following day. Subsequently collected in *Collected Essays*, Vol. II, pp. 172–5.

| — | November | **HAIG** (*Cosmopolitan; see* **C316b**) |

| C328 | November | **LORD MORLEY** |

Nash's—Pall Mall, Vol. LXXXIV, No. 438, 42–3, 141–2

The article was written aboard the *Empress of Australia* in early August. Churchill's letter of 8 August to Clementine, posted the following day at Rimouski, said, "I have written an article on John Morley, with which I am quite satisfied."[74] This article also served as the basis for 'John Morley: A Lamp of Wisdom' in the 1936 *News of the World* series 'Great Men of Our Time' (**C486.13**).

| C329 | Nov. 16 | **THE PERIL IN INDIA.** |

Daily Mail, 10

| C330 | | **MR. CHURCHILL'S IMPRESSIONS** |

The serialization of Churchill's impressions of the United States and Canada was first published in the United States, and thereafter in Great Britain in the *Daily Telegraph*.[75] Initial efforts to place the articles with the Hearst and *New York Times* syndicates failed, and attempts to secure interest in the

---

73. Letter of 9 August 1929 from Nancy Pearn of Curtis Brown Ltd. to Churchill, c/o the Canadian Pacific Railway in Montreal (CHAR 8/227/40).

74. *Speaking for Themselves*, pp. 335–6, at p. 336. Churchill was paid £450 for the article. See his letter of 19 September to Clementine (Gilbert, *WSC*, Vol. V, *C.V.* 2, pp. 85–8, at p. 87).

75. Churchill wrote that he had taken "care that the first refusal was made to *The Times* on account of the long and agreeable business we have done together" (letter of 4 April 1930 to Thornton Butterworth, Gilbert, *WSC*, Vol. V, *C.V.* 2, pp. 147–8, at p. 148).

Canadian market were also unsuccessful.[76] Finally, the Bell Syndicate agreed to pay $750 per article for a series of ten articles of 1500 to 2000 words each, for exclusive American and Canadian rights. "The subject matter of these articles is to be Mr. Churchill's impressions of the United States and Canada, as gathered on his tour, one or two articles possibly discussing Canada, but preferably these Canadian articles will not be published until the ninth or tenth of the series. We would also like to have him take up the subject of prohibition in one of his articles, if he will consent to it."[77] Churchill responded to the proposed contract that the "ten American articles ... will constitute a pithy and comprehensive commentary upon American themes and questions,— California, Prohibition, Hollywood, Grand Canyon, Chicago, Ford's work, the Canadian Development, American–Canadian Relations, American Newspapers, the great stock market craze [*sic*], The South, Washington, New York, and Anglo-American cooperation. ... The final selection can not be made until my tour is at an end, and I can review the whole scene in its proper proportion."[78]

In the end, Curtis Brown managed to modify the arrangements so as to obtain for Churchill 60% of the revenues for any Canadian syndication, apart from the guaranteed amount for the American rights.[79] The articles were also sold to South Africa,[80] Australia[81] and Malaya.[82] *De Telegraaf* offered £30 for the Dutch rights and *Le Figaro* Frs. 5000 for the French rights (on the basis of Frs. 500 per article).[83] Churchill succeeded in having a total

---

76. The word used by Curtis Brown in his letter of 16 July 1929 to Churchill was "feeble". He annexed a letter of 11 July from Kenneth Macmillan, the manager of the Star newspaper Service, which explained why they could not extend to anything close to the $200 per article which Curtis Brown sought from them. He added, "We would say confidentially that *The Toronto Star* gets the Lloyd George and Mussolini newspaper articles at $20 each and Lloyd George's, at least, runs to 2500 words. *The Toronto Star* incidentally pays a higher price for such material than any of the half dozen Canadian newspapers which represent the total Canadian market. You will appreciate that while we have more than sixty daily newspapers in Canada there are a mere handful which buy features of this nature" (CHAR 8/227/33–4).

77. Letter agreement of 29 August 1929 from John N. Wheeler of the Bell Syndicate to R. G. Rich of Curtis Brown (CHAR 8/227/4).

78. Letter of 20 September 1929 to E. G. Rich (CHAR 8/227/6–8).

79. Churchill was informed of this by Curtis Brown by a letter of 6 September 1929 sent to him "c/o Canadian Pacific Railroad, Montreal, Canada" (CHAR 8/227/5).

80. The Argus South African Newspapers paid £100 for the series.

81. The Australian Cable Newspaper Service paid £50 for the Australasian serialization rights.

82. The *Straits Times* paid £75 for the series.

83. Letter of 14 December 1929 to Churchill from the Foreign Department at Curtis Brown (CHAR 8/227/115).

of eight submitted by 6 November. At the same time, he advised his agents in New York that he would be "MAILING REMAINING TWO ARTICLES THREE WEEKS LATER. GLAD YOU LIKED FIRST TWO. THINK OTHERS BETTER." In that cabled night letter, he added that he could "MANAGE TWO MORE IF DESIRED MAKING TWELVE ON AMERICAN INDUSTRY AND NEGRO PROBLEM".[84] Churchill had hoped to publish the articles as a book, tentatively entitled *American Impressions*, but neither Thornton Butterworth nor Scribner's would agree to undertake publication.[85] Some of the articles were ultimately collected by Churchill's grandson, Winston S. Churchill, with other writings on the United States, in *The Great Republic* (**A301**).

C330a

The *Washington Post* serialization. There was no common heading for the articles in the *Washington Post*.

C330a.1   Nov. 17

CHURCHILL TELLS WHY VISIT OF MACDONALD WAS SIGNAL SUCCESS / Due Mainly, He Says, to New Feeling in U.S. toward Britain. / Four Reasons for Goodwill of America Given by Statesman.
Washington Post, 1, 4

C330a.2   Nov. 24

U.S. INCONSISTENT IN NAVAL POLICY, CHURCHILL AVERS / Vigorous against Neutral Rights When at War, for Them at Peace. / Divergence of Views on Building Traced / Cruiser Construction Led to Tri-cornered Race in Building.
Washington Post, 1, 16

C330a.3   Dec. 1

CHURCHILL CALLS PROHIBITION HERE COMIC SPECTACLE / Also Sees Pathetic Factor and Amazing Arrogance of Majority Rule. / Intolerant Idealism Costly, He Declares / Drunkenness and Crime Gain in U.S. While Decreasing in Great Britain.
Washington Post, 1, 18

C330a.4   Dec. 8

STOCK CRASH IN U.S. SEEN BY CHURCHILL AS PASSING EPISODE / Calls Titanic Market Fierce Experiment by People Hewing New Paths for Men. / Englishman Vividly Paints Wall Street / American

---

84. CHAR 8/227/53. The initial payment of $1500 for the first two articles (£275. 12*s*. 11*d*. in all, after deduction of the agency commission of 10%) was remitted to Churchill by Curtis Brown on 30 December 1929 (CHAR 8/227/135).
85. See Gilbert, *WSC*, Vol. V, at p. 351*n*.

Speculative Machine Built to Survive Crises, He Declares.
Washington Post, 1, 23

C330a.5   Dec. 15   CALIFORNIA'S CHARM AND HUGE WONDERS ASTOUND CHURCHILL / People amid Wealth Beheld as Best Anglo-Saxon Stock to Be Found in U.S. / Sees Stars Sparkle through Telescope / Gazes at the Redwood Firs and Talks over Continent and Ocean by Phone.
Washington Post, 1, 27

C330a.6   Dec. 22   CALIFORNIA TURNS ITS MAGIC ALLURE ON CHURCHILL TRIP / Principal Characteristics of Film Land Frugality, Hard Work and Discipline. / "Sacramental Wine" Flows in California / San Francisco and Los Angeles Contrasted by Former Cabinet Man.
Washington Post, 1, 18

C330a.7   Dec. 29   WEALTH OF CANADA AMAZES CHURCHILL, VISITING DOMINION / Former Harsh Regions Are Found Centers of Vast Deposits of Copper. / St. Lawrence River Is Fountain of Food / Fleet of Grain Ships and Enormous Elevators Encountered.
Washington Post, 1, 21

The rest of the serialization appeared in January 1930.

C330a.8   Jan. 5   WAR-TIME FIELDS OF OLD DOMINION THRILL CHURCHILL / Follows McClellan's Seven Days' Battles, Which He Paints as Masterful. / Visits "Bloody Angle" at Fredericksburg / World Famous Virginia Still Breathes Mellow Air of Ante Bellum Days.
Washington Post, 1, 16

C330a.9   Jan. 12   PROSPERITY IN U.S. ONLY AT BEGINNING, CHURCHILL STATES / Just Getting into Stride with No Limit in Sight, Says Visiting Englishman. / Impressed by Scale of Mass Production / American Mentality and Outlook Should Rivet European Attention, He Holds.
Washington Post, 1, 16

C330a.10   Jan. 19   **FAR NORTH CANADA TO BE FOOD CENTER, CHURCHILL STATES** / Hudson Bay Route Also to Supply World with Oil and Minerals. / Wealth of Country Only at Beginning. / Scenery of 20 Switzerlands at Disposal of Visitors; Climate Invigorating.
Washington Post, 1, 16

C330b   Serialization in the New York newspaper *The World*. There was no common heading for the articles in *The World*.

C330b.1   Nov. 17   **CHURCHILL WEIGHS AMERICAN FRIENDSHIP** / Former British Chancellor, Back Home, Sums up Present Friendly Anglo-American Relations / Declares 'Twisting Lion's Tail' Is Obsolete Sport—Spirit of Amity Is Spreading across the Entire Country
The World, 1E

C330b.2   Nov. 24   **CHURCHILL SCANS NAVAL PROBLEM** / Points out That Washington Conference Did Not Produce Hoped-for Results
The World, 1E, 7E

C330b.3   Dec. 1   **CHURCHILL DISCUSSES "DRY" AMERICA**
The World, 1E

C330b.4   Dec. 8   [On Wall Street—no copy located.]
The World

C330b.5   Dec. 15   [No copy located.]
The World

C330b.6   Dec. 22   **WINSTON CHURCHILL TOURS THROUGH CALIFORNIA** / Looks over Scenic Beauties— Discourses on Near Beer and Calls Hollywood the Peter Pan Township
The World, 5E

C330b.7   Dec. 29   **CHURCHILL DECLARES QUEBEC LIKE SCOTLAND** / Romantic Charm of Canadian City Is Matched by Beauty of the Surrounding Country, He Says
The World, 6E

The rest of the serialization appeared in January 1930.

C330b.8   Jan. 5   **TRACES OF CIVIL WAR ASTONISH CHURCHILL /**
Former Chancellor of the British Exchequer Visits Many
Battlefields of Historic Struggle on American Trip
The World, 7E

C330b.9   Jan. 12   **CHURCHILL SEES NO LIMIT TO CANADIAN**
PROSPERITY / Former British Cabinet Member Says
Essentials of Industrial Production Are Our Favorite
Gambling Counters
The World, 6E

C330b.10   Jan. 19   [No copy located.]
The World

C330c   The *Los Angeles Times* serialization. There was no common
heading for the articles in the *Los Angeles Times*.

C330c.1   Nov. 17   **ANCIENT ANGLO-AMERICAN ENMITY NOW**
FORGOTTEN / Battles in Common Cause Reunited
Long-sundered Family, Writes Winston Churchill for
'Times'
Los Angeles Times, 1–2

C330c.2   Nov. 24   **ANGLO-AMERICAN   NAVAL   ARGUMENTS**
ANALYZED / Winston Churchill Reviews Chain of
Events Since World War Leading to Arms Parley
Los Angeles Times, 1–2

C330c.3   Dec. 1   **PROHIBITION IN AMERICA DECRIED BY**
CHURCHILL / British Leader Regards Liquor Law as
Impractical Idealism Unthinkingly Adopted
Los Angeles Times, 4

C330c.4   Dec. 8   **CRASH OF STOCKS HELD NO CAUSE FOR**
WORRY / Churchill Views Market Slump as "Passing
Episode" in Nation's Progress
Los Angeles Times, 3

C330c.5   Dec. 15   **CALIFORNIA   WONDERFUL,   DECLARES**
CHURCHILL / Conditions Necessary to Health and
Happiness to Be Found in State
Los Angeles Times, 15

C330c.6   Dec. 22   **LOS ANGELES DESCRIBED AS GAY AND HAPPY**
CITY / Everyone Has Room to Live and Poverty
Missing, Finds Winston Churchill
Los Angeles Times, 2

C330c.7   Dec. 29   **CHURCHILL FINDS CANADA LAND OF OPPORTUNITY / Briton Charmed by Wild Beauty and Amazed by Great Natural Wealth**
Los Angeles Times, 5

The rest of the serialization appeared in January 1930.

C330c.8   Jan. 5   **HALLOWED GROUND TROD BY WINSTON CHURCHILL / Better Understanding of Civil War Gained by Visit to Historic Virginia**
Los Angeles Times, 11

C330c.9   Jan. 19   **AMERICAN MASS PRODUCTION AMAZING TO CHURCHILL / Gigantic Enterprises Spring up Overnight, Former British Cabinet Minister Says**
Los Angeles Times, 11

C330c.10   Jan. 26   **CANADA PUSHES BACK ITS NORTHERN FRONTIER LINE / Noted British Visitor Predicts Enormous Developments in Next Quarter Century**
Los Angeles Times, 6

C330d   The serialization in the *Daily Telegraph*, all the parts of which were subsequently published in *Collected Essays*. It was "part of the agreement with the *Daily Telegraph* that they shall be given sufficient notice of the date on which the Bell Syndicate plan to publish your articles on AMERICA to enable them to make arrangements for simultaneous publication."[86] The first eight articles for British syndication were sent by Churchill to his British literary agents on 8 November 1929. Receipt of the ninth and tenth articles was acknowledged by Curtis Brown's London office on 5 December.[87]

C330d.1   Nov. 18   **WHAT I SAW AND HEARD IN AMERICA. / Public Prayers for Our King. / Premier's Visit on the Tide of Good Feeling.**
Daily Telegraph, 10
Subsequently collected in *Collected Essays*, Vol. IV, pp. 31–4.

C330d.2   Nov. 25   **II. / What I Saw and Heard in America. / The Naval Misunderstanding. / Attempt by Two Nations to Reach a New Arrangement.**
Daily Telegraph, 10
All the articles in this series from this one on are under the superhead '*Mr. Churchill's Impressions—*' followed by the

---

86. Letter of 24 September 1929 from Curtis Brown to Churchill in Canada (CHAR 8/227/9).
87. Letter to Josephine Cummins (CHAR 8/227/102).

roman numeral indicating its order in the serialization. Subsequently collected in *Collected Essays*, Vol. IV, pp. 34–8.

C330d.3   Dec. 2   **III. / What I Saw in America of Prohibition. / Its Many Dangerous Evils. / "Amazing Exhibition of Arrogance and Impotence."**
Daily Telegraph, 10
Subsequently collected in *Collected Essays*, Vol. IV, pp. 38–41.

C330d.4   Dec. 9   **IV. / Fever of Speculation in America. / Wall Street during the Panic. / Machine Built Not to Prevent Crises but to Survive Them.**
Daily Telegraph, 10
Subsequently collected in *Collected Essays*, Vol. IV, pp. 42–5.

C330d.5   Dec. 16   **V. / Old Battlefields of Virginia. / Lee and Stonewall Jackson. / Memories of the Tremendous Fights between North and South.**
Daily Telegraph, 10
Subsequently collected in *Collected Essays*, Vol. IV, pp. 45–8.

C330d.6   Dec. 23   **VI. / Nature's Panorama in California. / A Bountiful Countryside. / Other Worlds Seen through the Great Lick Telescope.**
Daily Telegraph, 8
Subsequently collected in *Collected Essays*, Vol. IV, pp. 49–52.

C330d.7   Dec. 30   **VII. / Peter Pan Township of the Films. / Hollywood's Fantasy of Life. / Conquest of the "Talkie" over the Silent Picture.**
Daily Telegraph, 8
A selection of pictures entitled 'MR. CHURCHILL'S TOUR—FAMOUS CITIES OF THE PACIFIC COAST' can be found on p. 12. The article was subsequently collected in *Collected Essays*, Vol. IV, pp. 52–6.

The rest of the serialization appeared in 1930.

C330d.8   Jan. 6   **VIII. / World's Greatest Grain Emporium. / Waving Cornfields of Canada. / Wealth on the Deposit of a Vanished Inland Sea.**
Daily Telegraph, 8
Subsequently collected in *Collected Essays*, Vol. IV, pp. 56–9.

C330d.9   Jan. 13   **IX. / Across Canada to the Pacific. / Grandeur of the Rockies. / Roll to the North the Feature of the Future.**
Daily Telegraph, 8
Subsequently collected in *Collected Essays*, Vol. IV, pp. 59–62.

C330d.10   Jan. 20   **X. / Fleets of Britain and America. / Attaining Naval Parity. / Sea Power without Acceptance of Definite Inferiority.**
Daily Telegraph, 10
Subsequently collected in *Collected Essays*, Vol. IV, pp. 62–5.

C330d.11   Jan. 27   **XI. / Vastness of America's Industry. / Capital and Labour Banded. / No Limits Yet in Sight to Material Prosperity.**
Daily Telegraph, 10
Subsequently collected in *Collected Essays*, Vol. IV, pp. 65–9.

C330d.12   Feb. 3   **XII. / Industrial Conditions of America. / Business Leads the Nation. / Workshop Management Made Free of Labour Troubles.**
Daily Telegraph, 8
Subsequently collected in *Collected Essays*, Vol. IV, pp. 69–72.

C330e.1   Nov. 27   **WINSTON CHURCHILL ON AMERICA**
Family Herald and Weekly Star, Vol. LX, No. 48, 54

C330e.2   Dec. 4   **POINTS OF DIVERGENCE IN DISCUSSION OF NAVAL PACT DATE BACK TO 1921 TREATY**
Family Herald and Weekly Star, Vol. LX, No. 49, 55

C330e.3   Dec. 11   **CHURCHILL SCOFFS AT LAW DESIGNED TO MAKE U.S. DRY; COMPARISON WITH CANADA**
Family Herald and Weekly Star, Vol. LX, No. 50, 55

C330e.4   Dec. 18   **CHURCHILL THINKS SLUMP IN WALL STREET PASSING EPISODE IN MARCH OF VALIANT PEOPLE**
Family Herald and Weekly Star, Vol. LX, No. 51, 54

C330e.5   Dec. 25   **CALIFORNIA CAPTURES WINSTON CHURCHILL BY HER SUNNY PROSPERITY**
Family Herald and Weekly Star, Vol. LX, No. 52, 65

The rest of the serialization appeared in January 1930.

C330e.6   Jan. 1   **STUDIO LAND OF HOLLYWOOD SHOWS WINSTON CHURCHILL "WORLD'S QUEEREST FACTORY"**
Family Herald and Weekly Star, Vol. LXI, No. 1, 65

C330e.7   Jan. 8   **IMPRESSIONS OF DOMINION GATHERED BY A STATESMAN AFTER 30 YEARS' ABSENCE**
Family Herald and Weekly Star, Vol. LXI, No. 2, 57

C330e.8   Jan. 15   **BATTLEFIELDS OF VIRGINIA TELL BRITISH STATESMAN OWN TALES OF CIVIL WAR**
Family Herald and Weekly Star, Vol. LXI, No. 3, 57

C330e.9   Jan. 22   **STANDARDIZATION OF U.S. PEOPLE IN BUSINESS AND HOMES GREAT EXPERIMENT**
Family Herald and Weekly Star, Vol. LXI, No. 4, 56

C330e.10   Jan. 29   **QUARTER CENTURY OF PROSPERITY ASSURED CANADA BY NORTHLAND**
Family Herald and Weekly Star, Vol. LXI, No. 5, 57

C331a   December   **TROTSKY / The Ogre of Europe / Whose Fire-breathing Days Are Gone Forever**
Nash's—Pall Mall, Vol. LXXXIV, No. 439, 50–3, 122

C331b   March 1930   **THE OGRE OF EUROPE / A Study of a Living Dead Man Trotsky**
Cosmopolitan, Vol. LXXXVIII, No. 3, 72–3, 230

1930

C332   January   **LORD YPRES / Some Impressions of John French— the First Commander-in-Chief of the British Army in the World War**
Nash's—Pall Mall, Vol. LXXXIV, No. 440, 26–9
This article also served as the basis for 'French: The Man Who Came Back' in the 1936 *News of the World* series 'Great Men of Our Time' (**C486.4**).

C333   February   **CHAMBERLAIN— / The Radical Imperialist Statesman Who Sounded Trumpet Calls That Still Draw Stubborn Soldiers to the Field**
Nash's—Pall Mall, Vol. LXXXIV, No. 441, 30–2
This article also served as the basis for 'Chamberlain: The Prophet of Protection' in the 1936 *News of the World* series 'Great Men of Our Time' (**C486.12**).

C334   Feb. 15   *A GREAT BIG IDEA!* / **Mass Wealth: Mass Happiness**
John Bull, Vol. XLVII, No. 1235, 20–1

C335a   Feb. 15   **THE UNITED STATES OF EUROPE**
Saturday Evening Post, Vol. 202, No. 33, 25, 48, 51
As a result of approaches made by Mr Rich of Curtis Brown, Churchill was commissioned to write a series of six articles for the *Saturday Evening Post* on subjects specified by the magazine from time to time but in any event, Churchill hoped, to be

completed by the end of June. "Meanwhile they have specifically asked for an article on Monsieur Briand's project of a
'United States of Europe'. I propose to deliver this article in the
early days of December so that it can be published towards the
end of January. It is an article of 5000 words in length. I do not
wish to enter English monthly magazines before my contract
with *Nash's* expires or that with the *Strand* begins. It is therefore
a case of finding a weekly or daily publication which would take
this article in one or two instalments and publish it at the same
time as the *Saturday Evening Post*."[88] In the event, Curtis Brown
was not successful. *Answers* had contemplated the prospect at
£300 but decided that neither the subject matter nor the length
was suitable. Subsequently collected in *Collected Essays*, Vol. II,
pp. 176–86.

C335b	July/ August 1977	**DEALING IN FUTURES** *Saturday Evening Post*, Vol. 249, No. 5, 53 A portion of the original article.

C336	Feb. 28	**A STRAIGHT TALK ON OUR TASK FOR PEACE IN PALESTINE / CREATING JEWISH NATIONAL HOME PROMISE MADE IN BALFOUR DECLARATION.** *Evening News* (Glasgow), 5 Subsequently collected in *Collected Essays*, Vol. II, pp. 187–90, under the title 'Our Task for Peace in Palestine'.

—	March	**THE OGRE OF EUROPE** (*Cosmopolitan*; *see* **C331b**)

C337a.1	March 26	**MR. CHURCHILL ON THE ABUSE OF THE "DOLE" / I.—Fallacies of the Live Register / Britain's "Poverty Complex" and Its Effects Abroad** *Daily Telegraph*, 14 Subsequently collected in *Collected Essays*, Vol. II, pp. 191–6, under the title 'The Abuse of the Dole'.

C337a.2	March 27	**MR. CHURCHILL ON THE ABUSE OF THE "DOLE" / II.—Crying down British Credit / Wilful Misrepresentations That Magnify Our Unemployment Troubles** *Daily Telegraph*, 12 Subsequently collected in *Collected Essays*, Vol. II, pp. 196–201.

C337b	March 29	**THE DOLE** *Saturday Evening Post*, 6–7, 173, 177

88. Copy of letter of 9 November 1929 to Nancy Pearn (CHAR 8/227/63–5).

C338	April	**THE TRUTH ABOUT THE DARDANELLES / The Rt. Hon. Winston Churchill, M.P. States His Case in Giving the Facts about His Connection with Lord Fisher during the Momentous Years 1914–1915** *Nash's—Pall Mall*, Vol. LXXXV, No. 443, 18–21
—	April 6	**AT THE FRONT WITH THE GUARDS** (*Sunday Chronicle; see* **C306c**)
C339	April 12	***WHY MORE TAXES?* / Exclusive Budget Statement** *John Bull*, Vol. XLVII, No. 1243, 7 Subsequently collected in *Collected Essays*, Vol. II, pp. 202–5.
—	April 13	**BERNARD SHAW—SAINT, SAGE, AND CLOWN.** (*Sunday Chronicle; see* **C324b**)
—	April 20	**A MAN'S HOBBIES** (*Sunday Chronicle; see* **C305c**)
—	April 27	**MEN WHO CHANGE THEIR MINDS** (*Sunday Chronicle; see* **C311b**)
C340a		**CRUCIAL CRISES IN THE WAR** This title for a series of articles on the First World War is the one conceived in the original correspondence, but it was not used in the actual publication. The original hope was to publish them in the *Saturday Evening Post* but "the *Post* are not keen to commission, as they say that doing so is against their practice [and] Reynolds felt that you would not care to do articles on chance".[89] *Collier's* was, however, prepared to commission Churchill to write twelve articles at $2000 apiece, for a total of $24,000. By 9 October, that had been re-negotiated to six articles at the same price and it was intended that publication should begin in the first week of March. By 13 December, it was agreed that the articles would begin running on 3 May 1930, provided that two articles would be mailed by 25 January 1930.
C340a.1	May 3	**PANIC IN THE EAST** *Collier's*, Vol. 85, No. 18, 10–11, 55–6
C340a.2	May 17	**LUDENDORFF AT TANNENBERG** *Collier's*, Vol. 85, No. 20, 30, 84–7

89. Letter of 8 June 1929 from John Farquharson (London literary agent) to Churchill; Paul R. Reynolds was the New York agent trying to place the articles (CHAR 8/228/1).

C340a.3   May 31   **THE MAN WHO SAVED PARIS**
Collier's, Vol. 85, No. 22, 20–1, 54–5

C340a.4   June 14   **THE MYSTERY OF THE MARNE**
Collier's, Vol. 85, No. 24, 26, 29, 46, 49

C340a.5   July 5   **DREADNOUGHTS AT BAY**
Collier's, Vol. 86, No. 1, 14–15, 56–7

C340a.6   July 12   **LUDENDORFF'S LAST CARD**
Collier's, Vol. 86, No. 2, 24–5, 56–7
Subsequently collected in *Thoughts and Adventures* (**A95**), pp. 149–62.

C340b   **CRUCIAL CRISES OF THE WAR**
The series of articles on the First World War as they ran in the *Daily Telegraph*; some but not all of these were published in *Collected Essays*. In his letter to Curtis Brown of 9 November 1929, Churchill informed him that he had agreed to write the series of articles for *Collier's* and was "anxious to sell the English and Continental rights of these articles and should be glad to put this in your hands".[90] He thought that "it ought to be possible to obtain £250 apiece for these articles which of course if necessary could be reduced in length by me to suit an English publication". Curtis Brown succeeded and wrote to Churchill that the *Daily Telegraph* would take the articles at the £250 price but would divide them "in two parts, presumably on successive days".[91] The first article in the serialization appeared under the series title 'CRUCIAL CRISES OF THE WAR'; each of the others under a superhead '*Crucial Crises of the War.—[X.]*'.

C340b.1   May 5   **CRUCIAL CRISES OF THE WAR / Germany's Grave Peril at the Fierce Battle of Gumbinnen / Von Mackensen's Army Thrown Back**
Daily Telegraph, 10

C340b.2   May 6   **Preparations for Tannenberg / How Hindenburg and Ludendorff Were Brought upon the Scene / Inheriting a Ready Made Plan**
Daily Telegraph, 12

---

90. CHAR 8/227/63–5.
91. Letter of 15 November from Nancy Pearn of Curtis Brown Ltd. (CHAR 8/227/83).

C340b.12	July 14	**Ludendorff's All—Or Nothing / Council Which Decided to Undertake the Great Offensive / Onslaught of the British Army** *Daily Telegraph*, 10
C340b.13	July 15	**German Great Offensive / The Allies Holding Together under the Unified Command** *Daily Telegraph*, 10 Subsequently collected in *Collected Essays*, Vol. I, pp. 287–92.
—	May 4	**THE TRUTH ABOUT DOUGLAS HAIG.** (*Sunday Chronicle*; *see* **C316c**)
—	May 11	**A WILD PLOT OF MY YOUTH** (*Sunday Chronicle*; *see* **C308c**)
C341		**MEMORIES OF MY YOUTH.** The serialization of *My Early Life*. The rights were sold by Churchill to the *Daily News* for their *News Chronicle* for $7500. In a letter to Charles Scribner, Jr, Churchill stated, "Everyone here who has seen the copy seems very keen, and the Daily News have gone far beyond any price they have previously paid for serials."[92]
C341.1	Aug. 30	**MEMORIES OF MY YOUTH.** *News Chronicle*, 6
C341.2	Sept. 1	**Father and Son** *News Chronicle*, 6
C341.3	Sept. 2	**The Heart of a Boy** *News Chronicle*, 6
C341.4	Sept. 3	**The Call to Youth** *News Chronicle*, 6
C341.5	Sept. 4	**The Degradation of War** *News Chronicle*, 6
C341.6	Sept. 5	**The Lure of Adventure** *News Chronicle*, 6
C341.7	Sept. 6	**King Edward and "13"** *News Chronicle*, 6

---

92. Letter of 2 July 1930 to Charles Scribner, Jr (Scribners Archives, Box 31, Folder 3).

C341.8	Sept. 8	**A Subaltern in India / Ponies and Polo** *News Chronicle*, 4
C341.9	Sept. 9	**Mr. Churchill as the Scholar-Soldier. / The Hungry Mind.** *News Chronicle*, 4
C341.10	Sept. 10	**What I Believe** *News Chronicle*, 6
C341.11	Sept. 11	**Asking to Stop a Bullet / Refused by Kitchener** *News Chronicle*, 4
C341.12	Sept. 12	**Dawn on the Battlefield. / "The Hour to Live."** *News Chronicle*, 4
C341.13	Sept. 13	**"I Commend My Example to My Son"** *News Chronicle*, 4
C341.14	Sept. 15	**How Mr. Winston Churchill Entered Politics. / My First Speech.** *News Chronicle*, 4
C341.15	Sept. 16	**The Comedy of the Other Winston Churchill / Sharing a Reputation.** *News Chronicle*, 4 Churchill's famous letter of 7 June 1899 to the American novelist Winston Churchill is included in this part. Subsequently collected in *The Five Hundred Best English Letters* (**B44**).
C341.16	Sept. 17	**Mr. Winston Churchill & Lord Kitchener / How to Fight a War.** *News Chronicle*, 4
C341.17	Sept. 18	**My First £10,000.** *News Chronicle*, 6
C341.18	Sept. 19	**I Meet Lloyd George** *News Chronicle*, 4
C341.19	Sept. 20	**Winston Churchill's Final Article / 'Marriage & Happy Ever After'** *News Chronicle*, 6
C342a	Oct. 25	**THE TRUTH ABOUT THE EX-KAISER** *Collier's*, Vol. 86, No. 17, 16, 42, 45–6

C342b   November   **THE TRUTH ABOUT THE EX-KAISER**
Strand Magazine, Vol. LXXX, No. 479, 476–86

C342c   Jan. 28,   **THE TRUTH ABOUT THE EX-KAISER**
          1934   *Sunday Chronicle*, 10–11

C343a   Nov. 29   **TIGER OF FRANCE**
Collier's, Vol. 86, No. 22, 10, 62–4
Subsequently collected in *Thoughts and Adventures* (**A95**),
pp. 165–78.

C343b   December   **CLEMENCEAU—THE MAN AND THE TIGER**
Strand Magazine, Vol. LXXX, No. 480, 582–93
Published in German as "Clemenceau" in *Das Neue Tage-
Buch*, 21 May 1938, pp. 495–500.

C343c   May 1943   **CLEMENCEAU**
American Mercury, Vol. LVI, No. 233, 578–86
Reproduced here from the *Great Contemporaries* essay by
arrangement with Putnam's.

C344   December   **IF LEE HAD NOT WON THE BATTLE OF
GETTYSBURG**
Scribner's Magazine, Vol. LXXXVIII, No. 6, 587–97
The second in a series of "If" articles, speculations on
American history. The other pieces in the series were not
written by Churchill. Subsequently collected in *Collected
Essays*, Vol. IV, pp. 73–84.

C345   Dec. 4   **FANTASTIC TRIAL AT MOSCOW / Soviet's Appeal
to the Organised Ferocity of the Mob**
Daily Telegraph, 12
Subsequently collected in *Collected Essays*, Vol. II, pp. 209–12.

1931

C346a   February   **MEN WHO HAVE INFLUENCED OR IMPRESSED
ME**
Strand Magazine, Vol. LXXXI, No. 482, 132–41
Subsequently collected in *Thoughts and Adventures* (**A95**),
pp. 51–61.

C346b   Feb. 7   **PHILOSOPHERS AND FRIENDS**
Collier's, Vol. 87, No. 6, 22–3, 60

C347a	March	**IF I LIVED MY LIFE AGAIN**

Strand Magazine, Vol. LXXXI, No. 483, 243–51

Subsequently collected in *Thoughts and Adventures* (**A95**), pp. 11–19, under the title 'A Second Choice'.

C347b	April 4	**IF I LIVED MY LIFE OVER**

Collier's, Vol. 87, No. 14, 12, 47, 50

C347c	Feb. 3, 1934	**IF I COULD LIVE MY LIFE AGAIN**

Answers, Vol. XCII, No. 12 (2383), 3–4

C347d	December 1938	**A SECOND CHOICE**

Men Only, Vol. 10, No. 37, 23–6

C348	April	**ARTHUR JAMES BALFOUR**

Strand Magazine, Vol. LXXXI, No. 484, 345–56

C349	April 19	**MY BUDGET FORECAST**

Sunday Pictorial, No. 840, 8

Subsequently collected in *Collected Essays*, Vol. II, pp. 213–17.

C350	May	**MASS EFFECTS IN MODERN LIFE**

Strand Magazine, Vol. LXXXI, No. 485, 474–85

Subsequently collected in *Thoughts and Adventures* (**A95**), pp. 255–66.

C351	June	**CARTOONS AND CARTOONISTS**

Strand Magazine, Vol. LXXXI, No. 486, 582–91

Subsequently collected in *Thoughts and Adventures* (**A95**), pp. 23–35.

C352	June 18	**GOVERNMENT OF THE, BY THE, FOR THE DOLE-DRAWERS**

Daily Mail, 10

Subsequently collected in *Collected Essays*, Vol. II, pp. 218–21.

C353a	June 27	**UNLUCKY ALFONSO**

Collier's, Vol. 87, No. 26, 11, 46, 49

Subsequently published in *Great Contemporaries* (**A105**) under the title 'Alfonso XIII' and as the Preface to *Alfonso XIII* (**B185**).

C353b	July	**ALFONSO THE UNLUCKY**

Strand Magazine, Vol. LXXXII, No. 487, 15–23

C354   July 3   **NOTHING BUT HUMBUG!**
Daily Mail, 10
Subsequently collected in *Collected Essays*, Vol. II, pp. 222–4.

C355   July 11   **WILL AMERICANS AND THE ENGLISH EVER UNDERSTAND EACH OTHER?**
Liberty, 15–19
Subsequently collected in *The Liberty Years* (**B118**).

C356   **"PERSONALITIES"**
A series on British political and literary personalities.

C356.1   July 26   **No. 1 / Ramsay Macdonald**
Sunday Pictorial, No. 854, 8
Subsequently collected in *Collected Essays*, Vol. III, pp. 44–7.

C356.2   Aug. 2   **No. 2 / Philip Snowden**
Sunday Pictorial, No. 855, 8

C356.3   Aug. 9   **No. 3 / The Truth about "Jix"**
Sunday Pictorial, No. 856, 8
Re Lord Brentford. Subsequently collected in *Collected Essays*, Vol. III, pp. 47–50.

C356.4   Aug. 16   **No. 4 / Lady Astor and G. Bernard Shaw**
Sunday Pictorial, No. 857, 8

C356.5   Aug. 23   **No. 5 / H. G. Wells / Who Nurses a Grievance But for Which He Might Be of Great Help to Britain**
Sunday Pictorial, No. 858, 8
Subsequently collected in *Collected Essays*, Vol. III, pp. 50–4.

C356.6   Aug. 30   **No. 6 / "B.-P."**
Sunday Pictorial, No. 859, 10

C356.7   Sept. 6   **No. 7 / Lloyd George**
Sunday Pictorial, No. 860, 8
Subsequently collected in *Collected Essays*, Vol. III, pp. 54–7.

C356.8   Sept. 20   **No. 8 / Montagu Norman / The Man with a Load of Mystery**
Sunday Pictorial, No. 862, 8, 14
Subsequently collected in *Collected Essays*, Vol. III, pp. 57–60.

C356.9   Sept. 27   **No. 9 / J. H. Thomas**
Sunday Pictorial, No. 863, 8
Subsequently collected in *Collected Essays*, Vol. III, pp. 60–3.

C356.10 Oct. 11 **No. 10 / "UNCLE ARTHUR"**
Sunday Pictorial, No. 865, 8, 12
Re the Rt. Hon. Arthur Henderson. Subsequently collected in *Collected Essays*, Vol. III, pp. 64–6.

C356.11 Nov. 8 **No. 11 / Sir John Simon**
Sunday Pictorial, No. 869, 8, 14
Subsequently collected in *Collected Essays*, Vol. III, pp. 67–9.

C356.12 Nov. 15 **No. 12 / Sir Herbert Samuel**
Sunday Pictorial, No. 870, 8
Subsequently collected in *Collected Essays*, Vol. III, pp. 69–72.

C357 August **THE AMERICAN MIND AND OURS**
Strand Magazine, Vol. LXXXII, No. 488, 140–50

C358 Aug. 12 **WILL LLOYD GEORGE "COME BACK"?**
Daily Mail, 8
Subsequently collected in *Collected Essays*, Vol. II, pp. 225–7.

— September **G.B.S. SAGE OR CLOWN?** (*Cosmopolitan; see* **C324c**)

C359 September **SOME ELECTION MEMORIES**
Strand Magazine, Vol. LXXXII, No. 489, 236–47
Subsequently collected in *Thoughts and Adventures* (**A95**), pp. 201–15.

C360 Sept. 7 **INDIA INSISTENT. / Sir Harcourt Butler's Grave Warning.**
Daily Mail, 10
A review of Sir Harcourt Butler's book which bore that title. Subsequently collected in *Collected Essays*, Vol. II, pp. 228–32.

C361 Sept. 19 **THE EMPEROR FRANCIS JOSEPH**
Saturday Review, Vol. 152, No. 3960, 349–50

C362 Sept. 26 **THE VICTIM OF SERAJEVO** [*sic*]
Saturday Review, Vol. 152, No. 3961, 388–9

C363 Oct. 2 **THE WAY OUT OF THE CRISIS**
Daily Mail, 10
Subsequently collected in *Collected Essays*, Vol. II, pp. 233–5.

C364 Oct. 3 **THE 'PANTHER' AFFAIR**
Saturday Review, Vol. 152, No. 3962, 420
Subsequently collected in *Collected Essays*, Vol. I, pp. 293–5.

C365   Oct. 6   **THE TWO ISSUES NOW BEFORE THE NATION**
Daily Mail, 10
Subsequently collected in the *Collected Essays*, Vol. II, pp. 236–8.

C366   Oct. 10   *HOW WILL IT ALL END?*
Answers, Vol. LXXXVII, No. 2262, 3
Under the superhead 'THE TRUTH ABOUT THE CRISIS!' Subsequently collected in *Collected Essays*, Vol. II, pp. 239–42.

C367   Oct. 10   **A QUARREL IN VIENNA**
Saturday Review, Vol. 152, No. 3963, 451–2

C368   Oct. 17   **PRELUDE TO ARMAGEDDON**
Saturday Review, Vol. 152, No. 3964, 488

C369   Oct. 22   **THE WORLD LOOKS FOR OUR VICTORY**
Daily Mail, 10
Subsequently collected in *Collected Essays*, Vol. II, pp. 243–5.

C370   Nov. 8   **MOSES / The Leader of a People**
Sunday Chronicle, 7
Under the superhead 'Great Bible Stories Retold by the World's Best Writers'. Subsequently collected in *Thoughts and Adventures* (**A95**), pp. 283–94.

C371a   Nov. 15   **FIFTY YEARS HENCE**
Maclean's, 7, 66–7
Subsequently collected in *Thoughts and Adventures* (**A95**), pp. 269–80.

C371b   December   **FIFTY YEARS HENCE**
Strand Magazine, Vol. LXXXII, No. 492, 549–58

C371c   January 1932   **FIFTY YEARS HENCE**
Review of Reviews, Vol. LXXXV, No. 1, 58–9
Excerpts only from the *Maclean's* appearance.

C371d   March 1932   **FIFTY YEARS HENCE**
Popular Mechanics Magazine, Vol. 57, No. 3, 390–7

C371e   January 1952   **FIFTY YEARS HENCE**
Popular Mechanics Magazine, Vol. 97, No. 1, 144–5, 326

| C372 | Nov. 16 | **THE COUNTRY CALLS FOR VIRILITY, REALISM, ACTION / An Exhortation on the Morrow of Victory** |

Daily Mail, 12

Subsequently collected in *Collected Essays*, Vol. II, pp. 246–9.

| C373.1 | Nov. 16 | **GERMANY'S DESPERATE U-BOAT DECISION / Dramatic Events Which Led to the Naval Life and Death Struggle** |

Daily Telegraph, 10

This series of articles was edited for publication in *Thoughts and Adventures* (**A95**), the first four parts as 'The U-Boat War', pp. 123–38, and the fifth as 'The Dover Barrage', pp. 141–6. Colonel Fred Lawson, the General Manager of the *Daily Telegraph*, was unhappy about the overlap in the timing of the publication of this first article with that in the *Daily Mail* (**C372**). "We were naturally very annoyed to find that the *Daily Mail* had an article from you on the same day that we commenced our series of four articles. These articles have been costly to us, because in addition to the fee that we paid you for writing them, we spent a considerable amount of money on publicity. Obviously to have another paper giving an article from your pen on the same day detracts enormously from the value of our publication."[93] On the following day, Churchill explained the circumstances of the conflicting publication dates and apologized for the overlap. The original proposed publication date of the first of the fortnightly series in the *Daily Mail* had been delayed in order to accommodate the *Daily Telegraph* series; however, the latter series had itself been "held back for another week", with the result that the first article in each series appeared on the same day.[94] Each subsequent article in the serialization appeared under the superhead '*The U-Boat War—[X]*'.

| C373.2 | Nov. 18 | **Politicians Were Right and Admirals Wrong / Secret History of Struggle to Meet Growing U-Boat Menace** |

Daily Telegraph, 10

| C373.3 | Nov. 23 | **Jellicoe's Dramatic Decision at Admiralty / Convoy Plan of War Cabinet Adopted against Naval Resistance** |

Daily Telegraph, 10

---

93. Letter of 16 November from Fred Lawson to Churchill (Gilbert, *WSC*, Vol. V, *C.V.* 2, p. 373).

94. Response of 17 November from Churchill to Colonel Lawson, *ibid.*, at p. 374.

C373.4	Nov. 25	**Triumph of the Convoy System / U-Boats** [*sic*, no possessive apostrophe] **Daring Incursion into the Straits of Dover**

Daily Telegraph, 12

C373.5	Nov. 30	**Eleven U-Boats Destroyed in Dover Minefields / Seascape Illuminated "Bright as Piccadilly at Night"**

Daily Telegraph, 10

—	December	**FIFTY YEARS HENCE** (*Strand Magazine; see* **C371b**)

C374	Dec. 1	**BACK TO THE SPARTAN LIFE IN OUR PUBLIC SCHOOLS**

Daily Mail, 10
Subsequently collected in *Collected Essays*, Vol. IV, pp. 85–7.

1932

—	January	**FIFTY YEARS HENCE** (*Review of Reviews; see* **C371c**)

C375a.1	Jan. 4	**MY NEW YORK MISADVENTURE**

Daily Mail, 10
The account of Churchill's being struck by a car in New York City on 13 December 1931, just prior to the planned start of his North American lecture tour. The two parts were subsequently collected as a single essay in *Collected Essays*, Vol. IV, pp. 88–95.

C375a.2	Jan. 5	**I WAS CONSCIOUS THROUGH IT ALL .. / How It Feels to Be "Smashed Up"**

Daily Mail, 8, 11

C375b	Jan. 10	**CHURCHILL DESCRIBES CRASH / Statesman Tells How It Feels to Be Run Down.**

Sunday Star (Washington), Pt. 2, p. 6
The North American Newspaper Alliance paid $1500 for the article, which was commissioned by its President, John Wheeler.[95]

---

95. According to the account of John Wheeler (see *I've Got News for You*, New York: Dutton, 1961, p. 163). This version contrasts with those of Phyllis Moir in *I Was Winston Churchill's Private Secretary*, in which she reports at p. 205 that the article was sold for $2500, and Walter Thompson in *Assignment: Churchill*, in which he unreliably chronicles, at p. 109, that the article appeared in *Collier's* and fetched $3000. See also J. Richard Heinzkill, "Addenda to Woods' *A Bibliography of the Works of Sir Winston Churchill*", *Papers of the Bibliographical Society of America*, 1978, Vol. 72, No. 3, pp. 358–60.

C375c	Jan. 11	**FEELINGS OF AUTO VICTIM DESCRIBED BY CHURCHILL** / Glare of Light, Violent Shock and Practical Thoughts Recalled as Mishap Impressions *Los Angeles Times*, 4
—	March	**FIFTY YEARS HENCE** (*Popular Mechanics Magazine; see* **C371d**)
C376	March 23	**MY HAPPY DAYS IN THE "WET" BAHAMAS** *Daily Mail*, 10 Subsequently collected in *Collected Essays*, Vol. IV, pp. 96–9.
C377a	March 29	**PLAIN WORDS ON THE IRISH TREATY** *Daily Mail*, 8 Subsequently collected in *Collected Essays*, Vol. II, pp. 250–3.
C377b	Jan. 20, 1934	**HOW WE MADE THE IRISH TREATY** *Pictorial Weekly*, Vol. 1, No. 12 (New Series), 2–3
C378	May 7	**THE ACADEMY REVEALS BRITAIN'S BRAVE GAIETY** *Daily Mail*, 10 Subsequently collected in *Collected Essays*, Vol. IV, pp. 103–6.
C379	May 26	**SOME PLAIN SPEAKING ABOUT GENEVA** *Daily Mail*, 12 Subsequently collected in *Collected Essays*, Vol. I, pp. 296–9.
C380	June 30	**THE REAL ISSUE IN INDIA** *Daily Mail*, 8 Subsequently collected in *Collected Essays*, Vol. II, pp. 254–6.
C381	July 18	**THE FIRST SESSION—A SUMMING UP** *Daily Mail*, 10 Subsequently collected in *Collected Essays*, Vol. II, pp. 257–60.
C382a	Aug. 13	**THE SHATTERED CAUSE OF TEMPERANCE** *Collier's*, Vol. 90, No. 7, 20–1, 48–9
C382b	Aug. 14	**PROHIBITION** *Sunday Chronicle*, 8, 10 Subsequently collected in *Collected Essays*, Vol. IV, pp. 107–13.

C392a	Dec. 17	**DEFENSE IN THE PACIFIC**
		Collier's, Vol. 90, No. 25, 12–13, 30
		Subsequently collected in *Collected Essays*, Vol. II, pp. 269–75.

| **C392b** | March 10, | **[On defence in the Pacific; no copy located]** |
| | 1934 | *Pictorial Weekly* |

1933

C393a

THE WORLD'S GREAT STORIES
A series of classic literary works retold in individual articles. The idea was first proposed to Churchill by Lord Riddell, who suggested six articles in a series to be entitled 'Six Great Stories of the World Retold by Winston Churchill'. His suggestions included Anatole France's *Thais* and Rider Haggard's *She*, in addition to the first four actually published, their length to be 5000 words each.[96] Churchill thought the proposal a "brilliant idea", although he might "on reflection suggest a couple of alternatives [to the proposed titles]". He suggested £2000 for the series and agreed that, "while the series was coming out, I should not write *for money* in any other Sunday paper".[97] Churchill immediately contacted Eddie Marsh to seek his help in the task. "If I had read about 2,500 words of your ideas on each of the selected books it would be a foundation on which I could tell my story. I shall of course be reading them all again myself." He offered Marsh £25 "for each article you cared to help me with" and sought his views on the choice of the six books.[98] On 18 October 1932, he sent Lord Riddell the first three of the articles. As he said there, "The main difficulty is compressing these complicated stories accurately and yet dramatically within the limit of five thousand words."[99] On 9 November, after concluding a sale of the American rights to the *Chicago Tribune*, Churchill had to write to Riddell to persuade him to withhold initial publication of the series until 8 January to coincide with the anticipated first date of publication in the United States, no doubt out of fear that American copyright would not otherwise be secured and that the American publication rights might thus be turned down. His

96. Letter of 30 July 1932 (Gilbert, *WSC*, Vol. V, *C.V.* 2, p. 459).
97. Letter of 2 August to Riddell (*ibid.*, pp. 461–2).
98. Letter of 5 August (*ibid.*, p. 463). He sent Marsh £100 for the three drafts, as well as for his assistance on *Thoughts and Adventures* (**A95**) (letter of 11 November; *ibid.*, p. 489). As to Eddie Marsh's role in the series preparation, see also Christopher Hassall, *A Biography of Edward Marsh*, pp. 575–6 (**F146**).
99. Gilbert, *WSC*, Vol. V, *C.V.* 2, pp. 483–4, at p. 484.

entreaties succeeded. On 4 January, the publishers issued a postcard promoting the forthcoming series: "Six of the World's greatest stories re-told by Winston Churchill begin next Sunday Jan 8th in the News of the World—[a list of the titles follows]."

Even before the series began to run, the publisher advised Churchill that "they like them so much that they have ordered another half-dozen".[100] Having by mid-January decided on four of the six titles for the second series, on which he had "made considerable progress", Churchill advised Riddell that he needed a date for them; if they were desired to run immediately on conclusion of the first series, a decision which Churchill considered "wise" from a business promotion perspective, he would "have to lay aside Marlborough in which I am breast–high".[101]

C393a.1	Jan. 8	**1. "Uncle Tom's Cabin" / Book That Shook the Shackles from the Slave / Fearless Woman's Challenge to Her Country**

News of the World, 5–6
Subsequently collected in *Collected Essays*, Vol. IV, pp. 123–33.

C393a.2	Jan. 15	**No. 2. "The Count of Monte Cristo" / The Man Who Lived for Exquisite Revenge / Store of Riches to Destroy His Enemies**

News of the World, 5–6
Subsequently collected in *Collected Essays*, Vol. IV, pp. 133–45. Notes for the article were supplied by Eddie Marsh, but Churchill explained in bold and vivid terms what his view of the series was. "I have read your Monte Cristo, which is very careful and thorough, but we are not writing great stories *summarised*, but great stories *retold*. It is essential to seek the salient features of the tale and make them live in all their fullness, leaving the rest in darkness. ... I want to point out how hopeless it is to try and reduce these great works proportionately chapter by chapter to a smaller compass. Hundreds of pages have to be obliterated as if they had never been written. Only the salient counts and must be told fully enough to hold their full dramatic interest."[102]

---

100. Letter of 3 December to Eddie Marsh, in which Churchill solicited his collaboration in the choice and preparation of the material as in the first proposed series (*ibid.*, p. 500).
101. Letter of 13 January 1933 to Riddell (*ibid.*, p. 518).
102. Letter of 17 September to Marsh (*ibid.*, pp. 473–4, at p. 473).

C393a.3	Jan. 22	**No. 3. "The Moonstone" / Ill-starred History of a Stolen Jewel / Pseudo Saint Unmasked in Death** *News of the World*, 5–6 Subsequently collected in *Collected Essays*, Vol. IV, pp. 145–57.
C393a.4	Jan. 29	**No. 4. "Ben-Hur" / Galley Slave to National Hero / Chariot Race for Destiny of an Empire** *News of the World*, 5 Notes for the article were supplied by Eddie Marsh, who wrote, "Golly what a book! The seafight is really fun, so I'm making that a 'high-light', & there will be another in the chariot race; but there are terrible unmanageable tracts between—I don't think I've ever read a book in such bad English."[103] Churchill replied, "I think it is only necessary to select the main episodes and not to tell the story evenly or conscientiously throughout."[104] Subsequently collected in *Collected Essays*, Vol. IV, pp. 157–66.
C393a.5	Feb. 5	**No. 5. "Tess of the D'Urbervilles" / The Classic of "The Woman Always Pays" / Black Flag Flies over Immortal Nobility** *News of the World*, 5–6 Subsequently collected in *Collected Essays*, Vol. IV, pp. 166–77. Notes for the article were supplied by Eddie Marsh, who wrote, "I hope you like my Tess, which gave me less dissatisfaction than any of my others!"[105] On the file copy of Churchill's request of 23 December 1932 to Macmillan, the publishers, for permission to write this article, there is a pencilled notation: "We gave permission for the article to appear in England. The Executors could hardly object to such valuable publicity."[106]
C393a.6	Feb. 12	**No. 6. "A Tale of Two Cities" / A Very Gallant Gentleman of England / Sidney Carton's Choice of the Only Way** *News of the World*, 5–6 Subsequently collected in *Collected Essays*, Vol. IV, pp. 177–90.

103. Letter of 12 November 1932 from Marsh to Churchill (*ibid.*, pp. 491–2, at p. 491).
104. Letter of 14 November (*ibid.*, p. 492).
105. *Ibid.*
106. MACM 55245, document 191.

C393a.7	Feb. 19	**No. 7. "Jane Eyre" / A Secret Bared at the Altar / The Man Who Married a Maniac**

News of the World, 5

Subsequently collected in *Collected Essays*, Vol. IV, pp. 190–200.

C393a.8	Feb. 26	**No. 8. "Adam Bede" / Tragedy Springs from a Village Idyll / Girl Who Was Snatched from the Gallows**

News of the World, 5

Notes for the article were supplied by Eddie Marsh, who wrote that "for once I have got in within 5,000 words! I hope you won't find anything I've left out indispensible [*sic*]."[107] Subsequently collected in *Collected Essays*, Vol. IV, pp. 201–10.

C393a.9	March 5	**No. 9. "Vice Versa" / The Man Who Became a Boy Again / A Jewel, a Wish, and an Era of Chaos**

News of the World, 5–6

Subsequently collected in *Collected Essays*, Vol. IV, pp. 211–24.

C393a.10	March 12	**No. 10. "Ivanhoe" / Spacious Days of Lance and the Arrow / Gallants Fight for Love of a Lady**

News of the World, 5–6

Written by Churchill and submitted to Marsh for his "careful revision as usual".[108] Subsequently collected in *Collected Essays*, Vol. IV, pp. 224–35.

C393a.11	March 19	**No. 11. "Westward Ho!" / Men Who Made This England Mistress of the Seas / Life, Love and Gay Adventure out on the Spanish Main**

News of the World, 5–6

Notes for the article were supplied by Eddie Marsh, who wrote, "I hope it will pass muster, but it's rather hard to manage such a rambling book."[109] Subsequently collected in *Collected Essays*, Vol. IV, pp. 235–45.

C393a.12	March 26	**No. 12. "Don Quixote" / Rise and Fall of a Bold Knight Errant / Satire That Smiled Spain's Chivalry Away**

News of the World, 5–6

Subsequently collected in *Collected Essays*, Vol. IV, pp. 246–56.

---

107. Letter of 21 January 1933 (Gilbert, *WSC*, Vol. V, *C.V.* 2, p. 520).
108. Letter of 25 February from Violet Pearman to Marsh (*ibid.*, p. 532).
109. Letter of 24 February (*ibid.*, p. 531).

C393b   **CELEBRATED ROMANCES OF THE**
             NINETEENTH CENTURY
             The *Chicago Sunday Tribune* paid Churchill $1000 apiece for
             the American rights to this series of six articles, a then record
             total of $6000.[110] Encouraged by this, C. R. Everitt, of Curtis
             Brown's New York office, offered a second series of six re-
             told stories, "but Mary King had had enough; the first, *Adam
             Bede*, was returned with thanks".[111] Everitt then proposed to
             Charles Scribner that the six or seven articles sold to the
             Chicago Tribune and the "six or seven further parts … are
             rather good and should make an interesting book. Do you
             want to consider making an offer for the volume rights?"[112]

C393b.1   Jan. 8   **Winston Churchill Tells the Story of Uncle Tom's
                        Cabin by Harriet Beecher Stowe / Uncle Tom, Little
                        Eva, Topsy, Eliza, and All the Others Come to Life
                        Again in This Thumbnail Version of a History-making
                        Masterpiece**
                        Chicago Sunday Tribune, Pt. 6, p. 7

C393b.2   Feb. 5   **Winston Churchill Tells the Story of A Tale of Two
                        Cities by Charles Dickens**
                        Chicago Sunday Tribune, Pt. 6, p. 5

C393b.3   March 5   **Winston Churchill Tells the Story of The Count of Monte
                        Cristo by Alexandre Dumas / One of the Great Novels of
                        the Past Century Is Condensed by One of the Great
                        Writers of the Present Century, and Published Complete
                        in This Issue**
                        Chicago Sunday Tribune, Pt. 6, pp. 7–8

C393b.4   April 2   **Winston Churchill Tells the Story of The Moonstone
                        by Wilkie Collins / This Absorbing Tale of an Huge
                        Yellow Diamond Is Called by Many the Greatest
                        Detective Story in All Fiction.**
                        Chicago Sunday Tribune, Pt. 6, pp. 5–6

---

110. According to a letter of 23 September 1932 from Curtis Brown (see J. Richard Heinzkill and
     Martin Schmitt, 'Sir Winston's Potboilers', *Imprint: Oregon*, Vol. I, No. 2, Fall 1974, 3).
     Reported by Churchill to Lord Riddell, his British publisher for the series, as £1800. "The
     contract is a very valuable one to me" (letter of 9 November 1932; Gilbert, *WSC*, Vol. III,
     C.V. 2, pp. 486–7, at p. 487).
111. Heinzkill and Schmitt, 'Sir Winston's Potboilers', at p. 9.
112. Scribner Archives, Box 31, Folder 5.

C393b.5   May 7   **Winston Churchill Tells the Story of Tess of the D'Urbervilles by Thomas Hardy / This Sublime Old Tragedy of a Young Country Girl Whose Life Was Badly Twisted by Fate Is Set Forth Complete in This Issue.**
Chicago Sunday Tribune, Pt. 6, p. 4

C393b.6   June 4   **Winston Churchill Tells the Story of Jane Eyre / This Classic Tale of the Quiet, Unassuming Little English Woman and Edward Rochester, the Strange Lord of the Manor, Is Given in Tabloid Form Complete in This Issue**
Chicago Sunday Tribune, Pt. 6, pp. 5–6

C394   Jan. 27   **GORDON: A CHRISTIAN HERO'S SACRIFICE**
Daily Mail, 10
Subsequently collected in *Collected Essays*, Vol. III, pp. 79–81.

C395   Feb. 15   **WHAT ISOLATION MEANS TO THE FREE STATE**
Daily Mail, 10
Subsequently collected in *Collected Essays*, Vol. II, pp. 276–8.

C396a   Feb. 25   **WHO'LL PAY THE JOBLESS?**
Collier's, Vol. 91, No. 8, 10–11, 32
Churchill sent this article and 'Land of Corn and Lobsters' (**C404**) to Eddie Marsh with the request that he "put the grammar etc to rights". He also acknowledged that "they are awful stuff I fear, but it is what they like and what they pay for. They help to pay the American debt—with a vengeance."[113]

C396b.1   March 19   **NOBODY STARVES.**
Sunday Chronicle, 10
Under the heading 'Here Is the First of Three Important Articles in Which Mr. Winston Churchill Tells the Truth about Unemployment Relief, for Which He Is Largely Responsible.' Subsequently collected in *Collected Essays*, Vol. II, pp. 279–81.

C396b.2   March 26   **BRITAIN WAS RIGHT ABOUT THE "DOLE"**
Sunday Chronicle, 10
Subsequently collected in *Collected Essays*, Vol. II, pp. 282–5.

---

113. Letter of 5 December 1932 (Gilbert, *WSC*, Vol. V, *C.V.* 2, p. 501).

C396b.3	April 2	**UNEMPLOYMENT—THE WAY OUT / Six Wise Men Could Liberate Mankind**

Sunday Chronicle, 10
Subsequently collected in *Collected Essays*, Vol. II, pp. 285–7.

C396c	Feb. 17, 1934	**BRITAIN IS RIGHT ABOUT UNEMPLOYMENT**

Pictorial Magazine, Vol. 2, No. 16 (New Series), 18–19

C397	March	**GREAT FIGHTERS IN LOST CAUSES**

Strand Magazine, Vol. LXXXV, No. 507, 246–55
Subsequently collected in *Collected Essays*, Vol. III, pp. 82–9.

C398	March 18	**LIFE—THE GREATEST SECRET OF ALL. / And How to Tackle Its Trials and Problems.**

Answers, Vol. XC, No. 2337, 3–4
Under the superhead ' "WINSTON" BRILLIANTLY SUMS UP AN ARRESTING *ANSWERS*' SERIES.' Subsequently collected in *Collected Essays*, Vol. IV, pp. 257–61.

C399	April 6	**LIFE OF LORD BIRKENHEAD BY HIS SON: FOREWORD**

Daily Telegraph, 12
There was a second instalment entitled 'Lord Birkenhead's Youth' by his son, the Earl of Birkenhead. It ran the following day in the *Daily Telegraph* at p. 12.

C400	April 20	**BRITAIN'S ANSWER TO SOVIET HATE**

Daily Mail, 10
Subsequently collected in *Collected Essays*, Vol. II, pp. 288–91.

C401	April 25	**GLADSTONE'S GRIM BATTLE WITH CHAMBERLAIN**

Daily Mail, 12

—	June	**MY ADVENTURES WITH A PAINT BRUSH** (*Reader's Digest*; *see* **C267b**)

C402		**MARLBOROUGH: HIS LIFE AND TIMES**

The serialization of Volume I (**A97**). On 5 July 1929, Churchill offered to *The Times* the United Kingdom serialization rights to *Marlborough*. In his letter to William Lints Smith, he said, "Perhaps you will let me know whether *The Times* is interested in this new project, and whether you would care to repeat your previous offer [for *The World Crisis*], or what offer you would wish to make." He added, as a negative inducement, that "Lord Camrose, whom I met at dinner last night, has authorised me to say that he would like to purchase these Rights for the *Daily Telegraph*, in the event of *The Times* not wishing to do so."[114] *The Times* declined the offer six days later.[115] Churchill then turned to Lord Camrose and proposed the same £5000 to him for serialization in the *Daily Telegraph*.[116] While there is no "formal" documentary record of the offer, there is a typed transcript of a telegram from Camrose, which reads, "Sorry great pressure this week has prevented my replying. ... Please take this message as confirmation of my offer of figures mentioned in your letter for all serial rights outside America ..."[117] In the end, Camrose decided to publish the serialization in his *Sunday Times* rather than the *Daily Telegraph*.[118] On 2 August, Churchill acknowledged receipt of the offer. He assured the publisher that "I shall do my utmost to produce a story which will command the interest of a wide circle of readers. It would be a great disappointment to me if the results did not justify the price you are paying me."[119] The publisher was proud of the work and advertised it in the *Sunday Times* of the week before as "unquestionably one of the most important biographies of our time. ... It is a thrilling story which readers of the *Sunday Times* will follow with growing interest week by week."[120] Except for the first issue in the serialization, each part was published under the superhead '*Marlborough: His Life and Times—[X]*'.

C402.1   June 11   **THE GREAT MARLBOROUGH / His Life and Times / Calumny Exposed: Honour Vindicated**
Sunday Times, 16, 12
Churchill sent proofs of the first two parts to Maurice Ashley on 3 June. He wrote with resignation that "There is not much use in worrying them about what they select. It is their affair, and of course an author does not like this 'skeletonising'."[121] He nonetheless sought Ashley's verification for accuracy and the insertion of the latest volume revisions.

---

114. Gilbert, *WSC*, Vol. V, *C.V.* 2, pp. 12–13, at p. 13.
115. *The Times*: Sir Winston Churchill, Managerial File, 1929–66.
116. By letter of 28 July (Gilbert, *WSC*, Vol. V, *C.V.* 2, pp. 26–7).
117. CHAR 8/225/170.
118. The Berry brothers, William Ewert, the first Lord Camrose (he was created a baron in 1929), and Gomer, had purchased the *Sunday Times* in June 1915 for £75,000. It was only on 9 January 1928 that they added the *Daily Telegraph* to their Allied Newspapers group.
119. Gilbert, *WSC*, Vol. V, *C.V.* 2, p. 32.
120. *Sunday Times*, 4 June 1933, p. 13.
121. Gilbert, *WSC*, Vol. V, *C.V.* 2, pp. 610–11.

C402.2   June 18   **Courtier and Courtesan / Desperate Fighting in Flanders / How D'Artagnan Met His Death**
Sunday Times, 16, 13

C402.3   June 25   **Marlborough's Romance / His Love for Sarah Jennings / Counter-Attack on Macaulay**
Sunday Times, 16, 13

C402.4   July 2   **Protestant or Catholic / A Great Historic Struggle / Churchills behind the Scenes**
Sunday Times, 16, 12

C402.5   July 9   **Rebellion That Failed / Summer Campaign in Dorset / Desperate Hazard at Sedgemoor**
Sunday Times, 16, 12

C402.6   July 16   **Why James Lost His Throne / People's Dread of Romanism / On the Eve of Rebellion**
Sunday Times, 16, 13

C402.7   July 23   **English Throne the Stake / The Invasion by Request / Rival Armies Take the Field**
Sunday Times, 12, 9

C402.8   July 30   **The Bloodless Revolution / Ignominious Exit of James II / London's Night of Terror**
Sunday Times, 12, 9

C402.9   Aug. 6   **Marlborough's Irish Campaign / Cork and Kinsale Captured / A Great Achievement**
Sunday Times, 10, 7

C402.10   Aug. 13   **Deceit as a Policy / Marlborough and the Exiled Stuarts / Promise without Performance**
Sunday Times, 10, 5

C402.11   Aug. 20   **The Flowerpot Conspiracy / Marlborough in the Tower / A Wicked Plot Exposed**
Sunday Times, 12, 9

C402.12   Aug. 27   **The Hour of Triumph / Marlborough's Call to Power / He Forms the Great Alliance**
Sunday Times, 12, 9

C403   Aug. 4   **AUGUST 4, 1914: A NATION TRANSFORMED**
Daily Mail, 8
Subsequently collected in *Collected Essays*, Vol. I, pp. 309–11.

C404	Aug. 5	**LAND OF CORN AND LOBSTERS**

Collier's, Vol. 92, No. 6, 16–17, 45

Subsequently collected in *Collected Essays*, Vol. IV, pp. 262–7.

C405	Aug. 7	**COMMON INTERESTS OF BRITAIN AND FRANCE / Mr. Churchill on Present Conditions**

The Times, 12

Prints part of an article to be published in the *Bulletin* of the Agence économique et financière of 8 August 1933.

C406	Aug. 12	**"ENGLAND, MY ENGLAND!"**

Answers, 3–4

C407	Sept. 7	**WINSTON CHURCHILL ON LLOYD GEORGE'S MEMOIRS PUBLISHED TO-DAY**

Daily Mail, 8

Subsequently collected in *Collected Essays*, Vol. III, pp. 90–2, under the title 'Lloyd George's War Memoirs: Vol. I'.

C408	Oct. 14	**INDIA: THE COMING CLASH**

Daily Mail, 10

Subsequently collected in *Collected Essays*, Vol. II, pp. 292–5.

C409	Oct. 19	**A BOOK OF TREMENDOUS FACTS / Lloyd George's War Memoirs, Volume 2: Out To-day**

Daily Mail, 10

Subsequently collected in *Collected Essays*, Vol. III, pp. 92–6, under the title 'Lloyd George's War Memoirs: Vol. II'.

C410	November	**SHAKESPEARE'S PLAYS AS SHORT STORIES / Nº 2 / Julius Caesar**

Strand Magazine, Vol. LXXXVI, No. 515, 471–80

Subsequently collected in *Six Stories from Shakespeare*, pp. 39–63 (**B55**), and *Collected Essays*, Vol. III, pp. 102–11.

C411	Nov. 4	**THE BOND BETWEEN US**

Collier's, Vol. 92, No. 19, 12–13

Churchill submitted the text of the article to William Chenery[122] on 15 September with the admonition that "there is no doubt that this Economic article is like a soufflé. It must be served while hot."[123] Subsequently collected in *Collected Essays*, Vol. II, pp. 296–302.

---

122. William Ludlow Chenery was the Editor of *Collier's Weekly* (later simply *Collier's*) from 1925 to 1943. He then served as Publisher of *Collier's* from 1943 until his death in 1949.

123. He noted earlier in the letter that he had "written the greater part of [the article] three times over, but every time the situation changed, and most that I had written was no longer apt" (Gilbert, *WSC*, Vol. V, *C.V.* 2, pp. 652–3).

C418   Feb. 24   **MUST CIVILISATION CRASH?**
                           Answers, Vol. XCII, No. 15 (2386), 3–4
                           Under the superhead 'THE ROAD TO WORLD SUICIDE'.

C419   March 3   **HOW BIG IS ROOSEVELT?**
                           Pictorial Weekly, 1

C420   March 6   **"BE   PREPARED"—AND   THE   MAN   WHO
                           THOUGHT OF IT.**
                           Daily Mail, 10

—   March 10   **CAN WE DEFEND OURSELVES?** (*Pictorial Weekly*; *see*
                           C388b)

C421   March 15   **CAVALCADE 1909–1934 / Whither Are We Being
                           Hurled at This Tremendous Pace?**
                           Daily Sketch, 7–8
                           Subsequently collected in *Collected Essays*, Vol. IV,
                           pp. 277–80.

C422   March 17   **THE TRUTH ABOUT WAR DEBTS.**
                           Answers, Vol. XCII, No. 18 (2389), 3–4
                           Under the superhead 'WE COULD PAY, BUT—'.
                           Subsequently collected in *Collected Essays*, Vol. II, pp. 313–17.

C423   March 24   **SINGAPORE—KEY TO THE PACIFIC**
                           Pictorial Weekly, Vol. 2, No. 21 (New Series), 16–17
                           Subsequently collected in *Collected Essays*, Vol. I, pp. 318–21.

C424   March 31   **IS THE PRIVATE MEMBER A PUBLIC NUISANCE?
                           / Penny-in-the-Slot Politics**
                           Answers, Vol. XCII, No. 20 (2391), 3–4
                           Subsequently collected in *Collected Essays*, Vol. II, pp. 318–21,
                           under the title 'Penny-in-the-Slot Politics'.

C425   April 13   **THE GREATEST HALF-HOUR IN OUR HISTORY**
                           Daily Mail, 12
                           Subsequently collected in *Collected Essays*, Vol. IV, pp. 281–3.

C426   April 14   **FILL UP THE EMPIRE!**
                           Pictorial Magazine, Vol. 2, No. 24 (New Series), 1–2
                           Subsequently collected in *Collected Essays*, Vol. IV, pp. 284–6.

C427   April 15   **WHAT NEVILLE OUGHT TO DO / Restore the
                           Salary Cuts Then Cut Income Tax**
                           Sunday Pictorial, No. 996, 10
                           Subsequently collected in *Collected Essays*, Vol. II, pp. 322–4.

C428   April 21   **HAVE YOU A HOBBY?**
Answers, Vol. XCII, No. 23 (2394), 3–4
Under the superhead 'HOW TO BE HAPPY THOUGH
WORRIED!' Subsequently collected in *Collected Essays*,
Vol. IV, pp. 287–90.

C429   April 28   **A SILENT TOAST TO WM. WILLETT**
Pictorial Weekly, Vol. 2, No. 26 (New Series), 2–3
Subsequently collected in *Collected Essays*, Vol. III,
pp. 116–19.

C430   April 28   **LET'S BOOST BRITAIN!**
Answers, Vol. XCII, No. 24 (2395), 3–4
Under the superhead 'A SPECIAL ST. GEORGE'S DAY
MESSAGE TO "ANSWERS."' Subsequently collected in
Collected Essays, Vol. IV, pp. 291–3.

C431   May 5   **WHAT'S WRONG WITH PARLIAMENT?**
Answers, Vol. XCII, No. 25 (2396), 3–4
Under the superhead 'PAVING THE WAY FOR A NEW
BRITAIN.'

C432   May 12   **I WANT NATIONAL SWEEPSTAKES**
Pictorial Weekly, Vol. 3, No. 28 (New Series), 11

C433   May 13   **WHERE ARE WE HEADING?**
Sunday Pictorial, No. 1000, 10
The article received high praise from the well-known suffra-
gette Christabel Pankhurst, who wrote to Churchill on the
following day that the article "is a masterly review of twenty
years. I appreciate your generous allusion to women's emanci-
pation and achievement."[124]

C434   May 16   **THIS YEAR'S ROYAL ACADEMY EXHIBITION IS
EXHILARATING**
Daily Mail, 10
Subsequently collected in *Collected Essays*, Vol. IV, pp. 294–7.

C435   May 19   **WILL THE KINGS COME BACK?**
Answers, Vol. XCIII, No. 1 (2398), 14–15
Under the superhead 'EUROPE'S NEW REPUBLICS IN
THE MELTING POT—AND THE ROYAL EXILES ARE
READY!'

---

124. Gilbert, *WSC*, Vol. V, *C.V.* 2, pp. 791–2, at p. 791.

C436	May 24	**GREAT DEEDS THAT GAVE US THE EMPIRE** *Daily Mail*, 12 Subsequently collected in *Collected Essays*, Vol. IV, pp. 298–300.
C437	May 26	**WHEN I "DRIED UP"** *Pictorial Weekly*, Vol. 3, No. 30 (New Series), 16–17
C438	June	**ARE PARLIAMENTS OBSOLETE?** *Pearson's Magazine*, Vol. LXXVII, No. 462, 554–9
C439	June 2	**DRAMATIC DAYS IN "THE HOUSE"** *Pictorial Weekly*, Vol. 3, No. 31 (New Series), 22–3
C440	June 2	**THE BLACKCOAT TRAGEDY** *Answers*, Vol. XCIII, No. 3 (2400), 13 Under the superhead 'BREAKING ENGLAND'S BACKBONE'.
C441		**THE LIFE OF MARLBOROUGH / VOLUME II** The serialization of the second volume of *Marlborough*.
C441.1	June 24	**I / Anne's Great Reign / England's Leadership of Europe / Marlborough in Power** *Sunday Times*, 16, 13
C441.2	July 1	**II / First Flanders Campaign / The Dutch Way in War / Decisive Battles Barred** *Sunday Times*, 16, 13
C441.3	July 8	**III / A Great Adventure / Planning Danube Campaign / Marlborough and His Wife** *Sunday Times*, 16, 13
C441.4	July 15	**IV / March to the Danube / The Scarlet Caterpillar / Puzzling the French** *Sunday Times*, 14, 7
C441.5	July 22	**V / Marlborough and Eugene / Their First Meeting / A "Glorious Brotherhood"** *Sunday Times*, 16, 7
C441.6	July 29	**VI / Shambles on the Danube / Storming the Schellenberg / Dearly Bought Victory** *Sunday Times*, 14, 7

C441.7	Aug. 5	**VII / The Story of Blenheim / Marlborough's Great Day / The Fight for Supremacy** *Sunday Times*, 10, 7

C441.8	Aug. 12	**VIII / How Blenheim Was Won / The French Crushed / Enemy's Heroic Last Stand** *Sunday Times*, 10, 5

C441.9	Aug. 19	**IX / The Conquering Hero / Marlborough in Berlin / London's Great Welcome** *Sunday Times*, 12, 4

C441.10	Aug. 26	**X / The Unfought Waterloo / Allies Foil Marlborough / Lost Opportunity** *Sunday Times*, 12, 10

C441.11	Sept. 2	**XI / Clearing the Decks / Dutch and Marlborough / The Duke's Triumph** *Sunday Times*, 14, 11

C442	June 30	**I *ALWAYS* TOOK CHANCES!** *Answers*, Vol. XCIII, No. 7 (2404), 3–4 Under the superhead 'WHEN LIFE HUNG IN THE BALANCE'. Subsequently collected in *Collected Essays*, Vol. IV, pp. 301–4.

C443	July 1	**MY FIGHT FOR LANCASHIRE** *Sunday Dispatch*, 12

C444	July 2	**A FRIEND'S TRIBUTE** *The Times*, 10 A tribute to Churchill's first cousin and great friend, Charles, ninth Duke of Marlborough, who died on June 20. Subsequently published separately as *Charles, IXth Duke of Marlborough K.G.* (**A98**) and collected in Gilbert, *WSC*, Vol. V, *C.V.* 2, pp. 819–22, and *Collected Essays*, Vol. III, pp. 120–3.

C445	July 9	**HOW I WOULD PROCURE PEACE** *Daily Mail*, 10 Subsequently collected in *Collected Essays*, Vol. I, pp. 322–5.

C446	July 21	**FAIR PLAY FOR LANCASHIRE!** *Answers*, Vol. XCIII, No. 10 (2407), 3–4 Under the superhead 'SHALL WE GIVE UP INDIA?'

C447	July 22	**OUR LAST CHANCE / Men of Lancashire Must Face the Truth** *Sunday Dispatch*, 12

C448a   August   **LAST NIGHT OF THE OLD WORLD**
Redbook, Vol. 63, No. 4, 20–3, 106

C448b   Aug. 5   **THE LAST NIGHT OF THE OLD WORLD**
Sunday Pictorial, 20
Subsequently collected in *Collected Essays*, Vol. I, pp. 330–3.

C449   Aug. 2   **HINDENBURG IN WAR AND PEACE**
Daily Mail, 8

C450   Aug. 4   **AUGUST 4, 1914**
Daily Mail, 8
Under the superhead '*Twenty Years Ago Today*—'.
Subsequently collected in *Collected Essays*, Vol. I, pp. 326–9.

C451   Aug. 4   **PREMIERS ON THE *SICK LIST***
Answers, Vol. XCIII, No. 12 (2409), 5
Under the superhead 'ARE POLITICS A "DANGEROUS
TRADE"?' Subsequently collected in *Collected Essays*, Vol. III,
pp. 124–6.

C452   [No entry.]

C453   Aug. 25   **OPEN LETTER TO A *COMMUNIST***
Answers, Vol. XCIII, No. 15 (2412), 3
Under the superhead 'FREEDOM IS EVERY BRITON'S
BIRTHRIGHT'. Subsequently collected in Gilbert, *WSC*,
Vol. V, *C.V.* 2, pp. 858–61.

C454   Aug. 25   **HOW WE CARRY LIQUOR**
Collier's, Vol. 94, No. 8, 10–11, 38
On 1 May, Churchill wrote to William Chenery that the
article was being sent to him by the *Bremen*, which was sailing
the next day.[125] Subsequently collected in *Collected Essays*, Vol.
IV, pp. 305–12.

C455   Sept. 7   **VISCOUNT SNOWDEN'S LIFE AND CHARACTER**
Daily Mail, 10

C456   Sept. 21   **LLOYD GEORGE'S TWO TERRIFIC YEARS**
Daily Mail, 12
Subsequently collected in *Collected Essays*, Vol. III, pp. 96–8,
under the title 'Lloyd George's War Memoirs: Volume III'.

---

125. Gilbert, *WSC*, Vol. V, *C.V.* 2, p. 779.

C457	Oct. 2	**SHIPS COULD HAVE FORCED THE DARDANELLES**

Daily Mail, 12

Subsequently collected in *Collected Essays*, Vol. I, pp. 334–6.

C458	Oct. 26	**LLOYD GEORGE'S BITTER FOURTH VOLUME**

Daily Mail, 12

Subsequently collected in *Collected Essays*, Vol. III, pp. 98–101, under the title 'Lloyd George's War Memoirs: Volume IV'.

C459		[No entry.]

C460a	Dec. 29	**WHILE THE WORLD WATCHES**

Collier's, Vol. 94, No. 26, 24–5, 49

C460b.1	Feb. 3, 1935	**THIS MAN'S GAMBLE MAY CHANGE YOUR WHOLE LIFE**

Sunday Chronicle, 10

C460b.2	Feb. 10, 1935	**EVERY WORKING MAN WILL BE AFFECTED IF ROOSEVELT FAILS**

Sunday Chronicle, 10

1935

C461		**MY LIFE**

Initial serialization in the *News of the World*. Only about 13,000 words of the material published here had previously been included in the volume publication of *My Early Life*. Churchill wrote to Clementine of the proposal from Lord Riddell that he "write 30–35,000 words of my Life to date for the News of the World: price £3,000–3,500. This will be v[er]y easy to do, and it makes next year as good as this."[126] That proposal, as initially made by Lord Riddell on 20 August 1934, was in the following terms: "Would you care to write a new and popular Story of your Life for the News of the World—say—30,000 words,

---

126. Letter of 25 August 1934 (*Speaking for Themselves*, pp. 360–1, at p. 361). Also collected in Gilbert, *WSC*, Vol. V, *C.V.* 2, p. 856. George Allardice Riddell, a solicitor to the Welsh *Western Mail*, left his position there to join Lascelles Carr, who had acquired the *News of the World* in 1891. Under Riddell's leadership, the circulation of the paper rose from 40,000 in 1892 to 2,500,000 in 1917. Riddell was knighted in 1909, became Baron Riddell in 1918, and was elevated to the peerage in 1920. Having made the arrangements with Churchill for the publication of the autobiographical series, he died on 5 December 1934, too soon to see the first of the articles in print.

price £2,500 . . . ; copy to be written by you personally, not too much politics. . . . To avoid controversy it might be well to finish at 1929. . . . The matter would have to be popular and suitable for the millions who read the NOW."[127] By 24 October, Churchill had written eight of the originally proposed ten articles and he advised his agent that "Newnes are so pleased with the series that they have commissioned twelve, instead of ten, which enables me to finish more satisfactorily."[128] The price ultimately settled on for the full series of twelve articles was £4200, which Churchill received on 2 January 1935. Much of the paraphrased material from *My Early Life*, which constituted just over one-third of the published text, albeit a greater percentage of Chapters II through VII, was prepared by Marshall Diston.[129]

C461a.1   Jan. 13   **1. Looking Back on Sixty Years**
News of the World, 5
Subsequently collected in *Collected Essays*, Vol. III, pp. 127–34.

C461a.2   Jan. 20   **2. Frontier Days in India**
News of the World, 5
Subsequently collected in *Collected Essays*, Vol. III, pp. 134–41.

C461a.3   Jan. 27   **3. Charge of the 21st Lancers**
News of the World, 5
Subsequently collected in *Collected Essays*, Vol. III, pp. 141–9.

C461a.4   Feb. 3   **4. Taken Prisoner by the Boers**
News of the World, 5
Subsequently collected in *Collected Essays*, Vol. III, pp. 149–56.

C461a.5   Feb. 10   **5. My Escape from Pretoria**
News of the World, 5
Subsequently collected in *Collected Essays*, Vol. III, pp. 156–63.

---

127. Gilbert, *WSC*, Vol. V, *C.V.* 2, pp. 851–2.
128. Letter of 24 October 1934 to C. R. Everitt (*ibid.*, pp. 888–90, at p. 888).
129. Adam Marshall Diston had been with the Amalgamated Press after the First World War and later served as assistant editor and then acting editor of *Answers*. He had also been an officer of the Trade and Periodical Branch of the National Union of Journalists. Politically a socialist, he once ran unsuccessfully for Parliament (Gilbert, *WSC*, Vol. V, *C.V.* 2, p. 725*n*). As will be clear from some of the entries in Section C, he assisted Churchill with the preparation of numerous articles in the 1930s.

C461a.6   Feb. 17   **6. My Entry into Politics**
News of the World, 5
Subsequently collected in *Collected Essays*, Vol. III, pp. 163–70.

C461a.7   Feb. 24   **7. Changing the Political Camp**
News of the World, 5
Subsequently collected in *Collected Essays*, Vol. III, pp. 170–6.

C461a.8   March 3   **8. Sidney Street and 'Peter the Painter'**
News of the World, 5
Subsequently collected in *Collected Essays*, Vol. III, pp. 176–83.

C461a.9   March 10   **9. How the Grand Fleet Went to War**
News of the World, 5
Subsequently collected in *Collected Essays*, Vol. III, pp. 183–90.

C461a.10   March 17   **10. The Dardanelles Held the Key to Peace**
News of the World, 5
Subsequently collected in *Collected Essays*, Vol. III, pp. 191–8.

C461a.11   March 24   **11. Back to the Wild Tumult of Peace**
News of the World, 5
Subsequently collected in *Collected Essays*, Vol. III, pp. 199–206.

C461a.12   March 31   **12. Rise and Fall of Parties and Politicians**
News of the World, 5
Subsequently collected in *Collected Essays*, Vol. III, pp. 206–12.

C461b   **"MY LIFE," AN AUTOBIOGRAPHY**
Serialization in the *Chicago Tribune*. The version differs in minor respects from that published in the *News of the World* and from the text of the manuscript.[130] Churchill was paid $6000 for all American and Canadian serial and syndication rights.[131] He had originally asked his agent to place the articles with *Collier's*, hoping for a total of "$10,000 for the series, or about $850 a piece". Optimistically, he advised Everitt, "Of course, if you can get more do so. However, if inevitable I

---

130. The original manuscript of *My Life* can be found in the University of Oregon Library.
131. See Heinzkill, 'Addenda to Woods', p. 359, and Heinzkill and Schmitt, 'Sir Winston's Potboilers', pp. 3–15.

would take as low as $500 each, or $6,000 for the series."[132] The full copy of the autobiographical serialization was forwarded to the agent in the United States on 3 December.

C461b.1   Feb. 4   **[PART I]**
Chicago Daily Tribune, 3

C461b.2   Feb. 5   **[PART II]**
Chicago Daily Tribune, 4

C461b.3   Feb. 6   **[PART III]**
Chicago Daily Tribune, 4

C461b.4   Feb. 7   **[PART IV]**
Chicago Daily Tribune, 6

C461b.5   Feb. 8   **[PART V]**
Chicago Daily Tribune, 8

C461b.6   Feb. 9   **[PART VI]**
Chicago Daily Tribune, 8

C461b.7   Feb. 11   **[PART VII]**
Chicago Daily Tribune, 6

C461b.8   Feb. 12   **[PART VIII]**
Chicago Daily Tribune, 11

C461b.9   Feb. 13   **[PART IX]**
Chicago Daily Tribune, 12

C461b.10   Feb. 14   **[PART X]**
Chicago Daily Tribune, 13

C461b.11   Feb. 15   **[PART XI]**
Chicago Daily Tribune, 18

C461b.12   Feb. 16   **[PART XII]**
Chicago Daily Tribune, 6

C461b.13   Feb. 18   **[PART XIII]**
Chicago Daily Tribune, 4

---

132. Letter of 24 October 1934 to C. R. Everitt (Gilbert, *WSC*, Vol. V, *C.V.* 2, pp. 888–90, at p. 889).

C461b.14 Feb. 19 **[PART XIV]**
Chicago Daily Tribune, 13

C461b.15 Feb. 20 **[PART XV]**
Chicago Daily Tribune, 18

C461b.16 Feb. 21 **[PART XVI]**
Chicago Daily Tribune, 8

C461b.17 Feb. 22 **[PART XVII]**
Chicago Daily Tribune, 12

C461b.18 Feb. 23 **[PART XVIII]**
Chicago Daily Tribune, 11

C461b.19 Feb. 25 **[PART XIX]**
Chicago Daily Tribune, 6

C461b.20 Feb. 26 **[PART XX]**
Chicago Daily Tribune, 9

C461b.21 Feb. 27 **[PART XXI]**
Chicago Daily Tribune, 18

C461b.22 Feb. 28 **[PART XXII]**
Chicago Daily Tribune, 11

C461b.23 March 1 **[PART XXIII]**
Chicago Daily Tribune, 10

C461b.24 March 2 **[PART XXIV]**
Chicago Daily Tribune, 8

C461b.25 March 4 **[PART XXV]**
Chicago Daily Tribune, 8

C461b.26 March 5 **[PART XXVI]**
Chicago Daily Tribune, 9

C461b.27 March 6 **[PART XXVII]**
Chicago Daily Tribune, 8

C461b.28 March 7 **[PART XXVIII]**
Chicago Daily Tribune, 11

C461b.29 March 8 **[PART XXIX]**
Chicago Daily Tribune, 13

C469		**THE KING'S 25 YEARS**

A series of articles published in the *Evening Standard* to coincide with King George V's Silver Jubilee. United Kingdom serial rights were also granted to the *Birmingham Evening Despatch, Manchester Evening News, Yorkshire Evening Post, Evening Advertiser* (Swindon), *Nottingham Evening News, Eastern Daily Press, Eastern Evening News* and *Glasgow Evening Times*. Churchill asked Percy Cudlipp: "I should be glad to know ... what you think the circulations are of these papers. I should suppose about one million people read these articles as they came out. I hope you were thus able to recoup yourselves fully."[133] On Friday, 5 April, he had written to Clementine that he was "very tired after this hard week, but have to finish up my articles for the *Evening Standard* on King George V's reign".[134]

C469.1   May 2   **No. 1—The Accession**
Evening Standard, 12
Subsequently collected in *Collected Essays*, Vol. III, pp. 213–16.

C469.2   May 3   **The King Faces His First Crisis / No. 2. "Peers v. People" Clash**
Evening Standard, 12–13
Subsequently collected in *Collected Essays*, Vol. III, pp. 216–20, under the title 'The King Faces His First Crisis'.

C469.3   May 4   **No. 3—The Coronation and the Agadir Crisis / War Clouds Gather**
Evening Standard, 21, 28
Subsequently collected in *Collected Essays*, Vol. III, pp. 221–5, under the title 'The Coronation and the Agadir Crisis'.

C469.4   May 6   **No. 4. / Royal Courage: / Durbar Splendour: / Frenzied Women**
Evening Standard, 12–13, 20
Subsequently collected in *Collected Essays*, Vol. III, pp. 225–30, under the title 'Royal Courage: Durbar Splendour: Frenzied Women'.

C469.5   May 7   **No. 5 / War—In the King's Name**
Evening Standard, 23, 27
Subsequently collected in *Collected Essays*, Vol. III, pp. 230–3.

---

133. Letter of 12 May 1935 (Gilbert, *WSC*, Vol. V, *C.V.* 2, p. 1170).
134. Chartwell Bulletin, No. 10 (*Speaking for Themselves*, pp. 396–7, at p. 397).

C469.6	May 8	**The King with His Troops**

Evening Standard, 23, 27
Under the superhead 'THE RT. HON. WINSTON S. CHURCHILL C.H. M.P. CONTINUES HIS STORY OF THE KING'S 25 YEARS'. Subsequently collected in *Collected Essays*, Vol. III, pp. 233–6.

C469.7	May 9	**Aftermath of War / Revenge of the Pygmies: The King's Illness / Economic Blizzard / Baldwin–Macdonald Regime**

Evening Standard, 23, 26
Under the superhead 'THE RIGHT HON. WINSTON S. CHURCHILL C.H. M.P. BRINGS HIS STORY OF THE KING'S 25 YEARS TO A CLOSE'. Subsequently collected in *Collected Essays*, Vol. III, pp. 236–40.

C470	May 4	**NATIONS ON THE LOOSE**

Collier's, Vol. 95, No. 18, 22, 30
Subsequently collected in *Collected Essays*, Vol. I, pp. 340–6.

C471	May 15	**THE MORAL OF THE JUBILEE**

Daily Mail, 12
Subsequently collected in *Collected Essays*, Vol. IV, pp. 313–15.

C472	May 26	**THIS IS THE ANSWER!**

Sunday Chronicle, 12–13

C473a	May 26	**LAWRENCE OF ARABIA'S NAME WILL LIVE! / "One of the Greatest Beings of Our Time" / "Bells of the Armistice Forestalled His Triumph" / Brilliant Pen-Picture by Mr. Winston Churchill / That Embarrassing Moment in the Royal Presence**

News of the World, 1, 12

C473b	December 1936	**LAWRENCE OF ARABIA**

English Race, No. 71, 13

C474	May 29	**ELECTION AHEAD—AND THE SAME OLD VOTING SYSTEM**

Daily Mail, 10

C475	June 6	**THE CONSTITUTIONS OF GREAT BRITAIN AND THE UNITED STATES**

Daily Mail, 12

C476a	June 29	**TO END WAR** *Collier's*, Vol. 95, No. 26, 12, 48–9 Subsequently collected in *Collected Essays*, Vol. I, pp. 347–53.
C476b	July 28	**TO END ALL THIS** *Sunday Chronicle*, 10–11
C477	July 29	**LAWRENCE'S GREAT BOOK PUBLISHED TODAY** **/ Grim War Realism of "Seven Pillars of Wisdom" /** **Mr. Winston Churchill's Review** *Daily Mail*, 8 Subsequently collected in *Collected Essays*, Vol. III, pp. 241–2.
C478	Aug. 4	**21 YEARS AGO TODAY—THE INSIDE STORY OF** **THE WAR / Mr. Churchill Tells of the Fateful Hours** **before Midnight, August 4, 1914** *Sunday Chronicle*, 6–7
C479	Oct. 3	**HAIG .. THE MAN THEY TRUSTED** *Daily Mail*, 5 Review of Volume I of the Duff Cooper biography. Volume II was reviewed by a different critic. Subsequently collected in *Collected Essays*, Vol. III, pp. 243–5.
C480a	Oct. 26	**EVERYBODY'S LANGUAGE** *Collier's*, Vol. 96, No. 17, 24, 37–8 Subsequently collected in *Collected Essays*, Vol. III, pp. 246–52.
C480b	Feb. 9, 1936	**HE HAS MADE THE WHOLE WORLD RICHER** *Sunday Chronicle*, 12–13
C480c	May 1936	**CHAPLIN—The Man Who Has Made the World Rich** **with Laughter** *Screen Pictorial*, 10–11, 56
C481	November	**THE TRUTH ABOUT HITLER** *Strand Magazine*, Vol. XC, No. 539, 10–21 This article was solicited by Reeves Shaw on behalf of the *Strand*, and was originally wanted for publication in the September number. Shaw offered Churchill £150 for first British Empire serial rights to an article 4000 words long in which, he said, "I should like you to be as outspoken as you possibly can in your appraisement of Hitler's personality and ambitions, and absolutely frank in your judgment of his methods."[135] The fee was settled at £250 and the article

---

135. Letter of 15 May 1935 (Gilbert, *WSC*, Vol. V, *C.V.* 2, p. 1175).

published two months later than originally planned. It was ready by the end of July, at which time Churchill wrote to his friend and adviser, Professor F. A. Lindemann, to see whether he could suggest any "other great [German] names" to the last paragraph.[136] That last paragraph, revised in consequence, was submitted to the *Strand* on 1 August.[137]

C482 Nov. 8 **MR. CHURCHILL ON HIS FIGHT / "More Elections Than Any Living Man" / Staunch Supporters—and a Very Conservative Dog!**
Daily Mail, 9

C483 Nov. 12 **BRITAIN'S SECURITY IS THE VITAL ISSUE**
Daily Mail, 10
Subsequently collected in *Collected Essays*, Vol. I, pp. 354–6.

C484a Dec. 28 **YOU GET IT IN BLACK AND WHITE**
Collier's, Vol. 96, No. 26, 32, 36–7
Subsequently collected in *Collected Essays*, Vol. IV, pp. 316–23.

C484b Jan. 12, 1936 **RADIO, NEWS-REEL OR THE PRESS**
Sunday Chronicle, 10, 15

1936

— January **CONSISTENCY IN LEADERSHIP** (*Rotarian*; *see* **C311c**)

C485 January **THE TRUTH ABOUT MYSELF**
Strand Magazine, Vol. XC, No. 541, 276–86

C486 **GREAT MEN OF OUR TIME**
A series of articles on British military and political figures, supplemented by articles on King George V and Clemenceau. Much of the work was done by Marshall Diston, whose "task was to piece together from Churchill's existing writings, from previously published books and articles by Churchill himself, and by means of short linking paragraphs or extra paragraphs, where necessary, coherent, unified pieces for re-publication" in this series.[138] Diston himself explained his method in the

---

136. Letter of 27 July from Violet Pearman to Professor Lindemann (*ibid.*, p. 1226).

137. The text, which was a part of the letter from Violet Pearman to Reeves Shaw, is incorporated as a part of her letter (*ibid.*, p. 1227).

138. As explained by Martin Gilbert (*ibid.*, pp. 1238–9*n*). According to Violet Pearman's monthly summary of literary expenses, Diston was paid £15 per article. See the extracts from the September, October and November accounts (*ibid.*, p. 1253*n*).

letter covering the dispatch of the articles on Clemenceau, Balfour, French and Curzon: "In doing them I did not attempt to put all the new matter in the introduction and follow on with the rest. I found that I could get much more satisfactory results, and that the unity of the articles was preserved much better, if I spread the new matter out and incorporated passages of the old in the introduction."[139] Churchill proposed to write on Kitchener and Haig himself, as well as Birkenhead, "as of course they were great friends for many years".[140] Diston was, however, paid for ten of the twelve articles and I am uncertain as to the identity of the two on which Churchill did the principal writing. Churchill did write the article on the King, which was not one of the numbered articles but was published on the Sunday between the second and third articles, on Fisher and French. Sir Elmsley Carr, Chairman of the paper, read the articles prior to publication and wrote enthusiastically to Churchill: "I have read with great interest your articles on Great Men of Our Times [*sic*], and I at once hasten to say that they are the most interesting series you have yet written for us."[141]

C486.1   Jan. 12   **1. Kitchener—The Empire's Man of Destiny**
News of the World, 5
Subsequently collected in *Collected Essays*, Vol. III, pp. 253–60.

C486.2   Jan. 19   **2. Fisher: The Warrior Who Went on Strike!**
News of the World, 5

C486.3   Jan. 26   **King George V., The Beloved of His People**
News of the World, 5
This article is unnumbered, although published under the same 'Great Men of Our Time' series title.

C486.4   Feb. 2   **3. French: The Man Who Came Back**
News of the World, 5
This is thus the fourth article in the series, although the *News of the World* numbering does not reflect that. Based on 'Lord Ypres', first published in *Nash's—Pall Mall* (**C332**).

---

139. Letter of 17 September 1935 to Churchill (*ibid.*, pp. 1260–1, at p. 1260). Detailed explanations of the structuring of each of the four articles are also provided in that letter. Churchill sent along material and instructions for the articles on Morley, Chamberlain, Asquith and Fisher on 24 September. On 12 October, Violet Pearman, on Churchill's behalf, added Lloyd George to the list.
140. Letter of 12 October from Violet Pearman to Marshall Diston (*ibid.*, p. 1292).
141. Letter of 19 November 1935, in which he also congratulated Churchill on his victory at Epping in the general election of 13 November (*ibid.*, pp. 1329–30).

C486.5   Feb. 9   **4. Haig: The Prop of the British Army**
News of the World, 5
Substantially the text as previously published in *Nash's Magazine* (**C316a**) and *Cosmopolitan* (**C316b**) but revised by Marshall Diston.

C486.6   Feb. 16   **5. Asquith: The Unflinching Patriot**
News of the World, 5

C486.7   Feb. 23   **6. Lloyd George: The War Leader**
News of the World, 5
In this instance Violet Pearman wrote to Diston that this article was "the one he [Churchill] likes the least, as the fitting in of the reviews does not hang at all well with your own material. Would you therefore please put in much more of your own composition, as it is good."[142] Subsequently collected in *Collected Essays*, Vol. III, pp. 261–8.

C486.8   March 1   **7. Birkenhead: The Pilot Who Weathered the Storm**
News of the World, 5

C486.9   March 8   **8. Curzon: Majestic, But He Never Led**
News of the World, 5
Based on 'George Curzon', first published in *Nash's Magazine* (**C317**).

C486.10   March 15 **9. Clemenceau: The Tiger**
News of the World, 5

C486.11   March 22 **10. Balfour: The Statesman Who Saw Life from Afar**
News of the World, 5

C486.12   March 29 **11. Chamberlain: The Prophet of Protection**
News of the World, 5
Based on 'Chamberlain', first published in *Nash's—Pall Mall* (**C333**).

C486.13   April 5   **12. John Morley: A Lamp of Wisdom**
News of the World, 5
Based on 'Lord Morley', first published in *Nash's—Pall Mall* (**C328**).

C487   Feb. 6   **I WAS ASTONISHED BY MOROCCO**
Daily Mail, 12
Subsequently collected in *Collected Essays*, Vol. IV, pp. 324–6.

---

142. Letter of 26 October (*ibid.*, p. 1303).

—   Feb. 9   **HE MADE THE WHOLE WORLD LAUGH** (*Sunday Chronicle*; *see* **C480b**)

C488   Feb. 12   **WHY NOT A CHANNEL TUNNEL?**
Daily Mail, 10
Subsequently collected in Peter Haining, *Eurotunnel* (**B197**), and *Collected Essays*, Vol. I, pp. 357–9.

C489   March 13   **BRITAIN, GERMANY AND LOCARNO**
Evening Standard, 7
Subsequently collected in *Step by Step* (**A111**), pp. 13–16.

C490   April 3   **STOP IT NOW!**
Evening Standard, 7
Subsequently collected in *Step by Step* (**A111**), pp. 17–20.

C491   April 8   **NAPOLEON LIVES AGAIN IN "ST. HELENA" / The Play of Plays**
Daily Mail, 12
Subsequently collected in *Collected Essays*, Vol. III, pp. 269–71.

C492   April 17   **WHERE DO WE STAND?**
Evening Standard, 7
Subsequently collected in *Step by Step* (**A111**), pp. 21–4.

—   May   **CHAPLIN—The Man Who Has Made the World Rich with Laughter** (*Screen Pictorial*; *see* **C480c**)

C493   May   **QUEEN OF THE SEAS**
Strand Magazine, Vol. XCI, No. 545, 42–53
Subsequently collected in *Collected Essays*, Vol. IV, pp. 327–34.

C494   May 1   **HOW GERMANY IS ARMING**
Evening Standard, 7
Subsequently collected in *Step by Step* (**A111**), pp. 25–8.

C495   May 15   **OUR NAVY *MUST* BE STRONGER**
Evening Standard, 7
Subsequently collected in *Step by Step* (**A111**), pp. 29–32.

C496   May 29   **ORGANISE OUR SUPPLIES**
Evening Standard, 7
Subsequently collected in *Step by Step* (**A111**), pp. 33–6.

—   June   **THE BATTLE OF SIDNEY STREET** (*Men Only*; *see* **C277c**)

C497	June 12	**HOW TO STOP WAR**

Evening Standard, 7
Subsequently collected in *Step by Step* (**A111**), pp. 37–40.
Translated into German as 'Wie der Krieg Vermieden Werden
Kann' and published in the 20 June issue of *Das Neue Tage-
Buch*, pp. 589–90.[143]

C498a June 20 **SOAPBOX MESSIAHS**
Collier's, Vol. 97, No. 25, 11, 44, 46
Subsequently collected in *Collected Essays*, Vol. IV,
pp. 335–43.

C498b June 28 **MONEY FOR NOTHING**
Sunday Chronicle, 10, 15

C499 June 26 **WHY SANCTIONS FAILED**
Evening Standard, 7
Subsequently collected in *Step by Step* (**A111**), pp. 41–4.
Translated into German as 'Das Ende der Sanktionen', in the
4 July issue of *Das Neue Tage-Buch*, pp. 635–6.

— June 28 **MONEY FOR NOTHING** (*Sunday Chronicle*; see **C498b**)

C500a July 11 **OLDEST AND RICHEST**
Collier's, Vol. 98, No. 2, 21–2, 28
Subsequently collected in *Collected Essays*, Vol. III, pp. 272–8.

C500b July 12 **MONEY-GRABBER—BUT MONEY-GIVER TOO**
Sunday Chronicle, 10–11
Published on John D. Rockefeller's ninety-seventh birthday,
under the heading 'Do you know the only thing that gives me
pleasure? It is to see my dividends coming in, just to see my
dividends coming in.'

C501 July 13 **DUSK APPROACHES**
Evening Standard, 7
Subsequently collected in *Step by Step* (**A111**), pp. 45–8.
Translated into German as 'Götterdämmerung in England', in
the 18 July issue of *Das Neue Tage-Buch*, pp. 683–4.

143. The translation of this article and several others (**C499**, **C501**, **C516**, **C520**, **C521**, **C536** and
C539) prior to the establishment of the contractual arrangements between Emery Reves and
Churchill (see **C541a**) was accomplished by a Dr Meyer, an émigré journalist, apparently
without charge or commission of any kind. When Reves began to represent Churchill for the
publication of his bi-weekly articles on the European continent and, indeed, around the
world, Meyer was understandably miffed; however, Reves's Cooperation Press Service took
over that agency function and that was the end of the matter. (See the letter of 12 July 1937
from Reves to Churchill, in *Winston Churchill and Emery Reves* (**A297**), pp. 44–5.)

C502	July 19	**THE LIFE OF MARLBOROUGH**

The serialization of the third volume of *Marlborough* in the *Sunday Times*, advertised in the issue of 12 July (at p. 19). On 1 January 1934, Churchill proposed to Lord Camrose that their original understanding be modified. He explained that the initial arrangement, which was for a 200,000-word work, from which the newspaper could extract 40,000 words for the sum of £5000, had been increased to 400,000 words, from which the *Sunday Times* would publish an additional 40,000 words in 1934, at no extra cost. As of the date of that letter, though, he asked, "If I decide to extend the work to say six hundred thousand words, would you agree to purchase the third similar series for the year 1935?"[144] If so, he said that he "should be content with £1,250 or one quarter of the rate of our original agreement, for the extension." Camrose replied that he would much prefer the work to be completed in two volumes. "Two serials of a work which is not contemporary matter is, in our judgment, as much as we should give our readers. The addition of a third volume, to be published a year later than the second, would not, therefore, I am sorry to say, appeal to us."[145] In the end, a compromise was reached and Camrose advised Churchill: "In confirmation of our conversation last night, I have told the *Sunday Times* people that you are making *Marlborough* into a three volume book and that the price we pay you is to be increased to £5,500."[146] Except for the first issue in the serialization, each part was published under the superhead ' *"MARLBOROUGH"*–[X]'.

C502.1	July 19	**Marlborough at Ramillies / One of the Greatest of Battles / British Leader's Supreme Genius** *Sunday Times*, 16, 13
C502.2	July 26	**A Wonderful Month / Swift Conquest of Belgium / Sieges of Ostend and Menin** *Sunday Times*, 14, 12
C502.3	Aug. 2	**Sarah and Abigail / Story of Palace Intrigue / Effect on Marlborough** *Sunday Times*, 8, 6
C502.4	Aug. 9	**Queen and Marlborough / A Grave Political Crisis / Cabinet and Commons Strike** *Sunday Times*, 12, 10

144. *Ibid.*, pp. 694–5, at p. 694.
145. Letter of 5 January (*ibid.*, pp. 697–8, at p. 698).
146. Letter of 9 February (*ibid.*, p. 718).

C502.5	Aug. 16	**The Victory at Oudenarde / Marlborough's Military Genius / A "Glorious Debt" Repaid** *Sunday Times*, 10, 9
C502.6	Aug. 23	**The Siege of Lille / "A Prodigy of Human Effort" / Louis XIV's War Weariness** *Sunday Times*, 12, 10
C502.7	Aug. 30	**The End of a Campaign / Marlborough Forces the Scheldt / An "Elaborate Strategic Farce"** *Sunday Times*, 12, 10
C502.8	Sept. 6	**The Transformation / One Man and Three Battles / Triumph of the League** *Sunday Times*, 16, 13
C503	July 24	**RELIEF COMES AT LAST** *Evening Standard*, 7
C504	Aug. 10	**THE SPANISH TRAGEDY** *Evening Standard*, 7 Subsequently collected in *Step by Step* (**A111**), pp. 50–3.
C505	Aug. 21	**KEEP OUT OF SPAIN** *Evening Standard*, 7 Subsequently collected in *Step by Step* (**A111**), pp. 54–7.
C506	Aug. 22	**WHAT GOOD'S A CONSTITUTION?** *Collier's*, Vol. 98, No. 8, 22, 39–40
C507	Sept. 4	**ENEMIES TO THE LEFT** *Evening Standard*, 7 Subsequently collected in *Step by Step* (**A111**), pp. 59–61.
C508	Sept. 18	**THE TESTING TIME FOR FRANCE** *Evening Standard*, 7 Subsequently collected in *Step by Step* (**A111**), pp. 62–5, under the title 'A Testing Time for France'.
C509	October	**THE TRAGIC STORY OF PARNELL** *Strand Magazine*, Vol. XCI, No. 550, 600–10
C510	Oct. 2	**SPAIN—OBJECT LESSON FOR RADICALS** *Evening Standard*, 7 Subsequently collected in *Step by Step* (**A111**), pp. 66–9, under the title 'An Object Lesson from Spain'.

C511 Oct. 16 *WE* **ARE STILL FREE**
Evening Standard, 7
Subsequently collected in *Step by Step* (**A111**), pp. 70–3, under the title 'The Communist Schism'.

C512 Oct. 24 **I ASK YOU—WHAT PRICE FREEDOM?**
Answers, Vol. XCVII, No. 2525, 3–4
Subsequently collected in *Collected Essays*, Vol. I, pp. 360–4.

C513 Oct. 30 **GATHERING STORM**
Evening Standard, 7
Subsequently collected in *Step by Step* (**A111**), pp. 74–7.

C514 Nov. 13 **IN MEDITERRANEAN WATERS**
Evening Standard, 7
Subsequently collected in *Step by Step* (**A111**), pp. 78–81.

C515 Nov. 27 **GERMANY AND JAPAN**
Evening Standard, 7
Subsequently collected in *Step by Step* (**A111**), pp. 83–6.

— December **LAWRENCE OF ARABIA** (*English Race*; *see* **C473b**)

C516 Dec. 11 **FRANCE'S PLEDGE TO US**
Evening Standard, 7
Subsequently collected in *Step by Step* (**A111**), pp. 87–90, under the title 'The Pledge of France'. Translated into German as 'England und Frankreich Hand in Hand', in the 19 December issue of *Das Neue Tage-Buch*, pp. 1213–14.

C517 Dec. 28 **1936 IN PARLIAMENT**
Evening Standard, 7
Subsequently collected in *Step by Step* (**A111**), pp. 91–4, under the title 'Mr. Baldwin's Revival'.

1937

C518 Jan. 3 **MY PROPHECIES FOR 1937**
Sunday Pictorial, 8
Subsequently collected in *Collected Essays*, Vol. IV, pp. 344–6.

C519 Jan. 8 **NO INTERVENTION IN SPAIN FOR US!**
Evening Standard, 7
Subsequently collected in *Step by Step* (**A111**), pp. 95–7, under the title 'No Intervention in Spain'. For the individual articles

written for the *Evening Standard* in the first six months of 1937, Churchill was paid a total of £1440.[147]

C520   Jan. 22   **HOW YOU WILL HELP TO MEET THE BILL**
Evening Standard, 7
Subsequently collected in *Step by Step* (**A111**), pp. 98–101, under the title 'How to Meet the Bill'. Published in German as 'Die Fortsetzung der englischen Rüstung', in the 30 January issue of *Das Neue Tage-Buch*, pp. 109–10.

C521   Feb. 5   **EUROPE'S PEACE**
Evening Standard, 7
The title falls within the sentence: "EUROPE'S PEACE is to-day threatened with relapse into the insecurity of the dark ages, declares the Rt. Hon. Winston Churchill, P.C., M.P." Subsequently collected in *Step by Step* (**A111**), pp. 102–5. Published in German as 'Nach Hitlers Rede' in the 13 February issue of *Das Neue Tage-Buch*, pp. 157–9.

C522   Feb. 19   **FRANCE FACES A NEW CRISIS**
Evening Standard, 7
Subsequently collected in *Step by Step* (**A111**), pp. 106–9.

C523   Feb. 20   **THE MISSION OF JAPAN**
Collier's, Vol. 99, No. 8, 12–13, 42, 44
Subsequently collected in *Collected Essays*, Vol. I, pp. 365–72. For this and the five subsequent articles for *Collier's*, Churchill was paid £1800.[148]

C524   Feb. 21   **BIG NAVY**
Sunday Chronicle, 12–13

C525   March 5   **GERMANY'S CLAIM FOR COLONIES**
Evening Standard, 7
Subsequently collected in *Step by Step* (**A111**), pp. 110–13.

C526   March 22   **REBUILDING THE BATTLE FLEET**
Evening Standard, 7
Subsequently collected in *Step by Step* (**A111**), pp. 114–17.

C527   April 2   **CAN THE POWERS BRING PEACE TO SPAIN?**
Evening Standard, 7
Subsequently collected in *Step by Step* (**A111**), pp. 118–21.

---

147. According to his letter of 28 December 1936 to Stanley Williams, then first clerk at Lloyds Bank, Pall Mall Branch (Gilbert, *WSC*, Vol. V, *C.V.* 3, pp. 517–18, at p. 517).
148. *Ibid.*

C528	April 16	**THE NEW PHASE IN INDIA**

Evening Standard, 7

Subsequently collected in *Step by Step* (**A111**), pp. 122–5.

C529		**THE GREAT REIGNS**

A series of articles on British monarchs. For what Churchill referred to as the "Coronation series", he was paid the sum of £1250.[149]

C529.1	April 26	**THE HEROIC STORY OF ALFRED THE GREAT /**

The Creation of the Fleet: The Birth of a Nation

Evening Standard, 7, 10

Subsequently collected in *Collected Essays*, Vol. III, pp. 279–82, under the title 'I. Alfred the Great'.

C529.2	April 27	**William, Our Last Invader**

Evening Standard, 23

Subsequently collected in *Collected Essays*, Vol. III, pp. 282–5, under the title 'II. William the Conqueror'. Note that the date of publication is erroneously given there as 26 April.

C529.3	April 28	**Conqueror of Wales / Hammer of the Scots / From**

Edward I a United Kingdom Grew

Evening Standard, 7, 23

Subsequently collected in *Collected Essays*, Vol. III, pp. 285–8, under the title 'III. Edward I'.

C529.4	April 29	**Here Was a Man for the People / His Wisdom, His**

Lusts, His Crimes, Helped to Bring England Security

Evening Standard, 22

Subsequently collected in *Collected Essays*, Vol. III, pp. 288–92, under the title 'IV. Henry VIII'.

C529.5	April 30	**A Queen Indeed**

Evening Standard, 22–3

Subsequently collected in *Collected Essays*, Vol. III, pp. 292–6, under the title 'V. Queen Elizabeth I'.

C529.6	May 1	**A Reign of Splendour / Dazzling Victories Made**

Britain Supreme

Evening Standard, 14–15

Subsequently collected in *Collected Essays*, Vol. III, pp. 296–9, under the title 'VI. Queen Anne'.

---

149. *Ibid.*

C529.7	May 3	**"Mother of Many Nations"**

Evening Standard, 26

Subsequently collected in *Collected Essays*, Vol. III, pp. 299–302, under the title 'VII. Queen Victoria'.

C530	May	**HIS MAJESTY KING GEORGE VI**

Strand Magazine, Vol. XCIII, No. 557, 14–16, 18–23

Subsequently collected in *Collected Essays*, Vol. III, pp. 303–10. The article was prepared by Marshall Diston. As Gilbert points out, "Churchill accepted Diston's draft for the article, but he did add several sentences."[150] Churchill himself found the Diston draft "so very helpful that instead of the usual fee, I hope you will let me increase it to £20".[151]

C531	May 7	**GERMANY AND THE LOW COUNTRIES**

Evening Standard, 7

Subsequently collected in *Step by Step* (**A111**), pp. 126–9.

C532a	May 9	**A KING IS CROWNED**

Sunday Chronicle (Coronation supplement), 12–13

Subsequently collected in *Collected Essays*, Vol. IV, pp. 347–54.

C532b	May 15	**A KING IS CROWNED**

Collier's, Vol. 99, No. 20, 12–13, 57

C533	May 13	**DEFENDING THE EMPIRE**

Evening Standard, 7

Subsequently collected in *Step by Step* (**A111**), pp. 130–3.

C534	May 16	**LET US PRAISE A DOUR BUT GREAT MAN**

Sunday Express, 12

A tribute to Sir Philip Snowden,[152] which Lady Snowden described as "your beautiful article on my husband. It is the finest thing which has appeared and bears the brand of sincerity. ... Your generosity to a political opponent marks you for ever in my eyes the 'great gentleman' I have always thought you."[153]

---

150. *Ibid.*, p. 519*n*.

151. Letter of 29 December (*ibid.*, p. 519).

152. Snowden was a Labour M.P. and Chancellor of the Exchequer both immediately before and immediately after Churchill's tenure in that Cabinet post (1924 and 1929–31). He was a principal critic of Churchill while the latter held the position (6 November 1924 to June 1929).

153. Letter of 20 May 1937 from Ethel Snowden to Churchill (Gilbert, *WSC*, Vol. V, *C.V.* 3, pp. 675–6, at p. 675).

C535 **GREAT EVENTS OF OUR TIME**
A series of articles on historical events and future projections which are thematically unconnected. The commissioning of these articles was broached by Sir Elmsley Carr following his pre-publication reading of the 1936 series on 'Great Men of Our Time' (**C486**). Carr was so enthusiastic that he immediately requested the contribution of "a further series of articles next year" even though he had no idea at the time what the subject matter might be. "The nature of the articles can be discussed later, but it might be a convenience to both of us if we now entered into a definite arrangement."[154] Churchill accepted the offer the next day, allowing that they might consider the subject matter on both sides and arrive at a decision after Christmas. "It is a great help always to look ahead and let a literary project ripen slowly."[155] For these twelve articles Churchill was paid £4200.[156]

C535.1 May 30 **The Awful Crime That Shook Civilisation / Hope of Peace Died with a Pistol Shot**
News of the World, 12–13
Subsequently collected in *Collected Essays*, Vol. IV, pp. 355–62. The draft of the article was prepared by Marshall Diston, and was based on the first five chapters of *The Eastern Front* (**A69.2(V)**). "After the introduction, the story is told very largely in the words of the book, but the arrangement is different. Naturally, there has been a good deal of condensation."[157]

C535.2 June 6 **Tragedy of the Torpedoed Lusitania / Blunder Which Sealed the Fate of Germany**
News of the World, 12
Subsequently collected in *Collected Essays*, Vol. IV, pp. 362–8. The draft of this article was also prepared by Marshall Diston but was based on Volume II of *The World Crisis* (**A69.2(II)**) and, more specifically, the chapter 'The Intervention of the United States in 1916–1918'. "For the actual sinking I have supplemented the *Evening Standard* information with another account. And I have taken quotations from House, Roosevelt and Spring-Rice from the Lloyd George *War Memoirs*."[158]

154. Letter of 19 November 1935 (Gilbert, *WSC*, Vol. V, *C.V.* 2, pp. 1329–30, at p. 1329).
155. *Ibid.*, p. 1330.
156. *Ibid.*
157. Letter of 18 September 1936 from Adam Marshall Diston to Churchill (*ibid.*, pp. 345–6, at p. 345).
158. *Ibid.*

C535.3a   June 13   **The Decisive Factor in the Allied Victory / Defeat of U–Boats Was Our Navy's Supreme Service**
News of the World, 12
Subsequently collected in *Collected Essays*, Vol. IV, pp. 368–74.

C535.3b   May 10,   **THE U-BOAT MENACE**
           1941   *Liberty*, 10–11, 51–3

C535.3c   Fall 1971   **THE U-BOAT MENACE**
Liberty, the Nostalgia Magazine, 28–31, 95

C535.4   June 20   **When the Crash Came to the United States / Road to Recovery from Economic Collapse**
News of the World, 10–11
Subsequently collected in *Collected Essays*, Vol. IV, pp. 374–81. The draft was prepared by Marshall Diston. "I have drawn on two articles, written, I think, during the earlier period of the depression, 'The American Mind and Ours' and 'Gold versus Wealth', and have added about 2,500 words of new matter."[159]

C535.5   June 27   **The Dominions Are Partners of Empire / The Statute of Westminster Was a Guarantee of Equality**
News of the World, 12
Subsequently collected in *Collected Essays*, Vol. IV, pp. 381–7.

C535.6   July 4   **Chief Factors in Our Social Revolution / State Insurance and a Modernised Market for Labour**
News of the World, 12–13
Subsequently collected in *Collected Essays*, Vol. IV, pp. 387–93.

C535.7   Oct. 10   **This Age of Government by Great Dictators / Dynasties Have Gone and War Lords Are the Idols in the Shrines of Europe**
News of the World, 12–13
Subsequently collected in *Collected Essays*, Vol. IV, pp. 393–400.

C535.8   Oct. 17   **Japan's Swift Rise to Her Place in the Sun / Our Famous Treaty and Its Influence in the War against Russia**
News of the World, 12

---

159. Letter of 26 September (*ibid.*, p. 350).

Subsequently collected in *Collected Essays*, Vol. IV, pp. 400–4.
The draft was prepared by Marshall Diston and acknowledged
by Churchill in his letter of 5 October 1936: "The Japanese
outline is very good. ... [Except for one point] I think the
picture extremely well drawn."[160]

| C535.9 | Oct. 24 | **Will Japan Decide to Accept the Olive Branch? / Reasons Why War with China Cannot Go on Indefinitely** |

News of the World, 12
Subsequently collected in *Collected Essays*, Vol. IV, pp. 404–10.

| C535.10 | Oct. 31 | **Vision of the Future through Eyes of Science / March of Time and Progress to the Era of the Elusive Atom** |

News of the World, 12
Subsequently collected in *Collected Essays*, Vol. IV, pp. 410–14.

| C535.11 | Nov. 7 | **Life in a World Controlled by the Scientists / A Vision of the Future When Nature Is Subservient to Man** |

News of the World, 12
Subsequently collected in *Collected Essays*, Vol. IV, pp. 414–18.

| C535.12 | Nov. 14 | **Mankind Is Confronted by One Supreme Task / Let Us Make a Blessing and Not a Curse of Material Progress** |

News of the World, 12
Subsequently collected in *Collected Essays*, Vol. IV, pp. 418–22.

| C535.13 | Nov. 21 | **A Federation for Peace Is the Hope of the World / Nations Divided in Politics May Yet Welcome a United League** |

News of the World, 12
Subsequently collected in *Collected Essays*, Vol. IV, pp. 422–6.

| C536 | May 31 | **AMERICA LOOKS AT EUROPE** |

Evening Standard, 7
Subsequently collected in *Step by Step* (**A111**), pp. 134–7.
Published in German as 'Amerikas Augen Sind auf Europa
Gerichtet', in the 5 June issue of *Das Neue Tage-Buch*,
pp. 541–3.

---

160. Letter of 5 October to Diston (*ibid.*, p. 356).

| C537 | June 5 | **EDWARD THE EIGHTH** |

Collier's, Vol. 99, No. 23, 27, 39–40

Subsequently collected in *Collected Essays*, Vol. III, pp. 311–17. Of this critical view of Hector Bolitho's biography, *Edward VIII, His Life and Reign*, Churchill said to the Duke of Windsor, "I have written a review of his book … which I think will amuse you when it is printed."[161]

| C538 | June 11 | **THE ROME–BERLIN AXIS** |

Evening Standard, 7

Subsequently collected in *Step by Step* (**A111**), pp. 138–41.

| C539 | June 25 | **"VIVE LA FRANCE!"** |

Evening Standard, 7

Subsequently collected in *Step by Step* (**A111**), pp. 143–6. Published in German as 'Ewiges Frankreich', in the 3 July issue of *Das Neue Tage-Buch*, pp. 636–8.

| C540a.1 | June 27 | **THE CREEDS OF THE DEVIL** |

Sunday Chronicle, 10–11

| C540a.2 | July 4 | **THE BETTER WAY** |

Sunday Chronicle, 10

| C540b | July 3 | **THE INFERNAL TWINS** |

Collier's, Vol. 100, No. 1, 12–13, 28

| C541a | July 9 | **THE EBBING TIDE OF SOCIALISM** |

Evening Standard, 7

Subsequently collected in *Step by Step* (**A111**), pp. 147–50. This was the first of the articles sold by Emery Reves to foreign periodicals. Details of the arrangements between Churchill and Reves can be found in Martin Gilbert, *Winston Churchill and Emery Reves: Correspondence 1937–1965* (**A297**). The volume also provides a full list of the foreign periodicals that carried each of Churchill's articles and the price obtained by Reves for each published piece.[162]

| C541b | Oct. 16 | **THE EBBING TIDE OF SOCIALISM** |

Answers, Vol. XCIX, No. 2576, 3

---

161. Letter of 30 April 1937 to the Duke of Windsor (Gilbert, *WSC*, Vol. V, *C.V.* 3, pp. 659–60, at p. 659).

162. Gilbert's book does not, of course, make any attempt to provide details of the date and pagination of each of the articles, which would have been far removed from the *raison d'être* of his work. While such information is closer to the purpose of *this* work, any attempt on my part to locate the details of those foreign appearances would have further delayed the publication of this bibliography and would have added considerably to its length.

C542	July 23	**PARTITION PERILS IN PALESTINE**

Evening Standard, 7
Subsequently collected in *Step by Step* (**A111**), pp. 151–4, under the title 'Palestine Partition'.

C543   Aug. 6   **ANGLO-ITALIAN FRIENDSHIP—HOW?**
Evening Standard, 7
Subsequently collected in *Step by Step* (**A111**), pp. 155–8.

C544   Aug. 20   **A PLAIN WORD TO THE NAZIS**
Evening Standard, 7
Subsequently collected in *Step by Step* (**A111**), pp. 159–62.

C545   Sept. 3   **WHY I AM AGAINST PARTITION**
Jewish Chronicle, No. 3569, 24–5

C546   Sept. 3   **THE WOUNDED DRAGON**
Evening Standard, 7
Subsequently collected in *Step by Step* (**A111**), pp. 163–6.

C547   Sept. 12   **[WAR AND PEACE]**
New York News, 79–80
Churchill was paid $1000 for this re-telling of Tolstoy's novel.[163] This article was apparently republished in the *New York News* of 9 May 1943.

C548   Sept. 17   **FRIENDSHIP WITH GERMANY**
Evening Standard, 7
Subsequently collected in *Step by Step* (**A111**), pp. 167–70.

—   Sept. 19   **G.B.S.** (*Sunday Chronicle*; *see* **C324d**)

C549   Oct. 1   **THE DICTATORS HAVE SMILED / —But They Have Missed an Opportunity**
Evening Standard, 7
Subsequently collected in *Step by Step* (**A111**), pp. 172–5.

C550   Oct. 2   **CAN AMERICA KEEP OUT OF WAR?**
Collier's, Vol. 100, No. 14, 14–15, 38–9
Subsequently collected in *Collected Essays*, Vol. I, pp. 373–9.

C551   Oct. 15   **WAR IS NOT IMMINENT**
Evening Standard, 7
Subsequently collected in *Step by Step* (**A111**), pp. 176–9.

---

163. Heinzkill, 'Addenda to Woods', p. 360.

C552 Oct. 16 **ENGLAND'S "NO" MAN**
Collier's, Vol. 100, No. 16, 18, 79–81
Subsequently collected in *Collected Essays*, Vol. III, pp. 318–24, under the title 'England's "No Man" (Neville Chamberlain)'. Note that the date is erroneously given there as 14 October. Marshall Diston did a major part of the drafting of this article. In his cable back to Diston via Violet Pearman, Churchill said: "Article received, thanks. Publication date late August. Can you send insert three or four hundred words description aloof personality and anecdotes of man."[164]

— Oct. 16 **THE EBBING TIDE OF SOCIALISM** (*Answers; see* **C541b**)

C553 Oct. 17 **MENACE OVER EUROPE**
Sunday Chronicle, 12–13

C554 Oct. 24 **JELLICOE / He Could Have Lost the War in 2 Hours**
Sunday Chronicle, 6, 16
Subsequently collected in *Collected Essays*, Vol. III, pp. 325–30.

C555 Oct. 29 **A KEY STATE IN EUROPE**
Evening Standard, 7
Subsequently collected in *Step by Step* (**A111**), pp. 180–3, under the title 'Yugoslavia and Europe'.

C556 Oct. 31 **KITCHENER / "He Comforted His Countrymen in Their Darkest Hours."**
Sunday Chronicle, 6, 14
Subsequently collected in *Collected Essays*, Vol. III, pp. 331–6.

C557 Nov. 11 **ARMISTICE—OR PEACE?**
Evening Standard, 7
The headline runs over two contributions, which occupy the full page. That on the left is by Churchill and that on the right by George Bernard Shaw (in fact an interview with Shaw by Ormsby Lennon, updating an interview twelve months earlier on the question "Will there be another world war?"). Subsequently collected in *Step by Step* (**A111**), pp. 184–7.

C557/1 Nov. 13 **MUST THERE BE WAR? / "Shall We All Be Nakedly Exposed to the Challenge of the Two Harassed Dictators at the Head of Their Two Impoverished Nations Armed to the Teeth?"**

---

164. Gilbert, *WSC*, Vol. V, *C.V.* 3, p. 709.

Answers, Vol. C, No. 2580, 3
Under the superhead 'The Right Hon. Winston Churchill, P.C., M.P. Answers the Question of the Hour—'.

C558	Nov. 26	**SPAIN'S ROAD TO PEACE**

Evening Standard, 7
Subsequently collected in *Step by Step* (**A111**), pp. 188–91.

C559	Nov. 26	**HOMAGE TO KIPLING**

John O'London's Weekly and the Outline, 341–2, 348
This article is based on, but is not the same text as, Churchill's proposal of the toast of "The Rudyard Kipling Memorial Fund" (**E46a**). Subsequently published separately as *Homage to Kipling* (**A106**) and collected in *Collected Essays*, Vol. III, pp. 337–9.

C560		**MY LIFE AND TIMES**

A series in the *Sunday Chronicle*.

C560.1	Dec. 5	**My Childhood**

Sunday Chronicle, 6

C560.2	Dec. 12	**Under Fire / "A Bullet Passed within a Foot of My Head. I Was under Fire at Last!"**

Sunday Chronicle, 6

C560.3	Dec. 19	**Charge! / My Do-or-Die Attack with the Lancers**

Sunday Chronicle, 6

C560.4	Dec. 26	**I Was a Prisoner of War**

Sunday Chronicle, 6–7

The rest of the series appeared in 1938.

C560.5	Jan. 2	**I ESCAPE / From the Horrors of a Boer Prison Camp to a Life of Vivid Interest**

Sunday Chronicle, 6

C560.6	Jan. 9	**1914: THE BLUNDER THAT BEAT GERMANY**

Sunday Chronicle, 4, 12

C560.7a	Jan. 16	**THE TRUE STORY OF THE TANK**

Sunday Chronicle, 4

C560.7b	May 17, 1941	**TANK TACTICS**

Liberty, 12–13, 61

C560.8   Jan. 23   **WHEN BRITAIN NEARLY STARVED**
Sunday Chronicle, 4

C560.9   Jan. 30   **DRAMA OF THE DARDANELLES**
Sunday Chronicle, 4, 15

C560.10   Feb. 6   **MY SPY CHASE**
Sunday Chronicle, 4

C560.11   Feb. 13   **WOULD I LIVE MY LIFE AGAIN?**
Sunday Chronicle, 4

C561   Dec. 10   **EUROPE'S PLEA TO ROOSEVELT**
Evening Standard, 7
Subsequently collected in *Step by Step* (**A111**), pp. 193–6, under the title 'What We Ask of the United States'.

C562   Dec. 23   **PANORAMA OF 1937**
Evening Standard, 7
Subsequently collected in *Step by Step* (**A111**), pp. 197–200.

1938

C563   Jan. 7   **BRITAIN REARMS**
Evening Standard, 7
Subsequently collected in *Step by Step* (**A111**), pp. 201–4.

C564   Jan. 21   **WHAT JAPAN THINKS OF US**
Evening Standard, 7
Subsequently collected in *Step by Step* (**A111**), pp. 205–8.

C565a   February   **WOMEN IN WAR**
Strand Magazine, Vol. XCIV, No. 566, 406–14
Subsequently collected in *Collected Essays*, Vol. I, pp. 380–7.

C565b   March 27   **WOMEN CAN WIN WARS / 1938—Without Firing a Shot**
Sunday Chronicle, 8

C566   Feb. 4   **THE LEAGUE IS NOT DEAD YET / Though a Surgical Operation Just Now Might Prove Fatal**
Evening Standard, 7
Subsequently collected in *Step by Step* (**A111**), pp. 209–12, under the title 'The Dusk of the League'.

C567   Feb. 17   **IT'S NOT ALL OVER YET**
Evening Standard, 7
Subsequently collected in *Step by Step* (**A111**), pp. 214–17.

C568   March 4   **CARRY ON!**
Evening Standard, 7
Subsequently collected in *Step by Step* (**A111**), pp. 219–22.

C569   March 13   **DEFENCE / Our Air Force Is Two Years out of Date**
Sunday Chronicle, 10
Under the superhead '*Crisis!—And What of Our Air Defences?*'
Subsequently collected in *Collected Essays*, Vol. I, pp. 388–90,
under the title 'What of Our Air Defences?'

C570   March 18   **THE AUSTRIAN EYE-OPENER**
Evening Standard, 7
Subsequently collected in *Step by Step* (**A111**), pp. 223–6.

—   March 27   **WOMEN CAN WIN WARS** (*Sunday Chronicle*; *see* **C565b**)

C571   **THE LIFE OF MARLBOROUGH**
The serialization of the fourth and final volume of *Marlborough*.

C571.1 March 27   **MARLBOROUGH'S   LAST   GREAT   BATTLE /
Victory out of the Jaws of Defeat**
Sunday Times, 16, 13

C571.2 April 3   **THE DUCHESS AND ABIGAIL / Fierce War of the
Factions at Queen Anne's Court**
Sunday Times, 14

C571.3 April 10   **GREAT   COMMANDER   WEAKENED   BY
INTRIGUE / Duchess Sarah and the Queen**
Sunday Times, 14

C571.4 April 17   **"POISONED DAGGERS" OF THE PRESS / Swift's
Attack on Marlborough**
Sunday Times, 7

C571.5 April 24   **GREAT COMMANDER DISMISSED FROM ALL
OFFICES / Prince Eugene in London**
Sunday Times, 15

C571.6 May 8   **THE FIRST KING GEORGE / How the Whig Chiefs
Averted Civil War**
Sunday Times, 15

C571.7   May 15   **MARLBOROUGH'S LAST DAYS / Blenheim and Its Memorials**
Sunday Times, 15

C572   April 5   **RED SUNSET IN SPAIN**
Evening Standard, 7
Subsequently collected in *Step by Step* (**A111**), pp. 227–30. This was the last of Churchill's fortnightly contributions to the *Evening Standard* which had begun with his article of 13 March 1936 (**C489**). The notice of the newspaper's intention "to end an association which has been most agreeable to us, and from a literary point of view has given our columns a rare lustre" was given in R. J. Thompson's letter of 24 March 1938.[165] He provided two reasons for the rupture. First, the newspaper found "it necessary to have articles based, as far as possible, on the news of the day. As your articles have to be written some days in advance of publication, it occasionally happens that there is little difference—so far as argument goes—between the speech you make in the House of Commons on an important issue and the article based on the same subject which you write for us." Second, "as it is my duty to be completely frank, it has been evident that your views on foreign affairs and the part which this country should play are entirely opposed to those held by us." Churchill expressed his surprise to Thompson in a letter of 11 April (written after the conclusion of his arrangements with the *Daily Telegraph* to continue the series of articles on foreign affairs "without any intermission").[166] His tone was very measured in response to arguments that he clearly found to be baseless. Among other things, he pointed out that "it was always understood that, if circumstances changed and an emergency arose, you could have a new topic chosen up till almost the last moment." On the other principal issue, he added: "With regard to the divergence from Lord Beaverbrook's policy, that of course has been obvious from the beginning, but it clearly appears to me to be less marked than in the case of the Low cartoons. I rather thought that Lord Beaverbrook prided himself upon forming a platform in the *Evening Standard* for various opinions including of course his own." A letter of 18 April from W. H. Robertson, Manager of the Syndication Department of the *Evening Standard* (and other Beaverbrook papers), expressed his personal regret at the severance of the relationship, as well as his "great pleasure to have been associated even in a small way with such a brilliant series".[167]

---

165. CHAR 8/600/17.
166. CHAR 8/600/22–3. The articles began to appear nine days later, on 14 April 1936 (see **C573** on).
167. CHAR 8/600/27–8.

C573	April 14	**FRANCE'S NEW GOVERNMENT / Significance to Europe of M. Daladier's Bid for Era of Internal Stability** *Daily Telegraph and Morning Post*, 12 Subsequently collected in *Step by Step* (**A111**), pp. 231–4, under the title 'The New French Government'.

C574	April 24	**HOW WARS OF THE FUTURE WILL BE WAGED / Mechanical Invention May Be Impotent against Great Lines of Fortifications** *News of the World*, 12–13 Subsequently collected in *Collected Essays*, Vol. I, pp. 391–7. The first eight of the twelve articles to be published in the "1938 series" were sent by Churchill to Major Percy Davies[168] on 6 November 1937. He hoped to have the remaining four "before the end of the month".[169]

C575	April 28	**BRITAIN'S DEFICIENCIES IN AIRCRAFT MANUFACTURE / Disquiet over Weakness of Home Resources / Orders from U.S. as Part of a Settled Policy** *Daily Telegraph and Morning Post*, 16 Subsequently collected in *Step by Step* (**A111**), pp. 235–9.

C576	May 1	**FUTURE SAFEGUARDS OF NATIONAL DEFENCE / Navy Alone Can Fill our Granaries and Keep Invading Legions from Our Shores** *News of the World*, 12–13 Subsequently collected in *Collected Essays*, Vol. I, pp. 398–405.

C577	May 8	**EFFECT OF AIR TRANSPORT ON CIVILISATION / Flying Has Made Our World Smaller and Caused the Globe to Shrink** *News of the World*, 12–13 Subsequently collected in *Collected Essays*, Vol. IV, pp. 427–34.

C578	May 12	**PREMIER'S WORK FOR A NON-WAR SYSTEM IN EUROPE / Significance of Pact with Italy and Closer Collaboration with France** *Daily Telegraph and Morning Post*, 16 Subsequently collected in *Step by Step* (**A111**), pp. 240–4, under the title 'Britain and Italy'.

---

168. David Percy Davies was, at the time, deputy editor and a director of the *News of the World*. He succeeded Sir Emsley Carr as Editor in 1941.
169. Gilbert, *WSC*, Vol. V, *C.V.* 3, pp. 830–1.

C579   May 15   **THE UNION OF THE ENGLISH-SPEAKING PEOPLES / The Greatest Tie of All Is Language, and Words Alone Last for Ever**
News of the World, 12–13
Subsequently collected in *Collected Essays*, Vol. IV, pp. 435–42.

C580   May 22   **PEOPLING THE WIDE, OPEN SPACES OF THE EMPIRE / There Is a Threat in Foreign Invasion of Our Dominions Overseas**
News of the World, 12–13
Subsequently collected in *Collected Essays*, Vol. IV, pp. 443–9.

C581   May 26   **HOW JAPAN'S MILITARY ENTERPRISE IS SHACKLED / Shock of Resistance by a Unified China / The "Russian Anxiety" a Perpetual Danger**
Daily Telegraph and Morning Post, 16
Subsequently collected in *Step by Step* (**A111**), pp. 245–8, under the title 'Japan Entangled'.

C582   May 29   **WHY NOT "THE UNITED STATES OF EUROPE"? / Away with Those Barriers Which Divide Their Common Interests**
News of the World, 12–13

C583   June 9   **PERFECTING BRITAIN'S STRENGTH BY NATIONAL SERVICE / How a Sacrifice of 1914–18 Serves Peace To-day? Laying Plans Now to Avoid Past Mistakes**
Daily Telegraph and Morning Post, 14
Subsequently collected in *Step by Step* (**A111**), pp. 250–4, under the title 'National Service'.

C584   June 23   **FACTORS WHICH SWAY EUROPE'S FATE OVER CZECHOSLOVAKIA / Berlin's Advantage from a Peaceful Issue**
Daily Telegraph and Morning Post, 16
Subsequently collected in *Step by Step* (**A111**), pp. 255–8, under the title 'Shadows over Czechoslovakia'.

C585   July 6   **GERMANY'S DISCIPLINE FOR THE OLD AUSTRIA / Ruthless Penalties on Unwanted Elements / Workers' First Taste of Nazi Doctrines**
Daily Telegraph and Morning Post, 16
Subsequently collected in *Step by Step* (**A111**), pp. 259–62, under the title 'The Rape of Austria'.

C586   July 26   **WHAT FREEDOM MEANS TO FRANCE / Amid Flash of Arms in Paris, the Nation's Peaceful Genius Called out to Europe**
Daily Telegraph and Morning Post, 14
Subsequently collected in *Step by Step* (**A111**), pp. 263–6, under the title 'Thoughts on the Royal Visit'.

C587   July 30   **JAPAN GUESSES WRONG**
Collier's, Vol. 102, No. 5, 12–13, 45
Drafted by Marshall Diston for Churchill. Subsequently collected in *Collected Essays*, Vol. I, pp. 406–12.

C588   Aug. 4   **INFLUENCE THE U.S. MAY WIELD ON EUROPE'S DESTINY / A People Deeply Moved by World Issues**
Daily Telegraph and Morning Post, 10
Subsequently collected in *Step by Step* (**A111**), pp. 267–71, under the title 'The United States and Europe'.

C589   Aug. 18   **THOUGHTS ON GERMANY'S BIG-SCALE MANOEUVRES / Duty of Prudence in Neighbour Countries**
Daily Telegraph and Morning Post, 10
Subsequently collected in *Step by Step* (**A111**), pp. 272–5, under the title 'German Manoeuvres'.

C590   Sept. 1   **IS AIR POWER DECISIVE IN WAR? / Lessons of the Bomber's Failures in Spain / Britain's Special Need of Strong Defences**
Daily Telegraph and Morning Post, 12
Subsequently collected in *Step by Step* (**A111**), pp. 276–80, under the title 'Is Air-Power Decisive?'

C591   **LONDONER'S DIARY**
Paragraphs written for the column 'Londoner's Diary' in the *Evening Standard*.

C591.1   Sept. 1   **Sport at Balmoral**
Evening Standard, 6
Subsequently collected in Gilbert, *WSC*, Vol. V, *C.V.* 3, pp. 1133–4.

C591.2   Sept. 1   **Enough**
Evening Standard, 6
Subsequently collected in Gilbert, *WSC*, Vol. V, *C.V.* 3, p. 1134.

| C591.3 | Sept. 1 | **War at Churt**
Evening Standard, 6
Subsequently collected in Gilbert, *WSC*, Vol. V, *C.V.* 3, p. 1134. |

| C592 | | **LONDONER'S DIARY**
Paragraphs written for the column 'Londoner's Diary' in the *Evening Standard* but unattributed to Churchill there. |

| C592.1 | Sept. 2 | **Civil Service Leaders**
Evening Standard, 6
Subsequently collected in Gilbert, *WSC*, Vol. V, *C.V.* 3, pp. 1134–5. |

| C592.2 | Sept. 2 | **Then Too**
Evening Standard, 6
Subsequently collected in Gilbert, *WSC*, Vol. V, *C.V.* 3, p. 1135. |

| C592.3 | Sept. 2 | **Rebel**
Evening Standard, 6
Subsequently collected in Gilbert, *WSC*, Vol. V, *C.V.* 3, p. 1136. |

| C593 | Sept. 3 | **DICTATORS ON DYNAMITE**
Collier's, Vol. 102, No. 10, 16–17, 26
Subsequently collected in *Collected Essays*, Vol. I, pp. 413–20. Drafted by Marshall Diston for Churchill. |

| C594 | Sept. 4 | **SPORT IS A STIMULANT IN OUR WORKADAY WORLD / The Effect of Modern Amusements on Life and Character**
News of the World, 12–13
Subsequently collected in *Collected Essays*, Vol. IV, pp. 450–7. Note that, although this and seven other articles were announced as part of a series and were reproduced in *Collected Essays* as a single serialization, they were not numbered as Parts I, II and so on, and therefore they appear to me to be sufficiently disparate in terms of their subject matter to justify their inclusion as separate main entries (see **C596**, **C598**, **C601**, **C604**, **C606**, **C607** and **C609**). |

| C595 | | **LONDONER'S DIARY**
Paragraphs written for the 5 September 'Londoner's Diary' in the *Evening Standard* but unattributed to Churchill there. |

C595.1	Sept. 5	**Taken His Wings**

Evening Standard, 6

A brief piece on Lord Lloyd taking his "Wings" and on Lord Lloyd before the war.[170] The draft paragraphs, very close to the final version, were subsequently collected in Gilbert, *WSC*, Vol. V, *C.V.* 3, p. 1147.

C595.2   Sept. 5   **Grow More Food**

Evening Standard, 6

A brief piece on Prime Minister Neville Chamberlain's Birmingham speech. The draft paragraph, very close to the final version, was subsequently collected in Gilbert, *WSC*, Vol. V, *C.V.* 3, pp. 1147–8.

C596   Sept. 11   **PREVENTION OF CRIME IS AS VITAL AS PUNISHMENT / Reform of the Penal Code Restores Men to Society and Citizenship**

News of the World, 12–13

Subsequently collected in *Collected Essays*, Vol. IV, pp. 457–65.

C597   Sept. 15   **CAN EUROPE STAVE OFF WAR? / Menace of Unprecedented German Preparations / Joint Warning by Powers the Strongest Hope**

Daily Telegraph and Morning Post, 12

Subsequently collected in *Step by Step* (**A111**), pp. 281–4, under the title 'The European Crisis'.

C598   Sept. 18   **SYSTEM THAT GUARANTEES "THIS FREEDOM" / Our Democratic Parliament Is an Example to the World**

News of the World, 12–13

Subsequently collected in *Collected Essays*, Vol. IV, pp. 465–72.

C599   Sept. 20   **AIR AGE**

Evening Standard, 6

Written for the 'Londoner's Diary' of the *Evening Standard* but unattributed to Churchill there. Draft paragraphs for the published piece were subsequently collected in Gilbert, *WSC*, Vol. V, *C.V.* 3, pp. 1168–9.

---

170. Lord Lloyd's first exposure to flying had been in 1911 but his engagement to Blanche Lascelles (then Maid of Honour to the Queen) led him to drop the hazardous pastime until 1934. At the age of 56, he secured his pilot's certificate and then, in 1938, after "a strenuous nine months of work learning to fly by military standards", he acquired his "Wings" (letter of September 1938 to Blanche, *Life of Lord Lloyd* [**B107**], at pp. 279–80).

C600   Sept. 24   **ENGLAND LEARNS ABOUT LABOR**
                        Collier's, Vol. 102, No. 13, 13, 25

C601   Sept. 25   **THE CHILDLESS MARRIAGE THREATENS OUR RACE / A Falling Birth-rate Must Inevitably Lead to Extinction**
                        News of the World, 12–13
                        Subsequently collected in *Collected Essays*, Vol. IV, pp. 472–8.

C602   Sept. 28   **A Move Ahead**
                        Evening Standard, 6
                        Written for the 'Londoner's Diary' of the *Evening Standard* but unattributed to Churchill there. Draft paragraphs for the published piece were subsequently collected in Gilbert, *WSC*, Vol. V, *C.V.* 3, p. 1188 (and referred to and quoted in part in Vol. V, at p. 985). The first four paragraphs of the draft version were not included in the published version.

C603a   October   **WHAT CAN ENGLAND DO ABOUT HITLER?**
                        Current History, 13–15

C603b   June 1940   **WINSTON CHURCHILL ONCE REMARKED:**
                        Current History, 50–1
                        Extracts from the previous article.

C603c   January   **WHAT CAN ENGLAND DO ABOUT HITLER?**
            1989   *Toward the 21st Century*, 24–5, 50

C604   Oct. 2   **WORKERS OF BRITAIN HAVE COME INTO THEIR OWN / Let Us Review the Expansive Field of Our Social Services**
                        News of the World, 12
                        Subsequently collected in *Collected Essays*, Vol. IV, pp. 479–83.

C605   Oct. 4   **FRANCE, BRITAIN AND THE FUTURE FATE OF EUROPE / Western Democracies' Loss of Prestige / How Shaken Confidence May Be Repaired**
                        Daily Telegraph and Morning Post, 16
                        Subsequently collected in *Step by Step* (**A111**), pp. 285–8, under the title 'France after Munich'.

C606   Oct. 9   **HEALTH COMES FIRST IN SOCIAL PROGRESS / The State's Contribution to Our Modern Standard of National Fitness**
                        News of the World, 12
                        Subsequently collected in *Collected Essays*, Vol. IV, pp. 483–7.

Subsequently collected in *Step by Step* (**A111**), pp. 304–7, under the title 'France and England'.

C615   Dec. 15   **EASTERN EUROPE ON THE MORROW OF MUNICH / Poland May Have to Pay Dearly for Teschen / Can the Balkans Unite in Self-Preservation?**
Daily Telegraph and Morning Post, 14
Subsequently collected in *Step by Step* (**A111**), pp. 308–11, under the title 'New Lights in Eastern Europe'.

C616   Dec. 18   **MEMORIES OF PARLIAMENT AS A NOVITIATE MEMBER / The Inviolate Strip of Carpet That Marked the Party Gulf**
News of the World, 10–11

C617   Dec. 25   **ON MAKING A MAIDEN SPEECH IN THE HOUSE / Of Three Different Formulas Spontaneity Is the One to Be Preferred**
News of the World, 10–11

C618   Dec. 30   **LET THE SPANIARDS MAKE PEACE, LEST SPAIN LOSE ALL / The Moment Not for Victory But for Reunion**
Daily Telegraph and Morning Post, 10
Subsequently collected in *Step by Step* (**A111**), pp. 312–16, under the title 'The Spanish Ulcer'.

1939

C619   Jan. 1   **PARLIAMENT IS THE STAGE OF EMPIRE DRAMA / Historic Scenes in Moments of National Crisis**
News of the World, 10–11

C620a   Jan. 12   **IS THERE A PRICE FOR OUR NAVAL PACT WITH GERMANY? / Danger in Consenting to Limit Air Strength as a Return Gesture**
Daily Telegraph and Morning Post, 12
Subsequently collected in *Step by Step* (**A111**), at pp. 317–21, under the title 'The Anglo-German Naval Agreement'.

C620b   March 23   **ANGLO-GERMAN NAVAL AGREEMENT**
Ken, Vol. 3, No. 6, 13–14

C621   Jan. 14   **LET THE TYRANT CRIMINALS BOMB!**
Collier's, Vol. 103, No. 2, 12–13, 36
Subsequently collected in *Collected Essays*, Vol. I, pp. 421–7.

C629a   March 24   **HERR HITLER FACED WITH A NEW SPIRIT OF RESISTANCE** / Can Europe's Reaction Disillusion Him?
Daily Telegraph and Morning Post, 16
Subsequently collected in *Step by Step* (**A111**), pp. 341–5, under the title 'The Crunch'.

C629b   March 24   **WORLD REACTION SEEN AS UGLY SHOCK TO HITLER** / Winston Churchill Says Czech Grab Cause of Changed Opinion on Peace Possibility
Los Angeles Times, 4

C630   [No entry.]

C631a   April 13   **WOULD PEACE OR WAR BETTER SERVE MUSSOLINI'S INTERESTS?** / Hazardous Choice That Is Still Open Despite Albanian Adventure
Daily Telegraph and Morning Post, 14
Subsequently collected in *Step by Step* (**A111**), pp. 347–50, under the title 'Mussolini's Choice'.

C631b   April 14   **ITALY CERTAIN TO BE LOSER IN WAR AS GERMANY'S ALLY** / With Armies Scattered, French and British Fleets Could Punish Nation, Says Churchill
Los Angeles Times, 8

C632a   April 20   **SHADOW OF THE AXIS OVER FRANCO'S NEXT MOVES** / Is Spain to Gamble away Her Much-needed Respite from Devastating War?
Daily Telegraph and Morning Post, 14
Subsequently collected in *Step by Step* (**A111**), pp. 352–6, under the title 'After President Roosevelt's Message'.

C632b   April 21   **CHURCHILL SIGHTS HOPES IN ROOSEVELT PEACE APPEAL** / United States Will Not Intervene in Any European Row, Says British Statesman
Los Angeles Times, 12

C633   **[GREAT OFFICES OF STATE]**
A series of four articles on the great Cabinet positions of the Exchequer, the Home Office, the Admiralty and the War Office.

C633.1   April 30   **THE MINISTER WHO HAS TO SAY "NO"** / Treasury Is the Most Thankless of the Great Offices of State
News of the World, 12–13

C638   June 8   **TOWARDS A PACT WITH RUSSIA / Common Interests Which Must Overcome Obstacles to New Peace Alliance**
Daily Telegraph and Morning Post, 16
Subsequently collected in *Collected Essays*, Vol. I, pp. 444–6.
An advance copy of the article was sent to Sir Alexander Cadogan at the Foreign Office.

C639a   June 17   **BOMBS DON'T SCARE US NOW**
Collier's, Vol. 103, No. 24, 11, 56–8
Subsequently collected in *Collected Essays*, Vol. I, pp. 447–53.

C639b   June 18   **AIR BOMBING IS NO ROAD TO WORLD DOMINATION / The Answers to Enemy Attempts at Mass Terror Are in Our Hands**
News of the World, 12–13

C639c   November   **CHURCHILL'S PROPHECY**
          1940   *Parade*, Vol. 4, No. 2, 9
Note that the title on the cover is 'A PROPHECY'.

C640a   June 22   **GERMANY'S USE OF TACTICS OF ENCIRCLEMENT / Paradox of Her Pose as Aggrieved Party / Too-Clever Propaganda by Dr. Goebbels**
Daily Telegraph and Morning Post, 14
Subsequently collected in *Collected Essays*, Vol. I, pp. 454–6.

C640b   June 22   **GOEBBELS CONSIDERED BEST PROPAGANDIST FOR ANTI-NAZIS / Winston Churchill Declares His Utterances Should Bring Pay from People He Derides**
Los Angeles Times, 7
With not-insignificant deletions from the *Daily Telegraph* piece.

C641a   July 13   **NO BLOOD WILL FLOW—UNLESS …**
Daily Mirror, 16–17
The awkward headline reads: 'Churchill writes for us now, warns Hitler: "No blood will flow, unless—" '. Subsequently collected in *Collected Essays*, Vol. I, pp. 457–9.

C641b   July 14   **NAZIS' WAR OF NERVES DOOMED, SAYS CHURCHILL / British Pictured Calm but Resolute in Face of Threat as Hitler Holds Key to Peace in Hands**
Los Angeles Times, 2
The final two and a half paragraphs of the *Daily Mirror* version of the article have been excised.

C642a   July 27   **HITLER SELLS THE PASS!**
Daily Mirror, 15, 19
Subsequently collected in *Collected Essays*, Vol. I, pp. 460–2.

C642b   July 30   **BRITON SCOFFS AT NAZI 'PEACE' / Churchill Says Hitler Aims at Continental Control Despite Denial**
Los Angeles Times, 8
With not–insignificant deletions from the *Daily Mirror* piece.

C643   August   **THE RT. HON. ANTHONY EDEN, P.C.**
Strand Magazine, Vol. XCVII, No. 584, 358–66
Subsequently collected in *Collected Essays*, Vol. III, pp. 340–7.

C644   August   **IF WAR COMES**
P.T.O., Vol. 1, No. 2, 1–9
Said to be condensed from *News of the World*.

C645   Aug. 5   **HOW THE WAR BEGAN**
Picture Post, 11–18
Subsequently collected in *Collected Essays*, Vol. I, pp. 463–6.

C646a   Aug. 11   **A WORD TO JAPAN!**
Daily Mirror, 15, 19
Subsequently collected in *Collected Essays*, Vol. I, pp. 467–9.

C646b   Aug. 15   **CHURCHILL DECLARES JAPAN CAN'T RISK FIGHTING BRITAIN / Predicts Singapore Could Withstand Siege and Navy Would Cut off Lines to China**
Los Angeles Times, 7

C647   Aug. 19   **THE ANSWER TO ENCIRCLEMENT**
Picture Post, Vol. 4, No. 7, 33
Note that a German translation of this article, entitled 'Einkreisung', appears on p. 34. Subsequently collected in *Collected Essays*, Vol. I, pp. 470–2.

C648a   Aug. 24   **.. AT THE ELEVENTH HOUR!**
Daily Mirror, 14–15
The headline reads: "Churchill's Opinion! Winston Churchill Returned from France Last Night / Here He Sums Up the World Crisis .. AT THE ELEVENTH HOUR!"
Subsequently collected in *Collected Essays*, Vol. I, pp. 473–5.

C648b   Aug. 25   **HITLER ALONE CAN PREVENT CATASTROPHE, SAYS CHURCHILL / Events Moving from Every Quarter and along All Roads toward War, Munich Bloc Foe Declares**
Los Angeles Times, 7

C649   Sept. 30   **THE TERRIBLE TWINS**
Collier's, Vol. 104, No. 14, 22, 49–50
Subsequently collected in *Collected Essays*, Vol. I, pp. 476–82.

C650   **THE WORLD CRISIS**
A new serialization of different extracts from *The World Crisis* (**A69**). There is no single heading for the series.

C650.1   Oct. 1   **WAR—FROM INSIDE THE ADMIRALTY**
Sunday Chronicle and Sunday Referee, 6–7

C650.2   Oct. 8   **U-BOATS / How the Navy Beat Them**
Sunday Chronicle and Sunday Referee, 4

C650.3   Oct. 15   **WAR ON THE WESTERN FRONT**
Sunday Chronicle and Sunday Referee, 4

C650.4   Oct. 22   **THE COURAGE OF THE BRITISH SOLDIER**
Sunday Chronicle and Sunday Referee, 4

C650.5   Oct. 29   **LIGHTNING WAR / It Failed in 1914—It Will Fail Again Now**
Sunday Chronicle and Sunday Referee, 4

C650.6   Nov. 5   **HOW GERMANY INVADED BELGIUM**
Sunday Chronicle and Sunday Referee, 4

C650.7   Nov. 12   **SEA RAIDERS AT LARGE**
Sunday Chronicle and Sunday Referee, 6

C650.8   Nov. 19   **THE HUN**
Sunday Chronicle and Sunday Referee, 4

C650.9   Nov. 26   **HUNS AT SEA**
Sunday Chronicle and Sunday Referee, 6

C650.10   Dec. 3   **THREATS!**
Sunday Chronicle and Sunday Referee, 6

C650.11 Dec. 10 **THE NELSON SPIRIT / Beatty—They Advised Me against Him, but I Promoted Him over the Heads of All**
Sunday Chronicle and Sunday Referee, 6

C650.12 Dec. 17 **MIGHTIER YET / .. God Who Made Thee Mighty, Make Thee Mightier Yet ..**
Sunday Chronicle and Sunday Referee, 4

C650.13 Dec. 24 **STRANGLEHOLD / Britain's Navy Has Seized and Kept Control of All the Oceans of the World**
Sunday Chronicle and Sunday Referee, 8

C650.14 Dec. 31 **READY FOR ANYTHING! / The British Navy Can Well Defend Itself against All Forms of Attack—as the Past Few Weeks Have Shown**
Sunday Chronicle and Sunday Referee, 7

The rest of the serialization appears in the first half of 1940.

C650.15 Jan. 7 **ESCORT / From the Ends of the Earth the Navy Brings the Empire's Fighters**
Sunday Chronicle and Sunday Referee, 4

C650.16 Jan. 14 **SPRING OFFENSIVE**
Sunday Chronicle and Sunday Referee, 4

C650.17 Jan. 21 **40 DAYS OF HELL**
Sunday Chronicle and Sunday Referee, 4

C650.18 Jan. 28 **THE DRAMA OF RUMANIA / Germany's Vital Bid to Beat Blockade / What 1916 Did to Rumania**
Sunday Chronicle and Sunday Referee, 9

C650.19 Feb. 4 **Q-BOATS VERSUS U-BOATS**
Sunday Chronicle and Sunday Referee, 4

C650.20 Feb. 11 **GERMANY'S FATAL MISTAKE**
Sunday Chronicle and Sunday Referee, 4

C650.21 Feb. 18 **ANZACS / Day and Night They Fought with Fury, Asking No Quarter, Giving None**
Sunday Chronicle and Sunday Referee, 4

C650.22 Feb. 25 **THE NAVY STRIKES / We Risked Our Ships on a Bold Plan and Won Through**
Sunday Chronicle and Sunday Referee, 4

C650.23   March 3   **THE MAN WHO SCARED THE U-BOATS**
Sunday Chronicle and Sunday Referee, 4

C650.24   March 10   **THE GERMAN ARMY MYTH / They Said Once Before It Was an Invincible Army—But It Was Smashed**
Sunday Chronicle and Sunday Referee, 6

C650.25   March 17   **THE FRENCH / They Fight with the Same Indomitable Courage as Their Fathers at Verdun**
Sunday Chronicle and Sunday Referee, 6

C650.26   March 24   **THE BLACK DAY OF THE GERMAN ARMY**
Sunday Chronicle and Sunday Referee, 6

C650.27   March 31   **THE VALIANT HEART OF MAN**
Sunday Chronicle and Sunday Referee, 6

C650.28   April 7   **PLAN FOR VICTORY / Strategy That Won the Great War**
Sunday Chronicle and Sunday Referee, 6

C650.29   April 14   **BATTLE AT SEA**
Sunday Chronicle and Sunday Referee, 6

C650.30   April 21   **LANDING UNDER FIRE**
Sunday Chronicle and Sunday Referee, 4

C650.31   April 28   **MY FIGHT FOR SEA POWER**
Sunday Chronicle and Sunday Referee, 4

C650.32   May 5   **INTO THE JAWS OF DEATH / Our Brave Submarine Men Terrorized the Enemy by Their Courage**
Sunday Chronicle and Sunday Referee, 4

C650.33   May 12   **INVASION / Our Men Broke the Legend of German Might**
Sunday Chronicle and Sunday Referee, 4

C650.34   May 19   **BATTLE OF THE TANKS**
Sunday Chronicle and Sunday Referee, 4

C650.35   May 26   **ONCE BEFORE ... / The German Army Broke through, but We Smashed It in the End**
Sunday Chronicle and Sunday Referee, 4

C650.36	June 2	**SKY HEROES**

Sunday Chronicle and Sunday Referee, 4

C650.37	June 9	**THAT OTHER SOMME BATTLE**

Sunday Chronicle and Sunday Referee, 4

C650.38	June 16	**GUNS .. TANKS PLANES ..** [*sic*, no points after 'TANKS']

Sunday Chronicle and Sunday Referee, 4

C650.39	June 23	**ENDURANCE**

Sunday Chronicle and Sunday Referee, 4

C650.40	June 30	**POWER OF THE NAVY**

Sunday Chronicle and Sunday Referee, 4

C650/1	Oct. 7	**I WAS A PRISONER OF WAR**

Tit-Bits, No. 3023, pp. 4–6

C651	Oct. 7	**TODAY'S BATTLES**

Collier's, Vol. 104, No. 15, 12, 62–3
Subsequently collected in *Collected Essays*, Vol. I, pp. 483–8.

C652	Oct. 7	**DIE ENTSTEHUNG DER TANKS**

Das Neue Tage-Buch, 951–5
The German translation of Chapter IV, 'The Origin of Tanks and Smoke', of Volume II of *The World Crisis* (**A69.2(II)**). This is the only periodical appearance of a part of the actual chapter of the volume. In its serialized form in *The Times*, it appeared as 'Origin of Tanks. / Lord Dundonald's Smoke Secret' (**C270a.11**).

C653	November	**AVIATION—MAN'S BANE OR BOON?**

Rotarian, Vol. LV, No. 5, 8–12
The editors note that "This article was prepared before the outbreak of the hostilities in Europe and, of course, before the author became Britain's First Lord of the Admiralty." Subsequently collected in *Peace Is a Process* (**B93**).

C654	Dec. 9	**DER SPRINGENDE PUNKT IN EUROPA**

Das Neue Tage-Buch, 1164–8
The German translation of a section of Chapter XI, 'The Peace Treaties', of Volume IV of *The Aftermath* (**A69.2(IV)**). This is the only periodical appearance of a part of the actual chapter of the volume.

1940

C655	Jan. 13	**EIN KRIEGMINISTER TRITT ZURÜCK** *Das Neue Tage-Buch*, 38–40 The German translation of a section of Chapter IV, 'Verdun', of Volume III of *The World Crisis* (**A69.2(III)**). This is the only periodical appearance of a part of the actual chapter of the volume.
—	June	**WINSTON CHURCHILL ONCE REMARKED:** (*Current History*; see **C603b**)
C656	June 23	**AMERICA, LAND OF HOPE** *Sunday Dispatch*, 5
C657	June 30	**POWER OF THE NAVY** *Sunday Chronicle*, 4 Excerpted from *The World Crisis* (**A69**).
C658	July	**A ROVING COMMISSION** *Reader's Digest*, 152–92 Excerpted from the 1939 second American issue of *A Roving Commission* (**A91.5.a**).
—	November	**CHURCHILL'S PROPHECY** (*Parade*; see **C639c**)
C659	Dec. 10	**THE INFLUENZA** *Harrovian*, Vol. LIV, No. 11, 38–9

1941

—	May 10	**THE U-BOAT MENACE** (*Liberty*; see **C535.3b**)
—	May 17	**TANK TACTICS** (*Liberty*; see **C560.7b**)
C660	May 31	**OUR FRIENDSHIP WITH AMERICA** *Liberty*, 12–13, 48
C661	August	**A ROVING COMMISSION** *Omnibook Magazine*, Vol. 3, No. 9, 67–98

1942

—	Jan. 4 to March 1	**SAVROLA** (For this *Sunday Dispatch* serialization see **C73b**.)

C662   March 8   **ARE THERE MEN IN THE MOON?**
Sunday Dispatch, 7
Written before the war but published here for the first time.
Subsequently collected in *Collected Essays*, Vol. IV, pp. 493–8.

C663   March 15   **IDES OF MARCH**
Sunday Dispatch, 7

C664   March 22   **INDIA—AS I KNEW IT**
Sunday Dispatch, 7

C665   March 29   **I PRAYED**
Sunday Dispatch, 4
The narration runs from the moment of Churchill's escape
from prison to his being taken in by John Howard.

C666   April 5   **WHAT DO YOU KNOW ABOUT YOURSELF?**
Sunday Dispatch, 7
Written before the war but published here for the first
time. Subsequently collected in *Collected Essays*, Vol. IV,
pp. 499–503.

C667   April 12   **THE OTHER WINSTON CHURCHILL BY
WINSTON S. CHURCHILL**
Sunday Dispatch, 4
This is the exchange of correspondence between Churchill
and the American novelist of the same name. Previously
published in *My Early Life* (**A91**, pp. 230–3) and *The Five
Hundred Best English Letters* (**B44**, pp. 919–20) and
subsequently in R. Churchill, *WSC*, Vol. I, *C.V.* 2,
pp. 1026–7.

C668   April 19   **PRIMROSE DAY**
Sunday Dispatch, 6

C669   April 26   **LIFE UNDER THE MICROSCOPE**
Sunday Dispatch, 4
Written before the war but published here for the first time.

C670   **MEN & MEMORIES**
A series of articles on political and literary figures and political
and other memorable moments, most of which appear under
this title as a superhead. For those which do not have this
superhead, their principal title is given below in full capitals.

C670.1   May 3   **"THE FOUR MOST PLEASING AND BRILLIANT MEN TO WHOM I HAVE EVER LISTENED" / No. 1 / John Morley**
Sunday Dispatch, 6

C670.2   May 10   **MEMORIES / A Man Who 'Set Death in Its Proper Place'**
Sunday Dispatch, 4
On Lord Rosebery.

C670.3   May 17   **The Best-mannered Man I Ever Met**
Sunday Dispatch, 6
On Arthur James Balfour.

C670.4   May 24   **Joseph Chamberlain, the Political Piebald**
Sunday Dispatch, 4

C670.5   May 31   **Writing a Book**
Sunday Dispatch, 6

C670.6   June 7   **A Colonel of the Old School**
Sunday Dispatch, 4

C670.7   June 14   **Curzon—Magnificent Failure**
Sunday Dispatch, 6

C670.8   June 21   **H. G. WELLS**
Sunday Dispatch, 4

C670.9   June 28   **DON QUIXOTE AND SANCHO PANZA**
Sunday Dispatch, 6

C670.10   July 5   **Montagu Norman: Man of Mystery**
Sunday Dispatch, 4

C670.11   July 12   **Miner's Son Became Lord Chancellor**
Sunday Dispatch, 6
On Lord Birkenhead.

1943

—   May   **CLEMENCEAU** (*American Mercury*; *see* **C343c**)

1944

C671   November   **ARMISTICE!**
World Digest, Vol. 11, No. 67, 48–9
Reprinted from the *The World Crisis, 1916–18*, by permission
of Macmillan & Co.

1945

C672a   May?   **THE BIG JOB AHEAD**
Popular Illustrated, Vol. 2, No. 1, 2
The paper is 8 pages long and *undated*; however, it is clearly
post-VE-Day and pre-election.

C672b   June   **THE BIG JOB AHEAD**
National Magazine, 14–15
There is also an article on Churchill, on pp. 4–6, entitled
'Winston Churchill the Record .. and the Man', and a small
photo-essay at p. 7 entitled 'Five Years of Leadership'.

C673   June   **HOW I EDUCATED MYSELF**
Encore, Vol. VII, No. 40, 649–56
Excerpted from *My Early Life* (**A91**).

1946

—   July   **PAINTING AS A PASTIME** (*Strand Magazine; see*
C267c.1)

—   August   **WINSTON   CHURCHILL'S   PAINTINGS: A
FURTHER SELECTION** (*Strand Magazine; see* **C267c.2**)

C674   August   **THE AMAZING GEORGE BERNARD SHAW**
Adam International Review, Year XIV, No. 161, 1–4

1947

C675a   Jan. 4   **THE HIGH ROAD OF THE FUTURE**
Collier's, Vol. 119, No. 1, 11–12, 64
Churchill was paid $25,000 for this article, which
had the unintended effect of upsetting the tentative
1-million-dollar offer that *Collier's* was then about to make for
the American serial rights to his war memoirs. For reasons
recounted by Emery Reves, the offer was finally made at
$500,000, which sum was simply ignored by Lord Camrose

during a meeting with William L. Chenery, the editor.[171] The article was separately published as *A United Europe: One Way to Stop a New War* (**A231**).

| C675b | January 1973 | **THE HIGH ROAD OF THE FUTURE**
Uniropa, 8–9 |

C676   February   **ONE WAY TO STOP A NEW WAR**
World Digest, Vol. 16, No. 95, 7–10
Condensed from two articles in the *Daily Telegraph*.

C677a.1   April 11   **CHURCHILL SAYS BRITAIN SAVED GREECE FROM COMMUNISM / Recalls His Order to Fight Reds in Athens in December, '44, as Background of Truman's Democratic Security Plan**
New York Times, 1, 27

C677a.2   April 12   **CHURCHILL HAILS U.S. POLICY AS STABILIZING MIDDLE EAST / Russia's Aims to Control Whole Balkan Area and Turkey, in His View, Face Restraint Short of War in Truman Plan**
New York Times, 1, 19

C677b.1   April 12   **THE NEW AMERICAN POLICY / What Aid to Greece and Turkey Means to World Peace**
Daily Telegraph, 4

C677b.2   April 14   **THE NEW AMERICAN POLICY—II. / Soviet Expansionist Ambitions / Russia Does Not Want War, but Only Its Fruits**
Daily Telegraph, 4

C677b.3   April 15   **THE NEW AMERICAN POLICY—III. / The Oceans No Longer Isolate America / Facing the Facts of the Post-War World**
Daily Telegraph, 4

C677c   April 14   **IF I WERE AN AMERICAN / A Great British Statesman Examines the New U.S. Foreign Policy as His Country Retires from a World Role and America Moves In**
Life, Vol. 22, No. 15, 107–8, 110, 112, 115–16, 118, 121, 123
Subsequently collected in *Collected Essays*, Vol. II, pp. 468–77.

---

171. The circumstances of those negotiations are cited in Gilbert, *Reves*, p. 268.

1948

— February– **SAVROLA** (*France Illustration Littéraire et Théâtrale*; *see* **C73c**)
April

C678a   **THE SECOND WORLD WAR**
The *Daily Telegraph* serialization. Robin Barrington-Ward had apparently intended to raise the question of the serialization of the war memoirs at the last recorded meeting between him and Churchill in December 1946 at 28 Hyde Park Gate.[172] Barrington-Ward's biographer, Donald McLachlan, speculates that "no chance for *The Times* [to obtain the serialization rights] was ever open", the "negotiations with Camrose [having] begun before Churchill had ever started writing." The price which Barrington-Ward had heard mentioned was £250,000, "which was to go into a trust for the grand-children".[173] Except for the first number of the serialization, each article is preceded by the superhead '*"The Second World War" —[Part No.]*'.

C678a.1   April 16   **THE SECOND WORLD WAR: FOLLIES OF THE VICTORS OF 1918**
Daily Telegraph & Morning Post, 4

C678a.2   April 19   **"The Final Safeguard of Peace Cast Away"**
Daily Telegraph & Morning Post, 4

C678a.3   April 20   **The Baldwin–MacDonald Regime: Locarno**
Daily Telegraph & Morning Post, 4

C678a.4   April 21   **Germany under Hitler Arming Apace**
Daily Telegraph & Morning Post, 4

C678a.5   April 22   **Friends and Advisers in "The Locust Years"**
Daily Telegraph & Morning Post, 4

C678a.6   April 23   **Unheeded Warnings of Our Air Peril**
Daily Telegraph & Morning Post, 4

C678a.7   April 26   **Hitler's Challenge and the Response**
Daily Telegraph & Morning Post, 4

C678a.8   April 27   **Condoning Germany's Treaty-Violation**
Daily Telegraph & Morning Post, 4

---

172. See Donald McLachlan, *In the Chair: Barrington-Ward of* The Times, *1927–1948* (London: Weidenfeld and Nicolson, 1971), p. 211.
173. *Ibid.*

C678a.41   June 16   **A Damaging Debate and Division on Norway**
Daily Telegraph & Morning Post, 4

C678a.42   June 17   **Called to Premiership in Critical Days**
Daily Telegraph & Morning Post, 4

C678b   **THE SECOND WORLD WAR / Volume I—The Gathering Storm**
The *New York Times* (illustrated) serialization of Volume I, the first 13 parts being under the additional subtitle **Book I— From War to War** and the final 17 under the additional subtitle **Book II—The Twilight War**. At this time, it was expected that the history would be published in five volumes. The serialization was published daily except Sunday, and the series runs from Vol. XCVII, No. 32,956 to No. 32,989. There is a note from the editors on printing style at p. 25 of the first instalment which explains that the *New York Times* "is reproducing Mr. Churchill's own spellings, punctuation and capitalization. Many words will thus be found to conform with the British rather than the American spellings. A few geographical names likewise will be at variance with forms familiar to TIMES readers." The *New York Times* paid $400,000 to Henry Luce for the daily newspaper rights and was the only daily newspaper to serialize the work in the United States.

C678b.1   April 16   **Installment 1: / The Follies of the Victors**
New York Times, 1, 25

C678b.2   April 17   **Installment 2: / Peace at Its Zenith**
New York Times, 1, 17

C678b.3   April 19   **Installment 3: / The Locust Years**
New York Times, 1, 25

C678b.4   April 20   **Installment 4: / Air Parity Lost**
New York Times, 1, 29

C678b.5   April 21   **Installment 5: / Problems of Air and Sea (1935–1939)**
New York Times, 1, 29

C678b.6   April 22   **Installment 6: / Sanctions against Italy; Hitler Strikes**
New York Times, 1, 29

C678b.7   April 23   **Installment 7: / The Loaded Pause; Germany Armed**
New York Times, 1, 25

C678b.8	April 24	**Installment 8—Mr. Eden at the Foreign Office; Resignation** *New York Times*, 17 The presentation format changes slightly with this number, as the serialization no longer begins on page 1.
C678b.9	April 26	**Installment 9—Czechoslovakia and the Tragedy of Munich** *New York Times*, 25
C678b.10	April 27	**Installment 10—Munich Winter** *New York Times*, 27
C678b.11	April 28	**Installment 11—Prague, Albania and the Polish Guarantee** *New York Times*, 29
C678b.12	April 29	**Installment 12—The Soviet Enigma** *New York Times*, 25
C678b.13	April 30	**Installment 13—On the Verge** *New York Times*, 25
C678b.14	May 1	**Installment 14—War** *New York Times*, 17
C678b.15	May 3	**Installment 15—The Admiralty Task** *New York Times*, 23
C678b.16	May 4	**Installment 16—The Ruin of Poland** *New York Times*, 27
C678b.17	May 5	**Installment 17—War Cabinet Problems** *New York Times*, 27
C678b.18	May 6	**Installment 18—The Front in France** *New York Times*, 27
C678b.19	May 7	**Installment 19—The Combat Deepens** *New York Times*, 25
C678b.20	May 8	**Installment 20—The Magnetic Mine** *New York Times*, 17 Note that, in the same issue of the *New York Times*, Churchill's address at the opening of the Congress of Europe in The Hague is reported at p. 6, under the title 'Text of Churchill Plea for European Unity'.

C678b.21   May 10   **Installment 21—Surface Raiders**
New York Times, 23

C678b.22   May 11   **Installment 22—The Action of the River Plate**
New York Times, 27

C678b.23   May 12   **Installment 23—Scandinavia; Finland**
New York Times, 29

C678b.24   May 13   **Installment 24—A Dark New Year**
New York Times, 27

C678b.25   May 14   **Installment 25—Before the Storm**
New York Times, 25

C678b.26   May 15   **Installment 26—The Class of the Fleets**
New York Times, 17

C678b.27   May 17   **Installment 27—Narvik**
New York Times, 21

C678b.28   May 18   **Installment 28—Trondheim**
New York Times, 25

C678b.29   May 19   **Installment 29—Frustration in Norway**
New York Times, 29

C678b.30   May 20   **Installment 30—The Fall of the Government**
New York Times, 31

C678c   **THE WAR MEMOIRS OF WINSTON CHURCHILL**
The American magazine *Life* serialized *The Gathering Storm* in six profusely illustrated parts, which ultimately became, with the material used in the serialized publication of the other volumes, the basis for Time-Life's two-volume illustrated edition of *The Second World War* (**A240.10**). The principal title of the first part of this serialization was the slightly more formal **WAR MEMOIRS OF THE RT. HON. WINSTON CHURCHILL O.M., C.H., M.P.** Until at least some forty years after the date of the *War Memoirs*, Churchill remained the "man who was unquestionably *Life*'s best-rewarded author", having earned "more than $1 million for assorted memoirs, histories, speeches".[174]

---

174. Loudon Wainwright, *The Great American Magazine: An Inside History of* Life (New York: Knopf, 1986), p. 199.

C678c.1	April 19	**The Gathering Storm: Part I** *Life*, 28–41, 114–24
C678c.2	April 26	**The Gathering Storm: Part II** *Life*, 48–55, 57–8, 60, 63–4, 66, 71–2, 74, 77–8, 80
C678c.3	May 3	**The Gathering Storm: Part III** *Life*, 72–8, 81–2, 84, 87–8, 91–2
C678c.4	May 10	**The Gathering Storm: Part IV** *Life*, 60–75
C678c.5	May 17	**The Gathering Storm: Part V** *Life*, 66–70, 72, 74, 77–8, 81–2, 87–8
C678c.6	May 24	**The Gathering Storm: Part VI** *Life*, 64–75

1949

C679.1	January	**SPARKS FROM THE ANVIL** *Atlantic*, 23–5
C679.2	February	**SPARKS FROM THE ANVIL** *Atlantic*, 52–3
C680a		**THE SECOND WORLD WAR, Volume II** The serialization of the second volume of *The Second World War* (**A69.2(II)**) by the *Daily Telegraph & Morning Post*. Except for the first issue of the serialization, each article is preceded by the superhead ' *"The Second World War" (Vol. II)—[Part No.]*'.
C680a.1	Feb. 4	**THE SECOND WORLD WAR: THEIR FINEST HOUR** *Daily Telegraph & Morning Post*, 4
C680a.2	Feb. 5	**War Direction: The Men and the Machinery** *Daily Telegraph & Morning Post*, 4
C680a.3	Feb. 7	**The Battle of France: Sudden Disaster** *Daily Telegraph & Morning Post*, 4
C680a.4	Feb. 8	**Gamelin Says He Has No Strategic Reserve** *Daily Telegraph & Morning Post*, 4
C680a.5	Feb. 9	**B.E.F.'s Peril: Mobilising the Little Ships** *Daily Telegraph & Morning Post*, 4

C680a.38   March 24   **Days of Danger: A Frank Letter to Roosevelt**
Daily Telegraph & Morning Post, 4

C680a.39   March 25   **Lend–Lease Transformed the Entire Scene**
Daily Telegraph & Morning Post, 4

C680a.40   March 26   **Growing U-Boat Menace Was Frightening**
Daily Telegraph & Morning Post, 4

C680a.41   March 29   **Italian Forces in Libya Ripe for the Sickle**
Daily Telegraph & Morning Post, 4

C680a.42   March 30   **Heads High as Our Year of Peril Closes**
Daily Telegraph & Morning Post, 4

C680b   **THE SECOND WORLD WAR / Volume II—Their Finest Hour**
The *New York Times* (illustrated) serialization of Volume II, the first 15 parts being under the additional subtitle **Book I— The Fall of France** and the final 17 under the additional subtitle **Book II—Alone**. The serialization was published daily except Sunday, and the series runs from Vol. XCVIII, No. 33,249 to 33,283.

C680b.1   Feb. 4   **Installment 1: / The National Coalition**
New York Times, 1, 25–6

C680b.2   Feb. 5   **Installment 2: / The Battle of France**
New York Times, 1, 17

C680b.3   Feb. 7   **Installment 3: / The March to the Sea**
New York Times, 1, 21

C680b.4   Feb. 8   **Installment 4: / The Deliverance of Dunkirk**
New York Times, 1, 27

C680b.5   Feb. 9   **Installment 5: / The Rush for the Spoils**
New York Times, 29

C680b.6   Feb. 10   **Installment 6: / Back to France**
New York Times, 1, 29

C680b.7   Feb. 11   **Installment 7: / The French Agony**
New York Times, 1, 25

C680b.8   Feb. 12   **Installment 8—The Bordeaux Armistice**
New York Times, 19

C680b.24   March 3   **Installment 24—Dakar**
                        New York Times, 27

C680b.25   March 4   **Installment 25—Relations with Vichy and Spain**
                        New York Times, 23

C680b.26   March 5   **Installment 26—Mussolini Attacks Greece**
                        New York Times, 19

C680b.27   March 7   **Installment 27—A Letter to the President**
                        New York Times, 23

C680b.28   March 8   **Installment 28—Lend-Lease**
                        New York Times, 27

C680b.29   March 9   **Installment 29—Ocean Peril**
                        New York Times, 27

C680b.30   March 10   **Installment 30—Desert Victory**
                        New York Times, 29

C680c   **THE WAR MEMOIRS OF WINSTON CHURCHILL**
                        The continuation of the profusely illustrated *Life* serialization. As in the case of the first volume, the principal title of the first part of the serialization of *Their Finest Hour* was the slightly more formal **WAR MEMOIRS OF THE RT. HON. WINSTON CHURCHILL O.M., C.H., M.P.**

C680c.1   Feb. 7   **Their Finest Hour**
                        Life, 58–73, 75–8, 80, 82–3

C680c.2   Feb. 14   **Their Finest Hour: Part II**
                        Life, 38–52, 55–6, 61–2

C680c.3   Feb. 21   **Their Finest Hour: Part III**
                        Life, 48–55, 57–60, 63–4

C680c.4   Feb. 28   **Their Finest Hour: Part IV**
                        Life, 42–52, 54, 56, 61–5

C680c.5   March 7   **Their Finest Hour: Part V**
                        Life, 48–53, 55–6, 61–4, 66

C680c.6   March 14   **Their Finest Hour: Part VI**
                        Life, 82–7, 91–4, 97–8, 100

C680c.7	March 21	**Their Finest Hour: Part VII** *Life*, 54–62, 65–6

C681	August	**A Troublesome Boy** *Reader's Digest*, Vol. 55, No. 328, 101–4 *Reader's Digest* purchased the rights "to publish a condensed version of the first four chapters of said book in not over 1700 words in the United States edition of The Reader's Digest" for the sum of $1000.[175] Subsequently collected in *Reader's Digest 50th Anniversary Treasury* (**B196**).

C682	Sept. 3	**THE FIRST DAY OF THE WAR** *Picture Post*, Vol. 44, No. 10, 11–17 An excerpt from *The Gathering Storm*, reprinted here with the permission of the *Daily Telegraph*.

1950

C683a		**THE SECOND WORLD WAR** The serialization of the third volume of *The Second World War* by the *Daily Telegraph & Morning Post*. Except for the first issue of the serialization, each article is preceded by the superhead ' *"The Second World War" (Vol. III)—[Part No.]*'.

C683a.1	Jan. 26	**THE SECOND WORLD WAR: THE GRAND ALLIANCE** *Daily Telegraph & Morning Post*, 4

C683a.2	Jan. 27	**Threat to Balkans Sets Us a Grim Problem** *Daily Telegraph & Morning Post*, 4

C683a.3	Jan. 28	**1941 Blitz and Anti-Blitz: London's Worst Raid** *Daily Telegraph & Morning Post*, 4

C683a.4	Jan. 30	**The True Story of the Hess Mission** *Daily Telegraph & Morning Post*, 4

C683a.5	Jan. 31	**Aiding Greece: A Gamble with Big Stakes** *Daily Telegraph & Morning Post*, 4

C683a.6	Feb. 1	**No Hesitation or Division in Cabinet on Greece** *Daily Telegraph & Morning Post*, 4

---

175. Letter of 9 June 1949 from Ralph Henderson of *Reader's Digest* to Whitney Darrow of Scribner's (Scribner Archives, C0101, Author Files III, Box 12, Folder 9).

C683a.7	Feb. 2	**Revolution in Belgrade against Hitler Pact**
		Daily Telegraph & Morning Post, 4
C683a.8	Feb. 3	**Jugoslavia's One Chance of a Major Victory**
		Daily Telegraph & Morning Post, 4
C683a.9	Feb. 4	**Germans Press Japan to Attack Singapore**
		Daily Telegraph & Morning Post, 4, 6
C683a.10	Feb. 6	**Rommel Was a Splendid Military Gambler**
		Daily Telegraph & Morning Post, 4
C683a.11	Feb. 7	**Our Campaign in Greece: Rescue by the Navy**
		Daily Telegraph & Morning Post, 4
C683a.12	Feb. 8	**Tanks for Wavell: Vital Convoy Got Through**
		Daily Telegraph & Morning Post, 4
		Publication of the serialization was suspended during the course of the General Election campaign.
C683a.13	March 2	**Bold Action Foils Rashid Ali's Revolt in Irak**
		Daily Telegraph & Morning Post, 4, 6
C683a.14	March 3	**Overwhelming Air Force Hurled upon Crete**
		Daily Telegraph & Morning Post, 4, 7
C683a.15	March 4	**Navy Smashes Seaborne Invasion of Crete**
		Daily Telegraph & Morning Post, 4, 6
C683a.16	March 6	**Crete a Pyrrhic Victory for the Germans**
		Daily Telegraph & Morning Post, 4, 7
C683a.17	March 7	**The Bismarck's Sortie: Loss of the Hood**
		Daily Telegraph & Morning Post, 4, 6
C683a.18	March 9	**Drama of the Bismarck: The Hunt and the Kill**
		Daily Telegraph & Morning Post, 4, 3
C683a.19	March 10	**Gen. Auchinleck Relieves Gen. Wavell**
		Daily Telegraph & Morning Post, 4, 3
C683a.20	March 13	**Blunders of the Kremlin before Hitler Struck**
		Daily Telegraph & Morning Post, 4
C683a.21	March 15	**Russia Invaded: No Doubt Where Our Duty Lay**
		Daily Telegraph & Morning Post, 4, 6

C683a.38   April 10   **A Memorable Christmas at the White House**
Daily Telegraph & Morning Post, 4

C683a.39   April 11   **American Confidence in General Wavell**
Daily Telegraph & Morning Post, 4

C683a.40   April 12   **Stalin Accepts Religious Freedom as a War Aim**
Daily Telegraph & Morning Post, 4

C683a.41   April 13   **Safely Home: A Long Hop from Bermuda**
Daily Telegraph & Morning Post, 4, 7

C683b   **THE SECOND WORLD WAR / Volume III—The Grand Alliance**
The *New York Times* (illustrated) serialization of Volume III, the first 14 parts being under the additional subtitle **Book I—Germany Drives East** and the final 16 under the additional subtitle **Book II—War Comes to America**. The serialization was published daily except Sunday. The series runs from Vol. XCIX, No. 33, 605 to No. 33, 639.

C683b.1   Jan. 26   **Installment 1: / The Widening War**
New York Times, 1, 29

C683b.2   Jan. 27   **Installment 2: / Blitz of 1941; Arrival of Hess**
New York Times, 1, 25

C683b.3   Jan. 28   **Installment 3: / The Mediterranean War**
New York Times, 1, 15

C683b.4   Jan. 30   **Installment 4: / The Battle of the Atlantic, 1941**
New York Times, 1, 19

C683b.5   Jan. 31   **Installment 5: / Yugoslavia**
New York Times, 1, 25

C683b.6   Feb. 1   **Installment 6: / The Japanese Envoy**
New York Times, 1, 31

C683b.7   Feb. 2   **Installment 7: / The Desert Flank: Rommel: Tobruk**
New York Times, 1, 29

C683b.8   Feb. 3   **Installment 8: / The Greek Campaign**
New York Times, 1, 25

C683b.9   Feb. 4   **Installment 7—The Revolt in Iraq**
New York Times, 17

C683b.25   Feb. 23   **Installment 25—Pearl Harbour!**
New York Times, 29

C683b.26   Feb. 24   **Installment 26—A Voyage amid World War**
New York Times, 25

C683b.27   Feb. 25   **Installment 27—Proposed Plan and Sequence of the War**
New York Times, 19

C683b.28   Feb. 27   **Installment 28—Washington and Ottawa**
New York Times, 21

C683b.29   Feb. 28   **Installment 29—Anglo-American Accords**
New York Times, 31

C683b.30   March 1   **Installment 30—Return to Storm**
New York Times, 29

C683c   **THE WAR MEMOIRS OF WINSTON CHURCHILL**
The continuation of the profusely illustrated *Life* serialization. In the case of *The Grand Alliance*, the title of the first part is **WINSTON CHURCHILL'S WAR MEMOIRS**.

C683c.1   Feb. 6   **The Grand Alliance**
Life, 46–58, 63–4

C683c.2   Feb. 20   **The Grand Alliance: Part II**
Life, 66–76, 79–80, 82

C683c.3   Feb. 27   **The Grand Alliance: Part III**
Life, 62–76

C684a   **THE SECOND WORLD WAR, Volume IV**
The serialization of the fourth volume of *The Second World War* by the *Daily Telegraph & Morning Post*. Except for the first issue of the serialization, each article is preceded by the superhead ' *"The Second World War" (Vol. IV)—[Part No.]*'.

C684a.1   Oct. 10   **THE SECOND WORLD WAR: THE HINGE OF FATE**
Daily Telegraph & Morning Post, 4

C684a.2   Oct. 11   **The Frightful Dilemma of Singapore**
Daily Telegraph & Morning Post, 4

1951

C686a   **THE SECOND WORLD WAR / Volume V—Closing the Ring**
The *New York Times* (illustrated) serialization of Volume V, the first ten parts being under the additional subtitle **Book I—Italy Won** and the final 14 under the additional subtitle **Book II—Teheran to Rome**. The serialization was published daily except Sunday, and the series runs from Vol. CI, No. 34,222 to No. 34,249.

C686a.1   Oct. 5   **Installment 1: / The Command of the Seas**
New York Times, 1, 29

C686a.2   Oct. 6   **Installment 2: / The Fall of Mussolini**
New York Times, 1, 21

C686a.3   Oct. 8   **Installment 3: / The Quebec Conference "Quadrant"**
New York Times, 1, 23

C686a.4   Oct. 9   **Installment 4: / Italy: The Armistice**
New York Times, 1, 31

C686a.5   Oct. 10   **Installment 5: / At the White House Again**
New York Times, 1, 29

C686a.6   Oct. 11   **Installment 6: / Tensions with General de Gaulle**
New York Times, 1, 39

C686a.7   Oct. 12   **Installment 7: / Hitler's Secret Weapon**
New York Times, 1, 29

C686a.8   Oct. 13   **Installment 8—Arctic Convoys Again**
New York Times, 19

C686a.9   Oct. 15   **Installment 9—Foreign Secretaries Conference in Moscow**
New York Times, 27

C686a.10   Oct. 16   **Installment 10—Advent of the Triple Meeting**
New York Times, 33

C686a.11   Oct. 17   **Installment 11—Cairo**
New York Times, 33

C686a.12   Oct. 18   **Installment 12—Teheran: The Opening**
New York Times, 31

C686c   **THE SECOND WORLD WAR, Volume V**
The serialization of the fifth volume of *The Second World War* by the *Daily Telegraph & Morning Post*. Except for the first issue of the serialization, each article is preceded by the superhead ' *"The Second World War" (Vol. V)—[Part No.]* '.

C686c.1 Nov. 5 **Closing the Ring: How the Battle of the Atlantic Was Won**
Daily Telegraph & Morning Post, 4

C686c.2 Nov. 6 **II / The Conquest of Sicily: A 38-Day Campaign**
Daily Telegraph & Morning Post, 4

C686c.3 Nov. 7 **III / Mussolini's Fall: "This Is a Time to Dare"**
Daily Telegraph & Morning Post, 4, 6

C686c.4 Nov. 8 **IV / Putting the Screw on to Save Our Prisoners**
Daily Telegraph & Morning Post, 4

C686c.5 Nov. 9 **V / Synthetic Harbours for Normandy Invasion**
Daily Telegraph & Morning Post, 4, 7

C686c.6 Nov. 12 **VI / Why Normandy Command Went to an American**
Daily Telegraph & Morning Post, 4

C686c.7 Nov. 13 **VII / Italy Secretly Signs Allies' Terms of Surrender**
Daily Telegraph & Morning Post, 4, 6

C686c.8 Nov. 14 **VIII / Italian Fleet Fights Its Way to Surrender at Malta**
Daily Telegraph & Morning Post, 4, 6

C686c.9 Nov. 15 **IX / Salerno Recalls Suvla but Alexander Is on the Spot**
Daily Telegraph & Morning Post, 4, 6

C686c.10 Nov. 16 **X / Tensions with Gen. de Gaulle That Left Their Mark**
Daily Telegraph & Morning Post, 4, 7

C686c.11 Nov. 19 **XI / Co-Belligerent Italy Begins to Work Her Passage**
Daily Telegraph & Morning Post, 4, 7

C686c.12 Nov. 20 **XII / A Difference with America: Aegean Prizes Lost**
Daily Telegraph & Morning Post, 4, 6

C686c.13 Nov. 21 **XIII / How Hitler's Secret Weapon Was Blunted by R.A.F.**
Daily Telegraph & Morning Post, 4, 6

The last two articles in the serialization appeared in January 1952.

In the month of November, there was also some question of a serialization of *A Roving Commission* (**A91.2**) by North American Newspaper Alliance Inc., initiated and discussed between John Wheeler of that organization and Whitney Darrow of Scribner's. It led to some very testy correspondence between Charles Scribner himself and C. H. Parsons and G. C. Piper of Odhams Press over the question of which company had the rights to serialize works such as *My Early Life/A Roving*

Commission and derivative works such as 'My Story', which was running in *Illustrated*. The issue ultimately came to nought and this series did not run in any American publication, although Randolph Churchill, who had compiled and edited the series at the request of *Illustrated*, was trying to find a sale for the serialization in the United States. When seeking the permission of *Life*, since a small part of the articles involved the war years, he wrote that "Nearly everything in the series is very old stuff written twenty or thirty years ago."[176]

C688.2	Nov. 24	**MY STORY**
		Illustrated, 16–21, 43, 45

C688.3	Dec. 1	**MY STORY**
		Illustrated, 31–6, 45

C688.4	Dec. 8	**MY STORY**
		Illustrated, 26–30, 32–3

C688.5	Dec. 15	**MY STORY**
		Illustrated, 19, 21–3, 41, 43, 45

C688.6	Dec. 22	**MY STORY**
		Illustrated, 13–17

C688.7	Dec. 29	**MY STORY**
		Illustrated, 17, 20, 22

This article is excerpted from *Painting as a Pastime* (**A242**). Reproductions of Churchill paintings occupy pp. 18–19.

1952

C688.8	Jan. 5	**MY STORY / Winston Churchill in War ... in Peace**
		Illustrated, 24–7

1953

C689a   **THE SECOND WORLD WAR, Volume VI**

The serialization of the sixth and final volume of *The Second World War* by the *Daily Telegraph & Morning Post*. Except for the first issue of the serialization, which does not include the

176. Letter of 22 November 1951 to Daniel Longwell (Sir Winston Churchill Collection, 1908–1954, Daniel Longwell Bequest, Rare Book and Manuscript Library, Columbia University).

part number, each article is preceded by the superhead ' *"The Second World War" (Vol. VI)—[Part No.]*'.

C689a.0   Oct. 22   **SIR WINSTON CHURCHILL'S WAR MEMOIRS**
Daily Telegraph & Morning Post, 1
Churchill's Preface of 30 September 1953 appears as part of the *Daily Telegraph*'s announcement of the publication of the last volume of the war memoirs to begin the following day.

C689a.1   Oct. 23   **D-Day Surprise: We Had Expected to Lose "About 10,000 Men"**
Daily Telegraph & Morning Post, 6

C689a.2   Oct. 24   **From Caen to Paris: Eight Nazi Divisions Trapped in Pocket**
Daily Telegraph & Morning Post, 6

C689a.3   Oct. 26   **How the Flying Bombs Were Mastered**
Daily Telegraph & Morning Post, 6, 9

C689a.4   Oct. 27   **Freak Error Warned Us of V2 Assault**
Daily Telegraph & Morning Post, 6

C689a.5   Oct. 28   **Conflict over Landing in Southern France**
Daily Telegraph & Morning Post, 6, 8

C689a.6   Oct. 29   **Tito on Communism and the Future of Istria**
Daily Telegraph & Morning Post, 6

C689a.7   Oct. 30   **Shorn Forces in Italy Just Not Enough**
Daily Telegraph & Morning Post, 6, 9

C689a.8   Nov. 2   **Vain Appeals to Stalin to Aid Warsaw Rising**
Daily Telegraph & Morning Post, 6, 9

C689a.9   Nov. 3   **Moscow Quest for "Common Mind" about the Balkans**
Daily Telegraph & Morning Post, 6, 9

C689a.10   Nov. 4   **Lublin Poles Seen as "Mere Pawns of Russia"**
Daily Telegraph & Morning Post, 6, 9

C689a.11   Nov. 5   **Talks with de Gaulle and France's Future Role**
Daily Telegraph & Morning Post, 6, 8

C689a.12   Nov. 6   **Civil War in Greece Called for Firm British Action**
Daily Telegraph & Morning Post, 6, 9

C689a.29   Dec. 8   **Firmness with Tito and Washington Reactions**
Daily Telegraph & Morning Post, 6, 8

C689a.30   Dec. 9   **Shock of Truman Plan to See Stalin Alone**
Daily Telegraph & Morning Post, 6, 8

C689a.31   Dec. 10   **Choice of Election Date: A Difficult Decision**
Daily Telegraph & Morning Post, 6, 9

C689a.32   Dec. 11   **Best Chance of Peace Was Lost as Armies Withdrew**
Daily Telegraph & Morning Post, 6, 9

C689a.33   Dec. 14   **First Talk with Mr. Truman: "Why Not Share Bases?"**
Daily Telegraph & Morning Post, 6, 9

C689a.34   Dec. 15   **Use of Atomic Bomb against Japan Was Never in Doubt**
Daily Telegraph & Morning Post, 6, 9

C689a.35   Dec. 16   **Potsdam's Legacy: Plea for Exiled Poles in Britain**
Daily Telegraph & Morning Post, 6, 9

C689a.36   Dec. 17   **Stalin's Excuse for Polish Inroad on East Germany**
Daily Telegraph & Morning Post, 6, 9

C689a.37   Dec. 18   **Parting of the Three: Stalin Told about Atomic Bomb**
Daily Telegraph & Morning Post, 6, 9

C689b   **THE SECOND WORLD WAR / Volume VI— Triumph and Tragedy**
The *New York Times* (illustrated) serialization of Volume VI, the first 11 parts being under the additional subtitle **Book I— The Tide of Victory** and the final 14 under the additional subtitle **Book II—The Iron Curtain**. The serialization was published daily except Sunday, and the series ran from Vol. CIII, No. 34,971 to No. 35,005.

C689b.1   Oct. 23   **Installment 1: / Normandy to Paris**
New York Times, 1, 25

C689b.2   Oct. 24   **Installment 2: / The Pilotless Bombardment**
New York Times, 1, 17

C689b.3   Oct. 26   **Installment 3: / Attack on the South of France?**
New York Times, 1, 23

1954

C689/1   March   **MY SPY STORY**
                          Sea Stories, 46–54

C690   Nov. 28   **IF I HAD A SECOND CHANCE**
                          Observer, 3
                          Excerpted from *Thoughts and Adventures* (**A95**).

—   Nov. 28–   **SAVROLA** (For this serialization in the *Sunday Dispatch*, *see*
           Jan. 30   **C73d**.)

1955

—   July 16   **SAVROLA** (For this serialization in *Star Weekly*, *see* **C73e**.)

C691   November   **"THE CHARTERED SURVEYOR—HIS TRAINING
                          AND HIS WORK"**
                          Chartered Surveyor, 241
                          Includes a 192-word excerpt from the Churchill Foreword.

C691/1   December   **THE MOST FAMOUS GENERAL I HAVE KNOWN**
                          Scouting, 2–3, 22
                          On Lord Baden-Powell.

1956

C692   **A   HISTORY   OF   THE   ENGLISH-SPEAKING
                          PEOPLES**
                          The American magazine *Life* serialized *A History of the English-
                          Speaking Peoples* (**A267**) under the editorial leadership of Jay
                          Gold, its top articles editor, and his assistant Ralph Graves.
                          "Graves made his selections for each installment from the full
                          Churchill manuscripts, had them approved or modified by
                          Gold and then sent the choices to Sir Winston's office in
                          London, along with whatever connective writing was
                          necessary to string the selections together. There were rarely
                          hitches of any kind."[177]

---

177. Wainwright, *op. cit.*, p. 199. On a subject of interest, albeit not bibliographic, to some users of
     this bibliography, Wainwright records, at p. 339, that *Life*'s coverage of the pageantry of
     Churchill's funeral was accomplished "by chartering a jet airliner, outfitting it as a photo lab
     and makeshift city room and flying a working crew of forty direct from London to the plant
     in Chicago even as the story was being developed, printed, laid out and written in the air".

C692a.1   March 19   **THE BIRTH OF BRITAIN**
Life, 75–94, 97–8, 102–3, 106–7

C692a.2   March 26   **THE NORMAN CONQUEST**
Life, 86–100, 103–4, 107–8, 111–12, 115, 118

C692a.3   April 2   **BARONS AGAINST THE KING**
Life, 64–6, 68–73, 77–8, 80, 83–6, 91

C692a.4   April 9   **TRIAL AND TORMENT**
Life, 178–88, 190–2, 194, 199, 203–4, 207–8

C692b.1   April 28   **A HISTORY OF THE ENGLISH-SPEAKING PEOPLES / The Lost Island**
Everybody's, 16–20, 29, 31

C692b.2   May 5   **DESPERATE INHERITANCE**
Everybody's, 16–20, 40

C692b.3   May 12   **WOE TO THE CONQUERED!**
Everybody's, 20–3, 42–4

C692b.4   May 19   **YEARS OF GLORY**
Everybody's, 20–3, 42–4

C692b.5   May 26   **'THE HAMMER OF THE SCOTS'**
Everybody's, 20–2, 42–3

C692b.6   June 2   **THE GLEAMING KING OF AGINCOURT**
Everybody's, 24–6, 38–9

C692b.7   June 9   **THE ADVENTURES OF EDWARD IV**
Everybody's, 28–9, 45–7

C692b.8   June 16   **'USURPER OF THE REALM'**
Everybody's, 26–7, 39–40

C692/1   May 19   **JEANNE D'ARC**
Paris Match, 48, 57–60
The French translation of a section of Part 6 of the *Everybody's* serialization, which was published two weeks before the first English-language appearance of that part.

C693   Sept. 6   **SIR WINSTON CHURCHILL IN HOLLYWOOD FILM / "Prophetic" Foreword on East Africa**
The Times, 5

In researching the film *Something of Value*, the Hollywood studio MGM came across "some prophetic words written by Sir Winston Churchill in 1907". When asked permission to use the words in a prologue, he agreed and also allowed himself to be filmed speaking them. They are published here.

C693/1   Sept. 9   **GIOVANNA D'ARCO**
Epoca, 34, 42–3
The Italian translation of that section of the *History of the English-Speaking Peoples* (**A267**) dealing with Joan of Arc. Not otherwise separately published in Italian.

C694a.1   Oct. 29   **THE NEW WORLD**
Life, 76–93, 95–6, 98, 101, 104, 107

C694a.2   Nov. 5   **DAYS OF GLORY, GOOD QUEEN BESS**
Life, 144–61, 165–6, 168, 170, 172

C694a.3   Nov. 12   **HIGH VENTURE AND CIVIL WAR**
Life, 178–82, 184, 186, 189–93, 195–6, 199–200, 203–4

C694b.1   Nov. 3   **A HISTORY OF THE ENGLISH-SPEAKING PEOPLES, Volume II / King Henry the Eighth**
Everybody's, 16–17, 37

C694b.2   Nov. 10   **THE TRAGEDY OF ANNE BOLEYN**
Everybody's, 20–3

C694b.3   Nov. 17   **QUEEN ELIZABETH THE FIRST**
Everybody's, 24–6

C694b.4   Nov. 24   **'GLORIANA' AND THE SPANISH ARMADA**
Everybody's, 19–21

C694b.5   Dec. 1   **'I AM A MARTYR TO THE PEOPLE'**
Everybody's, 20–1, 42

C694b.6   Dec. 8   **THE MERRY MONARCH**
Everybody's, 20–1, 30–1

1957

C694/1   **MY EARLY LIFE**
The first of a series of 24 articles to appear in nine instalments. Taken from the Odhams *My Early Life* (**A91.9**) and the Scribners *A Roving Commission* (**A91.2**).

C695	April 13	**LENIN: THE MUMMIFIED SYMBOL OF COMMUNISM**

Everybody's, 10–11

This is Churchill's only separate biographical piece on Lenin. Interestingly, spurred by a letter to the Editor in the *Standard*,[178] Curtis Brown had written to Miss Fisher at Chartwell more than a quarter-century before to express his belief that Churchill ought to write a full biography of the Russian leader. "I expect Mr. Churchill saw this in the *Standard*. How I wish he would follow that suggestion and write a Life of Lenin."[179]

C696a.1	April 15	**AMERICA'S WAR OF INDEPENDENCE**

Life, 120–30, 133–4, 137–8, 143–4, 147–8

This is the first article in the serialization of Volume III of *A History of the English-Speaking Peoples (see* **A267.3(III)**).

C696a.2	April 22	**THE NEW NATION**

Life, 84–6, 88–94, 96, 99–100, 104, 107–8, 110, 115

C696a.3	April 29	**FAMOUS MEN IN A CENTURY OF WARS**

Life, 86–8, 90–7, 99–100, 102, 104, 106, 111

C696b.1	Oct. 19	**A HISTORY OF THE ENGLISH–SPEAKING PEOPLES, Volume III / The Great Duke of Marlborough**

Everybody's, 10–11, 28

C696b.2	Oct. 26	**COMING OF THE GEORGES**

Everybody's, 16–17, 30

C696b.3	Nov. 2	**THE AMERICAN WAR OF INDEPENDENCE**

Everybody's, 14–15, 27

C696b.4	Nov. 9	**CLIVE OF INDIA**

Everybody's, 18–19, 31

---

178. The letter, under the heading 'An Opportunity', is but a fragment in the Churchill Archives (CHAR 8/227/20), in which the unknown author writes, "Incidentally, I do not see why great soldiers and great statesmen, who have a gift for writing, should not make the best biographers. Mr. Churchill, for instance, would make a far better biographer than Ludwig. He told me the other night that he had been reading a good deal of Mongol history and had found an interesting parallel between Lenin and Jhengiz Khan, the ruthless Mongol conqueror. I hope one day he will carry it out to its logical conclusion and complete his brilliant portrait of Lenin in his last work by a full life of the Bolshevist leader."

179. Letter of 13 March 1929 (CHAR 8/227/21).

C696b.5   Nov. 16   **NAPOLEON AND NELSON**
Everybody's, 16–17, 30

C696b.6   Nov. 23   **NAPOLEON AND WELLINGTON**
Everybody's, 22–3, 25, 33, 35

1958

C697a.1   Feb. 24   **THE NOBLEST WAR**
Life, 76–84, 86, 89–90, 93–4, 96
This is the first article in the serialization of Volume IV of
A History of the English-Speaking Peoples (*see* **A267.3(IV)**).

C697a.2   March 3   **AN AGE OF UNREST**
Life, 58–60, 62–8, 70, 73–6

C697b.1   March 22   **A HISTORY OF THE ENGLISH-SPEAKING
PEOPLES, Volume IV / Victoria the Great**
Everybody's, 6–8

C697b.2   March 29   **THE MIGRATION OF THE PEOPLES**
Everybody's, 8–10

C697b.3   April 5   **BIRTH OF A CONTINENT**
Everybody's, 16–18

C697b.4   April 12   **"THE NOBLEST OF ALL THE MASS-CONFLICTS"**
Everybody's, 16–18

C697b.5   April 19   **THE DAWN OF THE TWENTIETH CENTURY**
Everybody's, 16–17

C698   **SIR WINSTON WRITES A POSTSCRIPT**
The Epilogue to *The Second World War*. First published in
volume form in the abridged edition (**A240.8**) but separately
published only in Italian (**A269**).

C698a.1   April 21   **I / Soviet Shadow over Europe / Convincing America
of the Danger**
Daily Telegraph, 8, 14

C698a.2   April 22   **II / Design for the Defence of Freedom**
Daily Telegraph, 8

C698a.3   April 23   **III / The H-Bomb and Our Future / "Certain Hopeful
Features": West's Task Is to Reach the Russian Mind**
Daily Telegraph, 8, 16

C698a.4	April 24	**IV / "We Have Not Tried in Vain" / If the Free World Holds Together, Russia Will Find That Peace Offers More Than War** *Daily Telegraph*, 10

C698b	April 29	**THE COLD "PEACE" AND OUR FUTURE** *Look*, Vol 22. No. 9, 21–32 Churchill's text begins on p. 23. Page 26 contains only photographs.

1961

—	March	**"I RIDE MY HOBBY"** (*Cosmopolitan; see* **C305d**)

C699	April	**OVER THE TOP AT OMDURMAN** *Argosy* (US), Vol. 352, No. 4, 22–3, 96–8 Chapter XV of the 1960 Scribner issue of *My Early Life* (**A91.13**), pp. 182–96.

1963

C700	January	**ESCAPE** *Argosy* (UK), 14–31 Chapters XXI and XXII of the Odhams edition of *My Early Life* (**A91.9**), pp. 264–94.

1965

C701	March 8	**CHURCHILL, ON ANCIENT ENGLISH JUSTICE** *Weekly Law Digest*, 10a The cover jacket for Vol. 29, No. 10, of the *Weekly Law Digest*. Not meant to be retained in the loose-leaf binder or bound in at the end of the year with the rest of the *Digest*. Nor is the item included in the *Weekly Law Digest* index. Excerpted from Volume II, Chapter 13, of the Dodd, Mead *A History of the English-Speaking Peoples* (**A267.3(II)**).

C702	March 8	**CHURCHILL, ON THE JURY SYSTEM** *Weekly Law Digest*, 10a The cover jacket for Vol. 29, No. 10, of the *Weekly Law Digest*. Not meant to be retained in the loose-leaf binder or bound in at the end of the year with the rest of the *Digest*. Nor is the item included in the *Weekly Law Digest* index. Excerpted from Volume II, Chapter 13, of the Dodd, Mead *A History of the English-Speaking Peoples* (**A267.3(II)**).

| C703 | March 8 | **CHURCHILL, ON THE ENGLISH COMMON LAW** |

Weekly Law Digest, 10b–d

The cover jacket for Vol. 29, No. 10, of the *Weekly Law Digest*. Not meant to be retained in the loose-leaf binder or bound in at the end of the year with the rest of the *Digest*. Nor is the item included in the *Weekly Law Digest* index. Excerpted from Volume II, Chapter 13, of the Dodd, Mead *A History of the English-Speaking Peoples* (**A267.3(II)**).

| C704 | April 19 | **AMERICAN "RECONSTRUCTION"** |

Weekly Law Digest, 16b–d

The cover jacket for Vol. 29, No. 16, of the *Weekly Law Digest*. Not meant to be retained in the loose-leaf binder or bound in at the end of the year with the rest of the *Digest*. Nor is the item included in the *Weekly Law Digest* index. Excerpted from Volume IV of the Dodd, Mead *A History of the English-Speaking Peoples* (**A267.3(IV)**).

| — | June | **MAN OVERBOARD** (*Argosy* (UK); *see* **C72b**) |

1966

| C705 | Jan. 30 | **THE DREAM / His Last Story—Locked away in a Box for Years—Now Published for the First Time.** |

Sunday Telegraph, 4–5

Subsequently collected in *Collected Essays*, Volume IV, pp. 504–11, and published separately for the first time in 1988 by the Churchill Literary Foundation (**A288**). A promotional postcard was sent to potential readers on 28 January, announcing that a "so far unpublished story written by Sir Winston Churchill entitled 'The Dream' has been acquired by the Sunday Telegraph and will appear exclusively this Sunday (January 30)".

1969

| C706 | February | **KING HENRY VIII** |

Mankind, Vol. 1, No. 11, 10–17, 70–1

Reprinted from the chapter on Henry VIII in *Heroes of History* (**A278**), at pp. 74–89.

1971

| — | Fall | **THE U-BOAT MENACE** (*Liberty, the Nostalgia Magazine*; *see* **C535.3c**) |

1972

| — | Spring | **PAINTING AS A PASTIME** (*Saturday Evening Post*; *see* **C267d**) |

1977

| — | July/
August | **DEALING IN FUTURES** (*Saturday Evening Post*; *see* **C335b**) |

1980

| — | Spring | **ZIONISM VERSUS BOLSHEVISM** (*Conspiracy Digest*; *see* **C258b**) |

SECTION D

Reports of Speeches in Books, Pamphlets and Leaflets

This section contains titles in which speeches by Churchill appear in a book, pamphlet or leaflet written, compiled or edited by someone else, together with sufficient other material that the work may reasonably be said not to be wholly or substantially by Churchill. The titles are arranged chronologically. Items including speeches previously unpublished in volume form are so identified; references to previous appearances in periodical, volume, pamphlet or leaflet form are provided. All British, American, Canadian and Australian editions, issues and states are described and subsequent printings are noted.

SECTION D

Reports of speeches to Books, Pamphlets and Leaflets.

D1 YEAR BOOK OF THE PENNSYLVANIA SOCIETY OF NEW YORK — 1901

Year Book | of | The Pennsylvania Society | of New York | [device of the Society, 29 × 40.8 mm] | New York | 1901

PUBLICATION: New York: Pennsylvania Society of New York, 1901.

PAGINATION: [2], 70, 1 leaf of plates.

CONTRIBUTION: Speech at the dinner of 12 December 1900: pp. 37–9.

LOCATIONS: RIC, USDLC, USMH

D1/1 TORY M.P.'S ON MR. BRODRICK'S ARMY CORPS SCHEME — 1903

[Dropped-head title only:] TORY M.P.'S | ON | MR. BRODRICK'S | ARMY CORPS SCHEME. | [39-mm rule]

PUBLICATION: London: Liberal Publication Department, 1903.

PAGINATION: 4. Leaflet, folded. This is Liberal Leaflet No. 1923. Copies were sold at 4s. 6d. per 1000.

CONTRIBUTION: Two separate excerpts from speech of 24 February 1903: pp. 3–4. The full text of the address was subsequently collected in Rhodes James, Vol. I, at pp. 164–75, under the title 'Army Organisation'; and the excerpts appear on pp. 167 and 173.

LOCATIONS: CaOOP, MLW

D2 PROCEEDINGS OF THE FIFTY-EIGHTH FESTIVAL OF THE ROYAL GENERAL THEATRICAL FUND — 1903

[Royal arms, 10.6 × 19.2 mm] | PROCEEDINGS | OF THE | Fifty-Eighth Festival | OF THE | ROYAL | General Theatrical Fund | HELD AT THE | Whitehall Rooms, Hôtel Métropole, | 𝕺𝖓 𝕿𝖍𝖚𝖗𝖘𝖉𝖆𝖞, 21st 𝕸𝖆𝖞, 1903. | [50.7-mm wavy rule] | Mr. J. FORBES=ROBERTSON, | IN THE CHAIR. | [50.7-mm wavy rule] | 𝕷𝖔𝖓𝖉𝖔𝖓: | Printed by G. HARMSWORTH & Co., Floral Street, Covent Garden. | [5.4-mm rule] | 1903.

PUBLICATION: London: Harmsworth, 1903.

PAGINATION: 32.

CONTRIBUTION: The Chairman toasted the King and other members of the Royal Family. Churchill then proposed 'The Drama': pp. 14–16. This is the only published appearance of this address.

LOCATION: RIC

REFERENCE: Woods D(b)22.

D3   PREFERENTIAL TARIFFS   1903

D3.1.a   First edition, first printing (1903)

[Cover title:] [above a thick–thin rule box, enclosing 187.5 × 114.1 mm] "LIBERAL MAGAZINE" EXTRA No. 3. | [within the thick–thin rule box] PREFERENTIAL TARIFFS. | [37.5-mm double rule] | FACTS, FIGURES, AND ARGUMENTS. | [29-mm double rule] | "To rob the public, it is necessary to deceive them. To | deceive them, it is necessary to persuade them that they are | robbed for their own advantage." – (BASTIAT.) | [29-mm double rule] | PUBLISHED BY | THE LIBERAL PUBLI-CATION DEPARTMENT | (*In connection with the National Liberal Federation* | *and the Liberal Central Association*), | 42, PARLIAMENT STREET, LONDON, S.W. | [3-mm rule] | 1903 | [below the thick–thin rule box] PRICE TWOPENCE.

PUBLICATION: London: Liberal Publication Department, 1903.

PAGINATION: 40. Pamphlet in self-wrappers.

CONTRIBUTION: Under the heading 'IV—UNIONISTS ON PREFERENTIAL TARIFFS', an extract from Churchill's 28 May 1903 speech in the House: p. 24. The full text of the speech was subsequently collected in Rhodes James, Vol. I, at pp. 191–2; the excerpt is taken from p. 192.

NOTE: When included in the volume *Pamphlets and Leaflets for 1903*[1] or disbound therefrom, the pamphlet will be stamped '4'; it bears no Liberal Publication number.

LOCATION: MLW

D3.1.c   First edition, third printing (1903)

As the first printing except for slight modifications on the title page, which now reads:

[Cover title:] [above a thick–thin rule box, enclosing 187.5 × 114.1 mm] "LIBERAL MAGAZINE" EXTRA No. 3. *Third Edition.* | [within the thick–thin rule box] PREFERENTIAL TARIFFS. | [37.5-mm double rule] | FACTS, FIGURES, AND ARGUMENTS. | [29-mm double rule] | "To rob the public, it is necessary to deceive them. To | deceive them, it is necessary to persuade them that they are | robbed for their own advantage." – (BASTIAT.) | [29-mm double rule] | PUBLISHED BY | THE LIBERAL PUBLICATION DEPARTMENT | (*In connection with the National Liberal Federation* | *and the Liberal Central Association*), | 42, PARLIAMENT STREET, LONDON, S.W. | [3-mm rule] | 1903 | [below the thick–thin rule box] PRICE TWOPENCE. | (For prices of quantities see page 40.)

LOCATION: CaOOP

D4   EIGHT YEARS OF TORY GOVERNMENT   1903

EIGHT YEARS | OF | TORY GOVERNMENT. | 1895—1903. | HOME AFFAIRS. | [46.8-mm rule] | A HANDBOOK | FOR THE | USE OF LIBERALS. | [21.3-mm rule] | "*In spite of the changes which have taken place, in spite of the great loss* | *we have sustained in the withdrawal of Lord Salisbury's riper experience from* | *our Councils, it is still the same party*

---

1. London: Liberal Publication Department, 1904. These annual collections are nothing more than the various pamphlets and leaflets published in the year bound together. There is no revised or additional sequential page numbering associated with the volume.

and the same Government which is in | *power.*"—Mr. AUSTEN CHAMBERLAIN *at Birmingham, January 6ᵗʰ, 1903.* | [13.4-mm rule] | *"Promising is the very air o' the time . . . To promise is most courtly and* | *fashionable : performance is a kind of will or testament which argues a great* | *sickness in his judgement that makes it.*"—TIMON OF ATHENS. | 1903. | THE LIBERAL PUBLICATION DEPARTMENT | 41 & 42, PARLIAMENT STREET, | LONDON, S.W.

PUBLICATION: London: Liberal Publication Department, September 1903. Price 3*s*.

PAGINATION: xii, 244.

CONTRIBUTIONS: Excerpts from Churchill's speeches on the Army Corps Scheme of 12 February 1903 at Wallsend, and 13 May 1901 and 24 February 1903 in the House of Commons: pp. 92–4.

NOTE: A supplement to this volume, entitled *The Ninth Year of Tory Government*, was published in 1904 (**D7**).

LOCATION: RIC

D5   THE FREE TRADE MEETING AT BIRMINGHAM 1903

PUBLICATION: London: Unionist Free Food League, 1903.

I have been unable to locate a copy of the pamphlet.

CONTRIBUTION: Speeches delivered by Mr Winston Churchill, M.P., and Lord Hugh Cecil, M.P., on 11 November 1903 at the Town Hall in Birmingham. Churchill's address was subsequently collected in Rhodes James, Vol. I, at pp. 220–4, under the title 'Free Speech and Free Trade'.

REFERENCE: Woods D(b)23.

D6   PROCEEDINGS IN CONNECTION WITH THE TWENTY-SIXTH ANNUAL MEETING OF THE FEDERATION   1904

NATIONAL LIBERAL FEDERATION. | [23.4-mm French rule] | PROCEEDINGS | IN CONNECTION WITH THE | TWENTY-SIXTH ANNUAL MEETING | OF THE FEDERATION, | HELD IN MANCHESTER, | MAY 12th, 13th, and 14th, 1904, | WITH | *The Annual Report and the Speeches,* | INCLUDING THOSE DELIVERED BY | THE RIGHT HON. | JOHN MORLEY, M.P. | THE RIGHT HON. | HERBERT J. GLADSTONE, M.P. | AND | MR. WINSTON S. CHURCHILL, M.P. | [32.8-mm double rule] | 1904. | THE LIBERAL PUBLICATION DEPARTMENT, | 42, PARLIAMENT STREET, LONDON, S.W.

PUBLICATION: London: Liberal Publication Department, 1904. Price 6*d*.

PAGINATION: 108, plus paper wrappers.

CONTRIBUTION: Churchill's speech of 13 May 1904 in the Free Trade Hall: pp. 98–101. Subsequently collected in Rhodes James, Vol. I, at pp. 291–4, under the title 'The Policy of Birmingham'. Note, however, that the motion ending the report in Rhodes James begins the report in the *Proceedings*.

NOTE: Most surviving copies of the pamphlet will be found with the number '1' hand-stamped in the upper right-hand corner of the title page, signifying that it has been disbound from the volume of *Pamphlets and Leaflets for 1904.*[2] Furthermore, the pamphlet was originally published in blue fibre-flecked light grey paper wrappers, with a thickness of 0.11 mm, on which the title page is reproduced framed in a thick–thin-rule box, enclosing 184 × 114.2 mm, below which the words 'PRICE SIXPENCE.' appear.

LOCATIONS: CaOOP, FBW, RIC, RPH (in wrappers), USIU, USNhD (in wrappers)

D7   THE NINTH YEAR OF TORY GOVERNMENT   1904

THE NINTH YEAR | OF | TORY GOVERNMENT | (THE SESSION OF 1904) | HOME AFFAIRS. | [47.7-mm rule] | *A Supplement to the Handbook* | "EIGHT YEARS OF TORY GOVERNMENT, | 1895–1903." | [48-mm rule] | 1904. | THE LIBERAL PUBLICATION   DEPARTMENT, | 41   &   42,   PARLIAMENT   STREET, | LONDON, S.W.

PUBLICATION: London: Liberal Publication Department, October 1904. Price 6*d.*

PAGINATION: vi, 74. Pamphlet in grey card wrappers.

CONTRIBUTION: Excerpt of 26 lines from Churchill's speech in the House of Commons on 2 August 1904: p. ii. The isolated text appears as an epigraph, facing the 'EDITOR'S NOTE' on p. iii. The full text of the speech can be found in Rhodes James, Vol. I, at pp. 343–7, under the title ' "A Most Miserable Session" '.

NOTE: Copies which bear a hand-stamped '2' in the upper right-hand corner of the cover title have been disbound from the collected *Pamphlets and Leaflets for 1904.*[3] The handbook, *Eight Years of Tory Government, 1895–1903*, referred to on the title page, is **D4**.

LOCATIONS: CaOOP, MLW (separate), PMW, RIC, RPH

D8   THE ISSUES AT STAKE   1904

[Cover title:] AUTHORISED EDITION. | [all of the following within a single-rule box, enclosing 179 × 111.4 mm] THE ISSUES AT STAKE. | [29.4-mm double rule] | A SPEECH | DELIVERED BY THE | RT. HON. JOHN MORLEY, M.P. | together with a Speech delivered by | MR. WINSTON CHURCHILL, M.P. | *On MAY 13th, 1904,* | AT MANCHESTER. | [38.3-mm double rule] | PUBLISHED BY | THE LIBERAL PUBLICATION DEPARTMENT | (*In connection with the National Liberal Federation | and the Liberal Central Association*), | 42, PARLIAMENT STREET, LONDON, S.W. | [3.5-mm rule] | 1904. | [beneath the single-rule box] PRICE ONE PENNY.

PUBLICATION: London: National Liberal Federation, May? 1904. Price 1*d.*; 1*s.* 9*d.* for 25 copies; 3*s.* for 50 copies; 4*s.* 6*d.* for 100 copies; 10*s.* 6*d.* for 250 copies; and £1. 15*s.* 0*d.* for 1000 copies.

PAGINATION: 20. Pamphlet in self-wrappers.

---

2. London: Liberal Publication Department, 1905.

3. London: Liberal Publication Department, 1905.

CONTRIBUTION: Speech of 13 May 1904: pp. 17–20.

NOTE: Copies of the pamphlet found with the number '10' hand-stamped in the upper right-hand corner of the title page have been disbound from the volume of *Pamphlets and Leaflets for 1904.*[4]

LOCATIONS: CaOOP, FBW, RIC, RPH, UKScNL, USIU

REFERENCE: Woods D(b)25.

D9   IMPROVED TRANSPORT FACILITIES IN NORTHERN NIGERIA   1906

[Ranged upper left] No. 10.—[MAY, 1906.] [*sic*, immediately preceding brackets original] | [centred]   THE | BRITISH   COTTON   GROWING | ASSOCIATION. | [INCORPORATED BY ROYAL CHARTER.] [*sic*, immediately preceding brackets original] | [publisher's device, 35.1 mm in diameter] | IMPROVED TRANSPORT FACILITIES | IN | NORTHERN   NIGERIA. | [23.6-mm   rule] | DEPUTATION | TO   THE | PRIME MINISTER, | *May   17th,   1906.* | [24.1-mm   rule] | THE   BRITISH   COTTON GROWING ASSOCIATION | (INCORPORATED BY ROYAL CHARTER), | 13, ST. ANN STREET, MANCHESTER

PUBLICATION: Manchester: The British Cotton Growing Association, 1906.

PAGINATION: 88. Pamphlet in paper wrappers, 1 map (folding).

CONTRIBUTION: 'RAILWAY AND RIVER DEVELOPMENT IN WEST AFRICA', speech of 5 May 1906 at the banquet of the Liverpool Chamber of Commerce in the Adelphi Hotel: pp. 71–9. Subsequently collected in Rhodes James, Vol. I, at pp. 618–24, under the title 'Development of the Crown Colonies'.

LOCATIONS: SF, USNhD

REFERENCE: Woods D(b)25/5.

D10   YOUR SAFETY *V.* THEIR POCKETS   1906?

[Dropped-head title only] [ranged upper left] L.U.C. – No. 89. | YOUR SAFETY | *v.* | THEIR POCKETS. | [double 42.5-mm rule] | [text]

PUBLICATION: London: McCorquodale & Co. Limited, n.d. [1906?].

CONTRIBUTION: Excerpt from a speech at Manchester of 19 October 1906, the text taken from the *Manchester Guardian.*[5]

LOCATION: MLW

---

4. London: Liberal Publication Department, 1905.

5. The speech does not appear to have been collected in Rhodes James, although two speeches of 18 October 1906 are found in Vol. I, at pp. 681–3.

D11   NATIONAL DEMONSTRATION IN FAVOUR OF LAND AND HOUSING REFORM   1907

[Cover title:] AUTHORISED EDITION. | [all of the following within a thick–thin rule box, enclosing 185.8 × 115.7 mm] | NATIONAL DEMONSTRATION | IN FAVOUR OF | LAND & HOUSING REFORM | Held in LONDON, | On APRIL 20th, 1907. | [double 37.7-mm rule] | REPORT OF SPEECHES | BY | The Rt. Hon. Sir Henry Campbell-Bannerman, | G.C.B., M.P. | (Prime Minister); | The Rt. Hon. The Earl Carrington, K.G., | (President of the Board of Agriculture); | AND | The Rt. Hon. Winston Churchill, M.P., | (Under-Secretary for the Colonies). | [double 38.5-mm rule] | 1907. [3.1-mm rule] | THE LIBERAL PUBLICATION DEPARTMENT | (*In connection with the National Liberal Federation and the* | *Liberal Central Association*), | 42, PARLIAMENT STREET, | LONDON, S.W. | [below the thick–thin rule box] PRICE ONE PENNY.

PUBLICATION: London: Liberal Publication Department, 1907. Price 1*d*.

PAGINATION: 20. Pamphlet in self-wrappers.

CONTRIBUTION: 'Speech by Mr. Churchill', address of 20 April 1907: pp. 12–19. Subsequently collected in Rhodes James, Vol. I, at pp. 779–82, under the title 'Land Reform'.

NOTE: Copies which bear a hand-stamped '7' in the upper right-hand corner of the cover title have been disbound from the collected *Pamphlets and Leaflets for 1907*.[6]

LOCATIONS: FBW, RIC, RPH, USNhD, USNNC

REFERENCE: Woods A10.

D12   THE GREAT PREFERENCE DEBATE AT THE IMPERIAL CONFERENCE   1907

D12.1.a   First edition, first printing (1907)

[Ranged left] THE GREAT | PREFERENCE | DEBATE | [centred] AT THE COLONIAL CONFERENCE, 1907. | [32-mm rule] | Reprinted from the Blue Book (Cd. 3523), containing the | Minutes of the Proceedings of that historic gathering, and | comprising over 200 of its pages, with the speeches of | the Premiers and His Majesty's Ministers, and the many | interruptions for discussion, all amply reported | [32-mm rule] | Published at the offices of THE PLANET, | 22, Henrietta Street, Covent Garden, W.C [*sic*, no point]

PUBLICATION: London: The Planet, August 1907. Price 6*d*.

PAGINATION: 194, plus moderate orange paper wrappers.

CONTRIBUTION: Churchill's speech "as a representative of the Colonial Office" on 7 May, the fifth day of the Conference: pp. 165–73. Subsequently collected in Rhodes James, Vol. I, at pp. 788–9, under the title 'Imperial Preference'.

LOCATION: RIC

REFERENCE: Woods D(b)25/2.

---

6. London: Liberal Publication Department, 1908.

D12.1.b   First edition, second printing (1907?)

There is also a self-described second "edition", in which I have detected no differences from the first except that: 1) the volume is bound in moderate red paper wrappers, with a thickness of 0.20 mm; and 2) the words 'Second Edition.]' are included on the front wrapper.

LOCATIONS: CaOONL, RIC

D12.1.c   First edition, third printing (1907?)

As the second "edition" except that the words 'THIRD EDITION.' replace 'Second Edition.]' on the front wrapper.

LOCATION: USMoFuWc

D13   PEERS OR PEOPLE?   1907

PEERS OR PEOPLE? | THE HOUSE OF LORDS WEIGHED IN THE | BALANCES AND FOUND WANTING | AN APPEAL TO HISTORY | BY | WILLIAM T. STEAD | "Now a little before it was day, good Christian as one half amazed | brake out in this passionate speech : What a fool, quoth he, am I, thus | to be in a stinking dungeon, when I may walk as well at liberty! | I have a key in my bosom, that will, I am persuaded, open any lock | in Doubting Castle. Then said Hopeful, That is good news, good | brother, pluck it out of thy bosom and try."—BUNYAN'S "Pilgrim's | Progress." | LONDON | T. FISHER UNWIN | ADELPHI TERRACE | 1907

PUBLICATION: London: T. Fisher Unwin, January 1907. Price 3*s.* 6*d.* or 2*s.* 6*d.* net.

PAGINATION: [4], viii, 264, plus paper wrappers.[7]

CONTRIBUTION: Excerpt from address of 17 December 1906: p. 18. This is the first published appearance of any excerpt of this address. The entire speech was subsequently collected in *Liberalism and the Social Problem* (**A29**), at pp. 45–66, and in Rhodes James, Vol. I, at pp. 703–7, under the title 'Transvaal and Orange River Colonies Constitutions'.

LOCATIONS: CaOONL, CaOTTC, UKScNL

D14   THE COBDEN CLUB DINNER HELD AT THE HÔTEL MÉTROPOLE ON THE 4TH JULY, 1907   1907

THE | COBDEN CLUB | DINNER | HELD AT | THE HÔTEL MÉTROPOLE | ON THE 4th JULY, 1907 | THE RIGHT HON. LORD WELBY, G.C.B. | IN THE CHAIR | *REPORTS OF SPEECHES* | [publisher's device, 24.4 mm in diameter] | CAXTON HOUSE, WESTMINSTER | LONDON, S.W. | 1907

PUBLICATION: London: Cobden Club, 1907.

PAGINATION: 38, [2]. Pamphlet in paper wrappers.

---

7. This information is provided with trepidation since the copy held by Library and Archives Canada was damaged and *may* not have been complete, and that held by the National Library of Scotland was rebound.

CONTRIBUTION: Speech of 4 July 1907: pp. 6–19. Subsequently collected in Rhodes James, Vol. I, at pp. 788–9, under the title 'Free Trade'.

LOCATIONS: CaOKQ, USDLC

REFERENCE: Woods D(b)25/3.

D15 PROCEEDINGS OF THE ROYAL COLONIAL INSTITUTE 1908

PROCEEDINGS | OF THE | ROYAL COLONIAL INSTITUTE | EDITED BY THE SECRETARY | [59-mm rule] | VOLUME XXXIX | 1907–1908 | [59-mm rule] | *All Rights Reserved* | 𝔓𝔲𝔟𝔩𝔦𝔰𝔥𝔢𝔡 𝔟𝔶 | THE INSTITUTE, NORTHUMBERLAND AVENUE, LONDON, W.C. | [3-mm rule] | Telegraphic Address: "RECITAL, LONDON" | Telephone No. 5537, "GERARD"

PUBLICATION: London: Royal Colonial Institute, 1908.

PAGINATION: xii, 492, 1 leaf of plates.

CONTRIBUTIONS: Churchill, chairing the Fifth Ordinary General Meeting of the Session on Tuesday, 10 March 1908, made a brief statement about a resolution passed by the Council of the Institute regarding the death of Lord Linlithgow: p. 197. He then introduced Archibald R. Colquhoun, whose address was entitled 'On Our East African Empire'. Churchill's reply appears on pp. 211–18. First published in the *Journal of the Royal Colonial Institute* (**E9**) and subsequently collected in Rhodes James, Vol. I, at pp. 907–8, under the title 'East African Development'.

LOCATIONS: CaOONL, RIC

REFERENCE: Woods D(b)25/4.

D16 REPORT OF THE PROCEEDINGS OF THE INTERNATIONAL FREE TRADE CONGRESS 1908

[Ranged left] REPORT OF THE | PROCEEDINGS OF | THE INTERNATIONAL | FREE TRADE CONGRESS | [centred] LONDON, AUGUST, 1908 | [ranged right] Chairman | THE RIGHT HON. LORD WELBY, G.C.B. | Treasurer | RUSSELL REA, ESQ., M.P. | Secretary | J. A. MURRAY MACDONALD, ESQ., M.P. | [ranged left, device of the Cobden Club] | CAXTON HOUSE, | WESTMINSTER, S.W.

PUBLICATION: London: The Cobden Club, October 1908. Price 5*s*.

PAGINATION: xx, 652.

CONTRIBUTION: Speech entitled 'Free Trade in Its Bearing on International Relations', delivered on 4 August, the opening day of the Congress: pp. 1–9. For the first publication of the speech in separate form, see **A26**. Subsequently collected in Rhodes James, Vol. II, at pp. 1078–82, under the title 'Free Trade'.

LOCATIONS: CaOTTC, RIC, USIU

REFERENCE: Woods D(b)26.

D17   THE SHORTHAND GAZETTE   1908

Volume II

[All of the following within a single-rule box, with decorative corners, the whole enclosing 199 × 114.7 mm; ranged left] The | [centred] Shorthand Gazette. | [fancy 13.1-mm decorative rule] | LITHOGRAPHED IN | PITMAN'S SYSTEM OF SHORTHAND | [fancy 13.1-mm decorative rule] | EDITED BY | A. BENJAMIN, F.I.P.S. (Hon.), and E. PIKE, F.I.P.S. (Hon.) | [13.1-mm decorative rule] | VOLUME II. | OCTOBER 1907—SEPTEMBER 1908. | [13.1-mm decorative rule] | London: | SIR ISAAC PITMAN & SONS, LTD., 1 AMEN CORNER, E.C.

PUBLICATION: London: Isaac Pitman, 1908.

PAGINATION: [4], 200.

CONTRIBUTION: Under the heading 'Gems of Oratory. | Mr. Winston Churchill's Tirade against Socialism.', there is an unidentified address in shorthand: pp. 166–9. It is, in fact, an excerpt from 'Liberalism and Socialism', the speech of 4 May 1908 at Kinnaird Hall, Dundee, which begins "There are a great many Socialists whose opinions and whose views I have the greatest respect for" and ends "No man can be either a collectivist or an individualist. He must be both; everybody must be both a collectivist and an individualist. For certain of our affairs we must have our arrangements in common. Others we must have sacredly individual and to ourselves."[8] First published in Pitman shorthand in the *Shorthand Gazette* (**E8**). The entire speech was subsequently collected in Rhodes James, Vol. I, pp. 1025–35, under the title 'Liberalism and Socialism', and the excerpt runs from p. 1028.15 to p. 1029.36.

LOCATIONS: RIC, UKBL

D18   A PARLIAMENT OF THE PRESS   1909

A PARLIAMENT | OF | THE PRESS: | THE FIRST | Imperial Press Conference. | *Written and Compiled* | *by* | THOS. H. HARDMAN. | *With Preface by the Rt. Hon.* | THE EARL OF ROSEBERY, K.G. | *ILLUSTRATED.* | LONDON: | HORACE MARSHALL & SON. | 1909.

PUBLICATION: London: Horace Marshall, July 1909. Price 2s. 6d.

PAGINATION: xii, 248, 23 leaves of plates, 2 maps.

CONTRIBUTION: Speech, delivered on 10 June 1909, the fourth day of the conference: pp. 194–6. Subsequently collected in Rhodes James, Vol. II, at pp. 1261–3, under the title 'English and the Empire'.

LOCATIONS: CaOONL, CaOTTC, RIC

REFERENCE: Woods D(b)27/1.

---

8. For the transcription of this Pitman shorthand, without which I would have been unable to identify the address, I am indebted to Audrey Elmes.

D19   PEERS OR PEOPLE?   1909?

PEERS OR PEOPLE ? | [triple 116.5-mm rule with decoration beneath the bottom rule] | A Record of Wrong. | BY HECTOR MACPHERSON. | [lily-in-the-water decorative device, 10.5 × 27.1 mm] | Peers and the Budget. | By "Constitutionalist." | [lily-in-the-water decorative device, 10.5 × 27.1 mm] | [57.2-mm decorative rule] | Dundee and London: John Leng & Co., Ltd.

PUBLICATION: Dundee: John Leng, 1909?

PAGINATION: 40. Pamphlet in self-wrappers.

CONTRIBUTION: Excerpt from speech of 13 November 1909 at Bristol under the title: 'REVOLUTION OF THE RICH' | 40.5-mm decorative rule | 'MR. CHURCHILL'S WEIGHTY WORDS.': pp. 18–19. The full text of the speech was subsequently collected in Rhodes James, Vol. II, at pp. 1346–55, under the title 'The Budget'; this excerpt appears at p. 1353.

LOCATIONS: MLW, UKChT, UKScNL

D20   INTERNATIONAL ASSOCIATION FOR LABOUR LEGISLATION. SPEECHES BY THE RT. HON. WINSTON CHURCHILL, THE EARL OF LYTTON, MR ARTHUR HENDERSON   1910

[Cover title, printed very deep red on light olive grey paper wrappers:] [ranged upper right] *PRICE FOURPENCE* | [all of the following within a thick–thin rule box, enclosing 88.6 × 96.8 mm; centred] *INTERNATIONAL* | *ASSOCIATION* FOR | LABOUR | LEGISLATION | [three acorn devices] | SPEECHES BY THE Rt. | Hon. WINSTON CHURCHILL | THE EARL OF LYTTON | Mr. ARTHUR HENDERSON | [below the box and ranged lower left] GARDEN CITY PRESS LTD | LETCHWORTH ; AND | 6, YORK BUILDINGS | ADELPHI, LONDON

PUBLICATION: Letchworth and London: Garden City Press, 1910.

PAGINATION: 24. Pamphlet in paper wrappers; thickness: 0.21 mm.

CONTRIBUTION: Speech of 13 April 1910 at the meeting of the British Section of the International Association for Labour Legislation, held at the Caxton Hall, Westminster: pp. 3–11. Subsequently collected in Rhodes James, Vol. II, at pp. 1549–51, under the title 'Labour Legislation'.

NOTE: In addition to the speeches noted on the title page, one was given by Stephen Bauer, General Secretary of the International Association.

LOCATIONS: NeRoEU, USNNC

D21   CROWNED MASTERPIECES OF ELOQUENCE   1910

D21.1.a   First edition containing the Churchill address (1910)

[All of the following within a single-rule box, enclosing 170.3 × 109.3 mm; three vivid orange single-rule boxes, respectively enclosing 52.5 × 103.4 mm, 78.1 × 103.4 mm, and 33.4 × 103.4 mm; within the first interior box, black] *Victoria Edition* | [vivid orange] 𝕮𝖗𝖔𝖜𝖓𝖊𝖉 𝕸𝖆𝖘𝖙𝖊𝖗𝖕𝖎𝖊𝖈𝖊𝖘 | [black] OF | [vivid orange] 𝕰𝖑𝖔𝖖𝖚𝖊𝖓𝖈𝖊 | [black] REPRESENTING THE ADVANCE OF CIVILIZATION | [within the second interior box, black, a double-rule box, the bottom double rule of which is divided at the centre by a decorative device, within which] As Collected in | [vivid orange] 𝕿𝖍𝖊 𝖂𝖔𝖗𝖑𝖉'𝖘 𝕭𝖊𝖘𝖙 𝕺𝖗𝖆𝖙𝖎𝖔𝖓𝖘 | [black] From the Earliest Period | to the Present Time | [vivid orange, decorative device] | [black] DAVID J. BREWER | Justice, United States Supreme Court | Editor | With Special Introductions by | Rt. Hon. AUGUSTINE BIRRELL, M.P., K.C. | SIR GILBERT PARKER, Kt., D.C.L., M.P. | [within the third interior box] NOTTINGHAM NEW YORK TORONTO | [vivid orange] 𝕴𝖓𝖙𝖊𝖗𝖓𝖆𝖙𝖎𝖔𝖓𝖆𝖑 𝖀𝖓𝖎𝖛𝖊𝖗𝖘𝖎𝖙𝖞 𝖘𝖔𝖈𝖎𝖊𝖙𝖞 | [black] 1910 | [below the last interior box] J. B. LYON CO., PRINTERS, ALBANY, N.Y., U.S.A.

PUBLICATION: Nottingham: International University Society, 1910.

PAGINATION: [2], viii, [2], 384 [numbered 11–394], [6], 5 leaves of plates, 1 facsimile.

CONTRIBUTION: Excerpt from speech of 6 December 1909 at the Free Trade Hall, Manchester: pp. 325–9 of Volume III, under the title 'Free Trade and the "Unearned Increment"'. The full text of the speech was subsequently collected in Rhodes James, Vol. II, at pp. 1378–90, under the title ' "Union among Progressive Forces" '.

NOTE 1: There is an introduction of Churchill at pp. 324–5.

NOTE 2: There should be descriptive tissues over all the plates and the facsimile.

NOTE 3: The printer's imprint on p. 394 of the volume indicates that the printing of the set examined by me was done by J. B. Lyon Company, Albany, New York.

NOTE 4: The copy I examined was bound in half-calf, with top edge gilt, and the fore and bottom edges were untrimmed.

LOCATION: CaMWU

D21.1.b   Second? edition containing the Churchill address (1912)

[All of the following within a single-rule box, enclosing 170.3 × 109.3 mm; three vivid orange single-rule boxes, respectively enclosing 52.5 × 103.4 mm, 78.1 × 103.4 mm, and 33.4 × 103.4 mm; within the first interior box, black] *Victoria Edition* | [vivid orange] 𝕮𝖗𝖔𝖜𝖓𝖊𝖉 𝕸𝖆𝖘𝖙𝖊𝖗𝖕𝖎𝖊𝖈𝖊𝖘 | [black] OF | [vivid orange] 𝕰𝖑𝖔𝖖𝖚𝖊𝖓𝖈𝖊 | [black] REPRESENTING THE ADVANCE OF CIVILIZATION | [within the second interior box, black, a double-rule box, the bottom double rule of which is divided at the centre by a decorative device, within which] As Collected in | [vivid orange] 𝕿𝖍𝖊 𝖂𝖔𝖗𝖑𝖉'𝖘 𝕭𝖊𝖘𝖙 𝕺𝖗𝖆𝖙𝖎𝖔𝖓𝖘 | [black] From the Earliest Period | to the Present Time | [vivid orange, decorative device] | [black] | With Special Introductions by | Rt. Hon. AUGUSTINE BIRRELL, M.P., K.C. | SIR GILBERT PARKER, Kt., D.C.L., M.P. | [within the third interior box] LONDON GLASGOW NOTTINGHAM | [vivid orange] 𝕴𝖓𝖙𝖊𝖗𝖓𝖆𝖙𝖎𝖔𝖓𝖆𝖑 𝖀𝖓𝖎𝖛𝖊𝖗𝖘𝖎𝖙𝖞 𝖘𝖔𝖈𝖎𝖊𝖙𝖞 | [black] 1912 | [below the last interior box] J. B. LYON CO., PRINTERS, ALBANY, N.Y., U.S.A.

PUBLICATION: London: International University Society, 1912.

PAGINATION: [2], viii, [2], 384 [numbered 11–394], [6], 5 leaves of plates, 1 facsimile.

CONTRIBUTION: As per the first edition.

NOTE 1: In the copy examined, there was no printer's imprint on p. 394.

NOTE 2: The copy examined was bound in the style of the first edition examined, except in cloth, with the top edge gilt and all edges trimmed.

LOCATIONS: CaACU, CaOONL

D22   HOME RULE FROM THE TREASURY BENCH   1912

HOME RULE FROM THE | TREASURY BENCH | SPEECHES DURING THE FIRST AND | SECOND READING DEBATES | WITH AN INTRODUCTION BY | THE RIGHT HON. H. H. ASQUITH, M.P. | T. FISHER UNWIN | LONDON: ADELPHI TERRACE | LEIPSIC: INSELSTRASSE 20 | 1912

PUBLICATION: London: T. Fisher Unwin, October 1912. Price 7s. 6d.

PAGINATION: 320, [4], 8 leaves of plates.

CONTRIBUTION: Address of 30 April 1912 on Second Reading of the Home Rule Bill: pp. 107–41. A photograph of Churchill with facsimile signature faces p. 107. Subsequently collected in Rhodes James, Vol. II, at pp. 1947–61, under the title 'Government of Ireland Bill'.

LOCATIONS: CaOONL, CaOTTC, RIC

REFERENCE: Woods D(b)29.

D23   A GUIDE TO LUGANDA PROSE COMPOSITION 1912

A GUIDE TO | LUGANDA PROSE COMPOSITION | [32-mm decorative rule] | PREPARED BY | THE REV. F. ROWLING, M.A., | C.M.S. UGANDA | [32-mm decorative rule] | LONDON | SOCIETY FOR PROMOTING CHRISTIAN KNOWLEDGE | NORTHUMBERLAND AVENUE, W.C. | 1912

PUBLICATION: London: Society for Promoting Christian Knowledge, 1912.

PAGINATION: [8], 148.

CONTRIBUTION: Extract from address of 20 November 1907 in Kampala: pp. 105–6, with the translation into Lugandan below each line of English text. This is the only volume appearance of the speech.

LOCATIONS: MLW, UKScNL, USNN

D24   FOREIGN POLICY   1912

[Cover title:] [within a thick–thin rule box, enclosing 180.8 × 115.1 mm] FOREIGN POLICY | *A Series of Extracts from* | *Ministerial Speeches and Declarations* | *on Foreign Affairs.* | [within a single-rule box, 60.3 × 82.6 mm] 1.–GENERAL. | 2.–ARBITRATION. | 3.–PERSIA AND THE ANGLO-RUSSIAN | AGREEMENT. | 4.–SECRECY. | 5.–PUTUMAYO. | 6.–CHINA LOAN. | 7.–RIGHT OF CAPTURE OF PRIVATE | PROPERTY AT SEA. | [below the single-rule box] PUBLISHED BY | THE LIBERAL PUBLICATION DEPARTMENT | (*In connection with the National Liberal Federation* | *and the Liberal Central Association*). | 42 PARLIAMENT STREET, LONDON, S.W. | 1912. | [below the thick–thin rule box] PRICE ONE PENNY.

PUBLICATION: London: Liberal Publication Department, 1912.

PAGINATION: 24. Pamphlet in self-wrappers.

CONTRIBUTION: Sheffield speech of 30 October 1912: pp. 9–11. Subsequently collected in Rhodes James, Vol. II, at pp. 2029–31, under the title 'Balkan Situation and Defence Preparedness'.

NOTE: Copies bearing a hand-stamped '10' in the upper right-hand corner of the cover title are a part of, or have been disbound from, the volume *Pamphlets and Leaflets for 1912*.[9]

LOCATIONS: MLW, RIC, USNhD

REFERENCE: Woods D(b)30.

D25   THE BOOK OF PUBLIC SPEAKING   1912?

D25.1   First? edition (1912?)

The set is complete in four volumes. There are Churchill speeches only in Volumes II and III of this edition.

Volume II

THE BOOK OF | PUBLIC SPEAKING | EDITED BY | ARTHUR CHARLES FOX-DAVIES | OF LINCOLN'S INN, BARRISTER-AT-LAW | VOLUME II | LONDON | CAXTON PUBLISHING COMPANY, LIMITED | CLUN HOUSE | SURREY STREET, W.C.

PUBLICATION: London: Caxton, 1912?

PAGINATION: xxviii, 274, [2], 8 leaves of plates.

CONTRIBUTION: 'THE PRESS', speech of 10 June 1909 at the Conference of the Press: pp. 83–5. Previously published in *A Parliament of the Press* (**D18**) and subsequently collected in Rhodes James, Vol. II, at pp. 1261–3, under the title 'English and the Empire'.

NOTE: There is also an address by Lord Randolph Churchill, 'Political Life and Thought in England' (given on 6 June 1885 at a University Carlton Club dinner, in Cambridge), at pp. 277–85 of Volume I.

LOCATION: RIC

Volume III

THE BOOK OF | PUBLIC SPEAKING | EDITED BY | ARTHUR CHARLES FOX-DAVIES | OF LINCOLN'S INN, BARRISTER-AT-LAW | VOLUME III | LONDON | CAXTON PUBLISHING COMPANY, LIMITED | CLUN HOUSE | SURREY STREET, W.C.

PUBLICATION: London: Caxton, 1912?

PAGINATION: xx, 288, 8 leaves of plates.

CONTRIBUTION: 'LIBERALISM *VERSUS* SOCIALISM', speech of 4 May 1908 at Kinnaird Hall, Dundee: pp. 32–40. Previously published separately in *Liberalism and Socialism* (**A24**) and collected in *For Liberalism and Free Trade* (**A25**) and *Liberalism and the Social Problem* (**A29**), and subsequently in Rhodes James, Vol. I, at pp. 1025–35, under the title 'Liberalism and Socialism'.

LOCATION: RIC

---

9. London: Liberal Publication Department, 1913.

D25.2   Second? edition (1913)

The set is complete in five volumes and is characterized by the following principal content distinctions from the first edition: Volume I includes an additional seven speeches (including the one by Churchill); Volume II an additional nine speeches; Volume III drops the speech by W. C. Bryant and adds four speeches; and Volume IV moves the location of the speech by Booker T. Washington and adds three speeches. There are Churchill speeches in Volumes I, II, III and V. The pagination of each of the volumes of this edition differs by the addition of one or more signatures plus plates; however, the Churchill contributions noted under **D25.1** are located in the same places as in the earlier edition. The National Library of Scotland holds two sets which I was unable to examine, the first being in seven volumes and noted in their catalogue as "1913–15" and the other in three volumes, noted as "[1919]".

Volume I

THE BOOK OF | PUBLIC SPEAKING | EDITED BY | ARTHUR CHARLES FOX-DAVIES | OF LINCOLN'S INN, BARRISTER-AT-LAW | VOLUME I | LONDON | CAXTON PUBLISHING COMPANY, LIMITED | CLUN HOUSE | SURREY STREET, W.C. | 1913

PUBLICATION: London: Caxton, April 1913. Price 8*s*. 6*d*.

PAGINATION: [2], xiv, 332, 13 leaves of plates.

CONTRIBUTION: 'WELSH CHARACTERISTICS', speech of 1 March 1911 at a St David's Day dinner, in London: pp. 295–8. Subsequently collected in Rhodes James, Vol. II, at pp. 1718–21, under the title 'The Welsh Character'. (The date of the speech is given there as 11 March 1911.)

NOTE: The name of the printer on the title-page verso of Volume I is incorrectly given as 'AZELL, WATSON AND VINEY, LD.' The printer's imprint is correctly given as Hazell, Watson and Viney on the last page of that volume and correctly on the last page of each of the other volumes in the set (but not at all on the title-page versos in the other volumes).

LOCATIONS: CaMWU, CaOTMCL, CaOTU, RIC, UKBL

Volume II

THE BOOK OF | PUBLIC SPEAKING | EDITED BY | ARTHUR CHARLES FOX-DAVIES | OF LINCOLN'S INN, BARRISTER-AT-LAW | VOLUME II | LONDON | CAXTON PUBLISHING COMPANY, LIMITED | CLUN HOUSE | SURREY STREET, W.C. | 1913

PUBLICATION: London: Caxton, April 1913. Price 8*s*. 6*d*.

PAGINATION: xviii, 322, [2], 13 leaves of plates.

CONTRIBUTION: 'THE PRESS', speech of 10 June 1909 at the Conference of the Press: pp. 83–5.

Volume III

THE BOOK OF | PUBLIC SPEAKING | EDITED BY | ARTHUR CHARLES FOX-DAVIES | OF LINCOLN'S INN, BARRISTER-AT-LAW | VOLUME III |

LONDON | CAXTON PUBLISHING COMPANY, LIMITED | CLUN HOUSE | SURREY STREET, W.C. | 1913

PUBLICATION: London: Caxton, April 1913. Price 8*s*. 6*d*.

PAGINATION: xiv, 322, 13 leaves of plates.

CONTRIBUTION: 'LIBERALISM *VERSUS* SOCIALISM', speech of 4 May 1908 at Kinnaird Hall, Dundee: pp. 32–40.

Volume V

THE BOOK OF | PUBLIC SPEAKING | EDITED BY | ARTHUR CHARLES FOX-DAVIES | OF LINCOLN'S INN, BARRISTER-AT-LAW | VOLUME V | LONDON | CAXTON PUBLISHING COMPANY, LIMITED | CLUN HOUSE | SURREY STREET, W.C. | 1913

PUBLICATION: London: Caxton, April 1913. Price 8*s*. 6*d*.

PAGINATION: [2], 324, 9 leaves of plates.

CONTRIBUTIONS: '"DERRY"', speech of 11 February 1913 at the Hotel Cecil, London: pp. 64–7; 'NAVAL VOLUNTEERS', speech of 14 December 1912 in Commercial Road, Lambeth: pp. 151–2. The speeches of 11 February 1913 and 14 December 1912 are published here for the first time in volume form. They were subsequently collected in Rhodes James, Vol. II, respectively at pp. 2065–7, under the title 'Ulster Problem', and 2039–40, under the title 'Royal Naval Volunteer Reserve'.

D26 THE PRIME MINISTER'S APPEAL TO THE
NATION   1914

[Cover title:] [ranged upper right] No. 5. | [centred, a thick–thin rule box, enclosing 164.9 × 98.4 mm, within which all of the following] *"To a Victorious Conclusion!"* | The Prime Minister's | Appeal to the Nation | Speeches delivered at the | Guildhall, London, on | September 4th, 1914, by | [ranged right] MR. ASQUITH, | MR. BONAR LAW, | MR. BALFOUR and | MR. CHURCHILL. | [centred] 1914. | Parliamentary Recruiting Committee, | 12, Downing Street, London, S.W.

PUBLICATION: London: Parliamentary Recruiting Committee, 1914.

PAGINATION: 15, [1]. Pamphlet in self-wrappers. Wire-stitched.

CONTRIBUTION: Excerpt from Churchill's speech: p. 14. Subsequently collected in Rhodes James, Vol. II, at p. 2328, under the title 'The War'.

NOTE: There were two printings, distinguished by the parliamentary warrant number on p. 15.[10] The first printing of 50,000 copies took place in October 1914 and the second printing of 100,000 copies in November 1914.

LOCATIONS: AuVM, RIC (2nd printing), UKLo, USIU (2nd printing), USNN (2nd printing; microform)

---

10. In first-printing copies, the warrant line reads: '(2204.) Wt. 6999/71. 50,000. 10/14. C.P. Ltd.'

D27   THE WAR: PROSPECT AND RETROSPECT   1914

[Cover title:] [all of the following within a thick–thin rule box, enclosing 200 ×
112.8 mm] THE WAR. | PROSPECT AND RETROSPECT. | [42-mm rule] |
REPORTS OF SPEECHES | DELIVERED BY | The Rt. Hon. WINSTON
CHURCHILL, M.P., | First Lord of the Admiralty | (*House of Commons, 27 November,
1914*) : | Field-Marshal The Rt. Hon. EARL KITCHENER, | Secretary of State for
War | (*House of Lords, 26 November, 1914*) : | AND | The Rt. Hon. DAVID LLOYD
GEORGE, M.P., | Chancellor of the Exchequer | (*House of Commons, 27 November,
1914*).

PUBLICATION: London: Harrison and Sons, April 1915, 1000 copies.

PAGINATION: 24. Pamphlet in self-wrappers.

CONTRIBUTION: Speech of 27 November 1914: pp. 3–11. Subsequently collected in
Rhodes James, Vol. II, at pp. 2342–8, under the title 'The Royal Navy'.

TRANSLATIONS

Danish: *Den store krig*, Copenhagen: Forlagt af V. Pios Boghandel, 1915 (with rights for
the Danish and Norwegian markets), 40 pages in length plus card wrappers; thickness:
0.20 mm.

Dutch: *De Oorlog: hoe wij er voor staan en wat wij deden*, London: Nelson, 1915?

French: *La Guerre actuelle, son passé, son avenir*, London: Harrison, 1915.

German: *Der Krieg ein vor- und Rückblick*, Lausanne: Payot, 1915, 32 pages in length;
London: Harrison, 1915.

Spanish: *La guerra: su perspectiva y retrospeccion*, London: Harrison, 1915.

Swedish: *Storbrittaniens militära och ekonomiska ställning*, Stockholm: Bonnier, 1915, 52
pp. plus wrappers.

LOCATIONS: AuVM (Swedish), BeNL (Dutch; French; German, both Lausanne and
London; Spanish), NeRoEU (Dutch), RIC (German, Lausanne; Swedish), SvNL
(Swedish), UKChT, UKLeU, UKMaU, USNN (microform; German, microform),
ZACtU

REFERENCE: Woods D(b)31.

D28   THE NATIONAL POLICY   1914?

D28.1   First edition, first issue

[Cover title:] [ranged left] No. 6 | [all of the following within a single-rule box, 179.3 ×
105 mm, the words centred between a design consisting of two single-rule boxes ranged
left and right, each 169 × 14.8 mm] [83.2-mm thin–thick rule] | THE NATIONAL |
POLICY | [83.2-mm thin–thick rule] | As set forth by | Mr. Asquith, Sir Edward | Grey,
Mr. Churchill, Mr. | Lloyd George, Mr. Austen | Chamberlain, Mr. Balfour, Mr. Bonar
Law, Mr. Arthur | Henderson, and others. | [12.2-mm single rule] Price One Penny. |
[12.2-mm single rule] | Published by | THE UNION OF DEMOCRATIC
CONTROL | 37, NORFOLK STREET, STRAND, | LONDON, W.C.

PUBLICATION: London: Union of Democratic Control, 1914?

PAGINATION: 16, plus paper wrappers.

CONTRIBUTIONS: Excerpt from speech of 11 September 1914 at the London Opera House: pp. 2–3; excerpt from interview with Signor Calza-Bedolo in the *Giornale d'Italia*: p. 3.

NOTE: The number '16490' is ranged lower right on p. 14; the subscription form at p. 15 includes a list of 20 branches of the organization; and p. 16 is blank.

LOCATIONS: USCSt,[11] PC, UKOxB, USNN

D28.2   First edition, second issue

As the first issue, except that the number ranged lower right on p. 14 is '17796'; the subscription form on p. 15 has the following instruction in the second line: '*Please fill in this and post to address below.*'; and p. 16 provides the names of the members of the General Council and the Executive Committee and lists all of the 50 branches in England, Ireland, Scotland and Wales and the 12 local groups of the London branch.

LOCATION: CaAEU

D29   DEBATES ON NAVAL AFFAIRS   1915

Debates on Naval Affairs. | [two rules, the first 35.5 mm and the second 38.4 mm] | HOUSE OF LORDS | SESSION 1914 | 4 AND 5 GEORGE V. | [*From 10th February to 18th September*, 1914.] [*sic*, immediately preceding brackets original] | COMPRISING EXTRACTS   FROM | THE   PARLIAMENTARY   DEBATES | (*OFFICIAL REPORT*) | OF ALL QUESTIONS, PROCEEDINGS AND DEBATES RELATING | TO NAVAL AFFAIRS | [37.9-mm double rule] | LONDON | PRINTED FOR THE COMPTROLLER OF HIS MAJESTY'S STATIONERY OFFICE | BY | HARRISON AND SONS | ST. MARTIN'S LANE, W.C. | PRINTERS IN ORDINARY TO HIS MAJESTY. | [11-mm rule] | 1915.

PUBLICATION: London: HMSO, 1915.

PAGINATION: [4], 544 [numbered, however, to 1088, using column rather than page numbers, in the style of Hansard], xvi, 44.

CONTRIBUTIONS: As First Lord of the Admiralty, Churchill spoke frequently in the House of Commons. His participations in the debates, which are indexed, are found *passim*.

LOCATION: RIC

D30   THE CONDUCT OF THE WAR BY SEA   1915

[Cover title:] [all of the following within a double-rule box, enclosing 202.8 × 109 mm] THE CONDUCT | OF THE | WAR BY SEA. | [two rules, the first 38.7 mm and the second 27.7 mm] | [small acorn device, 3.4 × 3.4 mm] | LONDON: | DARLING & SON, LIMITED. | [8.2-mm rule] | 1915.

PUBLICATION: London: Ministry of Information, March 1915, 13,000 copies.

PAGINATION: 24. Pamphlet in self-wrappers.

---

11. I have not examined either the New York Public Library or Stanford University copies personally and am unsure whether they are first or second issue.

CONTRIBUTION: Speech of 15 February 1915: pp. 3–12. Subsequently collected in Rhodes James, Vol. III, at pp. 2363–74, under the title 'British Command of the Sea'.

TRANSLATIONS

Dutch: *De Oorlog: de gang van zaken*, London: Nelson, 1915.

French: *La Guerre maritime*, London: Darling, 1915.

German: *Die Kriegführung zur See*, London: Harrison, 1915 (32 pp. pamphlet in self-wrappers).

Spanish: *La guerra en el mar*, Paris: Thomas Nelson, 1915?

LOCATIONS: BeNL (German), NeNL (Dutch), UKIWM (English and German), USMH (English and Spanish)

REFERENCE: Woods D(b)33(a).

D31 GREAT SPEECHES OF THE WAR 1915

D31.1 First edition, only printing (1915)

[All of the following within a single-rule box, enclosing 175 × 110.2 mm; the title only within another single-rule box, enclosing 38.5 × 103.8 mm] GREAT SPEECHES | OF THE WAR | [within another single-rule box, enclosing 89.5 × 103.8 mm, wreathlike device, 20.9 × 16.5 mm] | [within another single-rule box, enclosing 33.9 × 103.8 mm] LONDON | CAXTON PUBLISHING COMPANY, LIMITED | CLUN HOUSE, SURREY STREET, W.C. | 1915

PUBLICATION: London: Caxton Publishing, 1915.

PAGINATION: x, 312, 12 leaves of plates.

CONTRIBUTIONS: Speech of 3 June 1915 at a meeting held in Kinnaird Hall, Dundee: pp. 32–40. Subsequently collected in Rhodes James, Vol. III, at pp. 2378–84, where the date is given as 5 June. Speech of 15 February 1915 in the House of Commons: pp. 104–20. Subsequently collected in Rhodes James, Vol. III, at pp. 2363–74. Speech of 21 September 1914, wrongly dated 21 September 1915, at the Tournament Hall in Liverpool: pp. 216–19. Subsequently collected in Rhodes James, Vol. III, at pp. 2336–40. Speech of 11 September 1914 at the London Opera House: pp. 282–91. Subsequently collected in Rhodes James, Vol. III, at pp. 2328–34, where the speech is indicated as having taken place at the National Liberal Club.

LOCATION: RIC

D31.2 Second edition, only printing (1915)

Distinguished from the first edition on the title page by the removal of the publisher's name from the bottom single-rule box and its replacement by: 'PRINTED BY | HAZELL, WATSON & VINEY, LD. | LONDON AND AYLESBURY | 1915'.

There are other changes as well between the two volumes, the most important being the replacement of the first eleven speeches in the volume, occupying the first 74 pages, by ten addresses. Thus, Churchill's speech of 3 June 1915 at Kinnaird Hall is no longer present in this edition. In addition, the inaccurate date of his Liverpool address at p. 216 is corrected to 1914.

PAGINATION: x, 312, 12 leaves of plates.

LOCATIONS: CaOTTC, RIC, USIU

REFERENCE: Woods D(b)33(b).

D32 WAR SPEECHES BY BRITISH MINISTERS
1914–1916   1917

WAR | SPEECHES | BY | BRITISH | MINISTERS | 1914   —   1916 | T.   FISHER UNWIN, LTD. | 1 ADELPHI TERRACE, LONDON | [3.5-mm rule] | 1917

PUBLICATION: London: T. Fisher Unwin, June 1917. Price 1*s*.

PAGINATION: [*8*], 374, [*2*].

CONTRIBUTIONS: Speech of 27 November 1914 in the House of Commons: pp. 302–10. Speech of 15 February 1915: pp. 311–28. Subsequently collected in Rhodes James, Vol. III, at pp. 2363–74, and previously in *Great Speeches of the War* (**D31**).

LOCATIONS: CaOTTC, MLW, RIC, UKCaU, UKScGlU, USDLC, USIU

REFERENCE: Woods D(b)35/1.

D33 ENGLAND'S WELCOME TO VENIZELOS   1917

[Cover title:] [ranged upper left] No. 35. | [centred] ENGLAND'S WELCOME | TO | VENIZELOS | AT THE MANSION HOUSE | NOVEMBER 16, 1917 : | SPEECHES BY THE RIGHT | HON. A. J. BALFOUR, EARL | CURZON OF KEDLESTON, | —— MR. VENIZELOS, —— | MR. J. GENNADIUS, AND | DR. R. M. BURROWS | LONDON | THE   ANGLO-HELLENIC | LEAGUE | 43 ALDWYCH | 1917

PUBLICATION: London: The Anglo-Hellenic League, March 1918.[12] No. 35 of the League's publications. Price 3*d*.

PAGINATION: 20, 1 leaf of plates. Pamphlet in paper wrappers.

CONTRIBUTION: Speech at the dinner of 16 November 1917 at the Mansion House: pp. 10–12. Subsequently collected in Rhodes James, Vol. III, at p. 2577, under the title 'M. Venizelos, Prime Minister of Greece'.

LOCATIONS: UKBL, USOU

REFERENCE: Woods D(b)35.

D34 SPEECHES AND DOCUMENTS ON BRITISH
COLONIAL POLICY, 1763–1917   1918

Volume II

D34.1.a First edition, first printing (1918)

SELECTED   SPEECHES   AND | DOCUMENTS   ON | BRITISH | COLONIAL POLICY | 1763—1917 | EDITED BY | ARTHUR BERRIEDALE KEITH, | D.C.L., D.LITT. | IN   TWO   VOLUMES | VOL.   II | [25.5 × 18.1 mm] | HUMPHREY

---

12. According to the *English Catalogue of Books*.

MILFORD | OXFORD   UNIVERSITY   PRESS | LONDON   EDINBURGH
GLASGOW | NEW YORK TORONTO MELBOURNE BOMBAY

PUBLICATION: Oxford: Oxford University Press, 1918. The two volumes were reprinted in 1944, 1948 and 1953. In 1961, the two volumes were reprinted in a single volume.

PAGINATION: viii, 424.

CONTRIBUTIONS: Speech of 17 December 1906 in the House of Commons on the Transvaal Constitution: pp. 1–24; speech of 17 March 1914 on the creation of an Imperial Squadron: pp. 343–56. The 1906 speech was subsequently collected in Rhodes James, Vol. I, at pp. 703–7, under the title 'Transvaal and Orange River Colonies Constitutions', and the 1914 speech in Vol. III, at pp. 2262–7, under the title 'Imperial Defence'.

LOCATIONS: CaOKQ, CaOONL, UKBL, USDLC

D34.1.e   First edition, fifth printing (1961)

SELECTED   SPEECHES | AND   DOCUMENTS   ON | BRITISH | COLONIAL
POLICY | 1763 – 1917 | Edited by | ARTHUR BERRIEDALE KEITH | OXFORD
UNIVERSITY PRESS | 1961

PUBLICATION: Oxford: Oxford University Press, 1961. Published in a single volume.

PAGINATION: xx, 382, 426, plus card wrappers.

LOCATIONS: CaOWA, CaQMU, RIC

D35   THE WAR CABINET REPORT FOR THE YEAR
1917   1918

[Cover title:] THE WAR CABINET | [45.7-mm double rule] | REPORT | FOR THE YEAR 1917. | [114.3-mm double rule] | Presented to Parliament by Command of His Majesty. | [114.3-mm   double   rule] | [royal   arms,   35.1 × 30 mm] | LONDON   : | PUBLISHED BY HIS MAJESTY'S STATIONERY OFFICE. | [33.6-mm rule] | 1918. | [ranged left] [Cd. 9005.] [*sic*, immediately preceding brackets original] [centred] *Price One Shilling Net.*

PUBLICATION: London: HMSO, 1918. Price 1*s*. Cd. 9005.

PAGINATION: xx, 236, 3 maps (2 folding).

CONTRIBUTION: Undated excerpt [from an address?] re the origins of the Ministry of Munitions: pp. 67–8.

LOCATIONS: CaOGU, RIC

D36   THE ANGLO-HELLENIC ALLIANCE   1918

[Cover title:] [all of the following printed deep purplish blue on light greenish blue] [ranged left] No. 36. | [centred] THE | Anglo-Hellenic Alliance | SPEECHES | OF | MR. WINSTON CHURCHILL | THE GREEK MINISTER | AND VISCOUNT BRYCE | AT THE MANSION HOUSE | JUNE 27, 1918 | THE ANNIVERSARY OF THE | ENTRY OF RE-UNITED | GREECE INTO THE WAR | WITH SOME ACCOUNT   OF | OTHER   CELEBRATIONS | LONDON | THE   ANGLO-HELLENIC LEAGUE | 1918

PUBLICATION: London: The Anglo-Hellenic League, 1918.

PAGINATION: 32. Pamphlet in light greenish blue paper wrappers.

CONTRIBUTION: Address: pp. 2–14. Subsequently collected in Rhodes James, Vol. III, at pp. 2611–13, under the title 'Greece and the War'.

LOCATIONS: MLW, RIC, UKBL, USNN

REFERENCE: Woods D(b)37.

D37   THE GREAT WAR IN VERSE AND PROSE   1919

THE GREAT WAR | IN VERSE AND PROSE | Selected and Edited by | J. E. WETHERELL, B.A. | With an Introduction by | HON. H. J. CODY, D.D., LL.D. | Minister of Education for the | Province of Ontario | [provincial arms, 16.2 × 19.6 mm] | RECOMMENDED FOR USE IN SCHOOLS | Printed by Order of | The Legislative Assembly of Ontario | TORONTO | Printed and Published by A. T. WILGRESS, Printer to the | King's Most Excellent Majesty | 1919

PUBLICATION: Toronto: King's Printer, 1919. Price 20¢.

PAGINATION: [2], xiv, 160.

CONTRIBUTIONS: Excerpt from speech of 11 September 1914: p. 16; 'On the Navy', excerpt from an unidentified article or speech of December 1918: pp. 144–6. The entire 1914 speech was subsequently collected in Rhodes James, Vol. III, at pp. 2328–34, under the title ' "The Ebb and Flow of Fortune" ', and the excerpt is found at pp. 2331.44–2332.10. I have been unable to locate another appearance of the 1918 excerpt.

LOCATIONS: CaOOCC, CaOONL, CaQMM, RIC, UKBL

D38   THE WAR CABINET REPORT FOR THE YEAR
1918   1919

[Cover title:] THE WAR CABINET | [50.5-mm double rule] | REPORT | FOR THE YEAR 1918. | [115.1-mm double rule] | Presented to Parliament by Command of His Majesty. | [115.1-mm double rule] | [royal arms, 34.8 × 30.1 mm] | LONDON : | PUBLISHED BY HIS MAJESTY'S STATIONERY OFFICE. | [33.5-mm rule] | 1919. | [ranged left] [Cd. 325.] [*sic*, immediately preceding brackets original] [centred] *Price 3s. 6d.*

PUBLICATION: London: HMSO, 1919. Price 3s. 6d.

PAGINATION: xv, [1], 338, [1], 7 maps (all folding).

CONTRIBUTIONS: Excerpts from addresses of 18 October, 7 November and 23 December: at pp. 121–2, 126 and 127, respectively.

NOTE: One copy I examined was a proof or master one on which the Command Paper number and price were blank.

LOCATIONS: CaOGU, CaOONL, RIC

D39   AMERICAN JOURNALISTS IN EUROPE   1919

AMERICAN | JOURNALISTS IN | EUROPE | AN ACCOUNT OF A VISIT TO ENGLAND AND FRANCE AT THE | CLOSE OF THE WAR MADE BY A PARTY OF EDITORS AND | PUBLISHERS OF AMERICAN INDUSTRIAL PAPERS | AS GUESTS OF THE BRITISH GOVERNMENT | UNDER THE AUSPICES OF THE | BRITISH MINISTRY OF | INFORMATION | [12.5-mm rule] | BY | H. M. SWETLAND | [12.5-mm rule] | Published by the | UNITED PUBLISHERS CORPORATION | New York | 1919

PUBLICATION: New York: United Publishers, 1919.

PAGINATION: [*10*], 116, [*6*], 31 leaves of plates.

CONTRIBUTIONS: The British Newspaper Conference gave a dinner at the Savoy on 13 November 1918 as a welcome to the party. Lord Burnham, Publisher of the *Telegraph*, was in the chair. Churchill proposed the toast to 'The Newspaper Press of America': pp. 21–3. (A photograph of Churchill faces p. 22.) Churchill spoke earlier that day at lunch and, although that speech is not reported here, brief excerpts from his lunchtime chat with his neighbour are given at p. 30. Finally, his statement "There will be more wars!" opens the fourth chapter at p. 59. A brief excerpt only of Churchill's toast was subsequently collected in Rhodes James, Vol. III, at p. 2641, under the title 'The Press'.

LOCATIONS: MLW, RIC, UKBL, USDLC, USMH

D40   REPORT OF THE SPEECHES AT THE DINNER
TO HIS EXCELLENCY THE AMERICAN
AMBASSADOR, 16 JANUARY 1919   1919?

The American Society in London. | [25.4-mm rule] | REPORT OF THE SPEECHES | at the DINNER to | His Excellency The American Ambassador, | January 16th, 1919. | [25.4-mm rule] | Held at the Savoy Hotel, Strand, W.C.

PUBLICATION: London?: American Society in London?, 1919?

PAGINATION: 29, [1].

CONTRIBUTION: Toast to the President: pp. 3–7. Subsequently collected in Rhodes James, Vol. III, at pp. 2663–4, under the title 'Comrades in War and Peace'.

LOCATION: UKChT

D41   DEMOSTHENES DEMOBILISED   1920

DEMOSTHENES | DEMOBILISED | A Record of Cambridge Union | Society Debates | February, 1919—June, 1920 | *By the* | FOUR PRESIDENTS | With a Preface by | THE RT. HON. AUSTEN CHAMBERLAIN, M.P. | And an Introduction by | DR. J. R. TANNER (St. John's) | CAMBRIDGE : | W. HEFFER AND SONS LTD. | 1920

PUBLICATION: Cambridge: Heffer, December 1920. Price 6*s*.

PAGINATION: xviii, 102, 1 leaf of plates.

CONTRIBUTION: Churchill's speech during the sixth debate, on Tuesday, 24 February 1920, on the motion "That this House considers that the time is now ripe for a Labour Government": pp. 67–8. This is the only published appearance of this speech.

LOCATIONS: CaOTTC, UKBL, USMH

REFERENCE: Woods D(b)39/1.[13]

D42 SPEECHES AT BANQUET GIVEN TO THE RT.
HON. WINSTON SPENCER CHURCHILL M.P.   1921

No. 74. JULY, 1921. | THE BRITISH COTTON GROWING | ASSOCIATION. [INCORPORATED BY ROYAL CHARTER.] [*sic*, immediately preceding brackets original] | [British Cotton Growing Association device, 35.4 mm in diameter] | SPEECHES AT BANQUET | GIVEN TO THE | RT. HON. WINSTON S. CHURCHILL, M.P., | H. M. Secretary of State for the Colonies, | 7th JUNE, 1921. | [33.3-mm rule] | ALSO | REPORT | OF THE | Sixteenth Annual Meeting of Shareholders. | [33.3-mm rule] | *Head Offices:* 333 to 350 THE ROYAL EXCHANGE, MANCHESTER.

PUBLICATION: Oldham: The British Cotton Growing Association, 1921.

PAGINATION: 36, plus light bluish grey fibre-flecked paper wrappers.

CONTRIBUTION: Speech: pp. 11–17. Subsequently collected in Rhodes James, Vol. III, at pp. 3088–90, under the title 'The Government and Empire Cotton Growing'.

LOCATION: SF

REFERENCE: Woods D(b)39/3.

D43 CONFERENCE OF PRIME MINISTERS AND
REPRESENTATIVES OF THE UNITED
KINGDOM, THE DOMINIONS, AND INDIA   1921

[Cover title:] CONFERENCE | OF PRIME MINISTERS AND REPRESENTATIVES | OF THE | UNITED KINGDOM, THE DOMINIONS, | AND INDIA, | HELD IN | June, July, and August, 1921. | [35.2-mm rule] | SUMMARY OF PROCEEDINGS | AND | DOCUMENTS. | [151-mm double rule] | 𝔓𝔯𝔢𝔰𝔢𝔫𝔱𝔢𝔡 𝔱𝔬 𝔓𝔞𝔯𝔩𝔦𝔞𝔪𝔢𝔫𝔱 𝔟𝔶 𝔠𝔬𝔪𝔪𝔞𝔫𝔡 𝔬𝔣 𝔥𝔦𝔰 𝔐𝔞𝔧𝔢𝔰𝔱𝔶. | *August*, 1921. | [151-mm double rule] | [royal arms, 47 × 40.2 mm] | LONDON: | PUBLISHED BY HIS MAJESTY'S STATIONERY OFFICE. | [54.4-mm rule] | To be purchased through any bookseller or directly from | H. M. STATIONERY OFFICE at the following addresses : | IMPERIAL HOUSE, KINGSWAY, LONDON, W.C.2, and 28, ABINGDON STREET, LONDON, S.W.1; 37, PETER STREET, MANCHESTER; 1, ST. ANDREW'S CRESCENT, CARDIFF; | 23, FORTH STREET, EDINBURGH; or from E. PONSONBY, LTD., 116, GRAFTON STREET, DUBLIN. | [23.1-mm rule] | 1921. | *Price 9d. Net.* | [ranged lower left] [Cmd. 1474.] [*sic*, immediately preceding brackets original]

PUBLICATION: London: HMSO, 1921. Price 9*d.*

PAGINATION: [2], 67, [3].

CONTRIBUTION: 'Statement by Mr. Churchill on the Colonies' on 21 June 1921: pp. 34–9.

LOCATION: RIC

---

13. Where it is incorrectly entitled *Demosthenes Demolished*.

D44   NATIONAL LIBERAL CONFERENCE   1922

[Cover title:] [all of the following within a double-rule box, enclosing 181 × 109.2 mm] NATIONAL LIBERAL | CONFERENCE | [oval half-tone photograph of the Prime Minister, David Lloyd George, in an oval single-rule frame, 74.7 × 62.6 mm] | [ranged right near the bottom of the photograph] [*Vandyk, Ltd* [sic, immediately preceding bracket original] | [centred below photograph] THE PRIME MINISTER, | *President of the National Liberal Council.* | Full Report of proceedings at Central Hall, | Westminster, on January 20th and 21st, 1922.

PUBLICATION: Tiptree (Essex): Anchor Press, 1922.

PAGINATION: 80. Pamphlet in self-wrappers.

CONTRIBUTION: Speech at the First Session: pp. 23–33. Subsequently collected in Rhodes James, Vol. III, at pp. 3159–65, under the title 'The Coalition's Social Policy'.

LOCATION: CaOTTC

REFERENCE: Woods D(b)39/4.

D44/1   THE DRAMA OF EIGHT DAYS   1922?

[Cover title:] [all of the following within a single-rule box, enclosing 155.2 × 97.6 mm] THE DRAMA | OF | EIGHT DAYS | [71.4-mm rule] | JUNE 22nd to JUNE 29th, 1922 | [71.4-mm rule] | *How war was waged on Ireland* | *with an economy of* | *English Lives* | AS RELATED BY | GENERAL SIR NEVIL MACREADY | MR. WINSTON CHURCHILL | AND | MR. LLOYD GEORGE | [25.2-mm rule]

PUBLICATION: New York?: American Association for the Recognition of the Irish Republic?, 1922?

PAGINATION: 8. Pamphlet in self-wrappers.

CONTRIBUTION: Excerpt from speech of 26 June 1922 in the House of Commons: p. 5. The full speech was subsequently collected in Rhodes James, Vol. IV, at pp. 3327–37, under the title 'British Policy in Ireland'; and the excerpt occurs at p. 3337.

LOCATIONS: RIC, SF

D44/2   THE CANADIAN HISTORY SOCIETY AND
ITS ORGANIZATION   1923?

[Cover title:] THE | CANADIAN HISTORY SOCIETY | AND ITS | ORGANIZATION

LONDON: The Times Publishing Company, 1923?

PAGINATION: 24, plus card wrappers.

CONTRIBUTION: Speech at the inaugural dinner of 7 November 1923 of the Canadian History Society in London, at which the Canadian Prime Minister Mackenzie King was welcomed.

LOCATION: RIC

D45 SOURCE RECORDS OF THE GREAT WAR 1923?

The following Churchill contribution exists in two separate sets of seven volumes each, one bearing the title *Source Records of the Great War* and the other the title *The Great Events of the Great War*. Apart from the title page and binding, the sets are apparently textually identical and the Churchill contribution is accordingly found at the same location in each. I have been unable to assign priority to either issue;[14] both indicate copyright as being held by "National Alumni"[15] in the United States and both were printed in that country.[16] To add to the confusion regarding both title and priority of issue, one of the sales blurbs accompanying the American Legion prospectus refers indifferently to *both* titles and I have seen one particularly curious reference to the title *Uncensored Source Records of the Great Events of the Great War*.[17]

Volume II

D45.1 Source Records of the Great War issue (1923?)

SOURCE RECORDS | OF | THE GREAT WAR | [the following 5 lines within a single-rule box, enclosing 21.6 × 96.3 mm] A COMPREHENSIVE AND READABLE SOURCE RECORD OF THE | WORLD'S GREAT WAR, EMPHASIZING THE MORE IMPORTANT | EVENTS, AND PRESENTING THESE AS COMPLETE NARRATIVES | IN THE ACTUAL WORDS OF THE CHIEF OFFICIALS AND MOST | EMINENT LEADERS | [below the box] NON-PARTISAN NON-SECTIONAL NON-SECTARIAN | [the following 4 lines within a single-rule box, enclosing 18.4 × 96.3 mm] PRESENTING DOCUMENTS FROM GOVERNMENT ARCHIVES AND | OTHER AUTHORITATIVE SOURCES, WITH OUTLINE NARRATIVES, | INDICES, CHRONOLOGIES, AND COURSES OF READING ON SOCIO- | LOGICAL MOVEMENTS AND INDIVIDUAL NATIONAL ACTIVITIES | [below the box] EDITOR-IN-CHIEF | CHARLES F. HORNE, PH.D. | DIRECTING EDITOR | WALTER F. AUSTIN, LL.M. | *With a staff of specialists* | VOLUME II | [two leaf decorative devices] | 𝔑ational 𝔄lumni

PUBLICATION: No city indicated: National Alumni, 1923?

PAGINATION: xxxvi, 449, [3], 4 leaves of plates.

CONTRIBUTION: Only Volume II of the seven-volume set contains a Churchill contribution. In the chapter titled 'Capture of Antwerp', there are untitled contributions by five authors. Churchill's appears on pp. 308–10. It is an excerpt from his speech to the House of Commons of 15 November 1915, in which he resigned as First Lord of the Admiralty. It begins with an assessment of his own role in the Antwerp events:

---

14. The Harvard Library catalogue indicates that *The Great Events of the Great War* was published *c.* 1920 [in New York City]; however, the only copy I have examined bears the same 1923 copyright notice on the title-page verso.
15. Apparently the National Alumni Association.
16. The Harvard Library catalogue indicates that *The Great Events of the Great War* was printed by J. J. Little & Ives Co., but it provides no corresponding information for *Source Records of the Great War*.
17. Stated to be a quotation from *The Providence News*.

> The project of sending a relieving army to the aid of Antwerp did not originate with me. It originated with Lord Kitchener and the French Government. I was not concerned or consulted in the arrangements until they had advanced a long way; and until large bodies of troops were actually moving or under orders to move.

It later disputes a common contemporaneous view of the British effort: "I think it is a great mistake to regard Lord Kitchener's efforts to relieve Antwerp—in which I played a subsidiary though important part—as an event which led only to misfortune." Finally, it gives Churchill's assessment of the value of the enterprise:

> I believe it will be demonstrated in history—certainly it is the opinion of many highly competent military officers at the present time—that the whole of this enterprise, the moving of those British troops and the French troops who were in association with them, though it did not save Antwerp, had the effect of causing the great battle to be fought on the line of the Yser instead of twenty or thirty miles further south. If that is so, the losses which were incurred by our naval division, luckily not very heavy in life, will certainly have been well expended in the general interest.

The text is 879 words in length and differs only in small and immaterial respects from the corresponding portion of that speech as collected in Rhodes James, Vol. III, at pp. 2392–4.

NOTE: I have examined a prospectus for the set issued by the American Legion in which the Legion provides its enthusiastic "endorsement of *THE UNCENSORED OFFICIAL SOURCE RECORDS*, a work intended to increase the public knowledge of the causes, events and consequences of the War". The prospectus, modestly entitled '*ANNOUNCEMENT* TO THE PEOPLE OF THE UNITED STATES OF AMERICA', includes endorsements from Col. E. M. House, General John J. Pershing, General Douglas MacArthur, Clemenceau, Joffre, French, Haig, Lloyd-George and others, as well as numerous press comments. In one of the accompanying sales blurbs, a quoted excerpt from the *St. Petersburg* (Florida) *Times* provides a further explanation of the link between the National Alumni Association and the American Legion:

> The original intention was to keep these records in Washington for departmental archives. The demand however for authentic information led to their being turned over to the National Alumni, who in turn are distributing the records with the endorsement of the American Legion.

LOCATIONS: RIC (boxed), USMH

D45.2   Great Events of the Great War issue (1923?)

The title page differs only in that the first line reads: 'THE GREAT EVENTS'.

LOCATIONS: RIC (boxed), USMH

D46   THE WORLD'S BEST ORATIONS   1923

The orations are collected in a ten-volume set. It is only Volume III which contains a Churchill speech.

Volume III

[All of the following within a double-rule box, enclosing 168 × 104 mm] *Revised Edition* | [12.2-mm rule] | The World's Best | Orations | *Representing the Development of Civilization* | *from the Earliest Times to the Present* | [12.2-mm rule] | DAVID J. BREWER, LL.D. | *Editor in Chief* | [12.2-mm rule] | *Managing Editor* | WILLIAM VINCENT BYARS | *Associate Editors* | EDWARD A. ALLEN—WILLIAM SCHUYLER | *With Special Introductions by* | SIR GILBERT PARKER and AUGUSTINE BIRRELL | [12.2-mm rule] | FERD. P. KAISER PUBLISHING CO. | CHICAGO

PUBLICATION: Chicago: Kaiser, 1923.

PAGINATION: [2], 394 (numbered [i–v] vi–viii [ix–x] 11–394), [6], 3 leaves of plates, 1 facsimile.

CONTRIBUTION: 'Free Trade and the Unearned Increment', an excerpt from the speech of 6 December 1909 at the Free Trade Hall, Manchester. The full speech was subsequently collected in Rhodes James, Vol. II, at pp. 1378–90, under the title ' "Union among Progressive Forces" '.

LOCATIONS: CaQML, USDLC

REFERENCE: Woods D(b)39/2.

D47   MODERN ELOQUENCE   1923

The set consists of twelve volumes. Churchill's only contribution is found in Volume VII. There are also three supplementary volumes, one of which contains an article by Churchill (**B34**).

Volume VII

[All of the following within a double-rule box, enclosing 161.8 × 94.2 mm] MODERN ELOQUENCE | FOUNDED BY THOMAS B. REED | VOLUME SEVEN – ADDRESSES | [94.2-mm double rule] | ASHLEY H. THORNDIKE, EDITOR | *Professor of English, Columbia University* | [8.1-mm rule] | ADVISORY EDITORIAL BOARD | BRANDER MATTHEWS, CHAIRMAN | *Professor, Dramatic Literature, Columbia University* | SIR ROBERT LAIRD BORDEN | *Formerly Prime Minister of Canada* | NICHOLAS MURRAY BUTLER | *President, Columbia University* | JOHN W. DAVIS | *Formerly U.S. Ambassador to England* | HENRY CABOT LODGE | *Senator from Massachusetts* | ELIHU ROOT | *Formerly Secretary of State, Secretary of War, Senator* | OSCAR S. STRAUS | *Formerly Secretary of Commerce, Ambassador to Turkey* | AUGUSTUS THOMAS | *Playright [sic], Chairman, Producing Managers' Association* | HENRY VAN DYKE | *Professor of English Literature, Princeton University* | *Formerly U.S. Minister to the Netherlands* | [94.2-mm double rule] | MODERN ELOQUENCE CORPORATION | NEW YORK

PUBLICATION: New York: Modern Eloquence Corporation, 1923.

PAGINATION: [2], xxii, 442, [2], 6 leaves of plates.

CONTRIBUTION: 'American Independence Day': pp. 105–10. Speech of 4 July 1918 at the Anglo-Saxon Fellowship Meeting at Central Hall, London. First published in *Current History*, September 1918 (**E19**), and subsequently collected in Rhodes James, Vol. III, at pp. 2613–16, under the title ' "The Third Great Title-Deed" of Anglo-American Liberties'.

LOCATIONS: RIC, USMH

D48   ACROSS WITH THE "AD-MEN"   1924

ACROSS | WITH   THE   "AD-MEN" | INTERNATIONAL | ADVERTISING | CONVENTION | LONDON,   1924 | BY | THE   BUCKEYE   COVER   MAN | (CARL RICHARD GREER) | Author of: *What a Buckeye Cover Man Saw in Europe* | [publisher's device, 15.5 mm in diameter] | THE BECKETT PAPER COMPANY | MAKERS OF GOOD PAPER IN | HAMILTON, OHIO, SINCE 1848

PUBLICATION: Hamilton (Ohio): Beckett Paper, 1924.

PAGINATION: [*16*], 238, [2], 41 leaves of plates.

CONTRIBUTION: Speech of 17 July 1924 at the main conference hall, Palace of Industry, Wembley: pp. 86–93. Subsequently collected in Rhodes James, Vol. IV, at pp. 3464–6, under the title 'The International Financial Situation'.

LOCATIONS: CaOTTC, RIC, USDLC, USMH

REFERENCE: Woods D(b)40.

D49   THE ROYAL NAVAL DIVISION UNVEILING
AND DEDICATION OF WAR MEMORIAL   1925

[Cover title:] [all of the following within a single-dotted-rule box, enclosing 179.7 × 105.1 mm] THE | ROYAL NAVAL DIVISION. | [Royal Naval Division device, 34.3 × 45.1 mm] | UNVEILING AND DEDICATION | OF | WAR MEMORIAL. | [ranged lower right] ADMIRALTY, LONDON. | 25th April, 1925.

PUBLICATION: London: Royal Naval Division, 1925.

PAGINATION: 14. Pamphlet in paper wrappers.

CONTRIBUTION: Address: pp. 12–14. Separately published in *Address by the Right Honourable Winston Spencer Churchill, C.H., M.P. at the Unveiling of the Royal Naval Division Memorial* (**A78**). Subsequently collected in *Present-Day Prose* (**D55**) and in Rhodes James, Vol. IV, at pp. 3554–6, under the title 'Royal Naval Division War Memorial'.

LOCATION: PC

REFERENCE: Woods D(b)40/2.

D50   THE DORSET YEAR BOOK FOR 1925   1925

The Society of | *Dorset Men in London.* | FOUNDED JULY 7th, 1904. | [arms of the Society, 23.9 × 24.2 mm] | [set in a curved line] "A Silver Tower, Dorset's Red Banner Bears." | [set horizontally] *PRESIDENT :* | THE EARL OF SHAFTESBURY, K.P., G.C.V.O. | (H. M. Lieutenant for the Counties of Dorset and Poole.) | [list of eight past-presidents in 9 lines within a single-rule box, 65.2 × 117 mm] | THE DORSET YEAR

BOOK for 1925. | Honorary Editor : STANLEY I. GALPIN, 40/43, Fleet Street, E.C.4. | *Containing also* | List of Members, Rules and Objects and other Information.

PUBLICATION: London: Society of Dorset Men in London, November? 1925. Price 2*s*. 6*d*.

PAGINATION: [*4*], 272, 1 map, plus moderate purplish blue wrappers.

CONTRIBUTION: Speech: pp. 123–5.

LOCATIONS: RIC, UKBL, UKScNL, USNhD

D51   THE GENERAL STRIKE   1926?

The General Strike | [17-mm rule] | *Extracts from Speeches by the Prime* | Minister and Mr. *Winston Churchill,* | *House of Commons, May 3rd, 1926*

PUBLICATION: No publisher, city or date indicated [1926?].

CONTRIBUTION: Mr. Baldwin's speech occupies pp. 3–11. Churchill's appears at pp. 11–14. Subsequently collected in Rhodes James, Vol. IV, at pp. 3946–53.

LOCATIONS: MLW, USNN (but apparently missing)

REFERENCE: Woods D(b)41.

D52   THE GENERAL STRIKE, MAY, 1926   1926

D52.1   First edition, first printing (1926)

THE GENERAL STRIKE | [decorative device] MAY 1926: [decorative device] | ITS ORIGIN & HISTORY | Prepared by | R. PAGE ARNOT | for the | LABOUR RESEARCH DEPARTMENT | 162 Buckingham Palace Road, London, S.W.1 | 1926

PUBLICATION: London: Labour Research Department, 1926. Price 2*s*.

PAGINATION: [*8*], 245, [3].

CONTRIBUTION: Speech of 10 December 1925: pp. 58–9. Subsequently collected in Rhodes James, Vol. IV, at pp. 3800–7, under the title 'Coal Mining Industry Subvention'.

LOCATION: UKBL (rebound with front paper wrapper preserved)

D52.2   American issue, photo-reproduced from first-edition sheets (1967)

THE GENERAL STRIKE | [decorative device] MAY 1926: [decorative device] | ITS ORIGIN & HISTORY | Prepared by | R. PAGE ARNOT | [publisher's device, 9.5 × 8.7 mm] | REPRINTS OF ECONOMIC CLASSICS | [81.8-mm rule] | AUGUSTUS M. KELLEY • PUBLISHERS | NEW YORK • 1967

PUBLICATION: New York: Augustus Kelley, 1967.

LOCATIONS: CaOONL, UKBL

D53   WOLFE BI-CENTENARY CELEBRATION   1927?

[Cover title:] [all of the following within a thick (2.1-mm) decorative frame box, enclosing 168.1 × 105.7 mm] WOLFE | BI-CENTENARY CELEBRATION | LONDON | JANUARY 3rd, 1927 | [drawing of a torch, 63.1 × 9.1 mm] | *By* JOHN CLARENCE WEBSTER | SHEDIAC, N.B., CANADA

PUBLICATION: Shediac (NB)?: no publisher indicated, 1927?

PAGINATION: [*12*].

CONTRIBUTION: Toast to 'The Dominion of Canada', on 3 January 1927 at the Savoy Hotel, London: pp. 6–8. Subsequently collected in Rhodes James, Vol. IV, at pp. 4123–4, under the title 'Canada'.

NOTE: The tradition of celebrating the birth of General James Wolfe, who was born on 2 January 1727 in Westerham, Kent, was moved to the Savoy Hotel for the two-hundredth anniversary. The event was attended by H.R.H. The Prince of Wales, General Viscount Byng of Vimy, The Rt. Hon. The Earl of Minto and others. Dr Webster attended from Canada, representing various historical societies and others. Churchill's remarks are paraphrased in the style of Hansard.

LOCATIONS: CaOONL, CaQMM, RIC, UKChT

REFERENCE: Woods D(b)41/2.

D54   MEMORIES AND REFLECTIONS   1928

Volume I contains first-appearance speech material; Volume II, which contains first-volume-appearance correspondence only, can be found at **F34**.

Volume I

D54.1   First edition (1928)

MEMORIES AND REFLECTIONS | *1852–1927* | BY | THE EARL OF OXFORD AND ASQUITH, K.G. | VOL 1 | *With Eight Plates* | [publisher's device, 19.7 × 13.1 mm] | CASSELL AND COMPANY LIMITED | LONDON TORONTO MELBOURNE AND SYDNEY

PUBLICATION: London: Cassell, September 1928. Price 42*s*. the set.

PAGINATION: [*2*], xvii, [1], 284, 7 leaves of plates, 1 facsimile.

CONTRIBUTION: First volume appearance of any portion of Churchill's address of 17 February 1908 to the Authors' Club (undated excerpt published here): pp. 241–2. Subsequently collected in Rhodes James, Vol. I, at pp. 903–5, under the title 'The Joys of Writing', where, nonetheless, the text differs considerably from that quoted here.

NOTE: There are other non-oratorical contributions in Volume II (*see* **F34**).

LOCATIONS: CaOKQ, CaOONL, UKBL (rebound), UKScNL

REFERENCE: Woods D(b)42.

D54.2   American edition (1928)

[Dark bluish green, 100-mm wavy double rule] | [black] MEMORIES | AND REFLECTIONS | 1852 [decorative hyphen] 1927 | [dark bluish green, 100-mm wavy double rule] | [black] BY | THE EARL OF OXFORD | AND ASQUITH, K.G. | VOLUME ONE | [dark bluish green, 100-mm wavy double rule] | [black] LITTLE, BROWN, AND COMPANY | BOSTON [publisher's device] 1928

PUBLICATION: Boston: Little, Brown, September 1928. Reprinted 1928.

PAGINATION: [*2*], xix, [1], 337, [1], 6 leaves of plates, 1 facsimile.

CONTRIBUTION: Address of 17 February 1908 to the Authors' Club: pp. 286–7.

LOCATIONS: CaQMM, USDLC

D54.3 Canadian issue of American sheets (1928)

[Dark bluish green, 100-mm wavy double rule] | [black] MEMORIES | AND REFLECTIONS | 1852 [decorative hyphen] 1927 | [dark bluish green, 100-mm wavy double rule] | [black] BY | THE EARL OF OXFORD | AND ASQUITH, K.G. | VOLUME ONE | [dark bluish green, 100-mm wavy double rule] | [black] TORONTO | McCLELLAND AND STEWART | 1928

PUBLICATION: Toronto: McClelland & Stewart, 1928. Two volumes, boxed. Price $10.00.

LOCATIONS: CaOONL, CaOTTC, RIC (dj), UKBL

D55   PRESENT-DAY PROSE   1928

Present-Day Prose | chosen by | E. A. Greening Lamborn | Author of *The Rudiments of Criticism,* | *Expression in Speech and Writing,* | &c., &c. | London: Sidgwick & Jackson, Ltd. | 44 Museum Street, W.C.ɪ

PUBLICATION: London: Sidgwick & Jackson, November 1928. Price 2*s.* 6*d.*

PAGINATION: xii, 244.

CONTRIBUTION: 'Lest We Forget' [speech of 25 April 1925 at the unveiling of the Royal Naval Division Memorial at the Royal Horse Guards Parade]: pp. 241–4. Previously published in *Address by the Right Honourable Winston Spencer Churchill, C.H., M.P. at the Unveiling of the Royal Naval Division Memorial* (**A78**) and *The Royal Naval Division Unveiling and Dedication of War Memorial* (**D49**) and subsequently in Rhodes James, Vol. IV, at pp. 3554–6, under the title 'Royal Naval Division War Memorial'.

LOCATIONS: CaOHM, CaOTMCL, CaOTU, DAT, RIC, UKBL, UKOxB

D56   TRANSACTIONS OF THE INSTITUTION OF
NAVAL ARCHITECTS   1928

TRANSACTIONS | OF THE | INSTITUTION OF NAVAL ARCHITECTS. | VOLUME LXX. | EDITED BY | R. W. DANA, O.B.E., M.A., M.Inst.C.E. | SECRETARY OF THE INSTITUTION | [62-mm rule] | 1928 | PUBLISHED AND SOLD BY THE INSTITUTION OF NAVAL ARCHITECTS | 2, ADAM STREET, ADELPHI TERRACE, W.C.2. | ALSO | SOLD BY HENRY SOTHERAN & CO., 43, PICCADILLY, LONDON, W.1; AND | 140, STRAND, LONDON, W.C.2. | [*All rights reserved.*] [*sic,* immediately preceding brackets original]

PUBLICATION: London: Institution of Naval Architects, 1928.

PAGINATION: [2], lvi, 283, [1], 7 leaves of plates, 1 map (folding), 1 table (folding), 18 diagrams (all folding).

CONTRIBUTION: 'Presentation of Bust of the Late Sir Philip Watts, K.C.B.': pp. 86–7.

NOTE: Speech of 29 March 1928. Separately published by the Institution in a 4-page pamphlet entitled *Presentation of Bust of the Late Sir Philip Watts* (**A83**) but not subsequently collected in Rhodes James.

LOCATIONS: CaACU, RIC

D57   SOCIALISTS AND REPUDIATION OF WAR DEBTS POLICY   1929

[Dropped-head title only:] [ranged upper right] G. E. Memo No. 4. | [centred] Socialists and Repudiation of | War Debts Policy.

PUBLICATION: London: National Union of Conservative and Unionist Associations, 1929.

PAGINATION: 16. Pamphlet in self-wrappers.

CONTRIBUTIONS: Extracts from Churchill speeches in 1928 and 1929 *passim*.

LOCATION: UKOxB

REFERENCE: Woods D(b)44.

D58   TRADE UNION DOCUMENTS   1929

TRADE UNION DOCUMENTS | Compiled and Edited with an Introduction | *by* | W. MILNE-BAILEY | *Secretary of the Research and Economic Department* | *of the Trades Union Congress* | LONDON | G. BELL & SONS LTD. | 1929

PUBLICATION: London: Bell, February 1929. Price 8*s*. 6*d*.

PAGINATION: xxviii, 552.

CONTRIBUTION: Excerpt from address of 30 May 1911 in the House of Commons, Item 164, under the title 'Political Activities of Trade Unions': pp. 380–1. The entire address was subsequently collected in Rhodes James, Vol. II, at pp. 1822–8, under the title 'Trade Unions (No. 2) Bill'.

LOCATIONS: CaOKQ, CaOOCC, RIC (dj), UKBL, USDLC, USMH

D59   EMPIRE CLUB OF CANADA: ADDRESSES DELIVERED TO THE MEMBERS DURING THE YEAR 1929   1930

[All of the following within a single-rule box, enclosing 151 × 96.4 mm] EMPIRE CLUB | OF | CANADA | ADDRESSES   DELIVERED   TO   THE | MEMBERS DURING THE | YEAR 1929 | *Twenty-seventh Year of Issue* | [publisher's device, 27 × 29.5 mm] | GOD SAVE THE KING | TORONTO : | T. H. BEST PRINTING CO., LIMITED

PUBLICATION: Toronto: Empire Club of Canada, 1930.

PAGINATION: ix [there is no leaf i/ii], [1], 380, 1 leaf of plates.

CONTRIBUTION: 'British Imperial Interests, an address by Right Honourable Winston Churchill, C.H., M.P., before a joint meeting of The Empire Club, The Canadian Club, and the Board of Trade': pp. 203–14. Although undated in the volume, the address is that given on 16 August 1929. Also collected in *Addresses Delivered Before the Canadian Club of*

Toronto, Season of 1929–30 (**D60**). An extract from the address was subsequently collected in Rhodes James, Vol. IV, at pp. 4670–1, under the title 'Imperial Ties'.

LOCATIONS: CaOONL, CaOTTC, RIC

D60   ADDRESSES DELIVERED BEFORE THE CANADIAN CLUB OF TORONTO, SEASON OF 1929–30   1930

ADDRESSES | DELIVERED   BEFORE | The   Canadian   Club | of   Toronto | VOLUME   XXVII | Season   of   1929–30 | [publisher's   device,   33.6 × 32.4 mm] | TORONTO | WARWICK BROS. & RUTTER, LIMITED | 1930

PUBLICATION: Toronto: Warwick & Rutter, 1930.

PAGINATION: [2], xiv, 322, [2].

CONTRIBUTION: 'Address' of 16 August 1929: pp. 15–26 (the introductions at p. 15; the Churchill address begins at p. 16). Also collected in *Empire Club of Canada: Addresses Delivered to the Members During the Year 1929* (**D59**). An extract from the address was subsequently collected in Rhodes James, Vol. IV, at pp. 4670–1, under the title 'Imperial Ties'.

LOCATION: FBW

D60/1   INTERNATIONAL UNIVERSITY READING COURSE   [1932]

There is more than one edition of this set; however, the two I have examined give no indication of their year of publication and I have been unable to assign priority. Of the nine-volume set at the Vancouver Public Library (conjecturally dated 1932), only Volume 2 contains Churchill material. It is described by the publisher as Section 2, 'Text Matter'.

Volume 2

[All of the following within a thick (11.8-mm) decorative-border box, enclosing 170.7 × 93.1 mm]   Text   Matter | INTERNATIONAL | UNIVERSITY | Reading   Course | [publisher's   device,   28.3 × 34.4 mm] | A   DISTINCTIVE   AND | INDEPENDENT LIBRARY | OF REFERENCE | ADVISORY EDITOR: ERNEST BARKER, M.A., LL.D. | SPECIAL INTRODUCTIONS BY | RT. HON. AUGUSTINE BIRRELL, K.C. | SIR GILBERT PARKER, K.T. [*sic*], D.C.L. | International University Society | OFFICES: I.U.S. HOUSE, ARBORETUM STREET, NOTTINGHAM; AND AT | LONDON   BELFAST   GLASGOW   SYDNEY, AUSTRALIA

PUBLICATION: Nottingham: International University Society, [1932].

PAGINATION: [*10*], iv, 407, [3], 1 leaf of plates.

CONTRIBUTIONS: 'The Work of the Navy' (speech of 15 February 1915): pp. 166–77; 'Return to the Gold Standard' (speech of 28 April 1925): pp. 177–82; 'Widows' Pensions' (undated speech): pp. 182–91.

NOTE: I have examined a photocopy of the Churchill section in another edition of Volume 2. It includes only the Gold Standard speech at pp. 108–14.

LOCATIONS: CaBVA, UKBL

D61 SPEECHES AND DOCUMENTS ON THE BRITISH DOMINIONS, 1918–1931 1932

D61.1.a First edition, first printing (1932)

SPEECHES AND | DOCUMENTS | ON THE BRITISH DOMINIONS | 1918–1931 | *FROM SELF-GOVERNMENT TO* | *NATIONAL SOVEREIGNTY* | EDITED WITH AN INTRODUCTION AND NOTES BY | ARTHUR BERRIEDALE KEITH | D.C.L., D.LITT. | OF THE INNER TEMPLE, BARRISTER-AT-LAW, AND OF THE | SCOTTISH BAR; REGIUS PROFESSOR OF SANSKRIT AND | COMPARATIVE PHILOLOGY, AND LECTURER ON THE | CONSTITUTION OF THE BRITISH EMPIRE AT THE | UNIVERSITY OF EDINBURGH | [publisher's device, 33.2 × 22.2 mm] | OXFORD UNIVERSITY PRESS | LONDON : HUMPHREY MILFORD

PUBLICATION: Oxford: Oxford University Press, October 1932. Price 2*s*.

CONTRIBUTION: Speech of 20 November 1931: pp. 274–85. Subsequently collected in Rhodes James, Vol. V, at pp. 5097–104, under the title 'Statute of Westminster Bill'.

LOCATIONS: CaOKQ, UKBL, UKScNL (accession-dated 27 October 1932), USDLC, USMH

D61.1.b First edition, second printing (1938)

Title page as first printing.

PUBLICATION: Oxford: Oxford University Press, 1938.

LOCATIONS: CaOTY, UKBL, USMH

D61.1.c First edition, third printing (1948)

SPEECHES AND | DOCUMENTS | ON THE BRITISH DOMINIONS | 1918—1931 | *FROM SELF-GOVERNMENT TO* | *NATIONAL SOVEREIGNTY* | EDITED WITH AN INTRODUCTION AND NOTES BY | ARTHUR BERRIEDALE KEITH | D.C.L., D.LITT. | OF THE INNER TEMPLE, BARRISTER-AT-LAW, AND OF THE | SCOTTISH BAR; REGIUS PROFESSOR OF SANSKRIT AND | COMPARATIVE PHILOLOGY, AND LECTURER ON THE | CONSTITUTION OF THE BRITISH EMPIRE AT THE | UNIVERSITY OF EDINBURGH | *Geoffrey Cumberlege* | OXFORD UNIVERSITY PRESS | *London New York Toronto*

PUBLICATION: Oxford: Oxford University Press, 1948.

LOCATIONS: CaOME, CJZ (dj), UKBL

D61.1.d First edition, fourth printing (1961)

SPEECHES AND | DOCUMENTS | ON THE BRITISH DOMINIONS | 1918—1931 | *FROM SELF-GOVERNMENT TO* | *NATIONAL SOVEREIGNTY* | EDITED WITH AN INTRODUCTION AND NOTES BY | ARTHUR BERRIEDALE KEITH | D.C.L., D.LITT. | OF THE INNER TEMPLE, BARRISTER-AT-LAW, AND OF THE | SCOTTISH BAR; REGIUS PROFESSOR OF SANSKRIT AND | COMPARATIVE PHILOLOGY, AND

LECTURER ON THE | CONSTITUTION OF THE BRITISH EMPIRE AT THE | UNIVERSITY OF EDINBURGH | OXFORD UNIVERSITY PRESS | 1961

PUBLICATION: Oxford: Oxford University Press, 1961.

PAGINATION: xlviii, 504, plus card wrappers.

LOCATIONS: CaOOU, RIC

D62 MONETARY POLICY   1932

MONETARY POLICY | [26.2-mm double rule] | Extracts from Speeches | on the | BUDGET DEBATE | 20th and 21st April, 1932 | BY THE | RT. HON. SIR ROBERT HORNE, M.P. | RT. HON. L. S. AMERY, M.P. | RT. HON. WINSTON CHURCHILL, M.P.

PUBLICATION: London: HMSO, 1932.

PAGINATION: 12. Pamphlet in self-wrappers.

CONTRIBUTION: Speech of 21 April 1932: pp. 10–12.

LOCATIONS: AuNL, UKChT

REFERENCE: Woods D(b)44/2.

D63 SPEECHES AT THE DINNER TO CELEBRATE THE BI-CENTENARY OF THE BIRTH OF GEORGE WASHINGTON   1932?

[Cover title:] [ranged upper left, device of the Pilgrims Society, 24.3 × 18.9 mm; ranged opposite the device in 2 lines] THE | PILGRIMS | [centred and below the device] SPEECHES | at the | DINNER | TO CELEBRATE | The Bi-Centenary of the Birth of | GEORGE WASHINGTON. | THE RT. HON. THE EARL OF DERBY, K.G. | in the Chair. | HOTEL VICTORIA, LONDON, W.C.2, | Tuesday, 12th July, 1932. | (*And a report of the Annual Meeting of the Society | held on the 19th July, 1932*).

PUBLICATION: London?: The Pilgrims?, 1932?

PAGINATION: 19, [1]. Pamphlet in card wrappers.

CONTRIBUTION: Churchill's welcome of Dr Murray Butler, the President of Columbia University: pp. 2–5. The speech to the Pilgrims' Society dinner in London was also broadcast to the United States. Subsequently collected in Rhodes James, Vol. V, at pp. 5195–7, under the title 'Anglo-American Relations'.

LOCATIONS: USDLC, USMH, USNNC

D64 CELEBRATED AND HISTORICAL SPEECHES   1933

CELEBRATED AND | HISTORICAL SPEECHES | *An Anthology of Ancient and Modern Oratory* | Compiled and Edited | by | WILLIAM HENRY BEABLE | *Author of "Epitaphs, Graveyard Humour and Eulogy", | "Romance of Great Businesses", "On the Square", | "Stories for Speeches", etc.* | With a Foreword by | THE RT. HON. LORD CAMROSE | ILLUSTRATED | HEATH CRANTON LIMITED | [ranged left] 6 FLEET LANE [ranged right] LONDON E.C.4 | [centred] 1933

PUBLICATION: London: Heath Cranton, October 1933. Price 25*s*.

PAGINATION: xii, 434, 39 leaves of plates.

CONTRIBUTION: Speech of 30 March 1909 in the House of Commons under the title 'Fiscal Retaliation': pp. 117–23. Subsequently collected in Rhodes James, Vol. II, at pp. 1197–202.

LOCATIONS: CaOTMCL, CaQMM, RIC (dj), UKBL, USDLC, USMH

REFERENCE: Woods D(b)46/1.

D65   THE HOUSE OF COMMONS AND GERMAN REARMAMENT   1934

[Cover title:] [ranged left] "FRIENDS OF EUROPE" PUBLICATIONS [ranged right] No.   19 | [centred]   THE | HOUSE   OF   COMMONS | AND | GERMAN | REARMAMENT | *Speeches of* | THE RT. HON. STANLEY BALDWIN, M.P. | THE RT. HON. WINSTON CHURCHILL, M.P. | ISSUED BY FRIENDS OF EUROPE | 122, St. STEPHEN'S HOUSE, | WESTMINSTER S.W.

PUBLICATION: London: Friends of Europe, 1934. No. 19 of the Society's publications. Price 2½d. Printed by Robert Arnold, 43 Johnson Street, London S.W.1.

PAGINATION: 20. Pamphlet in self-wrappers.

CONTRIBUTION: Churchill's speech of 28 November 1934 in the House of Commons during the debate on the King's Address: pp. 3–10. (That of Mr Baldwin appears at pp. 10–19.) Subsequently collected in Rhodes James, Vol. V, at pp. 5440–9, under the title 'The German Air Menace'.

LOCATIONS: BeNL, RIC, UKChT, UKScNL, USNN

REFERENCE: Woods D(b)47.

D66   THE HOUSE OF COMMONS AND THE GERMAN SITUATION   1935

[Cover title:] [ranged left] "FRIENDS OF EUROPE" PUBLICATIONS [ranged right] No.   23 | [centred]   THE | HOUSE   OF   COMMONS | AND   THE | GERMAN | SITUATION | [33.6-mm rule] | Speeches by | The Rt. Hon. J. Ramsay Macdonald, M.P. | The Rt. Hon. Winston Churchill, M.P. | The Rt. Hon. Sir Austen Chamberlain, M.P. | The Rt. Hon. Sir John Simon, M.P. | [33.6-mm rule] | ISSUED BY FRIENDS OF EUROPE | 122, St. STEPHEN'S HOUSE, | WESTMINSTER, LONDON, S.W.1

PUBLICATION: London: Friends of Europe, 1935. No. 23 of the Society's publications. Price 3d. Printed by Dilliway Printing Company, 75 Ebury Street, London S.W.1.

PAGINATION: 32. Pamphlet in self-wrappers.

CONTRIBUTION: Speech of 2 May 1935 in the House of Commons: pp. 9–17. Subsequently collected in Rhodes James, Vol. V, at pp. 5590–6, under the title 'Air Parity Lost'.

LOCATIONS: BeNL, UKChT, UKScNL

REFERENCE: Woods D(b)48.

D66/1 SOME MEMORIES, 1901–1935   1935

D66/1.1 First edition (1935)

SOME MEMORIES | 1901–1935 | *A Publisher's Contribution to* | *the History of Publishing* | by | GEORGE G. HARRAP | [publisher's device] | GEORGE G. HARRAP & CO. LTD. | LONDON   BOMBAY   SYDNEY

PUBLICATION: London: Harrap, 1935.

PAGINATION: 175, [1], 16 leaves of plates.

CONTRIBUTION: Speech of 14 February 1935 at the new Harrap building: pp. 164–7.

LOCATIONS: CaQMM, RIC (dj), UKBL, USDLC, USMH

D66/1.2 American issue of British sheets (1935)

SOME MEMORIES | 1901–1935 | *A Publisher's Contribution to* | *the History of Publishing* | by | GEORGE   G.   HARRAP | NEW   YORK | HARCOURT,   BRACE   & COMPANY | 1935 *New York: Harcourt, Brace, 1935*

PUBLICATION: New York: Harcourt, Brace, 1935.

LOCATIONS: CaOHM, CaOONL

D67   STANLEY BALDWIN: MAN OR MIRACLE?   1936

D67.1 First edition (1936)

STANLEY BALDWIN: | MAN OR MIRACLE? | BY | BECHHOFER ROBERTS | "EPHESIAN" | ILLUSTRATED | [publisher's   device,   22.3 × 17 mm] | London | ROBERT HALE & COMPANY | 102 Great Russell Street W.C.1 | MCMXXXVI

PUBLICATION: London: Hale, September 1936. Price 12*s*. 6*d*.

PAGINATION: 288, 16 leaves of plates.

CONTRIBUTIONS: Excerpts from unidentified speeches by Churchill in the House of Commons: [17 March 1909]: p. 37; [1935 or 1936] on Coalitions: p. 220; and [1936?] on the India reforms: p. 222. The speech of 17 March 1909 was subsequently collected in Rhodes James, Vol. II, at pp. 1188–91, under the title 'Foreign Investments'.

LOCATIONS: CaOOP, CaOTU, RIC, UKBL, USDLC

D67.2 American edition (1937)

STANLEY BALDWIN: | MAN OR MIRACLE? | BY | BECHHOFER ROBERTS | "EPHESIAN" | *ILLUSTRATED* | [publisher's device, 14.3 × 10.2 mm] | NEW YORK | GREENBERG : PUBLISHER

PUBLICATION: New York: Greenberg, 1937.

PAGINATION: 287, [1], 16 leaves of plates.

CONTRIBUTIONS: As the first edition.

LOCATIONS: CaOHM, CaOTTC, RIC (dj), USDLC, USMH

D68   THE ABDICATION OF EDWARD VIII   1937

J. Lincoln White | THE ABDICATION OF | EDWARD | VIII | *A Record with all* | *the Published   Documents* | LONDON | GEORGE   ROUTLEDGE   &   SONS, LTD. | BROADWAY HOUSE: 68–74 CARTER LANE, E.C. | 1937

PUBLICATION: London: Routledge, January 1937. Price 2*s*. 6*d*.

PAGINATION: xiv [in which the front free endpaper is counted as pp. i–ii], 150 [numbered as 15–164].

CONTRIBUTIONS: Excerpts from the debate of Thursday, 3 December 1936, in the House of Commons: pp. 46–7; statement of 5 December to the press: pp. 55–9; address of 10 December in the House: pp. 115–18.

LOCATIONS: CaOONL, RIC, UKBL, USDL, USIU, USMH

D69   RESPONSIBILITIES OF EMPIRE   1937

RESPONSIBILITIES | OF   EMPIRE | [25-mm   rule] | EARL   BALDWIN   OF BEWDLEY | LORD SNELL | Rt. Hon. WINSTON CHURCHILL, M.P. | Hon. R. G. CASEY | *Treasurer of the Commonwealth of Australia* | SIR MUHAMMED ZAFRULLAH KHAN | *Member of the Executive Council of the* | *Governor-General of India* | Rt. Hon. W. G. A. ORMSBY GORE, M.P. | *Secretary of State for the Colonies* | Rt. Hon. D. LLOYD GEORGE, M.P. | HON. C. A. DUNNING | *Minister of Finance for Canada* | HON. H. T. ARMSTRONG | *Minister of Labour and of Immigration* | *in New Zealand* | VISCOUNT HALIFAX | [25-mm rule] | LONDON | GEORGE ALLEN & UNWIN LTD | MUSEUM STREET

PUBLICATION: London: George Allen & Unwin, November 1937. Price 3*s*. 6*d*.

PAGINATION: 86, [2-page catalogue].

CONTRIBUTION: 'FREEDOM AND PROGRESS FOR ALL': pp. 21–9. Reprinted from *The Listener* of 5 May 1937 (**E44**).

LOCATIONS: CaOOP, CaOTMCL, CaOTTC (dj), UKBL, USDLC, USIU (dj)

REFERENCE: Woods B28.

D70   THE AUSTRIAN CRISIS AND BRITISH
FOREIGN POLICY   1938

[Cover title:] [ranged upper right] PRICE 3d | [ranged left] "FRIENDS OF EUROPE" PUBLICATIONS [ranged right] *No 62* | [centred, the following 6 lines within a single-rule box, 21.3 × 66.7 mm] OBJECTS: | 1. To encourage effective co-operation for the prevention | of war and the establishment of peace. | 2. To provide accurate information about Nazi Germany | for use throughout Great Britain, the British Empire, the | U.S.A., Europe and wherever the English tongue is known. | [below the box] THE AUSTRIAN CRISIS | AND | BRITISH FOREIGN POLICY. | SPEECHES BY | The Rt. Hon. ANTHONY EDEN, M.P., | The Prime Minister | The Rt. Hon. NEVILLE   CHAMBERLAIN,   M.P. | AND | The   Rt.   Hon.   WINSTON CHURCHILL, M.P. | ISSUED BY FRIENDS OF EUROPE, | 122, ST. STEPHEN'S HOUSE, | WESTMINSTER, LONDON, S.W.1

PUBLICATION: London: Friends of Europe, 1938. No. 62 of the Society's publications.

PAGINATION: 24. Pamphlet in self-wrappers.

CONTRIBUTION: Speech of 24 March 1938: pp. 15–21.

LOCATIONS: BeNL, UKIWM, UKScNL, USMH, USNN

REFERENCE: Woods D(b)51.

D71   CEUX QUI OSENT RÉPONDRE A HITLER   1938

APRÈS   MUNICH | CEUX | QUI   OSENT | RÉPONDRE | A   HITLER | PAROLES | DE   MM.   DUFF   COOPER,   ATTLEE,   EDEN, | WINSTON CHURCHILL,   SIR   ARCHIBALD | SINCLAIR,   LORD   CECIL,   LORD CRANBORNE, | ETC. | PRÉFACE DE Ed. VERMEIL | Professeur à la Sorbonne | ÉDITIONS NANTAL | 9, Rue Louis-le-Grand | PARIS

PUBLICATION: Paris: Éditions Nantal, October 1938. Price 10 fr.

PAGINATION: 192.

CONTRIBUTION: Speech of 5 October 1938 in the House of Commons (translated into French): pp. 63–75. This is the first appearance of the speech in volume form. It was subsequently collected in *Into Battle* (**A142**), at pp. 41–53, under the title 'The Munich Agreement', and in Rhodes James, Vol. VI, at pp. 6004–13, under the title ' "A Total and Unmitigated Defeat" '.

LOCATIONS: RIC, USDLC

D72   THE TOTALITARIAN STATE   1939?

[Cover title:] [borders of thick and thin rules at head and foot] | LEAGUE FOR THE MAINTENANCE | OF DEMOCRACY | • | THE | TOTALITARIAN | STATE | Addresses by | THE RT. HON. WINSTON CHURCHILL, M.P. | PROFESSOR PHILIP NOEL-BAKER, M.P. | The two outstanding debaters in the British | House of Commons | and | PASTOR NIEMOLLER, | The German preacher arrested by the Nazis | for the stand he took in defence | of Christianity.

PUBLICATION: Johannesburg: League for the Maintenance of Democracy, 1939?

PAGINATION: 16. Pamphlet in paper wrappers.

CONTRIBUTION: Broadcast address of [16 October 1938], under the title 'The New Menace': pp. 1–6. The address was subsequently collected in *Into Battle* (**A142**), at pp. 54–9, under the title 'The Defence of Freedom and Peace', and in Rhodes James, Vol. VI, at pp. 6015–17, under the title 'Defence of Freedom and Peace'.

LOCATION: ZAPrU

D73   BRITISH WAR AIMS   1940

[Royal arms, 43.4 × 49.7 mm] BRITISH WAR AIMS | *A collection of Extracts* | *from Speeches delivered* | *by H. M. Ministers in* | *the United Kingdom* | *between 3rd September,* | *1939, and 31st March,* | *1940*

PUBLICATION: London: Ministry of Information, 1940.

PAGINATION: 44.

CONTRIBUTION: Excerpt from speech of 3 September 1939 in the House of Commons: p. 4. Subsequently collected in Rhodes James, Vol. VI, at pp. 6152–3, under the title 'War'.

LOCATIONS: CaNBFU, UKBL, USMH

D74   A DAILY TELEGRAPH MISCELLANY   1940

J. B. FIRTH | ★ | A DAILY TELEGRAPH | MISCELLANY | HUTCHINSON & CO. (Publishers) LTD. | LONDON AND MELBOURNE

PUBLICATION: London: Hutchinson, October 1940. Price 3s. 6d.

PAGINATION: 460.

CONTRIBUTIONS: Under the heading 'The Hour and the Man', excerpts from the speeches of 13 May 1940:[18] pp. 44–5; 4 June: pp. 45–6; and 18 June: p. 46; and, under the heading 'A Neglected Warning', an excerpt from *Step by Step* (A111): pp. 421–2.

NOTE: Julian Grenfell's poem "Into Battle" is re-published here at pp. 90–1.

LOCATIONS: UKBL, USDLC

D75   THE PENGUIN HANSARD   1940

Published in six volumes. There are Churchill contributions in each one, except for Volume 2.

Volume 1: From Chamberlain to Churchill

THE | PENGUIN HANSARD | VOL. I. [*sic*, point]—FROM CHAMBERLAIN TO CHURCHILL | [publisher's device, 20.5 × 16.6 mm] | PENGUIN BOOKS | HARMONDSWORTH MIDDLESEX ENGLAND | 41 EAST 28TH STREET, NEW YORK, U.S.A.

PUBLICATION: London: Penguin, 1940.

PAGINATION: 304.

CONTRIBUTIONS: Speeches *passim*.

LOCATIONS: CaBVAS, CaQMHE, RIC, UKBL, USMH

Volume 3: Britain Gathers Strength

THE | PENGUIN HANSARD | VOLUME III—BRITAIN GATHERS STRENGTH | [publisher's device, 20.5 × 16.6 mm] | ALLEN LANE | PENGUIN BOOKS | HARMONDSWORTH MIDDLESEX ENGLAND | 41 EAST 28TH STREET, NEW YORK, U.S.A.

PUBLICATION: London: Penguin, 1940.

PAGINATION: 288.

CONTRIBUTIONS: Speeches *passim*.

Volume 4: The Second Winter

THE | PENGUIN HANSARD | VOLUME IV—THE SECOND WINTER | [publisher's device, 20.5 × 16.6 mm] | PENGUIN BOOKS | HARMONDSWORTH MIDDLESEX ENGLAND | 41 EAST 28TH STREET, NEW YORK, U.S.A.

PUBLICATION: London: Penguin, 1941.

---

18. Here misdated 14 May 1940.

PAGINATION: 288.

CONTRIBUTIONS: Speeches *passim*.

Volume 5: The Deepening Struggle

THE | PENGUIN HANSARD | VOLUME V | THE DEEPENING STRUGGLE | SPRING 1941 | [publisher's device, 20.5 × 16.6 mm] | PENGUIN BOOKS | HARMONDSWORTH MIDDLESEX ENGLAND | 41 EAST 28TH STREET, NEW YORK, U.S.A.

PUBLICATION: London: Penguin, March 1942.

PAGINATION: 320.

CONTRIBUTIONS: Speeches *passim*.

Volume 6: The War Moves East

THE | PENGUIN HANSARD | VOLUME VI | THE WAR MOVES EAST | 22 JUNE TO 7 DECEMBER 1941 | [publisher's device, 20.5 × 16.6 mm] | PENGUIN BOOKS | HARMONDSWORTH MIDDLESEX ENGLAND | 300 FOURTH AVENUE NEW YORK U.S.A.

PUBLICATION: London: Penguin, 1942.

PAGINATION: 288.

CONTRIBUTIONS: Speeches *passim*.

D76   KING AND COUNTRY   1940?

[All of the following within a single-rule frame, within a decorative-rule frame, within a thick–thin rule box, the last enclosing 135.1 × 84.6 mm] KING AND COUNTRY | SELECTIONS FROM BRITISH | WAR SPEECHES 1939–1940 | [publisher's device, 14.3 mm in diameter] | 1940 | Chatto and Windus | LONDON

PUBLICATION: London: Chatto and Windus, December 1940? Price 1s. The book was reprinted once.

PAGINATION: 64.

CONTRIBUTIONS: This slim little volume contains eight speeches by Churchill (as well as twenty-one other speeches by the King, the Queen, Princess Elizabeth, the heads of the Anglican and Catholic Churches in England, other major political figures and J. B. Priestley). Of Churchill's speeches/broadcasts, five appear here for the first time and one, the speech of 15 February 1940 on the return of H.M.S. *Exeter* after the battle with the *Graf Spee*, at pp. 22–3, is not even included in *Into Battle* (**A142**), although it was subsequently collected in Rhodes James, Vol. VI, at pp. 6191–2.

    Extract from the speech of 13 May 1940: pp. 25–6. Previously published as *Mr. Churchill's First Speech as Prime Minister* (**A120**) and subsequently in *Into Battle*, at pp. 207–8. Extract from the broadcast of 19 May: pp. 26–7. Previously published as *Conquer We Shall* (**A121**) and subsequently in *Into Battle*, at pp. 209–12. Extract from the speech of 4 June: pp. 40–1. Previously published as **A124** and subsequently in *Into Battle*, at pp. 215–23. The broadcast address of 17 June: p. 46. Subsequently collected in *Into Battle*, at p. 224. A lengthy excerpt from the 20 August address: pp. 51–4. Previously published as **A131** and subsequently in *Into Battle*, at pp. 252–62. An excerpt from the broadcast of

11 September: pp. 55–7. Subsequently collected in *Into Battle*, at pp. 272–5. An excerpt from the speech of 8 October: p. 62. Subsequently collected in *Into Battle*, at pp. 279–91.

LOCATIONS: CaOHM, CaOONMC, RIC (dj), RPH, UKBL

REFERENCE: Woods D(b)52.

D77 CHRISTMAS DAY MESSAGE FROM HIS MAJESTY KING GEORGE VI TO HIS PEOPLE 1940

[Cover title:] [all of the following within a thick–thin rule box, enclosing 131.5 × 69.6 mm] Christmas Day Message | from | His Majesty | KING GEORGE VI | to his people | Broadcast from London, England | December 25th, 1940 | [decorative device, 2.2 × 8.7 mm] | Christmas Day Message | from | PRIME MINISTER | MACKENZIE KING | to the Canadian Army | Abroad and At Home | [decorative device, 2.2 × 8.7 mm] | Prime Minister Churchill's | Address | to the Italian People | December 23rd, 1940

PUBLICATION: Winnipeg: Universal Life Assurance and Annuity Company, n.d. [1940?].

PAGINATION: 16. Pamphlet in self-wrappers.

CONTRIBUTION: Broadcast of 23 December 1940: pp. 8–14.

LOCATION: RIC

REFERENCE: Henderson L34.

D78 "TILL THE HOUR OF VICTORY" 1941

D78.1 First English-language edition (1941)

"TILL THE HOUR OF VICTORY" | [24.6-mm double rule] | *Addresses by* | Right Honourable W. L. MACKENZIE KING | *Prime Minister of Canada* | Right Honourable WINSTON | CHURCHILL | *Prime Minister of Great Britain* | Right Honourable ERNEST LAPOINTE | *Minister of Justice* | [24.6-mm double rule] | Delivered over the national network of the | Canadian Broadcasting Corporation | 1st June, 1941 | [24.6-mm double rule] | [arms of Canada, 16.4 × 11.8 mm] | OTTAWA | EDMOND CLOUTIER | PRINTER TO THE KING'S | MOST EXCELLENT MAJESTY | 1941

PUBLICATION: Ottawa: Director of Public Information, 1941.

PAGINATION: 12. Pamphlet in self-wrappers.

CONTRIBUTION: Broadcast address: pp. 8–9. Subsequently collected in Rhodes James, Vol. VI, at pp. 6407–8, under the title 'To the People of Canada'.

LOCATIONS: CaOKQ, CaOONL, CaOOP, CaOOU, RIC

REFERENCE: Henderson F125.

D78.2 First French-language edition (1941)

VERS LA VICTOIRE | [24.7-mm double rule] | *Discours des* | Très honorable W. L. MACKENZIE KING | *Premier ministre du Canada* | Très honorable WINSTON CHURCHILL | *Premier ministre de la Grande-Bretagne* | Très honorable ERNEST LAPOINTE | *Ministre de la Justice* | [24.7-mm double rule] | Discours prononcés à la radio, | le 1er juin 1941 | [24.7-mm double rule] | [arms of Canada, 16.4 × 11.8 mm] | Ottawa | EDMOND CLOUTIER | IMPRIMEUR DE SA TRÈS EXCELLENTE MAJESTÉ LE ROI | 1941

PUBLICATION: Ottawa: Imprimeur du Roi, 1941.

PAGINATION: 12. Pamphlet in self-wrappers.

CONTRIBUTION: Broadcast address: pp. 8–9.

LOCATIONS: CaOONL, CaOOP

REFERENCE: Henderson F126.

D79 INTER-ALLIED MEETING HELD IN LONDON AT ST JAMES'S PALACE ON JUNE 12, 1941   1941

[Cover title:] [royal arms, 42.6 × 49.4 mm] Miscellaneous No. 1 (1941) | INTER-ALLIED MEETING | HELD IN LONDON AT ST. JAMES'S PALACE | ON JUNE 12, 1941 | REPORT OF PROCEEDINGS | *Presented by the Secretary of State for Foreign Affairs* | *to Parliament by Command of His Majesty* | LONDON | PRINTED AND PUBLISHED BY HIS MAJESTY'S STATIONERY OFFICE | To be purchased directly from H. M. STATIONERY OFFICE at the following addresses : | York House, Kingsway, London, W.C.2 ; 120 George Street, Edinburgh 2 ; | 39–41 King Street, Manchester 2 ; 1 St. Andrew's Crescent, Cardiff ; | 80 Chichester Street, Belfast ; | or through any bookseller | 1941 | Price 3*d.* net | [ranged lower left] Cmd. 6285

PUBLICATION: London: HMSO, June 1941, 5000 copies. Price 3*d.*

PAGINATION: 16. Pamphlet in self-wrappers.

CONTRIBUTION: Speech of 12 June 1941, opening the Inter-Allied Meeting: pp. 3–5. The Churchill speech was also separately published by the British Library of Information in New York (see **A148**) and subsequently collected in Rhodes James, Vol. VI, at pp. 6423–5, under the title ' "Our Solid, Stubborn Strength" '.

LOCATIONS: CaOOE, CaOTMCL, CaOTYL, RIC, USDLC

D80 ADDRESSES BY WINSTON CHURCHILL AND OTHERS AT THE NINETY-FIRST ANNUAL COMMENCEMENT OF THE UNIVERSITY OF ROCHESTER   1941

[Cover title:] [device of the University of Rochester, 32.9 × 26.4 mm] | [between two single rules running the width of the front wrapper] ADDRESSES BY WINSTON CHURCHILL AND OTHERS | AT THE NINETY-FIRST ANNUAL COMMENCEMENT | OF THE UNIVERSITY OF ROCHESTER | [below the bottom rule] ROCHESTER, NEW YORK | JUNE 16, 1941

PUBLICATION: Rochester: University of Rochester, 1941.

PAGINATION: 24, plus laid watermarked ('*Linweave Text*') card wrappers.

CONTRIBUTION: Address upon the acceptance of the degree of Doctor of Laws: pp. 7–9. Subsequently collected in Rhodes James, Vol. VI, at pp. 6425–7, under the title ' "The Old Lion" '.

LOCATIONS: CaOTTC, RIC, RPH, USNhD

REFERENCE: Woods D(b)53/1.

D81   THE LORD MAYOR'S LUNCHEON   1941

D81.1   First English-language edition (1941)

CANADA AND THE WAR | [24.8-mm rule] | THE LORD MAYOR'S LUNCHEON | IN HONOUR OF | THE PRIME MINISTER OF CANADA | [24.8-mm rule] | *Addresses by* | Right Hon. SIR GEORGE HENRY WILKINSON, | *Lord Mayor of London* | Right Hon. W. L. MACKENZIE KING, M.P., | *Prime Minister of Canada* | AND | Right Hon. WINSTON S. CHURCHILL, C.H., M.P. | *Prime Minister of Great Britain* | [24.8-mm rule] | THE MANSION HOUSE | LONDON, ENGLAND, SEPTEMBER 4, 1941 | [24.8-mm rule] | *Issued by the Director of Public Information, Ottawa, under authority of* | Hon. *J. T. Thorson, Minister of National War Services* | [arms of Canada, 15.9 × 11.8 mm] | OTTAWA | EDMOND CLOUTIER | PRINTER TO THE KING'S MOST EXCELLENT MAJESTY | 1941

PUBLICATION: Ottawa: King's Printer, 1941.

PAGINATION: 16. Pamphlet in self-wrappers.

CONTRIBUTION: Address of 4 September 1941: pp. 14–16. Subsequently collected in Rhodes James, Vol. VI, at pp. 6478–80.

LOCATIONS: CaOKQ, CaOONL, CaOOP, CaOOU, DLJ, RIC, USIU

REFERENCE: Henderson F131.

D81.2   First French-language edition (1941)

LE CANADA ET LA GUERRE | [21.5-mm rule] | DÎNER OFFERT PAR LE LORD-MAIRE | EN L'HONNEUR | DU PREMIER MINISTRE DU CANADA | [21.5-mm rule] | *Discours des* | Très Honorable SIR GEORGE-HENRY WILKINSON | *Lord-maire de Londres* | Très Honorable W.-L. MACKENZIE KING, M.P., | *Premier Ministre du Canada* | ET DU | Très Honorable WINSTON CHURCHILL, C.H., M.P., | *Premier ministre de Grande-Bretagne* | [21.5-mm rule] | À MANSION HOUSE | LONDRES, ANGLETERRE, LE 4 SEPTEMBRE 1941 | [21.5-mm rule] | *Publié par le Service de l'Information, Ottawa, avec l'autorisation de* | l'Honorable *J. T. Thorson, C.R., ministre des* | *Services nationaux de Guerre* | [arms of Canada, 16.5 × 11.5 mm] | OTTAWA | EDMOND CLOUTIER | IMPRIMEUR DE SA TRÈS EXCELLENTE MAJESTÉ LE ROI | 1941

PUBLICATION: Ottawa: Imprimeur du Roi, 1941.

PAGINATION: 16. Pamphlet in self-wrappers.

CONTRIBUTION: Address of 4 September 1941: pp. 14–16. This is the only French-language publication of this address.

LOCATIONS: CaOOE, CaOONL, CaOONMC, USIU

REFERENCE: Henderson F132.

D82   PEACE AIMS   1941

[Cover title:] [ranged in an arc over the title, five half-tone photographs, approximately 38 × 31.5 mm each, of, clockwise from lower left, Neville Chamberlain, Viscount Halifax, Anthony Eden, Arthur Greenwood and Clement Attlee] | PEACE | AIMS | [circular photograph of Churchill, 81.8 mm in diameter] | "In war, Resolution. In defeat,

Defiance. | In victory, Magnanimity. In peace, Goodwill." | *Winston Churchill: "My Early Life", published in 1930.* | [154-mm rule] | BRITISH OFFICIAL STATEMENTS | [154-mm rule] | A Chronological Record, from September 2, 1939, to September 24, 1941.

PUBLICATION: New York: British Library of Information, 1941.

PAGINATION: 30, [2]. Pamphlet, plus glossy paper wrappers.

CONTRIBUTIONS: There are excerpts from addresses by numerous British political figures as well as the King. Included are excerpts from eleven Churchill addresses: speeches in the House of Commons of 13 May and 18 June 1940: p. 10; speech in the House of 20 August 1940: pp. 10–11; speech in the House of 5 September 1940: p. 12; broadcast to the Czecho-Slovak People of 30 September 1940: pp. 12–31; speech at the Mansion House of 9 November 1940: p. 14; speech in the House of 21 November 1940: pp. 14–15; speech in the House of 22 January 1941: p. 18; speech in the House of 11 February 1941: pp. 18–19; the text of the Atlantic Charter of 14 August 1941: pp. 24–5; broadcast of 24 August 1941: p. 25; and speech in the House of 9 September 1941: pp. 26–7.

The excerpts from the speeches of 5 September, 9 and 21 November 1940, 22 January and 11 February 1941 and the broadcast of 30 September 1940 had not been previously published separately, although they were collected in *The War Speeches of the Right Hon. Winston Churchill (First Series)* (**A130**), *The War Speeches of the Right Hon. Winston Churchill (Second Series)* (**A135**), or *Their Finest Hour* (**A136**).

NOTE: Printed in Concord, NH, at the Rumford Press.

LOCATIONS: RIC, RPH, USMH

D83   THE POCKET BOOK OF THE WAR   1941

[All of the following within a single-rule box, enclosing 131.3 × 80.9 mm, the top and bottom of the frame being decorative rules] THE *Pocket* | BOOK OF | THE WAR | *Edited by Quincy Howe* | [double rule running the width of the box] | *Pocket* BOOKS, Inc. [within a circle 16.7 mm in diameter, the publisher's device of a bespectacled kangaroo reading a pocket book] NEW YORK, N. Y.

PUBLICATION: New York: Pocket Books, October 1941. There was a second printing in October, a third in November and a fourth in December.

PAGINATION: x, 372, [2].

CONTRIBUTIONS: Broadcast [of 22 June 1941], under the title ' "This Is No Class War" ': pp. 347–53; the Atlantic Charter, under the title 'The Eight Point Program': pp. 357–9. The broadcast was separately published by the British Library of Information (see **A149**) but this is the first volume in which it has been collected. Subsequently collected in Rhodes James, Vol. VI, at pp. 6427–31, under the title 'The German Invasion of Russia'.

LOCATION: RIC (1st, 3rd and 4th printings)

D84 WHY THE GERMAN REPUBLIC FELL   1941

WHY THE GERMAN | REPUBLIC FELL | AND OTHER STUDIES | OF THE CAUSES AND CONSEQUENCES | OF ECONOMIC INEQUALITY | EDITED BY | A. W. MADSEN, B.Sc. | *(Editor of "Land & Liberty")* | THE HOGARTH PRESS | 37 MECKLENBURGH SQUARE | LONDON W.C.1

PUBLICATION: London: Hogarth Press, July 1941. Price 2*s*. 6*d*. The volume was reprinted in August.

PAGINATION: x, 182.

CONTRIBUTIONS: 'Winston Churchill on the Land Monopoly', comprising extracts from the following speeches: at the Drury Lane Theatre, London, 20 April 1907; at the King's Theatre, Edinburgh, 17 July 1909; and in Dundee, 12 September 1912: pp. 98–102. The full addresses were subsequently collected in Rhodes James, Vol. I, at pp. 779–82, under the title 'Land Reform'; Vol. II, at pp. 1277–86, under the title 'The Budget'; and Vol. II, at pp. 2021–3, under the title 'Irish Home Rule and Local Government'.

LOCATIONS: CaACU, CaOHM, CaOOCC, UKBL, USMH

D85 NORWAY AND THE WAR   1941

DOCUMENTS ON | *INTERNATIONAL AFFAIRS* | [79.2-mm thin–thick rule] | NORWAY | AND THE WAR | September 1939—December 1940 | EDITED BY | MONICA CURTIS | OXFORD UNIVERSITY PRESS | LONDON NEW YORK TORONTO | *Issued under the auspices of the Royal Institute of* | *International Affairs* | 1941

PUBLICATION: London: Oxford University Press, 1941.

PAGINATION: x, 154.

CONTRIBUTIONS: Extracts from speech of 11 April 1940: pp. 68–72; extracts from speech of 8 May: pp. 111–17.

LOCATIONS: CaOOE, CaOTMCL, RIC (dj), UKBL, USDLC, USMH

D86 DAILY TELEGRAPH SECOND MISCELLANY   1941

J. B. FIRTH | ✷✷ | DAILY TELEGRAPH | SECOND | MISCELLANY | HUTCHINSON & CO. (Publishers) LTD. | LONDON : NEW YORK : MELBOURNE

PUBLICATION: London: Hutchinson, December 1941. Price 4*s*. 6*d*.

PAGINATION: 462, [2].

CONTRIBUTIONS: Excerpt from broadcast of 20 August 1940, under the title ' "Let It Roll!" ': p. 39; excerpt from broadcast of 16 June 1941 upon Churchill's receipt of the Doctor of Laws at Rochester University, under the title 'The Stars Proclaim Mankind's Deliverance': pp. 39–41; excerpt from the speech of 12 June 1941 to the Conference of Dominion High Commissioners and Allied Countries' Ministers at St James's Palace, under the title ' "Our Solid Stubborn Strength" ': pp. 42–3; excerpt from broadcast of 24 August 1941, under the title 'The Atlantic Meeting of President Roosevelt and Mr.

Churchill':[19] pp. 44–5; and 'Marlborough's Last Days', excerpted from *Marlborough: His Life and Times* (**A97**):pp. 60–2. This is the first volume appearance of any portion of the 16 June broadcast. The excerpt from *Marlborough* is taken from the paragraphs that run from p. 647.27 to p. 648.27. Note that a somewhat overlapping excerpt was subsequently separately published as *The Last Days of Marlborough* (**A189**).

LOCATIONS: RIC (dj), UKBL

D87   AMERICA GOES TO WAR   1941

D87.1   First edition (1941)

[Dark greyish brown, within a blank shield set on a background of an American eagle and the date 'DEC 7ᵀᴴ 1941'] AMERICA | GOES TO | WAR | [below the shield] President Franklin D. Roosevelt's | Message to Congress | Declarations of War | The President's First Report of War | The First White Paper | *Official Documents, Events, and Negotiations Leading | to War, and a Background for Understanding How and | Why We Went to War and What We Are Fighting For.* | CORDELL HULL   WINSTON CHURCHILL | FRANK KNOX   JAMES MONROE | COMPILED AND EDITED by HAROLD L. HITCHENS, B.A., M.A. | Copyright 1941 by | COLUMBIA EDUCATIONAL BOOKS, INC. | 153 No. Michigan Ave., Chicago, Illinois

PUBLICATION: Chicago: Columbia Educational Books, 1941.

PAGINATION: 128.

CONTRIBUTIONS: ' "THE GREAT DEMOCRACIES FACE | THEIR TASK WITH WHATEVER | STRENGTH GOD MAY GIVE | THEM" ', speech of 8 December 1941: pp. 43–8; Atlantic Charter: pp. 73–4.

LOCATIONS: CaOONL, CaOTTC, RIC, USDLC, USMH

D87.2   Second edition (1942)

[Dark greyish brown] THE AMERICAN THEATRE WING WAR SERVICE, inc. | [eagle with wings spread over a shield, 69.1 × 75.9 mm, within which] *AMERICA* | *GOES TO* | *WAR* | [below the shield] *SPECIAL EDITION* | [ranged left] ★ PRESIDENT ROOSEVELT'S MESSAGES | [centred] ★ THE DECLARATIONS OF WAR | [ranged left] ★ NEGOTIATIONS LEADING TO WAR | [centred] ★ OFFICIAL DOCUMENTS ★ EVENTS | A background for understanding how and why | we went to war and what we are fighting for | Edited by HAROLD LEE HITCHENS, B.A., M.A. | [printer's wartime union device, 3 × 7.9 mm] 3 | Copyright 1942 by | COLUMBIA EDUCATIONAL BOOKS, INC. | 153 No. Michigan Ave., Chicago, Illinois

PUBLICATION: Chicago: Columbia Educational Books, 1942.

PAGINATION: 192 (glossy paper), plus [64] (ordinary paper). Illustrated.

CONTRIBUTIONS: In addition to Churchill's speech and the Atlantic Charter of the first edition, there is added the speech to Congress of 26 December 1941, under the title ' "What Kind of People Do They Think We Are?" ': pp. 123–33.

LOCATIONS: RIC, RPH, USDLC, USMH

---

19. Incorrectly dated 27 August in the volume.

D88   ROOSEVELT'S FOREIGN POLICY, 1933–1941   1942

[All of the following within a double-rule box, enclosing 193 × 113.2 mm] *ROOSEVELT'S* | FOREIGN   POLICY | *1933–1941* | *Franklin   D.   Roosevelt's* | *Unedited Speeches and Messages* | ★ | *WILFRED FUNK, INC.* | [ranged left] *Publishers* [ranged right] *New York*

PUBLICATION: New York: Funk, 1942.

PAGINATION: xv, [1], 634, [6].

CONTRIBUTIONS: Broadcast address of 24 August 1941: pp. 454–60; message of 24 December from the White House: pp. 614–15.

LOCATIONS: CaOTMCL, CaQMM, RIC, USDLC

D88/1 BEST BROADCASTS OF 1940–41   1942

Best Broadcasts | of 1940–41 | *Selected and Edited by* | MAX WYLIE | *Radio Department* | *N. W. Ayer & Son, Inc.* | [101.6-mm decorative rule] | *New York* WHITTLESEY HOUSE *London* | MCGRAW-HILL BOOK COMPANY, INC.

PUBLICATION: New York: Whittlesey House, 1942.

PAGINATION: vi, 344, [2].

CONTRIBUTION: Broadcast address of 26 December from the White House: pp. 11–18.

LOCATIONS: CaOTMCL, CaOONL, RIC (dj), USDLC, USMH

D89   VOICES OF HISTORY: GREAT SPEECHES AND   PAPERS OF THE YEAR 1941   1942

[Within a frame made up of an outer thick–thin rule and an inner wavy-rule box, enclosing 174 × 97.9 mm] VOICES OF | HISTORY | Great Speeches and Papers | of the Year 1941 | *Introduction by* | CHARLES A. BEARD | *Edited by* | FRANKLIN WATTS | FRANKLIN WATTS, INC. | NEW YORK

PUBLICATION: New York: Franklin Watts, 1942. Projected to be published on 4 November 1942; however, a letter of 6 November from the publisher to Little, Brown indicates that the "first edition is off the press, folded and gathered", so it is clear that the publication date must have been a week or two after the anticipated date.

PAGINATION: xxv, [1], 669, [1].

CONTRIBUTIONS: Includes Churchill's principal speeches and broadcasts from 9 January to 30 December 1941 as well as the Atlantic Charter.

ANNOTATIONS: When Little, Brown, the publishers of *The Unrelenting Struggle* (**A172.2**) and the other war speech volumes, became aware of the forthcoming publication of this volume, they became concerned and Alfred McIntyre of their Boston office sent a memo to Raymond Everitt, the company President, on 28 September saying, "I am wondering ... whether or not the speeches contained in it [*The Unrelenting Struggle*] are protected by copyright."[20] A cable was sent to Cassell on 7 October advising the British publisher of

---

20. All quotations from, and references to, correspondence in this 'Annotations' section, are from the Little, Brown Archives, "Churchill, Winston 1942".

this forthcoming volume and asking whether Churchill's speeches were copyrighted in the United States and whether permission had been given to any other publisher. It concluded: "STRONG ACTION NECESSARY." A follow-up cable the next day reiterated the questions and observed: "EFFECT ON SALES UNRELENTING STRUGGLE MAYBE [*sic*] SERIOUS. HOPE STRONG ACTION CAN BE TAKEN." Cassell's reply (of 16? October) was brief: "NO PERMISSIONS GRANTED SUGGEST YOU CONTACT MCCLELLAND WHO KNOWS COPYRIGHT POSITION."

On 16 October, Everitt sent Franklin Watts a registered letter in which he advised the publisher of *Voices of History* of Little, Brown's rights and asking "from whom [do] you have permission for book publication rights to the speeches and what position you take in the matter?" I have been unable to review the intervening correspondence from Franklin Watts; however, the Little, Brown letter of 30 October advised that Little, Brown would be including a "Copyright 1942, by Winston S. Churchill" notice and recommending that Watts do the same. That letter also advised that any Watts advertising of his volume should not imply that all of Churchill's 1941 speeches were included, "pointing out the small number of the Churchill speeches in your volume and that they are merely selected ones".

On 2 November, in a letter to Aubrey Gentry of Cassell, Raymond Everitt revealed the weakness of his legal position. "Our legal advice on the matter is that unless Mr. Churchill has individually copyrighted each speech in Washington, there are no legal steps we can take under the copyright law." While Everitt could not, of course, speculate about the effect of the Watts book on Little, Brown's sales, he advised Gentry that it was a "disturbing factor" since they had "the sole and exclusive right to publish in book form in the United States of America" and, on that account, had "paid a large advance and invested a great deal of money" in the work. He also observed that the Watts volume would become an annual publication and suggested that Cassell consider what they would be doing about Churchill's 1942 and future speech volumes.

It was the view of Franklin Watts in his letter of 6 November to Raymond Everitt that "all of the [Churchill] material in this book is in the public domain" and that there was "no conflict in sales or appeal between [the Little, Brown] book and mine, and I can't conceive of a single person not buying your book and buying mine instead." He offered as a courtesy but "not because there is any legal compulsion" that, in future volumes, he would include a statement providing that Churchill's speeches were reprinted "through the courtesy of his publishers, Little Brown & Company" but the Boston publishers cautiously refused that concession on 10 November.

LOCATIONS: CaOONL, CaOOP, CaQMM, RIC (dj), UKScGlU, USDLC, USMH

D90   INDIA (LORD PRIVY SEAL'S MISSION)   1942

[Royal arms, 43.6 × 49.8 mm] | INDIA | (Lord Privy Seal's Mission) | Statement and Draft Declaration by | His Majesty's Government with correspondence | and Resolutions connected therewith | *Presented by the Secretary of State for India to Parliament* | *by Command of His Majesty* | *April,* 1942 | LONDON | PRINTED AND PUBLISHED BY HIS MAJESTY'S STATIONERY OFFICE | To be purchased directly from H.M.

STATIONERY OFFICE at the following addresses : | York House, Kingsway, London, W.C.2 ; 120 George Street, Edinburgh, 2 ; | 39–41 King Street, Manchester 2 ; 1 St. Andrew's Crescent, Cardiff ; | 80 Chichester Street, Belfast ; | or through any bookseller | 1942 | Price 6*d*. net | [ranged lower left] Cmd. 6350

PUBLICATION: London: HMSO, April 1942, 5,050 copies. Price 6*d*.

PAGINATION: 30. Pamphlet in self-wrappers.

CONTRIBUTION: Statement of 11 March 1942 in the House of Commons: pp. 3–4. Subsequently collected in Rhodes James, Vol. VI, at pp. 6601–3, under the title 'The Cripps Mission'.

LOCATIONS: CaOOE, UKScNL, USDLC, USMH

D91   REPRESENTATIVE AMERICAN SPEECHES: 1941–1942   1942

THE REFERENCE SHELF | [92.7-mm rule] | [ranged left] Vol. 16 [ranged right] No. 1 | [centred] REPRESENTATIVE AMERICAN | SPEECHES: 1941–1942 | Selected by | A. CRAIG BAIRD | *Department of Speech, State University of Iowa* | [publisher's device, 11.5 mm in diameter] | THE H. W. WILSON COMPANY | [ranged left] NEW YORK [ranged right] 1942

PUBLICATION: New York: H. W. Wilson, 1942.

PAGINATION: [*2*], 297, [5].

CONTRIBUTION: 'Address to Congress' of 26 December 1941: pp. 19–29.

LOCATIONS: CaOKQ, CaQML, RIC, USDLC, USMH

D92   DAILY TELEGRAPH THIRD MISCELLANY   1942

J.   B.   FIRTH | ✹✹✹ | DAILY   TELEGRAPH | THIRD | MISCELLANY | HUTCHINSON & CO. (Publishers) LTD. | LONDON : NEW YORK : MELBOURNE

PUBLICATION: London: Hutchinson, December 1942.

PAGINATION: xvi, 422.

CONTRIBUTIONS: Excerpt from broadcast of 10 May 1942 (the date is not given in this volume), under the title 'We Have Only to Persevere to Conquer': pp. 2–3; excerpt from speech of 8 September 1942 in the House of Commons, under the title 'The Coming Hour of Retribution': pp. 3–4; and another excerpt from the same speech (although there is no such indication in this volume) dealing specifically with Stalin, under the title 'Churchill's Impression of Stalin': pp. 6–7.

LOCATIONS: RIC, UKBL

D93 ADDRESSES OF FRANKLIN D. ROOSEVELT AND WINSTON CHURCHILL 1942

𝔄𝔡𝔡𝔯𝔢𝔰𝔰𝔢𝔰 | OF FRANKLIN D. ROOSEVELT | AND | WINSTON CHURCHILL | [device of intertwined American and British flags in vivid red, deep blue and light olive grey, 54.1 × 51.4 mm] | 𝕿𝖍𝖊 𝖂𝖍𝖎𝖙𝖊 𝕳𝖔𝖚𝖘𝖊 • 𝖂𝖆𝖘𝖍𝖎𝖓𝖌𝖙𝖔𝖓 | Christmastide • 1942

PUBLICATION: Washington: Government Printing Office, 1942. Only 100 copies were printed for President Roosevelt.

PAGINATION: 64.

CONTRIBUTIONS: Christmas greetings of the Prime Minister: pp. 27–8; and his address of 26 December to the U.S. Congress: pp. 29–40.

LOCATIONS: RIC, USDLC, USMiU

REFERENCE: Woods D(b)56.

D94 THE WORLD'S GREAT SPEECHES 1942

[All of the following within a double-rule frame, enclosing 157.5 × 96.4 mm; the title within an elaborate frame, enclosing 43.8 × 65.1 mm] *The World's | Great Speeches* | [below the title frame] EDITED BY | LEWIS COPELAND | GARDEN CITY PUBLISHING CO., INC. | GARDEN CITY, N.Y.

PUBLICATION: Garden City (NY): Garden City Publishing, 1942.

PAGINATION: xx, 748.

CONTRIBUTIONS: '"Blood, Sweat and Tears"', speech of 13 May 1940: pp. 459–61; 'Dunkirk', speech of 4 June: pp. 461–7; '"Their Finest Hour"', speech of 18 June: pp. 467–74; 'The War on Russia', speech of 22 June 1941: pp. 475–8; 'Address before United States Congress', speech of 26 December: pp. 720–6.

LOCATIONS: CaOOE, CaOTMCL, RIC (dj), USDLC

D95 VOICES OF HISTORY, 1942–43 1943

[Within a frame made up of an outer thick–thin rule and an inner wavy-rule box, enclosing 174 × 97.9 mm] VOICES OF | HISTORY | 1942–43 | Speeches and Papers of | ROOSEVELT, CHURCHILL, | STALIN, CHIANG, HITLER | AND OTHER LEADERS | Delivered During 1942 | FRANKLIN WATTS, *Editor* | BARBARA E. LEIGHTON, *Associate Editor* | GRAMERCY PUBLISHING COMPANY | NEW YORK

PUBLICATION: New York: Gramercy, 1943. Price $3.50.

PAGINATION: xx, 759, [3].

CONTRIBUTIONS: Includes Churchill's principal speeches and broadcasts from 27 January to 5 December 1942 as well as his message to Stalin of 11 June.

LOCATIONS: CaOONL, CaOOP, CaOTMCL, RIC (dj), UKScGlU, USDLC, USMH

D96   WINSTON CHURCHILL, PRIME MINISTER   1943

D96.1   First edition (1943)

WINSTON CHURCHILL | [decorative rule running the width of the page] | [ranged right] PRIME MINISTER | *A SELECTION FROM SPEECHES* | *MADE BY WINSTON CHURCHILL* | *DURING THE FOUR YEARS* | *THAT BRITAIN HAS BEEN AT WAR.* | [ranged left] PUBLISHED DECEMBER, 1943, BY | BRITISH INFORMATION SERVICES | *An Agency of the British Government* | 30 ROCKEFELLER PLAZA • NEW YORK CITY, 20, N.Y.

PUBLICATION: New York: British Information Services, 1943.

PAGINATION: [*52*], plus paper wrappers.

CONTRIBUTIONS: On the versos, excerpts from speeches from 12 November 1939 to 6 September 1943; on the rectos, wartime photographs of Churchill.

LOCATIONS: CaMWU, CaOKQ, RIC, USDLC, USMH

D96.2   Canadian issue of American sheets (1943?)

WINSTON CHURCHILL | [decorative rule running the width of the page] | [ranged right] PRIME MINISTER | *A SELECTION FROM SPEECHES* | *MADE BY WINSTON CHURCHILL* | *DURING THE FOUR YEARS* | *THAT BRITAIN HAS BEEN AT WAR.* | [ranged left] DISTRIBUTED BY | [centred] UNITED KINGDOM INFORMATION OFFICE | [ranged left] 75 SPARKS STREET • OTTAWA • CANADA

PUBLICATION: Ottawa: United Kingdom Information Office, n.d. [1943?].

LOCATIONS: CaOONL, RIC

D97   NATIONAL CONFERENCE OF WOMEN
CALLED BY H. M. GOVERNMENT   1943

[Cover title:] [printed dark blue on moderate yellow green paper wrappers; thickness: 0.14 mm] [royal arms, 27.3 × 31.3 mm] | NATIONAL | CONFERENCE *of* WOMEN | *called by* | H. M. GOVERNMENT | REPORT OF PROCEEDINGS | Tuesday, 28th September, 1943 | ROYAL ALBERT HALL • LONDON

PUBLICATION: London: HMSO, December 1943, 7500 copies.

PAGINATION: 45, [1].

CONTRIBUTION: Speech of 28 September 1943: pp. 5–7. Subsequently collected in Rhodes James, Vol. VII, at pp. 6854–6, under the title 'The Women of Britain'.

LOCATIONS: RIC, UKChT

REFERENCE: Woods D(b)60/1.

D98 PARALLEL PASSAGES ON POSTWAR PROBLEMS 1943

[Typed text] RESEARCH BULLETIN SERIES ON POSTWAR PROBLEMS | PARALLEL PASSAGES ON POST-WAR [*sic*] PROBLEMS | WINSTON CHURCHILL'S SPEECH OF MARCH 21, 1943 | and | NATIONAL RESOURCES PLANNING BOARD, REPORT FOR 1943, | PART I, POSTWAR PLAN AND PROGRAM | APRIL, 1943 | BX-232 | Published by | THE COUNCIL OF STATE GOVERNMENTS | 1313 EAST 60th STREET | Chicago, Illinois

PUBLICATION: Chicago: Council of State Governments, 1943.

PAGINATION: 12 leaves, mimeographed and numbered on rectos only: [*1*], 11. Side-stitched in pale yellow watermarked laid paper wrappers.

CONTRIBUTION: Speech of 21 March 1943: pp. 1–11.

LOCATIONS: RIC, USDLC

REFERENCE: Woods D(b)61.

D99 OUR NEW ORDER—OR HITLER'S? 1943

A PENGUIN SPECIAL | OUR NEW ORDER— | OR HITLER'S? | A Selection of Speeches by *Winston Churchill, The Arch-* | *bishop of Canterbury, Anthony Eden, Sir Stafford Cripps,* | *Sir Richard Gregory, Sir William Beveridge, Sir Richard* | *Acland, Franklin D. Roosevelt, Henry A. Wallace, Cordell* | *Hull, John G. Winant, Sumner Wells, Milo Perkins, Paul* | *H. Appleby, Herbert Agar and Pearl S. Buck.* | EDITED BY PHYLLIS BOTTOME | [publisher's device, 20.3 × 17.1 mm] | PENGUIN BOOKS | HARMONDSWORTH MIDDLESEX ENGLAND | 245 FIFTH AVENUE NEW YORK U.S.A.

PUBLICATION: London: Penguin Books, 1943.

PAGINATION: 192. Perfect-bound.

CONTRIBUTION: Under the divisional heading, 'PART ONE: VOICES OF BRITAIN', the first contribution, entitled 'Objectives after the War', is an extract from Churchill's broadcast address of 21 March 1943: pp. 11–17.

LOCATIONS: CaAEU, CaBVAS, RIC, UKScNL, USDLC, USMH

D100 ENGLAND IS HERE 1943

[102.9-mm rule] | ENGLAND IS HERE | [102.9-mm rule] | a selection | from the Speeches and Writings of | THE PRIME MINISTERS OF ENGLAND | from *Sir Robert Walpole* to | the *Rt. Hon. Winston Spencer Churchill* | [102.9-mm rule] | edited and with an Introduction by W. L. HANCHANT | [102.9-mm rule] | [a 2-line excerpt from Robert Browning's "Strafford" and a 3-line excerpt from Robert Burton's *The Anatomy of Melancholy*] | ILLUSTRATED | [102.9-mm rule] | LONDON John Lane The Bodley Head MDCCCCXLIII

PUBLICATION: London: John Lane The Bodley Head, May 1943. Price 10*s.* 6*d.*

PAGINATION: 256, 5 leaves of plates.

CONTRIBUTIONS: Excerpts from *The River War* (**A2**) and 13 speeches: pp. 243–56.

LOCATIONS: RIC (dj), UKBL, USIU, USMH

D101 REPRESENTATIVE AMERICAN SPEECHES: 1942–1943   1943

THE REFERENCE SHELF | [92.7-mm rule] | [ranged left] Vol. 16 [ranged right] No. 6 | [centred] REPRESENTATIVE AMERICAN | SPEECHES: 1942–1943 | Selected by | A. CRAIG BAIRD | *Department of Speech, State University of Iowa* | [publisher's device, 11.5 mm in diameter] | THE H. W. WILSON COMPANY | [ranged left] NEW YORK [ranged right] 1943

PUBLICATION: New York: H. W. Wilson, 1943.

PAGINATION: [*2*], 319, [*4*].

CONTRIBUTION: Address of 19 May 1943 to Congress: pp. 30–46. Previously separately published in Great Britain, the United States and Switzerland (see **A181**) and subsequently collected in Rhodes James, Vol. VII, at pp. 6775–84, under the title 'To the U.S. Congress'.

LOCATIONS: CaAEP, RIC, USDLC, USMH

D101/1 NEW YUGOSLAVIA   1944?

[Cover title:] [deep purplish blue on light bluish grey wrappers] NEW [ranged right, thin–thick–thin rule] | YUGOSLAVIA | Declaration and decisions of the | Anti-Fascist Council of National | Liberation of Yugoslavia. | Composition of the Provisional | National Government. | Parliamentary debates. | Churchill's speech in the | House of Commons | 1/- | [thin–thick rule] | Published by THE UNITED SOUTH SLAV COMMITTEE, | Cornwall House, Flat 5, Cornwall Gardens, London, S.W.7

PUBLICATION: London: United South Slav Committee, 1944?

PAGINATION: 36.

CONTRIBUTION: Extract from the speech of 22 February 1944, on the opening of the war debate: pp. 33–6. The full speech was subsequently collected in Rhodes James, Vol. VII, at pp. 6881–94, under the title 'The Progress of the War'.

LOCATIONS: RIC, UKBL, USDLC, USMH

D102 SPEECHES BY THE RT. HON. WINSTON S. CHURCHILL, C.H., M.P., AND THE RT. HON. LORD MORAN   1944

[Cover title:] [ranged upper right] *With the President's Compliments.* | [centred] ROYAL COLLEGE OF PHYSICIANS | OF LONDON | *SPEECHES BY* | The RT. HON. WINSTON S. CHURCHILL, C.H., M.P. | Prime Minister | *and* | The RT. HON. THE LORD MORAN | President of the College | MARCH 2, 1944 | *Reprinted from* THE LANCET, *March* 11, 1944.

PUBLICATION: London: The Lancet for the Royal College of Physicians, March 1944, probably 750 to 1000 copies. Distributed free to the (approximately) 650 Fellows of the College and to an undetermined number of guests at the luncheon and others.

PAGINATION: 8. Pamphlet in paper wrappers.

CONTRIBUTION: Address of 2 March 1944 to a College-sponsored luncheon: pp. 5–8. The address was previously published in its entirety in *The Lancet* of 11 March (**E109**) and in excerpted form in the *British Medical Journal* of 11 March. It was subsequently collected in Rhodes James, Vol. VII, at pp. 6895–7, under the title 'The Royal College of Physicians'.

LOCATIONS: RIC, UKLRcp, ZACtU

REFERENCE: Woods D(b)61/2(b).

D103 PROCEEDINGS ON THE OCCASION OF AN ADDRESS BY THE RT. HON. W. L. MACKENZIE KING   1944

There were two editions of this pamphlet, one in English and one in French. While it is likely that the English edition preceded the French, the two editions may have been issued simultaneously. On the basis of information currently available, I cannot assign priority.

D103.1   English-language edition (1944)

CANADA AND THE WAR | [17-mm rule] | *Proceedings on the Occasion of* | AN ADDRESS | *by* | Rt. Hon. W. L. MACKENZIE KING, M.P. | *Prime Minister of Canada* | *to* | *The Members of Both Houses of* | THE PARLIAMENT OF THE UNITED KINGDOM | [16.8-mm rule] | *Addresses by* | The Right Honourable WINSTON CHURCHILL, C.H., M.P. | *Prime Minister of the United Kingdom* | The Right Honourable W. L. MACKENZIE KING, M.P. | *Prime Minister of Canada* | The Right Honourable VISCOUNT SIMON, G.C.S.I., G.C.V.O. | *Lord Chancellor of the United Kingdom* | The Right Honourable CLIFTON BROWN, M.P. | *Speaker of the House of Commons of the United Kingdom* | [16.6-mm rule] | WESTMINSTER, LONDON, ENGLAND | MAY 11, 1944 | [arms of Canada, 19.2×13.6 mm] | OTTAWA | EDMOND CLOUTIER | PRINTER TO THE KING'S MOST EXCELLENT MAJESTY | 1944

PUBLICATION: Ottawa: King's Printer, 1944.

PAGINATION: 22, [2]. Pamphlet in self-wrappers.

CONTRIBUTIONS: 'Introduction by Right Honourable Winston Churchill, Prime Minister of the United Kingdom': pp. 3–5; brief words calling upon the Lord Chancellor and the Speaker to propose votes of thanks to the Prime Minister of Canada: pp. 20–2.

LOCATIONS: CaOKQ, CaOOE, CaOONL, CaSSU, RIC

REFERENCE: Henderson F179.

D103.2   French-language edition (1944)

LE CANADA ET LA GUERRE | [18.5-mm rule] | *Cérémonie tenue à l'occasion* | D'UN DISCOURS PRONONCÉ | *par* | Le Très Honorable | W. L. MACKENZIE KING, M.P., | *Premier Ministre du Canada* | *devant* | LES DEUX CHAMBRES DU PARLEMENT DE | WESTMINSTER | [18.5-mm rule] | *Discours prononcés par* | Le très honorable WINSTON CHURCHILL, C.H., M.P., | *Premier ministre du Royaume-Uni* | Le très honorable W. L. MACKENZIE KING, M.P. [*sic*, no comma] | *Premier Ministre du Canada* | Le très honorable VICOMTE SIMON, G.C.S.I., G.C.V.O., | *Lord*

Chancelier | Le très honorable CLIFTON BROWN, M.P., | *Président de la Chambre des Communes du Royaume-Uni.* | [18.5-mm rule] | WESTMINSTER, LONDRES, ANGLETERRE | LE 11 MAI 1944. | [arms of Canada, 21.1 × 13.9 mm] | OTTAWA | EDMOND CLOUTIER | IMPRIMEUR DE SA TRÈS EXCELLENTE MAJESTÉ LE ROI 1944

PUBLICATION: Ottawa: Imprimeur du Roi, 1944.

PAGINATION: 23, [1]. Pamphlet in self-wrappers.

CONTRIBUTION: Speech of 11 May 1944: pp. 3–5.

LOCATION: CaOOP

REFERENCE: Henderson F180.

D104 VICTORY ON THE MARCH   1944

VICTORY ON THE MARCH | [American eagle device, 58 × 55 mm] | *reports on the Progress of the War by* | PRESIDENT FRANKLIN D. ROOSEVELT | PRIME MINISTER WINSTON CHURCHILL | GENERAL GEORGE C. MARSHALL | *and the* | U.S. NAVY | 1944 | NATIONAL EDUCATIONAL ALLIANCE, INC. | New York

PUBLICATION: New York: National Educational Alliance, 1944.

PAGINATION: viii, 200.

CONTRIBUTION: 'Churchill before the House of Commons' (speech of 21 September 1943): pp. 15–42.

LOCATIONS: CaOHM, USDLC

D105 REPRESENTATIVE AMERICAN SPEECHES:
1943–1944   1944

THE REFERENCE SHELF | [92.7-mm rule] | [ranged left] Vol. 17 [ranged right] No. 4 | [centred] REPRESENTATIVE AMERICAN | SPEECHES: 1943–1944 | Selected by | A. CRAIG BAIRD | *Department of Speech, State University of Iowa* | [publisher's device, 11.5 mm in diameter] | THE H. W. WILSON COMPANY | [ranged left] NEW YORK [ranged right] 1944

PUBLICATION: New York: H. W. Wilson, 1944.

PAGINATION: [2], 360, [6].

CONTRIBUTION: 'British-American Co-operation', speech of 6 September 1943 at Harvard University: pp. 27–36.

ANNOTATIONS: It is interesting that A. Craig Baird, of the State University of Iowa and editor of the series, wrote to Little, Brown to ask permission to publish the Harvard address in this volume, since no such permission had apparently been requested by him with respect to the two addresses to the Congress published in the *Representative American Speeches* volumes of 1941–42 and 1942–43 (**D91** and **D101**). He likely viewed those speeches as being in the public domain. In any event, he explained the purpose of the series in the following terms in his letter of 24 February 1944:[21]

---

21. "Churchill, Winston 1944" file, Little, Brown Archives.

The Wilson Company, as you know, is primarily a library reference publishing house. It does not compete in the textbook field nor in the general publishing field. My proposed volume has a limited library distribution. ... The volume includes only addresses given by Americans or those delivered in this country.

Little, Brown replied on 1 March that the speech had not yet been copyrighted but that they were planning to include it in their forthcoming volume of speeches (*Onwards to Victory*, **A194.2**). In the event that Baird was paying fees to others, Little, Brown proposed $10, but allowed that, if no fees were being paid, the speech could be used *gratis*. In such circumstances there should be no reference to its being published with the permission of Little, Brown.

LOCATIONS: CaAEP, RIC, USDLC, USMH

D106 WINNING THE PEACE   1944

[Cover title:] [on moderate greenish blue paper wrappers; with a white rectangle, 95.8 × 113.6 mm, centred 13.5 mm from the head] WINNING | THE | PEACE | [below the white rectangle and ranged right] EXTRACTS FROM | SPEECHES BY | MEMBERS OF | THE BRITISH GOVERNMENT

PUBLICATION: New York: British Information Services, 1944.

PAGINATION: 12. Pamphlet in self-wrappers.

CONTRIBUTIONS: Extracts from broadcast of 21 March 1943: p. 4; Lord Mayor's Luncheon address of 10 November 1942: p. 5; speeches in the House of Commons of 11 February and 17 March 1943: p. 6; and the Lord Mayor's Luncheon address of 9 November 1943: p. 8.

LOCATIONS: CaOONL, RIC, RPH, USMH

D107 MARSHAL TITO AND HIS GALLANT BANDS   1944

Two editions by separate publishers are known. On the basis of information currently available, I have been unable to assign priority.

D107.1   American edition (1944)

[Cover title:] MARSHAL TITO | AND HIS GALLANT BANDS | *By* WINSTON CHURCHILL, SERGEANT WALTER BERNSTEIN, | FRANK GERVASI, STOYAN PRIBICHEVICH | *and* LOUIS ADAMIC | [119-mm swelled rule] | [a 14-line text followed by:] (*Signed*) MARSHAL TITO. | [119-mm swelled rule] | UNITED COMMITTEE OF SOUTH-SLAVIC AMERICANS | 1010 Park Avenue, New York 28, N.Y.

PUBLICATION: New York: United Committee of South-Slavic Americans, 1944.

PAGINATION: 16. Pamphlet in self-wrappers, 2 leaves of plates.

CONTRIBUTION: 'Marshal Tito and His Gallant Bands': pp. 3–5. An excerpt of Churchill's statement to the House of Commons on the progress of the war. On the basis of information currently available, it is impossible to determine whether this edition or the *Address of 22 February 1944* (**A191**) constituted the first volume appearance of any significant portion of the address. The entire address was subsequently collected in

Rhodes James, Vol. VII, at pp. 6881–94, under the title 'The Progress of the War'. The cited portion is taken from pp. 6889.23 to 6891.18.

NOTE: The Library of Congress copy was donated by the publisher on 29 March 1944.

LOCATIONS: CaAEU, RIC, USDLC, USMiU, USNN

D107.2   Australian issue (1944)

[Cover title:] MARSHAL TITO | AND HIS GALLANT BANDS | By WINSTON CHURCHILL, SERGEANT WALTER BERNSTEIN, | FRANK GERVASI, STOYAN PRIBICHEVICH | LIEUT-GENERAL MILOVAN DZILAS, and LOUIS ADAMIC | [triple rule, two thin 96.1-mm rules with a thicker 108.6-mm rule between] | [a 14-line text followed by:] (Signed) MARSHAL TITO. | [triple rule, two thin 96.1-mm rules with a thicker 108.6-mm rule between] | Published by the | JUGOSLAV IMMIGRANTS' ASSOCIATION OF AUSTRALIA, | 641 George Street, Sydney. | PRICE 9d.

PUBLICATION: Sydney: Jugoslav Immigrants' Association of Australia, 1944.

CONTRIBUTION: As the American edition.

LOCATIONS: AuNL, USNN

D108   VOICES OF HISTORY 1943–44   1944

[Within a frame made up of an outer thick–thin rule and an inner wavy-rule box, enclosing 174 × 97.9 mm] VOICES OF | HISTORY | 1943–44 | Speeches and Papers of | ROOSEVELT, CHURCHILL, | STALIN, CHIANG, HITLER | AND OTHER LEADERS | Delivered During 1943 | FRANKLIN WATTS, *Editor* | NATHAN AUSUBEL, *Associate Editor* | GRAMERCY PUBLISHING COMPANY | NEW YORK

PUBLICATION: New York: Gramercy, 1944.

PAGINATION: xviii, 621, [1].

CONTRIBUTIONS: Includes Churchill's principal speeches and broadcasts from 11 February to 9 November 1943, as well as the Casablanca Communiqué, the joint message with Roosevelt to the Italian people of 16 July, their joint statement following the Quebec Conference, their joint message of 11 September to Marshal Badoglio, the joint message with Roosevelt and Stalin on Italy and their joint declaration at Teheran.

As N. Wartels of Gramercy Publishing explained in a letter of 10 February 1944 to Raymond Everitt of Little, Brown,[22]

> The 1943–44 volume will contain, in fact, all the public speeches of Churchill, as the 1942–43 volume contained all of Churchill's public speeches of that year. A comparison of *The End of the Beginning* with the 1942–43 volume will demonstrate that there was nothing of any consequence whatever contained in your book that was not contained in ours.

LOCATIONS: CaOONL, CaOOP, CaQMM, RIC, UKBL, USDLC, USMH

---

22. From the "Churchill, Winston 1944" file in the Little, Brown Archives.

D109 "AN HONOUR TO SERVE" 1945?

"AN HONOUR TO SERVE" | [battalion's device, 23×27.3 mm] | A SHORT HISTORY | OF THE | 8th SURREY (Reigate) BATTALION | HOME GUARD | MAY, 1940–DECEMBER, 1944 | BY | N. R. BISHOP, Ph.D., B.Com. (Lond.)

PUBLICATION: No city indicated: no publisher indicated [8th Surrey (Reigate) Battalion?], no date [1945?].

PAGINATION: [6], iii, [1], 68, [2], 4 leaves of plates.

CONTRIBUTION: Speech broadcast from Washington on 14 May 1943: pp. 63–6.

LOCATION: UKBL

D110 VOICES OF HISTORY 1944–45 1945

[Within a frame made up of an outer thick–thin rule and an inner wavy-rule box, enclosing 174×97.9 mm] VOICES OF | HISTORY | 1944–45 | Speeches and Papers of | ROOSEVELT, CHURCHILL, | STALIN, CHIANG, HITLER | AND OTHER LEADERS | Delivered During 1944 | NATHAN AUSUBEL, *Editor* | GRAMERCY PUBLISHING COMPANY | NEW YORK

PUBLICATION: New York: Gramercy, 1945. Price $3.50.

PAGINATION: xviii, 660, [2].

CONTRIBUTIONS: Includes Churchill's principal speeches and broadcasts from 22 February to 15 December 1944 as well as his messages to the Prime Minister of Greece and the People of Italy, and his joint statement with Roosevelt on Italy.

LOCATIONS: CaOONL, RIC (dj), USDLC, USMH

D111 MR CHURCHILL AND THE PARTIES 1945?

[Dropped-head title:] MR. CHURCHILL | AND THE PARTIES

PUBLICATION: London: Liberal Publication Department, 1945?

PAGINATION: 2. Leaflet.

CONTRIBUTIONS: Excerpts from Churchill's speeches of 3 April 1939 (63 words) and 23 July 1943 (41 words): p. 2.

NOTE: The small leaflet (126.5×126 mm) is an election document (549 words of text), clearly destined to be distributed to the electorate during the 1945 election. It closes with the exhortation: "The best thing that can happen to Churchill at the election is that he should be returned—with as few Tories and as many Liberals as possible."

LOCATION: CB

D112 10 DOWNING STREET 1945

10 | DOWNING STREET | THE ROMANCE OF A HOUSE | *by* | EGON JAMESON | [triangular publisher's device, 19.1×20.8 mm] | FRANCIS ALDOR

PUBLICATION: London: Aldor, October 1945. Price 18s. Reprinted in January 1946.

PAGINATION: 536, 4 leaves of plates.

CONTRIBUTION: Major portion of the address of 4 June 1940 (undated in this volume) to the House of Commons: pp. 531–5.

LOCATIONS: CaOHM, CaOTU, RIC (dj), UKBL, USDLC, USMH

D113 WAS CHURCHILL RIGHT IN GREECE?   1945

[All of the following within a decorative-rule box, enclosing 143 × 89 mm] WAS | CHURCHILL RIGHT | IN GREECE? | PRESS REPORTS | and | EDITORIAL COMMENT | *Compiled by* | CHRIS J. AGRAFIOTIS | PRINTED BY GRANITE STATE PRESS | MANCHESTER, N.H., U.S.A.

PUBLICATION: Manchester (NH): Granite State Press, 1945.

PAGINATION: [*8*], 152, 1 leaf of plates.

CONTRIBUTION: Speech of 18 January 1945, under the title 'Events in Greece: "Our Simple Policy"': pp. 79–102. Two additional interventions by Churchill in the debate are found at pp. 103 and 104. This is the first appearance of the address, which was subsequently collected in Rhodes James, Vol. VII, at pp. 7083–103, under the title 'Review of the War'. The lengthy excerpt published here is not the complete address, which dealt with subjects other than Greece, although it does incorporate portions of the debate which are not contained in Rhodes James, for example the section of the debate regarding the tabling of a telegram which Churchill quotes. Rhodes James notes this omission on p. 7091. The Agrafiotis excerpt begins at p. 7085.27 and ends at p. 7095.21.

LOCATIONS: USMH, USNhD, USOrU

REFERENCE: Woods D(b)65.

D114 BRITAIN AND TOMORROW   1945

Britain | *and* | *Tomorrow* | [17.6-mm rule] | BRITISH OFFICIAL STATEMENTS | VOLUME IV | September 1943 to December 1944 | BRITISH INFORMATION SERVICES | *An Agency of The British Government* | [123-mm rule] | NEW YORK 20 .... 30 ROCKEFELLER PLAZA .... CIRCLE 6-5100 | WASHINGTON 5, D.C. . 1336 NEW YORK AVE., N.W. . EXECUTIVE 8525 | CHICAGO 1 ..... 360 NORTH MICHIGAN AVENUE . ANDOVER 1733 | SAN FRANCISCO 8 ... 391 SUTTER STREET ..... SUTTER 6634

PUBLICATION: New York: British Information Services, 1945.

PAGINATION: 145.

CONTRIBUTIONS: Statements in the House of Commons of 21 September 1943: p. 3; and 22 February 1944: pp. 22–3; broadcast of 26 March: pp. 36–8; statements in the House of 21 April: p. 44; 24 May: pp. 46–9; 2 August: pp. 89–90; 28 September: pp. 96–8; 27 and 31 October: pp. 107–10; 17, 29 and 30 November: pp. 120–4; 8 December: pp. 127–8; 15 December: pp. 135–9; and 27 December: p. 140.

LOCATIONS: RIC, USMH

REFERENCE: Woods D(b)62/1.

D115 REPRESENTATIVE AMERICAN SPEECHES: 1944–1945 1945

THE REFERENCE SHELF | [92.7-mm rule] | [ranged left] Vol. 18 [ranged right] No. 3 | [centred] REPRESENTATIVE AMERICAN | SPEECHES: 1944–1945 | Selected by | A. CRAIG BAIRD | *Department of Speech, State University of Iowa* | [publisher's device, 11.5 mm in diameter] | THE H. W. WILSON COMPANY | [ranged left] NEW YORK [ranged right] 1945

PUBLICATION: New York: H. W. Wilson, October 1945. Price $1.25.

PAGINATION: [2], 328, [6].

CONTRIBUTIONS: 'Germany Surrenders', speech on V-E Day: pp. 40–2; and 'Humanity's Loss', speech on the death of Roosevelt: pp. 170–3. The text of the first speech was taken from a recording of the radio broadcast made by a member of the speech department at the State University of Iowa; that of the second from *Vital Speeches of the Day* (**E133b**).

LOCATIONS: RIC, USDLC, USMH

D116 ŠEST LET EXILU 1945

D116.1 First edition (1945)

PUBLICATION: London: "Čechoslavák", 1945.

No copy examined.

LOCATIONS: UKBL, UKLse, UKScNL

D116.2 Second edition (1946)

DR. EDVARD BENEŠ | ŠEST LET EXILU | A DRUHÉ | SVĚTOVÉ VÁLKY | *Řeči, projevy a dokumenty z r. 1938–45* | 1946 | [53.7-mm rule] | Družstevní práce – Praha

PUBLICATION: Prague: Družstevní práce, 1946.

PAGINATION: 493, [3].

CONTRIBUTION: Broadcast address of 30 September 1940 to the Czech people: pp. 443–4. First volume appearance of this broadcast address; it has here been translated into Czech. The only volume appearance of the address in English is in Rhodes James, Vol. VI, at pp. 6283–4, under the title 'To the People of Czechoslovakia'.

LOCATIONS: CaOTU, RIC (dj), UKBL, UKOxB, USDLC, USMH

D116.3 Second edition, second issue (1947)

DR. EDVARD BENEŠ | ŠEST LET EXILU | A DRUHÉ | SVĚTOVÉ VÁLKY | *Řeči, projevy a dokumenty z r. 1938–45* | 1946 | [53.7-mm rule] | Orbis – Praha

PUBLICATION: Prague: Orbis, 1947. Price 160 Kčs (cloth) and 130 Kčs (wrappers).

LOCATIONS: RIC (dj), USDLC

D117 THE SECOND GREAT WAR   1946?

Published in nine volumes. Every volume includes Churchill speech material, generally abridged to some extent, plus occasional statements, messages and other communiqués.

Volume I

[All of the following within a deep reddish orange double-rule frame, within which a wide black crenellated border, enclosing 221.2 × 157.8 mm] THE SECOND | GREAT WAR | [deep reddish orange] 𝔄 𝔖𝔱𝔞𝔫𝔡𝔞𝔯𝔡 ℌ𝔦𝔰𝔱𝔬𝔯𝔶 | [black] Edited by | SIR JOHN HAMMERTON | Editor of The Great War, World War 1914–19, Europe's Fight for Freedom, etc. | Military Editor | Maj.-Gen. SIR CHARLES GWYNN, K.C.B., C.M.G., D.S.O. | [within a double ring, white on deep reddish orange, circular publisher's device, 19.3 mm in diameter] | [black] 𝔙𝔬𝔩𝔲𝔪𝔢 𝔒𝔫𝔢 | Pages 1–400 | Published by | THE WAVERLY   BOOK   COMPANY   LTD. | in   association   with | THE AMALGAMATED PRESS LTD. | Farringdon Street, London, E.C.4.

PUBLICATION: London: Waverly Book Company, 1946?

PAGINATION: viii, 400, 9 leaves of plates.

CONTRIBUTIONS: 'The First Lord on the U–Boat War' (speech of 26 September 1939): p. 94; 'Mr. Churchill on the First Month of the War' (broadcast of 1 October): p. 95; extract from statements in the House of Commons, on 17 October: p. 232; on 8 November: p. 351; and 'Carry on and Dread Nought' (speech of 6 December): p. 385.

LOCATIONS: CaOHM, CaOOU, RIC (dj), UKBL

Volume II

As the title page of Volume I, except as follows: substitute '𝔙𝔬𝔩𝔲𝔪𝔢 𝔗𝔴𝔬 | Pages 401–816'.

PAGINATION: viii, 416, 5 leaves of plates.

CONTRIBUTIONS: 'The First Ten Weeks of War' (speech of 12 November 1939): p. 403; 'From River Plate to North Sea' (broadcast of 18 December 1939): p. 474; and 'Offence and Defence round Britain's Coasts' (speech of 27 February 1940): p. 643.

Volume III

As the title page of Volume I, except as follows: substitute '𝔙𝔬𝔩𝔲𝔪𝔢 𝔗𝔥𝔯𝔢𝔢 | Pages 817–1240'.

PAGINATION: x, 424, 5 leaves of plates.

CONTRIBUTIONS: Speech of 13 May 1940: p. 835; statement of 28 May: p. 858; ' "The Miracle of Deliverance" ' (statement of 4 June in the House of Commons): pp. 898–9; message of 10 June to M. Paul Reynaud, the Prime Minister of France: p. 982; excerpt from broadcast of 17 June: p. 983; excerpt from speech of 18 June in the House: p. 990; statement of 23 June and excerpt from speech of 25 June in the House: p. 1002; ' "Conquer We Must—Conquer We Shall" ' (broadcast of 19 May): p. 1030; 'How Britain Secured the French Fleet' (speech of 4 July): p. 1094; ' "Men Will Say, This Was their Finest Hour" ' (speech of 18 June in the House): p. 1123; ' "The War of the Unknown Warriors" ' (broadcast of 14 July): p. 1124; excerpt from a broadcast of 20 January: p. 1144; excerpt from a broadcast of 11 September, message of 16 September to the Fighter Command, and excerpt from a speech of 17 September in the House: p. 1216.

Volume IV

As the title page of Volume I, except as follows: substitute '𝔙𝔬𝔩𝔲𝔪𝔢 𝔉𝔬𝔲𝔯 | Pages 1241–1636'.

PAGINATION: ix, [1], 396, 3 leaves of plates.

CONTRIBUTIONS: Excerpt from speech of 8 October 1940 in the House of Commons: pp. 1253 and 1265; 'The Premier on Britain's Home Front' (excerpts from speeches of 5 and 12 November in the House): pp. 1274 and 1309; ' "One Man and One Man Only" ' (broadcast of 23 December to the Italian people): p. 1364; broadcast message of 21 October: p. 1394; and excerpts from speeches of 20 August and 5 September: p. 1428.

Volume V

As the title page of Volume I, except as follows: substitute '𝔙𝔬𝔩𝔲𝔪𝔢 𝔉𝔦𝔳𝔢 | Pages 1637–2096'.

PAGINATION: x, 360, 8 leaves of plates.

CONTRIBUTIONS: Excerpts of 31 January 1941 at Portsmouth and broadcast of 27 April: pp. 1711 and 1736; 'Beating the Invader: Rules for Civilians in 1941': p. 1712; 'New Collaboration of the Free Peoples' (speech of 12 June to a meeting of representatives of Great Britain and the Allied governments at St James's Palace in London): p. 1785; excerpt from a broadcast speech of 22 June: p. 1819; joint message of Roosevelt and Churchill to Stalin during the Atlantic Conference and excerpt of statement of 30 September in the House of Commons: p. 1856; the Atlantic Charter, excerpt of broadcast address of 24 August, and speech of 9 September in the House: p. 1920; 'Premier's Address to Congress at Washington' (speech of 26 December): p. 1968; communication of 8 December to the Japanese Chargé d'Affaires in London: p. 1997. *Beating the Invader* was separately published in May 1941 (**B76**).

Volume VI

As the title page of Volume I, except as follows: substitute '𝔙𝔬𝔩𝔲𝔪𝔢 𝔖𝔦𝔵 | Pages 2097–2588'.

PAGINATION: x, 492, 9 leaves of plates.

CONTRIBUTIONS: ' "A Heavy Defeat" and "A Remarkable Victory" ' (broadcast of 15 February 1942 on the fall of Singapore and excerpt from speech of 10 November at the Mansion House): p. 2515.

Volume VII

As the title page of Volume I, except as follows: substitute '𝔙𝔬𝔩𝔲𝔪𝔢 𝔖𝔢𝔳𝔢𝔫 | Pages 2589–3084'.

PAGINATION: x, 496, 13 leaves of plates.

CONTRIBUTIONS: ' "We Should Make and Proclaim a 4 Years' Plan" ' (broadcast of 21 March 1943 and excerpt of speech of 9 November at the Mansion House): p. 2599; Teheran Declaration of 1 December and the official announcement related thereto: p. 2636; broadcast message of 16 July by Roosevelt and Churchill to the Italian people: p. 2819; speech of 21 September in the House of Commons: p. 2866; and speech of 6 June 1944 in the House on the liberation of Rome and the invasion of France: p. 3016.

Volume VIII

As the title page of Volume I, except as follows: substitute '𝔙𝔬𝔩𝔲𝔪𝔢 𝔈𝔦𝔤𝔥𝔱 | Pages 3085–3576'.

PAGINATION: x, 492, 15 leaves of plates.

CONTRIBUTIONS: Explanation of 26 December 1944 to Greek representatives in Athens of the presence of the British in Greece: p. 3358; and announcement of the end of the War in Europe on 8 May 1945: p. 3506.

Volume IX

As the title page of Volume I, except as follows: substitute '𝔙𝔬𝔩𝔲𝔪𝔢 𝔑𝔦𝔫𝔢 | Pages 3577–4076'.

PAGINATION: x, 500, 12 leaves of plates.

CONTRIBUTION: Statement of 2 May 1945 in the House of Commons on the German surrender in Italy: p. 3708.

D118 VOICES OF HISTORY, 1945–46   1946

[Within a frame made up of an outer thick–thin rule and an inner wavy-rule box, enclosing 184.2 × 104.5 mm] VOICES OF | HISTORY | 1945 – 46 | Speeches and Papers of | ROOSEVELT, TRUMAN, CHURCHILL, | ATTLEE, STALIN, DE GAULLE, CHIANG | AND OTHER LEADERS | Delivered During 1945 | NATHAN AUSUBEL, *Editor* | GRAMERCY PUBLISHING COMPANY | NEW YORK

PUBLICATION: New York: Gramercy Press, 1946.

PAGINATION: xix, [1], 810, [2].

CONTRIBUTIONS: Address of 18 January 1945 in the House of Commons: pp. 19–38; address of 27 February in the House: pp. 75–92; excerpts from address to the Annual Meeting of the Conservative Party of 15 March: pp. 121–3; eulogy to President Roosevelt delivered in the House on 17 April: pp. 154–7; text of a leaflet dropped on Germany on 23 April, consisting of a warning signed by President Truman, Marshal Stalin and Churchill: pp. 160–1; announcement of the surrender of Germany of 8 May 1945 in the House: pp. 193–4; speech of the same day to the V-E Day crowds: p. 195; broadcast address of 13 May on 'Five Years of War': pp. 203–8; letter of 22 May to Deputy Prime Minister Clement Attlee on the Labour Party's refusal to continue the Coalition Government: pp. 216–17; speech of 5 June on Syria and Lebanon in the House: pp. 257–61; reply of 12 June in the House to the allegations made by Marshal Pétain: pp. 287–8; Potsdam Proclamation by President Truman, Generalissimo Chiang Kai-Shek and Churchill defining the terms for Japanese surrender: pp. 388–9; and Statement on the Atomic Bomb, prepared by Churchill before the change of government, but released by Prime Minister Attlee on 6 August 1945: pp. 413–15.

LOCATIONS: CaOONL, RIC, UKBL, USDLC, USMH

REFERENCE: Woods D(b)69.

D119 BRITAIN'S MEMORIAL TO FRANKLIN ROOSEVELT   1946

[Cover title:] [vivid reddish orange] BRITAIN'S MEMORIAL TO | FRANKLIN ROOSEVELT | [black, sketch model of the proposed statue, set against, but extending above and below, a black-framed background, 123 × 91 mm, the proposed statue being 142 mm in height] | [ranged right below the background] *Sketch model of | the proposed statue* | [14 lines, set in two columns, explaining the souvenir book and the memorial]

PUBLICATION: London: *The Times* (and the Franklin Roosevelt Memorial Committee and the Pilgrims?), 1946.

PAGINATION: [2], 22.

CONTRIBUTION: Churchill's 'Tribute', being his comments in the House of Commons upon the second reading of the Bill establishing the Roosevelt Memorial: p. 5.

REFERENCE: Woods D(b)65/1.

LOCATIONS: CaOWTU, CaOTTC, RIC, UKBL, UKOxB

D120 BRITAIN AT WAR   1946

BRITAIN AT WAR | GREAT DESCRIPTIONS AND SPEECHES | FROM THE SECOND WORLD WAR | EDITED AND ANNOTATED BY | HENNING KRABBE | [ranged right] *Be great in act, as you have been in thought; | Be stirring as the time; be fire with fire; | Threaten the threatener, and outface the brow | Of bragging horror —* | SHAKESPEARE: KING JOHN | [centred] KØBENHAVN | [71.4-mm rule] | GYLDENDALSKE BOGHANDEL | NORDISK FORLAG | 1946

PUBLICATION: Copenhagen: Gyldendalske Boghandel/Nordisk Forlag, 1946.

PAGINATION: VIII, 288.

CONTRIBUTIONS: Contains 11 speeches by Churchill.

LOCATIONS: DkNL, USMH

D121 DINNER GIVEN BY THE CITY OF NEW YORK IN HONOUR OF THE RIGHT HONOURABLE WINSTON LEONARD SPENCER CHURCHILL P.C., C.H., O.M.   1946

[Deep purplish blue] DINNER | GIVEN BY THE CITY OF NEW YORK | IN HONOUR OF | THE RIGHT HONOURABLE | WINSTON LEONARD SPENCER CHURCHILL | P.C., C.H., O.M. | THE WALDORF-ASTORIA | FRIDAY, MARCH FIFTEENTH | NINETEEN HUNDRED AND FORTY-SIX

PUBLICATION: New York?: City of New York?, 15 March 1946.

PAGINATION: 12, plus card wrappers.

CONTRIBUTIONS: Excerpts from speeches of 13 May and 4 June 1940: p. 5.

LOCATION: RIC

D122 REPRESENTATIVE AMERICAN SPEECHES: 1945–1946   1946

THE REFERENCE SHELF | [92.7-mm rule] | [ranged left] Vol. 19 [ranged right] No. 4 | [centred] REPRESENTATIVE AMERICAN | SPEECHES: 1945–1946 | Selected by | A. CRAIG BAIRD | *Department of Speech, State University of Iowa* | [publisher's device, 11.5 mm in diameter] | THE H. W. WILSON COMPANY | [ranged left] NEW YORK [ranged right] 1946

PUBLICATION: New York: H. W. Wilson, 1946.

PAGINATION: [2], 287, [3].

CONTRIBUTION: 'The Sinews of Peace', speech of 5 March 1946: pp. 20–32.

LOCATIONS: USDLC, USMH

D123 THE FORCED CEDING OF SOUTH TYROL TO ITALY   1946?

The Forced Ceding of | SOUTH TYROL | to Italy through the | Peace Treaty of St. Germain,   1919 | CONDEMNED | by | AMERICAN,   BRITISH,   FRENCH, ITALIAN | Statesmen   and   Scholars | Statements | by | WOODROW   WILSON, DAVID   LLOYD   GEORGE,   GEORGES   CLEMENCEAU,   WINSTON CHURCHILL, | COLONEL HOUSE, LORD BRYCE, LORD VANSITTART, LORD ROBERT CECIL, LUIGI LUZZATI, LEONIDA BISSOLATI | and others | COMMITTEE ON SOUTH TYROL | 165 West 46th Street (Suite 1109) | New York 19, N.Y.

PUBLICATION: New York: Committee on South Tyrol, 1946?

PAGINATION: 28, plus title page. Roneoed.

CONTRIBUTION: Excerpt from speech of 5 June 1946 in the House of Commons: p. 18.

LOCATION: UKLse

D124 MINUTES AND PROCEEDINGS OF THE TOWN COUNCIL, 1945–1946   1947

[Cover title:] [arms of the city of Aberdeen, 25 × 32.3 mm] | City of Aberdeen. | [42.6-mm double rule] | MINUTES AND PROCEEDINGS | OF THE | TOWN COUNCIL. | [47.6-mm   rule] | 1945–1946. | [47.6-mm   rule] | Aberdeen   : | PRINTED   BY   G. CORNWALL & SONS. | [10.4-mm rule] | MCMXLVII.

PUBLICATION: Aberdeen: Town Council, 1946.

PAGINATION: 8.

CONTRIBUTION: Speech of 27 April 1946 on receiving the freedom of the City of Aberdeen: pp. 526–8.

LOCATION: UKScAb

REFERENCE: Woods D(b)66/1.

D125 VOICES FROM BRITAIN 1947

VOICES | FROM BRITAIN | *BROADCAST HISTORY 1939–45* | [25-mm thick–thin rule] | Compiled and Edited by | HENNING KRABBE | FORMER DANISH ANNOUNCER, B.B.C. | With a Foreword by | NOEL F. NEWSOME, O.B.E. | FORMER DIRECTOR OF EUROPEAN BROADCASTS | LONDON | GEORGE ALLEN & UNWIN LTD

PUBLICATION: London: George Allen & Unwin, May 1947. Price 18s.

PAGINATION: 304, 13 leaves of plates.

CONTRIBUTIONS: Speeches of 5 October 1938: pp. 14–17; 19 May 1940: pp. 32–5; 17 June: p. 50; 18 June: pp. 50–5; 14 July: pp. 56–8; 11 September: pp. 62–4; 21 October: pp. 74–6; 27 April 1941: pp. 85–91; 22 June: pp. 102–7; 24 August: pp. 110–15; 8 December: pp. 121–2; 15 February 1942: pp. 123–4; 8 May 1945: p. 270; and 13 May: pp. 286–94; the Atlantic Charter: pp. 109–10; and the Teheran Declaration: pp. 178–9.

LOCATIONS: CaOHM, RIC, UKScNL, USDLC, USMH, USNN

D126 HONOURED IN SCOTLAND'S CAPITAL 1947

HONOURED IN | SCOTLAND'S CAPITAL | Freemen or "Burgesses and Gild Brothers-Gratis" | of the City of Edinburgh, 1459 to 1946 | with extracts from their Speeches | Compiled by | C. J. COUSLAND, F.R.S.E., A.R.P.S. | With an Historical Note by | MARGUERITE WOOD, Ph.D. | [publisher's device, 18.6 × 39 mm] | 1946 | PUBLISHED BY C. J. COUSLAND & SONS LTD. | AND PRINTED AT THE PRESS OF THE PUBLISHERS

PUBLICATION: Edinburgh: Cousland, July 1947. Price 12s. 6d.

PAGINATION: viii, 132.

CONTRIBUTION: Speech of 12 October 1942 upon his acceptance of a freedom for the first time: pp. 118–26.

LOCATIONS: MLW, RIC (dj), UKBL, UKScNL, USDLC, USNN

D127 WE HAPPY FEW 1947

WE HAPPY FEW | AN ANTHOLOGY BY | OWEN RUTTER | I: Britain at War | II: Britain at Sea | III: Britain in the Air | *'We few, we happy few, | we band of brothers ....'* | [ranged right] *Shakespeare* | [centred] Printed in Great Britain, | with eleven engravings by John O'Connor, | at the Golden Cockerel Press | 1946

PUBLICATION: London: Christopher Sandford at the Golden Cockerel Press, July 1947. Price 30s.

PAGINATION: [4], 150, [6].

CONTRIBUTIONS: 'The First Non-stop Flight across the Atlantic': pp. 127–8. Churchill, as Secretary of State for War, spoke at a luncheon at the Savoy Hotel, London, on 30 June 1919, given in honour of Captain John Alcock, D.S.C., and Lieutenant A. Whitten Brown, R.A.F., who first flew across the Atlantic non-stop (from Canada to Ireland) on 14–15 June 1919, and presented them with the *Daily Mail* prize for their efforts. This is an excerpt from that address, which was subsequently collected in its entirety in Rhodes James, Vol. III, at pp. 2808–10, under the title 'The Advance of

Aviation'. Other material, not appearing for the first time in volume form, includes: 'England at Bay', pp. 44–7 (excerpts from Churchill's addresses of 14 May, 4 June and 18 June 1940); 'Our Navy', p. 115 (excerpt from Churchill's speech of 20 August 1940); and 'The Splendid Tribute' (another excerpt from the August 20 speech).

LOCATIONS: CaOONL, CaOTTC, RPH, UKBL, USDLC, USMH

REFERENCE: Cockalorum 171.

D128 PAMĚTI   1947

D128.1   First edition (1947)

DR. EDVARD BENEŠ | PAMĚTI | Od Mnichova k nové válce | a k novému vítězství | 1947 | [45-mm rule] | ORBIS – PRAHA

PUBLICATION: Prague: Orbis, 1947. Price 195 Kčs (cloth) and 165 Kčs (wrappers).

PAGINATION: [8], 519, [1], 12 leaves of plates.

CONTRIBUTION: Statement of 23 July 1940 in the House of Commons: p. 445. First volume appearance of this statement; it has here been translated into Czech. Subsequently collected in Rhodes James, Vol. VI, at p. 6255, under the title 'Provisional Czechoslovak Government'.

LOCATIONS: CaOTU, CaQMM, RIC (dj), UKBL, USMH

D128.2   First English-language edition (1954)

MEMOIRS OF | DR EDUARD BENEŠ | *From Munich to New War* | *and New Victory* | TRANSLATED BY GODFREY LIAS | *George Allen & Unwin Ltd* | RUSKIN HOUSE   MUSEUM STREET   LONDON

PUBLICATION: London: Allen & Unwin, 28 October 1954. Price 30s.

PAGINATION: xiii, [1], 346.

CONTRIBUTIONS: Address to the Czech people on the second anniversary of Munich: pp. 116–17; excerpt from broadcast of 22 June 1941 (at the time of the German invasion of Russia): pp. 154–5; letter to Beneš thanking him for his telegram of 23 June 1941 regarding that broadcast: p. 166; the Teheran Declaration: pp. 250–1; and statement of 23 July 1940 on recognition of the Czech Government in exile: p. 301.

LOCATIONS: CaOKQ, CaOTMCL, RIC (dj), UKBL, USMH

REFERENCE: Woods D(b)95.

D128.3   First American issue of British sheets (1954)

MEMOIRS OF | DR EDUARD BENEŠ | *From Munich to New War* | *and New Victory* | TRANSLATED BY GODFREY LIAS | HOUGHTON MIFFLIN COMPANY, BOSTON | *The Riverside Press, Cambridge* | 1954

PUBLICATION: Boston: Houghton Mifflin, 1954.

LOCATION: CaOME

D128.4   Second American issue (1972)

MEMOIRS OF | DR EDUARD BENEŠ | *From Munich to New War* | *and New Victory* | TRANSLATED BY GODFREY LIAS | [publisher's device] | ARNO PRESS | A NEW YORK TIMES COMPANY | New York • 1972

PUBLICATION: New York: Arno Press, 1972.

PAGINATION: [4], xiii, [1], 348, [2].

LOCATIONS: CaACU, CaOHM, CaSRU, USDLC, USMH

D128.5   Third American issue (1978)

PUBLICATION: Westport, CT: Greenwood Press, 1978.

No copy examined.

LOCATIONS: CaOTY, CaOWTL, USDLC

D129   UNITED EUROPE   1947

[Cover title:] [strong reddish brown on light olive grey card wrappers; thickness: 0.25 mm; 109-mm thick–thin rule] | [ranged left] UNITED | [ranged right] EUROPE | [centred] SPEECHES | AT THE | ROYAL ALBERT HALL | 14th MAY, 1947 | BY | THE ARCHBISHOP OF CANTERBURY | Rt. Hon. WINSTON CHURCHILL, M.P. | Mr. GEORGE GIBSON, | LADY VIOLET BONHAM CARTER | Mr. VICTOR GOLLANCZ | MODERATOR OF FREE SPEECH COUNCIL | Rt. Hon. OLIVER STANLEY, M.P. | [109-mm thin–thick rule] | [ranged lower right] SIXPENCE

PUBLICATION: London: United Europe Movement, October 1947. Price 6d.

PAGINATION: 24. Pamphlet in card wrappers.

CONTRIBUTION: Speech of 14 May 1947: pp. 4–13.

ANNOTATIONS: Copies were sent *gratis* to persons "in view of the support [they had] already given to the United Europe Movement". In his covering letter of October 1947 to those persons, Duncan Sandys, Honorary Joint Secretary, added that additional copies could be obtained for 6d. plus 2½d. postage.

LOCATIONS: CaOTTC, RIC

REFERENCE: Woods D(b)69/4.[23]

D130   OFFICIAL REPORT, 68TH ANNUAL
(CONSERVATIVE PARTY) CONFERENCE   1947

NATIONAL UNION OF CONSERVATIVE | AND UNIONIST ASSOCIATIONS | [46-mm rule] | 68th Annual Conference | BRIGHTON | 2nd–4th October, 1947, | [46-mm rule] | ABBEY HOUSE, 2–8, VICTORIA STREET, WESTMINSTER, S.W.1 | [ranged left] *Telegrams:* Constitute, Sowest, London. [ranged right] *Telephone:* WHItehall 8181

PUBLICATION: London: National Union of Conservative and Unionist Associations, 1947.

PAGINATION: 124, plus card wrappers.

CONTRIBUTION: Speech: pp. 114–21.

LOCATIONS: UKOxB, USNhD

---

23. Note that Woods's reference to the date of the speech as 14 *August* 1947 is incorrect.

D130/1 INTERNATIONAL CONFERENCE OF PHYSICIANS 1947

INTERNATIONAL CONFERENCE | OF PHYSICIANS | The Royal College of Physicians of London | 8 th to 13 th SEPTEMBER, 1947 | [publisher's device, 21.7 × 30.8 mm] | *President* | THE RIGHT HON. THE LORD MORAN OF MANTON, M.C., M.D. | [33-mm rule] | *Reprinted (with additions) from* THE LANCET, *September* 13 *and* 20, 1947

PUBLICATION: London: *The Lancet*, 1947.

PAGINATION: 64.

CONTRIBUTION: Speech (toast of the medical profession) of 10 September 1947: pp. 4–6. Subsequently collected in Rhodes James, Vol. VII, at pp. 7521–3, under the title 'The Medical Profession'.

LOCATIONS: RIC, UKBL, USMH

D131 ORDER OF CEREMONY AT THE UNVEILING OF THE MEMORIAL TO PRESIDENT ROOSEVELT BY MRS ROOSEVELT 1948?

Order of Ceremony | AT THE | Unveiling of the Memorial | TO | PRESIDENT ROOSEVELT | BY MRS. ROOSEVELT | IN | GROSVENOR SQUARE, LONDON | Monday, April 12th, 1948

PUBLICATION: London?: The Pilgrims?, 1948?

PAGINATION: 48. Pamphlet in card wrappers.

CONTRIBUTION: Speech: pp. 34–7. Subsequently collected in Rhodes James, Vol. VII, at pp. 7624–5, under the title 'Pilgrims' Dinner to Mrs. Roosevelt'.

LOCATIONS: RIC, UKBL

D132 THE LAYING OF THE FOUNDATION STONE OF THE NEW CHAMBER OF THE HOUSE OF COMMONS BY THE SPEAKER, 26TH MAY 1948 1948

[Dark green] THE LAYING OF THE | FOUNDATION | STONE OF THE | NEW CHAMBER | OF THE HOUSE | OF COMMONS | BY THE SPEAKER | 26TH MAY 1948

PUBLICATION: London: HMSO, October 1948.

PAGINATION: [4], 20, [2].

CONTRIBUTION: Speech of 26 May 1948: pp. 5–7.

NOTES: The normal edition of the work, for distribution to the Members of Parliament, was in wrappers. By order of the Speaker, however, 24 copies were printed (by Curwen Press Ltd., Plaistow) and bound in full green morocco by Sangorski and Sutcliffe, for presentation to His Majesty the King, the Library of the House of Commons and those who took part in the ceremony. I have also examined a cloth-bound copy. A folder of loose photographs of the occasion (reproduced by collotype at the Chiswick Press) was attached to the inside back cover.

LOCATIONS: CaOTTC, RIC, USNhD

REFERENCE: Woods D(b)70/2.

D133 BRITISH FOREIGN AFFAIRS   1948

Two issues have been noted. It has not been possible, on the basis of information currently available, to assign priority.

D133.1   Canadian issue (1948)

[Cover title:] BRITISH | FOREIGN AFFAIRS | DEBATE IN | THE HOUSE OF COMMONS | EXCERPTS FROM THE SPEECHES OF | MR. BEVIN, MR. EDEN, MR. MCNEIL, | MR. CHURCHILL AND MR. ATTLEE | JANUARY 22 AND 23, 1948 | [33.5-mm thick–thin rule] | *FEBRUARY 1948* | UNITED KINGDOM INFORMATION OFFICE | 10 ALBERT STREET, OTTAWA

PUBLICATION: Ottawa: United Kingdom Information Office, 1948.

PAGINATION: 56. Pamphlet in self-wrappers.

CONTRIBUTIONS: Speech in the House of Commons of 23 January 1948, untitled: pp. 40–9. Other brief interventions in the debate: pp. 52–6. This is the first separate appearance of the principal Churchill speech during the debate and the only appearance of the subsequent brief interventions (at pp. 52–6). Subsequently collected in *Europe Unite* (**A246**), at pp. 224–37, and in Rhodes James, Vol. VII, at pp. 7581–90, in both cases under the title 'Foreign Affairs'. Note that lines 7586.36–44, 7587.01–21 and parts of 7588.16–19 in the Rhodes James are not included in this pamphlet. Correspondingly, lines 47.43–5 of the pamphlet do not appear in Rhodes James.

LOCATIONS: CaOHM, CaOONL, RIC

D133.2   American issue (1948)

[Cover title:] BRITISH INFORMATION SERVICES | AN AGENCY OF THE BRITISH GOVERNMENT | REFERENCE DIVISION | *I.D. 807, FEBRUARY 1948* | [33.4-mm thick–thin rule] | BRITISH | FOREIGN AFFAIRS | DEBATE IN | THE HOUSE OF COMMONS | EXCERPTS FROM THE SPEECHES OF | MR. BEVIN, MR. EDEN, MR. MCNEIL, | MR. CHURCHILL AND MR. ATTLEE | JANUARY 22 AND 23, 1948 | [33.4-mm thin–thick rule] | 30 ROCKEFELLER PLAZA, NEW YORK 20, N.Y. | 607 FIFTEENTH STREET, N.W., WASHINGTON 5, D.C. | 360 NORTH MICHIGAN AVENUE, CHICAGO 1 | 310 SANSOME STREET, SAN FRANCISCO 4

PUBLICATION: New York: British Information Services, 1948.

LOCATIONS: RIC, RPH

D134 OFFICIAL REPORT, 69TH ANNUAL
(CONSERVATIVE PARTY) CONFERENCE   1948

NATIONAL UNION OF CONSERVATIVE | AND UNIONIST ASSOCIATIONS | [46.6-mm rule] | 69th Annual Conference | LLANDUDNO | 6th–9th October, 1948 | [46.6-mm rule] | ABBEY HOUSE, 2–8, VICTORIA STREET, WESTMINSTER, S.W.1 | *Telegrams:* Constitute, Sowest, London. *Telephone:* WHItehall 8181

PUBLICATION: London: National Union of Conservative and Unionist Associations, 1948.

PAGINATION: 160, plus card wrappers.

CONTRIBUTION: Speech of 9 October 1948: pp. 149–56. Subsequently collected in *Europe Unite* (**A246**), at pp. 409–24, under the title 'Conservative Mass Meeting', and in Rhodes James, Vol. VII, at pp. 7707–17, under the title 'Perils at Home and Abroad'.

LOCATIONS: CaOTTC, UKChP, UKLo, UKOxB

REFERENCE: Woods D(b)70/1.

D135 WHAT IS THE DIFFERENCE BETWEEN A LIBERAL AND A CONSERVATIVE? 1948

[Dropped-head title only:] [vivid reddish orange] WHAT IS THE DIFFERENCE | BETWEEN A LIBERAL AND | A CONSERVATIVE?

PUBLICATION: London: Conservative & Unionist Central Office and Liberal-National Organization, 1948.

PAGINATION: 2. Leaflet.

CONTRIBUTION: Excerpt, black, in 8 lines, from speech of 8 August 1947: p. 1.

LOCATION: UKScNL

D135/1 THE NORTH ATLANTIC TREATY 1949

[Cover title:] BRITISH INFORMATION SERVICES | AN AGENCY OF THE BRITISH GOVERNMENT | REFERENCE DIVISION | *I. D. 923, MAY 1949* | [33.6-mm thick–thin rule] | THE | NORTH ATLANTIC TREATY | DEBATE IN THE HOUSE OF COMMONS | EXCERPTS FROM THE SPEECHES OF | MR. BEVIN, MR. CHURCHILL, MR. DAVIES, | MR. ZILLIACUS AND MR. NOEL-BAKER | MAY 12, 1949 | [33.6-mm thick–thin rule] | 30 ROCKEFELLER PLAZA, NEW YORK 20, N.Y. | 1910 K STREET, N.W., WASHINGTON 6, D.C. | 39 SOUTH LA SALLE STREET, CHICAGO 3 | 310 SANSOME STREET, SAN FRANCISCO 4

PUBLICATION: New York: British Information Services, 1949.

PAGINATION: 31, [1].

CONTRIBUTION: Speech of 12 May 1949: pp. 11–17.

LOCATION: RIC

D136 REPRESENTATIVE AMERICAN SPEECHES: 1948–1949 1949

THE REFERENCE SHELF | [92.7-mm rule] | [ranged left] Vol. 21 [ranged right] No. 2 | [centred] REPRESENTATIVE AMERICAN | SPEECHES: 1948–1949 | Edited, and with introductions, | by | A. CRAIG BAIRD | *Department of Speech, State University of Iowa* | [publisher's device, 11.5 mm in diameter] | THE H. W. WILSON COMPANY | [ranged left] NEW YORK [ranged right] 1949

PUBLICATION: New York: H. W. Wilson, September 1949.

PAGINATION: [2], 252, [2]

CONTRIBUTIONS: 'United We Stand Secure', speech of 31 March 1949: pp. 35–50. This is the first volume appearance of the Massachusetts Institute of Technology address. Subsequently collected in *Mid-Century: The Social Implications of Scientific Progress* (**D142**), and in Rhodes James, Vol. VII, at pp. 7801–10, under the title 'The Twentieth Century—Its Promise and Its Realization'.

LOCATIONS: RIC, USDLC, USMH

D137 OFFICIAL REPORT, 70TH ANNUAL (CONSERVATIVE PARTY) CONFERENCE   1949

NATIONAL UNION OF CONSERVATIVE | AND UNIONIST ASSOCIATIONS | [46-mm rule] | 70th Annual Conference | LONDON | 12th–14th October, 1949 | [46-mm rule] | ABBEY HOUSE, 2–8 VICTORIA STREET, WESTMINSTER, S.W.1 | *Telegrams:* Constitute, Sowest, London. *Telephone:* WHItehall 8181

PUBLICATION: London: National Union of Conservative and Unionist Associations, 1949. Price 2*s*. 6*d*.

PAGINATION: 128, plus card wrappers.

CONTRIBUTIONS: Churchill delivered a 90-minute address from 8 p.m. on October 14 to a mass meeting of about 10,000 people assembled in the Empress Hall, Earls Court, London. The address appears at pp. 117–25. Hugh Linstead, M.P., moved the vote of thanks. Churchill's reply is at p. 126. Subsequently collected in *In the Balance* (**A255**), at pp. 105–18, and in Rhodes James, Vol. VII, at pp. 7860–71, in both cases under the title 'Conservative Annual Conference'.

LOCATIONS: CaOTTC, RIC, UKChP

D138 OFFICIAL REPORT, 71ST ANNUAL (CONSERVATIVE PARTY) CONFERENCE   1950

NATIONAL UNION OF CONSERVATIVE | AND UNIONIST ASSOCIATIONS | [50.4-mm rule] | 71st Annual Conference | BLACKPOOL | 12th–14th October, 1950 | [50.4-mm rule] | ABBEY HOUSE, 2–8 VICTORIA STREET, WESTMINSTER, S.W.1 | *Telegrams:* Constitute, Sowest, London. *Telephone:* WHItehall 8181

PUBLICATION: London: Conservative Central Office, 1950. Price 2*s*. 6*d*.

PAGINATION: 116, plus card wrappers.

CONTRIBUTIONS: Speech of 14 October 1950: pp. 107–13. Churchill's reply to the vote of thanks: pp. 113–14. Subsequently collected in *In the Balance* (**A255**), at pp. 389–402, under the title 'Conservative Annual Conference', and in Rhodes James, Vol. VIII, at pp. 8096–106, under the title 'Situation at Home and Abroad'.

LOCATIONS: CaOTTC, RIC, UKChP

D138/1 CONSERVATIVE PARTY CONFERENCE 1950   1950

[Cover title:] CONSERVATIVE | PARTY | CONFERENCE | 1950 | [16.2-mm rule] | A Summary of the Principal Speeches | together with the Text of the Resolutions | adopted. | [16.2-mm   rule] | Edited   by | CONSERVATIVE   RESEARCH DEPARTMENT | PRICE 6d.

PUBLICATION: London: Conservative Central Office, November 1950. Price 6d.

PAGINATION: 36. Pamphlet in self-wrappers.

CONTRIBUTION: 'Points from Mr. Churchill's Speech', significant extracts from Churchill's speech of 14 October 1950, presented under subject headings: pp. 3–10.

LOCATION: RIC

D139 CONSERVATISM 1945–1950   1950

[All of the following within a triple-rule box, enclosing 179.5 × 107 mm] CONSER-VATISM | 1945–1950 | [Conservative and Unionist Party device, 28.9 mm in diameter] | CONSERVATIVE POLITICAL CENTRE

PUBLICATION: London: Conservative Central Office, October 1950. Price 2s. 6d. cased and 1s. 6d. sewn.

PAGINATION: [8], 248.

CONTRIBUTIONS: Excerpts from Churchill's speeches of 5 October 1946, 23 July 1949 and 28 March 1950: pp. 81–4, 106–8, and 158–64, respectively; address of February 1950 to the electors of Woodford: pp. 168–70; Foreword to *The Right Road for Britain* (**B111**): p. 173; Introduction of 19 January 1950 to *This Is the Road* (**B117**): p. 225.

LOCATIONS: DAT, CaOTTC, RIC, UKOxB, USMH

REFERENCE: Woods D(b)77.

D140 INDEPENDENT MEMBER   1950

D140.1   First edition, first printing (1950)

INDEPENDENT | MEMBER | *by* | A. P. HERBERT | *With 17 illustrations* | *and 2 maps* | [publisher's device, 20.3 × 17.2 mm] | METHUEN & CO. LTD. LONDON | *36 Essex Street, Strand, W.C.2*

PUBLICATION: London: Methuen, 19 October 1950. Price 21s. There were at least three subsequent printings: in December 1950, May 1951 and in 1952.

PAGINATION: [2], xiii, [1], 504, 12 leaves of plates.

CONTRIBUTIONS: Excerpts from speech in the House of Commons of 2 July 1940: pp. 238–41; very brief extract from the debates of 22 April 1943: p. 243. Note also that Sir Alan Herbert's 10-line poem written for Churchill's seventy-sixth birthday is printed at p. 242.

LOCATIONS: CaOOP, CaOTMCL, UKBL (rebound), USDLC, USMH

D140.2   American edition (1951)

[Within an elaborately designed artistic frame] *Independent | Member | By | A. P. Herbert |* [below the frame] 1951 | DOUBLEDAY & COMPANY, INC., GARDEN CITY, NEW YORK

PUBLICATION: Garden City (NY): Doubleday, 1951. Price $5.00.

PAGINATION: [*4*], xii, 363, [3].

CONTRIBUTION: Speech: pp. 188–90. Note also that Sir Alan Herbert's 10-line poem written for Churchill's seventy-sixth birthday is printed at p. 193.

LOCATIONS: RIC (dj), USMH, USNNC

D140.3   Second British issue, photo-reproduced from the American edition (1970)

INDEPENDENT | MEMBER | A. P. HERBERT | [publisher's device] | HOWARD BAKER, LONDON | [83.8-mm rule]

PUBLICATION: London: Baker, 1970.

PAGINATION: xi, [1], 363, [1].

CONTRIBUTIONS: Excerpts from speech of 2 July 1940: pp. 188–90; extract from the debates of 22 April 1943: p. 193. Sir Alan Herbert's poem: p. 193.

LOCATION: UKBL

D141   BRITAIN AND EUROPE   1950

D141.1   First edition (1950)

PUBLICATION: London: N. Kaye, November 1950. Price 16*s.*

No copy examined.

LOCATION: USMH

D141.2   First edition, second issue (with minor corrections) (1961)

BRITAIN AND EUROPE | PITT TO CHURCHILL | 1793–1940 | EDITED BY | JAMES JOLL | FELLOW OF ST. ANTONY'S COLLEGE, OXFORD | ADAM & CHARLES BLACK | LONDON

PUBLICATION: London: Black, 29 March 1962. Price 21*s.*

PAGINATION: xv, [1], 385, [3].

CONTRIBUTIONS: Participation in the debate of 3–5 October 1938 in the House of Commons: pp. 354–66; excerpt from the speech of 4 June 1940 in the House: p. 371; excerpt from the speech of 20 August: pp. 372–4; and broadcast address of 11 September: pp. 375–8. The excerpt from the debate of October 1938 differs from the text in *Into Battle* (**A142**),[24] where the text is longer but misses, at least, the repartee with Viscountess Astor.

LOCATIONS: CaOTTC (dj), RIC (dj), UKLse, UKScNL

---

24. At pp. 41–53.

D141.3   First paperback issue (1967)

BRITAIN AND EUROPE | PITT TO CHURCHILL | 1793–1940 | EDITED BY | JAMES JOLL | FELLOW OF ST. ANTONY'S COLLEGE, OXFORD | [publisher's device, 38.6 × 32.4 mm] | OXFORD | AT THE CLARENDON PRESS

PUBLICATION: Oxford: Oxford University Press, 1967. Price 6s. 6d.

PAGINATION: xiv, 385, [1].

LOCATIONS: CaOKQ, RIC, UKOxB, USDLC

D142   MID-CENTURY: THE SOCIAL IMPLICATIONS OF SCIENTIFIC PROGRESS   1950

MID-CENTURY | *The Social Implications of* | *Scientific Progress* | ❧ Verbatim account of the discussions held | at the Massachusetts Institute of Technology | on the occasion of its Mid-Century Convoca- | tion, March 31, April 1 and April 2, 1949 | EDITED AND ANNOTATED BY | JOHN ELY BURCHARD | DEAN OF HUMANITIES, M.I.T. | [university device, 32.2 × 28.4 mm] | *CAMBRIDGE • 1950* | Published jointly by THE TECHNOLOGY PRESS | OF THE MASSACHUSETTS INSTITUTE OF TECHNOLOGY | and JOHN WILEY & SONS, INC., NEW YORK | CHAPMAN & HALL, LIMITED, LONDON

PUBLICATION: Cambridge (MA): Massachusetts Institute of Technology Press, 1950.

PAGINATION: xx, [2], 551, [3].

CONTRIBUTION: Speech of 31 March 1949 at M.I.T.: pp. 50–74. Subsequently collected in Rhodes James, Vol. VII, at pp. 7801–10, under the title 'The Twentieth Century— Its Promise and Its Realization'.

ANNOTATIONS: The invitation to speak was arranged by Churchill's longtime friend, Bernard Baruch, who fretted two days before the speech that it would be a disaster. The story is recounted by Fleur Cowles.[25]

LOCATIONS: RIC (dj), USMH

REFERENCE: Woods D(b)79/1.

D143   105 GREATEST LIVING AUTHORS PRESENT THE WORLD'S BEST STORIES, HUMOR, DRAMA, BIOGRAPHY, HISTORY, ESSAYS, POETRY   1950

105 GREATEST LIVING AUTHORS | *PRESENT* | *The World's Best* | STORIES • HUMOR • DRAMA • BIOGRAPHY | HISTORY • ESSAYS • POETRY | *Edited by* | WHIT BURNETT | *The Dial Press* [publisher's device, 10.7 × 13 mm] *New York • 1950*

PUBLICATION: New York: Dial Press, 1950.

PAGINATION: xxv, [1], 1186, [4].

CONTRIBUTION: 'Dunkirk: The Miracle of the Evacuation', speech of 4 June 1940: pp. 541–7.

LOCATIONS: CaMWU, CaOTMCL, RIC (dj), USDLC, USMH

---

25. In *Friends and Memories* (London: Jonathan Cape, 1975), at p. 152.

D144 THE NEW CHAMBER OF THE HOUSE OF COMMONS: OPENING CEREMONY   1950

[Dark green] THE | NEW CHAMBER | OF THE HOUSE | OF COMMONS | IN THE PALACE | OF WESTMINSTER | AN ACCOUNT OF | THE OPENING | CEREMONY | 26 OCTOBER 1950

PUBLICATION: London: HMSO, May 1951.

PAGINATION: [2], 65, [5], 4 leaves of plates.

CONTRIBUTIONS: Address of 24 October 1950 seconding the motion of the Prime Minister in reply to the message from His Majesty: pp. 12–14; statement of 25 January 1945 commending the Report from the Select Committee on the Rebuilding of the House of Commons: p. 30; and address of 26 October seconding the motion of the Prime Minister welcoming the "Speakers, Presiding Officers and other representatives" of the Commonwealth and Empire countries: pp. 39–41. The address of 26 October was subsequently collected in Rhodes James, Vol. VIII, at pp. 8109–10.

LOCATIONS: CaOOP (rebound), UKMaU, UKOxB

REFERENCE: Woods D(b)79/2.

D145 PRESENTATION OF PORTRAIT TO LORD MORAN   1951

[Cover title:] ROYAL COLLEGE OF PHYSICIANS | [arms of the College, 43.1 × 62.3 mm] | PRESENTATION OF PORTRAIT | TO | LORD MORAN | [16-mm rule] | *July 10th, 1951*

PUBLICATION: London: Royal College of Physicians, 1951. Supplied *gratis* to subscribers to the portrait.

PAGINATION: 12. Pamphlet in self-wrappers.

CONTRIBUTION: Address of 10 July 1951 at a dinner held in the Library of the College: pp. 5–7. Not published in the *British Medical Journal* and only mentioned in *The Lancet* of 21 July 1951, at pp. 111–12. Subsequently collected in Rhodes James, Vol. VIII, at pp. 8223–5, under the title 'Lord Moran'.

LOCATION: UKLRCP

D145/1 THE REIGN OF GEORGE VI   1952

[Cover title:] [against a full-bleed half-tone photograph of a royal procession down Pall Mall; ranged upper left, strong greenish blue] THE REIGN OF | GEORGE VI | [white] A NEWS CHRONICLE PUBLICATION | [ranged lower left, strong greenish blue and strong red, the Union Jack; ranged lower right, against a strong greenish blue background, white] PRICE TWO SHILLINGS

PUBLICATION: London: *News Chronicle*, 1952.

PAGINATION: [24]. Pamphlet in self-wrappers.

CONTRIBUTION: Broadcast address of 7 February 1952: pp. 1–4.

LOCATION: RIC

D145/2 MEMORIES   1952

MEMORIES | [66.5-mm French rule] | *By* | THOMAS JOHNSTON | COLLINS | ST JAMES'S PLACE, LONDON | 1952

PUBLICATION: London: Collins, 1952. There was a second printing in the same year.

PAGINATION: 255, [1], 1 leaf of plates.

CONTRIBUTION: Principal portion of the speech of 14 November 1922 at Broughty Ferry Parish Church Hall: pp. 219–20. This is the first appearance in volume form of these remarks delivered on the last day of the campaign to an audience of 300 women. No part of the speech was collected in Rhodes James's *Complete Speeches*; however, the full text of this important critique of the D. C. Thomson Dundee newspapers was later included in *A Seat for Life* (**F248**), at pp. 267–70.

LOCATIONS: CaOOP, RIC, UKBL, USDLC, USMH

D146   OFFICIAL REPORT, 72ND ANNUAL
(CONSERVATIVE PARTY) CONFERENCE   1952

NATIONAL UNION OF CONSERVATIVE | AND UNIONIST ASSOCIATIONS | [50.4-mm rule] | 72nd Annual Conference | SCARBOROUGH | 9th–11th October, 1952 | [50.4-mm rule] | ABBEY HOUSE, 2–8, VICTORIA STREET, WESTMINSTER, S.W.1 | [ranged left] *Telegrams:* Constitute, Sowest, London. [ranged right] *Telephone:* ABBey 9000

PUBLICATION: London: Conservative Central Office, 1952. Price 5*s*.

PAGINATION: 116, plus card wrappers.

CONTRIBUTIONS: Speech of 11 October 1952: pp. 110–14. Churchill's reply to the vote of thanks: p. 115. Subsequently collected in *Stemming the Tide* (**A264**), at pp. 339–49, under the title 'Conservative Annual Conference', and in Rhodes James, Vol. VIII, at pp. 8410–18, under the title 'The First Year'.

LOCATION: RIC

D147   REPRESENTATIVE AMERICAN SPEECHES:
1951–1952   1952

THE REFERENCE SHELF | [92.7-mm rule] | [ranged left] Vol. 24 [ranged right] No. 3 | [centred] REPRESENTATIVE AMERICAN | SPEECHES: 1951–1952 | Edited, and with introductions, | by | A. CRAIG BAIRD | *Department of Speech, State University of Iowa* | [publisher's device, 11.5 mm in diameter] | THE H. W. WILSON COMPANY | [ranged left] NEW YORK [ranged right] 1952

PUBLICATION: New York: H. W. Wilson, 1952.

PAGINATION: [2], 197, [9].

CONTRIBUTION: 'Address to Congress', 17 January 1952: pp. 30–41.

LOCATIONS: RIC, USMH

D148 THE CROWNING OF ELIZABETH II   1953

THE | *CROWNING OF ELIZABETH II* | [132.6-mm rule] | *a diary of the Coronation Year* | by L. A. NICKOLLS | *Author of Royal Cavalcade, The First Family, The | Royal Story, The Reign of Elizabeth II.* | MACDONALD & CO. (PUBLISHERS) LIMITED | 16 MADDOX STREET, LONDON, W.1

PUBLICATION: London: Macdonald, 27 June 1953. Price 10*s.* 6*d.*

PAGINATION: 128, 4 leaves of plates.

CONTRIBUTIONS: Broadcast tribute of 25 March 1953 to Queen Mary: pp. 67–8. Subsequently collected in *The Unwritten Alliance* (**A273**), at pp. 24–5, under the title 'The Death of Queen Mary', and in Rhodes James, Vol. VIII, at pp. 8464–5, under the title 'Queen Mary'. Speech of 27 May 1953 at the Commonwealth Parliamentary Association Luncheon at St Stephen's Hall, Westminster. Subsequently collected in *The Unwritten Alliance*, at pp. 26–7, under the title 'Commonwealth Parliamentary Association Luncheon', and in Rhodes James, Vol. VIII, at pp. 8485–6, under the title 'The Crown and Parliament'.

LOCATION: RIC

D149 OFFICIAL REPORT, 73RD ANNUAL
(CONSERVATIVE PARTY) CONFERENCE   1953

NATIONAL UNION OF CONSERVATIVE | AND UNIONIST ASSOCIATIONS | [50.5-mm rule] | 73rd Annual Conference | MARGATE | 8th–10th October, 1953 | [50.5-mm rule] | ABBEY HOUSE, 2–8, VICTORIA STREET, WESTMINSTER, S.W.1 | [ranged left] *Telegrams:* Constitute, Sowest, London. [ranged right] *Telephone:* ABBey 9000

PUBLICATION: London: Conservative Central Office, 1953. Price 5*s.*

PAGINATION: 120, plus card wrappers.

CONTRIBUTIONS: Speech of 10 October 1953: pp. 112–16. Churchill's reply to the vote of thanks: pp. 117–18. Subsequently collected in *The Unwritten Alliance* (**A273**), at pp. 57–67, under the title 'The Conservative Party Conference', and in Rhodes James, Vol. VIII, at pp. 8489–97, under the title 'Conservative Party Conference'.

LOCATION: RIC

D150 POWER AND INFLUENCE   1953

D150.1 First edition, first issue (1953)

POWER | AND INFLUENCE | by | LORD BEVERIDGE | [publisher's device, 21.9 × 19.3 mm] | HODDER AND STOUGHTON | LONDON

PUBLICATION: London: Hodder & Stoughton, 19 November 1953. Price 30*s.*

PAGINATION: xi, [1], 448, 1 leaf of plates.

CONTRIBUTION: Extract from speech of March 1943 on social security: p. 436.

LOCATIONS: CaOTTC (dj), RIC (dj), USMH

REFERENCE: Woods D(b)88.

D150.2 American issue from British plates (1955)

POWER | AND INFLUENCE | by | LORD BEVERIDGE | [publisher's device, 21.8 × 15.5 mm] | NEW YORK: THE BEECHHURST PRESS

PUBLICATION: New York: Beechhurst Press, 1955.

PAGINATION: xi, [1], 448, [4], 1 leaf of plates.

LOCATIONS: RIC, USMH

D151 OFFICIAL REPORT, 74TH ANNUAL (CONSERVATIVE PARTY) CONFERENCE   1954

NATIONAL UNION OF CONSERVATIVE | AND UNIONIST ASSOCIATIONS | [50.3-mm rule] | 74th Annual Conference | BLACKPOOL | 7th–9th October, 1954 | [50.3-mm rule] | ABBEY HOUSE, 2–8, VICTORIA STREET, WESTMINSTER, S.W.1 | [ranged left] *Telegrams:* Constitute, Sowest, London. [ranged right] *Telephone:* ABBey 9000

PUBLICATION: London: Conservative Central Office, 1954.

PAGINATION: 120, plus card wrappers.

CONTRIBUTIONS: Speech of 9 October 1954: pp. 113–17. Churchill's reply to the vote of thanks: pp. 118–19. Subsequently collected in *The Unwritten Alliance* (**A273**), at pp. 181–91, under the title 'The Conservative Party Conference', and in Rhodes James, Vol. VIII, at pp. 8593–601, under the title ' "Peace through Strength" '.

LOCATIONS: UKLo, USNhD

D152 SPEECHES AT THE DINNER IN HONOUR OF GENERAL ALFRED M. GRUENTHER   1954

SPEECHES | AT THE DINNER IN HONOUR OF | GENERAL ALFRED M. GRUENTHER | UNDER THE AUSPICES OF THE | ENGLISH-SPEAKING UNION OF THE | COMMONWEALTH, JUNE 8, 1954 | *With an Introductory Note* | By LIONEL CURTIS | OXFORD • BASIL BLACKWELL | 1954

PUBLICATION: Oxford: Blackwell, 1954.

CONTRIBUTION: Churchill's remarks: pp. 17–19.

LOCATION: UKChP

D153 THE COLONIAL AND IMPERIAL CONFERENCES FROM 1887 TO 1937   1954

The set is published in three volumes. Only Volumes I and II contain Churchill addresses.

Volume I

THE COLONIAL | AND | IMPERIAL CONFERENCES | FROM 1887 TO 1937 | COMPILED AND EDITED | BY | MAURICE OLLIVIER, Q.C., LL.D., F.R.S.C. | Law Clerk of the House of Commons of Canada. | VOLUME I | COLONIAL

CONFERENCES | OTTAWA | EDMOND CLOUTIER, C.M.G., O.A., D.S.P., | QUEEN'S PRINTER AND CONTROLLER OF STATIONERY, | 1954

PUBLICATION: Ottawa: Queen's Printer, 1954.

PAGINATION: viii, 330, [2].

CONTRIBUTIONS: Question re the secretariat of a proposed Imperial Council on the second day of the 1907 Colonial Conference, 17 April 1907: pp. 232–3; remarks re political and parliamentary aspects of the Preference question on the twelfth day of the Conference, 7 May 1907: pp. 299–302.

LOCATIONS: CaOONL, RIC

Volume II

THE COLONIAL | AND | IMPERIAL CONFERENCES | FROM 1887 TO 1937 | COMPILED AND EDITED | BY | MAURICE OLLIVIER, Q.C., LL.D., F.R.S.C. | Law Clerk of the House of Commons of Canada. | VOLUME II | IMPERIAL CONFERENCES | PART I | OTTAWA | EDMOND CLOUTIER, C.M.G., O.A., D.S.P., | QUEEN'S PRINTER AND CONTROLLER OF STATIONERY, | 1954

PAGINATION: viii, 474, [2].

CONTRIBUTIONS: Comments re uniformity of naturalization laws on the eighth day of the 1911 Imperial Conference, 13 June 1911: pp. 86–8 and 155–6; motion re undesirable aliens: p. 89; speeches at the 1921 Imperial Conference, 21 June 1921: pp. 432 and 437–42.

LOCATIONS: CaOONL, RIC

D154 DOCUMENTS ON INTERNATIONAL AFFAIRS, 1939–1946   1954

DOCUMENTS ON | INTERNATIONAL AFFAIRS | 1939—1946 | VOLUME II HITLER'S EUROPE | SELECTED AND EDITED | BY | MARGARET CARLYLE | *Issued under the auspices of the* | *Royal Institute of International Affairs* | OXFORD UNIVERSITY PRESS | LONDON   NEW YORK   TORONTO | 1954

PUBLICATION: Oxford: Oxford University Press, 24 June 1954. Price 38*s*.

PAGINATION: [2] xxi [1] 363 [1].

CONTRIBUTIONS: 'Churchill's Speech Broadcast to the Italian People, 23 December 1940': pp. 103–7; message of 18 January 1943 to President de Gaulle: pp. 152–3; letter of 7 August 1940 to de Gaulle, the text taken from Cmd. 6220, together with the Memorandum of Agreement "governing the organisation, employment and conditions of service" of de Gaulle's Free French Force: pp. 167–70; 'Statement by Churchill in the House of Commons on the Establishment of the French National Committee of Liberation, 8 June 1943': pp. 186–7; statement of 18 January 1945 in the House: pp. 342–3; statement made by Churchill in the House on the future government of Greece, 9 November 1943: p. 345. All of the foregoing speeches, statements, messages and letters had previously been published, with the exception of the statement of 9 November 1943, of which this is the only published appearance (apart, of course, from that in Hansard).[26]

---

26. Both *Victory* and Rhodes James include Churchill's speech of that date at the Mansion House but neither includes this statement.

LOCATIONS: CaNBSAM, USMH

D155 VISCOUNT SOUTHWOOD 1954

VISCOUNT | SOUTHWOOD | [75.8-mm swelled rule] | BY | R. J. MINNEY | [publisher's device, 31.5×17 mm] | ODHAMS PRESS LIMITED | LONG ACRE, LONDON

PUBLICATION: London: Odhams, 8 November 1954. Price 25*s*.

PAGINATION: 384, 33 leaves of plates.

CONTRIBUTION: Excerpt from Churchill's tribute to Julius Salter Elias, later Viscount Southwood, at a dinner of 26 October 1931: pp. 258–9. This is the only published appearance of any portion of the speech.

LOCATIONS: RIC (dj), USIU (dj), USMH

D156 A TREASURY OF THE WORLD'S GREAT SPEECHES 1954

D156.1 First edition (1954)

A | TREASURY OF THE WORLD'S | *Great Speeches* | EACH SPEECH PREFACED WITH | ITS DRAMATIC AND BIOGRAPHICAL SETTING | AND PLACED | IN ITS FULL HISTORICAL PERSPECTIVE | *Selected and edited by* | HOUSTON PETERSON | [100.7-mm swelled rule] | SIMON AND SCHUSTER | NEW YORK

PUBLICATION: New York: Simon and Schuster, 1954. There were at least five printings of the first edition.

PAGINATION: xxix, [1], 857, [9].

CONTRIBUTIONS: Speech of 13 May 1940, under the title 'Prime Minister Churchill Presents His Program': pp. 773–4; speech of 4 June 1940, under the title Churchill Reports the Miracle of Dunkirk': pp. 774–80; speech of 18 June 1940, under the title 'Churchill Anticipates the Battle of Britain': pp. 781–2; and speech of 5 March 1946, under the title 'The Sinews of Peace: Ex-Prime Minister Churchill Perceives an Iron Curtain': pp. 803–6.

LOCATIONS: RIC, USIU (5th printing), USMH

D156.2 Spencer Press issue from first-edition plates (1955?)

A TREASURY | OF THE WORLD'S | Great Speeches | [67.2-mm rule] | Each speech prefaced with its | dramatic and biographical | setting and placed in the full | historical perspective | *Selected and edited by* | HOUSTON PETERSON | [67.2-mm rule] | *Chicago* | SPENCER PRESS, *Inc.*

PUBLICATION: Chicago: Spencer Press, n.d. [1955?].

LOCATION: RIC

D156.3 Second edition (1965)

A | TREASURY OF THE WORLD'S | *Great Speeches* | EACH SPEECH PREFACED WITH | ITS DRAMATIC AND BIOGRAPHICAL SETTING | AND PLACED | IN ITS FULL HISTORICAL PERSPECTIVE | *Selected and edited by* | HOUSTON

PETERSON | [98.6-mm swelled rule] | [publisher's device, 10.7 × 12 mm] | [ranged right of the device in 3 lines] Grolier | INCORPORATED | New York

PUBLICATION: New York: Grolier, 1965.

PAGINATION: xxx [numbered to xxxii, but really only 30, no leaf i/ii], 866.

LOCATION: RIC

D157 BRITISH POLITICAL SPEECHES AND DEBATES FROM CROMWELL TO CHURCHILL   1954

BRITISH POLITICAL | SPEECHES AND DEBATES | FROM CROMWELL TO CHURCHILL | SELECTED AND EDITED, WITH AN INTRODUCTION AND NOTES, | by | HILDEGARD   GAUGER | and | HERMANN   METZGER | [publisher's device, 15.1 × 14.8 mm] | MAX NIEMEYER VERLAG | TÜBINGEN

PUBLICATION: Tübingen: Max Niemeyer, 1954.

PAGINATION: 64. Booklet in fibre-flecked yellowish grey card wrappers.

CONTRIBUTIONS: First speech, of 13 May 1940, as Prime Minister: pp. 40–1; and broadcast address on the death of King George VI, on 7 February 1952: pp. 51–5.

LOCATION: USWaU

REFERENCE: Woods D(b)96/1.

D158 CANADA'S TRIBUTE TO SIR WINSTON CHURCHILL   1954

Canada's Tribute | to | SIR WINSTON CHURCHILL | on the eve of | His Eightieth Birthday | [publisher's device, 22.2 × 22.2 mm] | The Canadian Club of Toronto | DINNER MEETING | Royal York Hotel | NOVEMBER 29th, 1954

PUBLICATION: Toronto: Canadian Club, 1954.

PAGINATION: 24. Pamphlet in paper wrappers.

CONTRIBUTION: Text of recorded excerpt of Churchill's thanks to the Canadian Club (read at the dinner of 29 November) for their honouring of him and in anticipation of the gift of a painting purchased for him but not yet seen by him at the time of the recording: p. 20. This is the only published appearance of those remarks.

LOCATIONS: CaOTTC, RIC

REFERENCE: Woods D(b)90.

D159 THE EIGHTIETH BIRTHDAY OF SIR WINSTON LEONARD SPENCER CHURCHILL   1954

A RECORD | of the proceedings in | WESTMINSTER HALL | Tuesday, November 30, 1954 | when men and women representing all sides | of British political life gathered to witness | THE PRESENTATION OF GIFTS | from | BOTH HOUSES OF PARLIAMENT | to | SIR WINSTON CHURCHILL | on his | Eightieth Birthday

PUBLICATION: London: Times Publishing Co., 1954.

PAGINATION: 8, plus card wrappers.

CONTRIBUTION: Response to the presentation of gifts: pp. 7–8.

LOCATION: RIC

REFERENCE: Woods D(b)91.

D160 THE SPOKEN WORD   1955

THE SPOKEN | WORD | [62.3-mm swelled rule] | *A Selection from Twenty-Five Years* | *of 'The Listener,' chosen and* | *introduced by* | RICHARD CHURCH | COLLINS | ST JAMES'S PLACE, LONDON | 1955

PUBLICATION: London: Collins, 1955. Price 16*s*.

PAGINATION: 318, [2].

CONTRIBUTIONS: 'A Sterner War', broadcast on 30 March 1940 and published in *The Listener* of 4 April (**E53a**): pp. 207–8; 'This Was Their Finest Hour', broadcast on 18 June 1940 and published in *The Listener* of 20 June (**E56a**): pp. 212–15; and ' "Never Your Foes Till Now" ', broadcast to the Italian people on 23 December 1940 and published in *The Listener* of 2 January 1941 (**E64a**): pp. 225–6.

LOCATION: USIU (dj)

D161 EXPANSION OR EXPLOSION   1955

ANTHONY VICKERS | [67.8-mm thin rule and 72.5-mm thick rule] | EXPANSION | or | EXPLOSION | *A solution to the vital* | *problem of the Machine Age* | [publisher's device, 19.6 × 21.7 mm] | [72.5-mm thick rule and 67.8-mm thin rule] | THE BODLEY HEAD

PUBLICATION: London: The Bodley Head, 7 March 1955. Price 6*s*.

CONTRIBUTION: Statement during the debate on the budget proposals of 21 April 1932 on the Gold Standard: p. 77 (Appendix I). A brief excerpt from the statement is quoted at p. 33.

LOCATIONS: CaBVIP, CaNBFU, CaOOP, RIC (dj)

REFERENCE: Woods D(b)99.

D162 BOOKS, LIBRARIES, LIBRARIANS   1955

BOOKS | LIBRARIES | LIBRARIANS | Contributions   to   Library   Literature | Selected   by | John   David   Marshall | Wayne   Shirley | Louis   Shores. | HAMDEN, CONNECTICUT | THE SHOE STRING PRESS | 1955

PUBLICATION: Hamden (CT): Shoe String Press, 1955.

PAGINATION: xv, [1], 432.

CONTRIBUTION: 'Books in Your Life', extract from Churchill's speech upon receiving the *Sunday Times* Literary Award[27] in 1949: pp. 3–4. Another extract was subsequently

---

27. This was awarded to Churchill for his two volumes of war memoirs, *The Gathering Storm* and *Their Finest Hour*, both of which were published during the twelve months ending 30 June 1949, the period of eligibility for the Award. "In this country the year's books have been overshadowed by them; they bear the mark of enduring literature, and were an inescapable choice for the award," said the *Sunday Times* in *The Sunday Times National Book Exhibition Catalogue and Magazine*, p. 48.

collected in Rhodes James, Vol. VII, at pp. 7883–4, under the title 'Riches of English Literature'. A brief, textually slightly different, extract also appears in Gilbert, *WSC*, Vol. VIII, at p. 494.

REFERENCE: Woods D(b)103.

LOCATIONS: CaOONL, RIC, USMH

D163 THE NEW CONSERVATISM   1955

The New Conservatism | [101.1-mm decorative rule] | AN ANTHOLOGY OF POST-WAR THOUGHT | *With an Introduction by The Rt. Hon. R. A. Butler*, C.H., M.P. | [decorative device, 15.8 × 12.8 mm] | Conservative Political Centre | [69.6-mm rule] | *LONDON*

PUBLICATION: London: Conservative Political Centre, October 1955. Price 3s. 6d.

PAGINATION: 203, [1], 3 leaves of plates.

CONTRIBUTIONS: Excerpts from: speech of 16 October 1945 in the House of Commons: p. 29; speech of 5 October 1946 at Blackpool: pp. 12–13 and 32–4; speech of 4 October 1947 at Brighton: pp. 116–17; speech of 9 October 1948 at Llandudno: pp. 154–5; speech of 23 July 1949: pp. 51–3; speech of 14 October 1950 at Blackpool: pp. 123–4; broadcast address of 8 October 1951: pp. 24–5; speech of 3 November 1953 in the House: p. 83; speech of 1 March 1955 in the House: pp. 159–62; and the 1951 *Manifesto of the Conservative and Unionist Party* (for the separate published appearance of which, see **A259**): pp. 128–9.

LOCATIONS: CaOTTC, DAT, FBW, RIC, UKLo, UKOxB, USMH

REFERENCE: Woods D(b)101.

D164 DOCUMENTS ON GERMANY UNDER
OCCUPATION 1945–1954   1955

DOCUMENTS ON | GERMANY UNDER | OCCUPATION | 1945–1954 | SELECTED AND EDITED BY | BEATE RUHM VON OPPEN | *Issued under the auspices of the* | *Royal Institute of International Affairs* | GEOFFREY CUMBERLEGE | OXFORD UNIVERSITY PRESS | LONDON NEW YORK TORONTO | 1955

PUBLICATION: London: Oxford University Press, 17 November 1955. Price 63s.

PAGINATION: xxviii, 660, 1 map (folding).

CONTRIBUTIONS: 'Statement by Churchill on the Principle of Unconditional Surrender', an excerpt from his speech of 18 January 1945 in the House of Commons: pp. 3–4; 'Report of the Crimea (Yalta) Conference, 4–11 February 1945' (co-signed by Churchill, Roosevelt and Stalin): pp. 4–6; brief excerpt from the debate of 30 June 1948 in the House: p. 310; 'Statement by Churchill on the Origins of the "Unconditional Surrender" Formula: Extracts from a Debate in the House of Commons' (21 July 1949): pp. 409–12; and 'Further Statement by Churchill on the Origins of the "Unconditional Surrender" Formula' (17 November 1949 in the House): pp. 437–9. Most of the statements in the House were subsequently collected in Rhodes James, Vol. VII, as follows: that of 18 January 1945 in its entirety at pp. 7083–103, under the title 'Review of the

War', the excerpted portion being from pp. 7100.36–7101.15; that of 21 July 1949 in its entirety at pp. 7826–31, under the title 'Foreign Affairs'; that of 17 November 1949 in its entirety at pp. 7888–99, under the title 'Foreign Affairs', the excerpted portion being from pp. 7888–7890.16. This is the only volume appearance of the excerpt from the speech of 30 June 1948.

LOCATIONS: CaOOP, CaOTMCL, RIC (dj), UKBL, USDLC, USMH

D165 GEOFFREY KEYES   1956

GEOFFREY KEYES | V.C., M.C., CROIX de GUERRE | ROYAL SCOTS GREYS | LIEUT.-COLONEL 11th SCOTTISH COMMANDO | *By* | ELIZABETH KEYES | LONDON | GEORGE   NEWNES   LIMITED | TOWER   HOUSE, SOUTHAMPTON STREET | STRAND, W.C.2

PUBLICATION: London: Newnes, 12 July 1956. Price 21s.

PAGINATION: x, 278, 17 leaves of plates.

CONTRIBUTION: Text of the allocution of 27 April 1950 at the unveiling of the memorial tablet to Lord Keyes and Geoffrey Keyes in the Crypt of St Paul's Cathedral: pp. 264–5. The allocution has been subsequently collected in Rhodes James, Vol. VIII, at pp. 7997–8, under the title 'Lord Keyes and His Son'.

LOCATIONS: CaOONL, CaOTMCL, CaOTTC (dj), RIC (dj), UKBL, USDLC, USMH

REFERENCE: Woods D(b)106.

D166 THE LIBERAL TRADITION FROM FOX TO
KEYNES   1956

D166.1 First edition (1956)

THE LIBERAL TRADITION | FROM FOX TO KEYNES | EDITED BY | ALAN BULLOCK | CENSOR OF ST. CATHERINE'S SOCIETY, OXFORD | AND | MAURICE SHOCK | FELLOW OF UNIVERSITY COLLEGE, OXFORD | LONDON | ADAM & CHARLES BLACK

PUBLICATION: London: Black, 11 October 1956. Price 25s.

PAGINATION: lv, [1], 288.

CONTRIBUTION: Speech of 11 October 1906: pp. 209–11. Excerpted from *Liberalism and the Social Problem* (**A29**). First published in *Liberalism and Socialism* (**A19**).

LOCATIONS: CaOONL, RIC (dj), UKBL, USDLC, USMH

D166.2 American issue (1957)

PUBLICATION: New York: New York University Press, 1957.

No copy examined.

LOCATIONS: CaOME, CaQMU, USDLC, USMH

D166.3 Paperback issue (1967)

PUBLICATION: Oxford: Clarendon Press, 1967.

No copy examined.

LOCATIONS: CaMWU, CaOTMCL, UKBL, USDLC

D167 PROCEEDINGS OF THE PRESENTATION OF THE WILLIAMSBURG AWARD TO SIR WINSTON CHURCHILL   1957

Proceedings of the Presentation of | THE WILLIAMSBURG AWARD | By the Trustees of Colonial Williamsburg | To The Rt. Hon. Sir Winston S. Churchill | At Drapers' Hall, London, | December 7, 1955 | [arms of Colonial Williamsburg, 29.7 × 28.9 mm] | COLONIAL WILLIAMSBURG | WILLIAMSBURG, VIRGINIA | 1957

PUBLICATION: Williamsburg: Colonial Williamsburg, 1957.

PAGINATION: 48.

CONTRIBUTION: Speech of 7 December 1955: pp. 19–21.

LOCATIONS: CaOHM, CaOONL, RIC, UKBL, USMH

REFERENCE: Woods D(b)110.

D168 BRITAIN IN EUROPE   1957

[Ranged right] Britain | in Europe | ADDRESSES AND MESSAGES | GIVEN AT A MEETING IN CENTRAL | HALL WESTMINSTER ON | 9TH JULY, 1957 | THE UNITED KINGDOM COUNCIL | OF THE EUROPEAN MOVEMENT

PUBLICATION: London: United Kingdom Council of the European Movement, August 1957.

PAGINATION: 39, [1], 1 leaf of plates.

CONTRIBUTION: Address of 9 July 1957: p. 11.

LOCATIONS: RIC, UKBL, USDLC, USMH

REFERENCE: Woods D(b)108/1.

D169 THE LEGISLATOR   1958

[Dropped-head title only:] A MEMORABLE | OCCASION IN A | MEMORABLE | YEAR.

PUBLICATION: London: Keighley Printers, Ltd., 1958. Bulletin No. 10 of *The Legislator*. Published and printed by Keighley but sent with the "compliments and good wishes of the UNITED KINGDOM ALLIANCE". Issued in commemoration of the fiftieth anniversary of the wedding of Winston and Clementine on 12 September 1908.

PAGINATION: [8].

CONTRIBUTIONS: Speech of 13 October 1908 on the occasion of the Churchills' "first public engagement on returning from their honeymoon", at the Free Trade Hall, Manchester: p. 2; speech at an overflow meeting in the Friends' House: pp. 2–3.

NOTE: Churchill was the Chairman of the Annual Meeting of the Kingdom Alliance and he was introduced by Leif Jones, M.P. (later Lord Rhayader).

LOCATION: CaOTTC

REFERENCE: Woods D(b)115.

D170 LONDON'S ROLL OF FAME   1959

LONDON'S | ROLL | OF FAME | *Being Records of Presentations* | *of the Freedom of the City* | *and Addresses of Welcome* | *from the Corporation of London* | *to Royal and other Distinguished Personages* | *A.D.   1885–1959* | PRINTED BY ORDER OF THE CORPORATION | UNDER   THE   DIRECTION   OF   THE   LIBRARY COMMITTEE

PUBLICATION: London: Corporation of London, November 1959. 500 copies.

PAGINATION: [2], xvi, 466, 17 leaves of plates.

CONTRIBUTION: At a Court of Common Council on 18 March 1943, it was resolved that Churchill be admitted to the Freedom of the City. The ceremony took place on 30 June 1943, at which time Sir Adrian Donald Wilde Pollock, the Chamberlain, addressed Churchill: pp. 284–6. Churchill's reply: pp. 286–93.

LOCATIONS: RIC, RPH

D171 THE IRON CURTAIN, FIFTEEN YEARS AFTER   1960

The Iron Curtain, | Fifteen Years After | BY | THE VISCOUNT HAILSHAM | 1960 | WITH   A   REPRINT   OF | The   Sinews   of   Peace | BY | SIR   WINSTON CHURCHILL | 1946 | JOHN FINDLEY GREEN FOUNDATION LECTURES | WESTMINSTER COLLEGE | FULTON, MISSOURI

PUBLICATION: Fulton: Westminster College, 1960.

PAGINATION: 48. Pamphlet in card wrappers.

CONTRIBUTION: 'The Sinews of Peace', Churchill's address of 5 March 1946: pp. 33–45.

LOCATIONS: CaOTTC, RIC, RPH, USMoFuWc

D172 THE POWER OF ELOQUENCE   1961

The | Power of Eloquence | A TREASURY OF BRITISH SPEECH | Selected and edited by | ANDREW SCOTLAND | [publisher's device, 24.9 × 16.5 mm] | CASSELL • LONDON

PUBLICATION: London: Cassell, 11 May 1961. Price 21*s*.

PAGINATION: ix, [1], 256, [2].

CONTRIBUTIONS: Speech of March 1936 on British policy and Europe, here titled 'The Loaded Pause': pp. 180–3; speech of 4 June 1940, 'A Colossal Military Disaster': pp. 184–94; speech of 18 June 1940, 'Their Finest Hour': pp. 194–204; speech of 8 October 1940, 'The Air Raids on London': pp. 204–11; broadcast address of 21 October 1940, 'To the French People': pp. 212–14; address of 5 March 1946 at Westminster College, Fulton, Missouri, 'The Iron Curtain': pp. 215–18.

This is the first volume appearance of the speech of March 1936, which was subsequently collected in Rhodes James, Vol. VI, at pp. 5694–6, under the title 'British Policy and Europe'.

LOCATIONS: RIC (dj), RPH (dj), UKScNL

D173 THE WESTERN WORLD IN THE TWENTIETH CENTURY   1961

THE Western World in the | Twentieth Century | A SOURCE BOOK FROM THE | CONTEMPORARY CIVILIZATION PROGRAM IN | COLUMBIA COLLEGE, COLUMBIA UNIVERSITY | *Edited by* Bernard Wishy | NEW YORK • Columbia University Press | [publisher's device] 1961

PUBLICATION: New York: Columbia University Press, 1961.

PAGINATION: [*8*], 518, [2].

CONTRIBUTION: Broadcast to the United States of 16 October 1938 on the Munich Crisis, under the title 'The Lights Are Going Out': pp. 387–93.

LOCATION: CaOONL

D174 COLD WAR DIPLOMACY   1962

COLD WAR DIPLOMACY | American Foreign Policy, 1945–1960 | [82.2-mm rule] | NORMAN A. GRAEBNER | *Professor of History* | *University of Illinois* | [21.1-mm rule] | AN ANVIL ORIGINAL | *under the general editorship of* | LOUIS L. SNYDER | [21.1-mm rule] | D. VAN NOSTRAND COMPANY, INC. | PRINCETON, NEW JERSEY | TORONTO   LONDON | NEW YORK

PUBLICATION: Princeton (NJ): Van Nostrand, 1962.

PAGINATION: viii, 248.

CONTRIBUTION: 'Churchill's Speech at Fulton, Missouri, March 5, 1946': pp. 144–8. The text used was that published in *Vital Speeches of the Day* (**E152a**).

LOCATIONS: CaOHM, CaOONL, CaQMM, USDLC, USMH

D175 SPEECHES FOR ILLUSTRATION AND EXAMPLE 1965

SPEECHES   FOR   ILLUSTRATION | AND   EXAMPLE | GOODWIN   F. BERQUIST, JR. | UNIVERSITY OF WISCONSIN – MILWAUKEE | SCOTT, FORESMAN AND COMPANY | CHICAGO, ATLANTA, DALLAS, PALO ALTO, FAIR LAWN, N.J.

PUBLICATION: Chicago: Scott Foresman, 1965.

CONTRIBUTION: Address of 26 December 1941 to the U.S. Congress, under the title 'Address to the Congress' and this under the broader superheading 'Speaking on Behalf of a Nation in Time of War': pp. 91–8. Note that the text used was that which appeared in the *New York Times*.

LOCATIONS: CaQWSMM, CaSSU, CJZ, USDLC, USMH

D176 AN HISTORICAL ANTHOLOGY OF SELECT BRITISH SPEECHES   1967

An Historical Anthology of | Select British Speeches | [ranged right, with a decorative device ranged right of the first and second names and another ranged left of the third name] *Edited by* | DONALD C. BRYANT | THE UNIVERSITY OF IOWA | CARROLL C. ARNOLD | THE PENNSYLVANIA STATE UNIVERSITY |

FREDERICK W. HABERMAN | UNIVERSITY OF WISCONSIN | RICHARD MURPHY | UNIVERSITY OF ILLINOIS | KARL R. WALLACE | UNIVERSITY OF ILLINOIS | [centred] THE RONALD PRESS COMPANY • NEW YORK

PUBLICATION: New York: Ronald Press, 1967.

PAGINATION: [2], xii, [2], 542, [2].

CONTRIBUTION: Speech of 10 December 1936 on the abdication of King Edward VIII: pp. 502–5; speech of 5 October 1938, under the title 'On the Munich Agreement': pp. 523–34; broadcast address of 19 May 1940, under the title 'A Solemn Hour': pp. 534–6.

LOCATIONS: CaOHM, CaOONL, RIC, UKBL, USDLC

D177 NOBEL LECTURES INCLUDING PRESENTATION SPEECHES AND LAUREATES' BIOGRAPHIES: LITERATURE 1901–1967   1969

NOBEL LECTURES | INCLUDING PRESENTATION SPEECHES | AND LAUREATES' BIOGRAPHIES | LITERATURE | 1901 – 1967 | *Edited by* | HORST FRENZ | *Professor of English and Comparative Literature,* | *Indiana University, Bloomington, Indiana, U.S.A.* | [publisher's device, 13 × 10.1 mm] | PUBLISHED FOR THE NOBEL FOUNDATION | IN 1969 BY | ELSEVIER PUBLISHING COMPANY | AMSTERDAM—LONDON—NEW YORK

PUBLICATION: Amsterdam: Elsevier for the Nobel Foundation, 1969.

PAGINATION: [2], XXI, [1], 640.

CONTRIBUTION: Churchill's acceptance speech as read by Lady Churchill: pp. 493–4.

LOCATIONS: UKScNL (accession-dated 30 September 1969), USMH

D178/1 MODERN BRITISH ELOQUENCE   1969

Modern | British | Eloquence | [100.1-mm rule] | [ranged right] *EDITED BY* | DAVID B. STROTHER | *FUNK & WAGNALLS New York*

PUBLICATION: New York: Funk & Wagnalls, 1969. Price $12.50.

PAGINATION: xv, [1], 492, [4].

CONTRIBUTIONS: 'Government Policy', speech of 5 October 1938 in the House of Commons: pp. 468–79; 'Parliament in the Air Raids', speech of 17 September 1940: pp. 481–6.

LOCATION: RIC (dj)

D179 THE DEBT WE OWE   1969

D179.1 First edition (1969)

The Debt We Owe | *The Royal Air Force Benevolent Fund 1919–1969* | Edward Bishop | [publisher's device, 16 × 12.8 mm] | Longmans

PUBLICATION: London: Longmans, September 1969. Price 36s.

PAGINATION: xii, 162, [2], 8 leaves of plates.

CONTRIBUTIONS: Broadcast of 16 September 1951: pp. 63–4. There is also a letter of 26 July 1951 from Churchill to Princess Marina, who had requested that he make this appeal on behalf of the R.A.F. Benevolent Fund: p. 62; and an excerpt from Churchill's telephone enquiry a few days later to Air Vice-Marshal Sir John Cordingley: p. 64. The speech was previously published as a leaflet entitled *Broadcast Appeal on Behalf of the Royal Air Force Benevolent Fund* (**A253**) and collected in *Stemming the Tide* (**A264**), at pp. 116–17, under the title 'R.A.F. Benevolent Fund'. It was also subsequently collected in Rhodes James, Vol. VIII, pp. 8243–4. This is the only published appearance of the letter to Princess Marina and the snippet of conversation with Cordingley.

LOCATIONS: CaACU, CaOKQ, RIC (dj), UKBL, USDLC

D179.2   Second edition (1979)

The Debt We Owe | *The Royal Air Force Benevolent Fund 1919–1979* | by Edward Bishop | London | GEORGE ALLEN & UNWIN | Boston   Sydney

PUBLICATION: London: Allen & Unwin, November 1979. Price £7.50.

PAGINATION: xix, [1], 202, [2], 8 leaves of plates.

CONTRIBUTIONS: The broadcast address: pp. 67–8; the letter: p. 67; the telephone enquiry: p. 69.

LOCATIONS: CaOLU, RIC (dj), UKBL, USDLC

D179.3   Third edition (1989)

The Debt | We Owe | *The* | *Royal Air Force* | *Benevolent Fund 1919–1989* | Edward Bishop | Airlife Publications | Shrewsbury

PUBLICATION: Shrewsbury: Airlife Publications, November 1989. Price £14.95.

LOCATIONS: CaOONMA, RIC (dj), UKBL

D180 A GUIDE FOR VISITORS TO THE WINSTON CHURCHILL MEMORIAL AND LIBRARY   1970?

[Cover title:] [all of the following within a single-rule frame, enclosing 251 × 188 mm; ranged upper right, a photograph of the statue of Churchill by Franta Belsky; ranged left of that photograph in 4 lines] A GUIDE FOR VISITORS TO THE | WINSTON CHURCHILL | MEMORIAL AND LIBRARY | IN THE UNITED STATES | [below the statue] WESTMINSTER COLLEGE/FULTON/MISSOURI | [photograph of the church at Westminster]

PUBLICATION: Fulton (MO): Westminster College?, 1970.

PAGINATION: [*32*], plus paper wrappers.

CONTRIBUTION: 'Sinews of Speech' (speech of 5 March 1946): pp. 25–31.

LOCATIONS: RIC, USMoFuWc

D181 THE WISDOM OF CONSERVATISM   1971

Issued as a four-volume set in slipcase. Excerpts from Churchill's speeches are included in Volume IV only.

Volume IV

THE | WISDOM OF | CONSERVATISM | [fancy 101.3-mm rule] | EDITED BY | PETER WITONSKI | Volume IV | [fancy 101.3-mm rule] | [ranged left] *ARLINGTON HOUSE* [ranged right] *New Rochelle, N.Y.*

PUBLICATION: New Rochelle (NY): Arlington House, July? 1971. Price $40.00 the set, boxed.

CONTRIBUTIONS: 'On the Dangers of Russian Communism', excerpt from speech of 5 March 1946: p. 2099; and 'The Basic Minimum', excerpt from speech of 4 October 1947: p. 2100.

NOTE: There are also excerpts from Lord Randolph Churchill's speeches 'Tory Democracy' (of 6 November 1885) and 'Trust the People' (of 16 April 1884) in Volume III, at pp. 1369 and 1370–4, respectively.

LOCATION: RIC (boxed)

D182 POINTS DE REPÈRE   1973

POINTS DE REPÈRE | [publisher's device, 25.1 mm in diameter] | CENTRE DE RECHERCHES EUROPÉENNES | LAUSANNE | 1973

PUBLICATION: Lausanne: Centre de Recherches Européennes, 1973.

PAGINATION: 22, [2], 1 leaf of plates.

CONTRIBUTION: Speech of 17 September 1946 at Zurich University, in French translation: pp. 7–12.

LOCATION: RIC

D183 THE WAR MAGICIAN   1983

The War | Magician | *David Fisher* | *Coward-McCann, Inc.* | *New York*

PUBLICATION: New York: Coward McCann, 17 February 1983.

PAGINATION: [2], 315, [1], 4 leaves of plates.

CONTRIBUTION: Address of 16 November 1941 to the troops in North Africa: p. 164.

LOCATIONS: RIC (dj), USMH

D184 CHURCHILL SONGS   1990

[Cover title:] [Harrow School device, 24 × 17.5 mm] | *50th Anniversary* | CHURCHILL SONGS | [line drawing of the older Churchill, 76.3 × 62.1 mm, over the lower left-hand corner of which is superimposed an oval half-tone photograph from his days at

Harrow, 49 × 35.8 mm] | [ranged right below the photograph] *"One by one—and as they name us, | Forth we go from boyhood's rule | Sworn to be renown'd and famous | For the honour of the School"* | [centred] *Thursday 22 November 1990* | ROYAL ALBERT HALL

PUBLICATION: Harrow: Harrow School, November 1990. Price £10.00.

PAGINATION: [76], plus paper wrappers.

CONTRIBUTIONS: Speech at the Harrow Songs of 18 December 1940: pp. 29–30; selected quotations from Churchill speeches at Harrow Songs from 1941 to 1955: pp. 54–7. Also included are a facsimile of Churchill's telegram of 5 October 1940 to Head Master A. P. Boissier: p. 25; letter of 20 October to Boissier: p. 32; facsimile note of thanks, sent to Boissier, dated 25 December 1940: p. 33; and the facsimile of a telegram from Winston and Clementine of about 30 October 1941: p. 33; as well as other bits of quoted material *passim*.

LOCATIONS: RIC, UKBL

D185 LEND ME YOUR EARS   1992

D185.1 First edition (1992)

[Within a frame made up of horizontal rules at the top and bottom and triple rules at the sides, enclosing 193 × 97 mm] LEND ME | YOUR EARS | GREAT SPEECHES | IN HISTORY | *Selected and Introduced by* | WILLIAM SAFIRE | W. W. NORTON & COMPANY | *New York London*

PUBLICATION: New York: Norton, October 1992. Price in the United States $35.00, and in Canada $42.00.

PAGINATION: 957, [3].

CONTRIBUTIONS: Speech of 13 May 1940, under the title 'Winston Churchill Braces Britons to Their Task': pp. 130–2; and speech of 5 March 1946, under the title 'Winston Churchill Warns the West of the Soviet "Iron Curtain"': pp. 783–95.

LOCATIONS: CaOHM, CaOTU, RIC (dj), UKBL, USMH

D185.2 Second (revised and expanded) edition (1997)

PUBLICATION: New York: Norton, 1997.

No copy examined.

LOCATIONS: CaOTU, CaSSU, UKBL, USMH

D185.3 Third (updated and expanded) edition (2004)

PUBLICATION: New York: Norton, 1997.

No copy examined.

LOCATIONS: UKBL, USMH

D186 WINSTON WINS! 1994

[All ranged flush right] WINSTON WINS! | Winston Churchill | and the | University of Edinburgh | Rectorial Elections | of 1908 and 1929 | a selection of original documents | from the Special Collections of Edinburgh University Library | to commemorate the visit to the University of Edinburgh | of the International Churchill Society of the United States | 21 May 1994 | Edinburgh | Edinburgh University Library | 1994

PUBLICATION: Edinburgh: Edinburgh University Library, May 1994.

PAGINATION: [*21*]. Mimeographed (one-sided) booklet, plus paper wrappers.

CONTRIBUTION: Speech of 5 March 1931 upon his installation as Rector of the University: pp. 15–21.

LOCATION: RIC

D187 BLUT, SCHWEISS UND TRÄNEN 1995

WINSTON CHURCHILL | Blut, Schweiß und Tränen | Antrittsrede im Unterhaus nach der | Ernennung zum Premierminister | am 13. Mai 1940 | Mit einem Essay von | HERFRIED MÜNKLER | Europäische Verlagsanstalt

PUBLICATION: Hamburg: Europäische Verlagsanstalt, 1995.

PAGINATION: 70, [2].

CONTRIBUTIONS: Speech of 13 May 1940 in the House of Commons: pp. 7–9; the same speech in German translation: pp. 11–14.

LOCATION: RIC

D188 WORDS THAT CHANGED AMERICA 2003

[Between 9-mm-thick horizontal grey borders at the head and foot] [black] WORDS | THAT | CHANGED | AMERICA | *Great Speeches that Inspired,* | *Challenged, Healed,* *and Enlightened* | ALEX BARNETT | [publisher's device] | The Lyons Press | Guilford, Connecticut | An imprint of The Globe Pequot Press

PUBLICATION: Guilford (CT): Lyons Press, 2003. Price $14.95.

PAGINATION: x, 324, [2].

CONTRIBUTIONS: Speech of 4 June 1940, 'Dunkirk': pp. 233–9; speech of 5 March 1946, 'The Iron Curtain': pp. 255–9.

LOCATIONS: RIC (dj), USDLC

SECTION E

Reports of Speeches in Serial Publications

This section contains all reports of speeches by Churchill in periodical publications appearing no more frequently than weekly and no less frequently than quarterly. It includes first and subsequent appearances of speeches arranged chronologically on the basis of the first periodical appearance of the Churchill speech.

1901

E1   May   **ANNUAL LADIES' BANQUET.**
Whitefriars Journal, No. 5, 11–13
Address to the meeting of 4 May at the Hotel Cecil, for which Friar Winston S. Churchill was in the chair. Note that Churchill had written to his mother on 26 March to ask whether she "would care to help me receive the guests at the Whitefriars Club annual banquet—at which I am to preside on the 3rd [*sic*] of May."[1]

E2   July   **SOME IMPRESSIONS OF THE WAR IN SOUTH AFRICA.**
Journal of the Royal United Service Institution, Vol. XLV, No. 281, 835–48
Address of 17 April (Gen. the Right Hon. Sir Redvers Buller in the chair).[2] Subsequently collected in *Collected Essays*, Vol. I, at pp. 68–80, and in rather abbreviated form in Rhodes James, Vol. I, at pp. 74–6, under the title 'The War in South Africa', where the address is incorrectly dated 27 April.[3]

1904

E3   April   **"IRELAND AND THE FISCAL QUESTION."**
Journal of the Institute of Bankers in Ireland, 99–108
Address of 25 January at the Annual Public Meeting of the Institute held in the Rotunda, Dublin. The list of those present and the introductory remarks of the Chairman are found at pp. 97–8. The motion of thanks, the seconding and the reply to Churchill's speech are found at pp. 108–12 and a third-party rendering of Churchill's reply is given at p. 112. Subsequently collected in Rhodes James, Vol. I, at pp. 239–42, under the title 'Ireland and Protection against England'.

---

1. R. Churchill, *WSC*, Vol. II, *C.V.* 1, at p. 49.

2. Bullers's own flattering comments about Churchill and his observations on the substance of the issue discussed occupy pp. 847–8.

3. See Churchill's own appointments diary, which indicates 17 April as the date of the R.U.S.I. speech at Bedford. On 27 April, Churchill was at the Stafford Club at Oxford University (R. Churchill, *WSC*, Vol. II, *C.V.* 1, at p. 31).

E4   April   **COMPLIMENTARY SUPPER TO MR. WINSTON S. CHURCHILL, M.P.**
Journal of the Institute of Bankers in Ireland, 113–14
Following Churchill's address (**E3**), a complimentary supper took place and, after the remarks of Maurice E. Dockrell, D.L., Churchill replied.

1907

E5   January   **EDITORIAL NOTES**
Journal of the African Society, Vol. VI, No. XXII, 212–13
Excerpt from Churchill's address at the annual banquet of the British Cotton-Growing Association on 6 December 1906. Subsequently collected in Rhodes James, Vol. I, at pp. 695–9, under the title 'Cotton'.

E6   April   **THE DEVELOPMENT OF AFRICA**
Journal of the African Society, Vol. VI, No. XXIII, 291–6
Address at the twelfth monthly dinner of the Society, held on 8 March. Subsequently collected in Rhodes James, Vol. I, at pp. 756–7, under the title 'Africa (Colonial Development)'.[4]

E7   April   **MONTHLY DINNERS OF THE SOCIETY**
Journal of the African Society, Vol. VI, No. XXIII, 305
Churchill's response to the toast at the twelfth monthly dinner of the Society on 8 March. Subsequently collected in Rhodes James, Vol. I, at pp. 907–8, under the title 'East African Development'.

E8   July   **GEMS OF ORATORY. / Mr. Churchill's Tirade against Socialism.**
Shorthand Gazette, Vol. II, No. 10, 166–8
Churchill's speech is reproduced in Pitman shorthand. Subsequently collected in Pitman shorthand in Volume II of *The Shorthand Gazette* (**D17**). The entire speech has been collected in Rhodes James, Vol. I, at pp. 1025–35, and the excerpt runs from p. 1028.15 to p. 1029.36.

---

4. Rhodes James notes the date of the dinner as 6 March.

1908

E9   April   **ON OUR EAST AFRICAN EMPIRE**
Journal of the Royal Colonial Institute, Vol. XXXIX, Part V, 295–302
Discussion by the Chairman of Archibald R. Colquhoun's paper 'On Our East African Empire'. Subsequently collected in *Proceedings of the Royal Colonial Institute* (**D15**) and in Rhodes James, Vol. I, at pp. 907–8, under the title 'East African Development'.

1911

E10   December   **THE FIRST LORD AT THE GUILDHALL.**
Navy, 316
Speech of 9 November at the Lord Mayor's Banquet at the Guildhall, London. Subsequently collected in Rhodes James, Vol. II, at pp. 1891–3, under the title 'Naval Defence'.

1913

E11   Oct. 11   **TOPICS OF THE DAY. / Mr. Churchill's Speech.**
Spectator, 552
Speech [of 8 October?] at Dundee.

1914

E12   May   **RT. HON. WINSTON CHURCHILL ON THE EMPIRE AND THE NAVY**
Britannic Review, Vol. I, No. 1, 104–9
Excerpt from the lengthy speech of 17 March. Subsequently collected in Rhodes James, Vol. III, at pp. 2233–62, under the title 'Navy Estimates'. The excerpted section runs from p. 2255.40 to p. 2260.23.

E13   October   **MR. CHURCHILL'S INSPIRING CALL.**
Navy, 283
Speech of 21 September at Tournament Hall, Liverpool. Subsequently collected in Rhodes James, Vol. III, at pp. 2336–40, under the title ' "Rats in a Hole" '.

E14   December   **THE WORK OF THE NAVY. / Our Increasing Superiority. / Important Statement by the First Lord.**
Navy, 357–60

Speech of 27 November in the House of Commons. Subsequently collected in Rhodes James, Vol. III, at pp. 2342–8, under the title 'Royal Navy'.

E15   Dec. 26   **NOW THE WAR HAS COME.**
Current History, 330–6
Speech of 11 September to the National Liberal Club at the London Opera House. Subsequently collected in Rhodes James, Vol. III, at pp. 2328–34, under the title ' "The Ebb and Flow of Fortune" '.

1915

E16   April   **THE NAVY ESTIMATES**
Britannic Review, Vol. II, No. 2, 263–8
Under the heading 'From the Parliaments'. Speech of 15 February in the House of Commons. Previously separately published as *Navy Estimates in the Great War* (**A45**) and collected in *The Conduct of the War by Sea* (**D30**), at pp. 3–12; subsequently collected in Rhodes James, Vol. III, at pp. 2363–74, under the title 'British Command of the Sea'.

E17   July   **THE   DARDANELLE'S   [*sic*]   CAMPAIGN— PROGRESS OF THE ALLIES IN JUNE—SLOW AND DIFFICULT / A Few Miles from Victory.**
Current History, 716–17
Excerpts from speech of 5 June at Dundee. Subsequently collected in Rhodes James, Vol. III, at pp. 2378–84, under the title 'The War'.

1916

E18   January   **BRITAIN'S SEA WAR**
Current History, Vol. III, No. 4, 691–705
Speech of 15 November 1915 in the House of Commons. Subsequently collected in Rhodes James, Vol. III, at pp. 2390–403, under the title 'Resignation as First Lord of the Admiralty'.

1918

E19   September   **AMERICAN INDEPENDENCE DAY**
Current History, 535–8
Address delivered on 4 July in Central Hall, Westminster, at the Liberty Day meeting of the Anglo-Saxon Fellowship. Subsequently collected in Rhodes James, Vol. III, at

pp. 2613–16, under the title ' "The Third Great Title-Deed" of Anglo-American Liberties'.

1921

E20 April 1 **MR. CHURCHILL IN PALESTINE. / Great Demonstration on Mount Scopus. / Mr. Churchill's Striking Statement.**
Jewish Chronicle, 25
Churchill's remarks following his receipt of a Scroll of the Law on Mount Scopus.

E21a April 8 **MR. CHURCHILL IN JERUSALEM. / His Speech to the Arabs.**
Jewish Chronicle, 23, 25
Churchill's replies to Jewish and Arab delegations in Jerusalem.

E21b April 15 **MR. CHURCHILL IN PALESTINE. / His Jerusalem Speeches.**
Jewish Chronicle, 26–8
More from these speeches, this time taken from the official transcripts. Extracts were subsequently collected in Rhodes James, Vol. III, at pp. 3083–5.

E22 June 17 **THE GOVERNMENT AND PALESTINE. / Mr. Churchill's Statement.**
Jewish Chronicle, 17–18
Extracts from statement of 14 June in the House of Commons on Middle Eastern affairs. Subsequently collected in Rhodes James, Vol. III, at pp. 3095–111, under the title 'Middle East (Government Policy)'.

E23 October **UNEMPLOYMENT AND MR. CHURCHILL**
Scottish Home Rule Association News Sheet, 14
Excerpt from address of 23 September at Dundee. Subsequently collected in Rhodes James, Vol. III, at pp. 3128–31, under the title 'Unemployment', the excerpted portion running from p. 3130.14 to p. 3130.27.

1924

E24 May **SINGAPORE.**
Navy, 132–9
Report of a public meeting held under the auspices of the Navy League at Winchester House, E.C., on 28 March. Churchill's speech appears at pp. 137–9. Subsequently

collected in Rhodes James, Vol. IV, at pp. 3450–1, under the title 'Singapore (Naval Base)'.

1926

E25   March   **THE CHAMBER'S LUNCHEON MEETINGS. / Finance and Trade of the Empire. / Address by the Rt. Hon. Winston S. Churchill.**
Belfast Chamber of Commerce Journal, Vol. 3, No. 36, 178–83
Address of 2 March, being the third of a series of luncheon meetings organized by the Chamber. Subsequently collected in Rhodes James, Vol. IV, at pp. 3847–50, under the title 'National Finance'.

1929

E26   May 8   **A CONSERVATIVE ADDRESS**
Listener, 654–5
Broadcast of 30 April from London. Subsequently collected in Rhodes James, Vol. V, at pp. 4614–16, under the title 'The General Election'.

E27   July   **"EQUAL FLEETS NOT EQUALITY" / The Right Hon. Winston Churchill, M.P., at Chingford.**
Navy, 193
Speech of 14 June at Chingford. Subsequently collected in Rhodes James, Vol. V, at pp. 4632–5, under the title 'Constituency Address'.

1930

E28   April   **NAVY LEAGUE PUBLIC MEETING. / 26th February, 1930.**
Navy, 101–4
Churchill's speech at a Navy League meeting held at the Cannon Street Hotel, 26 February. Separately published in pamphlet form as *The Navy League* (**A89**) and subsequently collected in Rhodes James, Vol. V, at pp. 4710–11, under the title 'London Naval Conference'.

E29   June–July   **BRITISH STATESMEN DEBATE THE LONDON TREATY / Ramsay MacDonald vs. Winston Churchill**
Congressional Digest, Vol. 9, Nos 6–7, 179–80, 189

E30	Dec. 12	**STARK TRUTHS ABOUT INDIA**

Daily Mail, 10

Speech of 11 December at the meeting of the Indian Empire Society at the Cannon Street Hotel in London. Subsequently collected in Rhodes James, Vol. V, at pp. 4934–8, under the title 'India (The Round Table Conference)'.

1931

E31	March 10	**ADDRESS BY THE RIGHT HONOURABLE WINSTON SPENCER CHURCHILL, P.C., M.P., LL.D. ON THE OCCASION OF HIS INSTALLATION AS RECTOR OF THE UNIVERSITY**

Student, Vol. XXVII, No. 9, 304, 307–10, 312

Address of 5 March. Subsequently collected in Rhodes James, Vol. V, at pp. 4987–90, under the title ' "The Present Decline of Parliamentary Government in Great Britain" ' and in *Winston Wins!* (**D185**).[5]

1932

E32	March	**THE WORLD ECONOMIC CRISIS**

Consensus, Vol. XVII, No. 1, 5–25

Address of 8 February before the Economic Club of New York. A small part only of the address has been subsequently collected in Rhodes James, Vol. V, at pp. 5132–3, under the title 'Deflation and War Debts'.

E33	July	**THE MONEY PROBLEM. / Mr. Winston Churchill and Sir Robert Horne.**

Journal of the Royal Empire Society, Vol. XXIII (New Series), No. 7, 385–93

Churchill and Sir Robert Horne, both ex-Chancellors of the Exchequer, spoke at a special City Luncheon of the Royal Empire Society at the Cannon Street Hotel in London on 15 June. Their remarks are published here. Churchill's are found at pp. 385–90, and were subsequently collected in Rhodes James, Vol. V, at pp. 5181–3, under the title ' "The Money Problem" '.

---

5. Churchill served as Lord Rector of the University of Edinburgh, an elected office, from 1929 until 1932. He was succeeded in the position by General Sir Ian Hamilton.

1933

E34   July–   **BANQUET ANNUEL DE L'ASSOCIATION EN**
          August   **L'HONNEUR DE MR. WINSTON CHURCHILL**
                    France–Grande Bretagne, 472–5
                    Churchill, accompanied by his daughter Sarah, was received
                    by the Association France–Grande Bretagne at a special dinner
                    in his honour, the proceedings of which are recorded at
                    pp. 469 *et seq.* Churchill's remarks, in English, occupy
                    pp. 472–5. Upon his reception to the Senate, he made a few
                    further remarks in French, which are recorded at p. 482.

E35   August   **'THE ANNUAL BANQUET OF THE PARENT**
                    SOCIETY'
                    English Race, No. 128, 20–1
                    The report of proceedings at the annual banquet of 24 April is
                    found beginning at p. 19. Churchill's speech, in proposing the
                    toast of England, is reported at pp. 20–1.

1934

E36a   Jan. 17   **WHITHER BRITAIN? – II / Complete Text of the**
                    Talk Broadcast by Mr. Winston Churchill on
                    January 16
                    Listener, Vol. XI, No. 262, 85–6, 126
                    H. G. Wells and George Bernard Shaw also gave broadcast
                    talks as a part of this series. Subsequently collected in Rhodes
                    James, Vol. V, at pp. 5319–20. The notes for the speech in
                    Churchillian reverse-pyramid format have been collected in
                    Gilbert, *WSC*, Vol. V, *C.V.* 2, pp. 702–13.

E36b   Nov. 2,   **VOICES FROM THE ARCHIVES / –1. Winston**
          1972   **Churchill in 1934**
                    Listener, Vol. 88, No. 2275, 591–3

E37   April   **MARLBOROUGH: HIS LIFE AND TIMES**
                    Lecture Recorder and Meeting Reporter, Vol. 3, No. 9, 209–12
                    Report of a lecture given in aid of the YWCA at University
                    College, Gower Street, London, W.C.1, on 21 February.
                    Subsequently collected in Rhodes James, Vol. V, at
                    pp. 5327–8.

E38a   Nov. 21   **CAUSES OF WAR**
                    Listener, Vol. XII, No. 306, 841–2, 872
                    Broadcast of 16 November. Subsequently collected in Rhodes
                    James, Vol. V, at pp. 5433–6.

E38b	Dec. 3	**CAUSES OF WAR**

Vital Speeches of the Day, Vol. I, No. 5, 133–5

E39	Dec. 31	**REARMAMENT OF GERMANY AND ENGLAND'S AIR STRENGTH**

Vital Speeches of the Day, Vol. I, No. 7, 194–8

Address of 28 November in the House of Commons. Previously published in *The House of Commons and German Rearmament* (**D65**) and subsequently collected in *Arms and the Covenant* (**A107**), at pp. 171–86, and in Rhodes James, Vol. V, at pp. 5440–9, in both cases under the title 'The German Air Menace'.

1935

E40	Feb. 6	**THE GREAT BETRAYAL**

Listener, Vol. XIII, No. 317, 213–15

Note that the article title is under the general rubric 'INDIA', which does not properly form a part of the title, although it is so listed in the table of contents. Separately published in *India: "The Great Betrayal"* (**A99**). An extract from the broadcast was subsequently collected in Rhodes James, Vol. V, at pp. 5467–8, under the title 'India—The Betrayal'. The full set of notes for the broadcast address, presented in Churchill's reverse-pyramid format, is published in Gilbert, *WSC*, Vol. V, *C.V.* 2, pp. 1053–61.

E41	November	**NELSON DAY DINNER**

Navy, 326–32

Contains the text of a toast by Churchill at the Navy League's 'Nelson Day Dinner' held at Grosvenor House on 17 October. Churchill's contribution appears on p. 330.

1936

E42	December	**PROCEEDINGS AT THE UNVEILING OF THE MEMORIAL TO LAWRENCE OF ARABIA**

City of Oxford High School Magazine, 77–81

Address delivered at the unveiling of a memorial plaque to T. E. Lawrence at Oxford High School. Churchill's allocution of 3 October appeared subsequently in the J. Thornton 1937 publication *Proceedings at the Unveiling of the Memorial to Lawrence of Arabia*, which was issued in two formats (see **A104**), in *The Home Letters of T. E. Lawrence and His Brothers* (**B145**), and in Rhodes James, Vol. VI, at pp. 5791–3, under the title 'Lawrence of Arabia'.

E43   December   **MR. WINSTON CHURCHILL AND THE NEW COMMONWEALTH**
New Commonwealth, 38–40
Speech of 25 November at the New Commonwealth Society Luncheon at the Dorchester Hotel. Subsequently published separately in pamphlet form as *Speech at a Luncheon at the Dorchester Hotel, London on November 25th, 1936* (**A103**) and in Rhodes James, Vol. VI, at pp. 4632–5, under the title 'Defence'.

E43/1   January   **MR. WINSTON CHURCHILL AT THE ANNUAL DINNER**
Leeds Chamber of Commerce Journal, Vol. 13, No. 8, 131–6
Speech of 25 January, delivered as chief guest at the annual dinner of the Leeds Chamber of Commerce. Subsequently collected in abridged form in Rhodes James, Vol. VI, at pp. 5823–4, under the title 'Fascism and Communism'.

1937

E44   May 5   **FREEDOM AND PROGRESS FOR ALL**
Listener, Vol. XVII, No. 434, 849–50, 887
Under the superhead 'Responsibilities of Empire'. Broadcast of 30 April. Subsequently collected in *Responsibilities of Empire* (**D69**), at pp. 21–9, and in Rhodes James, Vol. VI, at pp. 5854–5, under the title 'Imperial Defence'.

E45   November   **NAVY LEAGUE DINNER / Stirring Speech by Mr. Winston Churchill / Lord Nuffield and the Sea Cadets**
Navy, 331–7
Report of the Navy League Annual Dinner, 19 October, at Grosvenor House, Park Lane. Churchill's speech: pp. 333–6. Subsequently collected in Rhodes James, Vol. VI, at pp. 5896–7, under the title 'Rearmament'.

E46a   Nov. 25   **THE KIPLING MEMORIAL SCHEME. / Mr. Churchill's Eloquent Commendation.**
Great Britain and East, 711
Churchill proposed the toast of "The Rudyard Kipling Memorial Fund" at an inaugural dinner held at Grosvenor House on 17 November. Subsequently published separately in *Homage to Kipling* (**A106**) and collected in Rhodes James, Vol. VI, at pp. 5903–6, under the title 'Kipling'. Note also the 'Homage to Kipling' in *John O'London's Weekly and the Outline* (**C559**).

| E46b | December | **[CHURCHILL TOAST]** |
| | | *Kipling Journal*, No. 44, 111–12 |

1938

| E47 | Nov. 1 | **THE LIGHTS ARE GOING OUT / We Should Consult Together** |

Vital Speeches of the Day, Vol. V, No. 2, 50–2
Broadcast of 16 October. Subsequently collected in *Into Battle* (**A142**), at pp. 54–9, under the title 'The Defence of Freedom and Peace', and in Rhodes James, Vol. VI, at pp. 6015–17, under the title 'Defence of Freedom and Peace'.

1939

| E48 | April 15 | **ENGLAND SPEAKS / Views of Her Leading Statesmen** |

Vital Speeches of the Day, Vol. V, No. 13, 391–5
Speeches by Churchill, Chamberlain *et al.* in the House of Commons on 3 April. Churchill's address: pp. 393–4. Subsequently collected in Rhodes James, Vol. VI, at pp. 6090–6, under the title ' "Do Not Yield Another Yard" '.

| E49a | Oct. 5 | **THE FIRST MONTH OF THE WAR** |

Listener, Vol. XXII, No. 560, 647–8, 679
Broadcast address of 1 October. Subsequently collected in *Into Battle* (**A142**), at pp. 130–5, and in Rhodes James, Vol. VI, at pp. 6160–4.

| E49b | Oct. 15 | **WE WILL DEAL IN PERFORMANCES, NOT PROMISES / It Is Not for Hitler to Say When the War Will End** |

Vital Speeches of the Day, Vol. VI, No. 1, 12–13

| E50 | Nov. 16 | **TEN WEEKS OF WAR** |

Listener, Vol. XXII, No. 565, 947–8
Broadcast address of 12 November. Subsequently collected in *Into Battle* (**A142**), at pp. 142–6, and in Rhodes James, Vol. VI, pp. 6171–5.

| E51 | Dec. 21 | **THE BATTLE OF THE RIVER PLATE** |

Listener, Vol. XXII, No. 571, 1224
Broadcast of 18 December. Separately published in pamphlet form as *The Glorious Battle of the River Plate* (**A114**). Subsequently collected in *Into Battle* (**A142**), at pp. 154–7,

under the title 'The Battle of the Plate', and in Rhodes James, Vol. VI, at pp. 6179–82, under the title 'Battle of the River Plate'.

1940

E52a   Jan. 25   **THE STATE OF THE WAR**
Listener, Vol. XXIII, No. 576, 151–2
Broadcast of 20 January. Separately published in pamphlet form as *The State of the War* (**A115**). Subsequently collected in *Into Battle* (**A142**), at pp. 158–62, under the title 'A House of Many Mansions' and in Rhodes James, Vol. VI, at pp. 6183–6, under the title 'The War Situation: "A House of Many Mansions"'.

E52b   Feb. 15   **WAR PROSPECTS / It Will Rage and Roar Ever More Loudly**
Vital Speeches of the Day, Vol. VI, No. 9, 272–3

E53a   April 4   **A STERNER WAR**
Listener, Vol. XXIII, No. 586, 659–60, 680
Broadcast of 30 March. Separately published in pamphlet form under the same title (see **A118**). Subsequently collected in *Into Battle* (**A142**), at pp. 180–3, and in Rhodes James, Vol. VI, at pp. 6190–201, under the title ' "A Hideous State of Alarm and Menace" '.

E53b   April 15   **THE SITUATION IN EUROPE / Dwelling in the Cage with the Tiger**
Vital Speeches of the Day, Vol. VI, No. 13, 392–4
The broadcast is here described in error as being of 31 March.

E54a   May 23   **'BE YE MEN OF VALOUR'**
Listener, Vol. XXIII, No. 593, 997–8
Broadcast of 19 May. Separately published in pamphlet form under the title *Conquer We Shall* (**A121**). Subsequently collected in *Into Battle* (**A142**), at pp. 104–11, under the title 'The New Army', and in Rhodes James, Vol. VI, at pp. 6220–3, under the title ' "Arm Yourselves and Be Ye Men of Valour" '. It is worth noting here that it was Churchill's view that "*The Listener* gives the most accurate reports of the broadcast speeches."[6]

---

6. Letter of 16 May 1941 from Kathleen Hill to Charles Eade (CHAR 8/804/152).

E54b	Spring 1986	**"ARM YOURSELVES, AND BE YE MEN OF VALOUR"**

Finest Hour, back cover

Notes for the speech presented in the reverse-pyramid format used by Churchill for his speaking notes.

E55a	June 15	**THE RETREAT FROM FLANDERS / We Shall Defend Our Island Whatever the Cost**

Vital Speeches of the Day, Vol. VI, No. 17, 516–19

Speech of 4 June in the House of Commons. Previously separately published as *Prime Minister Churchill's Address before the House of Commons* (**A124.1**) and subsequently as *Speech of June 4th 1940* (**A124.3**) and *A Speech by the Prime Minister the Right Honourable Winston Churchill in the House of Commons, June 4th, 1940* (**A124.4**) and collected in *Into Battle* (**A142**), at pp. 215–23, under the title 'Dunkirk', and in Rhodes James, Vol. VI, at pp. 6225–31, under the title ' "Wars Are Not Won by Evacuations" '.

E55b	Summer 1986	**DUNKIRK**

Finest Hour, No. 52, back cover

Notes for the speech presented in the reverse-pyramid format used by Churchill for his speaking notes.

E56a	June 20	**'THIS WAS THEIR FINEST HOUR'**

Listener, Vol. XXIII, No. 597, 1147–8, 1173

Broadcast of 18 June. Separately published as *Speech by the Prime Minister Mr. Winston Churchill Delivered in the House of Commons* (**A125**), and subsequently collected in Rhodes James, Vol. VI, at pp. 6231–8, in both cases under the title ' "Their Finest Hour" '.

E56b	July 1	**THE BATTLE FOR BRITAIN / Let Us Brace Ourselves to Our Duty**

Vital Speeches of the Day, Vol. VI, No. 18, 559–62

E56c	Autumn 1986	**FINEST HOUR**

Finest Hour, No. 53, back cover

Notes for the speech presented in the reverse-pyramid format used by Churchill for his speaking notes.

E57	July 15	**THE ATTACK ON THE FRENCH FLEET / The British Position**

Vital Speeches of the Day, Vol. VI, No. 19, 589–92

Speech of 4 July in the House of Commons. Separately published as *Speech by the Prime Minister Mr. Winston Churchill on the Taking of the French Fleet Delivered in the House of*

Commons July 4, 1940 (**A127**) and subsequently collected in *Into Battle* (**A142**), at pp. 239–46, under the title 'The Tragedy of the French Fleet', and in Rhodes James, Vol. VI, at pp. 6241–7, under the title 'Destruction of the French Fleet'.

E58   July 18   **'THE WAR OF THE UNKNOWN WARRIORS'**
Listener, Vol. XXIV, No. 601, 75–6
Broadcast of July 14. Separately published as *Speech Broadcast by the Prime Minister Mr. Winston Churchill July 14, 1940* (**A128**) and subsequently collected in *Into Battle* (**A142**), at pp. 247–51, under the title 'The War of the Unknown Warriors', and in Rhodes James, Vol. VI, at pp. 6247–50, under the title ' "War of the Unknown Warriors" '.

E59   Sept. 1   **GREAT BRITAIN WILL NOT FAIL / We Are Stronger Than Ever**
Vital Speeches of the Day, Vol. VI, No. 22, 692–6
Speech of 20 August in the House of Commons. Separately published as *A Speech by the Prime Minister, the Right Honourable Winston Churchill in the House of Commons, August 20th, 1940* (**A131.1**), as *Britain's Strength* (**A131.2**) and as *Britain, Champion of the World's Liberties* (**A131.3**), and subsequently collected in *Into Battle* (**A142**), at pp. 252–62, under the title 'The War Situation', and in Rhodes James, Vol. VI, at pp. 6260–8, under the title ' "The Few" '.

E60a   Sept. 19   **EVERY MAN TO HIS POST**
Listener, Vol. XXIV, No. 610, 403
Broadcast of September 11. Subsequently collected in *Into Battle*, at pp. 272–5, under the title 'Every Man to His Post', and in Rhodes James, Vol. VI, at pp. 6275–7, under the title 'Night Bombing of London: "Every Man to his Post" '.

E60b   Oct. 1   **A MESSAGE OF GOOD CHEER / Our Victory Will Come**
Vital Speeches of the Day, Vol. VI, No. 24, 750–1

E60c   Jan. 14,   **EVERY MAN TO HIS POST**
           1954   *Listener*, Vol. LI, No. 1298, 91–2

E61a   Oct. 24   **'GATHER STRENGTH FOR THE MORNING'**
Listener, Vol. XXIV, No. 615, 575–6
Broadcast of 21 October. Previously separately published in pamphlet form as *Speech Broadcast by the Prime Minister Mr. Winston Churchill to the People of France, October 21, 1940* (**A132.1**) and then as *'Our Whole People and Empire Have Vowed Themselves to the Task of Cleansing Europe of the Nazi*

Pestilence' (**A132.2**), and subsequently collected in *Into Battle* (**A142**), at pp. 295–7, under the title 'To the French People', and in Rhodes James, Vol. VI, at pp. 6296–8, under the title ' "Le Dieu protége [*sic*] la France" '.

E61b   Nov. 1   **VIVE LA FRANCE! / Sleep to Gather Strength for the Morning**
Vital Speeches of the Day, Vol. VII, No. 2, 48
The date of the speech is incorrectly indicated as 19 October.

E62   Dec. 1   **THE PROGRESS OF THE WAR / We Will Do Our Best**
Vital Speeches of the Day, Vol. VII, No. 4, 108–11
Speech of 5 November in the House of Commons. Separately published in pamphlet form as *Speech by the Prime Minister Mr. Winston Churchill on War Problems Facing Britain Delivered in the House of Commons, November 5, 1940* (**A134**), and subsequently collected in *Into Battle* (**A142**), at pp. 301–9, under the title 'The War Situation', and in Rhodes James, Vol. VI, at pp. 6298–304, under the title 'The War Situation (The Autumn Balance Sheet)'.

E63   Dec. 24   **THE PRIME MINISTER'S VISIT**
Harrovian, Vol. LIV, No. 13, 45
Extracts from Churchill's speech of 18 December during the first of his annual visits to Harrow Songs. The tradition continued until 18 November 1955. Subsequently collected in *The Unrelenting Struggle* (**A172**), at pp. 16–17, under the title 'The Old School', and in Rhodes James, Vol. VI, at pp. 6315–16, under the title 'Britain's Public Schools'.

1941

E64a   Jan. 2   **'NEVER YOUR FOES TILL NOW' / Winston Churchill's Broadcast to the Italian People on December 23**
Listener, Vol. XXV, No. 625, 14–15
Broadcast of December 23. Separately published in pamphlet form as *Speech Broadcast by the Prime Minister Mr. Winston Churchill to the Italian People* (**A137**). Subsequently collected in *The Unrelenting Struggle* (**A172**), at pp. 27–31, under the title 'A Call to the Italian People', and in Rhodes James, Vol. VI, at pp. 6322–5, under the title 'To the People of Italy'.

E64b   February   **ADDRESS TO THE ITALIAN PEOPLE BY PRIME MINISTER CHURCHILL / December 23, 1940**
International Conciliation, No. 367, 84–8
From the text supplied by the British Library of Information.

E65a   Feb. 13   **'PUT YOUR CONFIDENCE IN US' / Broadcast by the Prime Minister on February 9**
Listener, Vol. XXV, No. 631, 225–6, 233
Broadcast of 9 February. Separately published in pamphlet form as *Mr. Winston Churchill's Broadcast to the British Commonwealth of Nations* (**A143.1**), *Speech Broadcast by the Prime Minister Mr. Winston Churchill, February 9th, 1941* (**A143.2**) and under other titles in New Zealand, Turkey and Canada. Subsequently collected in *The Unrelenting Struggle* (**A172**), at pp. 54–63, under the title 'Give Us the Tools and We Will Finish the Job', and in Rhodes James, Vol. VI, at pp. 6343–50, under the title ' "Give Us the Tools" '.

E65b   Feb. 21   **'GIVE US THE TOOLS, AND—WE WILL FINISH THE JOB!'**
Radio Times, 6–9

E65c   Feb. 15   **THE TIDE IS TURNING / Give Us the Tools and We Will Finish the Job**
Vital Speeches of the Day, Vol. VII, No. 9, 272–5

E65d   March   **ADDRESS BROADCAST BY PRIME MINISTER WINSTON CHURCHILL / February 9, 1941**
International Conciliation, No. 368, 172–81
Reprinted from the *New York Times* of 10 February 1941.

E66   March   **TEXT OF PRIME MINISTER WINSTON CHURCHILL'S ADDRESS TO THE PILGRIMS / January 9, 1941**
International Conciliation, No. 368, 182–4
Text supplied by the British Library of Information, which published the speech separately as *Speech by the Prime Minister Mr. Winston Churchill to the Pilgrims* (**A139**). Subsequently collected in *The Unrelenting Struggle*, at pp. 33–5, under the title 'A Tribute to Lord Halifax', and in Rhodes James, Vol. VI, at pp. 6327–9, under the title 'United States Cooperation'.

E67   April 1   **WE ARE NO LONGER ALONE / We Now Shall Surely Overcome the Enemy**
Vital Speeches of the Day, Vol. VII, No. 12, 357–8
Speech to the Pilgrims at the luncheon honouring the new Ambassador of the United States, John G. Winant, on

18 March. Separately published in pamphlet form as *Speech by the Prime Minister Mr. Winston Churchill to the Pilgrim Society* (**A144**). Subsequently collected in *The Unrelenting Struggle*, at pp. 80–2, and in Rhodes James, Vol. VI, at pp. 6361–2, in both cases under the title 'Welcome to Mr. Winant'.

E68   April 17   **'YOU HAVE SAVED THE FUTURE' / The Prime Minister's Message to the Yugoslav People, Broadcast in the B.B.C.'s Serbo-Croat Service on April 12**
Listener, Vol. XXV, No. 640, 557
Subsequently collected in *The Unrelenting Struggle*, at p. 103, and in Rhodes James, Vol. VI, at p. 6378, in both cases under the title 'To the People of Yugoslavia'. Churchill and Rhodes James both date the broadcast 13 April.

E69   May 1   **'WESTWARD, LOOK, THE LAND IS BRIGHT!' / The Prime Minister's Broadcast of April 27**
Listener, Vol. XXV, No. 642, 615–16, 640
Separately published in pamphlet form as *Speech Broadcast by the Prime Minister Mr. Winston Churchill April 27, 1941* (**A145**). Subsequently collected in *The Unrelenting Struggle*, at pp. 106–14, and in Rhodes James, Vol. VI, at pp. 6378–84.

E70   May 1   **REVIEW OF THE WAR / Everything Turns upon the Battle of the Atlantic**
Vital Speeches of the Day, Vol. VII, No. 14, 428–32
Speech of 9 April in the House of Commons. Subsequently collected in *The Unrelenting Struggle*, at pp. 93–102, and in Rhodes James, Vol. VI, at pp. 6369–76, in both cases under the title 'The War Situation'.

E71   May 8   **'POLAND WILL REMAIN UNCONQUERABLE' / Broadcast by the Prime Minister on May 3, the 150th Anniversary of the Polish Constitution**
Listener, Vol. XXV, No. 643, 656
Separately published in pamphlet form as *Broadcast by the Prime Minister Mr. Winston Churchill to the Polish People, May 3, 1941* (**A146**). Subsequently collected in *The Unrelenting Struggle*, at pp. 115–17, under the title 'A Message to the Polish People', and in Rhodes James, Vol. VI, at pp. 6385–7, under the title 'To the Polish People'.

E72   June 5   **TOGETHER WE SHALL SEE IT THROUGH / Broadcast Messages Exchanged between the Rt. Hon. Mackenzie King, Prime Minister of Canada, and the Rt. Hon. Winston Churchill, on the Occasion of the Launching on June 2 of Canada's '1941 Victory Loan'**

Listener, Vol. XXV, No. 647, 796
The actual date of the broadcast was 1 June. Subsequently collected in *The Unrelenting Struggle*, at pp. 147–8, and in Rhodes James, Vol. VI, at pp. 6407–8, in both cases under the title 'To the People of Canada'.

E73a   June 19   **'THIS IS NOT THE END OF THE TALE' / Broadcast by the Rt. Hon. Winston Churchill**
Listener, Vol. XXV, No. 649, 873
Broadcast of 16 June upon receiving an honorary degree at the University of Rochester Commencement. Churchill was not physically present to receive the Doctor of Laws, *honoris causa*, but he did transmit the text of this address live by short-wave radio to the event and, not incidentally, to the people of the United States. A charming description of the event can be found in 'Commencement Rites Span Atlantic as Winston Churchill Gets Degree'.[7] Subsequently published in *Addresses by Winston Churchill and Others at the Ninety-first Annual Commencement of the University of Rochester* (**D80**) and collected in *The Unrelenting Struggle*, at pp. 173–5, under the title ' "The Birth Throes of a Sublime Resolve" ', and in Rhodes James, Vol. VI, at pp. 6425–7, under the title ' "The Old Lion" '.

E73b   Spring
        1965   **ADDRESS BY WINSTON CHURCHILL IN ACCEPTING THE DEGREE OF DOCTOR OF LAWS FROM THE UNIVERSITY OF ROCHESTER**
University of Rochester Library Bulletin, Volume XX, No. 3, 42–4
In addition to the text of the Churchill address, the citation of Dr Alan Valentine, the President of the University, and a reminiscence of the day by Margaret B. Andrews, entitled 'A Churchill Episode', are provided at pp. 41 and 37–40 respectively.

E74a   June 26   **THE FOURTH CLIMACTERIC / Broadcast by the Prime Minister on June 22**
Listener, Vol. XXV, No. 650, 895–6
Separately published in pamphlet form as *Speech Broadcast by the Prime Minister Mr. Winston Churchill on the New War, June 22nd, 1941* (**A149**). Subsequently collected in *The Unrelenting Struggle*, at pp. 176–80, and in Rhodes James, Vol. VI, at pp. 6427–31, in both cases under the title 'The German Invasion of Russia'.

---

7. In the *Rochester Alumni–Alumnae Review*, June–July 1941, Vol. XIX, No. 5, at pp. 5–7. Other related stories appear on the immediately succeeding pages and there is a letter from the editors to 'Mr. Winston Churchill, '41 (Hon.)', at p. 20.

E74b   July 1   **THE NEW WAR / The Invasion of Russia**
Vital Speeches of the Day, Vol. VII, No. 18, 551–3

E75   Aug. 15   **THE BRITISH WAR EFFORTS / We Are Guarding the Treasures of Mankind**
Vital Speeches of the Day, Vol. VII, No. 12, 646–9
Speech of 29 July delivered in the House of Commons. Separately published in pamphlet form as *Statement by the Prime Minister Mr. Winston Churchill to the House of Commons, July 29, 1941* (**A150**). Subsequently collected in *The Unrelenting Struggle*, at pp. 200–21, and in Rhodes James, Vol. VI, at pp. 6455–71, in both cases under the title 'War Production'.

E76a   Aug. 28   **THE ATLANTIC CHARTER / The Prime Minister's Broadcast of August 24**
Listener, Vol. XXVI, No. 659, 287–8, 308
Separately published in pamphlet form only in Russian (**A171**) and subsequently collected in *The Unrelenting Struggle*, at pp. 229–37, under the title 'The Meeting with President Roosevelt', and in Rhodes James, Vol. VI, at pp. 6472–8.

E76b   Sept. 1   **SOMEWHERE IN THE ATLANTIC / A Meeting of Historic Importance**
Vital Speeches of the Day, Vol. VII, No. 22, 674, 676–8

E76c   October   **ADDRESS BROADCAST BY PRIME MINISTER WINSTON CHURCHILL / August 24, 1941**
International Conciliation, No. 373, 660–7
Reprinted from the *New York Times* of 25 August.

E77   Oct. 15   **A REVIEW OF THE WAR / The Menace of Invasion Is Still Present**
Vital Speeches of the Day, Vol. VIII, No. 1, 2–5
Speech of 30 September. Separately published in pamphlet form as *Statement by the Prime Minister Mr. Winston Churchill to the House of Commons, September 30, 1941* (**A156**). Subsequently collected in *The Unrelenting Struggle*, at pp. 258–66, and in Rhodes James, Vol. VI, at pp. 6490–6, in both cases under the title 'The War Situation'.

E78   Nov. 5   **THE PRIME MINISTER**
Harrovian, Vol. LV, No. 6, 19–20
Speech of 29 October at Harrow Songs. Subsequently collected in *The Unrelenting Struggle*, at pp. 274–6, and in Rhodes James, Vol. VI, at pp. 6498–500, in both cases under the title ' "These Are Great Days" '.

E79   Dec. 1   **BRITISH WILL SUPPORT U.S. AGAINST JAPAN /**
                        Would Declare War Within the Hour
                        Vital Speeches of the Day, Vol. VIII, No. 4, 104–6
                        Speech of 10 November at the Mansion House, London.
                        Separately published in folded leaflet form as *Speech by the*
                        Prime Minister Mr. Winston Churchill at the Mansion House,
                        November 10, 1941 (**A158**). Subsequently collected in *The*
                        Unrelenting Struggle, at pp. 282–6, and in Rhodes James,
                        Vol. VI, at pp. 6502–5, in both cases under the title 'A
                        Warning to Japan'.

E80a   Dec. 11   **THE GREAT ALLIANCE OF FREE PEOPLES / The**
                        Prime Minister's Broadcast of December 8
                        Listener, Vol. XXVI, No. 674, 775–6
                        The speech was originally delivered in the House of
                        Commons; it was repeated over the air with the addition of a
                        final paragraph. Separately published in pamphlet form as
                        Speech Broadcast by the Prime Minister Mr. Winston Churchill on
                        the Far East War, December 8, 1941 (**A161**). The entire text was
                        subsequently collected in *The Unrelenting Struggle*, at
                        pp. 316–19, and in Rhodes James, Vol. VI, at pp. 6523–6, in
                        both cases under the title 'War with Japan'.

E80b   January   **BRITAIN ANNOUNCES WAR AGAINST JAPAN**
           1942   *Current History*, 415–18

E81a   Dec. 27   **ADDRESS BY THE PRIME MINISTER OF GREAT**
                        BRITAIN BEFORE BOTH HOUSES OF CONGRESS
                        Department of State Bulletin, 573–8
                        Speech of 26 December before a Joint Session of the Congress.
                        Subsequently published separately in pamphlet form and cased
                        (see **A163**), and collected in *The Unrelenting Struggle*, at
                        pp. 333–40, under the title 'The Speech to Congress', and in
                        Rhodes James, Vol. VI, at pp. 6536–41, under the title ' "A
                        Long and Hard War" '.

E81b   Jan. 15,   **HERE WE ARE TOGETHER / Defending All That to**
           1942   **Free Men Is Dear**
                        Vital Speeches of the Day, Vol. VIII, No. 7, 197–9

E81c   February   **ADDRESS OF PRIME MINISTER WINSTON**
           1942   **CHURCHILL TO THE CONGRESS OF THE**
                        UNITED STATES / December 26, 1941
                        International Conciliation, No. 377, 62–9
                        Reprinted from the *New York Times* of 27 December 1941.

E81d   April 1942   **THE GREATEST MOMENT IN THE HISTORY OF
ANGLO-AMERICAN RELATIONS!**
Neptune, 11–15

1942

—   January   **BRITAIN ANNOUNCES WAR AGAINST JAPAN**
(*Current History; see* **E80b**)

—   Jan. 15   **HERE WE ARE TOGETHER** (*Vital Speeches of the Day*;
see **E81b**)

—   February   **ADDRESS OF PRIME MINISTER WINSTON
CHURCHILL TO THE CONGRESS OF THE
UNITED STATES** (*International Conciliation; see* **E81c**)

E82a   February · **COMMONWEALTH   LEADER   SPEAKS   TO
CANADIANS**
Canadian Geographical Journal, 73–9
Address of 30 December 1941 to the Canadian House of
Commons. Previously published separately in pamphlet form
(see **A164**) and subsequently collected in *The Unrelenting
Struggle*, at pp. 341–9, under the title 'Preparation—
Liberation—Assault', and in Rhodes James, Vol. VI,
at pp. 6541–7, under the title ' "Some Chicken! Some
Neck!" '

E82b   February   **ADDRESS OF PRIME MINISTER WINSTON
CHURCHILL TO THE CANADIAN PARLIAMENT /
December 30, 1941**
International Conciliation, No. 377, 70–8
Reprinted from the *New York Times* of 31 December 1941.

E82c   n.d.   **"IN GOOD HEART AND SOBER CONFIDENCE"**
War in Pictures, No. 21, 5–7

E83a   Feb. 19   **'INTO THE STORM AND THROUGH THE
STORM' / The Prime Minister's Broadcast of
February 15**
Listener, Vol. XXVII, No. 684, 227–8, 239
Separately published in pamphlet form as *Address by the Prime
Minister Mr. Winston Churchill Broadcast February 15, 1942*
(**A168.1**) and *Speech Broadcast by Mr. Churchill after the Fall of
Singapore* (**A168.2**). Subsequently collected in *The End of the
Beginning*, at pp. 50–6, under the title ' "Through the Storm" ',
and in Rhodes James, Vol. VI, at pp. 6583–7, under the title
'The Fall of Singapore'.

| E83b | March 1 | **THE STRUGGLE FOR LIFE** / "We Shall Not Fail Now"
Vital Speeches of the Day, Vol. VIII, No. 10, 295–7 |

— April **THE GREATEST MOMENT IN THE HISTORY OF ANGLO–AMERICAN RELATIONS!** (*Neptune*; *see* **E81d**)

E84a May 14 **A MESSAGE OF GOOD CHEER** / Broadcast by the Prime Minister on May 10
Listener, Vol. XXVII, No. 696, 611–12, 630–1
Separately published in pamphlet form in Portuguese, Russian, bilingually in Portuguese and English (**A169.1**) and as *Speech Broadcast by the Prime Minister Mr. Winston Churchill, May 10, 1942* (**A169.2**). Subsequently collected in *The End of the Beginning*, at pp. 100–7, and in Rhodes James, Vol. VI, at pp. 6629–35, in both cases under the title 'Prime Minister for Two Years'.

E84b May 15 **MY TWO YEARS OF STEWARDSHIP** / We Are Now Prepared for Aggressive Moments
Vital Speeches of the Day, Vol. VIII, No. 15, 453–6

E84c June **SPEECH OF PRIME MINISTER WINSTON CHURCHILL BROADCAST FROM ENGLAND, MAY 10, 1942**
International Conciliation, No. 381, 360–8
The text is as recorded by the *New York Times* and is reprinted by permission of that newspaper.

E85 Aug. 1 **THE BATTLE FOR EGYPT** / The Dangers of Unbridled Criticism
Vital Speeches of the Day, Vol. VIII, No. 20, 614–19
Speech of 2 July in the House of Commons. Subsequently collected in *The End of the Beginning*, at pp. 128–49, under the title 'The Central Direction of the War', and in Rhodes James, Vol. VI, at pp. 6645–61, under the title 'The Conduct of the War'.

E86 Sept. 15 **PROGRESS OF THE WAR** / Visits to Egypt and Moscow
Vital Speeches of the Day, Vol. VIII, No. 23, 710–14
Speech of 8 September in the House of Commons. Separately published in pamphlet form only in Russian (**A171**). Subsequently collected in *The End of the Beginning*, at pp. 163–76, and in Rhodes James, Vol. VI, at pp. 6665–75, in both cases under the title 'The War Situation'.

E87a	Oct. 15	**ALLIES' WAR GAINS / Fear Behind Hitler's Outrages** *Vital Speeches of the Day*, Vol. IX, No. 1, 11–13 Speech of 12 October delivered on a visit to Edinburgh. Subsequently collected in *The End of the Beginning*, at pp. 191–7, under the title ' "Keep Right on to the End" ', and in Rhodes James, Vol. VI, at pp. 6679–84, under the title ' "Our Greatest Glory" '.

E87b	July 15, 1943	**KEEP RIGHT ON TO THE END / "We must move forward together, united and inexorable"** *Vogue*, 32–3 Permission was requested of Little, Brown on 28 May to use 1500 to 2000 words from *The End of the Beginning*, which had not yet been published. Condé Nast Publications paid $200 for the rights, which were granted by Little, Brown before consultation with Cassell. Little, Brown kept 10% of the fee as its commission and remitted the balance, less the 30% foreign corporations tax, to Cassell on 16 September. The Editor's Note is worth quoting: "A living and lively legend, the Right Honourable Winston S. Churchill, Prime Minister of Great Britain, also happens to be a remarkably lucky man. Not the least of his luck is his native talent for speaking the King's English royally well. His small talk is literature. His more considered speech is both literature and history." Assignment of copyright was registered with the Register of Copyrights on 17 August 1943.

E88	Nov. 15	**VICTORY IN AFRICA / We Mean to Hold Our Own** *Vital Speeches of the Day*, Vol. IX, No. 3, 66–7 Speech of 10 November delivered at a luncheon for the Lord Mayor at the Mansion House, London. Subsequently collected in *The End of the Beginning*, at pp. 213–16, under the title ' "The End of the Beginning" ', and in Rhodes James, Vol. VI, at pp. 6692–5, under the title 'A New Experience—Victory'.

E89	Nov. 25	**THE PRIME MINISTER** *Harrovian*, Vol. LVI, No. 8, 15 Speech of 18 November at Harrow Songs. Subsequently collected in *The End of the Beginning*, at pp. 234–5, under the title 'Harrow School Songs', and in Rhodes James, Vol. VI, at pp. 6709–10, under the title 'The Harrow Songs'.

E90	Dec. 1	**VICTORY IN EGYPT AND AFRICAN CAMPAIGN / Military Technicalities Today** *Vital Speeches of the Day*, Vol. IX, No. 4, 98–104 Speech of 11 November in the House of Commons. Separately published in pamphlet form as *A Speech before the*

Parliament of England on 11th November 1942 (**A177**). Subsequently collected in *The End of the Beginning*, at pp. 218–33, and in Rhodes James, Vol. VI, at pp. 6696–709, in both cases under the title 'The War Situation'.

E91a   Dec. 3   **THE SPUR OF VICTORY / The Prime Minister's Broadcast of November 29**
Listener, Vol. XXVIII, No. 725, 707–8, 726
Separately published in pamphlet form as *Speech Broadcast by the Prime Minister Mr. Winston Churchill Broadcast November 29, 1942* (**A175**). Subsequently collected in *The End of the Beginning*, at pp. 237–43, under the title 'Victory as a Spur', and in Rhodes James, Vol. VI, at pp. 6710–15, under the title 'The Bright Gleam of Victory'.

E91b   Dec. 15   **WARNING TO ITALY / Grim Ordeals Ahead**
Vital Speeches of the Day, Vol. IX, No. 5, 131–4

1943

E92   March 1   **COMING ALLIED OFFENSIVE / The Casablanca Discussions**
Vital Speeches of the Day, Vol. IX, No. 10, 294–301
Speech of 11 February in the House of Commons. Separately published in pamphlet form as *The Casablanca Conference* (**A179**). Subsequently collected in *Onwards to Victory*, at pp. 13–29, and in Rhodes James, Vol. VII, at pp. 6742–55, in both cases under the title 'The War Situation'.

E93   March 20   **THE WAR / Statements by the Secretary of State Commending Speech of General Giraud**
Department of State Bulletin, 229
Statement in the House of Commons on 17 March regarding General Giraud's speech of 14 March. Subsequently collected in *Onwards to Victory* (**A194**), at p. 60, under the title 'General Giraud's Speech'.

E94a   March 25   **'NO PROMISES BUT EVERY PREPARATION' / The Prime Minister's Broadcast of March 21**
Listener, Vol. XXIX, No. 741, 347–8, 363–5
Separately published in pamphlet form as *A Four Years' Plan for Britain* (**A180.1**). Subsequently collected in *Onwards to Victory*, at pp. 33–45, under the title 'A Four Years' Plan', and in Rhodes James, Vol. VII, at pp. 6755–65, under the title 'Postwar Planning'.

E94b   March 29   **FOUR YEARS' PLAN FOR BRITAIN** / Tasks of the **Council of Europe** / **State Health and Insurance Schemes**
Crusader, Vol. 4, No. 48, 1–5

E94c   April 15   **POST-WAR COUNCILS ON WORLD PROBLEMS** / **A Four Year Plan for England**
Vital Speeches of the Day, Vol. IX, No. 13, 386–91

E94d   June   **SPEECH BY PRIME MINISTER WINSTON CHURCHILL** / **Broadcast from London, March 21, 1943**
International Conciliation, No. 391, 442–55
Reprinted by permission from the *New York Times* of 22 March 1943.

E94e   June 5   **AFTER THE WAR** / **The Prime Minister's Broadcast** / **(21st March, 1943)**
Current Affairs, 32–44

E95   May 20   **TWO MILLION RESOLUTE MEN** / **The Prime Minister's Message to the Home Guard Broadcast from Washington on May 14**
Listener, Vol. XXIX, No. 749, 589–90
Subsequently collected in *Onwards to Victory*, at pp. 87–90, and in Rhodes James, Vol. VII, at pp. 6772–4, in both cases under the title 'The Home Guard'.

E96   June 1   **FULL AID TO UNITED STATES AGAINST JAPAN** / **Weight off Russia This Year**
Vital Speeches of the Day, Vol. IX, No. 16, 482–7
Address of 19 May to the U.S. Congress. Separately published in pamphlet form by four different publishers (see **A181**). Subsequently collected in *Onwards to Victory*, at pp. 91–102, under the title 'The Speech to the U.S. Congress', and in Rhodes James, Vol. VII, at pp. 6775–84, under the title 'To the U.S. Congress'.

E97a   June 15   **AMPHIBIOUS OPERATIONS APPROACH** / **"Nothing Will Turn Us from Our Endeavor"**
Vital Speeches of the Day, Vol. IX, No. 17, 515–18
Speech of 8 June in the House of Commons. Subsequently collected in *Onwards to Victory*, at pp. 114–21, under the title ' "Brighter and Solid Prospects" ', and in Rhodes James, Vol. VII, at pp. 6786–92, under the title 'The War Situation'.

E97b	July	**[THE TUNISIAN VICTORY AND THE WAR AT SEA[8]]** *British Speeches of the Day*, [Vol. I], No. 5, 1–7

E98a	July	**ON RECEIVING THE FREEDOM OF THE CITY OF LONDON, JUNE 30, 1943** *British Speeches of the Day*, [Vol. I], No. 5, 8–14 Speech of 30 June at the Guildhall, London. Separately published in pamphlet form as *Marching to Victory* (**A182**). Subsequently collected in *Onwards to Victory*, at pp. 123–33, and in Rhodes James, Vol. VII, at pp. 6792–9, in both cases under the title ' "Before the Autumn Leaves Fall" '.

E98b	July 15	**"WE SEEK NO PROFIT" / "The Hard, Cold, Vindictive Truth"** *Vital Speeches of the Day*, Vol. IX, No. 19, 581–4

—	July 15	**KEEP RIGHT ON TO THE END** (*Vogue*; *see* **E87b**)

E99a	August	**[EVENTS IN ITALY]** *British Speeches of the Day*, [Vol. I], No. 6, 1–4 Speech of 27 July in the House of Commons. Subsequently collected in *Onwards to Victory*, at pp. 142–7, under the title 'Mussolini's Downfall', and in Rhodes James, Vol. VII, at pp. 6809–12, under the title 'The Fall of Mussolini'.

E99b	Aug. 15	**DEVELOPMENTS IN ITALY / Let Them "Stew in Their Own Juice"** *Vital Speeches of the Day*, Vol. IX, No. 21, 645–7

E100a	September	**[THE ALLIED ACHIEVEMENTS]** *British Speeches of the Day*, [Vol. I], No. 7, 22–8 Address of 31 August from the Citadel, Quebec City. Subsequently collected in *Onwards to Victory*, at pp. 173–80, under the title 'The Call for a Three-Power Talk', and in Rhodes James, Vol. VII, at pp. 6816–22, under the title 'The Quebec Conference'.

E100b	Sept. 2	**'LET US ALL GO FORWARD TOGETHER' / The Prime Minister's Broadcast from the Citadel, Quebec, on August 31** *Listener*, Vol. XXX, No. 764, 255–6, 270

---

8. Commonly in the case of *British Speeches of the Day*, there is not a title provided above the speech text. In such cases, I have included in brackets the title given on the wrapper of the number itself.

E100c   Sept. 15   **TROOPS WILL CROSS CHANNEL** / **Significant Events Are Taking Place**
                            Vital Speeches of the Day, Vol. IX, No. 23, 707–10

E100d   October   **CHURCHILL'S BROADCAST FROM QUEBEC**
                            Current History, 161–6

E101a   September   **[ON RECEIVING AN HONORARY DEGREE AT HARVARD UNIVERSITY]**
                            British Speeches of the Day, [Vol. I], No. 7, 1–5
                            Speech of 6 September at Harvard University. Subsequently published separately in pamphlet form (**A186**) and collected in *Onwards to Victory*, at pp. 181–6, and in Rhodes James, Vol. VII, at pp. 6823–7, in both cases under the title 'Anglo-American Unity'.

E101b   Sept. 15   **ALLIANCE WITH U.S. AFTER WAR** / **Common Tongue a Basis for Common Citizenship**
                            Vital Speeches of the Day, Vol. IX, No. 23, 713–15

E101c   Sept. 18   **ADDRESS BY PRIME MINISTER CHURCHILL IN RESPONSE TO THE AWARD OF THE HONORARY DEGREE OF DOCTOR OF LAWS, SANDERS THEATRE, SEPTEMBER 6, 1943**
                            Harvard Alumni Bulletin, Vol. 46, No. 1, 18–21

E102a   October   **[THE SURRENDER OF ITALY]**
                            British Speeches of the Day, [Vol. I], No. 8, 1–22
                            Speech of 21 September in the House of Commons. Separately published in pamphlet form as *The War Transformed* (**A187**). Subsequently collected in *Onwards to Victory*, at pp. 189–216, under the title 'The War: Past and Future', and in Rhodes James, Vol. VII, at pp. 6828–50, under the title 'The War Situation'.

E102b   Oct. 1   **RECENT WAR DEVELOPMENTS** / **Campaigns and Policies Skillfully Managed**
                            Vital Speeches of the Day, Vol. IX, No. 24, 743–54

E103   Oct. 15   **WOMEN'S PART IN THE STRUGGLE** / **"No Fear of the Future"**
                            Vital Speeches of the Day, Vol. X, No. 1, 2–3
                            Speech of 28 September to the National Conference for Women at the Albert Hall, London. Subsequently collected in *National Conference of Women Called by H.M. Government. Report of Proceedings* (**D97**), at pp. 5–7, and in *Onwards to Victory*, at pp. 222–5, and in Rhodes James, Vol. VII, at

pp. 6854–6, in both cases under the title 'The Women of Britain'.

E104   November   **[POLITICAL UNITY IN WAR; THE COAL SITUATION]**
British Speeches of the Day, [Vol. I], No. 9, 1–7
Speech of 13 October in the House of Commons. Subsequently collected in *Onwards to Victory*, at pp. 237–47, and in Rhodes James, Vol. VII, at pp. 6859–67, in both cases under the title 'The Coalmining Situation'.

E105   November   **[PARLIAMENTARY DEMOCRACY]**
British Speeches of the Day, [Vol. I], No. 9, 39
Speech of 28 October in the House of Commons. Separately published in pamphlet form as *The Prime Minister's Speech on the House of Commons Rebuilding* (**A188**) and subsequently collected in *Onwards to Victory*, at pp. 248–53, under the title 'Rebuilding the House of Commons', and in Rhodes James, Vol. VII, at pp. 6869–73, under the title ' "A Sense of Crowd and Urgency" '.

E106   Nov. 10   **THE PRIME MINISTER**
Harrovian, Vol. LVII, No. 6, 11
Speech of 5 November at Harrow Songs. Subsequently collected in *Onwards to Victory*, at pp. 261–2, and in Rhodes James, Vol. VI, at pp. 6873–4, in both cases under the title ' "Let Vision Guide Our Steps" '.

E107a   December   **[A YEAR OF VICTORY]**
British Speeches of the Day, [Vol. I], No. 10, 1–4
Speech of 9 November at the Lord Mayor's Day Luncheon at the Mansion House. Subsequently collected in *Onwards to Victory*, at pp. 263–7, under the title 'No Time to Relax', and in Rhodes James, Vol. VII, at pp. 6874–8, under the title 'The Task Ahead'.

E107b   December   **CHURCHILL'S LONDON SPEECH**
Current History, 344–6

E107c   Dec. 1   **MILESTONES OF OUR JOURNEY / This Is No Time for Relaxation**
Vital Speeches of the Day, Vol. X, No. 4, 103–5

1944

E108a   March   **[THE MILITARY AND POLITICAL SCENE]**
British Speeches of the Day, Vol. II, No. 3, 1–14
Speech of 22 February in the House of Commons. Separately published in pamphlet form as *Towards the Climax* (**A191.1**) and *The Eve of Action* (**A191.2**). Subsequently collected in *The Dawn of Liberation*, at pp. 3–20, under the title ' "Preparation, Effort, Resolve" ', and in Rhodes James, Vol. VII, at pp. 6881–94, under the title 'The Progress of the War'.

E108b   March 1   **HITLER'S FORCES STILL STRONG / Our Offensive and Cooperation Policies**
Vital Speeches of the Day, Vol. X, No. 10, 297–303

E108c   April   **CHURCHILL'S ADDRESS TO THE COMMONS**
Current History, 340–51

E109   March 11   **PREMIER AND PHYSICIANS**
Lancet, 348–9
Churchill's address of 2 March to the Royal College of Physicians in London. Note that Lord Moran's toast of Churchill and the guests is at pp. 347–8. Subsequently published in *Speeches by the Rt. Hon. Winston S. Churchill and Lord Moran* (**D102**) and collected in *The Dawn of Liberation*, at pp. 21–4, under the title 'A Tribute to Physicians', and in Rhodes James, Vol. VII, at pp. 6895–7, under the title 'The Royal College of Physicians'.

E110a   March 30   **'THE HOUR IS APPROACHING' / The Prime Minister's Broadcast of March 26**
Listener, Vol. XXXI, No. 794, 343–4, 359–60
Subsequently collected in *The Dawn of Liberation*, at pp. 38–49, and in Rhodes James, Vol. VII, at pp. 6907–16, in both cases under the title ' "The Hour of Our Greatest Effort Is Approaching" '.

E110b   April   **[WAR OVERSEAS: RECONSTRUCTION AT HOME]**
British Speeches of the Day, Vol. II, No. 4, 35–44

E110c   April 1   **THE WAR AND CONDITIONS IN ENGLAND / Our Greatest Effort Is Coming**
Vital Speeches of the Day, Vol. X, No. 12, 354–8

E111	May	**[WAR DECORATIONS AND MEDALS]**

British Speeches of the Day, Vol. II, No. 5, 1–6
Speech of 22 March in the House of Commons. Subsequently collected in *The Dawn of Liberation*, at pp. 28–36, and in Rhodes James, Vol. VII, at pp. 6900–5, in both cases under the title 'War Decorations'.

E112a	May	**[UNITY IN COMMONWEALTH AND EMPIRE]**

British Speeches of the Day, Vol. II, No. 5, 24–30
Speech of 21 April in the House of Commons. Subsequently collected in *The Dawn of Liberation*, at pp. 65–72, under the title ' "Spirit of the Empire" ', and in Rhodes James, Vol. VII, at pp. 6918–24, under the title 'The Future of the Empire'.

E112b	June	**[SPEECHES ON THE EMPIRE AND COMMON-WEALTH]**

British Speeches of the Day, Vol. II, No. 6 (Supp.), 29–34

E113a	June	**[FOREIGN AFFAIRS]**

British Speeches of the Day, Vol. II, No. 6, 37–51
Speech of 24 May in the House of Commons. Separately published in pamphlet form by three publishers (see **A193**). Subsequently collected in *The Dawn of Liberation*, at pp. 83–102, under the title 'A World Survey', and in Rhodes James, Vol. VII, at pp. 6930–45, under the title 'The World Situation'.

E113b	June 1	**BRITISH FOREIGN POLICY / Problems of Present; Hopes of Future**

Vital Speeches of the Day, Vol. X, No. 16, 482–90

E113c	July	**CHURCHILL ON FOREIGN POLICY**

Current History, 41–8
"Extensive excerpts" from the speech.

E114a	June 15	**START OF INVASION / Liberation of Rome**

Vital Speeches of the Day, Vol. X, No. 17, 515–16
Speech of 6 June in the House of Commons. Subsequently collected in *The Dawn of Liberation*, at pp. 104–7, and in Rhodes James, Vol. VII, at pp. 6945–8, in both cases under the title 'The Invasion of France'.

E114b	July	**[THE INVASION]**

British Speeches of the Day, Vol. II, No. 7, 1–2

E114c	July	**PRIME MINISTER CHURCHILL'S STATEMENTS TO THE COMMONS**

Current History, 37–8

E115a   July 15   **THE ROBOT BOMB CAMPAIGN / Casualties, Damage and Counter-Measures**
Vital Speeches of the Day, Vol. X, No. 19, 580–3
Speech of 6 July in the House of Commons. Subsequently collected in *The Dawn of Liberation*, at pp. 126–38, and in Rhodes James, Vol. VII, at pp. 6955–62, in both cases under the title 'The Flying Bomb'.

E115b   August   **[FLYING BOMBS]**
British Speeches of the Day, Vol. II, No. 8, 1–7

E116a   Aug. 15   **ALLIED WAR GAINS / Mastery Now Pronounced on All Fronts**
Vital Speeches of the Day, Vol. X, No. 21, 642–50
Speech of 2 August in the House of Commons. Separately published in pamphlet form as *The Hour of Decision* (**A195.1**). Subsequently collected in *The Dawn of Liberation*, at pp. 144–65, and in Rhodes James, Vol. VII, at pp. 6968–85, in both cases under the title 'The War Situation'.

E116b   Aug. 19   **REVIEW OF THE WAR**
World Press Review (Supplement to Issue 151), 1–6

E116c   September   **[THE WAR SITUATION]**
British Speeches of the Day, Vol. II, No. 9, 1–17

E117a   October   **[THE WAR AND THE ITALIAN SITUATION]**
British Speeches of the Day, Vol. II, No. 10, 20–36
Speech of 28 September in the House of Commons. Separately published in pamphlet form as *The Tide of Triumph* (**A196.1**). Subsequently collected in *The Dawn of Liberation*, at pp. 180–203, under the title 'A Review of the War', and in Rhodes James, Vol. VII, at pp. 6990–7007, under the title 'The War Situation'.

E117b   Oct. 7   **MR. CHURCHILL REVIEWS THE WAR / Foreign Affairs Are Involving "Heavy, Critical Work"**
World Press Review (Supplement to Issue 158), 1–6

E117c   Oct. 15   **CRITICAL PROBLEMS OF PAST, PRESENT AND FUTURE / Review of Military and Political Situations**
Vital Speeches of the Day, Vol. XI, No. 1, 2–11

E118a   November   **[DISCUSSIONS IN MOSCOW]**
British Speeches of the Day, Vol. II, No. 11, 1–6
Speech of 27 October in the House of Commons. Subsequently collected in *The Dawn of Liberation*, at pp. 220–7,

and in Rhodes James, Vol. VII, at pp. 7013–18, under the title ' "The Last Lap" '.

E118b Nov. 15 **THE LAST LAP / United Action Vital**
Vital Speeches of the Day, Vol. XI, No. 3, 66–9

E119 November **[ELECTIONS AT HOME]**
British Speeches of the Day, Vol. II, No. 11, 6–10
Speech of 31 October in the House of Commons. Subsequently collected in *The Dawn of Liberation*, at pp. 229–34, and in Rhodes James, Vol. VII, at pp. 7020–4, in both cases under the title 'Prolongation of Parliament'.

E120 December **[V–2]**
British Speeches of the Day, Vol. II, No. 12, 1
Speech of 10 November in the House of Commons. Subsequently collected in *The Dawn of Liberation*, at pp. 243–4, under the title 'V2 Rocket', and in Rhodes James, Vol. VII, at pp. 7029–30, under the title 'The V2 Rocket'.

E121 December **[HOME LEAVE; ASSASSINATION OF LORD MOYNE]**
British Speeches of the Day, Vol. II, No. 12, 2–4
Speech of 17 November in the House of Commons. Subsequently collected in *The Dawn of Liberation*, at pp. 251–2, under the title 'Palestine Terrorism', and in Rhodes James, Vol. VII, at pp. 7033–4, under the title 'Overseas Forces (Leave)'.

E122 December **FUTURE OF LEND-LEASE**
British Speeches of the Day, Vol. II, No. 12, 4–6
Speech of 30 November in the House of Commons. Subsequently collected in *The Dawn of Liberation*, at pp. 266–9, and in Rhodes James, Vol. VII, at pp. 7033–4, under the title 'Lend-Lease'.

E123 Dec. 1 **HIGH TIME FOR ANOTHER TRIPLE CONFERENCE / The American Election Results**
Vital Speeches of the Day, Vol. XI, No. 4, 105–6
Speech of 9 November at the Lord Mayor of London's Luncheon at the Mansion House, London. Subsequently collected in *The Dawn of Liberation*, at pp. 237–42, under the title 'The Fruits of 1944', and in Rhodes James, Vol. VII, at pp. 7025–9, under the title 'Review of 1944'.

E124   Dec. 6   **THE PRIME MINISTER**
Harrovian, Vol. LVIII, No. 10, 19
Speech of 1 December at Harrow Songs. Subsequently collected in *The Dawn of Liberation*, at pp. 271–2, under the title 'Britain's Public Schools', and in Rhodes James, Vol. VII, at pp. 7047–8, under the title 'The Public Schools'.

E125a   Dec. 15   **WAR'S END STILL DISTANT / Greatest Effort Needed for Last Lap**
Vital Speeches of the Day, Vol. XI, No. 5, 133–4
Speech of 29 November in the House of Commons. Subsequently collected in *The Dawn of Liberation*, at pp. 255–65, and in Rhodes James, Vol. VII, at pp. 7036–44, in both cases under the title ' "The Tasks Which Lie before Us" '.

E125b   January   **[THE NEW SESSION]**
        1945   *British Speeches of the Day*, Vol. III, No. 1, 1–9

E126a   Dec. 15   **PRIVATE ARMIES UNDERMINE DEMOCRATIC GOVERNMENT / Statement on Greece**
Vital Speeches of the Day, Vol. XI, No. 5, 134–6
Speech of 5 December in the House of Commons. Subsequently collected in Rhodes James, Vol. VII, at pp. 7049–50, under the title 'The Greek Situation'.

1945

E126b   January   **[SPEECH OF 5 DECEMBER 1944]**
British Speeches of the Day, Vol. III, No. 1, 9–10

E127   January   **[THE LIBERATED COUNTRIES]**
British Speeches of the Day, Vol. III, No. 1, 11–21
Speech of 8 December 1944 in the House of Commons. Subsequently collected in *The Dawn of Liberation*, at pp. 273–89, under the title 'The Crisis in Greece', and in Rhodes James, Vol. VII, at pp. 7050–64, under the title 'European Difficulties'.

E128a   January   **[THE RUSSO-POLISH BORDER]**
British Speeches of the Day, Vol. III, No. 1, 21–9
Speech of 15 December 1944 in the House of Commons. Subsequently collected in *The Dawn of Liberation*, at pp. 290–300, under the title 'The Future of Poland', and in Rhodes James, Vol. VII, at pp. 7064–72, under the title 'Poland's Future'.

E128b   Jan. 1   **SOVIET-POLISH   FRONTIERS / A   Working Agreement Necessary**
Vital Speeches of the Day, Vol. X, No. 6, 162–7

E128c   February   **THE POLISH PROBLEM / Churchill's Speech**
Current History, 157–65

E129   January   **[THE ATHENS PRESS CONFERENCE]**
British Speeches of the Day, Vol. III, No. 1, 29–31
Remarks of 27 December 1944 at the Press Conference in Athens. Subsequently collected in *The Dawn of Liberation*, at pp. 311–14, and in Rhodes James, Vol. VII, at pp. 7078–81, in both cases under the title 'The Greek Situation'.

E130a   February   **[THE WAR AND FOREIGN AFFAIRS]**
British Speeches of the Day, Vol. III, No. 2, 97–115
Speech of 18 January in the House of Commons. Note that the individual number is misidentified as Vol. IV, No. 2. Separately published in pamphlet form as *Bearing the Burden* (**A197.1**). Subsequently collected in *Victory*, at pp. 2–27, and in Rhodes James, Vol. VII, at pp. 7083–103, in both cases under the title 'Review of the War'.

E130b   Feb. 1   **THE SOLIDARITY OF THREE GREAT POWERS / The War and Foreign Policies**
Vital Speeches of the Day, Vol. XI, No. 8, 230–9

E131a   March   **[THE CRIMEA CONFERENCE]**
British Speeches of the Day, Vol. III, No. 3, 169–85
Speech of 27 February in the House of Commons. Separately published in pamphlet form by three publishers (see **A199**). Subsequently collected in *Victory*, at pp. 45–66, under the title 'Results of the Three Power Conference', and in Rhodes James, Vol. VII, at pp. 7107–24, under the title 'The Yalta Conference'.

E131b   March 15   **HOUSE OF COMMONS ON POLAND / Was Yalta an Act of Justice?**
Polish Fortnightly Review, No. 112/114, 1–3

E131c   April   **REPORT TO THE HOUSE OF COMMONS, LONDON, BY PRIME MINISTER WINSTON CHURCHILL**
International Conciliation, No. 410, 291–318
Reprinted from the Hansard text.

E132 April 1 **A FUTURE OF TOIL AND SWEAT / No Totalitarian System for England**
Vital Speeches of the Day, Vol. XI, No. 12, 354–7
Speech of 15 March at the Conservative Party Conference, Central Hall, Westminster. Separately published in pamphlet form as *'Here Is the Course We Steer'* (**A200**). Subsequently collected in *Victory*, at pp. 74–82, under the title 'The Conservative Policy', and in Rhodes James, Vol. VII, at pp. 7128–35, under the title ' "Imperium et Libertas" '.

E133a May **[PRESIDENT ROOSEVELT]**
British Speeches of the Day, Vol. III, No. 5, 329–31
Speech of 17 April in the House of Commons. Subsequently collected in *Victory*, at pp. 103–6, under the title 'Death of President Roosevelt', and in Rhodes James, Vol. VII, at pp. 7138–41, under the title 'President Roosevelt'.

E133b May 1 **"A BITTER LOSS TO HUMANITY" / The Greatest American Friend We Have Ever Known**
Vital Speeches of the Day, Vol. XI, No. 14, 421–2

E134 May **[EARL LLOYD-GEORGE OF DWYFOR]**
British Speeches of the Day, Vol. III, No. 5, 332–4
Speech of 28 March in the House of Commons. Subsequently collected in *Victory*, at pp. 87–90, under the title 'The Death of Earl Lloyd George', and in Rhodes James, Vol. VII, at pp. 7136–8, under the title 'Earl Lloyd George'.

E135a May 10 **'UNCONDITIONAL SURRENDER' / The Prime Minister's Announcement Broadcast at 3 p.m. on Tuesday, May 8**
Listener, Vol. XXXIII, No. 852, 508
Subsequently collected in *Victory*, at pp. 126–8, under the title 'Unconditional Surrender', and in Rhodes James, Vol. VII, at pp. 7152–3, under the title 'The End of the War in Europe'.

E135b May 15 **V-E / Unconditional Surrender / Prime Minister Churchill**
Vital Speeches of the Day, Vol. XI, No. 15, 451

E135c May 18 **THE MESSAGES, HERE AND AT HOME, PROCLAIMING THE END OF THE WAR IN EUROPE**
Yank, 3

E135d   June   **PRIME MINISTER CHURCHILL'S STATEMENT TO THE ENGLISH PEOPLE**
Current History, 506–7

E136a   May 17   **'FORWARD, TILL THE WHOLE TASK IS DONE' /**
The Prime Minister's Broadcast of May 13
Listener, Vol. XXXIII, No. 853, 535–6, 548
Separately published in pamphlet form in *A Timely Deliverance* (**A205**). Subsequently collected in *Victory*, at pp. 132–8, and in Rhodes James, Vol. VII, at pp. 7157–63.

E136b   June   **[FIVE YEARS]**
British Speeches of the Day, Vol. III, No. 6, 373–8

E136c   June 1   **REVIEW OF WAR, PLEDGE FOR FUTURE / De Valera Denounced**
Vital Speeches of the Day, Vol. XI, No. 16, 482–5

E137   June   **PRIME MINISTER CHURCHILL ADDRESSES BRITISH SUBJECTS IN THE FAR EAST**
Current History, 507
Broadcast of 8 May from London. Subsequently collected in Rhodes James, Vol. VII, at pp. 7155–6, under the title 'To the Peoples of the British Empire in the Far East'.

E138a   June   **[THE LEVANT STATES]**
British Speeches of the Day, Vol. III, No. 6, 378–81
Speech of 5 June in the House of Commons. Subsequently collected in *Victory*, at pp. 147–51, under the title 'Syria and Lebanon', and in Rhodes James, Vol. VII, at pp. 7175–8, under the title 'Anglo-French Dispute in Syria and Lebanon'.

E138b   June 15   **THE LEVANT INCIDENTS / The British Position**
Vital Speeches of the Day, Vol. XI, No. 17, 519–21

E139   June 7   **THE GENERAL ELECTION / The Rt. Hon. Winston S. Churchill's Broadcast of June 4**
Listener, Vol. XXXIII, No. 856, 629, 632
Subsequently collected in Rhodes James, Vol. VII, at pp. 7169–74, under the title 'Party Politics Again'.

E140   June 21   **POINTS FROM OTHER ELECTION BROADCASTS / Mr. Winston Churchill**
Listener, Vol. XXXIII, No. 858, 685, 688

E141 June 28 **POINTS FROM THE ELECTION BROADCASTS /**
Mr. Winston Churchill
Listener, Vol. XXXIII, No. 859, 713, 716

E142 July **[ALLEGED BRITISH AGREEMENT WITH PETAIN]**
British Speeches of the Day, Vol. III, No. 7, 429
Speech of 12 June in the House of Commons. Subsequently collected in *Victory*, at pp. 152–3, and in Rhodes James, Vol. VII, at pp. 7180–1, in both cases under the title 'Negotiations with Vichy'.

E143a August– **[DEBATE ON THE ADDRESS]**
September *British Speeches of the Day*, Vol. III, Nos. 8–9, 451–62
Speech of 16 August in the House of Commons. Subsequently collected in *Victory*, at pp. 227–39, under the title 'The Supreme Triumph', and in Rhodes James, Vol. VII, at pp. 7209–19, under the title 'The Iron Curtain Begins to Fall (Final Review of the War)'.

E143b Oct. 1 **WHERE DO WE STAND?**
Vital Speeches of the Day, Vol. XI, No. 24, 738–42
Only that part of the address dealing with foreign policy is included; the portion dealing with domestic affairs has been excised.

E144 August– **[TERMINATION OF LEND–LEASE]**
September *British Speeches of the Day*, Vol. III, Nos 8–9, 514
Speech of 24 August in the House of Commons.

E145 Sept. 1 **KING A SYMBOL OF UNITY / The Peoples** [*sic*] **Will**
Vital Speeches of the Day, Vol. XI, No. 22, 679–80
The article combines the resolution of Clement Attlee in the House of Commons on 15 August and Churchill's address on the resolution. Churchill's address alone was subsequently collected in *Victory*, at pp. 225–6, under the title 'The True Glory', and in Rhodes James, Vol. VII, at p. 7209, under the title ' "The True Glory": The Surrender of Japan'.

E146 Oct. 1 **WHERE DO WE STAND?**
Vital Speeches of the Day, Vol. XI, No. 24, 738–42
Most of Churchill's speech of 16 August.

E147 November **[DEMOBILISATION]**
British Speeches of the Day, Vol. III, No. 11, 581–8
Extracts from the address of 22 October in the House of Commons. Subsequently collected in *The Sinews of Peace*

(**A241**), at pp. 9–23, and in Rhodes James, Vol. VII, at pp. 7226–35, in both cases under the title 'Demobilisation'.

E148   Nov. 7   **MR. CHURCHILL'S VISIT**
Harrovian, Vol. LIX, No. 6
Speech of 31 October at Harrow Songs. Subsequently collected in Rhodes James, Vol. VII, at p. 7241, under the title ' "The Voice of Youth" '.

E149   December   **[PRESIDENT TRUMAN'S DECLARATION]**
British Speeches of the Day, Vol. III, No. 12, 669–77
Extracts from the speech of 7 November in the House of Commons. Subsequently collected in *The Sinews of Peace*, at pp. 26–36, under the title 'Foreign Policy [Motion for the Adjournment]', and in Rhodes James, Vol. VII, at pp. 7241–8, under the title 'The Anglo-American Alliance'.

1946

E150   Jan. 28   **SECRET WAR SPEECH**
Life, Vol. 20, No. 4, 27–31, 43–4, 46
Speech of 23 April 1942 to the House of Commons sitting in secret session. Subsequently collected in *Secret Session Speeches* (**A227**), at pp. 47–75, under the title 'The Fall of Singapore', and in Rhodes James, Vol. VI, at pp. 6611–27, under the title 'The War Situation'.

In order to stake his claim to the War Memoirs for publication in *Life*, Henry Luce bought and published the two secret session speeches as, he explained to *Life* editor Daniel Longwell, a "pig in a poke".[9] Churchill was paid $50,000 for the two speeches. A third had originally been contemplated but then was not selected by Longwell, to whom Churchill wrote, "I am much obliged to you for not seeking to reduce in any way the $50,000, on which we had agreed, because you do not wish to use the third article. Our relationship has certainly been most agreeable."[10] In response to Longwell's expression of concern regarding copyright in the speech, Churchill wrote,

> The paper to which you refer is not a State document. It is only the draft of what it was proposed to say and not a record of what was actually said. No such record

---

9. See Gilbert, *Reves*, p. 342, n.3. Note that David Reynolds, in his *In Command of History*, extends the Luce quotation thus: "a pig in a poke to keep a position in the meat market" (at p. 9).

10. Letter of 26 January 1946 to Daniel Longwell (Sir Winston Churchill Collection, 1908-1954, Daniel Longwell Bequest, Rare Book and Manuscript Library, Columbia University).

exists. It therefore belongs to me as much as any notes made by any other Member of the House of Commons for use in Secret Session Debates.[11]

E151	Feb. 4	**DARLAN / Second Secret Speech**

Life, Vol. 20, No. 5, 85–6, 88, 90, 93–4, 96–9
Speech of 10 December 1942 to the House of Commons sitting in secret session. Subsequently collected in *Secret Session Speeches*, at pp. 76–96, and in Rhodes James, Vol. VI, at pp. 6718–30, in both cases under the title 'Admiral Darlan and the North African Landings'. Published in French in *Le Littéraire* in May–June 1946.

E152a	March 15	**ALLIANCE OF ENGLISH-SPEAKING PEOPLE / A Shadow Has Fallen on Europe and Asia**

Vital Speeches of the Day, Vol. XII, No. 11, 329–32
The "Iron Curtain" speech of 5 March, given at Westminster College, Fulton, Missouri. Separately published in pamphlet form as *The Sinews of Peace* in various editions (see **A225**). Subsequently collected in *The Sinews of Peace*, at pp. 93–105, and in Rhodes James, Vol. VII, at pp. 7285–93, in both cases under the title 'The Sinews of Peace'.

E152b	April	**THE SINEWS OF PEACE**

Westminster College Bulletin, 11–17

E152c	Winter 1971	**THE SINEWS OF PEACE**

Westminster College Bulletin, Vol. 56, No. 2, 30–6

E153	April	**MR. CHURCHILL'S RESPONSE**

Westminster College Bulletin, Series 46, No. 1, 21–22
Churchill's response is to the conferring of the honorary degree of Doctor of Laws upon him by President McCluer.

E154	April 1	**BRITISH, AMERICAN AND RUSSIAN RELATIONS / "We All Have Much to Learn"**

Vital Speeches of the Day, Vol. XII, No. 12, 354–6
Speech delivered at a dinner in Churchill's honour at the Waldorf Astoria Hotel in New York City on 15 March. Subsequently collected in *The Sinews of Peace*, at pp. 115–20, under the title 'A Speech at the Reception by the Mayor and Civic Authorities of New York', and in Rhodes James, Vol. VII, at pp. 7299–305, under the title 'The Darkening International Scene'.

---

11. Letter of 30 January 1946 to Longwell (*ibid.*).

E155	May	**EDUCATION**

Association of American Colleges Bulletin, Vol. XXXII, No. 2, 287–90

Churchill's address at the University of Miami upon the conferment on him of a Doctor of Laws on 26 February. Subsequently collected in *The Sinews of Peace*, at pp. 89–92, under the title 'University of Miami', and in Rhodes James, Vol. VII, at pp. 7283–5, under the title 'Education'.

E156a	June	**THIS MIGHTY INSTRUMENT OF VICTORY**

Reader's Digest, 29–30

Speech of 9 March at the Pentagon in Washington. Subsequently collected in *The Sinews of Peace*, at pp. 111–14, under the title 'Address to American and British Service Members', and in Rhodes James, Vol. VII, at pp. 7296–9, under the title 'The Anglo-American Alliance'.

E156b	n.d.	**THIS MIGHTY INSTRUMENT OF VICTORY**

Field Artillery Journal, 324–5

E156/1	June	**BRITAIN, EGYPT AND THE SUEZ CANAL**

British Speeches of the Day, Vol. IV, No. 5, 323–5, 331–7

Extracts from Churchill's participation in the debate on Britain, Egypt and the Suez Canal of 7 and 24 May. Subsequently collected in *The Sinews of Peace*, at pp. 139–50, and in Rhodes James, Vol. VII, at pp. 7326–34, under the title 'Egypt (Treaty Negotiations)'.

E157	August	**[SPEECH OF 1 AUGUST 1946]**

British Speeches of the Day, Vol. IV, No. 7, 514–23

Speech of 1 August in the House of Commons. Subsequently collected in *The Sinews of Peace*, at pp. 185–96, and in Rhodes James, Vol. VII, at pp. 7372–9, in both cases under the title 'Palestine'.

E158a	Oct. 1	**A UNITED STATES OF EUROPE / France and Germany Must Lead the Way**

Vital Speeches of the Day, Vol. XII, No. 24, 741–2

Speech delivered at Zurich University on 19 September. Subsequently published separately in pamphlet form (**A253**), and collected in *The Sinews of Peace*, at pp. 198–202, under the title 'A Speech at Zurich University', and in Rhodes James, Vol. VII, at pp. 7379–82, under the title ' "The Tragedy of Europe" '.

E158b	December	**LET EUROPE ARISE**

Nineteenth Century and After, 297–301

E159   November   **[SPEECH OF 11 OCTOBER 1946]**
British Speeches of the Day, Vol. IV, No. 9, 652–5

E159/1   November   **CHURCHILL AT ABERDEEN**
Empire Digest, Vol. 4, No. 2, 96–8
Speech of 27 April in reply to the Latin address of the Vice Chancellor of Aberdeen University during the ceremony conferring the degree of Doctor of Laws (L.D.) on Churchill. This is the only published report of this speech.[12]

E160   Nov. 21   **BRITAIN'S TRIBUTE TO A GREAT AMERICAN / Appeals for the Franklin Roosevelt Memorial Fund / II – By Mr. Churchill**
Listener, Vol. XXXVI, No. 932, 699–700
The Churchill tribute follows one by Attlee. Broadcast on 18 November. Subsequently collected in *The Sinews of Peace*, at pp. 243–4, and in Rhodes James, Vol. VII, at pp.7408–9, in both cases under the title 'Roosevelt Memorial Fund'.

E161   December   **[DEBATE ON THE KING'S SPEECH]**
British Speeches of the Day, Vol. IV, No. 10, 686–95
Address of 12 November in the debate in the House of Commons on the King's Address. Subsequently collected in *The Sinews of Peace*, at pp. 230–42, under the title 'Debate on the Address', and in Rhodes James, Vol. VII, at pp. 7400–8, under the title 'The International Scene'.

E162   Dec. 4   **MR. CHURCHILL'S VISIT**
Harrovian, Vol. LX, No. 9, 33–4
Speech of 28 November at Harrow Songs.

1947

E163   January–
February   **THE INDIA DEBATE**
British Speeches of the Day, Vol. V, No. 1, 37–45
Speech in the course of the debate of 12 December 1946 on the motion of Sir Stafford Cripps regarding the settlement of difficulties between the Indian parties. Subsequently collected in *The Sinews of Peace*, pp. 245–56, and in Rhodes James, Vol. VII, at pp. 7410–17, under the title 'India'.

---

12. Churchill's other speech of that date, also made in Aberdeen, 'The Needs of a Sick World', is better known (see Rhodes James, Vol. VII, pp. 7306-8, and Gilbert, *WSC*, Vol. VI, pp. 228-9).

E164   June 1   **UNITED EUROPE / The Fourth Pillar of World Government**
Vital Speeches of the Day, Vol. XIII, No. 16, 482–5
Speech of 14 May delivered at the United Europe meeting at the Albert Hall in London. Subsequently collected in *Europe Unite*, at pp. 77–85, under the title 'United Europe Meeting', and in Rhodes James, Vol. VII, at pp.7483–8.

E165   Aug. 21   **A CRITICISM OF THE GOVERNMENT**
Listener, Vol. XXXVIII, No. 969, 307–8
Broadcast of 16 August. Published here under the superhead 'Party Political Broadcasts – III'. Subsequently collected in *Europe Unite*, at pp. 129–34, under the title 'Party Political Broadcast', and in Rhodes James, Vol. VII, at pp. 7517–21, under the title ' "No Easy Passage" '.

E166a   Oct. 20   **PROGNOSIS**
Time, 30
Portions of the speech of 14 October (previously recorded in London) broadcast to the Alfred E. Smith Memorial Foundation in New York. Subsequently collected in *Europe Unite*, at pp. 162–6, and in Rhodes James, Vol. VII, at pp.7538–40, in both cases under the title 'The Al Smith Memorial'.

E166b   Nov. 1   **SOVIET VIRULENT PROPAGANDA / What Is the Real Motive behind It?**
Vital Speeches of the Day, Vol. XIV, No. 2, 38–9
The full text of the speech.

E167   Nov. 1   **PEACE RESTS UPON STRENGTH / "Fundamental Dangers and Antagonisms Will Remain"**
Vital Speeches of the Day, Vol. XIV, No. 2, 44–6
Part of speech of 9 October. Subsequently collected in *Europe Unite*, at pp. 409–24.

E168   Nov. 12   **MR. CHURCHILL'S VISIT**
Harrovian, Vol. LXI, No. 7, 25–6
Speech of 4 November at Harrow Songs.

1948

E169   Feb. 19   **THE CONSERVATIVE CASE FOR A NEW PARLIAMENT**
Listener, Vol. XXXIX, No. 995, 302–3
Broadcast of 14 February. Published here under the superhead 'Party Political Broadcasts – XI'. Separately published in

pamphlet form as *Set the People Free* (**A235**). Subsequently collected in *Europe Unite*, at pp. 239–44, and in Rhodes James, Vol. VII, at pp. 7590–3, under the title 'A New Parliament'.

E170   March 1   **WILL THERE BE WAR? / Bring Matters to a Head with Soviet Government Now**
Vital Speeches of the Day, Vol. XIV, No. 10, 296–301
Speech of 23 January in the House of Commons. Subsequently collected in *Europe Unite*, at pp. 224–37, and in Rhodes James, Vol. VII, at pp. 7581–90, in both cases under the title 'Foreign Affairs'.

E171   May 15   **THE VOICE OF EUROPE / Plea for European Unity**
Vital Speeches of the Day, Vol. XIV, No. 15, 450–2
Speech of 7 May delivered at the opening of the Congress of Europe at The Hague. Separately published in pamphlet form in *The Grand Design* (**A237**). Subsequently collected in *Europe Unite*, at pp. 310–17, and in Rhodes James, Vol. VII, at pp. 7635–9, in both cases under the title 'The Congress of Europe'.

E172   Nov. 10   **MR. CHURCHILL'S VISIT**
Harrovian, Vol. LXII, No. 7, 25–6
Speech of 4 November at Harrow Songs.

1949

E173   Jan. 1   **NATIONALIZATION OF STEEL INDUSTRY / Not a Bill, But a Plot**
Vital Speeches of the Day, Vol. XV, No. 6, 183–9
Speech of 16 November 1948. Reprinted from Hansard. Subsequently collected in *Europe Unite*, at pp. 447–64, and in Rhodes James, Vol. VII, at pp. 7731–42, in both cases under the title 'Iron and Steel Bill'.

E174   Feb. 17   **RECRUITING FOR THE FORCES–III**
Listener, Vol. XLI, No. 1047, 259
Broadcast speech of 17 February. Subsequently collected in *In the Balance*, at pp. 23–5, and in Rhodes James, Vol. VII, at pp. 7789–90.

E175   April 1   **UNITED WE STAND SECURE / War Not Inevitable**
Vital Speeches of the Day, Vol. XV, No. 12, 380–4
Speech of 31 March. Subsequently collected in *In the Balance*, at pp. 40–51, and in Rhodes James, Vol. VII, at pp. 7801–10, in both cases under the title 'The Twentieth Century—Its Promise and Its Realization'.

E176   September   **PEACE IN DANGER**
Conservative Approach, No. 21, 1
Extracts from Churchill's speech of 15 July at Plymouth.

E177   [No entry.]

E178   Oct. 15   **STERLING EXCHANGE RATE / A Concession of Failure**
Vital Speeches of the Day, Vol. XVI, No. 1, 18–23
Speech of 28 September. Subsequently collected in *In the Balance*, at pp. 85–100, under the title 'Sterling Exchange Rate (Devaluation of £)', and in Rhodes James, Vol. VII, at pp. 7844–57, under the title 'Devaluation of the Pound'.

E179   Dec. 7   **MR. CHURCHILL'S VISIT**
Harrovian, Vol. LXIII, No. 11, 25–6
Speech of 1 December at Harrow Songs. A very brief excerpt only was subsequently collected in Rhodes James, Vol. VII, at p. 7902, under the title 'Exhortation for the Future'.

1950

E180   Jan. 26   **THE CONSERVATIVE POINT OF VIEW**
Listener, 156–7
Broadcast of 21 January. Subsequently collected in *In the Balance*, at pp. 155–60, and in Rhodes James, Vol. VIII, at pp. 7903–7.

E181   Feb. 23   **GENERAL   ELECTION   BROADCASTS / Mr. Winston S. Churchill**
Listener, Vol. XLIII, No. 1100, 339, 342–3
Broadcast of 17 February. Churchill's is the fourth election broadcast published here. Subsequently collected in *In the Balance*, at pp. 208–14, and in Rhodes James, Vol. VIII, at pp. 7946–51, in both cases under the title 'The Moment of Decision'.

E182   August   **PRESENTATION OF THE CHESNEY GOLD MEDAL TO THE RT. HON. WINSTON S. CHURCHILL, O.M., C.H., M.P.**
Journal of the Royal United Service Institution, Vol. XCV, No. 579, 371–5
The Chesney Award, in recognition of outstanding Service Literature, was given to Churchill on 4 July. His address upon receipt of it is given at pp. 372–5. Subsequently collected in *In the Balance*, at pp. 304–8, under the title 'Royal United

Services Institution', and in Rhodes James, Vol. VIII, at pp. 8028–31, under the title 'Military History'.

E183a   Aug. 31   **THE DANGER IN EUROPE**
Listener, Vol. XLIV, No. 1127, 308–9
Broadcast of 26 August. Published here under the superhead 'Party Political Broadcast'. Subsequently collected in *In the Balance*, at pp. 353–7, under the title 'The Peril in Europe', and in Rhodes James, Vol. VIII, at pp. 8069–73, under the title 'The Peril in Europe and Korea'.

E183b   Sept. 15   **THE SUPREME PERIL IN EUROPE / Improvidence and Want of Foresight**
Vital Speeches of the Day, Vol. XVI, No. 23, 706–8

E184   Nov. 29   **CHURCHILL SONGS**
Harrovian, Vol. LXIV, No. 8, 33–4
Speech of 23 November at Harrow Songs.

1951

E185   Jan. 1   **WORLD CAUSE WILL BE DECIDED IN EUROPE / The Need for Unity of Free Nations**
Vital Speeches of the Day, Vol. XVII, No. 6, 213–16
Speech of 30 November 1950. Subsequently collected in *In the Balance*, at pp. 435–42, under the title 'Foreign Affairs', and in Rhodes James, Vol. VIII, at pp. 8130–5, under the title 'The International Situation'.

E186a   March 22   **THE CONSERVATIVE CASE FOR AN ELECTION**
Listener, Vol. XLV, No. 1151, 462–3
Broadcast of 17 March. Published here under the superhead 'Party Political Broadcast'. Subsequently collected in Rhodes James, Vol. VIII, at pp. 8169–73.

E186b   April   **WHY WE NEED AN ELECTION**
Conservative Approach, 1
Excerpts only from the broadcast of 17 March.

E187   May 15   **A GRAVE HOUR / Britain's Influence Goes Down and Down**
Vital Speeches of the Day, 462–3
Speech of 27 April.

E188   Oct. 11   **GENERAL   ELECTION   BROADCASTS / Mr. Winston S. Churchill**
Listener, Vol. XLVI, No. 1180, 603, 605
Broadcast of 8 October. Churchill's is the second appearing here. Subsequently collected in Rhodes James, Vol. VIII, at pp. 8254–8, under the title 'Our Political Future'.

E189   Dec. 12   **CHURCHILL SONGS**
Harrovian, 39–40
Speech of 7 December at Harrow Songs. A brief excerpt only was subsequently collected in Rhodes James, Vol. VIII, at p. 8314, under the title ' "We Are One Country" '.

E190   Dec. 15   **GRAVE   RESPONSIBILITIES   FACE   NEW PARLIAMENT / Financial and Economic Situations**
Vital Speeches of the Day, Vol. XVIII, No. 5, 130–4
Speech of 6 November. Subsequently collected in *Stemming the Tide* (**A264**), at pp. 176–86, and in Rhodes James, Vol. VIII, at pp. 8289–97, under the title 'Debate on the Address'.

E191   Dec. 27   **THE   CONSERVATIVE   GOVERNMENT'S PROBLEMS**
Listener, Vol. XLVI, No. 1191, 1104–5
Broadcast of 22 December. Published here under the superhead 'Party Political Broadcast'. Subsequently collected in Rhodes James, Vol. VIII, at pp. 8314–18, under the title 'Party Political Broadcast'.

1952

E192a   Jan. 28   **CLOSE ANGLO-AMERICAN UNITY URGED FOR DEFENSE OF GLOBAL FREEDOMS / Address by the British Prime Minister, Winston Churchill, to the Congress.**
Department of State Bulletin, 116–20
Speech of 17 January. Reprinted from the *Congressional Record* of 17 January, at p. 279. Subsequently collected in *Stemming the Tide*, at pp. 220–7, and in Rhodes James, Vol. VIII, at pp. 8323–9, under the title 'Address to the United States Congress'.

E192b   Feb. 1   **BRITAIN NEEDS STEEL, NOT GOLD / United States and Commonwealth Must Tread the Same Path**
Vital Speeches of the Day, Vol. XVIII, No. 8, 231–4

E193   February   **MR. CHURCHILL'S OTTAWA SPEECH / Text of an address by the Prime Minister of the United Kingdom,**

the Right Honourable Winston S. Churchill, delivered
at a banquet given in his honour by the Government
of Canada in Ottawa, on January 14, 1952
External Affairs, Vol. 4, No. 2, 51–5
Subsequently collected in Rhodes James, Vol. VIII, at
pp. 8320–3, under the title 'Britain and Canada'.

E194a   Feb. 14   **KING GEORGE VI: THE PRIME MINISTER'S
                       TRIBUTE**
                       Listener, Vol. XLVII, No. 1198, 247–8
                       Broadcast of 7 February. Previously published separately in
                       pamphlet and miniature form (see **A262**), and subsequently
                       collected in *Stemming the Tide*, at pp. 237–40, and in Rhodes
                       James, Vol. VIII, at pp. 8336–8.

E194b   March 1   **KING GEORGE VI / The Crown Is the Magic Link
                       That Unites the Commonwealth**
                       Vital Speeches of the Day, 290–1

E195   May 8   **THE CONSERVATIVES' FIRST SIX MONTHS**
                       Listener, Vol. XLVII, No. 1210, 754–5
                       Broadcast of 3 May. Published here under the superhead 'Party
                       Political Broadcasts'. Subsequently collected in Rhodes James,
                       Vol. VIII, at pp. 8368–72.

E196   October?   **[SPEECH OF 13 JUNE 1952]**
                       Graya, Michaelmas Term issue, No. 36, 95–102
                       The Silver Jubilee Number.

E197   Oct. 9   **IN MEMORY OF KING GEORGE VI / The Rt. Hon.
                       Winston S. Churchill, O.M., Opens the National
                       Memorial Fund**
                       Listener, Vol. XLVIII, No. 1232, 589
                       Broadcast of 4 October. Subsequently collected in Rhodes
                       James, Vol. VIII, at pp. 8409–10, under the title 'King George
                       VI Memorial Fund Appeal'.

E198   Nov. 12   **CHURCHILL SONGS**
                       Harrovian, Vol. LXVI, No. 7, 21–2
                       Speech of 7 November at Harrow Songs.

1953

E199   March   **SPEECH AT THE ANNUAL DINNER OF THE
                       NATIONAL FARMERS' UNION, 17 FEBRUARY
                       1953**
                       Agriculture, 551–4

Subsequently collected in Rhodes James, Vol. VIII, at pp. 8449–52, under the title 'The Agricultural Industry'.

E200   April 2   **A GRACIOUS AND MUCH-LOVED QUEEN / Two Broadcast Tributes to Her Majesty Queen Mary**
Listener, Vol. XLIX, No. 1257, 545
Broadcast of 25 March. Churchill's is the first of the two; the other is by the Dowager Lady Ampthill. Subsequently collected in Rhodes James, Vol. VIII, at pp. 8464–5, under the title 'Queen Mary'.

E201   June 4   **TRIBUTES FROM THE COMMONWEALTH**
Listener, Vol. XLIX, No. 1266, 916
Broadcast of 2 June. The first of a series of tributes by Commonwealth prime ministers. The actual Churchill broadcast immediately preceded that of the Queen. Subsequently collected in Rhodes James, Vol. VIII, at p. 8487, under the title 'The Coronation of Queen Elizabeth II'.

E202   June 15   **SURVEY OF THE WORLD SCENE / Change of Attitude and Mood in the Kremlin**
Vital Speeches of the Day, Vol. XIX, No. 17, 522–6
Speech of 11 May in the House of Commons. Subsequently collected in *The Unwritten Alliance*, at pp. 42–54, and in Rhodes James, Vol. VIII, at pp. 8475–85, under the title 'Foreign Affairs'.

E203   Nov. 1   **PROGRESSIVE CONSERVATION / Trade Unions See Fallacy of Nationalization**
Vital Speeches of the Day, Vol. XX, No. 2, 36–40
Speech of 10 October at the Conservative Party Conference, Margate. Subsequently collected in *The Unwritten Alliance*, at pp. 57–67, and in Rhodes James, Vol. VIII, at pp. 8489–97, under the title 'Conservative Party Conference'.

E204   Dec. 2   **CHURCHILL SONGS**
Harrovian, Vol. LXVII, No. 10, 33–4
Speech of 27 November at Harrow Songs. A brief excerpt only was subsequently collected in Rhodes James, Vol. VIII, at p. 8515, under the title 'Harrow Songs'.

1954

—   Jan. 14   **EVERY MAN TO HIS POST** (*The Listener; see* **E60c**)

E205   June   **CANADIAN EULOGY**
External Affairs, Vol. 6, No. 7, 207

A brief address by Churchill during his trip to Ottawa of 29–30 June 1954. A photograph of Churchill with the Canadian Prime Minister Louis St Laurent appears at p. 206. Subsequently collected in Rhodes James, Vol. VIII, at p. 8576, under the title ' "Canada—The Master Link in Anglo-American Unity" '.

E206	Aug. 1	**BRITISH FOREIGN POLICY / Statement on Washington Talks**

Vital Speeches of the Day, Vol. XX, No. 20, 610–13
Speech of 12 July in the House of Commons. Subsequently collected in *The Unwritten Alliance*, at pp. 157–68, and in Rhodes James, Vol. VIII, at pp. 8576–85, under the title 'Visit to the United States and Canada'.

E207	Nov. 15	**PEACE THROUGH STRENGTH / The London Agreement**

Vital Speeches of the Day, Vol. XXI, No. 3, 836–8
Speech of 9 October at the Conservative Party Conference, Blackpool. Subsequently collected in *The Unwritten Alliance*, at pp. 181–91, and in Rhodes James, Vol. VIII, at pp. 8593–601, under the title ' "Peace through Strength" '.

E208	Nov. 17	**CHURCHILL SONGS**

Harrovian, Vol. LXVIII, No. 9, 33–4
Speech at the annual Harrow Songs on 12 November.

1955

E209	March 15	**DEFENCE THROUGH DETERRENTS / Free World Should Retain Superiority in Nuclear Weapons**

Vital Speeches of the Day, Vol. XXI, No. 11, 1090–4
Speech of 1 March in the House of Commons. Separately published as a pamphlet entitled *"Defence through Deterrents"* (**A265**) and collected in *The Unwritten Alliance*, at pp. 224–34, and in Rhodes James, Vol. VIII, at pp. 8593–601, under the title 'The Deterrent—Nuclear Warfare'.

E210	April 1	**TOP-LEVEL CONFERENCE / What We Have Done to Bring It About**

Vital Speeches of the Day, Vol. XXI, No. 12, 1127–31
Speech of 14 March in the House of Commons. Subsequently collected in *The Unwritten Alliance*, at pp. 235–45, and in Rhodes James, Vol. VIII, at pp. 8633–42, under the title 'World Disarmament'.

E211   Summer   **THE DUTIES OF A MEMBER OF PARLIAMENT**
Parliamentary Affairs, Vol. VIII, No. 3, 302
Churchill's comments on 26 March at the opening of the Sir
James Hawkey Hall at Woodford, Essex. Exceptionally, not
collected in either *The Unwritten Alliance* or in Rhodes James.

E212   July   **RESPONSE**
University of the State of New York Bulletin, No. 1436, 325–7
Churchill's Response "broadcast to the audience in
Chancellors Hall from a tape recording" at the Eighty-Seventh
Convocation of the University of the State of New York, 8
and 9 April 1954. It appears, according to Rhodes James, that
the recording of the remarks may have been made on 7 April,
but "publication" clearly did not occur until their "broadcast"
in New York. Subsequently collected in Rhodes James,
Vol. VIII, at pp. 8559–60, under the title 'America and
Britain'.

E213   Nov. 30   **CHURCHILL SONGS**
Harrovian, Vol. LXIX, No. 10, 39
Speech of 24 November at Harrow Songs.

1956

E214   June 1   **EUROPEAN UNITY / Russia and East European
States Should Be Included**
Vital Speeches of the Day, Vol. XXII, No. 16, 486–7
Speech of 10 May delivered at Aachen, Germany, after
receiving the Charlemagne Prize as a "Great European".
Subsequently collected in *The Unwritten Alliance*, at
pp. 289–91, and in Rhodes James, Vol. VIII, at pp. 8674–6, in
both cases under the title 'Grand Alliance of European
Powers'.

1959

E215   June 15   **THE UNION OF ENGLISH-SPEAKING PEOPLES /
We Understand Each Other**
Vital Speeches of the Day, Vol. XXV, No. 17, 526–7
Introduction of Churchill by President Eisenhower at a dinner
of 6 May in honour of Churchill, and Churchill's remarks at
that dinner. Subsequently collected in *The Unwritten Alliance*,
at pp. 316–17, and in Rhodes James, Vol. VIII, at pp. 8695–6,
under the title 'Union of English-Speaking Peoples'.

1962

E216   March   **WINSTON CHURCHILL SAID IT MUCH BETTER AND STRONGER FORTY YEARS AGO**
Land, 150–1
Speech on land monopoly.

1965

—   Spring   **ADDRESS BY WINSTON CHURCHILL IN ACCEPTING THE DEGREE OF DOCTOR OF LAWS FROM THE UNIVERSITY OF ROCHESTER**
(*University of Rochester Library Bulletin*; *see* **E73b**)

1971

—   Winter   **THE SINEWS OF PEACE** (*Westminster College Bulletin*; *see* **E152c**)

1972

—   Nov. 2   **VOICES FROM THE ARCHIVES** (*Listener*; *see* **E36b**)

1985

E217   Summer   **ON CIVILISATION**
Finest Hour, No. 48, back cover
Speech of 2 July 1938 as Chancellor of Bristol University. Previously collected in Rhodes James, Vol. VI, at pp. 5990–1, under the title 'Civilisation'.

E218   Winter   **LET US GO BOLDLY FORWARD**
Finest Hour, No. 50, back cover
Principal portion of the speech of 21 June 1955 at the unveiling of the Oscar Nemon statue of Churchill at the Guildhall, London. Previously collected in Rhodes James, Vol. VIII, at pp. 8658–60.

1986

—   Spring   **"ARM YOURSELVES, AND BE YE MEN OF VALOUR"** (*Finest Hour*; *see* **E54b**)

—   Summer   **DUNKIRK** (*Finest Hour*; *see* **E55b**)

— August **FINEST HOUR** (*Finest Hour*; *see* **E56c**)

E219 Winter **PERSIA**
Finest Hour, No. 54, back cover
Notes for the speeches of 30 July 1951 in the House of Commons and 6 October 1951 at Loughton County High School, presented in the reverse-pyramid format used by Churchill for his speaking notes.

1989

E220 September **LORD ROSSLYN AND HIS CONTROVERSIAL BOOK *TWICE CAPTURED: A RECORD OF ADVENTURE DURING THE BOER WAR***
Quarterly Bulletin of the South African Library, 12–25
Speech of 26 October 1900, at pp. 14–18.

1993

E221 Spring **THE SPIRIT OF ENGLAND**
This England, Vol. 26, No. 1, 43
Speech of 23 April 1953 to the Honourable Artillery Company at their St George's Day dinner. Previously collected in Rhodes James, Vol. VIII, at pp. 8471–3, under the title 'England'.

1995

E222 Autumn **DURBAN 1899: THE DESPERADO SPEAKS**
Finest Hour, No. 88, 15
Churchill arrived in Durban a free man, in triumph and "world famous overnight", in the words of his son Randolph (*WSC*, Vol. I, p. 489). His speeches of 23 December 1899 delivered from a rickshaw and at Durban Town Hall of the same date. The texts are taken from the *Natal Mercury* of that date. Neither was previously published other than in the daily press.

1997

E223 Summer **THE MAIDEN SPEECH, BATH, 1897**
Finest Hour, No. 95, 26–7
Speech of 26 July 1897 at the Habitation of the Primrose League, Claverton Down, Bath. Previously collected in Rhodes James, Vol. I, at pp. 25–8, under the title 'First Political Speech'.